PSALMS

BERIT OLAM
Studies in Hebrew Narrative & Poetry

Psalms

Konrad Schaefer, O.S.B.

David W. Cotter, O.S.B.
Editor

Jerome T. Walsh
Chris Franke
Associate Editors

A Michael Glazier Book
THE LITURGICAL PRESS
Collegeville, Minnesota

www.litpress.org

A Michael Glazier Book published by The Liturgical Press.

Cover design by Ann Blattner.

1   2   3   4   5   6   7   8   9

Library of Congress Cataloging-in-Publication Data

Schaefer, Konrad, 1951–
    Psalms / Konrad Schaefer ; David W. Cotter, editor.
        p.   cm. — (Berit Olam)
    Includes bibliographical references and index.
    ISBN 0-8146-5061-9 (alk. paper)
    1. Bible.   O.T.   Psalms—Criticism, interpretation, etc.   I. Cotter, David W.
II. Title. III. Series.

BS1430.52 .S33   2001
223'.207—dc21
                                                                00-062422

CONTENTS

Preface vii

Introduction. xi
    Imagery xii
    Repetition and Parallelism xiv
    The Psalms in Context and Sequence xix
    Shifting Address and Modes of Discourse xxi
    A School of Prayer xxv
    Disease, Death, and the Enemy xxxii
    Prayer and the Curse xxxviii

Book One, Psalms 1–41 1

Book Two, Psalms 42–72 105

Book Three, Psalms 73–89 175

Book Four, Psalms 90–106 223

Book Five, Psalms 107–150 265

Appendices 347
    Superscriptions 349
    Prehistory of the Psalter 352
    Literary Types 355

For Further Reading 359

Index of Scriptural References 363

General Index 387

Index of Hebrew Words 393

PREFACE

Some people never tire of reading the psalms. Recently a friend told me that she has read and listened to them repeatedly over the past few years. The phrases and images have become so familiar to her that they are almost memorized yet still unsettling. The content is always experienced in novel ways, and repeated contact awards surprisingly new insights.

Even so, recitation of the psalms can become tiring, the questions about them are in some respects unanswerable and the obstacles to their appropriation insurmountable. The images, phrases and ideas are sometimes far from the contemporary reader's life and interest. The present volume seeks to respond to this difficulty by adopting a particular focus in the appreciation of the psalms as poems which chart a profound and vital relationship with God, with all the ups and downs that such a relationship implies.

The psalms have a literary context, the Bible. As Sacred Scripture they share the historical and cultural milieu of the Ancient Near East. They have had pride of place in the liturgy since time immemorial. In commenting on each psalm, I will pay special attention to the poetic elements, while also respecting their historical context and liturgical use.

We do not know who composed these texts, whether they are the product of a single hand or various hands in successive stages of redaction, honed by continuous use in the life of a people at prayer. Tradition has honored an Israelite shepherd, musician, king, and messiah named David as the authority behind the psalms. To respect this and yet to honor the countless other hands and voices which contributed to their inspiration, I have dubbed the author "the poet" or "psalmist."

The aim in the Introduction is to synthesize some preliminary considerations. *The Psalms in Context and Sequence* represents a relatively new emphasis in the study of the book known in Hebrew as *Tehillim* or "Praises." Just as successive chapters may form a novel, so the Psalter taken as a whole has a shape analogous to a plot. Each psalm has a literary context within the Psalter, which has a design like that of a Jewish or Christian prayer book or hymnal. A hymnal, for example, may be arranged according to the liturgical cycle, in which a selection of hymns and prayers follows the sequence of the weekly or annual celebrations. It is instructive to locate a psalm in the plot of the Psalter as one studies or recites it, even though the psalms are usually read and prayed in isolation from that larger context.

The section on *Shifting Address and Modes of Discourse* shows an appreciation for the psalms as liturgical poems. That is how they are approached by many Jews and Christians who pray them. A psalm cannot be appreciated for its deepest meaning without acknowledging this aspect; otherwise, it may be too easily judged to be just a poem which is either fittingly well-done or untidy.

The remaining sections expound the hermeneutical considerations of the psalms. The Psalter was preserved in various forms, not just because it is a body of good classical Hebrew poetry, but because the reader has been interested in what he or she has read and prayed. Part of literary appreciation is the meaning of the text in the poet's context, and how this may be transposed and interpreted in the contemporary life of the reader who wishes to contact God and understand life in relation to God. The psalms, after all, represent the poet's efforts at self-expression in this relation. Thus, the Psalter is *A School of Prayer*. The section on *Disease, Death, and the Enemy* summarizes a theme which risks an overly literal interpretation, which in turn could divorce these texts from the author's intent and remove them from the reader's life. A sore spot in the Hebrew Psalter is violent rhetoric and the use of the curse in a religious context. The treatment of this theme is also hermeneutical. What does the poet mean by venting in this objectionable fashion? How can such harsh expressions be read and appreciated today? I suggest that the author was not as backward or surly as some readers might suppose. A benign judgment on the use of violence in the Psalter allows the reader freer scope in the appreciation of its poetry.

In the commentary I have not catalogued the psalms according to literary types. This is the slant of many other studies. Rather, I present a mental snapshot of the psalm and highlight some of the contours of the poetry, the phrases and images which otherwise may be lost on the reader who approaches the psalms in translation. Thus, a decision has been made in the commentary to identify the dynamics of the poetic discourse and thus enhance the reader's appreciation of the rhetoric and imagery, which are major keys to the meaning of the psalms.

The present commentary, based on the Hebrew text, is designed to be used alongside the NRSV translation with its chapter and verse divisions. This version does not count among the verses the psalm captions, like "To the leader: with stringed instruments; according to The Sheminith. A Psalm of David" (Psalm 6). Thus, the Hebrew verse numbering used in some versions may differ by one or two digits from that cited here. For example,

NRSV 6:1 = Hebrew 6:2

NRSV 60:1 = Hebrew 60:3

Where a comment hinges on the Hebrew verse in discussion, this is indicated. When appreciation of the inner dynamic of a psalm depends on the evidence of verbal or repetitive patterns in Hebrew, a more literal translation is offered, along with the NRSV's wording. The rendering "LORD" (in small capitals) represents the divine name *(yhwh)* in Hebrew; "Lord" translates the Hebrew *ʾădōnāy*.

The poet exploits repetition and double meanings to good effect, and these techniques result in a certain homogeneity of the text. As literary techniques, they create echoes that weave together what might otherwise appear to be disparate texts. Elements of Hebrew poetry like rhythm, alliteration, and assonance are difficult to represent in translation, and these will not be treated in the commentary, except in some instances where such a feature highlights the meaning or signals an inner dynamic in a poem. English composition requires the use of pronouns. This is not the case in Hebrew, where the verbal inflection includes the pronominal sense. The Hebrew pronoun is often employed for emphasis, in which case mention of it is made in the commentary.

Strophic division and the disposition of a psalm in paragraphs is a matter of conjecture and interpretation. Nonetheless, identifiable sections and successive movements are part of the drama and literary art of the poem. Sectional divisions are usually indicated by repetition (including the refrain) and framing devices or inclusion. Numerical patterns (for example, the sevenfold repetition of a word) and shifts of address or mood also help to delimit a section. In the few psalms which evidence a clear division, I apply the term *strophe* for the sections. In many psalms an alternate division from that in the NRSV is proposed, based on the literary and thematic factors identified in the commentary. Usually I refer to successive movements, in an effort to respect the flow of the composition and highlight the dramatic and liturgical action.

A considerable debt is owed to three people who inspired and taught me: Bonaventure Zerr, Luis Alonso Schökel, and Raymond Tournay. The study *Salmos I & II* by Luis Alonso Schökel, S.J., and Cecilia Carniti

(Estella: Ed. Verbo Divino, 1992-3), has influenced the approach taken in this present volume. Editor David Cotter, O.S.B. proved expert in scholarship and patient in friendship as the manuscript was nearing completion, and Chris Franke was generous in alerting me to details of content and style which called for attention. Thank you. By their collaboration, they became my teachers. Gratitude cannot be adequately expressed to confreres of two Benedictine monastic communities of Mount Angel Abbey in Oregon and Nuestra Señora de Los Ángeles in Cuernavaca, as well as to friends with whom I have shared the challenge of studying and living the sacred Word. May the divine Author of the psalms be honored by our lives of prayer, *lectio* and work, and may the Father who sees even your secret merit reward you who have helped bring this work to light.

INTRODUCTION

By its nature poetry intensifies human experience both for the poet and the reader. In a first reflection a poet steps back, surveys an experience, abstracts the universals, translates them into symbols (words and images) and transcribes them in poetic form. In the transaction between experience and poetry something of the particular experience is sacrificed, the symbol is shaped, so the poet might better appreciate life and others might comprehend it with a new scope. With respect to the poems known as the psalms, a community of faith adopted them as a fitting expression of their life. These poems chronicle both a poet's and a community's experience. Their religious basis is essential to their content and meaning. They express a personal relationship with God in a community context.

A second phase of reflection involves the reader, who enters the psalms through words and images, explores their meaning, acknowledges their unique cultural context, admires their beauty and relevance. Their spiritual side touches human sentiments about God translated into terms of struggling and exultant faith. The reader who savors the psalm forges a privileged relationship with the psalmist and the primitive community which brought it to light.

In principle poetry is approached as it is composed—calmly, so that it can be absorbed naturally, convincingly. A poem has its own voice, which communicates a poet's life and emotion. In addition, the psalms are conditioned by a cultural spirit different from that of most readers today. Because the Hebrew poem is both deeply personal and the patrimony of a flesh and bone community of faith, something about it evades scientific inquiry and critical investigation. Nonetheless such examination is necessary to appreciate the poem and adopt it as one's own.

As the mediation of experience the poem has its own identity, distinct from the poet's life and feeling. When a psalm is taken as the object of study, it does not matter what the author really felt but rather how he or she expressed the emotion and reshaped it in poetry. The imagery and literary patterns based on repetition are windows to the poetry of the psalms and are introduced here and identified in the commentary.

Imagery

The psalmist depicts reality, both actual and distorted, with a broad panorama of images. In the conception of a world of interconnected parts, human behavior has repercussions in the cosmic order. The unsteady moral climate reverberates in the collapse of the world's foundations. Geophysical and spatial imagery portrays the state of the poet's soul, and thus the poet reflects a universe wherein the physical and moral orders are interconnected. For example, Psalm 82 depicts God's deputies charged with the moral order who neither know nor understand. While they wander aimlessly in darkness they foment it. The critical situation is reflected in the world's tottering foundations (v. 5). It is as though the cosmos, as an extension of an unfair society, reverts to its chaotic, pre-creation state. To set it right, God assigns the death sentence to the authorities who acted irresponsibly (v. 7). Such a complex world view represents the theology of Genesis 3, where man and woman, charged with maintaining order in and cultivating the garden, merit capital punishment for transgressing the limit that distinguished them from God. The effects of their sin and its punishment disturbed the original balance and harmony enjoyed by the order of being.

Ephemeral images are common in the psalms: a slippery road (73:18), a dream which vanishes upon waking (73:20), withered grass or chaff blowing in the wind (35:5; 83:13), a forest fire (83:14), a breath or a passing shadow (144:4). Human plans are like puffs of air (94:11). The life span is a handbreadth (39:5). Emotions are fickle: weeping arrives and lodges in the evening but shouts of joy rise the following morning (30:5). Notably in the last two books of the Psalter, such images—a watch in the night, a dream upon waking, grass that sprouts and dies, a sigh (90:4-6, 9)—are applied to the swiftness of human life. The poet is almost obsessed with the theme: "I am gone like a shadow at evening; I am shaken off like a locust" (109:23). An eloquent use of imagery is found in the curses, which include a broad range of disasters, but with a preference for family calamities.

God is often described in metaphorical language. God is shepherd for the poet (23:1; 119:176) or the community (28:9; 80:1), and the people are the flock (74:1; 77:20; 78:52; 79:13; 95:7; 100:3). God is a farmer caring for a vineyard (80:8-12) or feeding livestock (145:15-16). God is a sun (84:11), a father (68:5; 89:26; 103:13), a warrior (68:1-2, 11, 17, 21-23; 89:10). God is compared to a person awaking from a hangover (78:65). The images for God are implied by functions: an archer who fires lightning bolts as arrows (7:12-13; 18:14; 21:12; 38:2; 77:17; 144:6), a bird who provides protection with its wings (17:8; 57:1; 63:7; 91:4), a builder (102:25; 104:5), a host (23:5), a knitter (139:13). The songs of ascent are rich in imagery for God—a provider of shade (121:5), a builder and guard (127:1), a master or a mistress (123:2), a mother (131:2), the mountains around Jerusalem (125:2).

The frequent recourse to plant imagery is remarkable given that much of Palestine is an arid dust bowl for most of the year. The person who meditates on the law is like a tree, deeply rooted and productive (1:3). The just are like the palm or cedar, flourishing and fertile even in old age (92:12-14). A family is blessed with a mother who is like a fruitful vine and children who sprout like olive shoots (128:3). The poet, trusting in God's love, is "like a green olive tree" (52:8). He or she asks for a blessing, including the wish that children "be like plants full grown" (144:12). The story of God's people is like the chronicle of a vine (80:8-16).

The poet adds vividness to a composition by using contrasting images, including primordial symbols: upwards, the heavens or the heights, and mountains, are God's residence; and the gravitational pull augurs evil and death. The metaphors of security and protection for God are extensive, as can be seen, for example, in Ps 18:1-3: rock, stronghold, refuge, fortress, strength, shield, deliverer. The stability of a person whom God steadies is set against the slippery footing of one without God. The perennial fecundity of the good is contrasted with the rootlessness of the godless. The transience of the wicked is compared with the security of the just in the land. Contrasting images of instability and stability are applied to the wicked and the just (Psalm 52); the wicked will be plucked from their tent (v. 5), while the just, like a well-watered olive tree, will stand forever (v. 8). Recurring contrasts are high and low, the abyss and the mountain, sea (or water) and the rock, the pit and firm ground, slippery mire and a steady path, entanglement (or a net) and freedom of movement, the dragon (a serpent) and a bird. Transitory images (102:3-4, 11, 23, 26) are contrasted with God's longevity (vv. 12, 24-27). Contrast is also evoked by the vocabulary. For example, the poet of Psalm 118 beautifully contrasts the sense of confinement with God's amplitude. Verse 5 is translated "Out of my distress I called on the LORD; the LORD answered me and set me in a broad place," which might be more literally rendered, "I called to the LORD from the narrow straits [*min-hammêṣar*]; the LORD answered me from the open plaza [*bammerḥāb*]."

Imagery, which is the poet's best friend, may be the reader's stumbling block. How many sensitive people pause at the expressions, "wife . . . like a fruitful vine . . . ; your children . . . like olive shoots around your table" (128:3), or "May . . . our daughters [be] like corner pillars, cut for the building of a palace" (144:12)? Another image which, if taken literally, might present difficulties for the reader: "I was born guilty, a sinner when my mother conceived me" (51:5). The curses present a wide repertoire of coarse and offensive images: "Happy shall they be who take your little ones and dash them against the rock" (137:9). But as with all poetry and every literary text, the reader may appreciate the rich cultural context out of which such images are born, yet take care against applying them literally. Imagery is always used with effect. This is not always positive, especially for today's reader separated by many leagues and centuries from the poet. But the author's intention and the sense of the poem can be appreciated and interpreted in the present context.

Repetition and Parallelism

Word and phrase repetitions are basic in Hebrew poetry. Framing or "inclusion" occurs when a literary unit begins and ends with a common element, be it a word, phrase or motif. The repetition of a word and its synonyms, sometimes according to numerical patterns (triplet, septet, decade), illustrates a point or makes an impression. What is less evident in translation is the sound and the melody of the Hebrew verse, what we know as alliteration, assonance, rhyme, and accent. These focus a composition and are used for emphasis.

The basic structural artifice of Hebrew poetry is termed parallelism, or the interrelation of two half-lines or hemistichs of poetry. James L. Kugel illustrates some of the usual ways in which the two hemistichs are related.[1] A minimal correspondence may exist between the two, as when the first part introduces a citation in the second line. Maximum correspondence is found when each term of the first hemistich is paralleled in the second.

The traditional understanding of parallelism is that it creates symmetry in a Hebrew poem. The phrases or words in two parts of a line of poetry may be balanced by synonymous parallelism, where the same

[1] James L. Kugel, *The Idea of Biblical Poetry: Parallelism and its History* (New Haven: Yale University, 1981) 4–7.

thought is repeated but with different words. An example is Ps 19:7-9, where the successive lines are arranged in a parallel sequence. Repeated six times in the same order is a synonym for law (A), an attribute (B), and its salutary effects (C): "The law of the LORD [A] is perfect [B], reviving the soul [C]." The word order in the balanced lines remains constant. The meditative effect is heightened in the two half-lines of v. 10 where the law is compared to a precious metal and to taste:

A	B	C
more desirable	than gold	even the finest gold
sweeter	than honey	even the sweetest honey

The conclusion is concise. The delicious taste of honey is not as flavorful as the law; the market value of gold fluctuates but the law is ever precious.

Synonymous parallelism is chiastic when the repeated members are inverted (in the order A + B followed by B' + A'). For example, Ps 89:30:

A	B
If his children abandon	my law
B'	**A'**
and if according to my decisions	they do not walk

This feature is often not apparent in translation.

When the second member contrasts with the first, antithetical parallelism results. For example, Ps 32:10:

> Many are the torments of the wicked,
> but steadfast love surrounds those who trust in the LORD.

Here "torments" are juxtaposed to "steadfast love" and "the wicked" are contrasted with "those who trust in the LORD."

Parallelism occurs in various ways. For example, there may be an interplay between a question and an answer, between a statement and a quotation; it may be of the form "A is better than B" (e.g., Ps 118:8-9); B may appear as a variation on A (e.g., Ps 136:2-3), or B may specify A (Ps 18:23), for example,

> I was blameless before him,
> and I kept myself from guilt.

Symmetry is created when two extremes embrace a totality, as with merism. For example, Ps 92:2:

> . . . to declare your steadfast love in the morning,
> and your faithfulness by night . . .

The extremes of morning and night embrace all time. This is a nice way of saying that one continually declares God's benefices. Parallel lines may formulate a simple comparison as in, for example, Ps 123:2:

> . . . as the eyes of a maid to the hand of her mistress,
> so our eyes look to the LORD our God.

Complete correspondence of the two parallel parts is relatively rare in Hebrew. As the basic structural pattern of Hebrew verse parallelism is quite versatile.

The alternation of and departure from parallel lines in the same composition is used with dramatic effect. This variation avoids boring repetition. But, more significantly, variations in parallel structure reinforce and illustrate the meaning of the poem. Robert Alter offers a good example from Ps 18:4-5,[2] where the "chiastic boxing in and the reversal of terms help reinforce the feeling of entrapment." The parallel lines of v. 4 are charted like this: encompassed me-the cords of death,-the torrents of perdition-assailed me (a-b-b-a). The verbs of assault, encompassed and assailed, enclose the assailing subjects, death and perdition. Verse 5 has the opposite pattern (b-a-a-b), where the two assailing subjects, Sheol and death, embrace the verbs, entangled and confronted. To reproduce this word order in English is clumsy, as can be seen here (18:4-5, redistributing the NRSV text):

> Encompassed me, the cords of death;
>   the torrents of perdition assailed me;
> the cords of Sheol entangled me;
>   confronted me, the snares of death.

The claustrophobic effect on the poet and the impression of formidable enemies are evident.

Alter identifies "elliptical syntactic parallelism" where a single verb is used for two poetic lines.[3] Ps 88:1 is translated literally:

> . . . by day I cry [in your presence],
> at night [I cry] in your presence.

This is an instance of a double-duty verb ("I cry out") as well as a double-duty preposition ("in your presence").

---

[2] Robert Alter, *The World of Biblical Literature* (New York: Basic Books, 1992) 175.
[3] Ibid., 175–76.

The dominant effect of parallel patterns is to intensify or focus images, ideas, and themes. What is initially general is specified; what is stated literally may be exaggerated in the repetition. The effect of focusing and intensification is illustrated in Ps 22:12-13:

> Many bulls encircle me,
>   strong bulls of Bashan surround me;
> they open wide their mouths at me,
>   like a ravening and roaring lion.

The bulls gradually come into focus as a herd; the lens narrows to their mouths, which resemble those of lions. The effect is terrifying. Elsewhere the psalmist pleads innocence and makes the point emphatically as, for example, in the parallel lines of Ps 139:21-22:

> Do I not hate those who hate you, O LORD?
>   And do I not loathe those who rise up against you?
> I hate them with perfect hatred;
>   I count them my enemies.

It would be enough to declare, soberly, "I hate them"; but the psalmist emphasizes the point even as he or she registers the fluctuating and intense emotion of hatred. Alter describes this as "the parallelism of intensification."[4]

Parallel lines may also represent a sense of narrative progression as the poem unfolds. The divine oracle of Ps 89:20-37 is a good example of an unfolding narrative sequence. God first "found" David, then anointed, protected, defended, accompanied, adopted him. In the end David's line receives a firm and lasting guarantee. The parallel lines add momentum to the narrative poem. The poetry of the Bible, by means of this intensifying, focusing, and narrative effect, represents a "dynamic process moving toward some culmination."[5]

Both Kugel and Alter point out that, rather than mere restatement, in most cases the second hemistich is a continuation or a specification of the first. Kugel's critique and correction of the classical schema of biblical parallelism expands the concept and its function in the poem. In fact, in relatively few instances does the second hemistich merely reproduce the first. More often, it adds to the first hemistich and thus complements it. For example, the extent that the poet experiences helplessness and nearness of death is illustrated in the complementary parallel lines of Ps 38:13-14:

---

[4] Ibid., 183.
[5] Ibid., 186.

[13] But I am like the deaf, I do not hear;
  like the mute, who cannot speak.
[14] Truly, I am like one who does not hear,
  and in whose mouth is no retort.

The result of the two hemistichs of v. 13 is a synthesis of deafness and the inability to speak, which is seconded in the repetition of v. 14. The point of Kugel's critique of the classical theory of parallelism is that more emphasis needs to be placed on the differentiation of the two parallel lines than on their synonymy. They do not represent mere repetition, but repetition with effect, which moves toward a synthesis and enhances the meaning of the poem.

After an extensive analysis of the phenomenon of parallel lines in Hebrew and Ugaritic poetry, Kugel determines that the essence of parallel lined composition in poetry is in the emphatic "seconding" character. The second line supports the first, develops it, echoes, defines, restates, completes, contrasts or surpasses it.[6] Parallel lines connect two separate statements and a synthesis is created.

Another aspect of repetition in Hebrew poetry is concentric symmetry, which occurs when two sequences are reversed around a single center (A-B-C-B'-A'). For example, the structure of Psalm 122 is concentric:

A the poet and companions pilgrimage toward God's house (vv. 1-2)

  B the city is the goal of the pilgrimage (vv. 3-4)

    C the thrones of judgment and David are found there (v. 5)

  B' prayer for the peace of Jerusalem, the city (vv. 6-7)

A' the poet and friends find peace in God's house (vv. 8-9)

In the present commentary special mention will be made of the repetition of words, images, and their contrasts, which are often couched in parallel structures.

Numerical sequences are another feature of Hebrew composition. A poem or text may be organized with a determined repetition of a word and its synonyms. Attention is often called to the use of the number seven and septenary patterns. Seven and its multiples signify wholeness. The fact that the name LORD occurs seven or fourteen times in a poem indicates that God is fully invoked or present, even when the

---

[6] Kugel, *Idea*, 51–52.

poet complains of the opposite. The appearance of numerical repetitions may not be noticeable, especially in translation. For example, the sevenfold use of the rare negative particle *bāl*, which bridges Psalms 16–17, argues for the deliberate juxtaposition of these two in the redaction of the Psalter. This is an arcane usage. On the other hand, the sevenfold repetition of the "voice of the LORD" in Psalm 29 is evident even in translation. The number four is also significant in the composition, as are three and ten. In addition to being a natural outcome of the composition of parallel lines, four suggests completeness; three and ten also point to a totality.

The Psalms in Context and Sequence

The Psalter begins with a wisdom psalm which blesses those who delight in the *tôrâh*. The believer may choose between the road which ends abruptly or the path of the *tôrâh* which leads to beatitude and endless praise. Although the structure and meter of Psalm 1 is different from Psalm 2, these form two different movements of a single introduction: the choice between two paths and the forecast of the final defeat of God's enemies. Furthermore, the first three books (Psalms 1–89) take their cue from two royal psalms (Psalms 2 and 89) which serve as book ends.[7] Book Four (Psalms 90–106) celebrates God's sovereignty with "the LORD is king" psalms (Psalms 93, 96–99). Psalm 110, a royal psalm, corresponds to Psalm 2; both speak of the universal king whom God appointed. The *hallelujah* psalms (Psalms 111–118) follow, which are brought to a close by Psalm 119, a meditation on the *tôrâh*. Thus, two *tôrâh* psalms frame the bulk of the Psalter (Psalms 1–119). Other segments follow, the Songs of Ascent (Psalms 120–134), a collection "Of David" (grouped by the caption, Psalms 138–145), and two series of *hallelujah* psalms (Psalms 135–136, 146–150). In this arrangement, one large collection (Psalms 1–118) and two smaller ones (Psalms 120–136; 138–150) end with *hallelujah* psalms, and Psalm 119 holds a special place. The following chart offers a synthetic view:

---

[7] Key psalms (41, 72, 89) were placed at major seams in the final edition of the Psalter. The strategic placement of the royal Psalm 72 in a corpus of mostly individual complaints (Psalms 51–72) transposes the private collection to the public domain. This is suggested also by the doxology in 72:18-20.

A View of the Psalter

Key psalms in the redaction of the Psalter	Books	Collections according to caption, theme or refrain	Doxology
	Pss 1–41		
Ps 1, *tôrâh* psalm			
Ps 2, royal psalm		Pss 3–41, mostly individual complaints	Ps 41:14
	Pss 42–72	Pss 51–71, mostly individual complaints	Ps 72:18-20
		Pss 42–83, preference for *ĕlōhîm*	
Ps 72, royal psalm			
	Pss 73–89	Pss 74–89, mostly communal complaints	
		Pss 73–83, "Of Asaph" collection	
		Pss 84–85,-87–88, "Sons of Korah" collection Ps 89:52	
Ps 89, royal psalm			
	Pss 90–106	Pss 93, 96-99, the LORD is sovereign	Ps 106:48
	Pss 107–150		
Ps 110, royal psalm		Pss 111–118, *hallelujah* psalms	
Ps 119, *tôrâh* psalm		Pss 120–134, Songs of ascent	
		Pss 135–136, *hallelujah* psalms	
		Pss 138–145, "Of David" collection; mostly individual complaints	
		Pss 146–150, *hallelujah* psalms	Ps 150

(This appreciation of the arrangement of the Psalter is complemented by Appendix Two on *The Prehistory of the Psalter*.)

From the captions, doxologies, and themes, one can distinguish collections of psalms.[8] In addition, the relation between consecutive psalms can be noted on the basis of characteristic vocabulary, style, and theme. The recurrence of connecting words and catch phrases may be the basis of the sequence (e.g., the images of strength attributed to God in Psalms 61 and 62). The concurrence of historical themes or different stages in a ritual may be why one psalm succeeds another. For example, what began as a complaint culminates in praise; or, in a legal procedure, Psalm 50 is the arraignment and Psalm 51 the confession of guilt.

The jerky, uneven text of some psalms leaves the impression that what were originally independent poems were fused into one. The best examples are Psalms 19 and 27. Psalm 19 is the composite of a nature hymn (vv. 1-6) and a eulogy of the law (vv. 7-10); these two may have been subsequently joined. Psalm 27 seems to be two poems patched together (vv. 1-6 and vv. 7-14). Conversely, a composition may have been

---

[8] Gerald H. Wilson, *The Editing of the Hebrew Psalter,* SBLDS 76 (Chico, CA: Scholars Press, 1985) 190–97, looks at thematic positioning of psalms (Psalms 65–68; 93 and 96–99; 105–106; 145–150) and groups the sequences on the basis of similar beginnings (Psalms 103–104; 105–106–107) and catch phrases (e.g., Psalms 7–8–9 or Psalms 32–33).

divided in two; e.g., Psalms 9 and 10; Psalms 42 and 43. Hebrew Psalms 116 and 147 are split in the LXX.

Consecutive psalms may be paired on the basis of theme or vocabulary. For example, Psalms 3 and 4 are both appropriate as night prayers, with references to lying down and sleeping (3:5; 4:8). Or, on the contrary, disjunction between two psalms may have played a part in their juxtaposition. Psalms 22 and 23 represent opposite experiences of God. Ps 22:1 begins, "My God, my God, why have you forsaken me?" and Ps 23:1, "The LORD is my shepherd, I shall not want" and continues "I fear no evil; for you are with me" (v. 4). Psalm 23 is the natural response to the exultant tone at the end of Psalm 22.

Although consecutive psalms may derive from different historical backgrounds and in many instances represent distinct concerns, a relationship exists between them. In the following commentary particular note will be made of paired and triplet psalm sequences, their verbal, thematic, and stylistic relation, and how the sense of one psalm complements its neighbor.

In summary, the evidence is scant that the positioning of consecutive psalms in the Psalter has a discernible logic. But words and catch phrases do connect many psalms, and some are grouped by numerical sequences, framed by repetitions, or appear as two movements of a process. Just as the superscriptions indicate psalm groupings (e.g., the Asaph or Korah guild psalms, the Hallel sections), so at some editorial stage many psalms were grouped together in the Psalter. A septenary pattern of words bridging two psalms indicates an editor's hand. Psalms which share a common theme or genre were grouped, and in a few cases psalms of similar theme and length appear together. The final forms of the Hebrew and Greek versions resulted from ongoing use and editorial activity on the entire collection.

Shifting Address and Modes of Discourse

Shifts of address, alternating speech to and about a person, are familiar in dramatic compositions. One can view a drama and appreciate the developing plot and character enhanced by the interchange of actors, the dialectic of problem and solution. One may read a play aloud and imagine the unfolding tension and resolution. The appreciation is aided by directional cues, which indicate changes of scene, tone, and time. Analogously, dramatic changes of mood and personal address are not infrequent in the psalms and in the liturgy.

   Shift of address occurs when in consecutive lines God is spoken about and addressed, when the enemy is alternately objectified and addressed, when an individual complains to God and suddenly rallies the community to hope. This feature may take any of various forms. The concluding apostrophe of Psalm 3, "may your blessing be on your people!" (v. 8) is one (cf. 31:21; 84:1; 93:5). Toward the end of Psalm 6 the poet addresses the wicked, "Depart from me, all you workers of evil." The last line of Psalm 97 addresses the just. The poet of Psalm 58 initially addresses the rulers, then writes about them. In such psalms the address shifts quite suddenly, leaving the reader to distinguish who is speaking, to and about whom. In the Hebrew no punctuation signals the change, and the benefits of paragraph indications, quotation marks, or even the telltale "thus says the Lord" are nonexistent. An apt example is the first strophe of Psalm 42 in which the poet alternately addresses God (v. 1), poses a question about God (v. 2), narrates the action and quotes the enemy (vv. 3-4), soliloquizes in questioning tones and exhorts the soul (v. 5): "Why are you cast down, O my soul, and why are you disquieted within me? Hope in God. . . ." Brief Psalm 24 shifts from narration (vv. 1-2), to question (v. 3), answer and assurance (vv. 4-6), invocation addressing the "gates" (vv. 7 and 9), and again to question and response (vv. 8 and 10).

   Shifts between third and second person discourse are frequent. Psalm 93:1, 4 speak about God (third person); vv. 2-3, 5 and address him (second person). The alternating voices of soloist and chorus in the liturgy can be heard. In Psalm 18 the poet addresses God (vv. 1-2) then narrates the trial, speaking about him (vv. 3-14). This is momentarily interrupted when the poet addresses God, "at your rebuke, O LORD, at the blast of the breath of your nostrils" (v. 15). This shift in person is evident in Hebrew; vv. 16-24, 28b, 29b-34, 46-48a, 50 speak in the third person about God and vv. 25-28a, 29a, 35-45, 48b-49 address him.[9] Although these shifts may jar the worshiper, they enhance the dramatic effect. Such changes of person where God speaks, is addressed, and spoken about are frequent in liturgical texts as well as in the prophetic writings.

   The shift from singular to plural can be equally startling. Psalm 31 laments personal affliction, as the poet urgently calls on God for rescue. The voice of the persecuted invalid undulates with pain, to the point that he or she feels abandoned: "I am the scorn of all my adversaries, a horror to my neighbors, an object of dread to my acquaintances" (v. 11). Then the prolonged anguish opens to a consideration of God's

   [9] This movement between the second and third person is not always reproduced in translation.

benefits "for those who fear you" (v. 19). As the poet celebrates rescue and relief, he or she addresses the community, "Be strong, and let your heart take courage" (v. 24), which was born of what began as an intensely personal drama.

Psalm 102 is entitled "A prayer of one afflicted, when faint and pleading before the LORD," and indeed much of it unfurls the personal complaint and confession (vv. 1-11). However, the mood changes (vv. 12-13), and the poet expresses confidence in God and ensures that Zion will be visited by God's mercy, that nations and rulers will turn to him (v. 15). It is as if the individual complaint embodied and gave voice to the national crisis. After the reassuring words about Zion (vv. 12-22) the poet resumes the impassioned prayer, speaking alternately about and to God, recalling the misery, comparing the brevity of life with God's longevity, and requesting long life for God's servants (vv. 23-28).

Another shift is the poet's disposition. Shifts in modes of discourse and mood occur with dramatic effect in Psalm 94. A recital of wicked acts culminates in the declaration, "The LORD does not see; the God of Jacob does not perceive" (v. 7), after which the psalmist, pushed to the brink of frustration, apostrophizes to the wicked, "Understand, O dullest of the people; fools, when will you be wise?" After a declaration of God's omniscience, the poet eulogizes, "Happy are those whom you discipline, O LORD, and whom you teach out of your law" (v. 12). In Psalm 20 the leader is apparently praying before a crisis, asking for divine aid (vv. 1-5); he or she then expresses the assurance of help (vv. 6-8). The final verse addresses God directly (v. 9). Something intervened to effect the mood change between vv. 5 and 6, possibly a prophetic oracle ensuring God's assistance, like the promises formulated in similar psalms (for example, 12:5; 21:8-12).

The reader gets the impression that a stage is missing, notably an assurance or divine oracle which answers the complaint. God's oracle can be explicit (60:6-8; 81:6-16), indirect (62:11; 85:8), or tacit, as in the example above, Psalm 20. In some instances, the poet declares that God has answered, or will do so (6:9; 28:6; 86:7). More often the brusque transition from complaint to assurance has no apparent cause (54:4; 64:7). Psalm 31 is a fine example. The poet pours out the venomous prayer, "Let the lying lips be stilled that speak insolently against the righteous with pride and contempt" (v. 18), after which he or she shifts to a eulogy, "O how abundant is your goodness that you have laid up for those who fear you" (v. 19). From an overwhelming sense of evil (vv. 1-18) the psalmist turns to thank God and encourage the community (vv. 19-24). The intervening oracle is missing.

Shifts in address and, more often, shifts in mood signal a change of theme, as from problem to resolution or from complaint to rejoicing. A description of an enemy siege or personal quandary which suddenly changes to an imperative "help," addressed to God, shifts toward solution. Psalms which have such a feature are likely to have other pivots, like the shift from indicative to imperative, the presence of an exclamation, or the change in person.

The shortest psalm may serve as the clearest example. Psalm 117 opens with two invitations to praise (v. 1), followed by two declarations of the motive (v. 2), introduced by *kî*, "for," the pivotal word. Or again, Psalm 20 may be divided into strophes of equal length, turning on the *ʿattāh*, "now" (v. 6), the central pivot. The repeated request for divine assistance (vv. 1-5) is absent from the second movement. Another example is the center of Psalm 23 where the psalmist declares "for you are with me" (emphatic "you," *kî-ʾattāh*, v. 4). This apostrophe thematically links the two images, the shepherd and the host. The divine presence is in the foreground of the extended metaphors, is named (LORD, vv. 1 and 6, an inclusion), and addressed with the pronoun (v. 4, the central pivot).

In some compositions a numerical pattern of repetitions spotlights a pivot, although this is often not evident in the translation. For example, in Psalm 92 the exclamatory address "but you, O LORD, are on high forever" (v. 8) is central in the poem. The name LORD appears seven times (a plenary motif), this being the fourth. Another example is the beatitude "Happy are those whom you discipline, O LORD," which is introduced by *ʾašrēy*, "Happy"; this is the central pivot of Psalm 94 (v. 12). It is further marked by eight direct references to the LORD or God in each half (vv. 1-11 and vv. 12-23). Psalm 22 also exhibits such a shift, marked by an emphatic pronoun and a mood change. The poet recounts the terrible distress (vv. 1-2, 6-8, 12-18), slightly relieved by recalling God's care on one's behalf or calling on God (vv. 9-11). Following the emphatic "But you," *wĕʾattâh* (v. 19), the discourse represents the union of God with the poet, with repercussions in the community. The sum of the appearances of the divine name (five) plus "your name" (v. 22) and *ʾădōnāy*, "the Lord" (v. 30), is seven in the latter half.

If we consider the psalms as liturgical texts, these sudden changes of discourse and mood are not so surprising. In the liturgy, shifts of address and modes of discourse are natural and necessary, as, for example, in the interchange between the various participants. In the offertory of the Roman Catholic mass, an interchange between the celebrant and the congregation ("The Lord be with you. And also with you," etc.) introduces a prayer addressed to God (the Preface), followed by congregational acclaim (the *Sanctus*), where God is spoken about. Similar shifts in address and modes of discourse are present in the penitential rite which culminates in the hymn of Glory to God.

Dynamic changes in discourse in the Roman Catholic and Eastern liturgies as well as in the Jewish ritual are analogous to the shifts in address and modes of discourse in the psalms. In the recitation of these texts today, confusion arises when the various parts of the liturgical drama are neither specified nor known, and the worshiper is left with the problem of interpretation even as he or she is praying with a text.

Confusion may occur around the use of the word "I." Does the personal pronoun indicate that a psalm was a personal prayer? The response must take account of the liturgical setting of the psalms. It would be as short sighted to understand every "I" as the community as it would be hasty to understand each one as an individual. The "I" could well manifest the strictly personal composition which, eventually, was accepted into the liturgical patrimony of Israel. In the ascription "Of David" to many psalms in the first two-thirds of the Psalter, the intent may have been to understand a text which appears to be intensely personal as a community prayer, presided over by the king or priest, David, who represents and in a sense embodies the people.

A School of Prayer

The psalms are reflected experience. Their cadences, words, and imagery reproduce the movements of the human spirit as it relates to God and thus make the experience accessible. The appreciation of the psalms may be aesthetic, the pure enjoyment of literature, or the reader's own experience may be analogous to the poet's, in which case sympathy is discovered between the two, and in their interaction a personal transformation may occur.

In the Psalter a believing poet speaks to God about God. Across the centuries worshiping communities and individuals have adopted this book to express their own faith and devotion. The poet's sentiments are intense, painful at times, as when he or she prays for revenge, in which case the violence may impress the *orante*, the devout person who prays them, as insensitive and indecent. The poems do not articulate theology, and the doctrinal hollows in the psalmist's faith are striking, especially when one looks for the expression of faith in eternal life. But the psalmist's original contribution is in the quality of poetry and prayer. The psalms open a door to the spiritual life of a believing community where both the poet and the *orante* find a home. Both are searchers. Each helps the other arrive at the richest meaning from the prayer. The poet provides the words and images, and the *orante* infuses them with new meaning and, in the case of the Christian, baptizes them in the experience of Christ. To appreciate the psalms is to understand them as the poetic expression of a religious experience, preserved by a worshiping faith community which extends to the present.

God takes the initiative in other books of the Bible, which give a slant on the history of God with people to effect salvation. But a unique value of the psalms is the way they record the human response to God. A friendship with God inspires the poet, who reaches out for the divine presence in the psalms, which in turn are adopted by later generations. Thus, the psalms chronicle the changing moods that condition men and women who seek God. They have always found meaning and were preserved in a communal setting where they were chanted and prayed. Through these inspired prayers God teaches the believer how to pray.

Each psalm can be understood and appreciated in context, and there are several. The first is the Hebrew poet's culture and experience. Today's reader may plumb this context by study. Another one has been applied to a number of psalms by the addition of a caption. The title of Psalm 59, "Of David. A Miktam, when Saul ordered his house to be watched in order to kill him," was added late, and it ascribes a setting to the psalm. Such a title draws the reader out of him or herself and suggests an analogous setting which can be adopted in prayer.

A third context emerges in the contemporary reader's experience. As he or she interacts with the text, its expressions may be transposed to the present and adopted to express his or her sentiments. The reader and the poet share the garden plot of human experience. Initially their experiences are not identical, but an analogy is forged between the two, and an ancient community which celebrated and preserved the poems as part of their liturgy offers them to the community of faith in which the *orante* is a participant.

An analogy illustrates the communion between the Hebrew poet and later generations who adopt the psalms as prayer, the contexts of poet and *orante*. An actress studies her role in order to duplicate another person, reincarnate another character on stage. She does more than mimic and memorize. She places her own voice, gestures, and actions at the service of her part. She mobilizes talents of imagination and concentration to embody the role, with all the strong and subtle, tender and violent emotions of her character. On stage the actress aims for a credible replica.

This happens when an individual prays the psalms. One aim of studying and praying them is to give them a home in the reader's context. In the process a person might use them to understand and articulate one's own experience. A desired effect: that the psalms become a catalyst to draw the reader out of the limited experience of the self and provide new possibilities for expression. The *orante* in search of a deeper religious experience adopts the psalms and thus allows them to guide him or her in recreating the experience. A transaction takes place where the ancient expressions become contemporary. The poet's sentiment is translated into the heart of the *orante*, and, ultimately, the poet's religious experience becomes vicarious. The effect is a happy one; the devout heart is deepened and horizons broadened to greater spiritual insight. And so a life today becomes richer than before one read and prayed the Psalter. This dynamic is termed transference.

It can occur in various ways. On one level a person has a powerful experience and then selects an appropriate psalm to articulate it, like the lover who selects a poem to express the emotion for which he or she does not have the words. The Psalter provides a repertoire of human sentiments and experiences with which we can match our own. A deeper level of transference occurs when the believer lets the psalm actually mediate the vicarious experience. On this level the Spirit who inspired the psalms effects a like condition in the *orante*. This transference occurs through symbol, which is the point of contact between two worlds.

The Psalter is packed with symbols which make the poet's experience accessible: narrowness or the sensation of being cramped, ups and downs, enemies and trying days, the sense of the loss of God or the failing of self. To arrive at a symbol, a poet abstracted from the particular experience, sacrificed what was personal, and translated it into an image or sign. Comprehension rests on the ability to crack the code, to comprehend the symbol and sympathize with the human condition logged in the psalm. Without the symbol, the passport to shared experience, and sympathy, the mode of transport, comprehension of poetry would be impossible. Transference presupposes a willingness and ability to allow the symbols their full value as they enter into commerce with the reader, who appropriates the poet's reflected experience insofar as he or she is open to the incentive of the symbol. As transference takes place, the horizons of the *orante* are expanded.

Every day in the human family people find that the deep sentiments of the psalms apply to their situation. Death's menace is no stranger, and its allies come in manifold forms: loneliness, political enemies, unfairness, sickness, depression, advanced years, fear. The psalms provide a panorama of the suffering all people undergo, even though one may feel chronically alone in the midst of one's own difficulties. The drama which the psalm lyrics play out is true to life when one considers the human condition yesterday and today.

The psalms touch the *orante* in their expression of joy, gratitude, desolation, alienation from God, hope. The poet at times wonders whether God's existence makes any difference, so empty is his or her experience. Similarly, these poems join people across the millennia in their articulation of awe; for what human at some time in his or her life does not pause, rather, is not awestruck at the mystery of the world, God, the human condition, or evil. The psalms may initially record personal experiences, awe, or desperation, but their expression flows easily into the community's typical experience. Psalm 8 is an apt example. I look up at the night sky, am struck by its magnificence and am captivated by the relation of the human to such a grand universe. Yet I exclaim as though I were not alone, "O LORD, *our* Sovereign." Awe is translated into a choral exclamation as a person discovers that he or she is neither the first nor the only. Then, turning within, the person questions, who am I? What is this mortal creature, that God should even think of him or her? It is amazing that God has appointed someone so fragile as caretaker of this grand environment.

Psalm 77 is another apt example, where the psalmist (singular, "I") poses the hard question, which unfolds into a reminiscence of God's mighty deeds on the people's behalf (vv. 7-9);

> Will the Lord spurn forever,
>   and never again be favorable?
> Has his steadfast love ceased forever?
>   Are his promises at an end for all time?
> Has God forgotten to be gracious?
>   Has he in anger shut up his compassion?

This questioning, so full of pathos, introduces a reflection on the celebrated moments of history (vv. 12-20). The supposition is that God can revisit the course of history and thus reinstate the community in their privileged status as God's people.

In the appreciation of a psalm, one asks whose voice is speaking. It is possible to distinguish between the "I" of the poet and the "I" of the poem, although at times these two coincide. The poet of Psalm 38 may have been enjoying health and prosperity, but he or she complains of a sense of guilt, physical and spiritual affliction, social disgrace. The voice may be that of David, a representative of the people, a sick person, a sage, or an innocent person who has been unfairly accused. Appreciation is enhanced by asking the questions, who is speaking? who is addressed? who is spoken about? who are the actors in the dialogue?

When we appropriate a psalm, we adopt the poet's stance yet bring our own personality to the poem. We can pray in our own name, in the name of our people, of a sister or brother persecuted or afflicted. In any case, we impress the psalm with our voice, the waves of our emotion.

At the same time its poetry informs and forms our person. For example, I enter Psalm 130 with

> Out of the depths I cry to you, O LORD;
> Lord, hear my voice!

I stand with the poet in the depths, crying for help. The psalm continues with a confession, and thus I articulate my guilt. The poet professes faith in God, who forgives iniquity, and sighs,

> my soul waits for the Lord
> more than those who watch for the morning.

Following the poet's lead, I profess the faith to which he or she ascends. In conclusion, I expand the human context and address the community,

> O Israel, hope in the LORD!
> For with the LORD there is steadfast love,
> and with him is great power to redeem.

In this transaction I may adopt the psalm's words for myself, or I may pray them for someone else in the human or faith community.

As in the case of the actress whose role places demands on her, the psalm makes demands on the *orante* for such a transaction to take place. A dialogue is created where two horizons approach each other, and the *orante* communes with the reflected experience of another. As the actress reincarnates her role, the *orante* can enter into and reenact the text. Excepting the interests of historical critical exegesis, which aims to eliminate the examiner's subjectivity, impersonal abstraction from these texts is a disservice to them. In the appreciation of religious poetry, it is important not so much to eliminate the examiner as for him or her to adapt to the poem and thereby transcend the limitations of the intellect in order to arrive at comprehension, insight, and prayer. The lover of poetry disposes him or herself to the initiative of the text, opens the door to its spirit. The *orante* captures the experience inasmuch as it invades him or her intellectually, emotionally, and spiritually. Appreciation grows at the same rate as personal involvement, and in this way the meaning the psalm bears for one's life expresses itself in prayer and is manifested in virtue.

This transaction is not just subjective, which would restrict the appreciation of the text to private devotion. The psalms were preserved because they were meaningful for the faith community. Thus, transference happens preeminently when an individual prays the liturgy. A psalm prayed on Friday, e.g., Psalms 22, 56, 51 or 62, eloquently places in the Christian's heart a prayer fitting for Jesus at the hour of his passion and death. Thus, to receive full personal and spiritual benefit in praying these poems, there is an intermingling of contexts: that of the Israelite poet, the *orante* who gives voice to this experience today, Jesus in his prayer to the Father, and the Church, in her struggle on earth to join the Father in heaven. Similarly, such a psalm may be prayed in any age by the Synagogue as she struggles to understand the plight of human suffering and alienation and welcomes God's interest and intervention. The Psalter shapes the lives of the faithful, deepens the believer's experience and comprehension, and offers a communal context for their appropriation.

What is taught about prayer in the Psalter? Some psalms refer to historical events of the Hebrew people, the crossing of the Red Sea and the entrance into the Promised Land. Others describe personal dramas, like conversion, betrayal, or personal weakness. The *orante* requests relief, prays for deliverance from aggressors, grapples with the mystery of suffering and affliction. Thus, the complaint is the expression of one who, conscious of his or her own misery, the sufferings of loved ones, and the suffering of the world, entrusts them to God. Such a prayer is purifying. It relieves the sufferer, transforms the *orante*, and transposes the pain into prayer.

The prayer may express praise, which lets go, relinquishes oneself to what is beyond the self. For example, the cadences of Ps 147:1-5 invade the *orante* and draw him or her out of the self,

> How good it is to sing praises to our God;
>   for he is gracious, and a song of praise is fitting.
> The LORD builds up Jerusalem;
>   he gathers the outcasts of Israel. . . .
> Great is our Lord, and abundant in power;
>   his understanding is beyond measure.

Praise does not pursue any objective except the inclination to let loose in praise. It expresses the handing over of the self, the liberation from self, and it is gratuitous. The Psalter ends with Psalm 150, wherein adoration reaches great heights and the self is eliminated as the poet and the created world are joined in the symphony of praise. The praises manifest the sensitivity of the poet, the ancient Hebrews, and their capacity to grasp, in harmony with creation, the powerful and delicate hand of God the creator.

Every human is marked for death from the time of his or her birth, and death's cancer infects the depth of one's being in an inexplicable way. The poet's cry to God, "Remember how short my time is—for what vanity you have created all mortals!" echoes in the human soul (89:47; cf. Pss 39:4-6; 62:9; 90:9-10; 144:3-4). With such expressions the psalms sound the human depths, survey their precarious reality and the threat of each day. The psalmist's tone may differ from the way people today express their concerns to God. But such sighs are not completely foreign. We hear expressions like "I'm dead tired" or ". . . sick to death," which express the same sort of exhaustion or despondency. Whether or not our misfortunes reach the same proportion as the poet's, they do find a resonance in these prayers.

How many people go to the theater or the movies, watch a drama on television or scan the Internet, and there contact misfortunes more terrible than those which face them? Are people attracted on some level by a deeper reality, which is preserved only invisibly in the soul's restless reaches? Such hidden realities exercise a fascination for people of all times, and the psalms project as vivid a panorama as any.

The psalms give ample room for trial. The roots of the poet's suffering intertwine with the roots of distress in the community of faith. The communal nature of these prayers is crucial for their understanding. They express the sentiments with which people almost instinctively pray for others. The psalms traverse the continents and mediate intercession for those who suffer, transposing the chronic condition of suffering to the person of the *orante*. Every time a person recites the complaints, he or she vicariously becomes one who faces injustice, who hungers, is sick and frightened. It is as if God does not narrow the focus to one particular case, but sees the whole drama of humanity, yesterday and today. The psalms open our ears, eyes, and hearts to human cries beyond us. Insofar as we accept this way of reciting them, the cry of the oppressed invades our space, occupies our prayer, and grounds our daily troubles in the misfortune of humanity. The prison, hospital, war zone, and slum invades our synagogue, church, or meditation and there is an exchange. Those for whom we pray, whose voice becomes ours, enlarge our hearts and transform us by their suffering. To pray and to say "I" in place of the persons who are most tested is an invitation to sympathize with them.

Successive generations adopt the psalms preeminently in the liturgy and devotional prayer. A Jew praying them places him or herself in the sandals of David, of the prophets and sages of the Hebrew Scriptures. Jesus appropriated the psalms for liturgical and personal prayer, and thus opened a new chapter in their appreciation as prayer. A Christian's prayer passes through the event and experience of Jesus. God hears the lament of the Jewish people or the cry Jesus offered in the face of injustice and death. Anyone who prays the psalms does so in the first person, yet as a representative voice of many, past and present, who relate to God.

The psalmist does not plead innocent. But even while confessing guilt he or she requests mercy, basing the claim on God's covenant loyalty with the people. The psalmist prays for health, deliverance, length of days. He or she expresses the basest of human passions, particularly in the thirst for vengeance. But rather than retaliating personally, the poet prays that the unjust aggressors might slip and get a just reward; that they get caught in their own snares. This opens another theme in the treatment of the Psalter, that of the enemy, death, and the related theme of violence as it is expressed in prayer.

Disease, Death, and the Enemy [10]

The psalmist presents a struggle between life and death. The symptoms of bodily affliction map the arena where the contest is waged under God's interested gaze. The poet complains of sickness and failing energies, and, given the passage of time and the foreign climate, the interpreter can do little more than list the symptoms and diagnose an underlying attitude towards illness.

Fever, loss of vision, and physical weakness are three such symptoms. References to thirst and dryness are associated with fever: the throat is parched as a potsherd; the tongue sticks to the palate (22:15; 69:3); the loins burn, the flesh is afflicted (38:7); the "bones burn like a furnace" (102:3). In sum, the individual is reduced to a hot desert-like state. The poet suffers eye trouble (6:7; 31:9; 38:10; 40:12; 69:3; 88:9); to have keen eyesight is to possess integrity of life, but impaired vision is like a plunge toward chaos. To make the contrast more explicit, God's enemy is in darkness (11:2; 82:5; 107:10-11; 143:3; cf. 23:4; 35:6; 44:19; 88:6, 10, 12, 18). The "bones" (ʿeṣem, variously translated), synonymous with "strength" or the ability to stand erect, recurs in the range of symptoms. A person is afflicted with weak bones. That the poet's "bones waste away" means the energies are depleted. Parallel lines demonstrate this (31:10):

> my strength fails because of my misery,
>   and my bones waste away.

---

[10] My debt to Paul Beauchamp, *Psaumes nuit et jour* (Paris: Éditions du Seuil, 1980), especially chapters 6–10, is evident in the following.

A similar complaint is imaged in the body wasting away, strength withering (32:3-4) or trembling bones (6:2). The compound symptoms in 38:6-10 include physical prostration, depression, fever, loss of vision, failing strength.

Rather than isolate a sickness, the poet stamps the impression of death's assault, so often couched in images. The physiological complaints—loss of appetite and sudden weight loss (102:4-5), insomnia (77:4, 6; 102:7), uncontrolled weeping and depression (6:6-7; 31:9-10; 69:3; 102:9)—are diagnosed as related to and imaging a critical spiritual state. As the life forces diminish, the poet complains that death is attacking. While a medical examiner may diagnose a benign tumor or an acute depression, the infirm poet complains (88:3-5),

> For my soul is full of troubles,
> and my life draws near to Sheol.
> I am counted among those who go down to the Pit;
> I am like those who have no help,
> like those forsaken among the dead,
> like the slain that lie in the grave. . . .

In these groans the last energy reserves are tapped, as the poet prays for a return to life and communion with God. The spiritual aspect of life is manifest in what he or she requests—reinstatement in the community, physical well-being, fairness in God's dealings, and prosperity.

The poet, drained of physical and spiritual energies, is socially stigmatized and rejected. A recurring complaint is the distancing of friends, family, and neighbors (31:11; 38:11; 41:9; 55:13-14; 69:8; 88:18). The memory of God's favors aggravates the pain as he or she likens himself to a worm, despised by people (22:4-6); neighbors' scorn 'increases the pain (vv. 7-8). The physical and psychological condition in Ps 102:3-11 includes both bodily ailments and social disgrace; the enemies use the poet's name as a curse (v. 8). Quarantine is not recommended for most illnesses today, because such isolation can be frankly depressing and delay the patient's recovery. But where we place afflictions in separate categories—one is either a social outcast, an accused, someone who is either acutely or terminally ill—the psalmist envisions all ills as interrelated. The criminal facing trial is like an invalid, and vice versa, and both are ostracized. This is illustrated in the eloquent, surrealistic tableau of Psalm 22 which is full of such images as the ambush of wild beasts tearing away at the flesh, a heart melting like wax, a throat dry as baked clay, the vicious crowd anticipating death by dividing the personal effects of the afflicted. The description evokes the most dire of physical weaknesses and social disgraces. The concurrence of all afflictions causes one to wonder whether God has rejected the poet, who pleads to be reinstated in the community.

Elsewhere the poet prays, "Be gracious to me, O LORD, for I am languishing; O LORD, heal me, for my bones are shaking with terror" (6:2). This invalid envisages the day when God, hearing the plea, will vindicate him or her against the enemies (v. 9). Or again, the poet suffers complications—eyes, "soul" (or throat, *nepeš*), "body" (or intestines, *beṭen*), life, strength, bones—while bystanders shun, fault, and plot his or her death (31:9-10, 13). In the description of an illness with multiple complications, the invalid complains that friends keep their distance, while oppressors plot against his or her life (38:5-12). Not only enemies condemn, but "Even my bosom friend in whom I trusted, who ate of my bread, has lifted the heel against me" (41:9). An insomniac who can no longer eat, reduced to skin and bones, is badgered by the enemies' taunts (102:3-5, 7-8).

Is this surprising? In business, under the stress of bosses' demands and the chafe of the competitor, people get sick. In a classroom where students are motivated more by the evaluative process than learning, sickness and the blues pay their visits. In a penitentiary criminals awaiting trial are prone to illness and depression. How many health-care facilities house patients who feel rejected or merely tolerated by society, even family and friends? The mere perception of scorn can cause sickness. Insidious, malignant is the power of rejection or hatred. And, true to the cultural milieu, the psalmist lumps all assaults of evil, including physical illness, under the category of death's inner workings. The psalms preserve a frank groan before God in the face of death's advances. The unbridled complaints confide one's misery to someone who is supposed to care.

Death and Sheol, the realm of the dead, are synonymous in the Psalter, and both assault and entangle the realm of life. Death, disguised as sorrow, sickness, sin, and defeat, encroaches on the living. The poet denounces these assailants as death's accomplices (55:4-5): "My heart is in anguish within me, the terrors of death have fallen upon me. Fear and trembling come upon me, and horror overwhelms me." He or she speaks of divine help as relief from grief, rescue from death, escape from its grasp, healing. The poet will thank God, "For you have delivered my soul from death, and my feet from falling, so that I may walk before God in the light of life" (56:13; see 30:1-3; 33:19; 49:14-15; 86:13).

The Hebrew poet is interested in life and its immediate future, not life after death. Sheol, existence without any loving contact with God, was thought of as non-life. The point is not that the dead escape God's all-encompassing greatness, but that the relationship the good might enjoy with God during life is annulled. Thus Sheol is a metaphor for any distress. On the contrary, release from Sheol means deliverance (30:3). Psalm 31:7-8 portrays a contrast between the narrow space, the affliction, of one who is assaulted by evil and the "broad place" reserved for one who has been rescued. The request becomes poignant when the consequences are considered, "for if you are silent to me, I shall be like those who go down to the Pit" (28:1; cf. 88:3-6; 143:7). The psalmist's descent bears consequences for the creator. God's love does not reach the dead, nor are thanksgiving songs heard in Sheol. Physical death and the underworld are images of final helplessness with regard to God. "The dead do not praise the LORD, nor do any that go down into silence" (115:17). The death of the faithful is "[p]recious in the sight of the LORD" (116:15), because when they die their praise is muted and their testimony to God among the living is lost (6:5; 30:9; 88:10-12).

The affinity between the wicked and death is evident from the phrase "their throats are open graves" (5:9). Typically the poet is the victim of social afflictions, the object of violence. He or she identifies the assailants and recounts their attacks. Mockery, gossip, and murmuring (22:17; 35:15-16; 41:5-7; 69:12; 70:3; 73:8-9)—inimical forces ranged against the poet and God—are all too close. Evil has a plan, and a physiognomy, but even more terrifying is its psychological grip on the soul. Appearances tell that the wicked are stronger than the just (18:17-18; 73:3-4; 142:6). The plots, conspiracies, the ambush, and intrigue are prepared secretly (10:7-10; 31:13; 36:4; 52:2; 56:5-6; 59:1-3; 83:5). The assault terrorizes the good and drains the poet's energies (13:3).

Some biblical metaphors for evil are constant throughout the Psalter. An image for radical evil which stretches over all creation and history is the flood or chaos, the sea which swallows and kills. The advance of deadly forces is likened to a raging storm (55:8) or rising floods where there is no foothold and drowning is imminent or threatening (18:4-5; 32:6; 40:2; 42:7; 69:1-2, 14-15; 88:7, 17; 144:7). Behind the image of the dragon is the power of the sea that wants to gulp down the earth (104:9). The symbol shows how evil encompasses everything, how it engulfs the cosmos. It hits like vertigo on the edge of a precipice (61:2). The descent into Sheol or the Pit is a typical image of the gravitational pull felt by the distressed poet (30:3; cf. 71:20; 130:1). The consequence of God's protracted aloofness is that the poet, counted among the faithful, will descend to Sheol and be hidden from God irretrievably (30:9). Evil is a project which aspires to the limit, as can be seen by the enemies' aim to take life (11:2; 31:13; 35:4; 37:14; 38:12; 40:14; 54:3). The poet, along with all the just, is caught in the critical struggle between good and evil.

The enemy spies, accuses, besieges, attacks. In its arsenal are offensive weapons, the sword, the bow and arrows, metaphors for offensive speech. But even more characteristic are the weapons suited for entrapment—nets, pits, traps and snares. The poet eloquently portrays the hunt of the defenseless with the snares and nets (10:8-9; cf. 64:5 and the use of *mistār*, "in secret" or "ambush"). To draw a sword or hurl a stone can be done on a violent impulse, but to dig a pit, set a trap, or lay a net implies premeditation, just as any type of hunting in which the predator keeps a distance from the prey.

In the psalms the deadly assaults are typically generated by speech, and thus it is no accident that the mouth is denounced so often as an arsenal of evil. Therein are contained all the mechanisms of violence— lying tongue, savage teeth, a gullet. Imaged like wild animals' fangs, the enemies want to "eat up my people as they eat bread" (53:4; cf. 14:4; 27:2; 35:25; 124:3). They are scavenging dogs in search of carrion (59:6, 14-15). They threaten to maul the poet (7:2; 17:12; 22:13, 16). The image of the lion is evocative. Does the poet allude to the nobility, imaged in the noblest of beasts, the lion? To be trapped among the wicked is to be among ravaging lions (57:4). Their mouths assault the innocent, as they circle in ambush, ready to pounce (17:9-12).

Two types of weaponry, those which aim for a direct hit and those which entrap, coalesce in the mouth, which is figured as a brandished sword that waves like lips, pierces like the tongue, devours like teeth. The gullet swallows like a pit; the tongue captures like a net. The mouth has a sword that does not kill on the spot but can leave one wounded and weakened (cf. Sir 28:18). Most often it destroys by lies, false witness, or flattery, which is the mechanism of death (5:9). In Psalm 50 the wicked profess to be religious while they work evil, and the sins of the mouth and tongue are prominent in the list of evils (vv. 16-20). The wicked reappear as the conspirator and deceitful tongue (52:1-4). In a plea of innocence the poet denies any complicity with the wicked, who are bloodthirsty (*ʾanšē dāmîm*, or "men of blood"), scheming, bribing people (26:9-10). The "company of evildoers" (26:5), whom the poet hates, assaults one to devour the flesh (27:2). These personal enemies are false witnesses and violent aggressors (v. 12).[11] The poet does not wish to be counted among the two-faced wicked, who speak peace yet harbor evil in their hearts (28:3). The image of honeyed

---

[11] In many psalms the use of *ḥāmās*, "violence," refers to social injustice rather than generic evil. *Ḥāmās* (11:5) would imply that the nature of violence is a deprivation of human rights. The wicked are called "violent," *ḥāmās* (140:1, 4, 11), planning evil in their hearts, with sharpened tongues and poison like vipers, plotting and setting traps, nets, and snares to fell the poet (vv. 1-5). They raise proud heads and slander (vv. 9, 11).

speech and slick, sword-like words with warring hearts recurs (55:21; cf. 62:4; 144:11). The wicked appear in full array in Psalm 109 with treacherous mouths, lying tongues, hateful words, and slander (vv. 2-4). They are false accusers who threaten death (vv. 20, 31). This assault is coupled with bodily affliction, the heart pierced, knees shaking, flesh wasted (vv. 22-24), while the accursed enemies mock the poet (v. 25). Lying lips and treacherous tongues appear again in 120:2-4, like sharpened arrows and a brush fire.

Both inner and outward troubles afflict the poet, who makes a connection between personal guilt and overwhelming distress (25:16-20). The connection between misfortune and guilt is a constant in the psalms and is treated in Psalm 37, which outlines the rewards for good and bad behavior. The implication is that the people's sinfulness has merited God's wrath (90:7-8). An aspect of the intrigue of evil is death, which is seductive. This is termed temptation in the Psalter, and it seduces one to favor death. Psalm 73:13-15 paints temptation in subtle hues. Its irresistible power is envisaged in Ps 141:4, where the poet admits to standing on the threshold of evil, tempted to cross over and eat of its delicacies. This provides a motive for God's immediate rescue.

The poet appeals to the law of retribution, according to which evil rebounds against itself. This corresponds to a frequent motif, the self-destruction of evil (5:10; 9:16; 35:8; 57:6; 59:12-13; 69:21-22; 94:23; 109:17-19; 141:10). The ironic yet welcome truth which the wisdom instructor espouses is that "Evil brings death to the wicked" (34:21). The poet declares that sinister plots will boomerang to their own destruction (7:14-16). His or her urgent cry for help is based on the idea that God has no effective allies on earth, lies and deceit having full rein (12:1-4). The weapons are lips and tongues, which have been whetted by the heart. The requested punishment? May God cut off their lips (v. 3). Elsewhere the enemies appear as stalkers of the poet's life, while he or she is an ardent seeker of God. The punishment? May they be victims of the sword and jackals (63:1, 9-10). It is not surprising that they should be reduced to the savage natures which characterize their beastly acts. Along the same lines, the insult is like a rock hurled against the innocent, and the psalmist's earnest plea is that this volley rebound on those who launched it (140:9-11). The mouth is the trapdoor which will eventually close over the one who opened it. It wields the sword, the tongue, which will pierce the one who used it to kill (64:8). The wicked are those who plot against the just and grind their teeth at them (37:12). Their typical weapons are swords and bows, which will ricochet and kill them (37:14-15).

The system of evil is clothed in evocative images, but as the psalmist unmasks its weapons, certain constants make its features recognizable, and thereby deprive it of its insidious power. The poet's strength is not in the definition of evil, but rather in the images of its power, which alert the reader to its mystery. Behind the complaints and petitions in the psalms were undoubtedly particular crises, but these have been transposed and projected through images to shed light on the universal crisis that each person faces, and herein the reader finds sympathy. To the extent that we can unmask these images, we may uncover and countermand the nefarious influences at work in our own lives. Such is the power of poetry.

The conflict with evil appears more intense in the earlier books of the Psalter (Psalms 1–72). In Book Three and beyond the struggle with evil diminishes in intensity. Although it never entirely disappears until Psalm 144, the struggle with evil in Books Three to Five expands to a universal battle, where the sovereign God is celebrated as triumphant and praise replaces complaint. This dynamic is anticipated already in Book One (Psalms 2 and 8). Surprisingly, in an anthem of praise and introspection, the poet pronounces the maxim that recognition of and proper relation to God is more powerful than God's adversaries (8:2). This anticipates the happy end of the drama, as the Psalter will conclude in unrestrained anthems of praise (Psalms 146–150). But praise is a weapon in itself, as the parallel lines of Ps 149:5-7 affirm:

> Let the faithful exult in glory;
>   let them sing for joy on their couches.
> Let the high praises of God be in their throats
>   and two-edged swords in their hands,
> to execute vengeance on the nations
>   and punishment on the peoples. . . .

In the end, the wicked and their evil schemes are vanquished in a re-created world where the only audible voice is praise.

Prayer and the Curse

The entire repertoire of human moods and passions is expressed in the psalms. The poet eloquently depicts both tranquility and stress. Following Psalm 136, a serene litany of God's abiding love, Psalm 137 jolts the reader with the desire that the wicked be rooted out, that Babylon and the children of evil be destroyed once and for all. This psalm, devoutly prayed, expresses passionate faith and hope in the defense of Jerusalem. It opens with a controlled prayer (vv. 1-6), then crescendos to unrestrained passion for revenge (vv. 7-9), a brutal articulation of the desire of the oppressed community. Paradoxically, this prayer also longs for Jerusalem and everything she represents—peace, security, union with God—as the psalmist cries out against the exploitation of the disadvantaged, displaced, and vulnerable of society, exploitation of which he or she has had personal experience.

Such a vindictive psalm calls for immediate action, because the world is in a state of emergency. Violent imagery articulates a hunger pang for a proper world order and a revulsion against the unjust. Psalm 58 petitions, in unabashedly vengeful terms, for the destruction of unfair rulers (vv. 6-10), because they foster violence on the earth and tip the balance in favor of wrong (v. 2). The poet asks that personified wickedness dissolve, that it be aborted. He or she requests the annihilation of the enemies, because they "did not remember to show kindness, but pursued the poor and needy and the brokenhearted to their death" (109:16). The curses in the Bible do not represent uncontrolled outbursts of human emotion, nor are they the abuse of a victim on the rampage. Given their liturgical, communal setting, they are the modulated, if vitriolic, articulation of the desire for the annihilation of evil forces against God's people.

Israel's liturgy included the curse of the foreign countries that fought against the people. Prophetic oracles against the nations formed part of the religious tradition (Isaiah 13–23; Ezekiel 25–32; 38–39; Amos 1–2). The ideology of extermination warfare was part of the religious patrimony (Deut 20:4, 10-20). Israel possessed ceremonies of excommunication for serious offenses or contagious diseases (Leviticus 13–14; Num 5:11-31; Deut 17:12-13; 19:16-21). Although these rituals may never have actually been put into effect, they remain the ideal of a people completely dedicated to God who radically deny any adulteration of that primary relation. Some psalms explode with the use of injurious language and imagery as horrifying as the violence they disclaim. It is hardly possible for the theologian, literary critic, or translator to soften these violent images and expressions without sanitizing the Bible. But both violent and pacific expressions are the Word of God; both have a home in the Bible. With these difficult prayers, the believing community appeals to God to attend to even the crudest level of human nature.

Imprecations are interspersed throughout the Psalter (12:3-4; 35:4-6, 8, 26; 40:14-15; 58:6-10; 59:11-13; 69:22-28; 70:2-3; 71:13; 79:12; 83:9-17; 109:6-19, 28-29; 137:8-9; 139:19-22; 140:9-11), and they must be understood in their cultural context. Semitic people are eloquent, and both praises and curses are formulated with elegant exaggeration. Some vindictive phrases are ghastly, like "Happy shall they be who take your little ones and dash them against the rock" (137:9). But this belongs to a conventional literary motif of the Near East. "Little ones" stands for the future generations of evil which must be destroyed if the enemy is to be eradicated. Or, in the case of Psalm 140, the accursed may be transposed to any of those in league with the devil, whose actions are diametrically opposed to the rule of God.[12] Curses like these represent indefatigable faith in God in the endurance test of life. There is no suggestion in Psalm 137 that the poet should take any action against Babylonian children. The vengeance is formulated generally, and its execution is left to other forces. When one submits to God by praying a curse, he or she is no longer free to take revenge, because vengeance is transferred from the heart of the speaker to God, who plays an interested role in the believer's life. Praying like this releases a person and admits that sooner or later, in accordance with God's steadfast love (109:26), justice will be done and right will prevail. This prayer acknowledges the violent reflex within and lets it go, placing it in God's hands.

It is healthy, on one level, to discern one's centers of anger and acknowledge vengeful sentiments. For some people such expressions are realistic. They attest to unfairness and exploitation that provoke rage. But even this is rightly carried to God whose rule is marked by majesty, faithfulness, compassion. Violence and the desire to get even are part of the sinful condition, and it is better to acknowledge this in a liturgical

---

[12] Sixth century Benedict may have been inspired by Ps 137:9 when he formulated the injunction to counteract temptation. He wrote, "While these temptations were still young, he caught hold of them and dashed them against Christ" (*Rule,* prol. 28; cf. 4.50). In the psalm the expression formulates the Israelite's hope that the future of the oppressor be eradicated. For the father of western monasticism, the rock is Christ. The appendix "The Role and Interpretation of Scripture in the Rule of Benedict" (*RB 1980. The Rule of St. Benedict;* ed., Timothy Fry [Collegeville, Minnesota: Liturgical Press, 1981]), 475, clarifies this and illustrates a principle in the Christian interpretation of biblical violence from the early Christian era: "The clue to this interpretation had been provided originally by 1 Cor 10:4, which interpreted 'the rock' (the one that Moses struck in the desert) as Christ. In 1 Pet 2:4-7 Christ was also described as 'a living stone.' Since the desire that real Babylonian babies be smashed on real rocks was both historically no longer relevant and hardly consistent with the teaching of Jesus, it was obvious to the Patristic interpreter that the verse must have a 'spiritual' meaning. There were spiritual rocks readily available in the New Testament; it remained only to spiritualize the babies into wrongful thoughts. It must also be remembered that for Christians the focus of the struggle between good and evil was no longer against the powers and principalities of this world but within the individual soul. It appeared natural, therefore, to seek the meaning of such a verse by applying it in a tropological sense. This interpretation of Ps 136(137):9 probably originated with Origen and had already appeared in the writings of Latin authors . . . before it reached the sixth-century monastic rules."

and prayerful setting than to excise it from prayer, while letting it, often unconsciously, inhabit other spheres of our lives. The curses signal a faith in God who is actively concerned for the well-being of people and who takes seriously the governance of the universe.

Expurgating the Bible of what is uncongenial has a disadvantage, because the reader, with an abridged version, is unable to appreciate the full range of its claims. Excising texts of a violent or vindictive flavor divorces the Bible from such contexts in human life which evoke an immediate response. To appreciate the poet's mind and the heart of the praying community, it is a challenge to understand where they stand and why they speak thus. The controlled liturgical curse can express a healthy outpouring of emotion which piety often denies. Such a psalm offers the believer the words to express the emotional reaction, while it acknowledges God as the judge and executor of justice.

The psalms touch a primal level in people that precedes conscience. Fear and anger respond to threats and violence, and they may be expressed in the impulse to destroy the perpetrator. Or the emotional response, which precedes reason, may find a release in psychological acupuncture. The poet of Psalm 140 voices that impulse. Threatened, he or she responds with anger and desires the adversary's destruction: "Deliver me, O LORD, from evildoers; protect me from those who are violent, who plan evil things in their minds and stir up wars continually" (vv. 1-2). In the end, though, personal revenge is relinquished, even as the poet unleashes the unholy wish: "Let burning coals fall on them! Let them be flung into pits, no more to rise" (v. 10). Is it not an error to label anger categorically as sinful and shameful? Censoring the psalms on such a fallacious basis impoverishes the prayer life of the Synagogue and the Church.

Biblical anthropology does not stress the theoretical distinction between wrong, which we hate, and the wrongdoer, who is in essence our neighbor whom theoretically we love. The Bible is more realistic. If wrong exists, there is a culprit. In appropriating such biblical prayers today, the worshiper can transfer the violent imagery onto the annihilation of evil or Satan's power. Thus, one is justified in praying for their downfall and an end to the wickedness they foment. But arguments like this do trouble a tender conscience formed by some of the more sublime texts of the first Testament and the Gospels.

Along with the discomfort which the reader may feel in the face of violence in the Bible, it is good to investigate, within oneself, whether the discomfort is born of a sincere fidelity to the Gospel which commands believers to love their enemies or whether it is rather a subtle, unconscious tactic of approbation of a dominant ideology which accepts and legitimizes the present politic and feels uncomfortable when someone appears to shake it up. The institutionalized violence of Pharaoh's system is uglier than the subtle, more acceptable forms of aggression which inhabit our own efforts to maintain the face of a peaceful society without oppression. And for devout and believing people, there is always the risk of allowing the rhetoric of forgiveness to conceal the dark areas of unforgiveness that lurk deep in their lives. The prayerful and liturgical adoption of these poems expresses one's necessary revulsion to evil in whatever form, even the most personal and deep-rooted.

The intense, violent language attests to a deep-seated aversion to wrong at human injustices. It is not to be understood at the literal level of malice and vituperation against personal opponents, or even, by application, to individual, class or national enemies. It belongs to the poet's critical concern over the messiness of life. What is expressed in hostile terms against those who seek to frustrate God's design is like the bitter speech with which Job expresses agonizing torment at the unfairness of human experience. The poet's direct onslaughts must be recognized as an exaggerated protest (109:8-10):

> May his days be few;
> > may another seize his position.
> May his children be orphans,
> > and his wife a widow.
> May his children wander about and beg;
> > may they be driven out of the ruins they inhabit.

No idle moralizing here. The poet expresses acute anguish in the face of systemic oppression. The metaphors are born of human bitterness, and they express a reflex reaction at the violence waged in life.

Vituperative language is not foreign to the ears or tongues of many who engage in the sports arena, the marketplace, and everyday society. In reality, competitors do not slaughter, maul, gouge, beat, crush, or strangle anyone, and fans know instinctively not to take these terms literally. People do understand violent language and exaggeration, given a context. So it is that not all the biblical expressions can be taken literally. When, for example, the poet asks that God's wrath annihilate the enemies, "consume them until they are no more" (59:13), he or she wishes their death, yes, but even more that their oppressive system be frustrated, that it not be regenerated, that there be no one left to foster it.

The curses in the Psalter address one's tenacious faith, one's capacity to hold up under severe trial. They represent a free-floating, emotional, undisciplined reaction to the wicked, a candid expression of the frayed edges of life that do not easily submit to piety and religious sentiment. For the Christian, the trouble with praying the cursing psalms has been the dichotomy between their horrendous pitch and Christ's teaching on loving enemies. It is for this reason that the Church has seen fit to use a bowdlerized version of these psalms in her liturgy,[13] when she has not omitted them entirely.

Most people daily encounter situations and events that are clearly unfair. Justifiable indignation wells up even in the devout who comes into contact with oppressive institutions and wicked perpetrators. Can he or she invoke God to destroy those people or institutions which oppose God's rule? Why should the believer not pray for the destruction of pornography and its promoters? Why not request the arrest of those who terrorize others? Does one pray to a God who tolerates persons or systems which treat people unjustly? The curse embedded in the complaint over Jerusalem articulates the underlying reason for any malediction: "For they have devoured Jacob and laid waste his habitation" (79:7). Because this is an assault on God's rule, the poet exclaims, "Return sevenfold into the bosom of our neighbors the taunts with which they taunted you, O Lord!" (v. 12). Perhaps such outbursts will be understood and valued first by those who have experienced or are enduring oppression and abuse.

A literal interpretation of the curse does no justice to the breadth of the poet's concern. Likewise, it is inappropriate to dismiss such sentiments as improper, sub-Christian, deriving from an environment that was violent and harsh. A prayer like Psalm 83, which pleads that God act against all who conspire against the divine rule, is no more shocking than the saying attributed to Jesus, calling for judgment: ". . . it would be better for you if a great millstone were hung around your neck and you were thrown into the sea" (Mark 9:42), a saying to be measured in terms of protest against evil rather than in terms of literal fulfillment. Jesus, who preached forgiveness and nonviolence eloquently, also preached judgment of evil in apocalyptic, including violent imagery. Even if a person finds such poetry unacceptable, he or she can still respect the emotional heat which ignites such protest and understand it as a witness to the intensity of the struggle against evil,

---

[13] All the verses of Psalm 35 that speak vindictively, and those which might be interpreted as such, have been removed from the Roman liturgy of the hours. Psalm 139 appears as a magnificent paean of the omnipresent, omniscient God, but its climax and probable intent has been excised from the official liturgical texts. In the abridged version the poet avows innocence, which must be evident to God (vv. 23-24), but refrains from calling down wrath on the wicked aggressor and idolater (vv. 19-22).

oppression, and dehumanization which can become so familiar that it arouses no more than passing interest. Even David, in his moral indignation at the conduct of the rich man in Nathan's parable (2 Samuel 12), pronounced the judgment that such a man merits death—only to discover that his anger must be directed against himself for his betrayal of the standards of right which a sovereign must uphold. Nathan's "You are the man" is a reminder that the unaware critic has to look more deeply into his or her own measure of complicity and blindness in regard to evil.

These so-called curse psalms were preserved and celebrated in the liturgy. The "I" of the poem loses some of its passion in the communal celebration, but it increases in theological value. Violence and vengeance may not befit personal piety, but in the liturgy the imprecations assume an instructional and ecclesial dimension. The solidarity of human abhorrence of violence is lifted up to God. These psalms are evidence of the individual's and community's faith that God is interested in the motions and emotions of every afflicted human heart.

Who is justified in praying like this? A victim of rape or assault, who is weary of awaiting a proper outcome of the clogged legal procedures. An Israeli taxpayer who is exasperated at the frustrated peace promises. A Palestinian refugee weary of war, resentful of displacement. A nun or social worker in the highlands of Chiapas who faces the tensions between military occupation and the struggle for basic human rights of the indigenous peoples. The curses in the psalms are the prayer of people, so oppressed and dehumanized by their suffering that they find it difficult to pray. People in concentration camps, prisons, and ghetto slums are turned into sub-human wrecks. Yet, if these people could pray, their words might be "God, destroy the oppressor who has done this to my parents, my spouse, my children, my bothers and sisters."[14] But such a personalizing effect would reduce these prayers to private devotion, whereas in reality they are the treasury of a community, and they find their real home in the liturgy, where they serve as both prayerful expression and education of the human heart in response to the critical condition of oppressed humanity. Through such psalms the worshiper voices the basic human hunger for God's justice as is done in the Lord's Prayer, "May your kingdom come"—the ardent

---

[14] There is a precedent for this in the Bible. The imprecations of the psalms were applied by Peter to Judas (Pss 69:25 and 109:8; cf. Acts 1:20). Paul applied Ps 69:22-23 to those who among God's people have remained hard of heart (Rom 11:7-10). What to make of the maledictions against Babylon the unjust (Rev 18:6-8)? Jesus delivered seven maledictions against the scribes and pharisees (Matt 23:13-29), and delivered a definitive judgment, "Get out of my sight" (Matt 25:41).

aspiration of all God's people, until the definitive cessation of the curse (Rev 22:3).

In the Christian liturgy, Psalm 95 is a morning prayer. "O that today you would listen to his voice! Do not harden your hearts as at Meribah, as on the day at Massah in the wilderness" (vv. 7b-8). The poet reviews the ancestors' tragic testing in the desert and the curse that befell them, and he or she applies the implicit curse of God's chosen people to the present generation who prays the psalm: if we do not hear and heed God's voice today, may we never enter into our promised rest.

Benedict advised his disciples to read all the Scriptures, but he also counsels them not to read certain scriptures at inappropriate times (*Rule* 42.4; 73.3). Such a selectivity with regards to the scriptural canon can be applied as well to psalms of imprecation. But that does not diminish their value, and as God's Word, as difficult as it is to comprehend at times, even such uncongenial expressions can find a corner in lives of faith.

Any explanation of the cursing psalms, like any justification for oppression, will leave one partially unsatisfied, for there is no adequate explanation for something as horrible as violence. But the very problem, as insoluble as it may seem, serves as an invitation to enter more deeply into the mystery of God's Word. The vexing problems and fearful insecurities of life, the travails that afflict every human being are all reflected in the Psalter. The poet who finds solace in adversity bequeaths that to the reader. Together, poet and reader, are sustained by faith and given the courage to proceed. And just as the poet's joys and sorrows were adopted by the community which preserved their expression, these poems voice the deepest aspirations of the contemporary community.

Book One

(PSALMS 1–41)

Psalm 1
Choice Between Two Ways

The word *tôrâh* (translated "law," v. 2) refers to the story of God's actions to create a people and guide them into the future, as described in Genesis and the first chapters of Exodus. Likewise it refers to the obligations, precepts and guidelines that shape the people's life, as in the rest of the first five books of the Bible, the Torah. These two dimensions, narration and obligation, or, in the Jewish tradition, *haggadah* and *halakah,* are complementary. The English word *law* suggests a restriction that limits freedom. But God's *tôrâh* as described in Scripture occasions rejoicing (see Pss 19:8; 112:1; 119:92), so it is better understood as God's will or design for the chosen people. *Tôrâh* is how God shapes the human soul, like a road map that guides and identifies landmarks toward a destination.

Psalm 1 must be interpreted as a psalm in its own right and in relation to the entire Psalter. As a preface to the Psalter it introduces themes which culminate in the praise at the end of Book Five. The *tôrâh* is the open door to praise through which one has access to interior rooms. Happy the wise person who meditates the *tôrâh* continually, enters through it to appreciate the riches of the Psalter and ends in praising God.

The Psalter opens with the word *ʾašrê,*[1] "happy," which has little to do with feeling and much to do with the lasting blessing held out to the person who pursues the good. Happiness results from a choice to participate in the divine life. This initial word begins with the first letter of

[1] The first word is fitting for its wordplay. The Semitic stem *(ʾšr)* from which *ʾašrê,* "happy," is derived yields a verb meaning "walk, advance" (cf. Isa 3:12; 9:15; Prov 4:14; 9:6; 23:19) and a noun denoting "footstep." One who walks or stops along a path is "happy" *(ʾašrê)* if his or her "steps" *(ʾašûrāy)* are not detained alongside those of the wicked (as in [Hebrew] Pss 17:5, 11; 37:31; 40:3; 44:19; 73:2; Prov 14:15; Job 23:11; 31:7).

the alphabet, *ʾaleph*. The last word in the psalm, "perish," begins with the final letter, *tav*. Opening or closing oneself to God's will *(tôrâh)* results in a choice between happiness and death. The contrast is sharpened by repeating *way* (v. 6; "path" in v. 1), and *righteous* and *wicked* (vv. 5-6). The repetition forms a chiasm:

A *"the wicked* will not stand"

   B "in the congregation of *the righteous*"

   B' "the LORD watches over the way of *the righteous*"

A' "the way of *the wicked* will perish"

The ruin of the wicked is on the periphery, and God's custody of the righteous is central. "Wicked" and "righteous" are opposite forensic terms with no mitigating degrees. One is either "guilty" or "acquitted." In the theology of Psalm 1 a person is either right with God or wrong.

Other repetitions form a thematic inclusion (vv. 1 and 6). The poet advises against following (literally, "walking in") the advice of *the wicked* or standing in their *way* (NRSV, "take the path"), for "the *way* of *the wicked* will perish" (cf. Prov 4:18-19; 15:9). The "way" is a metaphor for human behavior (for example, Ps 25:8-9; Prov 1:15; 2:8-9). That person is fortunate who, like the righteous of Ps 26:4-5, does not share the ideas, projects, and behavior of the wicked. Rather, this one benefits from constant reflection on the guide for behavior, God's *tôrâh*, received with affection and joy. The alternative route is introduced by "but" (Hebrew *kî*, v. 2 and *lôʾ-kēn*, v. 4), which introduces an emphatic denial, "The wicked are not so." In the end, the individual who shunned unwholesome company is included in community with the righteous, a "congregation," standing in a court of law (v. 5). The final scene is in diametric contradiction to the opening. At first the good person was advised to avoid *the session, môšab*, of scoffers. In the end the wicked have no place in *the righteous assembly, ʿēdâh*. The scene has changed completely. Once it is too late, the accounts cannot be adjusted; the sentence is pronounced. The decent individual who keeps honest in an immoral society thrives according to the divinely ordained *tôrâh*. An intransitive verb, "will perish," puts down "the way" of the wicked which leads to their ruin. In contrast, an active, transitive verb with God as the subject raises up the destiny of the good, "the LORD watches over the way of the righteous." The asymmetrical composition of v. 6 is calculated for its effect. In the first hemistich "the LORD" (subject) prospers "the way" (complement). In the second hemistich "the way" (subject) of its own accord turns to nothing.

A	B	C
The LORD	watches over	the way of the righteous
C	. . .	
the way of the wicked	will perish.	

God gives the righteous substance and durability. The wicked vanish. Success of the good depends on God; failure is a consequence of the wicked condition and behavior. God is occupied with the destiny of the person who occupies him or herself with "the law of the LORD." Along with other meanings, the verb, "perish," has the physical sense of going astray or getting lost—perdition, in its literal sense. A synonym of *Sheol*, the residence of the dead, is Abaddon (Ps 88:11; Job 26:6; 28:22; Prov 15:11), a cognate of *ᵓbd*. Some translators understand *tōᵓăbēd*, "will perish," as a present tense with a moral connotation (NEB, RNAB). Others understand it to refer to the future judgment (NRSV, JB), in which case it might be eschatological. The prospect of judgment is alluded to in the chaff image. This and the overarching structure evokes the liturgy of blessing and curse (see Joshua 24; Deut 27:11–28:68). Judgment separates and purges the worshiping community of ungodly elements. Given this connection, the wicked are idolaters, and their influence attempts to lead the faithful from God's way. Psalm 1 is a meditation on the final destiny of the wicked and God's accompaniment of the good. Anyone whose life is rootless and meaningless because he or she is godless will have no defense when arraigned in judgment. A reciprocal contrast is made between the other two parties; God will defend the lover of the law. Another contrast: the wicked scoffers, *seated* (v. 1), will not be able to *"stand* in the judgment . . . in the congregation of the righteous" (v. 5). This psalm shares the contrast with the wisdom school.

The symmetrical structure is formed by the opposite ways of the righteous and the wicked.

(positive)   "Happy are those who do not" (plus three negations, v. 1)
"but [rather] their delight is . . ." (v. 2)
the tree image of the good person (v. 3a)
the result: "they prosper" (v. 3b)

(negative)   "The wicked are not so"; a negation of what preceded
(v. 4a)
"but [rather]," followed by the chaff image (v. 4b)
the result: the recompense of the wicked (v. 5)

(summary)   the principle upon which the teaching is based (v. 6)

The Hebrew juxtaposes the righteous individual and the wicked class. The wicked are not a plurality, but rather a consolidated party; the word *ʿēṣâh*, "advice," reduces their counsel to a slogan (v. 1). This is also clear from *môšab* (NRSV, "seat"), "session" or "assembly," (cf. Ezek 28:2; Ps 107:32). In contrast, the term *tôrâh* is less formal, more attractive and relational. Clearly it includes the sacred writings, but it is more. It is the fine tuning to the divine will, and it is a source of pleasure, an object of desire. It is not imposed from without but inspired by the inclinations of the heart, which are free and loving. The logic of the text is "[h]appy is the person who . . ." maintains integrity and performs actions which conform to the meditation of the heart, ". . . like a tree planted by streams of water." On the other hand, the wicked are dismissed as a group.

The good person is described in relation to what he or she likes (v. 2). The Hebrew reads, "In the *tôrâh* of the LORD is his or her delight"; that is, God's law is a personal preference. An individual is formed by what one loves and reflects on continually. What delights us invades us. The verb *hgh*, translated "meditate," has a physical and auditory connotation, to mutter, to whisper with one's lips. This verb is applied to a young lion "growling" over its prey (Isa 31:4), the dove's "moaning" (Isa 38:14), and as a synonym of "speak" (Pss 37:30; 71:24) or "remember and muse on" (Ps 143:5). "They meditate" can mean "they mumble [to themselves] in a low tone." The aim of this practice is clear from Josh 1:8, "you shall meditate on it day and night, so that you may be careful to act in accordance with all that is written in it." The poet describes a person who continually ("day and night") relishes the law, feeds on and is nourished by it.

This person is compared to a tree planted beside running streams, which sinks its roots in the dampened earth, continually buds forth and produces seasonal fruits. After sketching the qualities of the good, the psalmist expands the material advantage that redounds on the individual who minds all that he or she does. The concise Hebrew formulation may also be translated, "God prospers all that he or she does" (v. 3b). The referent (NRSV), "In all that *they* do, *they* prosper," is ambiguous, as in Hebrew. Grammatically the poet speaks about a tree but is interested in the good person, who is resilient, stable, and fruitful because he or she is deeply rooted in the spiritual and ethical soil of the *tôrâh*. Imagery points inwards and outwards. A person is inwardly devoted to the law, "well-rooted" (the Hebrew verb *štl* is used, instead of *nṭʿ*, "plant") in the soil, stretching out roots for moisture. Outwardly such a person is fruit-bearing like a tree. The author mentions the tree's fruit before its leaves. In the stark and arid landscape of Palestine we would expect the greenery to catch the attention.

This deeply rooted, well watered, leafy tree with abundant fruit is compared to useless straw which the wind blows away after the grain has been sifted (cf. Pss 35:5; 92:12-14; Jer 17:7-8). Chaff portrays the lack of substance and the swift passing of the wicked. In the Hebrew Bible "chaff" is always used as a symbol of inconsistency and imperma- nence. A life lived apart from God is as empty, sterile, and worthless as chaff. Winnowing is repeatedly employed as a simile for God's judg- ment (Hos 13:3; Zeph 2:2; Isa 29:5; Matt 3:12). It was familiar to the poet's contemporaries who saw the grain threshed and winnowed every harvest. This simile describes both the people and their destiny, like chaff as long as they persist in wickedness. The economy of words matches the transitory image, in contrast to the elaborate portrayal of the ideal person like a tree.

The poet proposes as a constant practice the meditation on the *tôrâh*, by which a person shapes his or her conduct and from which flows everything else in life. The poet ably concentrates the integral life that comes from meditation on the law into a plant image; the scenery is remarkable. A tree—not a volunteer—is planted by a creek which guar- antees irrigation, foliage, and fruit in season. The person who absorbs the *tôrâh* produces fruit. The beauty of the tree comes from within. The antithesis, chaff, is curtly dismissed. Two comparisons result, a tree with chaff and the stream with the breeze. A gust of wind blows away the insubstantial; the steady flow of the stream nourishes the tree.

The psalmist concludes with the total failure of the wicked—forensic ("will not stand in the judgment"), religious (exclusion from "the con- gregation of the righteous"), life and practice ("the way of the wicked will perish"). The reason for the beatific end of the righteous is a recip- rocal relationship, God "watches over" (*ydᶜ*, literally "knows") the faithful, those who nourish themselves on the *tôrâh*. They are blessed because God protects their path. The poet invites the person who opens the Psalter to choose the blessed end and the means to attain it.

For the final verdict the poet employs the symbol of a path, which God traces and the good walk responsibly or, on the contrary, which the wicked design for themselves and which leads to perdition (cf. this theme in Psalms 37 and 73). God is absent from the life and destiny of the wicked, aptly formulated "the way of the wicked will perish." The contrast is evident. The wise person who lives by the *tôrâh* is successful, while the one who flouts it is a failure. However, the poem cannot be reduced to a simplistic equation. The psalmist contrasts two attitudes. Those who depend on God and seek the divine will by studying the *tôrâh* enjoy a relationship with God; they strive constantly and listen intently for God's word day and night. They are blessed by a sense of the meaning of life. In contrast are those who scorn the devout life and aim to live off their own resources. They are like chaff separated and burned after the threshing; their existence lacks substance.

The Psalter begins with a beatitude, typical of the wisdom style (see Pss 112:1; 119:1), promising happiness to the person devoted to God. The characteristics of such a person are described negatively as the avoidance of bad companions. The psalmist outlines progressive levels of collusion with the wicked. The first and least offensive is walking (NRSV "follow") according to "the advice of the wicked," then standing in (NRSV, "take") "the path that sinners tread," which means conforming to their example. The most corrosive evil would be to "sit" in the scoffers' assembly[2] and participate in their mockery. The wicked scoff at the trust of the good person, who is constantly, joyfully occupied with the study and observance of the *tôrâh* (v. 2). Psalm 1 is not a prayer in a usual sense. The poet neither praises nor complains to God, nor laments or rejoices in his or her situation. The major theme is the adhesion to God's *tôrâh* in a person's life, and its importance for the attainment of happiness. Beatitude is derived from the personal commitment to a course traced by God's *tôrâh*.

Psalm 2
Happy Those Who Submit to God's Rule

Psalm 2 reenacts a coronation ceremony which possibly took place during an annual feast. It celebrates a king enthroned by God's grace. In the conception of the author and the Jewish and Christian communities who adopted this poem for their liturgy, the Davidic dynasty is the fulfillment of the divine promise and the focus of God's covenant with the chosen people. The structure of the poem follows the ceremonial ritual. The poet dramatizes the nations' rebellion against God's "anointed" (*mĕšîaḥ*, vv. 1-3). In antiquity a change of throne signaled the flare for revolutionary activity. God is seated (*yôšēb*), enthroned over all in the heavens. The focus shifts to God's transcendent grandeur, and the king's installation in the temple, the "holy hill" of Zion (vv. 4-6). God's "decree," the protocol which endows the king with authority, is proclaimed. He is adopted as God's son, "begotten" on the day of anointing and elevated to universal dominion, which implies quelling dissident factions (vv. 7-9). The king issues the ultimatum that insur-

---

[2] "Session," *môšab*, implies a formal assembly (Ps 107:32; 1 Kgs 10:5; Ezek 28:2).

gent rulers and territories must either submit to the new authority or be annihilated (vv. 10-12a). A beatitude that commends those who take refuge in God closes the psalm.

The poet draws an antithesis between the king on Zion and other rulers. As in Psalm 1, the wicked form a conspiracy, and four verbs are used to describe it: "conspire," "plot," "set themselves," "take counsel together." Dramatic tension is imposed by the use of multiple speakers, persons addressed, and quotations. An anonymous voice, the "I" of the poem, frames it. This initial voice refers to rebels and poses a rhetorical question with mixed indignation and scorn. The allies against whom resistance is mounted are "the Lord and his anointed." The initial question registers amazement at the rebellion and condemns it to failure ("plot in vain"). God's opponents, an international coalition, talk big against the rightful successor to the throne: "let us burst their [literally, "his"] bonds asunder" (v. 3). The braggadocio indicates that these foreigners are Israel's vassals. God, nonplused, laughs at the insolent schemes (v. 4; cf. Pss 37:13; 59:8). The second reaction is anger at the mutiny. This is described beautifully. "Wrath," 'ap, refers to the nose as the place where rage is concentrated; "fury," ḥarôn, is the heat registered in the angry face. Understandably, considering who is angered, the adversary is scared. God speaks twice, first to broadcast the installation of the chosen king on Zion (v. 6) and then, in the voice of the newly elect, to quote the words God pronounced at his coronation, a promise still in effect (vv. 7-9). The images of an iron mace or scepter ("rod") and of smashing a jug illustrate the dissidents' defeat. The concluding voice takes stock of the situation and God's verdict and addresses the rebels to threaten them with an ultimatum, to surrender or perish. The four invitations have a wisdom flavor, "be wise," "be warned," "serve . . . with fear," "kiss." To "serve" the Lord, is a strange piece of advice for foreigners, unless this psalm belongs to a postexilic context like Ps 102:22, second Isaiah or Zechariah. The drama is intensified by an inversion of chronological order. The normal sequence would be coronation (vv. 7b-8), rebellion (vv. 1-3), God's reaction (vv. 4-6), verdict and ultimatum (vv. 10-12). But here the poet begins and ends in rebellion. The resolution stands outside the poem. The message is that God supports those who submit to divine authority.

The international setting into which the liturgy projects the modest proportions of the Judean kingship can be accounted for only by assuming that this is a copy of the etiquette of a foreign court. At no time in Israel's and Judah's history did a king rule the whole world. The ascent to the throne hearkens back to David's election and is equivalent to adoption, "I will be a father to him, and he shall be a son to me" (2 Sam 7:14, with echoes in 1 Chr 17:13; 22:10; 28:6; cf. Ps 89:26-27). This legitimized the king as God's son and most qualified representative. The adoption took place on the day of anointing, and it ascribed theological importance to the ruler's office. Zion's head of state was thereby understood to be a function and instrument of God. To obey the human sovereign was to obey God, and to rebel against human authority meant insurrection against God (vv. 2-3).

A privilege of adoption is that the king may request favors, and God can give nations and the earth for an inheritance (v. 8). This and the use of "rulers of the earth" (v. 10) to refer to the petty neighboring princes who were temporarily subjugated by Israel in real history is an exaggeration. The claim is understood as God's design for the Davidic dynasty. This is also the mainstay of the hope of the Hebrew scriptures for the consummation of all things at the end of time. Later this expanded horizon will express the people's messianic hope. Such a stylized form was used in the coronation liturgy and was adapted to messianic speculation, as is evident from this psalm's usage in the second Testament (cf. Acts 4:23-31).

This interpretation is corroborated by the last movement, where the psalmist draws a theological conclusion for the earth's rulers. The psalm thus postulates a theology of history according to which all will eventually submit to God's rule. The poet reverts to the beginning by addressing and warning earth's hostile rulers (vv. 10-12), and this is the logical consequence of what precedes. Against the mutiny God stands behind Zion's king as the true sovereign. If would-be earthly powers acknowledged this, they would humble themselves and worship God. The liturgy leaves no doubt about the seriousness of the human position in relation to God. It has one aim, to declare that God is sovereign of all and guarantee that he be recognized as such. Awe before God's universal reign dominates the final chord of the hymn. God's wrath threatens those who scorn him, but those who take refuge in God can be assured of divine aid. The author warns the rebels and all earth's governors to consider well before embarking on dangerous ventures. Best to submit to the true head of state ("Serve the LORD with fear, with trembling"), and thereby avoid drastic consequences—a good enough motive.

Psalm 1 is placed in relation to Psalm 2 and the rest of the Psalter (see the Introduction). The initial beatitude, "Happy [*ʾašrê*] are those who do not follow . . . or take the path . . . or sit . . ." (1:1), is echoed in the beatitude at the end of Psalm 2, "Happy [*ʾašrê*] are all who take refuge [*ḥsh*] in him" (v. 11),[3] thus bracketing these two psalms by an inclusion. Psalm 1 opens the Psalter presenting it as means of instruc-

---

[3] The root *ḥsh*, "take refuge," "trust," introduced in 2:12, is thematic in Psalms 1–10. Additional occurrences in 5:11 and 7:1, and synonyms, evidence that the motif

tion, and Psalm 2 introduces the content of the instruction, that God is sovereign. An analogous relation between consecutive psalms occurs with Psalms 118–119, but in reverse order. Psalm 118 is a thanksgiving liturgy celebrating a king's victory, and Psalm 119 a meditation on the law. Another verbal link between Psalms 1 and 2 is the repetition of the verb *hgh* (*yehgeh,* "meditate," 1:2; *yehgû,* "plot [in vain]," 2:1). The "advice of the wicked" (1:1) contrasts with the admonition to the kings (2:10) to "be wise" and "be warned." The beatitude and the clear option for the right way (Psalm 1) is countered by the experience that the choice is not so simple. Psalm 2 opens with the question "Why do the nations conspire?" which introduces an underlying plot of the Psalter, the threat of godlessness, which has its denouement in the psalms of God's reign. The destiny of God and the anointed is described in Psalm 2 with the same terms as in Psalm 1, and this places the instruction in an eschatological judgment context: "you will perish [*ʾbd*] in the way [*derek*]" (2:11, compare 1:6, "the way [*derek*] . . . will perish [*ʾbd*]"; see also 1:1, "path [*derek*] that sinners tread").

Psalm 3
Trust God in Times of Trouble

Psalm 2 posed an international affront to God's sovereignty. In Psalm 3 hostility overwhelms the individual. The poet opens by registering a complaint with God and quoting the aggressor (vv. 1-3). Of the three actors, the poet does not lose composure, even when adversaries rise up and speak against him or her, for God is an ally. The poet knows, and lets God know, that one is not alone even amidst oppression, that God, a shield (cf. 18:2; 28:7), provides protection, "glory," and strength ("the lifting of my head"; see 27:6). Then the poet summarizes the prayer, the divine response (v. 4), and personal confidence (vv. 5-6). God is addressed directly (v. 7). Finally, the poet addresses the audience with a theological premise, that salvation belongs to God, and invokes a blessing on the congregation (v. 8). This is a liturgical motif which may have been spoken by the priest or royal presider, as the individual complaint articulates a typical crisis of the people. Because the psalm was preserved in the liturgy, the individual voice is understood as the people's representative.

---

of trust is dominant at the beginning of the Psalter, and it continues throughout Books One and Two.

The triple repetition of *rab*, "many," sets the scene and creates the impression of an increasing number of enemies (vv. 1-2), which grow to "ten thousands [*ribĕbôt*, a cognate of *rab*] . . . against me all around" (v. 6). The ambush or a siege has a single target, but the LORD comes between the assailants and the victim. The rhyme in Hebrew calls attention to the presence of the enemies: *rabbîm qāmîm . . . rabbîm ʾōmerîm . . . ʾĕlōhîm* (vv. 2-3). But even with this insistence the psalmist is assured of God's presence and does not fear them.

Verbal cognates mark the poem with repetition and contrast. Alternate uses of *qwm* ("to rise") and *yšʿ* ("help," "save" or "deliverance") articulate the problem and the solution. "Many are *rising* against" the psalmist, saying "[t]here is no *help* for you in God"; may God *rise up* in defense *to deliver* (vv. 1-2, 7) him or her. Finally the psalmist affirms "*[d]eliverance* belongs to the LORD" (v. 8). The commensurate punishment for those who verbally antagonize the psalmist is a slap in the face and broken teeth (vv. 2, 7). The final request expresses the certainty of divine aid.

The enemies' initial self-assurance is based on the supposition that God has retired and will not intervene on the psalmist's behalf. This attitude contrasts with the act of faith during a crisis (vv. 3-7). Amidst the military assault, surrounded by innumerable enemies *rising up* to launch the final attack, the psalmist quietly *lies down*, falls asleep, and then awakes (v. 5). Life, with an accent on the most defenseless activity of resting, continues its normal rhythm. Sleep is a symbol of tranquility. While dawn approaches, the LORD *rises* to protect and sustain the besieged psalmist. From a countless army, a personal conflict of supernatural proportions, the battle takes the imaginative turn of a fist fight (cf. Exod 21:18; Isa 58:4). God is often depicted as a warrior in the Bible; here he engages in hand to hand combat, and knocking out the teeth of the enemy is an original touch. Could it be that the adversaries are verbal assailants, and thus the punishment is fitting so that they can no longer injure with their mouths? Amidst serious danger, surrounded by such a crowd, the poet's trust in God allows him or her to continue the natural rhythms of lying down, sleeping, and awaking, and this trust dispels all fear (vv. 5-6).

Psalm 4
Answer Me in My Distress; Night Prayer

Psalms 3 and 4 are joined by the verbal and thematic links of calling and answering (3:4; 4:1), lying down and sleeping (i.e., trusting God's protection, 3:5 and 4:8), and the expression "many are saying," *rabbîm 'ōmerîm* (3:2; 4:6). The poet of Psalm 4 opens and closes by addressing God (vv. 1, 6-8), who is both defender and protector. Within this frame two groups are addressed. The first is hostile (vv. 2-3), and the imperative "know" alerts them to God's defense of the faithful. The second is dispirited companions (vv. 4-5), whom the poet rallies to trust and worship, expressed with six more imperatives—"tremble" (the NRSV reads "When you are disturbed"), "do not sin," "ponder," "be silent," "offer" (sacrifices), and "trust." The imperatives chart the process of conversion desired of the adversary. At first one must recognize and marvel at the enormous distance between oneself and God, and stop sinning; the next step is quiet reflection, which is followed by liturgical offering and confidence. The poem ends with the poet's testimony of a trusting relationship with God (vv. 6-8).

The author deftly contrasts spatial images to describe the personal experience. The expression "You gave me room when I was in distress" stands out. Relief is described in terms of being in straits but then finding ample room. For a person accustomed to occupying a small apartment, a crowded barrio, a limited workspace, or moving about in compact cars and crowded public transport, malls, parks, mountains, fields and beaches make an unforgettable impression of free, open space. This physical roominess images a spiritual and emotional experience. The feeling of being closed in, bottled up, inhibited, stressed, anguished (a word derived from the concept "narrow" or "cramped") is relieved by an expanded heart or perspective. The psalmist taps into a basic human experience of narrowness and expanse, stress and relief. Cramped suddenly becomes roomy, an amplitude which is achieved in prayer. Thus, the poet recommends interior reflection and ritual sacrifices, which together restore trust in God (vv. 4-5). One without the other would be incomplete. He or she articulates the unrest of the "many" whose hopes are waning as they sigh, "O that we might see some good!" (v. 6a), and then requests a sign of God's presence to relieve the discouragement, "[l]et the light of your face shine on us" (v. 6b; cf. Num 6:25-26). The poet resumes the dialogue with God, the font of gladness, and tells how the divine company and action are more gratifying than an abundant harvest and the sense of security which that brings, "more than when their grain and wine abound" (v. 7; cf. Deut 33:28). A final brush stroke, that of sleep which comes quickly and brings peace, depicts the trust and tranquility of an intimate relation with God (v. 8; cf. v. 3). Sleep, even in the midst of adversity, is a basic symbol. The psalmist does not suffer from insomnia or nightmares. Restful sleep gives the space he or she needs to face trials and enemies. To lie down and sleep are one thing for the psalmist, but quite another for the adversary, who is restless and cannot sleep (v. 5). While others lay down to fret, repent of sin, or prepare for a liturgy, the poet falls fast asleep.

The "God of my right," which refers to a defense attorney, is credited with a past deliverance (v. 1). The anguish and the certainty of a happy outcome are personal. From between two opposing forces the poet addresses God, recalls his benefits, and speaks about him to others. The psalmist addresses two groups with rhetorical questions and seven imperatives (vv. 2-5). He or she does not let the adversary speak. Friends, on the other hand, speak indirectly, through the poet. Exasperation marks the address to the backsliders, with the repeated questioning, "[h]ow long . . .?" Faithfulness to God is a reward in itself, more precious than what people seek (vv. 2-3). They are attracted by vanity and falsehood, which is akin to idolatry. The psalmist confronts the adversary and encourages friends, "the LORD has set apart the faithful for himself"; this declaration is born of personal experience, "the LORD hears when I call." Material possessions ("grain and wine") pale in comparison to a relationship with God, which amounts to "gladness in my heart" and the splendor of God's face (vv. 6-7). In spite of personal distress and public discouragement, the dominant mood of Psalm 4 is confidence. The sheer joy of trusting in and being right with God testifies to a profound religious experience, as the poet of Psalm 73 also attests (cf. 73:17, 23-26, 28).

The sin referred to (vv. 4-5) comes to light when the parallel lines are considered. They look like this:

A	B
tremble	and "do not sin"
B'	A'
"Offer right sacrifices,	and put your trust in the Lord."

The middle member, "ponder it on your beds [literally, "speak in your hearts on your beds"], and be silent," can be summed up as "quiet down and think about it." This is framed by four members related to each other in chiastic form: "tremble" is related to "trust" and "do not sin" to "[o]ffer right sacrifices." The fault lies in adulterating the liturgies, not minding in the heart what is expressed in ritual. Furthermore, the psalmist addresses the "God of my *right*" who delights in "*right* sacrifices" (vv. 1 and 5, the repeated word *ṣedeq*). The psalmist counsels the priority of prayer and kosher ritual which restores trust in God. In response to these actions, God shows himself as defender and protector (vv. 1, 8).

Psalm 5
God Does Not Support Wickedness; Morning Prayer

If Psalm 4 is a night prayer, "I will both lie down and sleep in peace" (v. 8), Psalm 5 is a morning prayer (cf. v. 3). An innocent person complains to God, contrasts the practice of the faith with the adversaries' impiety, and requests deliverance. It is organized around the opposition between the psalmist and the wicked; God's incompatibility with evil (vv. 4-6) implies that the wicked are to be excluded from the temple; in contrast, the devout psalmist has sure access to it (vv. 7-8). The punishable wrongdoing has a double dimension. On the horizontal plane it amounts to false speech and rebellion; on the vertical axis it is rebellion against God (vv. 9-10). The poem is framed by an appeal to God and request for blessing for the righteous (vv. 1-3, 11-12). Two emphatic pronouns (Hebrew), "[b]ut I [the psalmist]" (v. 7) and "[f]or you [God]" (v. 12), forge a bond between God and the poet, who expects and requests equitable rewards for the good and the wicked. The repetition of the Hebrew *běrōb* juxtaposes the innocent psalmist's desire, "*abundance* of your steadfast love" (v. 7a), with the rebels' "*many* transgressions" (v. 10b). The personal complaint expresses an outcry against lawlessness and a request on behalf of the faithful community, whom the psalmist represents.

Psalm 5 opens with an insistent invocation which employs typical elements of the complaint: imperatives ("give ear," "give heed," "listen") and the address to the LORD and "my King and my God." The two titles imply different relations. The more intimate, "my God," means that this God and not some rival god is the one to whom allegiance is owed. Rather differently, a king is both sovereign and judge or defender. In ancient Israel these roles were not separate (cf. 2 Sam 14:1-24; Jer 21:12). The elliptical composition of v. 3b (NRSV translation, "in the morning I plead my case to you, and watch") may be translated literally, "at dawn I prepare . . . for you and wait." Morning is the normal time for the liturgy and legal proceedings (cf. Ps 59:16; Exod 29:38-40; Lev 6:12; 2 Kgs 3:20); dawn is also a symbol of deliverance (cf. Pss 46:5; 90:14; 143:8; Exod 14:24; Isa 33:2; 37:36). The psalmist prepares a legal defense that expects a final settlement and ritual sacrifice in the temple. The use of the legal term ("righteousness," *ṣĕdāqâh*, and "righteous," *ṣaddîq*, vv. 8 and 12) argues for this interpretation. The psalmist has been unjustly accused, which explains the request for acquittal, the punishment of accusers, and a return to the temple. The curse of the accusers is legal rhetoric and part of the appeal for justice. Their conniving leads to death and the poet reminds God of the rewards promised to people loyal to the covenant. God's righteousness, which rejects the criminal and protects the innocent, is the basis for the suppliant's trust. But this legal process is acted out in the liturgy. The poet's description places him or her at the entrance to the temple in the morning, appealing for a hearing with the invisible God, who was enthroned on the *kapporet* or mercy seat, the gold covering upon the ark. From this cherubim throne he judges with equity and saves the righteous (Exod 25:17-22; cf. Ps 9:7-8), which is graphically portrayed in the final phrase, "cover them with favor as with a shield" (v. 12).

The poet describes God with six statements, three negative and three positive, which definitively divorce the wicked and evil from God (vv. 4-6). Righteous God (v. 8) is incompatible with injustice and the unjust. The opposition to God is elaborated with general categories: "wickedness" and "evil" (synonyms *rešā‘* and *rā‘*), "the boastful," "evildoers," liars, "the bloodthirsty and deceitful" (vv. 5-6). These seven designations for evil represent a total threat. The last two, "bloodthirsty and deceitful," anticipate the case at issue (see v. 9). Once the grounds are laid, the specific appeal is expressed (v. 8). God's help is urgent because of "enemies," translating a Hebrew word (from *šwr*) that characterizes them as "watchers" who wait in ambush like a beast for prey. Their evil conduct consists in malicious intent and speech, designated by the mouth, heart, throat, and tongue (v. 9). What the calumniators say about the psalmist is false, destructive, and smells of death. "[T]heir throats are open graves" represents a Hebrew wordplay by an inversion of consonants, *qereb* ("the innermost parts," here, "throats") and *qeber* ("tomb"). "Open tomb" occurs in Jer 5:16-17 of foreign invaders, whose

> . . . quiver is like an open tomb. . . .
> They shall eat up your harvest and your food;
> they shall eat up your sons and your daughters.

"Throats" are likened to graves because corruption and calumny issue from them. The poet adverts to wicked behavior toward neighbor and God (vv. 9-10). He or she is confident of a just hearing ("righteousness"), based on "steadfast love," *ḥesed* (vv. 7-8). *Ḥesed* signals a turning point, after which the psalmist becomes more explicit about the personal enemies. The complaint is general, but the assault is death's working. In the pitch of the fray the poet is convinced that God will shield those who trust in him (v. 12).

The psalmist defends him or herself with an accusation and pleads innocent by denouncing the witnesses as false. He or she seeks acquittal from the enemies' charges and requests that their plans lead to their own destruction (v. 10). The "casting out" refers to the temple, where the righteous find asylum. In a larger scope it refers to punishment by exile or from the face of the earth, in which case the enemies would be cast out "from the land of the living" (Ps 52:5; cf. 37:9, 22, 28; Prov 2:22). The desired consequence is excommunication from the liturgical assembly.

Up until the last two verses the suppliant has thought and spoken about the personal situation—"my sighing," "my enemies," "my God," "my case." Finally the poet is identified as a member of the group of those who resort to and love God. His or her deliverance will have communal repercussions, which makes one think that the individual has been representing the community all along. As their spokesperson the poet requests their protection and relief. In the end everyone will rejoice at the acquittal and liberation. Psalm 5 bolsters the faithful to weather the worst crises of betrayal within family or community, of scandal within religious circles. As a morning prayer it brightens the day with hope in the LORD, a shield for the innocent accused.

Psalm 6
God Has Heard My Weeping

Psalm 6 opens with seven imperative requests for God's decisive action (vv. 1-4). The first is a stereotyped formula (v. 1; Ps 38:1; cf. Jer 10:24) in which divine displeasure and human suffering are associated and God's parental love is desired. The first four ("do not rebuke" nor "discipline me," "be gracious to" and "heal me") are followed by a twofold motive, "my bones" are *trembling* and "my soul *[nepeš]*" is *trembling* (the same Hebrew word, from the root *bhl*), which in turn is followed by the plaintive questioning "how long?" The last three requests ("turn," "save," and "deliver") are followed by *kî*, "for," which introduces the rhetorical question, "in Sheol who can give you praise?" (v. 5). After the sevenfold plea and the vague questioning, the psalmist is *worn out* (*ygꜥ*, v. 6; cf. Pss 31:11 [Hebrew]; 32:3; 69:4 [Hebrew]). Yet he or she, who is as close to Sheol as a living being can be, remembers God. A second description of the miserable state follows (vv. 6-7). Finally, God hears and rescues the psalmist from the enemies, and this is solemnized in three parallel lines (vv. 8b-9). This proclamation is framed between two appearances of the foes and it culminates in their certain downfall (v. 8a, 10). In the poet's experience, several factors surface: the illness with attendant aches and pains, psychological anguish and fear of death, the enemy, guilt feelings.

The two hemistichs of v. 1 are parallel, except for the initial "LORD," and thus the pattern can be charted a-b, a-b. The parallel hemistichs of v. 2 are more elaborate, adding LORD and the *kî* motive (a-b-c, a-b-c). The symmetry with which the poem begins gradually disintegrates as the poet prays and gets more entrenched in personal anguish. The final verses bring together previous parts. The "terror" *(bhl)* that is wished on the enemies (v. 10) was initially how the psalmist felt (bones "shaking" and soul "struck with terror," vv. 2-3). Bones and soul *(nepeš*, literally "breathing") comprise the person's consistency and the spiritual aspect. Any delay on God's part could be fatal, "how long?" (v. 3). The extreme difficulty of breathing, expressed with *nepeš*, is a matter of life or death, in "save my *life [nepeš]*" (v. 4). The subject of *šwb* changes. If God turns, *šwb*, to answer the plea, then the aggressor will be turned back, *šwb*, and disgraced, *bwš* (vv. 4, 10); *šwb* and *bwš* produce a chiastic alliteration with consonants in reverse order. The final word *rāgaʿ*, "in a moment" or "immediately," answers the question *ʿad-mātāy*, "how long" (vv. 3, 10). The divine name appears frequently, eight times in ten verses.

"Wrath" and "anger" express God's incompatibility with sin; thus a confession of sinfulness is implied (v. 1). The depleted physical energies and psychological terror are a consequence of guilt. The psalmist pleads, not for justice, but for mercy *(ḥnn*, "be gracious"). The anxiety and urgency are aptly expressed by the question, "how long?" (v. 3; see Ps 13:1-2). The psalmist seeks to change God's mind; indeed, mercy is the opposite of anger. The poet provides two reasons why God should intervene (vv. 4-5). The best reason is divine *ḥesed*, and the fact that the dead have no contact with God in Sheol (the descriptions are well-known; cf. Pss 30:9; 88:5, 10-12; 115:17; Isa 38:18). Lack of "remembrance" expresses the belief that liturgy is absent from among the dead. While a person is ill and, hence, practically in Sheol, he or she cannot participate in the liturgy. Thus, it is to God's advantage to restore the afflicted psalmist. The description of weeping strikes one as exaggerated, and aptly displays internal anguish and desperation. After a monologue of intense sadness (vv. 6-7), suddenly the psalmist commands the evildoers to depart (v. 8).[4] They were there all along, even though the psalmist did not advert to them and we did not notice them. The psalmist was so acutely aware of his or her own condition and the urgent need for God that they were momentarily out of range. Now that recovery and relief are on the way, the poet perceives their

---

[4] The role of the "foes" (v. 7) is not clear. They appear to think that the sufferer is getting what he or she deserves. As often in the Psalter, the one who is ill is also victim of social stigma, which adds to the grief (31:11-13; 38:11-12, 19-20; 41:9; 102:8).

sinister presence. Suddenly, the poet acknowledges God's help (vv. 8b-9). The description is a masterpiece. The afflicted poet spends nights in anguish, moaning and drenching the bed with tears. He or she is certain of God's benevolent hearing. In short, the psalmist pleads for release from sickness and death, describes the plight, and finally drives away the assailants. God intervenes and the wicked who delighted in the psalmist's humiliation are frustrated. Where does the astonishing certainty that "the LORD has heard" come from? These words are either recited in the temple after the psalmist has recovered or they are a reaction to the deliverance promised in a priestly oracle which is missing from the psalm.

The poet leaves an impression of three kinds of assault—corporal, spiritual, and social. Surrounded by hostility, curbed by pain and distress, the only way out is the LORD. Allusions to sin and death (vv. 1, 5) complete the picture of personal anguish. As often occurs both in reality and the psalms, personal suffering and enemies complicate the condition of the patient, who becomes more sensitive to hostility and rejection, even as the rivals or persons around take advantage of his or her weakness. The fear of death accompanies illness and intensifies the pain, and the premonition of death intensifies the poet's introspection and plight (vv. 4-7). The multiple complications and symptoms make it impossible to diagnose the illness—bones and respiratory problems, uncontrollable sighing, weeping, depression. Difficulty in breathing is an assault against life; trouble seeing implies that there is an obstacle to light; both light and life are from God.

True to his or her cultural milieu, not unlike popular thinking today, the psalmist perceives a causal relation between sin and sickness. Thus the query, "how much guilt?" or, in the psalmist's words, "how long?" Sickness and guilt can be treated. Pardon (relief from guilt) has favorable consequences in the body and spirit. In the request the poet treats every aspect of the affliction: for the sin, mercy, *ḥnn* (v. 2a); for the illness, healing, *rp$^>$* (v. 2b); and on the social front, that the adversaries be frustrated (v. 10). Just as personal anguish can provoke a change in the psalmist, prayer can provoke a change in God, an idea which is implicit in the *šwb*, "turn" (v. 4). One awaits God's transformation from "anger," *$^>$apĕkā*, to love, *ḥesed*, from correction and punishment to healing and salvation.

Physically and spiritually spent, the psalmist has reached the limit of human endurance. The frankness with which weakness is admitted prevents him or her from false claims of innocence. Justice pertains to God, as does mercy. Especially in the Hebrew, one notices a continuous tension between "I" (the poet) and "you" (God), between life and death, grace and sin. Despite the grim situation, the urgency of the plea, and the sense of God's distance, the divine presence is felt in the repeated invocation of the Name (vv. 1-4). The absence of the divine name in v. 5 is no accident, "For in death there is no remembrance of you." This silence of God is felt in the description of the poet's grave distress (vv. 6-7). The suppliant's last energies are spent pleading for help. The actual battle is waged in the body yet transcends it. Life and death are locked in combat, yet both are under God's dominion and the prize is the psalmist's life for whom prayer is the surety of God's presence and answer.

The superscription leaves one guessing about specific details, yet it hints about how this psalm was used in the liturgy. The reference to the "Sheminith" (meaning "eighth") led to theological speculation about circumcision among the Jews (on the eighth day after birth) and about the new creation and the Resurrection among both Jews and Christians. The "eighth" day is the day after God rested from creation. On that day all afflictions will be healed.

Psalm 7
Prayer of One Falsely Accused

In Psalm 7 an individual who has been falsely accused appeals to the ultimate judge, God, and in a strongly worded oath swears allegiance to the covenant and pleads innocence. The prayer invoking God's verdict and punishment is directed against his or her accusers. The poet treats the theme of adversaries who plot death and concludes by promising to worship God. The successive movements can be charted thus: request for divine help and deliverance from pursuers (vv. 1-2); examination of conscience and plea of innocence (vv. 3-5); appeal for the divine judge's intervention (vv. 6-8); description of how God frees the righteous by letting evil entrap the wicked (vv. 9-16); the pledge to thank God (v. 17). Cognates of the root *ṣdq* ("righteous-[ness]") occur five times from v. 8 on. In the early part of the poem, repeated reference is made to the poet's persecutors (vv. 1-6); in the last part the evildoers are general. The vague references and the rough condition of the Hebrew text give an impression of the poet's agitated state.

According to the popular theology of the day, afflictions resulted from sin. But the psalmist is innocent, which makes the plea similar to Job's (vv. 3-5; see Job 31:5-40; Pss 17:1-12; 26:1-10; 137:5-6) and the sufferings are not justified. The casuistic (if . . . then) style is typical of this kind of oath and reinforces the request: if I have done wrong, "then let the enemy pursue and overtake me." The psalmist does not pretend to be innocent, but pleads not guilty to the alleged crimes ("this," v. 3), which amount to the unfair treatment of friend or foe (v. 4). The request is that God (vv. 6-9), seated "on high," the judge of "peoples," "rise," pass sentence and thus vindicate the psalmist. The imperatives "[r]ise up," "lift yourself up," and "awake" derive from the battle cry in which the ark played a role (Num 10:35-36). God is expected to act in favor of the defenseless (Pss 9:18-19; 12:5); his enthronement "on high" on the ark mirrors the celestial throne.

God is not indifferent to oppression or calumny, and the poet presents the divine reaction as anger (v. 6; cf. Ps 6:1), a metaphor which aptly expresses the incompatibility between evil and God's goodness. The horizon widens from the particular to the universal, because God is judge of all the peoples (v. 7). Juridical language abounds in the appeal to the supreme judge, the plea of innocence (vv. 3-5, 9), an accusation (v. 14), the reprimand of the evil (vv. 6, 9), the postures of standing and sitting (vv. 6-7), punishment in terms of retribution (vv. 15-16), the justice and integrity of the judge (vv. 9, 11, 17). The psalmist relies on personal innocence (translated as "righteousness") as the best defense against calumny (v. 8). God examines a person's secret motives and defends the "righteous" or "innocent" (v. 9; as in Pss 17:3; 26:2-3; 139:23-24). The only escape from judgment and punishment is conversion (v. 12).

"I take refuge" (v. 1; see Pss 2:12; 5:11) relates to the hope of asylum from adversaries (Num 35:9-28; 1 Kgs 1:49-53; 2:28-34) and refers to the temple. The psalmist uses derivations of the root *nṣl* to convince God: "*deliver* me" or there will be "no one to *rescue*" (vv. 1-2). Masterful images portray the psalmist and articulate the request for a hearing. The poet's "life" or "soul" reverts to its prime matter of dust or clay (v. 5). The allusions to the psalmist are "me" (literally, "my soul," *nepeš*), "my life" *(ḥayyîm)*, and "my soul" *(kābôd)*, which connotes "glory" also, i.e. the weight of God's presence, and is synonymous with "me" and "my life." The imaginative sequence is true to life. The pursuer runs, catches up with the quarry, pushes the victim down, tramples him or her, pressing the belly on the ground. The contact with soil or dust is suggestive of death; the ground is the place of the grave. The sequence, *nepeš, ḥayyîm, kabôd*, magnifies the focus. The contact with the ground illustrates the critical condition. The distance between the psalmist and God is felt, "Rise up, O LORD" (v. 6).

Suddenly the scope expands to international proportions. The cruelty is likened to the behavior of wild animals. The enemy is often described like a beast, which is not surprising given the inhuman behavior (v. 2). The lion which stalks, attacks, and dismembers depicts the adversary's ferocity, and the image sheds light on human savagery manifest in certain conduct. The military imagery and language intensifies the judicial aspect and is in keeping with the range of images in a self-defense like this (vv. 10, 12-13). Since the wicked threaten the innocent like ferocious beasts who devour prey, God will hunt them down with weapons.[5] God will ambush the leonine accusers, and the punishment they intended for their victim will rebound on them (vv. 15-16; see Pss 9:16; 28:4; 35:7-8; 37:14-15; 57:6; 141:10; Prov 26:27). The poet depicts the adversary, who conceives evil, is pregnant and in labor with wickedness, gives birth to deceit (v. 14; Job 15:35; Isa 59:4). This almost cinematic image encapsulates the psychological process of crime from its conception to its execution. The procreative process illustrates the fecundity of evil. Two metaphors which illustrate the punishment are charted along the vertical axis, as though it descends from above, falling into the hole one has dug and evil which recoils on one's own head. By an unwritten law of commensurate returns the punishment fits the crime. The instrument of the self-destruction of evil is the gaping mouth, the pit that will close on those who open it for evil.

The poet is careful with numbers. Seven times the divine name Lord occurs, the last time with "the Most High" (v. 17). The appearance in the superscription is unusual. Six times the noun *ĕlōhîm* (in the form "God" or "my God") occurs (counting the contested Hebrew reading in v. 6, translated in the NRSV "O my God"). Thus, along with the term "the most High" there are fourteen explicit references to God. Four conditions of the poet's supposed guilt are answered by four violent consequences (vv. 3-5).

The psalmist anticipates God's pardon which will be manifest in praise and renewed participation in the liturgy. He or she is committed to a thanksgiving for liberation and God's righteousness (v. 17). Psalms of complaint frequently end with praise. Confident that God is interested, the psalmist vows to invoke God's name and testify before the community to what God has done (cf. Ps 13:6).

Psalm 8
How Admirable Is God Who Remembers Us

Psalm 7 ends, "sing praise to the *name* of the Lord, the Most High" (v. 17), which links to the acclamation framing Psalm 8, "O Lord, our Sovereign, how majestic is *your name* in all the earth." Psalm 8 is a gem,

---

[5] Textually v. 12 (Hebrew v. 13) is difficult; the subject is vague, "he." The NRSV and the ancient versions understand "he" to mean God. Some modern critics prefer to understand the wicked as the subject (as in vv. 14-16).

consisting of an introduction (vv. 1b-2), and the body (vv. 3-8), framed by a refrain (vv. 1a and 9).[6] The plural (*"our* Sovereign") of the refrain contrasts with the singular (*"I* look"), which signals the alternating voices of soloist and choir. The poet speaks for the liturgical assembly. Praise of God and contemplation of the natural world evokes wonder and the contemplation of humanity. The Hebrew word *māh* is translated in two ways, *"how* majestic" (vv. 1, 9), to express admiration, and *"what* is the human person?" (v. 4), to marvel and question. Thus attention is drawn from the frame to the center: how admirable is God! what is humanity? If contemplation of the created world provokes a chorus of admiration, the uniqueness of the human in this vast theater provokes a disconcerting question by the only creature capable of introspection, the only one able to verbalize the implicit praise of all creation. This awe and questioning is the distinction of Psalm 8 and the key to its interpretation. The worshiper gazes on eternity then targets the self. How small the human is when compared with divine greatness, yet how great by God's favor! What is tiny, like an infant, bursts in amazement. Human privilege is derived from and reflects the divine majesty. Like other psalms which treat of creation (Psalms 19, 65, 93, 104), this one starts from God, traverses earth and sky (a merism embracing all creation), enters human territory, and finishes its course in God, the source and goal.

The poet juxtaposes infants with rebels (v. 2). One group joyfully explores the world and praises the sovereign creator, while the other rebels. The praise of the powerless confounds those who, believing themselves self-sufficient, do not submit to God. Psalm 149:6-9 affirms the same, that praise is stronger than God's enemies. The most effective weapon against God's adversary is praise.

Overwhelmed by the spectacle of the night sky (v. 3), the poet reflects that such beauty and sublimity is God's handiwork, exquisite ornaments hung in the heavens. With the artistry and care of a sculptor or potter, he outfitted the detail of the cosmos with his fingers (v. 3) and hands (v. 6). "[T]he work of your fingers" projects the image of an artisan, who attends to details with precision and care. The thought is interrupted, leaving a subordinate clause unfinished, as if the poet were awestruck (an example of the rhetorical device called *aposiopesis*).

God and the human meet in creation. The sensitive poet perceives the palpable divine reality that breathes under the skin of creatures. God attends personally to the human, who can marvel at this personal attention (v. 4; cf. Pss 90:1-3, 5; 144:3-4). Rather than feeling belittled, the poet exclaims, "what are human beings that you are mindful of them?" In awe of one's immense smallness in this grandiose spectacle,

---

[6] The text (vv. 1b-2) presents problems and, consequently, different translations.

the gaze turns on the self as one becomes aware that the human, small and insignificant, a breath and a shadow, is a marvel of the universe. God is the subject and the human the object of six verbs (vv. 4-8). God remembers, cares for, makes, crowns, gives dominion, puts under [his] feet. He is personally involved in human existence from birth and he promotes man and woman to a privileged position. God invested them with glory, an attribute of the divine, and appointed them as co-regents of creation. The poet is in awe of God, creation, and his or her mysterious place therein: "little lower than God . . . all things under their feet." Even the birds and fish, so difficult to tame and manage, are beneath. The place of humans is minuscule in comparison with the creator, but they are endowed with awesome dignity and responsibility in regard to the rest of the created world. The privilege stems from God's creative initiative and rests on incomprehensible grace. As they discover and praise God they recognize their true dignity, a discovery which confounds God's enemies.

The focus flits to and fro: "Lord, our Sovereign," earth, heavens, babies, God's enemies, the natural world, humans, their exalted position, "all things under their feet," domestic and wild animals, birds, fish, and again "Lord, our Sovereign." A clue to the psalmist's intent is the repeated word *all* (Hebrew cognates of *kōl*, vv. 1, 6, 7, 9). Humans share God's marvelous sovereignty over all ("*all* things under their feet"). While the opening refrain, "Lord, our Sovereign" resonates with the covenant theology that Israel is God's chosen people and the Lord is Israel's God, the rest of the psalm marvels at his regard for humanity and the rest of creation.

Literally the second query in v. 4 could be translated "[what are] the children of Adam that you care for them," evoking not Abraham or Israel, but everyone tainted by sin—an even greater cause for wonder at God's esteem! When it comes to humans, even a giant is only a babe compared to the heavenly heights and the distant home of the stars. The term *ben ʾādām*, translated "mortals" (NRSV), is traditionally rendered "son of man," with the accent on lowliness; *ben ʾādām* alludes not only to God's creation of male and female in the divine image (Gen 1:27), but also to the origin of *ʾādām* from the earth (*ʾădāmâh;* cf. Gen 2:7). Humans are dirt, shaped by the divine potter's dexterous hands, yet we reach to the sky and are endowed with an inquisitive consciousness that reaches into the self. We are lowly in condition and origin, yet transformed into little less than God, whose self-revelation in the universe enables us to acquire a right understanding of self, someone who receives God's particular attentions.

God deputized humans as vice-regents who participate in the divine honor. "[L]ittle lower than God" (v. 5) reads in Hebrew "little less than gods [*ʾĕlōhîm*]," meaning the members of the divine assembly. The LXX translation established a tradition, "for a little while less than the angels." The translation of *ʾĕlōhîm* as "angels" removes the threat of polytheism from the translation "gods," while the phrase "a little while" focuses on the brief span which humans enjoyed before the advent of sin. The universal sovereign went so far as to install humans as superintendents of creation and "crown" them with the regalia of "glory and honor," God's attributes.

There is an affinity between Psalm 8 and Genesis 1. The poet focuses on creation, the role of the human in relation to the creator. In Gen 1:26-30 humans are the culmination of God's creative activity. They bear the divine imprint, from which flows the blessing and imperative of subduing the earth and caring for it. In the face of such a wondrous charge, what do humans do? They praise, gaze, contemplate, and weigh their privileged worth, which saves them from pride, which in turn would injure their right relation with God. In another meditation on human frailty and God's greatness the rhetorical question is expressed like this:

> Who considers the power of your anger?
> Your wrath is as great as the fear that is due you.
> So teach us to count our days
> that we may gain a wise heart.

(Ps 90:11-12; see also Job 7:17-21; 10:3-22; Sir 17:1-15). These reflections have a wisdom texture, which questions the mystery of humanity, which is both lofty and frail, yet related to the question of God. A proper appraisal of humanity in relation to the creator wards off sin and rebellion, which is the earnest plea with which the following Psalm 9 ends:

> Rise up, O Lord! Do not let mortals prevail. . . .
> Put them in fear, O Lord;
> let the nations know that they are only human.

Psalm 9
The Lord Judges the Peoples with Equity

Psalm 8 expresses amazement at God, creation, and human dignity in the world. Psalm 9 opens with thanksgiving for God's wonders. The two caution that mortals (*ʾĕnôš*, 8:4; 9:19-20), who possess an intrinsic greatness and enjoy God's predilection, not exceed their limits as creatures.

Psalm 9 is difficult to map. It alternates between thankful praise and recognition of God (vv. 1-2, 7-12), narrative (vv. 3-6, 15-18), and request (vv. 13-14, 19-20). Internal correspondences resonate. God does not *forget* (*lōʾ škḥ*) the afflicted, while the pagan nations *forget (škḥ)* God (vv. 12, 17-18), which will work for their downfall. Those who know the divine *name (šēm)* trust in God while the *name (šēm)* of the wicked is blotted out forever (vv. 5, 10). God dwells in *Zion*, liberates the poet at the *gates* of death, so that in the *gates* of *Zion* one may rejoice in deliverance (vv. 11, 13-14). Zion's "gates" are the center of civic life, but the "gates" of death or Sheol block the impious from life (v. 17; cf. Isa 38:10).

Rich imagery depicts God, who defends the psalmist and condemns the wicked, razes the enemies' cities and erases their memory forever. Thus personal oppression is widened to the international arena (vv. 3-6). The enemy is national ("the nations," v. 5) as in related psalms (e.g., Psalms 2 and 3, and the "ten thousands of people," 3:6), which shows that the individual "I" voices the nation's plight. The liturgical character of the Psalter argues for interpreting the psalmist's adversary as the aggressor of the people, even in the so-called individual complaints. God is a stronghold (v. 9), an avenger of blood (v. 12), invoked as sovereign and judge (vv. 4, 7-8, 19), and protector of the afflicted and the oppressed (*ʿănāwîm*, vv. 12, 18; cf. 10:17). The besieged poet bargains, save me "so that I may recount all your praises" (vv. 13-14; cf. 6:4-5). He or she articulates the law of retribution. God is behind this mechanism of justice which rights the violated order (vv. 15-16; cf. 7:15-16).

Psalms 9–10 show traces of an acrostic scheme of ascending letters of the Hebrew alphabet,[7] and the fact that Psalm 10 has no caption argues in favor of this. Psalms 3–9 and 11–32 all have captions, which make the void in Psalm 10 stand out. The text is badly preserved, which accounts for the conjectural translations particularly in the *l, m, n, s,* and *ṣ* lines, around the juncture of the two psalms. The general call for help changes to an urgent personal appeal at the center (the middle letter *lāmed*), with the plaintive tone, "Why, O LORD, do you stand far off? Why do you hide yourself in times of trouble?" (10:1). Such a change of tone is not unusual in an acrostic (for example, Ps 34:11). The repeated invocation to "Rise up, O LORD" also unifies the composition (9:19; 10:12).

The Greek and Latin tradition joins what in Hebrew are two psalms, and this explains in part the different numberings used in some translations from Psalm 9 to Psalm 147 (see Appendix II). Thanksgiving dominates in Psalm 9, and reference is made to the national enemies. In

---

[7] This breaks down with the absence of the fourth letter *dālet* and the missing letter lines of irregular meter between *kap* and *peh* (9:19–10:6).

Psalm 10 the genre of complaint dominates and the enemies are personal. The Jewish tradition and modern western Christian practice shows a preference for use of Psalms 9 and 10 as separate psalms. The traditional liturgical practice of Latin Christianity, based on the LXX translation, joined the two. Praying them either separately or together makes sense. What appear to be distinct compositions, like Psalms 42 and 43, with different backgrounds and literary textures, were linked by common vocabulary, and in the evolution of the Psalter an editor touched them up and elaborated on the alphabetical sequence. Analogously, the refrain was probably added to Psalm 43 to link it with Psalm 42. In psalm study the conjunction of Psalms 9 and 10 is a perennial question, which can be resolved in their liturgical use.

Psalm 10
Why, LORD, Do You Stand Far Off?

Psalm 10 has four movements: invocation (v. 1), description of the wicked (vv. 2-11), the request and motivations (v. 12-15), and trust in God's intervention (vv. 16-18). The initial question, "Why, O LORD, do you stand far off?" articulates the indignation, impatience, and complaint.

The poet offers a terrible description of the wicked and their deeds. Arrogance is the root of injustice and a trait of the wicked, which moves them to oppress the poor, blaspheme, deride God and the divine law, scorn their enemies, aggrandize themselves. They suppose that God is not interested (v. 4). The transgression is summarized, in thought (v. 6), word (vv. 3-4, 7), and deed (vv. 2, 8-10), and consists of crimes against the neighbor and particularly against the defenseless. The list of wrongs begins and ends with blasphemy (vv. 3-4, 11). Contempt for God is expressed in oppression of the afflicted. The stance of the wicked and their scorn for God is described: "God will not seek it out" which is akin to "There is no God" (v. 4), "We shall not be moved; . . . we shall not meet adversity" (v. 6), "God has forgotten . . . , he will never see" (v. 11), and "You will not call us to account" (v. 13).[8] The image of God hiding the face implies that he shows no concern (v. 11; cf. Pss 30:7; 44:24; 69:17; 88:14; 104:29, etc.). The scorn for God is a persuasive reason for him to intervene. This complaint is answered by the affirmation, that God *does* see (v. 14).

---

[8] The Hebrew of v. 13 exemplifies the ambivalent position of the wicked. After the previous denials of God's existence (v. 4), the wicked are quoted as addressing God (v. 13). Some ancient versions translate this in the third person.

The poet portrays the wicked—hiding, watchful, tensed, ready to pounce on victims, to seize and drag them off—"like a lion in its covert" (vv. 8-10). A plea wells up spontaneously, "Rise up . . ., do not forget the oppressed" (v. 12). God does notice the affliction of the defenseless who confide in him. The helpless, orphaned, and exploited will be consoled. Motivated by the belief that the divine sovereign takes interest in people's affairs, the poet requests that the wicked be obliterated, that the pagans "perish from his land," that terrorists be banished (vv. 15-16, 18b). This is in stark contrast to the vindication of the oppressed (vv. 17-18a). The contrast is phrased succinctly, evil perishes and God reigns forever (v. 16). The motif of divine sovereignty, the banishment of evil, and relief of the defenseless is reminiscent of Psalm 97.

Psalm 11
God Hates the Lover of Violence

Psalm 11 has two parts. First the psalmist, apparently in the midst of a crumbling society, questions whether there can be any refuge besides God (vv. 1-3); then he or she reaffirms confidence in God's righteousness and confirms the just deserts of the wicked (vv. 4-7). Two threats to the just order are introduced by *kî*, "*for* look, the wicked bend the bow" and "*[i]f* the foundations are destroyed" (vv. 2, 3). A final *kî* introduces the axiom "*[f]or* the LORD is righteous" (v. 7). The divine name LORD frames the psalm and is the first word of both vv. 4 and 5.

The poet is tranquil even in danger and treats unsolicited counsel with a reproach, "how can you say to me, 'Flee like a bird to the mountains'" (v. 1). This is not the advice one would expect from someone who confides in God. A bird fleeing from the archer hides in the mountain underbrush. The assailant is described as a hunter who aims an arrow from a hiding place, "in the dark" (v. 2; see Pss 10:8-9; 64:2-6). Darkness does not obstruct the all-seeing God, whose vision unmasks the camouflage and secrets (vv. 4-5; cf. Pss 14:2; 102:19; 139:1-3). The repetition of *ḥzh* is significant because as God *beholds* humankind, the upright "*behold* his face" (vv. 4, 7). First, God's *eyes* appear, then the penetrating gaze. The vision of the upright is toward the light, God's face. In Hebrew verse 5 is formulated with the verb couched between two objects, literally, "The LORD the righteous tests and the wicked." Actors are "the upright," *yāšār*, or "righteous," *ṣaddîq*, which are distributed in symmetrical order: upright, righteous, righteous, upright (vv. 2, 3, 5, 7). Both the LORD and the righteous are *ṣaddîq*. God is judge of humanity, which is divided in two: just and unjust or innocent and guilty. The opposition is underscored by hate and love (vv. 5, 7), which divides the world according to two agents. God, who "*loves [ʾhb]* righteous deeds," "hates the *lover [ʾhb]* of violence."

The wicked ready their arms, take aim, but shoot in the dark and miss. The LORD examines, looks carefully, and hits the target. "[H]e will rain coals of fire and sulfur; a scorching wind shall be the portion of their cup." The wicked are bombarded by a fiery rain, so that even the cover of night is useless. The crumbling foundations, which would leave everybody in the lurch (v. 3), and the rain of "coals of fire and sulfur" with "a scorching wind" (v. 6; Pss 7:13; 18:11-14; 144:5-6) are cosmic images. Tottering "foundations" refers to governors and judges responsible for ensuring law and order in society (cf. Ps 82:5). The wicked will be destroyed like Sodom and Gomorrah (Gen 19:24; cf. Deut 29:23; Isa 34:9; Ezek 38:22; Lk 17:29; Rev 9:17-18; 14:10; 19:20), a stylized image which has moral impact. Both the story of Sodom and Gomorrah and Psalm 11 have in common a cosmic punishment for a moral imbalance. Such descriptive language is employed in the apocalyptic tradition and is a characteristic way of presenting an eschatological judgment on history. Because personal meanness has repercussions on the world horizon, the commensurate punishment will be dealt out by cosmic weapons. The "cup" refers to the destiny of the wicked.

The final verse repeats vocabulary of the psalm: upright, *yšr* (vv. 2b, 7); righteous, *ṣdq* (vv. 3, 5, 7); behold, *ḥzh* (vv. 4, 7), love or lover, *ʾhb* (vv. 5, 7). The repetition creates a sequence of opposites which looks like this:

> LORD, the assault of the wicked *(ršʾ)*, the upright *(yšr)*, the righteous *(ṣaddîq)* (vv. 2-3); LORD, LORD, God's eyes behold *(ḥzh)*, humankind (v. 4); LORD, the righteous, the wicked, the lover *(ʾhb)* of violence, [God's] spirit (v. 5); the wicked, the righteous LORD, loves righteous deeds, the upright behold God's face (vv. 6-7)

The psalm begins and ends with the LORD and "his face." The wicked, centrally positioned and daunting, assault the good, but gradually their threat fades and they end up surrounded by the righteous and God.

The mountain offers the illusion of security in a world rocked to its foundations with evil. The psalmist finds support in God's stable presence which the good can contemplate. The destiny of the righteous is to see God's face, that is, celebrate the liturgy (vv. 5-7; cf. Pss 17:15; 24:6; 27:4, 8, 13; 42:2). Because the foundations of society are shaky, the righteous can only rely on God, enthroned in the temple, a reflection of the heavenly sanctuary. The mountain is a safe refuge, but a better option is God, a person, not a place. Fleeing from one place to another like a bird is juxtaposed to a stable relationship with God.

Psalm 12
Villainy Is Exalted Among Humankind

Psalm 12 is a community request. The composition is lively and alternating voices form a concentric structure. The elements correspond to each other in inverse order:

A   vv. 1-2, God is addressed; good people have disappeared

   B   vv. 3-4, God is spoken about (the wicked are quoted, v. 4)

      C   v. 5, God speaks an oracle

   B'   v. 6, God is spoken about ("promises of the LORD")

A'   vv. 7-8, God is addressed; evil is rampant

The major contrast is between human speech, vain and false, and God's words, sincere and trustworthy (**B** and **B'**). To the scarcity of good people corresponds the increase of evil (**A** and **A'**). The term "humankind," *běnê ʾādām*, frames Psalm 12 and sets it in a universal context. The translation of some verses (vv. 5, 6, 8) is conjectural.

Evil is relentless. A weighty vocabulary about speech makes an impression: "utter lies," "with flattering lips . . . they speak," "boasts," "say," lips and tongue (repeated), "promises" *(ʾimărôt)*. The psalmist makes an implicit connection between the disappearance of loyalty and vicious liars. The tongue is a formidable weapon of destruction, and the one who controls the media controls public opinion. The source of corruption—lying, flattery, and deceit—is the perverted heart. The "flattering lips" or divided speech is illustrated in the phrase "double heart" (*bělēb wālēb*, literally, "with heart and heart," v. 2), a neat way to describe double dealing. God's oracle relieves the tension of the opening lines. Ironically it is situated after the challenge of the scoffers, "who is our master?" (v. 4), and inspires confidence as it contradicts the falsifying lips and tongues. The poignant contrast with human speech is that God's promises are genuine, pure silver with no dross of falsity, as is expressed by the phrase "purified seven times." This signals completeness (v. 6; cf. the crucible in Ps 66:10; Prov 17:3). The vocabulary for communication and speech apparatus is replaced by terms from metallurgy, which develop an image of polishing, refining, removing the dross and tarnish. God's word and promises are pure, unalloyed silver with a quality guarantee.

The beginning and end is a pessimistic diagnosis of the emergency state (cf. Ps 14:1-4). The supply of good people has been exhausted and everyone is corrupt. The wicked boast about their lips and tongues with which they wield power ("will prevail," *gbr*); God, in contrast, will rise up *(qwm)* to defend the victims of evil speech. The poet petitions God to "cut off all flattering lips, the tongue that makes great boasts." This would effectively leave the adversary mute. The final appeal urges God to intervene and reminds him of the gravity of the situation.

Psalm 13
Impatience—How Long?

Both Psalms 12 and 13 underscore wicked speech (12:2-4; 13:4), which makes God's help urgent. Like its neighbor, Psalm 13 is a complaint and a request for deliverance from personal assailants. The poet mentions God in each of three movements: complaint (vv. 1-2); request with three persuasive reasons (vv. 3-4); expression of trust and thanks (vv. 5-6). The haunting questioning "[h]ow long?" is typical of this type of psalm (see Pss 6:3; 35:17; 74:10; 79:5; 80:4; 89:46; 90:13; 94:3), and illustrates mounting urgency. The psalmist, depressed and in mortal anguish, provoked by the enemies' actions, looks at God, the self, and the enemy (vv. 1-2). The triple optic is repeated in the request. The psalmist asks that God remember him or her and look. The distance between God, who "hides his face," and the poet is eliminated by calling upon God by name (LORD) and invoking him as "my God," which adds a note of intimacy. The poet asks to be freed from the onslaught of impaired vision and death. "[L]ight to my eyes" means life (cf. Pss 19:8; 38:10). This request is centrally positioned and reinforced by the threat of the foes' victory song (v. 4; see Pss 35:19; 38:16). The adversary is really death, and the psalm is an invalid's cry. To complicate matters, God hides in silence and seems to delay in giving aid, which intensifies the sense of alienation, more agonizing than physical illness. The affliction the psalmist suffers is typically vague, and thus the psalm may be easily appropriated in a liturgy and transferred to another group in a different context.

Effective repetition sets the tone. The repeated "[h]ow long?" illustrates the protracted suffering, and even the sound of this Hebrew
phrase, ⁅ad-⁆ānâh, is a plaintive moan over the loss of God's nearness.
Repetition expresses mounting panic and thus the impatience with
which the psalmist wishes God would act. The psalmist looks inward,
"in my soul" and "in my heart." In order to be free he or she requests
(external) "light to my eyes," so that the (interior) "heart" will rejoice.
Repetitions also produce contrasts. The author exchanges an anguished heart for a rejoicing [gll] one, *lēb* or *lēbāb* (vv. 2 and 5). This
jubilation contrasts with the threat that "my foes will rejoice [gll]" at
my downfall (vv. 4-5). Three imperatives, "[c]onsider and answer" and
"give light," which request relief, are followed by three negatives; so I
do not sleep in death, so my enemy does not gloat nor my foes rejoice
over my failing (vv. 3-4). To induce God to intervene, the poet uses the
motif of trust in divine *ḥesed* and offers to broadcast joyfully God's
intervention. The final expression, God "has dealt bountifully *with me*
[ʿālāy]," contrasts with the end of the complaint where the enemy is
"exalted *over me [ʿālāy]*."

Confident that God hears and answers, the poet promises to celebrate the divine rescue. This type of psalm almost invariably moves
from the minor key of complaint to the major key of thanksgiving. In
the certainty of being heard, the suppliant, whether community or
individual, anticipates God's deliverance, and thus the psalm ends
with a promise of praise (v. 6; cf. Pss 7:17; 22:22-31; 56:12-13; 57:9-11).
Psalm 13 is a marvelous example of how tension gradually disappears.
Initially a sense of haste or urgency dominates. God, eternal, has plenty
of time; while the anguished mortal has only a little. The enemy, so imposing at the beginning, gradually recedes as the psalmist continues to
pray confidently to God.

Psalm 14
The Good Is Absent Among Fools Who Deny God

Psalm 14 begins with the fool speaking, *ʾmr* (v. 1), which thematically links with the adversaries' speech of the previous two psalms.
The theme of rejoicing (cognates of *gll*) links 13:4-5 and 14:7; the poet's
desired rejoicing (Psalm 13) is placed in the communal context of Jacob
and Israel (Psalm 14).

Psalm 14 is comprised of three movements: the human situation
(vv. 1-4), trust in the divine protection (vv. 5-6), and the request for
Israel's salvation (v. 7). The psalmist paints a dark panorama. It ap-

pears that no one in all of humanity is just or seeks God. But reality is
not so grim. A group of people belongs to God ("my [or "his"] people,"
v. 4; cf. v. 7) and is identified as "the righteous" and "the poor" (vv. 5-6),
people who "call upon the LORD," in contrast to the wicked who ignore
God (v. 4). Does this "people" include only chosen Israel, or does it
embrace every one who is upright and honest? The poet contrasts oppressive humanity with the good who belong to God, those who are
humble and oppressed by the godless. No apparent difference exists on
the basis of blood or creed, except in the phrases "deliverance for
Israel" and "from Zion" (v. 7).

The "fool" who denies God's existence clashes with the image of
God looking down from heaven in vain for anyone who is wise and
seeks God. God "looks down [šqp] from heaven" to see (r'h) if anybody is
looking (drš) for God. The complete absence of anyone seeking God is
affirmed four times, "all [hakkōl] gone astray," all (yaḥdāw) perverse, no
one (ʾên), "not one" (ʾên gam-ʾeḥād). God's searching of Adam's race
("children of Adam" or NRSV "humankind") from heaven, contrasts
with the devout person in Psalm 8 who is looking heavenward, seeing
there God's reflected glory and asking about the intrinsic worth of
Adam's children. Initially the poet exaggerates in insisting that the
earth is destitute of anyone doing good. This sense of the unopposed
triumph of evil is replaced by confidence that God will act in favor of
the oppressed (vv. 5-6). The plaintive tone of the beginning changes to
confidence of a hearing by God and an allusion to return from exile
(v. 7; cf. Ps 126:1).

Psalm 14, like its nearly identical twin Psalm 53, has seven direct
references to God, which creates a sense of the fulness of the divine
presence in a psalm which complains of God's absence. The focus constantly shifts: fools denying God (v. 1), God looking down from heaven
(v. 2), everyone going astray (v. 3), evildoers eating up God's people,
ignoring him (v. 4), God in good company (v. 5), the offense against the
poor whose refuge is God (v. 6), Israel and Zion rejoicing (v. 7). The
wicked are sullen compared with the righteous poor, who are paradoxically fortunate and in the end rejoicing. The final wish, not addressed
to God directly, "O that deliverance for Israel would come from Zion,"[9]
transposes what had been the somber tone of the prelude to a major
key.

For the psalmist, fools are those who do not invoke God. Their characteristic refrain "[t]here is no God" is akin to saying that "God has no
clout," meaning that he is ineffective and disinterested, a premise born

---

[9] Alliteration and assonance mark the phrase "When the LORD restores the fortunes," běšûb yhwh šěbût (v. 7; Hebrew parallels, Pss 53:7; 85:2).

of the fool's senseless immorality (cf. 10:4). The poet paints a dismal
picture of humanity sunk in sin. The image of the wicked who "eat up
my people as they eat bread" is unforgettable. The formulation is neat,
literally, "Do they not know, all the evildoers, *eating* my people *as they
eat* bread, and they do not invoke the LORD." A double negation, "do
not know" and "do not invoke the LORD," frames the statement; "my
people" is tucked between the repeated verb "eat," as if to illustrate the
squeeze. The pattern looks like this (a–b–c–b'–a'):

> they do not know—eating—my people—eat—they do not invoke

The present state of God's people is suffering. The drama mounts as
the psalmist addresses the evildoers (v. 6), keeping a distance from
them, identifying him or herself with God's elect and thereby threatening the adversary. May God quickly send relief from the temple, so that
there may be rejoicing! Psalm 14, which has elements of a complaint,
gives moral guidance to the liturgical assembly about the fate of godless people.

Psalm 15
Morality and Worship: Who Can Dwell with God?

In Psalm 15 and its cousins, Psalms 24 and 101 (cf. Isa 33:14-16), the
poet sets down conditions for participation in the temple liturgy. Ritual
questions (v. 1) invite an examination of conscience (vv. 2-5). Twelve
traits identify the sincere worshiper who will never totter (v. 5b). The
last sentence affirms the soundness of people who fit this description.
The question about worthiness touches the heart of biblical morality
and its connection with liturgy. Personal integrity and innocence
demand harmony between action and conviction. In the hierarchy of
religious values material offerings are subordinate to the interior disposition of which they are an expression (cf. Ps 50:23). Lack of moral
character warrants excommunication. Every imperative stated in
Psalm 15 is concerned with the law toward the neighbor, which means
that a person who is responsible in a community context is fit to celebrate the liturgy.

Two initial questions about who can be God's guests are answered
by a description of qualities, both positive and negative. A progressive
three-step series responds to the double query—one who walks, acts,
and speaks "truth from their heart." The movement progresses from

external conduct to internal motivation (v. 2). These three positive stances are followed by actions to avoid ("not slander," nor do evil, "nor take up a reproach"), which in turn are followed by three more positive qualities (despise [the wicked], honor the devout, "stand by their oath"), and again three negative. What the NRSV translates as "even to their hurt" (v. 4b) can be translated literally "does not retract [an oath]," which is followed by "not lend money at interest," "not take a bribe" (v. 5). The positive and negative conditions are arranged nicely, as shown here:

v. 2	walk blamelessly	
	do what is right	
	speak the truth	
v. 3		do not slander
		do no evil
		do not take up a reproach
v. 4	despise the wicked	
	honor those who fear . . .	
	stand by their oath	[do not renege]
v. 5		do not lend
		do not take a bribe
v. 6	. . . do these things	shall not be moved forever

The outcome is summed up in the last line, formulated in positive and negative ways.

A seventh negation (Hebrew *lô'*) introduces the summary, "Those who do these things shall *never* be moved" (NRSV). The verb *mwṭ*, translated "be moved," also means "stumble" or "trip." With this association the list of prescriptions and prohibitions begins and ends with a person walking: "Those who walk blamelessly" (v. 2) and "will never stumble" (v. 5). A play on the word *rgl*, ("foot" or "to trip") continues the "walking" image; the phrase "who do not slander with their tongue" could be translated "who trips not over his tongue" (v. 3).[10]

The ethical conditions which deal with the neighbor need to be fulfilled for one to have permanent access to God's dwelling. The last word makes these conditions absolute, "never," *lĕ'ôlām*. The two initial verbs, "abide" *(gwr)* and "dwell" *(škn)*, embrace both temporary and stable dwelling; *gwr* is for people on the move or away from home, like Abraham in Canaan, Israel in Egypt, or a foreigner in Israel's midst; *škn* refers to a permanent dwelling. To dwell or abide in God's presence does not depend on an individual whim or decision; the one who offers

---

[10] See M. Dahood, *Psalms I*, Anchor Bible (Garden City, N.Y.: Doubleday, 1966) 84.

hospitality sets down specific conditions, as in a list of requirements for renting an apartment.

The third and fourth conditions deal with speaking the truth from the heart and avoiding slander with the tongue. Together they embrace both intention and speech. The seventh and eighth conditions, to despise the wicked and "honor those who fear the LORD," are also complementary. Human conduct leans either toward virtue or vice. A person who wishes to dwell with God must side with God's friends against God's enemies. The last two conditions, taking interest and bribery, are facets of the same offense (cf. Ezek 18:8; 22:12). The crime in charging interest on a loan is unfair profit from the poor, and usury with another Israelite was forbidden (Exod 22:25; Lev. 25:36-37). Bribery corrupts the course of justice. Taking advantage of the poor and obstructing justice undermine the foundations of a society.

The poet reflects on the obligations of God's guest, the conditions for entering the temple and participating in the liturgy, which is equivalent to keeping good relations with the neighbor and enjoying God's closeness. The mention of the "tent" evokes the place where the ark of the covenant was kept during its sojourn in the desert and the initial years in Canaan. The "holy hill" is Mount Zion, God's chosen dwelling among humans. To "abide" ("to stay over as a guest") in the tent and to "dwell" both portray God as host and homeowner; the tent and the hill are God's property and home. To abide in God's tent and dwell on the holy mount means to enter the temple. Because nearness to God is a sure refuge and Mount Zion is unshakable against any assault (cf. Pss 27:5; 31:1-3; 61:2-4; 125:1), those who fulfill certain conditions "shall never be moved."

To "dwell" symbolizes life in union with God. Regardless of what the initial meaning was, God's "tent" and "holy hill" are metaphors for living in the divine presence either while on the road or at home. This is clarified by the ending, a generalization, "Those who do these things shall never be moved." To "abide" or "dwell" on the holy hill or in God's tent is a guarantee of stability and security. During the Exodus the tent was well cushioned by the presence of the tribes gathered all around it. A hill or high place provides both defense in time of attack and a safe place from which to see those who are approaching. To approach and dwell in the divine presence is possible given certain conditions: upright conduct, honesty with oneself and others (avoiding slander), not harming others, avoiding contact with the wicked, honoring the faithful, standing by oaths even when it entails personal loss, not practicing usury nor accepting bribes. All these ethical conditions demand correct relations with the neighbor, which intimacy with God presupposes. These conditions apply to all people in general, not just

Israelites. The poet calls them "friend," "neighbor," "those who fear the LORD," "innocent." He or she also speaks of the "wicked," with whom correct behavior prohibits relations (cf. Pss 1:1; 26:4-5; 101:3-4; 139:21-22). The poet's formulation of the relationship between personal ethics and worship approximates that of Psalm 50 and prophetic texts (cf. Isa 1:10-20; Jer 7:3-23).

Psalm 16
The Lord is Everything for Me

Psalm 15 is a liturgical examination of life at the entrance to the shrine, a scrutiny which emphasizes neighborly virtues lacking among the wicked in Psalm 14. The confession of innocence (Psalm 16) places the poet among those who, having passed the scrutiny, are admitted into the temple. Psalm 17 bears traces of this scrutiny (vv. 3-5); once passed, the psalmist is worthy to request God's help (vv. 6-9). The concluding verse asks for reinstatement in God's presence, an apt conclusion to the liturgy begun in Psalm 15. The phrase "never [or "not"] be moved," expressed with a negative and the verb *mwṭ*, links these three psalms (15:5, *lōʾyimmôṭ;* 16:8, *bal-ʾemmôṭ;* 17:5, *bal-nāmôṭû,* translated "have not slipped"). In Psalms 16 and 17 the negation *bal-* is preferred (16:2, 4 [twice], 8; 17:3 [twice], 5)—seven times in all. The "right hand" is mentioned (16:8, 11; 17:7). The concluding lines of both share vocabulary: "In your presence *[pāneykā]* there is fullness *[śbʾ]* of joy" (16:11) and "I shall be satisfied *[śbʾ],* beholding your likeness *[pāneykā]*" (17:15). A cognate from *śbʾ,* "have more than enough," is used again in 17:14. Other verbal connections between the two are the following: the night setting (16:7; 17:3); path or ways (16:11; 17:4); hold, *tmk* (16:5; 17:5); "O God," *ʾēl* (16:1; 17:6); "faithful" and "steadfast love" (from *ḥsd,* 16:10; 17:7); "refuge" (16:1; 17:7); "portion" (16:5; 17:14); "life" (16:11; 17:14). The numerous points of contact between Psalms 16 and 17 make one wonder whether the poet intended a sequence as he or she composed them.

Psalm 16 is an intense, loving, joyful confession of trust. The text of vv. 2b-4a, difficult to interpret, reflects the situation of someone who had previously worshiped other gods or joined others in doing so. A question in translation arises when one tries to decide whether vv. 3 and 4 are disjunctive or conjunctive. According to the NRSV the poet lauds the noble ones in the land (v. 3), denounces the idolaters, and denies contact with them (v. 4). In another interpretation the implication is that the "holy ones in the land," the false gods, are carriers of death, and the psalmist has definitively separated from them. It is more reasonable to understand this as a past affinity, "in whom used to be all my delight," against the NRSV, "in whom is all my delight." It is ironic that the verses which most elude interpretation are those which refer to idolatry. The poet is innocent of sacrificing or praying ("pour out" and "take their names upon my lips") to false gods. He or she adheres exclusively to the LORD.

The poet asks God to watch ("protect") his or her life (*šmr*, v. 1; see Psalm 121). With the formula "in you I take refuge" life is entrusted to God's care. Calling on God grows progressively more intense and personal (vv. 1-2), "O God," "the LORD," and "*You* [emphatic] are my Lord." The dead are warehoused in "Sheol" and "the Pit" (v. 10, synonymous parallel lines; cf. Ps 30:3; Jon 2:2, 6) where no one remembers or praises God (see Pss 6:5; 30:9; 89:48).

God is the psalmist's permanent counselor ("in the night," v. 7). The "night" (in Hebrew, plural) could mean nights of prayer or it could be a metaphor for sickness, loneliness, or life threatening experiences, which amount to the absence of light (see above, Ps 4:6). The psalmist has God "always before" him or her, continually enjoys the divine company, and for that reason will never succumb ("not be moved," v. 8a). What is more, God, who holds delights in his right hand, is at the poet's right hand and gladdens him or her (vv. 8b-9, 11). The whole person participates in this security as trust and joy permeate "heart" (*lēb*), "soul" (*kabôd*, "liver," the spiritual aspect of the person), and "body" (*bāśār*, the physical aspect). Death includes the loss of the divine presence and joy. Another word translated "heart" (*kilyôt*, v. 7, literally, "kidneys," the conscience) is the instrument of God's instruction. The present life is full as long as it is lived in intimate friendship with God (vv. 10-11; see Pss 36:7-9; 41:12; 49:15; 63:2-4; 73:23-26, 28). By virtue of this primary relation the psalmist is assured of walking the path of life, of happiness in God's presence. The conclusion recapitulates the last part by repeating key words and concepts, "right hand," forever, "before me" or "in your presence," and words for rejoicing.

"I have no good apart from you" (v. 2) summarizes how the poet feels about the relationship with God, and this is made more explicit in vv. 8-11. The psalmist pledges allegiance to God, who is everything for him (vv. 5-6). This confident relationship is the psalmist's inheritance. The "chosen portion" and "lot" are echoed in the "boundary lines," "pleasant places," and "a goodly heritage," which is legal language for landed inheritance. The metaphors "chosen portion," "cup," and inheritance come from Joshua and describe Israel's occupation of the promised land (cf. Josh 14:1-3; 18:8-10; Ps 142:5). Tribes and individuals drew lots to determine their territory. What fortune, God is the prize for the lottery! The Levites' portion was not the land but the LORD (Num 18:20), which included intimacy with God even at night (v. 7). This implies that the psalmist enjoyed a relationship with God which transcended the liturgy. A sense of God's presence is the source of joy and security. From this intimate experience the author entrusts him or herself to the future (vv. 10-11).

Psalm 17
A Legal Plea: Protect Me in the Shadow of Your Wings

The scenario of Psalm 17, a personal complaint, is straightforward. The persecuted individual has been unjustly accused, and he or she appeals to the divine court, pleads innocence, accuses the adversary, and requests a hearing and investigation of the case. Throughout the night, until the sentencing, the poet finds asylum in the temple. Come the morning he or she will be admitted to God's presence. The repetition of "just" and "righteousness" (from ṣdq), "your face" (NRSV, "from you"), pāneykā, and "see" or "behold" (ḥzh) (vv. 1-2, 15) frame Psalm 17, which can be divided into three movements, each initialed by requests: divine justice with the oath of personal innocence (vv. 1-5), liberation from enemies (vv. 6-12), and punishment of the adversary with the certainty of God's hearing (vv. 13-15). Multiple requests, eleven in all, depict an emergency situation (vv. 1-2, 6-8). The first movement is dominated by the judge's investigation and the plea of innocence of any crime whether thought ("heart"), word ("mouth"), or deed ("my steps"). The second request repeats šmᶜ, "hear," and "ear" from the first (vv. 1, 6). In the third request seven imperatives represent an urgent plea for redress against the enemy (vv. 13-14). The repetition of ršᶜ, "wicked," (vv. 9, 13), and qwm ("adversaries" and "rise up," vv. 7, 13), weave the second and third movements together.

The poet unfolds a visual drama. God's "eyes see the right" (v. 2); the poet prays to be guarded "as the apple of the eye" (v. 8); enemies' eyes are spying on the poet (v. 11); finally, the poet prays to behold God's face (v. 15). The mouth is also prominent. The poet denies sinning with the lips and mouth (vv. 1, 3); indeed, God's lips have instructed him (v. 4). The enemies, in contrast, "with their mouths . . . speak arrogantly" (v. 10). The poet's footsteps on the right path are tracked by the enemy (repetition of ʾašûr, "steps," vv. 5, 11). The poet's heart is innocent, and the wicked hearts are closed to pity (vv. 3, 10). The "deadly enemies" leave a horrifying impression with their closed *hearts*, offensive *mouths*, and threatening *eyes*. All this is compressed in the image of the lion. The psalmist (literally) *keeps, šmr,* God's words, who *guards, šmr,* him or her as the pupil of the eye (vv. 4, 8). Verse 8 is eloquently formulated in Hebrew, with "guard" and "hide" framing the double declaration and illustrating the protection, like this:

> Guard me
>   as the apple of the eye; in the shadow of your wings
> hide me

Choice vocabulary draws the vertical axis and weaves the composition together: the lion ready to pounce, lurking (*ksp* and *yšb*, v. 12), adversaries (literally, "those who rise up," v. 7), "[r]ise up" (v. 13), "cast to the ground" (v. 11), overthrow them (*krʿ*, v. 13), arrogance (a word for "high," v. 10). The other theme repeated in different ways, either reassuring or threatening, is that of surrounding; the vocabulary is telling —pupil and wings (v. 8), surround and close (vv. 9-11), hide and guard. The reader can imagine the scene. An innocent person who is accused has gone to the temple ("the shadow of your wings," v. 8) for God's verdict. Night represents a time for investigation on the judge's part (v. 3; see Pss 16:7; 139:11-12). Morning is the time of deliverance (v. 15; see Pss 30:5; 46:5; 90:14; 101:8; 143:8), when the sentence is pronounced.

The poet, unjustly accused, requests divine justice. He or she is certain that God will attend to the case and pronounce a favorable verdict, on the grounds of personal innocence (vv. 1-5). The poet can pass any investigation God might apply (vv. 3-5; see Pss 7:9; 26:2). God's eyes, always watchful (see Ps 11:4-5), can attest to his or her unsullied conduct and word. God will attend to this matter (vv. 6-7) because he hears and saves those who take refuge in him. This certainty leads to the petition, "Guard me as the apple of the eye; hide me in the shadow of your wings" (v. 8), a metaphor for the temple, where God is enthroned on the wings of cherubim (cf. Pss 36:7; 57:1; 61:4; 63:7; 91:4). God's desired protection contrasts with the threat of the wicked who, like wild beasts, accuse, pursue, and attack the innocent. The description of the ambush is typical. The assailants oppress, besiege, are ruthless like prowling beasts (vv. 11-12; cf. Pss 10:8-10; 22:12-14, 20-21; 35:17; 57:4; 59:6, 14-15). The psalmist prays that the present and future generations of the wicked get even more than they deserve (vv. 13-14). He or she desires an immediate and well-deserved punishment for their evil. "Rise up," says the psalmist, as if requesting a judge or warrior to defend the rights of the innocent (see Pss 3:7; 7:6; 9:19; 10:12). The outcome of God's just sentence ("when I awake") implies intimacy with God (v. 15). In contrast to people content with this present life, the psalmist will only be satisfied with God's company in the temple. The phrase "behold your face in righteousness" expresses the favorable verdict the psalmist will receive (cf. Ps 11:7).

Psalm 18
I Love You, LORD, My All

The Hebrew title attributes Psalm 18 to David and gives it a setting, the expression of the king's gratitude for a military triumph. It may have been used in the Jerusalem liturgy, perhaps as an annual thanksgiving for deliverance. A version of Psalm 18 is found in 2 Samuel 22 with slight variations, a text which has not suffered the modifications of continued use in the liturgy as has Psalm 18.

The structure is easy to distinguish. It is framed by invocations with divine titles and a doxology (vv. 1-3, 46-50). What follows the introduction is an elaborate description. The desperate psalmist is assailed by misfortune and death's allies; God stormily intervenes (vv. 4-19). The psalmist declares his or her innocence and meditates on the reasons for God's intervention (vv. 20-32); this movement is framed by God's "way," *derek* (vv. 21, 30). Another description of the deliverance by God who trained the king (vv. 33-45) is followed by a summary of praise, the concluding rite (vv. 46-50). The sevenfold repetition of *yšʿ*, "rescue" and synonyms (vv. 2, 3, 27, 35, 41, 46, 50) is in contrast with the sevenfold repetition of two synonyms, *ʾōyēb* and *śnʾ*, adversary (vv. 3, 17 [twice], 37, 40 [twice], 48).

The theme of the first movement, deliverance from the enemy, is announced (v. 3). The danger and the cry for help is portrayed with metaphor (vv. 4-6). Cords of death and Sheol (personified) entangle the helpless swimmer, torrents swallow and ropes strangle the victim. The metaphors derive from myths about Sheol and death, conceived as powers that hunt down and snare humans (cf. Pss 30:3; 88:3-4; 116:3). Death is likened to a river or ocean (cf. Pss 69:1-2, 14-15; 88:6-7; Jon 2:2-3, 5). The deadly peril is emphatically couched in synonymous parallel (chiastic) lines (vv. 4-5, a literal translation):

A	B
Surged around me,	the breakers of death,
B¹	**A¹**
and the destroying floods	overwhelmed me.

B²   **A²**
The cords of the underworld   enmeshed me;

A³   **B³**
they overtook me,   the snares of death.

This danger dominates, but God in the sanctuary hears the cry for rescue (v. 6). The distance between God and the human is bridged; a cry from the depths reaches to heaven.

The description of the divine warrior is impressive (vv. 7-19; cf. Pss 29:3-9; 77:16-19; 97:2-5; Judg 5:4-5; Hab 3:3-15). He swoops down amidst a ravaging storm, accompanied by high winds, dark clouds, thunder and lightning, hail, earthquake, and tidal waves. To set the scene in motion and foreshadow the cosmic transformation, earthquakes are registered by four verbs followed by *kî*, and the reason is given: "reeled and rocked . . . trembled and quaked, *because* he was angry" (v. 7). The furious warrior's descent is dramatized like an aerial attack. Cloaked by darkness and clouds, he gallops on a "cherub" with wings of a hurricane, tosses lightning javelins right and left, scatters fiery coals, bellows and snorts like thunder, terrorizes and convulses the natural world. The cherub is a personification of the storm cloud (v. 10; cf. Pss 68:4, 33; 104:3; Deut 33:26). It is also related to the ark of the covenant where God was preeminently present among the people (see Exod 25:18-20; 37:7-9; 1 Kgs 6:23-28; Ps 80:1). The rescuer's face is fantastic and terrifying, smoke coming from the nose, fire from the mouth, burning coals radiating from him. Divine anger is depicted in terms of fire. Not surprisingly, flames from the mouth "devour." The images are magnified to distortion, for example, in the detail of the sea bottom becoming visible during the storm, the flared nostrils of God's anger (v. 15), or God exhaling smoke and blowing fire from the mouth (v. 8). The poet catches our attention by the combinations of water and fire, darkness and light (vv. 8-9, 11, 15), and, curiously, hailstones and fiery coals appear together (v. 12). The divine descent spans the cosmos: "He reached down from on high . . .; he drew me out of mighty waters" (v. 16). The scene quiets down as the author reflects on the rescue and puts it in a logical sequence. God reached out, took hold of me, lifted me from the drowning waters, put me in a roomy place (vv. 16-19). The waters portray the adversary's daunting strength. Seven verbs with the personal object "me" paint God's plenary intervention. Why? "[B]ecause he delighted in me" (v. 19), which corresponds to the initial avowal, "I love you."

It is too easily forgotten that Psalm 18 is a love poem, which opens with the declaration, "I love you, O Lord, my strength" (v. 1; cf. vv. 19,

35). The basis of the psalmist's "strength" is God's love.[11] This avowal tinges the psalm with the background hue of personal surrender to God. The psalmist's love draws its power from God's love. This is evident from "he delivered me, because he delighted in me" (v. 19) and the final verse, "Great triumphs he gives to his king, and shows steadfast love to his anointed" (v. 50). How can God resist the litany of titles which invoke personal strength and protection, following "I love you"? The repeated pronoun "my" emphasizes the personal relationship. The attributes are a caress of words, a plea born of love (cf. Song 2:13-14).

The psalmist's correct behavior is described (vv. 20-24; cf. Ps 17:1-5). God rewards innocence, which is asserted boldly with an accent on deeds. The repeated phrases "recompensed me," "according to my righteousness," and "according to the cleanness of my hands" frame the description (vv. 20, 24). Divine favor rewards loyalty to God and the covenant. The psalmist generalizes in four statements that human behavior determines God's action (vv. 25-26). Because God repays virtue with goodness and vice with correction, every humble person can rely on him for protection (v. 27). This does not mean that God's nature and sentiments are subject to change, but his abiding presence is conditioned by the human response. The devout person can be assured of God's reciprocity by loving God. On the contrary, the perverted, those unfaithful to the covenant, see God as "perverse," because he judges them and abandons them to their perversity. Thus divine action is constant and equitable, an axiom which the psalmist believes and demonstrates in the ensuing description.

The vigorous images review the rescue. God "lights up my darkness," strengthens the psalmist to crush opposing armies and "leap over a wall"; "he is a shield" (vv. 28-30). Darkness, death, and chaos are allies. Light is life, and stretches to the psalmist's battered existence. God will grant the same to "all who take refuge in him." Surprisingly, in the course of the description of an intense, personal plight, the psalmist speaks of "*our* God" (v. 31). God instructs and equips the psalmist for military triumph: a belt of strength, safe passage, fleetness of foot ("like the feet of a deer"), a stronghold out of reach, amazing strength (to "bend a bow of bronze"), and training for battle (vv. 31-35). Military vocabulary and images are preferred as the situation unfolds (vv. 36-42). In an attack and allied victory, the psalmist pulverizes the enemy (v. 42; chiastic parallel lines in Hebrew, a–b–b'–a'):

---

[11] The declaration "your *help* has made me great" (NRSV, v. 35) is better translated "your *gentleness* [or "humility"] has made me great" (cf. the word *ʿănāwâh* in Ps 45:5 [Hebrew]; Prov 15:33; 18:12; 22:4; Zeph 2:3).

I beat them fine,	like dust before the wind;
like the mire of the streets	I cast them out.

The description is thorough and evokes creation in reverse. "I pulverized them," made them like dust. This reduction to prime matter symbolizes the loss of real substance. The fact that the wicked cried to God (v. 41; cf. v. 6) indicates that they were Israelites. The mention of "foreigners" (v. 44) suggests that some were non-Israelites. Do these battles at home and abroad embrace all adversity which has been surmounted? The triumph belongs to God, but it redounds on his royal servant, so that both civil and foreign disturbances in the realm can be quelled (vv. 43-45).

Based on repeated vocabulary, the final verses are a summary of the whole: "give," *ntn* (vv. 13, 35, 40, 47), "under," *taḥat* (vv. 36, 38, 39, 47), "enemy" (see above), "exalted," *rwm* (vv. 27, 46, 48), *ḥesed* (vv. 25, 50), "delivered," *yṣl* (vv. 17, 48), "rise," *qwm* (vv. 38, 39, 48), "peoples" or "nations," *gôyîm* (43, 49), "save," *yšʿ* (see above). The last verse expands gradually:

great triumphs	to his king
showing *ḥesed*	to his anointed
	to David
	to his descendants
	forever

The psalmist is identified as the king, God's anointed of David's line (vv. 49-50). The lesson is clear; the righteous person, sovereign or subject, will enjoy divine help and protection. God's love is not just a present reality, confirmed by God's past intervention in the sovereign's case, but it is proclaimed as a promise to future generations. "Anointed" in Hebrew is literally "messiah," a royal title. After the extinction of the monarchy, this title was adopted for the ideal king of a future, awaited restoration. The last verse sharpens the focus on the Davidic dynasty and the covenant bond of God's *ḥesed*.

Psalm 19
Creation and the Law Announce God's Glory

Psalm 19 has several points of contact with Psalm 18. The pattern *ʾimrat–yhwh ṣĕrûpâh*, "the promise of the LORD proves [true]," followed by "a shield for all who take refuge in him" (18:30) is repeated in 19:7-9 (six times). Other verbal echoes are "[my] rock," *ṣûr* (18:1, 31, 46; 19:14), "blameless" and "perfect," *tāmîm* (18:23, 25, 30, 33 ["safe"]; 19:7). The expression "the ways of the LORD," *darĕkê yhwh* (18:21, 30), echoes the synonyms for God's law (19:7-9); "ordinances" and "statutes" (18:22) appear in Psalm 19. The poet's desire to be safeguarded against guilt, *ʿăwôn* (18:23-24), reflects the examination of conscience (19:12-13). God is the shining lamp, and the law has a luminous quality (18:28; 19:8). The appeal to God, "my rock" and "my redeemer," frames the two (18:1-2; 19:14).

Psalm 19 has four movements, differentiated from each other by their changing themes: space and time (vv. 1-4a); the sun (vv. 4b-6); the law (vv. 7-10); an examination of conscience and the final request (vv. 11-14). In the first two the heavens, the firmament, day, night, and the sun's orbit honor the creator. Then the psalmist meditates on the moral order (vv. 7-10). The natural and ethical sections are linked. The sun is to the natural world what the *tôrâh* is for the rational being. As the sun warms the world, God's will expressed in the *tôrâh* gives light, life, and warmth to the human spirit (cf. Ps 119:105, 130; Prov 6:23; Wis 5:6; 18:4). In the last movement the poet addresses God and prays that his or her life conform to God's will.

The psalmist paints an unforgettable scene of the horizon exploding in vigorous, radiant sunrise. The protagonist charges from his lover's tent, dashes across the ceiling of the world and regulates the pulse of day and night by coming and going (vv. 4b-6; cf. Sir 43:2-5). Suddenly a different theme interrupts. Six parallel sentences are chanted: a synonym for law, the divine name (LORD or *yhwh*), an adjective or equivalent. The Hebrew *qinah* rhythm (3 + 2 beats to the measure) imposes the cadence of a drumbeat on the praise of the *tôrâh*. There is another sudden change as the focus of the poem turns inward for an examination of conscience, when the poet addresses God for the first time.

In the first two movements the poet glimpses the cosmos and mentions God only once (v. 1). In the last two the focus narrows to the LORD's (seven times) instruction (vv. 7-9, 14). Together the two halves answer the question, what is the source of revelation? The response is twofold, nature and God's revealed law. The *tôrâh* embraces natural revelation, yet transcends it, as it restores the soul and teaches wisdom. The cosmic and moral orders are complementary spheres of God's design; the two can be contemplated in the visible world and within the moral fiber of the heart.

The opening lines are startling because, amidst so much communicating, silence awakens the ear. Poetic license allows inanimate beings to testify to the divine majesty. The vaulted ceiling of the sky is space personified. Days and nights, time personified, are separated in two choirs. All are engaged in communicating—"telling," "proclaiming," "pouring forth speech," and "declaring knowledge." Even without sound the message is intelligible to the limits of the earth. Space and time, divine artifacts, silently resonate with and mirror their creator's glory, as a sculptor is known by his or her craft. No corner of creation is left untouched, as three appearances of "end" demonstrate (vv. 4, 6). The subject of this universal hymn? The "glory of God," "his handiwork" (v. 1), and the perfection of the *tôrâh*. This global vision of God and the divine will inspires a person to ask for pardon, even from unwitting sins of omission (vv. 12-13). As the proclamation reaches the outer limits of the cosmos (v. 4), the psalmist seeks pardon to the innermost depths (v. 12). Just as nothing can escape the sun's heat, so too hidden sins need to be absolved. The final movement presents the paradox. The law is perfect; I am not. Law enlightens and energizes; I can stifle and hide. I value and savor the law, but do not fulfill it. Unexpectedly the poet addresses God and asks to be attuned to God's plan for the universe.

Obstacles exist in the moral realm. A person can depart from God's design inadvertently (the "hidden faults"; cf. Lev 5:2-4; Ps 90:8), by arrogance, and by "great transgression." The poet confesses four types of sin, distinguishable from each other by degrees of awareness on the part of the sinner—oversights, "hidden faults," "the insolent," and the "great transgression." Oversights are unconscious. They are sins insofar as we are responsible to form and inform the conscience. The "hidden faults" may be justifiable errors summarily dismissed. The Hebrew term translated "the insolent," *zēdîm* (plural) either refers to arrogant people or it can be an abstract noun and thus mean "insolence," a conscious rebellion against God. A related term which sheds light on the present is in Num 15:30-31, "But whoever *acts high-handedly* [or consciously, *bĕzēdîn*] . . . affronts the LORD, and shall be cut off from among the people. Because of having despised the word of the LORD and broken his commandment . . ." (cf. Deut 17:12). The LXX and the Latin translations of Ps 19:13 understood *zērîm* ("alien [gods]") instead of *zēdîm*, a confusion of the similar Hebrew letters *daleth* and *resh*. Whether arrogance or idolatry, the sin consists in opting for an authority other than God's. The "great transgression" is either the sum of sinfulness or a category in itself. The psalmist asks pardon for any deliberate or inadvertent act which may disturb the moral order.

Once absolved, the poet can unite his or her modest words with the wordless, voiceless hymn of creation and the revelation of the *tôrâh*, and hope thus to please God. The poet prays that his or her inner life harmonize with the music and order of the universe. A dramatic change of theme, language, and style contrasts the realms of creation and morality. What appear to be distinct poems with little interconnection—two nature hymns, the anthem extolling the law, and the examination of conscience—coalesce in the end, where God is named "my rock and my redeemer," a word each from creation and law.

There are meaningful repetitions in Psalm 19. Synonyms for "words" are used (vv. 3, 4, 14). The last verse summarizes the various movements: "the *words* of my mouth and the meditation of my heart" reflect the outward expression (vv. 1-6) and the interior disposition revealed in the *tôrâh* (vv. 7-10). The repetition of the word *hide* (Hebrew *str*, vv. 6 and 12) is intentional. The sun's heat penetrates invisible depths; likewise the divine law reaches the innermost regions of the conscience. The word rendered "blameless," *tmm* (v. 13), derives from the same root as "perfect," *tĕmîmâh* (v. 7). Three times the Hebrew *rāb* is used. God's ordinances are more desirable "than gold, *even much fine* gold" (v. 10); your servant is warned that "in keeping them there is *great* reward" (v. 11); honoring the *tôrâh* will restrain the poet from "*great* transgression" (v. 13). The value of the *tôrâh*, the rewards for keeping it, and the consequences of rejecting it are all illustrated in this repetition.

The *tôrâh*, rather than a collection of regulations and prohibitions, expresses God's loving, solicitous will. It is attractive, precious and delicious. It is valuable in itself, has a lasting guarantee (v. 9a) and salutary effects (vv. 7-8). Contrary to the experience of civil law, the *tôrâh* is neither oppressive nor threatening. Expressions like "reviving the soul," "making wise the simple," "rejoicing the heart," and "enlightening the eyes" awaken the desire for it (cf. Psalms 1 and 119), which amounts to a holistic, spiritual and physical experience. The *tôrâh* is more desirable than valuable goods and more satisfying than sweets (v. 10). This means that its acquisition, in theory and practice, is the most sublime goal. The poet prays that God's *tôrâh* be the guiding principle in life, that he or she find favor with God and not stray. It provides the means by which a person may be forgiven and saved from wrongdoing. If God bestows pardon and the grace of constancy, the poet will be blameless and the song acceptable to God.

The sky's quiet, eloquent beauty and the sun's heat penetrates everything. The brilliant light, the splendor of the law, reaches to the human depths. God, who makes the natural world echo and reflect his touch, who regulates the sun, who imposes order on cosmic and human existence, intervenes repeatedly to rescue the human from arrogance. The law—perfect, sure, right, clear, pure, true—has a dynamic aspect, as it revives, instructs, gladdens, illumines. Yet rooted in the human heart is the tendency to arrogate and hide from the all-encompassing and penetrating reaches of the *tôrâh*. This tendency might grow to critical proportions, a "great transgression." Law, which enlightens, makes one conscious of sin. But its delicious and precious quality can inspire one to confession, which also glorifies God.

The truth that God exists is accessible to anyone who contemplates nature and the heavens. Scientific study of the world alone, however, does not answer the deeper question of the meaning and order of human existence. Neither microscopic nor telescopic study of the created order, nor scientific or poetic endeavor can bring one to fully appreciate the divine intention. In Psalm 8 contemplation of the heavens and God's works turned the poet inward to question human nature and praise God. Psalm 19 extols the *tôrâh*, which orders life, reveals error, and readies a person to praise and live in harmony with God.

Psalm 20
Grant Victory to the King

In Psalm 20 a group addresses the king and presents a series of requests for help and victory (vv. 1-5), a soloist guarantees a benevolent divine hearing (v. 6); a chorus contrasts human and divine strength, confirms trust in God, and requests victory for the king (vv. 7-9). Repetitions frame the psalm and each movement, as shown here:

v. 1   LORD *answer* you *in the day* of trouble
v. 9   LORD . . . *answer* us *on the day* we call

v. 1   LORD . . . *the name of the God* of Jacob protect you
v. 5   . . . *in the name of our God* . . . LORD

v. 6   the LORD *will help [hôšîaᶜ]* his anointed
v. 9   *Give victory [hôšîᶜâh]* to the king, O LORD

The king will be the beneficiary of the blessings (v. 9) and, through him, the whole people. The psalm revolves around the verb "answer" (vv. 1, 6, 9). Its first appearance articulates a desire, for God to answer. The second articulates certainty, "he will answer." The poet closes with the request, "answer us," which seals the psalm with confidence in God. The bracketing inclusion *answer* is strengthened by the expression "in the day" or "when" *(bayyôm)* and LORD (vv. 1, 9). Repeated expressions, "I know that the LORD will *help* [or *"give victory* to"] his anointed" and *"[g]ive victory* to the king" (vv. 6, 9), form another inclusion. The divine name occurs five times (including the long form "the LORD our God," v. 7) and, in addition, "the name of [our] God" (vv. 1, 5)—a total of seven. Initially, eight verbs implore God's favor: may [God] *answer, protect, send help, give support, remember, regard with favor, grant, fulfill* (vv. 1-4). "Fulfill" is repeated (v. 5), giving a total of nine requests. What the NRSV translates "our pride is in the name of the LORD" (v. 7) in Hebrew is an intensive form of the verb *zkr* ("remember") which, in the Hiphil (an intensive) form, means "rely." Earlier this verb appears as "May he [God] *remember* all your offerings" (v. 3). Four cognates of *yšᶜ* (translated in the NRSV "victory," "help," and "victories," vv. 5-9) focus on the victory won in God's *name*.

Every verse is composed in parallel lines. The end of the first movement is marked by the lengthening of a verse, "May the LORD fulfill all your petitions" (v. 5b). The change of tone in v. 6 indicates that some liturgical action probably was performed after v. 5, like the proclamation of an oracle by a minister (see Ps 12:5); this would account for the sense of security, "Now I know . . ." (v. 6). The poet draws a colorful image of people who rejoice "over your victory" and unfurl banners to signal the feast in honor of God and the anointed king (v. 5). The speaker is alternately plural ("we," vv. 5 and 7-9) and singular ("I," v. 6). The parallel lines of the last verse illustrate the solidarity between the king and the people:

> Give victory to the king, O LORD;
> answer us when we call.

The two are frequently identified in the Hebrew scriptures, as the people's welfare is a reflection of the ruler's.

The author eloquently juxtaposes the two sources of power and their consequences (vv. 7-8). Military arsenals (chariots and horses) are opposed to "the LORD our God." People who trust in the former will "collapse and fall"; those who trust in God will "rise and stand upright." The antithesis between reliance upon human forces and trust in God is a recurrent theme in the Bible (Pss 33:16-19; 44:3-8; 118:6-9; 146:3-5; 147:10-11; cf. 1 Sam 17:45, 47; Isa 31:1-3; Hos 1:7). Trust in material resources is folly. Invocation of the divine name is the decisive weapon in battle.

The mention of "sanctuary" and "Zion" suggests that Psalm 20 is a liturgy for the Judean king ("you" singular, vv. 1-5) before battle. In the Ancient Near East it was believed that a god fought the battles of his people. For the Israelites this meant a holy war in which God, enthroned on the ark, accompanied the troops. After building the temple the king directed the battle, but God commanded the action from Zion, where he was enthroned in the temple (v. 2), a reflection of the heavenly palace (v. 6). The "God of Jacob" (v. 1; see Pss 46:7, 11; 75:9; 76:6; always in a military context, with the connotation of victory) dwells in the temple. From there God defends and favors the people (see Pss 14:7; 18:6; 110:2; 128:5; 132:13-18). Psalm 20 may have been composed to accompany a sacrifice before the battle (v. 3). "[Y]our burnt sacrifices" refers to the offering that accompanied this liturgy; 1 Sam 13:9-12 reflects an appropriate setting. The poet is confident that God will help his "anointed," the king or, in a later time, the ideal "messiah" (v. 6; cf. Ps 18:50).

Psalm 21
The Sovereign Rejoices in Your Favor

Psalms 20 and 21 celebrate the sovereign's dependence on God. The first requests God's protection in battle, which is followed in Psalm 21 by a thanksgiving and promise of success. Together they are analogous to 144:1-11 (petition, thanks, and desire for prosperity). Vocabulary and themes forge their relation, as seen here:

"heart's desire" (different Hebrew expressions, 20:4; 21:2)

"petitions" and "[h]e asked" (from *šʾl*, 20:5; 21:4; cf. 21:2b, "request of his lips")

"your victory" and "your help" (*yĕšûʿāteykā*, 20:5; 21:1)

"mighty" and "power" (*gĕbûrôt*, 20:6; 21:13)

"right hand" (*yāmîn*, 20:6; 21:8)

"king" (*melek*, 20:9; 21:7).

Psalm 21 has two movements (vv. 1-7, 8-13), framed by Lord and "in your strength" (vv. 1, 13). Words for "rejoice" frame the first movement (vv. 1, 6). Cognates of *šyt* illustrate the sovereign's benefits and the adversaries' frustration; God is the actor:

you *set* a crown of fine gold (v. 3)

you *bestow* on him blessings forever (v. 6)

you *will make* them like a fiery furnace (v. 9)

you *will put* them to flight (v. 12)

God's actions total fourteen, eight in the first part and six in the second. The monarch and the people react to God's attributes, as seen at the beginning, middle, and end of the poem:

	divine attribute	reaction
v. 1	strength, help	king rejoices, exults
v. 7	*ḥesed*	trust, stability
v. 13	strength, power	assembly sings, praises

In the center, the monarch's trust in God is based on divine *ḥesed*. At both extremes are the sovereign's and the assembly's celebration.

Psalm 21 opens as a thanksgiving for the sovereign's prosperity and for the request granted. The unique focus is God's benefactions to the sovereign. Then the poet summarizes the first part, giving the grounds for the blessing (v. 7). In the second movement the community addresses the sovereign and expresses confidence that God will grant victory over enemies, a fitting prayer for a royal accession or its anniversary. The liturgy ends by praising God (v. 13). The concluding acclamation, "Be exalted, O LORD, in your strength," echoes the first verse and forms an inclusion. The negative particle (Hebrew *bal*) appears three times, always to the monarch's benefit: "have *not* withheld" his request, "shall *not* be moved," and "they will *not* succeed" (vv. 2, 7, 11).

The victor is God (v. 1), who ensures the welfare of the sovereign who embodies the people's welfare. This theology is also operative in Ps 132:10-18. The gifts enumerated are benefits of the covenant, the basis of divine generosity: blessings, a crown, long life, fame, lasting beatitude, prosperity, and "the joy of your presence." The last is the best, a personal relationship with God (vv. 3-6; cf. Ps 73:23-26, 28). The motive for thanksgiving is that God granted the sovereign's request for "life" (*ḥayyîm*, v. 4), which connotes health and prosperity. In the original context "length of days forever" refers to the perpetual blessings for the royal descendants and the nation. Later this phrase came to be understood as a reference to life after death.

The center of the poem focuses on the ruler's essential action, trust in God, which merits God's benefits, foremost among which is *ḥesed*, which keeps the sovereign on a firm footing (v. 7). The sovereign's enemies likewise oppose God's plan (vv. 8-12). The people pray that the ruler, who enjoys God's favor, will hunt out and destroy all opposition. Depending on the interpretation of the tense of the verbs, the succession of victories is either a description of the past, a declaration of the present state (as in the NJPS), or a desire for the future (as in the NRSV, RNAB, and NJB). One is left with the impression that the adversaries are "consumed" by the sovereign's blazing fire and God's wrath (v. 9). When enemies conspire against the monarch, God will rout them and aim their weapons back on them (vv. 11-12). Suddenly the psalmist invokes God's strength and anticipates the benefits of the sovereign's relationship with God, which amounts to certain victory (v. 13). This description exceeds any ruler's triumph; the scope is eventually raised to the hope for the messiah.

Psalm 22
My God, Why Have You Forsaken Me?

Psalm 22 is divided into three movements, two which dramatize the complaint (vv. 1-11 and 12-21) and a third which celebrates victory (vv. 22-31). The main stylistic feature is doubling, beginning with the opening invocation "my God." Doubling magnifies the complaint and the praise. The repetition "do not be far" (vv. 11, 19) sets the tone and divides the complaint in two sections. In each, God is "far," *rḥq* (vv. 1, 11, 19), "trouble is near," and there is no relief in sight (vv. 11, 19-21). Corresponding to God's distance is the proximity of danger and the siege of the corralling, ambushing enemy (vv. 12, 16). The sense of God's distance is heightened by vocabulary like "abandon" or "forsaken," no answer, "no one to help" (vv. 1, 2, 11). The opposition between far and near is resolved in the third movement, where the poet celebrates the liturgy in a great assembly.

The first movement consists of two grievances about the poet's trouble (vv. 1-2 and 6-8), each one followed by remembering the past, God's rescue of the ancestors (vv. 3-5) and God's care of the psalmist from birth (vv. 9-10). This is concluded with a petition (v. 11). The second movement is composed of two grievances (vv. 12-15 and 16-18), which describes the ambushing savages and encroaching death. The concluding petition intensifies the earlier one by repeating "do not be far" and "help" (vv. 19-21). Previously the psalmist concluded that "there is no one to help" (v. 11); now God is addressed, "come quickly to my aid," a clue that vv. 19-21 are transitional. Further evidence for a division in two movements is the repetition of two verbs "deliver [nṣl]" and "save [yšˁ]." At first, the enemies' taunts imply that God cannot "deliver" (v. 8, nṣl), while the poet complains that God is "so far from helping" (v. 1, yšˁ). Invoking God's help and requesting that God "deliver" and "save" expresses faith during an otherwise hopeless situation.[12] The anguished cry which began "My God, my God, why have you forsaken me?" climaxes in the double plea.

Repetitions frame the last movement, *zrˁ*, "offspring" or "posterity," and *spr*, "tell" and "be told" (vv. 22-23, 30). This movement also has two parts (vv. 22-26 and 27-31). The poet summons the assembly to celebrate deliverance (vv. 22-23), and he or she gives the reason for praise

---

[12] The verb, translated "you have rescued me" (NRSV, v. 21; Hebrew v. 22) reads, in Hebrew, "you [have] answer[ed] me." The RSV follows the LXX with "my afflicted [soul]," which the context supports. Some commentators hypothesize that a salvation oracle was delivered after the complaint and preceding the celebration, that is, between vv. 21 and 22 (cf. Ps 12:5).

(vv. 24-26). The expanding circle of worship includes all humanity (v. 27), the dying (those who "go down to the dust," v. 29; cf. v. 15, "you lay me in the dust of death"), and people yet unborn (vv. 30-31).

Psalm 22 opens with "my God" and the direct address "you," *ʾattâh* (emphatic, vv. 1-3, 9, 10, 19). The name LORD *(yhwh)* is first heard in the adversaries' sarcastic challenge (v. 8) and is invoked in vv. 19, 26, 27, 28. The shift from "you" and "God" to the "LORD" (cf. v. 22, "your name") signals the deepening intimacy with God as the prayer progresses.

The first movement elaborates the opening cry, "why have you forsaken me?" Ironic as it may seem, God's absence makes him palpable. If God were really thought to be absent, why pray? The poet derives the sense of "my God" from the community's experience of "the holy one" who is enthroned in heaven and in the earthly temple and whose saving acts are the motive for Israel's praise (v. 3). *"My* God" shares the experience of *"our* ancestors," who trusted even when they were afflicted. They cried out *(zʿq)* and were saved (vv. 4-5), but the poet calls *(qrʾ)* day and night and receives no answer (v. 2). The soul is torn between past and present experience. The thrice repeated motif "[they] trusted" confirms the historical relationship between God and the people and, by implication, between God and the poet. The fact that the ancestors were not frustrated accentuates the sense of God's abandonment. The juxtaposition of individual and community reappears in reverse order in the last movement, where the poet announces that God has saved him or her (vv. 22-26) and addresses the international assembly (vv. 27-31). Thus, the accent in the first movement is how God responded in the past to ancestors in distress; why not now! The dilemma is that the faith based on experience has been ruptured. The poet addresses that rupture as God's desertion, "Why have you forsaken me?"

Yet, the poet senses that God has always been involved (vv. 9-10; cf. Ps 139:13; Job 10:9-10), like a midwife who assisted at birth and laid the child at the mother's breast to be nursed. The image gives the impression of a whole life dependent on God. The reproach is implicit. If since the womb I have been in your care, what happened? Birth imagery recurs at the end. This same God will bring forth future generations to praise him (v. 31). Deliverance is like a second birth for the poet.

The image of a worm depicts the poet's alienation from him or herself (v. 6). A worm is the opposite end of the animal scale from the human. The conjunction is adversative; "they" were not disappointed (v. 5), *but* I am scorned, like a worm (v. 6). The poet is perplexed. He or she was not born a worm, but rather by God's tender care. So how to account for God's desertion? Once again the clash between past and present is painful. One's life was an experience of God's "delight," but now the person is scorned for trust in God by "all who see" him or her (vv. 7-8). The psalmist is the object of mockery, people making faces, shaking their heads. The implied argument is that if the people ridicule me, in effect they ridicule God and question the divine power to intervene.

The second movement (vv. 12-21) unpacks the theme "trouble is near" (v. 11). Using the motif "surrounds" (*sbb*, vv. 12, 16), the poet paints a surrealistic picture of the vacancy left by God's retreat. One is surrounded and badgered to death by a pack of evildoers. Bashan bulls fade into ferocious lions which emerge as dogs (cf. Ps 7:2; 10:9; 17:12). These animal metaphors symbolize vicious threats to life. The conventional pair of lion and bull represents the epitome of power. Is the king of beasts an inference of royalty? Hounds evoke the sense of helpless prey, which is how the psalmist feels. In the second appearance the animals—bulls, lions, and dogs—are listed in reverse order (vv. 20-21), beginning with "the power [literally, paw] of the dog." The parallel lines demonstrate that the "dogs" are human agents of evil who hound the poet with drawn swords, their identity blurred behind animal masks. Both the poet, a helpless worm, and the enemy, ravaging beasts, are dehumanized.

The animal threats alternate with physiological symptoms of distress and death's nearness (vv. 14-15 and vv. 16c-18). "Bones" is the first and last anatomical member mentioned, and it brackets the heart, mouth, tongue, jaw, hands, and feet. Altogether this depicts failing physical energies, beginning with the heart, affecting the speech apparatus (mouth, tongue, jaws), and finally extending to the limbs—seven members in all.[13] Immobilizing hands and feet effectively restrains the psalmist from fighting back or fleeing. The parceling out of clothing indicates that onlookers regard death as certain. The first part concludes with the focus on the sword, claws, jaws, and horns of aggression, which only God can resolve.

As with other complaints in the Psalter, the reader is never sure what the real trouble is, and this is due primarily to the picturesque descriptions. The psalmist describes him or herself as encircled by "strong bulls of Bashan" (v. 12). Strength drains away "like water" and one's heart melts like wax (v. 14). One might wonder from this description whether the suppliant suffers from sickness, anxiety, approaching

---

[13] The elliptical clause in v. 16b (Hebrew, v. 17) reads "like a lion my hands and feet," which the NRSV reads "my hands and feet have shriveled." The RSV follows the LXX, "They have pierced my hands and feet," an interpretation that Christian interpreters connected with Jesus' crucifixion. The meaning of the Hebrew is conjectural.

death, stampeding animals, personal attack by ungodly people, or some other distress. Furthermore, the emotional impact is described in terms of physiological effects. What ought to be solid and consistent, the bone structure, is limp and "poured out like water" (v. 14; cf. 2 Sam 14:14). Water, which is necessary for life, is absent, "my mouth is dried up like a potsherd, and my tongue sticks to my jaws" (v. 15). Reality is distorted. God lays a person in the dust, one's primordial substance, which symbolizes the approach of death (v. 15). Paradoxically, with the sinking sensation the poet surmises the presence of the distant, enthroned God (v. 3), who allows the inimical forces to have their day. This is the same conviction found in Job 6:4; 7:20; 10:8-17; 16:7-14; Ps 74:10-11. The poet feels abandoned by God, ambushed from without and within, and suddenly he or she imagines that God is an ally of the adversary. Thus God's closeness deals a mortal blow. It is incomprehensible to the psalmist that God, who brought one from the maternal womb, now deposits him or her in the tomb. The poet feels as fragile as a potsherd, so brittle that it could be crumbled to bits. From the alternating descriptions of the actual and the internal experience results an intensely subjective portrayal, which perceives humans as animals and the human body as a foreign substance. In this and other psalms the poet creates a shifting montage which evokes violence and dying that never comes in focus. From across the chasm that separates life from death the poet appeals to divine providence to bridge the distance (v. 19). In the plea "Deliver . . . my life" (v. 20), NRSV's "my life" is in Hebrew "my only one," *yĕḥîdātî,* which is a nice way to express the solitude felt by the poet and the growing consciousness of the self that comes from suffering.

God answers the desperate cry. The transition from tears to joy is sudden and without apparent cause (v. 22). If isolation means the onslaught of death, life means communion, and the poet broadcasts the rescuer's name in ever-widening ripples to "brothers and sisters" (v. 22), to distant nations (v. 27), and to Israel's future as embodied in the yet unborn (vv. 30-31). The poet is joined by past, present, and future company in the proclamation of God's action in his or her behalf. The former social outcast threatened by evildoers is now surrounded by believers. A wish for long life in the community replaces the attack of death (v. 26). The worshiper fulfills the promises made when in distress, prepares a communal meal, and sings thanks. The motif of "praise" *(hll)* recurs (vv. 22-26, four times) and the reasons are given. This recalls the earlier expression, "enthroned on the *praises* of Israel" (v. 3), and removes the irony of that statement in its context of the first tragic movement. The repeated "despise" *(bzh,* v. 24; cf. v. 6) links the final movement to the earlier plight. People despised me; God does not. God inspires and grants the praise. The "vows" are liturgical sacrifices pledged during the distress. They have a communal aspect as the poor people share them together as at a potluck. The duo, eating and praise, is found in Isa 62:9.

In a final crescendo the frontiers disappear (vv. 27-31)—of space, because God's sovereignty extends to the limits of the earth; of the psalmist's situation, because God's dominion encompasses all peoples; of life, because God's rule reaches beyond death; of time, because the memory of deliverance will extend to future generations. The poet, who feels about as low as one can get, a worm, who has been laid "in the dust of death," envisions a beatific future for all those "who go down to the dust" (vv. 15, 29). This part connects the fate of the afflicted with the future of God's reign. People of every place and time will worship. This will occur through the proclamation that God has delivered (literally, "made righteous") the afflicted (v. 31, *ṣĕdāqâh* the NRSV translated "deliverance"). God's righteousness consists in rescuing the psalmist from distress. This will be the incentive of the nations' worship; they will "remember" (Hebrew *zkr*, v. 27) and celebrate. This last part identifies the poet as the one whose suffering and salvation are proclaimed to the world as a call to repent (*šwb* in v. 27, "turn") and believe in God's sovereignty.

The expression *"remember* and *turn*,*"* *zkr* and *šwb*, for the pagans, stands out. These two verbs are usually applied to the Israelites, who are supposed to recall God's benefits and return to God from whom they have strayed. How to remember or return when one has never been privy to the relation, as with the pagans? In light of this, *zkr* and *šwb* assume a liturgical connotation; to make present, *zkr*, and to "turn," *šwb*, and redirect oneself. Thus, the term *šwb* means a change of religion, rather than the process of conversion in which the chosen people are involved constantly. The "turning" or conversion culminates in worship. Recognition of God does not necessarily imply inclusion in the liturgy, as in the final chapters of Isaiah or Zechariah, unless "before him" (literally, "before you") refers to God's presence in the temple.

The difficult Hebrew of v. 30 (NRSV, v. 29) reads "they ate and they bowed down all the fat ones of the earth; before him shall bend all who go down to dust, the soul who cannot stay alive." The NRSV and other interpreters correct the *ʾākĕlû*, "they ate," to *ʾak lô*, "indeed, to him." Such surgery on the text is unnecessary and in any case does not iron out all the problems of an obscure verse, which can be seen in relation to v. 26, "the poor *shall eat* . . . May your hearts *live* forever." The "fat ones" refers to the comfortable class, the weighty people, and the verse restates the universal declaration of v. 27 that, finally, everybody will worship God, the well-situated and the poor who barely eke out a living.

Psalm 22 portrays a typical case of need which can be applied to any person's distress. To pray this psalm is to transpose oneself and one's suffering to a liturgical setting. The strength of the liturgy lies in its grasp of the entire process from distress to thanksgiving for relief. A person who appeals to God for help (vv. 1-21) ends by praising him (vv. 22-31); the final exultation clashes with the initial pathos. In this psalm the tension between the afflicted individual and the communal celebration is so beautifully sustained that we take the individual as the voice of the group. The afflicted psalmist describes the pathos, appeals to God, is rescued, and promises public celebration. Psalm 22 cannot be the prayer of just any afflicted Israelite. In its present form the afflicted poet shares Israel's corporate vocation and David's messianic role.

The echoes of Psalm 22 in the passion accounts of the gospels make it difficult for a Christian to recite it without recalling points of contact between the two. This invites a word of explanation about the messianic implications of the psalms. Within the Jewish tradition much of the first Testament was understood as the history of salvation and a prophecy of its fulfillment in the coming of the messiah. The Christian believes that fulfillment is embodied in Jesus of Nazareth. The story of the messiah cannot be told without reference to the first Testament. Early interpreters of Jesus' life and works, including the four evangelists, understood the details of his person to be a fulfillment of prophecies, notably Isaiah and the psalms. The passion narrative was taken as a chronicle of the fulfillment of the innocent sufferer's plight in Psalm 22. Jesus paved the way for this interpretation by praying the opening verse as he was dying (cf. Mark 15:34). Thus, he showed how to read Psalm 22 and texts like it as messianic and typological. It is clear, from the recorded words of Jesus on the cross, that he identified his own affliction with that of the psalmist. Subsequently, first generation Christians saw associations between the fate of the suppliant in Psalm 22 and Jesus. The evangelists interpreted the crucifixion in the light of this psalm, as they adopted its language and alluded to it in their narrative. Jesus or the evangelist understood the fulfillment in the details of his passion and death, and thus the text was adopted and cited as an interpretive key to the person of the messiah.

The narrators of the passion employed Psalm 22 and some companion pieces from the first Testament for their typological and theological value. According to the typological interpretation, the passion narrative recreates and specifies the innocent figure persecuted by his contemporaries, yet liberated by God in the resurrection of Jesus, which corresponds to the final movement of Psalm 22. In the messiah, the type becomes real. The innocent victim who is subsequently liberated is preeminently Jesus of Nazareth. According to this theological interpretation, the psalm interprets the experience of suffering and liberation in the light of faith, as it reflects on the mystery of suffering and its paradoxical fecundity. Poems of Isaiah (42:1-4; 49:1-6; 50:4-9; 52:13–53:12) or Psalm 22 are familiar texts to meditate, interpret, and explain Jesus' passion to generations of believers. Thus, in light of the belief that the life of Jesus as the long-awaited messiah is the fulfillment of the prophecies, it is no surprise that the evangelist was guided in his narrative by certain particulars from the psalms.

Psalm 23
You Are With Me

Psalm 23 is composed of a pastoral scene (vv. 1-4), a banquet (v. 5), and a summary (v. 6). God enters the poem as shepherd (cf. Pss 28:9; 80:1; 95:7; 100:3; Isa 40:11; 49:9-10; 63:14; Ezek 34:10-16) and exits as sheik or host. The sense of safety and tranquility dominates. The idyllic scene of the flock in green pastures, the steady guidance with the staff in the valley, and the comforting protection of the rod against would-be assailants opens onto the relaxing scene—the freshness and aroma of oil soothing the head and neck, congenial dining and drinking even in the sight of enemies. Though the reader may be foreign to nomadic life, these images are accessible to anyone who experiences uncertain paths and fears any assault.

The images can be paired off. Space is projected as open pastures and a meal inside a tent with the flaps up. The final two verbs, "follow" and "dwell," recall the images of shepherding and banqueting. "Goodness and mercy" find their counterpart in the shepherd's staff and rod, and dwelling "in the house of the LORD" replaces the tent banquet. Two scenes are parallel; the pasture, water, and restoring the flock corresponds to the table, the ointment, and wine. The "darkest valley" corresponds to "my enemies," both representing some undefined danger; however fear is dispelled because God is present. The final adverbial clauses sum up the journey and dwelling, flock and guest: "all the days of my life" and "my whole life long."

Psalm 23 begins and ends by speaking about the LORD. In the center the poet addresses God (vv. 4-5). In Hebrew the emphatic pronoun "you," *ʾattâh*, is pronounced as the divine shepherd accompanies the psalmist during the perilous passage "through the darkest valley." Confidence is unshaken because *"you* are with me" (v. 4; see Gen 26:3, 24; 28:15; 31:3; Deut 31:6; Josh 1:5, 9; Ps 91:15), which is what Psalm 23 is all about. The direct address of God intensifies the sense of intimacy.

This "you" is framed by the personal name LORD (third person) at the beginning and end. The poet underscores the relationship with God by the use of pronouns (which are suffixes in Hebrew), "*my* shepherd," "he makes *me* lie down," "leads *me*," and "restores *my* soul." The similarity between the Hebrew words for "evil" *(rāʾ)* and "my shepherd" *(rōʿî)* is noteworthy (the consonants that form the words are the same). This wordplay pits the shepherd against threatening evil, which is not to be feared. For the moment, God disappears from the text and the lone psalmist negotiates dark valleys (v. 4a). The emphatic declarations "you are with me" and "they comfort me" bring God and the psalmist together again. This intimacy is summarized in the last line, "I shall dwell in the house of the LORD my whole life long."

The poet projects his or her internal life in images from nature and everyday activity—pastures (v. 1), still waters (v. 2), the valley (v. 4), God's table (v. 5), and the temple (v. 6). These images project the psalmist's spiritual experience. The shepherd and sheep, for being first, dominate the others. The poet's relations with God are like animal husbandry. Beastliness is tamed and tended by God. Divine guidance brings one to pastures and fresh waters, divine protection provides safe conduct through the danger zones; God's table signifies relaxing in God's presence;[14] the temple symbolizes a whole life spent with God (cf. Ps 84:4). Both movement and rest are represented by a tranquil walk and a relaxing dinner hosted by God. Psalm 23 is the prayer of an intimate of God, and it was preserved for use in the liturgy. The poet voices the community sentiments. The "table for me" is not a meal in solitude, but a convivial banquet, and the "house of the LORD" is a public place where the community enjoys worship and public life.

Psalm 24
Lift Up Your Heads, O Gates

Psalm 24 may be divided into three stanzas. It presents God, creator and owner of the world (vv. 1-2), the ethical standards of those who would enter the temple (vv. 3-6), and a gate liturgy, which consists of questions and answers in antiphonal style (vv. 7-10). Six times the divine name is sounded, culminating in the full form "LORD of hosts" *(yhwh ṣĕbāʿôt,* v. 10). A seventh reference is "the God *[ʾĕlōhîm]* of their

---

[14] The "table," *šulḥān,* is a rug or carpet placed on the ground for eating and drinking as at a picnic.

salvation" (v. 5).[15] The divine epithet "King of glory," found nowhere else in the Hebrew Bible, is repeated five times (cf. Ps 29:3). Cognates of the verb *nśʾ* occur six times, declaring innocence ("who do not *lift up* their souls," v. 4), *receiving* blessing (v. 5), and bidding the gates to *lift up* their heads (vv. 7 and 9). To these may be added the synonym, *ʾlh*, "ascend," used to articulate the initial question, "Who shall *ascend* the hill of the LORD?" (v. 3). Thus appearances of the two synonyms total seven. Two questions ("who?") about the identity of worthy humans are matched by two about God (vv. 3, 8, 10), who is initially styled as the creator, and later as savior and warrior (vv. 2, 5, 8). The human is the only creature capable of posing the question, examining the self, and consciously making room for God.

The community knew of certain conditions necessary for worship (cf. Pss 50:14-23; 51:17) and of barriers between themselves and God. In response to the questions, requirements for participation in the liturgy are articulated. Personal integrity is defined by deeds and intentions toward God and humans: untainted by bribery, purity of heart, aversion to idols, and innocent of perjury (v. 4). The parallel lines are chiastic:

A	B
clean hands	and pure hearts
B¹	A¹
no false gods	nor false oaths

The hands and the heart, a merism, embraces action and intent. Thus, the requirements are hands unsoiled by dishonest practice or perjury and a heart free of insincerity or idolatry. The negative formulation of the second hemistich is more specific than the beginning. It bars the idolater and the perjurer from the liturgy.

Psalm 24 opens onto God's universal domain, with no distinction of peoples. From this macroscopic view the lens changes, as the poet focuses on one point on the horizon, the temple mount. Universal rule is juxtaposed to local presence, the earth and its inhabitants, the temple and its visitors. The poem which initially acclaims God's universal sovereignty and secure founding of the world approaches the temple and celebrates an entrance rite (see Isa 33:14-15; Mic 6:6-8). The liturgy reaches its climax in the acclamation of God's triumphal entrance. This provides

---

[15] The NRSV, following the LXX and Syriac versions, adds a reference to God in the translation "the face of the God of Jacob" (v. 6), literally "your face, O Jacob" (following the majority of Hebrew manuscripts). The Hebrew of this half-line is conjectural, but the total of seven references to LORD and God argue against this added appearance of "God" in the NRSV.

the context for question and answer about the admission requirements for God's presence, the holy place (v. 3). Another voice responds with a generic affirmation, to be innocent in deed and intention. This is followed by two negative conditions, one referring to God and another to the neighbor, which reflect two commandments of the decalogue (Exod 20:3-5, 16; Deut 5:7-10, 20), to refrain from idol worship and false swearing. Those who fulfill these conditions will receive a corresponding reward, God's blessing and the verdict of innocence (vv. 4-5).

This query about the basis of a relationship with God in the context of acclaiming the "King of glory" joins the awareness of God's supremacy and the believer's caution. As in Psalms 15 and 101, the objective is to awaken the worshiper's conscience, inspire self-examination, inculcate an understanding of God's demands on humankind. This provides the appropriate setting and frame of mind for worship. These psalms do not separate religion and morality; rather, religion encompasses morality, informs and helps define it. Furthermore, such psalms correct a false notion of worship. The basic requirement of Israel's faith was the adherence to the one God and the rejection of idolatry. This practice ensures a relationship with God which in turn guarantees well-being. Those who "seek the face of God," that is, desire to know the divine will and be in God's presence are, in effect, God's people.

The procession arrives at the temple gates and another hymn is intoned, this time addressing the sovereign God of history, the hero of battles. This corresponds to the hymn to the creator and savior earlier. The temple "gates" are more symbolic than real (cf. Ps 118:19-20), as is evident in the personification, "Lift up your heads, O gates." They have to open wide, expand, raise their lintels for the divine sovereign's entrance—the ardent wish of any believer who wishes to entertain the eternal God in his or her heart and life.

Psalm 25
For the Honor of Your Name, Pardon my Guilt

The same phrase "lift up . . . [the] soul," *ns² . . . nepeš*, is used in contrasting ways in Psalms 24 and 25. The poet who lifts the soul to God (25:1) is not counted among those who "lift up their souls to what is false" (24:4). Psalm 25, an acrostic (i.e. a poem which is composed so that the first words of lines follow the sequence of the Hebrew alphabet[16]),

---

[16] A trait sometimes found in wisdom composition is the alphabetic acrostic, which illustrates comprehensive instruction. In the Hebrew text of Psalm 25 the

weaves together various attitudes which include trust in and longing for God's response (vv. 1-2, 5b, 15, 16, 20-21), guilt over past sin (vv. 7, 11, 18), the enemy threat (vv. 2, 15, 19). The psalmist pleads for relief in a first and a third movement, the initial invocation and request (vv. 1-7) and the concluding request (vv. 16-21). The second movement is a wisdom reflection (vv. 8-15). The poet's personality shines through toward the end. At first he or she is pensive, self-assured. But the mention of "net" inspires an introspective confession (v. 15). He or she is "lonely and afflicted," troubled at heart, distressed, guilty, hated (vv. 16-19). The final verse is an ejaculatory prayer on Israel's behalf, which gives the poem a corporate dimension (v. 22).

The composition is concentric. The first and last movements correspond to each other. Repeated vocabulary frames the psalm (vv. 1-3 and 19-21): *God, my soul* or *my life (napšî), my enemies (ʿōyēb), wait for you (qwh), not . . . shame (lōʾ . . . bwš)*. The poet alternately speaks to (vv. 1-7, 11, 16-22) and about God (vv. 8-10, 12-15). The wisdom reflection is interrupted momentarily in the middle (*lamed* or "l") verse by the invocation, "For your name's sake, O LORD, pardon my guilt, for it is great" (v. 11). Framing this is the insistence that God teach the humble his way (vv. 9, 12). The theme of instruction, woven throughout, is the subject of petitions (vv. 4-5), the hymnic description of God (vv. 8-10), and wisdom teaching (vv. 12-14). Among the repetitions are cognates of *derek* ("the way," vv. 4, 8, 9, 12), a synonym *ʾōrĕḥôt*, "paths" (vv. 4, 10), and the verb *drk*, "lead" (vv. 5, 9). God's "ways" are like lines traced on a map which the poet asks to know. The two synonyms and the verb derived from *drk*, path or walk, appear a total of eight times, which illustrates the wisdom concern. The theme of God's memory (cognates of *zkr*) dominates the verses where the poet adverts to a sinful past (vv. 6-7). The divine name LORD occurs ten times and is absent from the requests (vv. 16-20).

Psalm 25 is the prayer of an elderly person, alone and afflicted (vv. 7, 16-17), who requests distance from enemies, pardon, and instruction in God's ways. The fine metaphor "to lift up the soul" (v. 1; cf. Ps 86:4) has a counterpart elsewhere in the uplifted hands at the evening sacrifice and the raised hands toward the temple (cf. Pss 28:2; 134:2; 141:2). This is synonymous with the expressions "in you I trust" (v. 2), "I take refuge in you" (v. 20), and "I wait for you" (in vv. 5b, 21; see v. 3). The

---

initials of the first, middle, and final verses (lines 1, 11, 22) spell the Hebrew root *ʾlp*, "teach" or "learn" (also Psalm 34). This summarizes the content of the psalm both for the individual and the community. The Hebrew initials *"w"* and *"ś"* do not occur; there are two lines initialed with *"r,"* and both vv. 16 and 22 begin with *"p."*

plea to be spared humiliation by enemies is followed by a similar request for those who "wait," *qwh*, for God (vv. 2-3; cf. Pss 27:14; 37:9, 34; 39:7; 40:1; 52:11 [Hebrew]; 69:6; 130:5-6). In a tender moment the poet declares, "My eyes are ever toward the LORD" (v. 15), and then prays to God, "Turn to me" or "Look at me" (v. 16). The eyes fixed on God expresses hope and longing. One prays with the eyes because the feet are knotted in the net (v. 15). May God turn his face to the psalmist's upturned face. The poet desires to be freed from the narrow space, set in a large space (v. 17). After looking toward the LORD, he or she considers the narrowness of the heart.

The initial invocation anticipates the dominant sentiments, longing and trust. The person who trusts in God will not meet with disillusionment, shame, or failure. The central movement reflects on God's ways which are the expression of the divine *ḥesed* and will, which the psalmist wishes to know to avoid danger and be protected and blessed. This part culminates with the rhetorical question, "Who are they that fear the LORD?" and the reflection which underscores God's benefits towards his adherents. To the initial desire for instruction in God's ways (vv. 4-5), the poet concludes by requesting pardon, freedom from enemies and tribulations, and Israel's deliverance.

Psalm 26
Vindicate Me, LORD, for I Have Walked in Integrity

Much of Psalm 26 describes the poet who examines his or her conduct and attitudes in a prayer for acquittal. The initial appeal, "judge" or "vindicate me" (NRSV), is followed by "I [have] *walk*[ed] in my integrity," which forms an inclusion and introduces the primary motif, the psalmist's innocence (vv. 1b, 11a, the verb *hlk*, cf. v. 3). The frame is solid, as shown here:

vv. 1-2	vv. 11-12
I walk in my integrity	I walk in my integrity
I trust *[bṭḥ]* in the LORD	I will bless *[brk]* the LORD
vindicate me *[špṭ]*	redeem me, be gracious *[pdh, ḥnn]*
without wavering *[mᶜd]*	stands *[ᶜmd]*

Petitions also frame the poem (vv. 1-2, 9, 11). A concentric pattern is evident:

A right walking (vv. 1-3)

    B the psalmist eschews the wicked company (vv. 4-5)

        C ritual purity and liturgical participation (vv. 6-8)

    B' may the psalmist not be destroyed with the wicked (vv. 9-10)

A' right walking and "My foot stands on level ground" (vv. 11-12)

As often in Hebrew composition, there is no clear strophic break. The declaration, "I do [will] *not sit*," *lôʾ yšb*, frames vv. 4-5 (cf. Ps 1:1).

To six appearances of the divine name ("LORD") is added "your glory" (v. 8), completing God's plenary (sevenfold) presence. There are two opposing groups, "the great congregation" with which the psalmist worships (v. 12) and the company of the wicked from which he or she wishes to be completely dissociated. Six synonyms designate the sinner (vv. 4-5, 9), "worthless," "hypocrites," "evildoers," "wicked," "sinners," and "the bloodthirsty" or, literally, "men of blood." These latter are specified (v. 10):

> . . . in whose hands are evil devices,
> and whose right hands are full of bribes.

Those who scheme and bribe refers to corrupt judges. The wicked have no spiritual side; their actions convict them. As in Psalm 139, an examination of conscience which culminates in a curse and divorce from the wicked (139:19-22), the poet asks to be kept from any complicity with evil and requests acquittal (vv. 9-11). Rather than request their punishment, the poet takes it for granted, "Do not sweep me away with sinners" (v. 9). Yet the poet insinuates that he or she may have been lumped together with the evil company; thus the vacillation between the declaration of loyalty, the willingness to submit to God's will, and the awareness of the precarious position. The poet is not presented as persecuted or a victim of the wicked and bloodthirsty. In the end he or she reaffirms integrity, upon which the initial plea is based (vv. 11-12). Finally the poet will broadcast the deliverance in the assembly. The "great congregation" (*maqĕhēlîm*, v. 12) where God is blessed contrasts with the hated "company" (the cognate *qāhāl*) of evildoers (v. 5). God's actions on behalf of the individual resonate in the worshiping assembly.

The poet asks to be scrutinized by God even to the secret motives ("my heart and mind," v. 2; cf. 17:3; 139:23). He or she affirms integrity in positive and negative ways (vv. 3-5) and keeps company, both in intention ("steadfast love is before my *eyes*") and behavior ("I *walk* in faithfulness"), with the divine attributes *ḥesed* and faithfulness (*ʾĕmet*).

Confidence lies in acknowledging God's loyalty to the faithful; this includes the repudiation of the wicked in every form. On the basis of personal innocence the poet is purified and joins the procession around the altar to commemorate what God has done (vv. 6-7). The affirmation of loyalty continues, formulated in opposite terms: the poet *hates* "the company of evildoers" and *loves* "the house in which you [God] dwell" (vv. 5, 8). Another word pair confirms the opposition, to *sit, yšb,* with the wicked (vv. 4-5), and to *"go around," sbb,* the altar of God. This implies that the wicked do not participate in the liturgy, and evil conduct is not found in the temple. The mood fluctuates, ranging between trust and uncertainty. The result is a poignant statement of the experience of God and the awareness that it is human nature to stand precariously between the hope of acquittal and the fear of being found guilty, in suspense between uncertainty and confidence.

Contrasts abound: good and bad conduct, presence with evil or at God's altar, "company of evildoers" and "great congregation." The poet's clean "hands" (innocence, v. 6) contrast with the evildoers' "hands" ("evil devices" and "full of bribes," v. 10). To the clean hands is added a firm footing, "[m]y *foot* stands on level ground" (v. 12); the two guarantee all-around good conduct. The final parallel lines confirm the blameless behavior, request God's intervention, and promise future recognition. After the emphatic "As for me," the psalmist continues like this:

A	B	C
in my integrity	I walk	redeem me, be gracious

B¹	A¹	D
my foot stands	on level ground	. . . I will bless the LORD

Once again the merism, walking and standing, embraces all activity. The verb *hlk,* walk (vv. 1, 3, 11), places the poet on the path; this is reinforced by *bwᵓ,* "consort," and *sbb,* "go around." Interestingly, the opposing camp is seated, *yšb* (v. 4). The sense of being on one's feet is sustained with expressions, "without tripping" or "wavering," and "[m]y foot . . . on level ground" (vv. 1, 12). The quatrain in vv. 4-5 is framed by *lōᵓ yšb;* it looks like this:

A	B
I do not sit *(lōᵓ yšb)*	with false people

B¹	A¹
and with hypocrites	I do not consort *(bwᵓ)*

A²	B²
I hate *(śnᶜ)*	the assembly of evildoers

$\mathbf{B^3}$	$\mathbf{A^3}$
and with [the] wicked	I do not sit *(lōʾyšb)*

The terms, "wicked" and "evildoers," are more general than the first two categories, the liars and hypocrites. The use of *yšb* and *bwʾ*, "sit" and, literally, "go," a merism, denies any association with the wicked. It is no accident that the wicked, worthless *company sit,* while the poet, who vigorously participates in right conduct, *walks* or *stands* amidst a worshiping *congregation* (vv. 1, 3-5, 11-12).

The psalmist details behavior with a double schema: I have done well; I am innocent of any evil. This is a confession similar to those in Psalms 7 and 17 (see also Ps 18:20-24; Job 31). On one hand, one has acted rightly, trusted in God, kept him always in view. On the other, he or she has avoided wicked company and behavior, like the just person of Psalm 1. Rather than keeping company with the perverse, for whom the poet professes an aversion, one has recourse to the temple, the object of affection because there God's "glory" resides. He or she joins in the liturgy, washes hands in innocence (action), praises and gives testimony (word), and loves "the house in which you dwell" (attitude).

Psalm 27
The LORD's Goodness in the Land of the Living

A remarkable attraction to the temple links 26:8 and 27:4, a connection reinforced by the literal usage of the rare word *mîšôr*, translated "level ground" or "level path" (26:12; 27:11). In Psalm 27 a discernible concentric pattern is formed by repeated themes. The central expression of intimacy with God (vv. 4-10) is framed by the enemies (vv. 2-3, 11-12) and declarations of confidence (vv. 1, 13-14). The poem can be charted like this:

A   confidence, repeated "LORD" and "[of] whom shall I fear" (v.1)

   B   the adversary threatens (vv. 2-3)

      C   intimacy with God (vv. 4-10)

   B'   the adversary threatens (vv. 11-12)

A'   confidence, "Wait for the LORD" (repeated) (vv. 13-14)

The divine name ("LORD") occurs thirteen times, and "God of my salvation" (v. 9) appears once, for a total of fourteen, which makes God fully present, even when the psalmist is under attack. The initial divine

name is followed by two rhetorical questions about fear. The concluding expression "wait for the LORD" is repeated. The rigorous parallel
hemistichs of vv. 1 and 3 reinforce confidence and dispel fear. The
psalmist's single-minded quest and consolation is the divine presence
in the temple, which orients all life (v. 4). Any other concern is of minor
import.

Changes of address reflect the agitated state of the poet who opens
with a confession of trust in God (third person, vv. 1-6), shifts to a
prayer addressing God (second person, vv. 7-9, 11-12), and again
speaks of God (third person, vv. 10, 13-14). An inner voice invites one to
seek God's presence, and he or she hesitates, "Do not hide your face
from me" (vv. 8-9). The imperative mood is prevalent in vv. 7-14, as one
pleads seven times addressing *yhwh*. Three imperative forms ("hear,"
"be gracious," "answer," v. 7) are followed by another four ("not hide,"
"not turn," "not cast," "not forsake," v. 9). These are followed by three
more ("[t]each," "lead," "not give . . . up," vv. 11-12). Thus a total of
ten jussives or imperatives articulate the urgent plea, five positive and
five negative. The sequence looks like this:

> hear
> be gracious
> answer me
>
> > do not hide
> > do not turn
> > do not cast me off
>
> do not forsake me
> teach me
> lead me
>
> > do not give me up

The image of an orphaned child is employed to stress God's faithful
attention. It is inadmissible for a parent to abandon a child or a mother
to forget her baby (v. 10; cf. Isa 49:15). God is more intimate and loving
(cf. Pss 103:13; 131:2) than father or mother, with all of their tender
affection. The poet trusts that he or she will enjoy the goodness and life
which God gives ("the land of the living," v. 13; see Pss 52:5; 116:9;
142:5; Isa 38:11). This reaffirms the desire for life and God's beauty (v. 4).
The psalmist rallies his or her soul (using a singular imperative) to
"wait" with the final repeated phrase, which amounts to an exhortation
to renew and maintain trust, the dominant sentiment in this prayer.

Verbal motifs weave the psalm together: "my salvation" (vv. 1, 9),
"my adversaries" (vv. 2, 12), "[my] heart" (vv. 3, 8, 14), the *rise* of an
assault (*qwm*, vv. 3, 12), "life" and "living" (*ḥayyîm*, vv. 4, 13). The poet
"seeks" God's face and favor, as earlier he or she "sought" to dwell in

his tent (*bqš*, vv. 4, 8; see Pss 24:6; 40:16; 69:6; 105:4). Repetitions include clusters of three appearances of "tent" (two Hebrew words, "shelter," *sūkkâh*, and "tent," *ʾōhel*, vv. 5-6), "face" (or "presence," *peh*, vv. 8-9), and "fear," *pḥd* or *yrʾ* (vv. 1 and 3). In addition, synonyms for "conceal" form another triplet (*"hide* me," *ṣpn*, *"conceal* me," *str*, and "do not *hide*," *str*, vv. 5, 9).

God is identified as light (v. 1; cf. Isa 60:19-20; Pss 36:9; 89:15; 104:2). Carnage depicts the enemy's savage nature, their verbal abuse (v. 2). This enemy is likened to an army (v. 3). The real trouble is false legal proceedings against the psalmist (v. 12), a recurring crime in the Psalter. A person can be threatened, have reason to fear, yet remain inwardly calm. The metaphor "to behold the beauty of the LORD" bespeaks visual contact in the temple (v. 4) and expresses the poet's desire for God's presence ("face," vv. 8-9; cf. Deut 31:11; Hos 5:15; Pss 11:7; 24:6; 42:2). The security of dwelling in God's house "all the *days* of my life" is contrasted with God's shelter "in the *day* of trouble" (vv. 4-5), a vague expression which can be applied to any threat. This means that, compared to God's lasting protection, trouble does not last long. Presence in the temple is akin to being safely out of reach *"high* [using a word derived from the verbal root *rwm*] on a rock." It offers asylum from danger. The high place on a rock folds into the image of "my head is *lifted up* [*rwm*] above my enemies all around" (v. 6); again the sanctuary comes into play. The "tent" (*ʾōhel*) embraces the repetition of *rwm*. The sequence looks like this (a–b–b–a):

"tent," *ʾōhel*—"set me high," *rwm*—"lifted up," *rwm*—"tent," *ʾōhel*

In this context the verb *sbb*, "surround" (i.e., "my enemies *all around*"), illustrates the sandwich effect of these words. What begins with safety and security in the sanctuary ("tent") is elevated to a high place, out of reach. These images, particularly the tent, are liturgical, like the sacrifices offered "with shouts of joy" (v. 6).

Relational terms bespeak the intimacy between God and the poet, "my light and my salvation," "the stronghold of my life," "your servant," "my help." To "see" or enjoy "the goodness of the LORD" connotes material benefits which derive from divine providence (v. 13). A vocabulary of trust shapes Psalm 27: "whom shall I fear" and "of whom shall I be afraid" (v. 1); "my heart shall not fear" and "I will be confident" (v. 3), "my head is lifted up" (v. 6), "I believe" (v. 13), "wait" (v. 14); "be strong, and let your heart take courage" (v. 14). God protects, provides shelter, hides, sets the poet out of danger, teaches, leads. Adverse situations corrode the psalmist's confidence—war (v. 3), family strife (v. 10), lawsuit (v. 12). The "heart," where fear resides, is spoken about and addressed, to bolster confidence: "my heart shall not fear" (v. 3), "my heart says" (v. 8), "let your heart take courage" (v. 14). Trust conquers fear. In the end the psalmist trusts, but residual fear remains. More than anything else, it is fear of the loss of God, which one counteracts with faith in the LORD's goodness, hope, courage, and waiting.

One of the last expressions results in a striking anacoluthon (an incomplete sentence) in Hebrew, "If only I were certain of seeing the goodness of the LORD in [the] land of living," the opening clause of a conditional sentence. This illustrates the state of the psalmist's soul. The first half of the poem is straightforward and confident. The personal crisis is reflected in the incomplete rhetoric. The text fragments, just as a person who prays may speak in ejaculations or unfinished thoughts (vv. 8, 13-14). The unique desire, "to live in the house of the LORD all the days of my life" (v. 4), is an analogy for enjoying God's ongoing presence. To dwell in the temple is the privilege of priests and Levites (cf. Pss 65:4; 84:4; 134:1) and serves as a metaphor for living spiritually close to God, contemplating the divine beauty (cf. 63:2). Here is the seed of a belief in eternal life. The "land of the living" (v. 13) arouses the instinct for a belief in the afterlife, a genuine union with God even after death.

Psalm 28
Hear My Voice

Psalm 28 has two movements, an urgent request (vv. 1-5) and praise (vv. 6-9). In more detail Psalm 28 can be charted like this:

vv. 1-2   the psalmist invokes God
vv. 3-5   the wicked get what they deserve
vv. 6-7   the psalmist thanks God
vv. 8-9   request on behalf of the people

The initial prayer is accompanied by a ritual gesture, uplifted hands toward the innermost sanctuary, *debîr* (only here in the Psalter; cf. 1 Kings 6–8). Instead of saying "hear me," the poet uses the negative, "do not refuse to hear me"; the alternative is drastic, death ("go down to the Pit"). God's silence would defer the innocent psalmist's acquittal. The thanksgiving embraces both verbal ("my song") and thought or intention ("my heart"). What is lacking in the first movement is the communal presence or participation. The expression "hear the voice of my supplication" *(šmᶜ qôl taḥănûnî)* is repeated and formulates both the petition and the answer (v. 2; the same phrase is translated differently in the NRSV of v. 6). Either God has already intervened or the psalmist is so certain of his eventual intervention that he or she regards it as an already accomplished fact.

The agitated psalmist of the first movement is suddenly relieved (v. 6), which indicates that a liturgical act or divine oracle (not present in the text) interrupted the prayer. What was requested for the individual is transferred to the assembly. The focus widens from the individual to the people. The ending is a prayer for God's flock. God is for the psalmist what he is for the people, "strength" and "the saving refuge of his anointed" (vv. 7, 8). The parallel lines argue that "his people" and "his anointed" are one and the same. This liturgical composition passes through the moments of invocation, confession of need, acknowledgment of the divine power and action, recognition of God's willingness to respond, thanksgiving, and renewed confidence.

A double repetition of terms (vv. 4-5), "their *work*" in opposition to "the *works* of the LORD" (the verb *p˓l*) and the "*work* of their [the wicked] hands" *(yĕdêhem)* in contrast to God's *handiwork (mā˒ăśēh yādâw)* expresses the polar tension. Meanwhile the poet raises *his hands* in prayer and is threatened by the "workers *[p˓l]* of evil" (vv. 2-3). The psalmist is pitted against the wicked. Everything he or she does is in relation to God; everything they do is divorced from God, which effectively reduces God to the silence or inaction which one wishes to avoid. The psalmist requests mercy for him or herself and for punishment of the wicked, who are just plain false, speaking one way and thinking another. The double expressions "break them down" and not "build them up" (v. 5; cf. Jer 1:10; 18:7-9; 31:28; 42:10; 45:4) are consistent with the doubling in v. 1, "do not refuse to hear me" and "if you are silent to me." The wicked should be punished both for their evil deeds and because they have not acknowledged God's deeds. If God is silent, the poet will be reduced to the silence of "the Pit" (v. 1). But the poet is not silent, cries out repeatedly while the wicked speak hypocritically, "peace with their neighbors" (v. 3). "Heart" is played back and forth. The wicked hearts engender evil, while the psalmist's heart trusts in God and rejoices (vv. 3, 7). The wicked are first of all neighbors, who abuse the greetings of "peace." The evil born in their hearts will be evidenced by the works of their hands.

The poet opens passionately, addressing God as "my rock," a secure and indestructible refuge (see Pss 18:2, 46; 19:14; 62:2, 6-7; 92:15; 144:1). In the end these sentiments are confirmed, "The LORD is my strength and my shield" (v. 7). As a result of misfortune and danger, the poet has one foot already in the grave and the pull of gravity is felt (v. 1). Without God's quick relief the psalmist risks descending to "the Pit," (a synonym for Sheol), in which case there will be no possibility for praise. The poet describes a person with hands uplifted in prayer, facing the temple. Words accompany the gesture of *raised* hands (the verb *nśʾ*, v. 2). In the end the poet asks God to "lift up" ("carry") the people (a repetition of *nśʾ*, v. 9). The psalmist's prayerful gesture anticipates God's sustenance, lifting up, of the community of believers. This hope on the psalmist's part is couched as an ejaculatory prayer, "be their shepherd, and carry them forever," an image of the shepherd carrying the sheep on the shoulder. The metaphors "heritage" and flock ("shepherd") strengthen the bond between God and the people.

Momentarily, remembering these wicked, the poet forgets the self, and with equal passion as at the beginning prays for strict justice according to their evil conduct and their incapacity to recognize God's actions (vv. 4-5; see Ps 54:5). The poet formulates a theology of retribution in traditional terms. In the world as God created and ordered it, wickedness works its own destruction, and the punishment will be commensurate with the nature of the sin. On the other hand, the poet and God's people who have prayed so earnestly deserve to be saved, blessed, and carried forever.

Psalm 29
God's Thunder Voice

Psalm 29 is a hymn to God's majesty and power. The three movements comprise an invitation to praise (vv. 1-2), a description of the theophany (vv. 3-9), and a concluding acclamation (vv. 10-11). God's powerful voice is manifest in tremendous natural phenomena, the storm and torrential rains. Repetition of words and phrases stamps the composition. The scope is vast and complex, and the locations are like lightning striking over an immense space: waters, cedars, Lebanon, Sirion (a poetic name for Mount Hermon), the desert, the Kadesh desert. The thunderstorm that comes from the sea, crashes against the forests of the coastal range, and even shakes the remote desert (vv. 3-7). The repetition *qôl yhwh*, "voice of the LORD," and geographic names map the advance of a storm from north to south, from Lebanon to the Kadesh of Sinai. This phrase thunders seven times at irregular intervals, like lightning. (Both "thunder" and "voice" translate the same Hebrew word; cf. Ps 68:33.) God appears as in a storm (see Pss 18:7-15; 68:4, 8; 77:16-18; 97:2-5; 104:3-4). The divine name (LORD) resounds eighteen times. The initial summons is addressed to supernatural rather than human beings, the heavenly court (cf. Ps 89:5-7). Four invitations to the "heavenly beings" to praise (vv. 1-2) and four statements (two declarative, two jussive, "May the LORD . . .") of God's action reinforce the frame (vv. 10-11). The psalm culminates in a prayer for the people. The glory is described in a sevenfold proclamation of the power (vv. 3-4) and effects (vv. 5-9) of "the voice of the LORD." To this voice a chorus responds, "Glory" (v. 9).

The first thunder resounds above the waters where God is enthroned (vv. 3, 10). It breaks through barriers, cuts loose a storm down below. God's raised voice dominates the flood and is like the cyclone which twists and uproots even Lebanon cedars, an image of stability and shade (see Pss 92:12-13; 104:16). With the waters unleashed, the earth convulses. What appeared to be stable mountains, Lebanon and Hermon, are turned into playful animals which scamper in the field, jolted by the terrible spasms (see Ps 114:4). Only after the fifth thunderclap does the poet allude to lightning, "flames of fire," which illuminate the scene (v. 7). This is true to experience, if not meteorology. One hears thunder, experiences the storm's ravages, then notices the lightning, which has flashed all along. God's voice is the cause, as the formidable spectacle of power and glory unfolds. The poet reproduces auditory and visual effects: the echoing crash of the thunder ("the voice of the LORD"), the flames of fire, and the quaking earth and twisting trees. The Hebrew of v. 9 reads, ". . . the LORD causes the deer to calve." The NRSV and other interpreters understand plant imagery, consistent with the second hemistich,

> the voice of the LORD twists the oaks,
> and strips the forests bare . . .

The searing ravages of a lightning bolt running down the trunk of a sturdy oak is an impressive image. The thunder is echoed in the liturgical acclamation "Glory!" God, manifest in the storm and in serene majesty, communicates strength and peace to the people (v. 11). Once the storm subsides, the still point is God, enthroned above the chaos, blessing the people with peace.

The skeleton of Psalm 29, based on repetitions, looks like this:

v. 1	ascribe to	the LORD	
	ascribe to	the LORD	glory and strength
v. 2	ascribe to	the LORD	glory
		the LORD	with splendor
v. 3	the voice of	the LORD	over the waters
			[God of] glory
		the LORD	over the mighty waters

v. 4	the voice of	the LORD	powerful
	the voice of	the LORD	with splendor
v. 5	the voice of	the LORD	breaks the cedars
		the LORD	breaks the cedars of Lebanon
v. 7	the voice of	the LORD	flashes flames
v. 8	the voice of	the LORD	shakes the wilderness
		the LORD	shakes the wilderness
v. 9	the voice of	the LORD	causes, strips glory
v. 10		the LORD	sits enthroned
		the LORD	sits enthroned
v. 11		the LORD	gives strength
		the LORD	blesses with peace

The organizing motif is "glory," which occurs at the beginning and end of the proclamation of God's voice (vv. 3, 9). Glory summarizes the divine attributes. The "God of glory" (v. 3, a unique variant of "king of glory"; see Ps 24:7-10) is a term for the display of God's divine majesty in the world. Both the heavenly palace and the earthly temple chant "glory." The effect is sound rather than speech, but sound that communicates.[17]

In addition to the other repetitions, *ʿōz*, "strength," is meaningful (vv. 1, 11). God is recognized for "strength" and, in turn, gives "strength to his people." Amidst all the dramatic action the last verse demonstrates that divine power is displayed with absolute serenity. What has been described is proper to God the eternal sovereign, who has dominion over all the forces. This divine power that appears with destructive force in nature redounds to the benefit of God's people in history. There is nothing to fear, neither cosmic powers nor historical forces, because "the LORD bless[es] his people with peace" (v. 11).

Psalm 30
Weeping Lingers at Night but Joy Dawns with the Morning

In captions where the words "A psalm. A song" appear together with a name (cf. Psalms 65, 68, 75, 76, 87) the addition "Of David" in the last position is unique. "A song" is unique among the captions of

---

[17] The dominant sound "*ō*" echoes throughout the Hebrew text and creates an auditory effect; aside from the seven echoes of *qôl* ("voice"), the "*ō*" resounds in

Book One; "at the dedication of the temple" in conjunction with "Of David" is perplexing because David did not dedicate the temple. According to the Talmud, Psalm 30 was prayed in the festival which celebrated the purification of the temple after its desecration by Antiochus Epiphanes (1 Macc 4:52; 2 Macc 10:1-8). It has verbal connections with King Hezekiah's prayer (Isaiah 38) and Psalm 6. Considering the subject matter, the caption gives a hermeneutical cue for the use of this prayer, and assigns a dramatic personal prayer to a liturgical celebration, transposing the "I" of the drama to corporate Israel.[18]

Flashback is employed. According to the unfolding drama, Israel was assaulted by personified Death and its cronies. After a near lethal blow, God intervened and joy was retrieved. Israel fell mortally ill, and enemies were poised to rejoice (vv. 1-2). Once recuperated, the poet offers this prayer, perhaps to accompany a thanksgiving sacrifice (vv. 3-4). The broadcast transforms personal relief into a general teaching (v. 5). Suddenly the mood changes as the poet reviews the illness. He or she had taken health and God's care for granted (vv. 6-7a, "I said in my prosperity, 'I shall never be moved'"). When the illusion collapsed, it caused a terrifying sense of the loss of God's favor (v. 7b) and the personal longing increased. God's name (LORD) echoes in the account of the crisis (vv. 7-8, 10), which intensifies the experience.[19] God's praise would diminish if the poet were reduced to dust, *ʿāpār* (v. 9; cf. Pss 6:5; 9:13-14; 88:10-12), his or her elemental state (cf. Gen 3:19; Ps 104:29; Job 10:9; Eccl 3:20; 12:7). Once the crisis is surmounted the psalmist committed to praise God (vv. 11-12). The poem concludes as it began.

The phrase "O LORD my God" and cognates of *śmḥ*, "rejoice" and "joy," frame the composition (vv. 1-2 and 11-12). This repetition draws a contrast; the *rejoicing* of the enemies was muted, and God "clothed me with *joy*." The theme is marked by the repetition of derivatives of *zmr*, "praise," and *hdh*, "thank" (vv. 4, 9, 12). The plural imperatives ad-

---

kābôd ("glory," four times), *ʾōz* (twice), *qodeš, koaḥ, lĕbayôn* (twice), *kĕmô* (twice), *śiryōn, lahăbôt, yeḥōlēl, ʾayyālôt, wayyeḥĕśop–yĕʾārôt*, the suffix *ô-* ("his"), *kûllô, lĕʿôlām, baššālôm*.

[18] The only other composition which the Hebrew caption assigns to a particular occasion is Psalm 92, for the Sabbath. The Greek titles of Psalms 24, 48, 93, and 94 assign them to other weekdays. According to the Greek versions, Psalm 29 was chanted in the feast of Tabernacles.

[19] The divine name (LORD) plus other designations ("my God," vv. 2 and 12; "his holy name," v. 4; "your face," v. 7) occur fourteen times. The second occurrence of LORD (NRSV, v. 8) represents the Hebrew *ʾădōnāy*, literally "my Lord," just as earlier it was "my God" (v. 2). The use of "my" expresses the sense of intimacy with God in prayer.

dressing "you his faithful ones" stamp the individual prayer with a communal context (v. 4).

A central verse summarizes the crucial predicament (v. 5). God's anger lasts but a moment, but divine goodness all life long. The verb *lyn* paints a nice picture. Weeping comes *to spend the night,* but rejoicing dawns with the morning. The poet understands that swift changes were brought on by God, who hid his face (v. 7), then suddenly changed the dirge into dancing (v. 11). The "mourning," *mispad,* is normally a dirge performed by relatives and friends. Here the image is exaggerated, as though the sick poet recited it for him or herself or others anticipated the death. The Hebrew verb translated "dancing," *hwl,* connotes writhing or whirling, and this terse formulation expresses the dramatic change from inertia to vigorous exercise.

The "moment," *rega^c,* is the opposite of a lifetime and describes God's anger versus God's pleasure (v. 5). The numerous polar contrasts are a stylistic trait of this psalm: God and the foes (v. 1), raising and descending, Sheol and life (v. 3), God's anger and favor, weeping and joy, night and dawn (v. 5), firm and shaken (vv. 6-7), mourning and dancing, sackcloth and festive clothes or disrobing and clothing (v. 11), praise and silence (v. 12). All this illustrates the tension between dying and rising, confusion and confidence. "I cried to you for help, and you have healed me" establishes the basic pattern (v. 2). The repetition of *lě^côlām* goes in two directions: "I shall *never* be moved" and "I will give thanks to you *forever*" (vv. 6, 12).

Contrasts or antitheses are expressed in reversals. The movement from divine anger to favor is given tension by the tug in the opposite direction from security to distress (vv. 5a, 7). The sense of security, "I shall never be moved" (v. 6 and Pss 10:6; 16:8; 62:2), vanished when God hid his face, which occurs when sin or unfaithfulness eclipses God's presence. "Hide your face" is a metaphor which portrays the divine reaction to sin (cf. Deut 31:17-18; 32:20; Isa 8:17; 54:8; 59:2-3; Jer 33:5; Ezek 39:23-24, 29; Mic 3:4; Job 13:24; 34:29; Pss 69:17; 143:7). The tears of affliction are dried in a fleeting night. God's wrath, the poet's suffering and weeping are transient guests which, once passed, leave room for joyful thanksgiving when God shows his face and favor (v. 5; see Pss 46:5; 90:14; 143:8). The alternation of weeping and rejoicing anticipates the move from mourning to dance. The threat that praise (verb *hdh,* v. 9) be muted by death is relieved when the soul breaks silence with thanks (*hdh,* v. 12).

The multiple reversals reinforce the theology. In essence, the poem represents a life-and-death struggle. Indeed, the images for death are obvious from the beginning. From this polarity other antitheses spring. The Hebrew root *dlh* (v. 1) connotes "to draw water from a well" (cf.

Exod 2:16, 19; Prov 20:5, and cognate *dělî*, "a bucket," Num 24:7; Isa 40:15). As a metaphor of the poet's situation it produces literary symmetry; a person "raises up" (*rwm*, "extols" or "praises") God in response to God's "drawing [him or her] up *[dlh]*." The image is consolidated with a verbal contrast (v. 3), "you *brought up [ʿlh]* my soul from Sheol, restored me to life from among those *gone down [yrd]* to the Pit." Sheol stands for the near fatal condition, synonymous with the Pit (*bôr*, v. 3) and the grave (*šaḥat*, v. 9, translated "death"), to which the poet descends (*yrd*, vv. 3 and 9) and for which God sends rescue. The "strong mountain," imaging stability and altitude, highlights the vertical axis (v. 7). Death is portrayed as descent; rescue is imaged by "drawing up" and results in praising God, which is the basis and the goal of prayer (vv. 9, 12).

Psalm 31
All My Hope Is in You; Let Me Never Be Put to Shame

The parallel sections of Psalm 31 (vv. 1-8 and 9-22) contain elements of complaint. It ends in an exhortation to the public (vv. 23-24). The design may be charted like this:

vv. 1-8, first movement	**vv. 9-22, second movement**
vv. 1-3, plea to the LORD for help	v. 9, plea to the LORD for help
v. 4, the psalmist's plight	vv. 10-13, the psalmist's serious plight
vv. 5-6, avowal of confidence, "Into your hand I commend my spirit"; LORD and "faithful God"; the verb *bṭḥ*, trust	vv. 14-15a, expression of confidence, LORD, "my times are in your hand"; , "my God"; the verb *bṭḥ*, trust
vv. 7-8, *ḥesed;* "you . . . have not delivered *[sgr]* me into the hand of the enemy *[běyyad–ʾôyēb]*"; confidence that God will help	vv. 15b-22, "deliver me *[nṣl]* from the hand of my enemies *[miyyad–ʾôyěbay]*"; final prayer for rescue and grateful recognition of God's *ḥesed*

The language is artful. Three times "steadfast love," *ḥesed* (vv. 7, 16, 21), and ten times the divine name ("LORD") are interspersed throughout the psalm. The poet says "faithful God," *ʾēl ʾěmet* (v. 5), because God can be counted on. His loyalty creates a faithful, loving people (*ḥāsîd*, v. 23). The repeated Hebrew particle *kî* introduces seven statements which focus the drama: "you are *indeed* my rock" (v. 3); "*for* you are my refuge" (v. 4); "*for* I am in distress" (v. 9); "*for* my life is spent" (v. 10); "*for* I hear the whispering of many" (v. 13); "*for* I call on you" (v. 17); "*for* he has wondrously shown his steadfast love" (v. 21). Forms of the verb *ḥsh,* "trust" or "seek refuge," articulate the plea for help (v. 1) and the assurance of God's favor, "for those *who take refuge in you*" (v. 19b). The tug-of-war is illustrated by the "hand" (a metaphor for "power") of opposing forces: "Into [God's] *hand*" one commits personal life (v. 5); God did not abandon him or her into the enemy's *hand* (v. 8); one's "times" are in God's *hand,* so he or she pleads for rescue from the assailant's *hand* (v. 15).[20] God's hands mean rescue; enemies' hands threaten. The soul's tension is aptly illustrated in the repetition of *ṣar,* "adversities" and "distress" (vv. 7, 9), which sandwiches the *merḥāb,* "broad place" (v. 8). Alone the sufferer is in straits, but God sets one's *feet* in the open. "Shame," *bwš,* articulates the initial petition, "do not let me ever *be put to shame*" and "let the wicked *be put to shame*" (vv. 1, 17). Thus the poet requests that disgrace fall upon the wicked, rather than on him or herself. In opposition to the poet's trust, *bṭḥ,* in God (vv. 6, 14) are the idolaters and those who plot against his or her life. *Neged* is employed in contrasting ways (vv. 19, 22). God's goodness is displayed *"in the sight of* everyone"; in contrast, the psalmist recalls the terrifying predicament, "I am driven far *from your sight."* Another repeated word, *ṣpn,* "laid up" or "hold safe," is consoling and might be translated God has *stored up* ("tucked away") abundant goodness for those who fear him and he *stores them up* (vv. 19-20). Two repetitions summarize the drama. The poet asks for a *hearing* (v. 2), speaks of God's *seeing* (v. 7), and reviews the drama, that God had lost *sight* of him or her but then *heard* the prayer (v. 22).

The poet paints distress with impressionist strokes ("take me out of the net that is hidden for me," v. 4), likening it to an animal getting tangled up in a net (cf. Pss 9:15; 10:9; 25:15; 35:7-8; 57:6; 140:5), an apt image for the anguish of one who feels isolated, sick, and disgraced. The affliction is physical, psychological, and social (vv. 9-13; cf. Pss 6:6-8; 22:14-18) and the invalid borders on collapse. The complications are impressive: eye trouble, depression ("soul"), belly ("body," *beṭen*), bones ("strength"), social disgrace, abandonment, presumed dead, target of insults, gossip, hostility. Physically and spiritually spent, the poet feels rejected and attacked. The lack of coherence in all these symptoms is typical of a sensitive, sick person, who imagines all kinds of torments. In the horrifying description the enemies poke fun, neighbors mock, and acquaintances avoid one like a corpse or discard him or her like a

---

[20] Two lofty expressions of trust are unique. "Into your hand I commit my spirit" (v. 5) entrusts the whole life to God's protection. Another way of saying the same is "[m]y times are in your hand" (v. 15), meaning the events in life are in God's care. The "spirit" (*rûaḥ,* v. 5) is the breath of life received from God and offered to him in return (cf. Gen 2:7, *nāpĕšâh;* Ps 104:29-30, *rûaḥ*).

shattered dish. Everybody talks bad, everything is scary, and the
wicked conspire against him or her. Can God resist such a reject crying
for help? The enemy gradually assumes a definite shape. Following the
initial vague descriptions, the assailants emerge as conspirators (v. 13),
armed with lying lips (v. 18), and quarrelsome tongues (v. 20). May
they receive a commensurate punishment and be struck dumb (v. 18).

The theme, expressed in the opening, "In you, O LORD, I seek
refuge," is reinforced with the metaphors "rock," "strong fortress,"
"refuge" (vv. 1-4; cf. Ps 71:1-3), and is resumed at the end ("shelter" and
"city under siege," vv. 19-21). The distressed poet depicts the soul with
mercurial temperatures and passions. He or she is tense, insecure,
apprehensive, a prisoner of the self; he or she glances at God but is
obsessed with the situation at hand. The tension and insecurity
crescendo: "do not let me . . . be put to shame," "deliver me," "incline
your ear to me," "rescue me speedily," "save me," "lead me and guide
me," "take me out of the net." In a single unforgettable breath he or she
expresses abandonment, suffering, trust, and freedom and enters
another orbit where God is the center of gravity (v. 5).[21] Thus, the emergency is resolved. Likewise in the second movement the poet approaches the limit of hopelessness (vv. 9-13) from which he or she
makes a quantum leap to profound security and peace (vv. 14-22). With
the adversative conjunction *vav*, "but" (v. 14), the poet finds solace in
God, as if to say, everybody is against me, "*But* I trust in you, O LORD."
This focus on God and forgetting the self stretches the horizons so that
thanksgiving can be heard. The poet generalizes about the rescue (vv.
19-22), admitting that human plots, poisoned arrows, and vipers' tongues
will not be wanting. The consolation is that "those who take refuge in
[God]" find peace in his presence. Following the exclamation "O how
abundant is your goodness" (v. 19), the psalmist does not return to the
self. Now with the gaze on God, terror will not threaten nor haunt him
or her. The psalmist records the experience as a teaching for others (vv.
23-24); hope is the invigorating force, a guarantee for assuring other
worshipers of the divine goodness.

Changes in addressee add to the drama. The poet addresses God
(vv. 1-5, 7-9), gazes inward, and soliloquizes about the suffering, personal and social (vv. 10-13). The poet again addresses God and requests
relief (vv. 14-20). God is spoken about (vv. 6, 21, 23-24) and, in the end,
the poet addresses the faithful and bolsters their hope.

Psalm 31 is true to life in the way it represents the emotional ebb
and flow of a person in distress. The content is clear. An innocent, un-

[21] Based on antithetical parallelism, the reading "I hate" (v. 6) of the Hebrew text
is preferable to "You hate" of some manuscripts and the NRSV.

justly persecuted, accused and—to complicate matters—sick person, seeks refuge in God, receives divine help, gives thanks, and encourages the assembly of the faithful.

Psalm 32
Happy Are Those Who Have no Deceit

Psalm 32 is a curious combination of thanksgiving and instruction. Two introductory beatitudes (vv. 1-2) are followed by teaching the benefit of confessing one's sin (vv. 3-5; addressing God) and relying on God (vv. 6-7). A change of address introduces the lesson (vv. 8-9; addressee, "you" singular). Interpreters disagree as to the speaker here; either the psalmist instructs the public or God instructs the psalmist. The concluding assurance urges the community to rejoice (vv. 10-11; addressee, "you" plural). Beatitude and rejoicing is offered to those who are "righteous" and "upright of heart" (v. 11), "those to whom the LORD imputes no iniquity" (vv. 1-2), which neatly frames this poem. A pivot in the celebration is signaled by "[t]herefore," ʿal-zōʾt, which introduces the positive consequences (vv. 6-11) of the confession. The lesson is clear. Pardon is a source of joy for the repentant individual, a fresh start under God's instruction, an example and encouragement for others. The finale resumes the theme of the initial beatitudes. In a nutshell, a person who is sick or disgraced because of guilt confesses this before God, requests pardon, and is saved.

The patient is weak and exhausted, like a plant scorched by the summer heat. According to popular belief, sickness was a result of personal sin and God's punishment: "your hand was heavy upon me" (v. 4; see Pss 38:2; 39:9-10). At first the poet was obstinate ("While I kept silence," v. 3), then he or she confessed the guilt ("I said," v. 5). Keeping quiet about one's guilt and pretending innocence aggravates the situation. The description of the effects of sin is typical. The person is distant, afflicted bodily and spiritually, separated from God (cf. similar descriptions in Psalms 6, 22, 30). The poet had sided with death, where silence rules. Confession is the first step toward pardon (see Psalms 38 and 51), which restores health and rescues the person, gladdening him or her with spiritual and physical relief (vv. 6-7). This corroborates the initial beatitudes and is articulated in the invitation that all the faithful, when in difficulty, invoke God, who does not let the flash flood drown his devotees (v. 6; see Pss 18:4-5, 16; 69:1, 15; 144:7). The autobiographical account of the struggle with guilt culminates in God's pardon. The similes are rich: God's heavy hand on me, one "dried up as by the heat of summer" (a plant image), a flood, a stubborn animal (vv. 4, 6, 9). The imagery is appropriate to the theme. The scorching summer wind saps the strength. The flood waters symbolize the life threat that besieges sinners. To manage horses or mules a person needs a bit and a bridle; one must be docile to God's guidance, not like an irrational animal (cf. Ps 73:22). Another impersonal testimony (v. 10) articulates the lesson. It will go badly for the wicked, but divine love will envelope those who trust in God—in this case, confessing their sins.

Each initial "Happy," *ʾašrē*, is followed by two qualifiers beatifying the one who is relieved of sin. This lesson is derived from the poet's experience. The second beatitude repeats the first and adds force. The intensity of the double beatitude and the triple synonymous categories (those whose fault is forgiven, "whose sin is covered," to whom God imputes no guilt) emphasize the pardon. Three statements show that the confession is a spoken interchange: "I acknowledged," "I did not hide," and "I said, 'I will confess'" (v. 5). Three affirmations focus attention directly on God; "[y]ou are a hiding place," "you preserve me," and "you surround me" (v. 7). The emphatic "you" introducing the triplet repeats the initial pronoun of the final hemistich of v. 5, "*you* forgave the guilt of my sin." In three affirmations, God is the actor and the beleaguered psalmist the beneficiary. The third, "you surround me with glad cries of deliverance," anticipates the ending, specifically in the word *surround* in the description that God's *ḥesed* "surrounds those who trust in the LORD" (v. 10). Finally, there is a triple invitation to rejoice. The psalm ends as the upright are invited to "shout for joy," which echoes the "glad cries" (v. 7).

Repeated vocabulary identifies the poet with the beatified. Four synonyms for sin occur nine times in the first verses (vv. 1-2 and 5) and form an inclusion: transgression *(pešaʿ)*, sin *(ḥăṭāʾâh)*, "deceit" *(rĕmiyyâh)*,[22] "iniquity" or guilt *(ʿawōn)*. The four synonyms are followed by *kî*, "while" (v. 3), and a description of the distress which results from sin. Sin is "covered," or removed *(ksh, v. 1)*. In a play on words those who do not "hide" *(ksh)* their iniquity will be the ones "whose sin is forgiven" (v. 5). The fault "forgiven" and the guilt "forgiven" are from the same verb *nśʾ*, which literally means "lift up, raise" (vv. 1, 5). This provides a gravitational contrast with the word *kbd*, "your hand *was heavy* [weighed down] upon me" (v. 4). Thus, both literally and theologically, God's forgiveness surrounds sin. The deft usage of *sbb* illustrates that God and divine *ḥesed surround* the faithful (vv. 7, 10). In the second half an inclusion is formed by the word *rabbîm*

---

[22] By virtue of the parallel lines (v. 2), "deceit," *rĕmiyyâh*, a reference to slackening or deceit, here designates sin.

("mighty" or "many") and cognates of *ḥsd* (vv. 6, 10). The "faithful" (*ḥāsîd*) derive their identity not from their own deeds but from God's *ḥesed* which forgives and restores them. The divine name occurs four times (vv. 2, 5, 10, 11), evenly divided between the two halves of the poem. No synonym for sin occurs in the second half, where relief is celebrated and the teaching generalized.

The poet was sorely afflicted and acknowledges that this came from God as a corrective. God's heavy-handedness, which is really love surrounding the poet, awoke him or her to confess guilt and open the door to God's pardon. The lesson is clear, confession of sin is part of prayer and one's relation to God. It is based on the poet's experience of silent torment which was relieved when sin was confessed to God. The experience of sin was like waters, swirling up to one's neck, but they receded with the confession. In the end, the poet generalizes and invites the community to accept this.

Psalm 33
Let Our Hope in You Be the Measure of Your Ḥesed

The beatitude introduced by *ʾašrê*, "Happy" (32:1-2; 33:12; cf. 34:8), links Psalms 32 and 33. The fact that Psalm 33 lacks a Hebrew superscription (the LXX supplies the superscription "of David") may indicate another phase of the penitential liturgy of Psalm 32, which ends as Psalm 33 begins, with the exhortation to "rejoice" *(rnn)*, addressing the "righteous," *ṣĕdîqîm,* and the "upright in heart," *yišrê–lēb* (32:11). The just and upright are invited to sing "a new song" (33:3), which is the appropriate response to God's renewing grace. The two psalms end similarly. The congregation is "glad," *śmḥ* (32:11; 33:21), affirming its "trust," *bṭḥ* (32:10; 33:21), in God's "steadfast love," *ḥesed* (32:10; 33:18, 22). God's watchful eye, *ʿên,* appears in both (32:8; 33:18). They are composed in didactic style: confession and instruction (Psalm 32), praise and instruction (Psalm 33).

Psalm 33, with hints of a wisdom reflection, is a hymn to the sovereign God, creator of all and owner of history. It is structured in three parts: initial invitation (vv. 1-3), the body with the grounds for praise (vv. 4-19), and the concluding request (vv. 20-22). With five imperatives the poet invites the congregation to praise. The motive is introduced by *kî,* "for" (v. 4; the imperative in v. 8 is also followed by *kî* and the motive). Five terms describe God's word and work—upright, faithfulness, "righteousness and justice," *ḥesed.* In the first place, God's word is efficacious (v. 4; see Ps 12:6). *Ḥesed* is listed last in the stunning affirmation, "the earth is full of the LORD's *ḥesed*" (v. 5; see Isa 6:3, "glory"). With his word God made heavens, stars, seas and earth. He was moved by *ḥesed*, two qualities of which are righteousness (*ṣĕdāqâh*) and justice (*mišpāṭ*), which are primordial and basic, practically constitutive of creation (see Pss 37:28-29; 99:4). The poet invites the earth and its inhabitants to worship the divine sovereign (vv. 6-9). In a progressively narrowing scope the poet focuses first on the nations, then the people whose God is sovereign (vv. 10-12). God's "heritage," *naḥălâh*, is a people, not a land (v. 12; cf. Pss 68:9; 74:2; 78:62, 71; 106:5). Then God surveys the human race (vv. 13-15) and focuses on those who fear him (vv. 16-19). In the end the poet is identified with the group, "we hope in you" (vv. 20-22). God helps and defends us, gladdens us (the psalm opened with an expression of gladness). In the final invocation the poet prays that divine *ḥesed* accompany the faithful and reward their hope (v. 22; cf. vv. 5, 18). Twenty-two poetic lines (verses) in Hebrew equals the sum of letters in the alphabet. The divine name occurs thirteen times, plus "his holy name," a sum of fourteen. Completeness in a composition is a wisdom trait.

The vertical axis is drawn by the mention of earth and heavens (vv. 5-6). For God creation is like filling a bottle with water. "He gathered the waters of the sea as in a bottle" and stored it in the cellar (v. 7). Five words or phrases express God's seeing or perception—"looks," *nbṭ*, "sees," *rʾh*, "watches," *šgḥ*, "observes," *byn*, "eye," *ʿên* (vv. 13-15, 18).[23] From the heavenly vantage point God surveys the human race and comprehends all people. God, sculptor of hearts, knows the innermost recesses of the human (cf. Pss 11:4; 14:2; 94:9-11; 102:19; 139:1-16). God keeps special watch on chosen Israel, "those who fear him," so nothing adverse happens to them.

Repetition is used effectively. The attribute *rāb* occurs three times, "*great* army," "*great* strength," and "*great* might" (vv. 16-17; cf. i.e., Ps 20:7-8, the futility of trusting in military arms). The battle imagery was anticipated by the use of *tĕrûʿâh*, a victory cry (v. 3, translated "with loud shouts," NRSV). God's trustworthy "work" contrasts with the human "deeds" (*maʿăśēh*, vv. 4, 15), among which is the king toying with his mighty army. The repetition of *ʿmd* ("it stood firm," v. 9; "stands forever," v. 11) illustrates God's ongoing creative work in history. God, whose command created the world, unravels history. The "*counsel* of the nations," *ʿăṣat–gôyîm*, and their "*plans*," *maḥšĕbôt*, are juxtaposed with the "*counsel* of the LORD," *ʿăṣat–yhwh*, and "the *thoughts* of his heart," *maḥšĕbôt* (vv. 10-11). God who frustrates the nations' time-

[23] The groups of five, five imperatives, five attributes, and five synonyms for perception recall the *tôrâh*, the first five books of the Bible.

conditioned schemes has a plan which will endure forever. *Nepeš* is repeated; God's watchful care rescues "their soul" from death, and "our soul" waits for God (vv. 19-20).

The call to praise (vv. 1-3) is replete with vocabulary for music, notably stringed instruments (cf. Ps 144:9), which will accompany this "new song" (*šîr ḥādāš*, cf. Pss 40:3; 96:1; 98:1; 144:9; 149:1)—is the old song obsolete? God's word corresponds to the theme of creation (vv. 4-9; cf. Psalm 19). It is portrayed in its efficacy, as in Genesis 1, able even to subdue the unstable sea (v. 7). The divine word made the heavens and arranged the created world. The beautiful exposé of God's work includes the "fashioning" of the human heart which thinks and decides (v. 15). Each heart was made unique; *yaḥad,* translated "of them all," separates the hearts, rather than lumps them together. A well-formed heart finds delight in its divine maker (v. 21).

The poet makes astonishing assertions. According to the parallel lines God's *ḥesed* is coupled with righteousness and justice, which shows that the human conception of righteousness and justice is not adequate to define God's plan (v. 5):

> He loves righteousness and justice;
> the earth is full of the LORD's *ḥesed.*

God's word and work are practically synonymous, and they are trustworthy (v. 4):

> For the word of the LORD is upright,
> and all his work is done in faithfulness.

This word is related to God's "breath," a concept coupled with God's "spirit" (v. 6):

> By the word *[dābār]* of the LORD the heavens were made,
> and all their host by the breath *[rûaḥ]* of his mouth.

This is an uncharacteristic treatment of creation. Elsewhere the divine word creates and the divine breath sustains life (cf. Ps 104:29-30). Here God's spirit, word, and *ḥesed* all conspire to convince the faithful congregation of God's trustworthiness (vv. 4-9, 18-19).

The scope moves from the liturgical assembly (vv. 1-3), to the cosmos (vv. 6-12, the deeds of the creator, and vv. 13-15, God enthroned in the cosmos), to divine protection (vv. 16-19), and again to the liturgical assembly which praises and awaits God (vv. 20-22). This wisdom hymn praises and teaches about God. The objective is to instill hope in the community. God is addressed in the last verse, as the poet requests that the measure of divine *ḥesed* correspond to the community's hope. Psalm 33 teaches that God is trustworthy, and encourages us to a life based on hope in God.

Psalm 34
Come, I Will Teach You the Fear of the LORD

As with Psalm 33, instruction dominates in Psalm 34. Psalm 33 has twenty-two lines but no acrostic sequence. Psalm 34, an acrostic, by adding a *peh* line at the end and collapsing the *śîn* and the *šîn* (two lines which correspond to Hebrew letters representing two different "s" sounds), results in twenty-two poetic lines and an added title. As with Psalm 25, the *vav* line is missing. The initial letters of the first, central, and concluding lines spell the word *ʾlp*, "teach" (vv. 1, 11, 22; cf. Psalm 25). The lengthy superscription, "Of David, when he feigned madness before Abimelech, so that he drove him out, and he went away," situates it in the context of 1 Sam 21:10-15. The king in Samuel is Achish, not Abimelech.

The psalm has two parts: praise and thanksgiving (vv. 1-11), followed by a wisdom reflection (vv. 12-22). At first the sage instructs the community. Repeatedly the assembly is invited to listen to God who has aided and inspired the psalmist (vv. 5, 8-9, 11). Four references to the fear of God (vv. 7, 9 [twice], 11) plus the two verbs *drš* ("seek," vv. 4, 10) and *nbṭ* ("contemplate, look," v. 5) result in a total of seven references to a personal search for God. The typical wisdom address "Come, O children, listen" (v. 11; cf. Prov 4:1; 5:7, etc.) anticipates the second part which contains warnings and maxims about the good being favored over the bad. The sage extols correct behavior and exhorts the poor and oppressed to behave. The alternative, to trust in what is not God, particularly through evil means, is to invite failure. The poet pledges to "bless the LORD *at all times*"; he or she insists on completeness (seven times *kōl*, "all" or "every," vv. 1, 4, 6, 10 ["*no* good thing"], 17, 19, 22 ["none"]).

There is evidence of a plot, which pivots on the initial *lamed*, the Hebrew letter "l" (v. 11), in the middle of the poem, "Come, O children, listen to me." The sage teaches "the fear of the LORD," which is the beginning, the crown, and the culmination of wisdom (see Sir 1:11-20). "Come" and "listen" are the sixth and seventh plural imperatives in the first part (cf. vv. 3, 5, 8 [twice], 9, 11 [twice]).[24] The imperatives in the

---

[24] The two words in the NRSV "let the humble *hear* and *be glad*" are jussive (third person) plural forms (v. 2).

second half (vv. 13 and 14) are singular. The address "children," wisdom's invitation to her disciples, is rare and appears only here in the plural; in Proverbs the address is usually singular ("my child," cf. Prov 1:8, 10; 2:1 and often). The question "Which of you desires life, and covets many days to enjoy good?" (v. 12) invites a personal response from what began as a general invitation. Given its central position, fear of the LORD is the safeguard and source of blessing for those who "do good." The consequences of this stance commit one to keeping the commandments. This implies the correct use of speech and action and the pursuit of peace (vv. 13-14). Appeal to God, modeled on personal testimony, is recommended repeatedly (vv. 4-10, 15, 17-18). The reward is a satisfying life. The style, topic, and promise of Psalm 34 are all characteristic of Proverbs.

The central invitation is followed by instruction (vv. 12-14) and the relation between fear of God, prayer, and deliverance (vv. 15-22). The sage expands the message, gives examples, and reassures the afflicted that God sides with the just, the innocent. Appearances can be deceiving, for "Many are the afflictions of the righteous" (v. 19), even to the threat of bodily injury (v. 20), but in the end God will redeem the loyal servants (v. 22), which constitutes true life and goodness (v. 12). The declaration that not one bone of the righteous will be broken alludes, intentionally or by coincidence, to the prescriptions about the paschal lamb in Exod 12:46. The righteous will be kept whole. Broken bones in Isa 38:13 and Lam 3:4 is a sign of distress under God's wrath. Even though the righteous may suffer physically or morally, God is close to them to help (vv. 4, 6, 17, 19). The poet is a proof of the general statement (v. 17),

> When the righteous cry for help, the LORD hears,
> and rescues them from all their troubles.

The sage bolsters the confidence of the innocent sufferer, the "humble" (*ʿănawîm*) or "poor" (*ʿānî*) (cf. vv. 2, 6), "the righteous" (vv. 15, 17, 19, 21), "those who take refuge in him" (vv. 8, 22).

The military image is appropriate for the afflicted wisdom devotee (v. 7). Human aggression will be foiled by divine protection (the "angel of the LORD"). God's goodness is projected as an experience like the sensation of taste. "Taste" and "hunger" embrace eating and famine (vv. 8-10). Those "who take refuge in" God, "who fear him," "who seek the LORD" are invited to taste; they will not want. The correspondence of the two hemistichs of v. 10 implies that those who do not cultivate a relation with God are like animals who "suffer want and hunger" while "those who seek the LORD lack no good thing." Elsewhere it is said that the law is delicious (Ps 19:10). One cultivates good taste by taking refuge in, lovingly fearing, and seeking the LORD. Just as a person may receive a vision or a locution, one may experience God through other senses, touch and taste. Again, two senses, taste and sight, describe the experience and appreciation of God which is open to everybody (the invitation is formulated in the plural). God's eyes and ears (v. 15), which watch and listen for the just, is an icon of God's interest and involvement with the devout. On the contrary, God will confront evildoers and "cut off the remembrance of them from the earth" (v. 16; cf. Pss 37:9, 22, 28, 38).

The opposition is evident (vv. 15-16a):

the eyes of the LORD	on the righteous
his ears	open to their cry
the face of the LORD	against evildoers

The result is that the fame, name, or memory of the wicked will be cut off (v. 16b). The downfall of the wicked and God's care of the good is reinforced by the conclusions in vv. 20-22, death to the wicked and rescue to the righteous. God acts for the benefit of the good; he does not forestall the death of the wicked.

The poet teaches "Many are the afflictions of the righteous" (v. 19) and tells how the afflicted paradoxically experience God's closeness. Appearances deceive, because even as a person suffers physically or spiritually God is near (vv. 17-20). This reassurance is framed by the declaration that the memory of the wicked will be erased and the aggressor condemned (vv. 16, 21), which amounts to a concise expression of the boomerang effect of evil. Those who fear God are not exempt from troubles. The ethical life must be lived in communion with God, who is close to the brokenhearted and crushed of spirit, those who know that they cannot help themselves and only God can save (v. 18).

Psalm 35
Do Not Let Them Rejoice Over Me

The militant "angel of the LORD," a figure from Exodus (e.g., Exod 14:19; 23:20; 33:2), appears in Pss 34:7 and 35:5-6 and nowhere else in the Psalter. In these and the following three psalms the poet confronts evil on different fronts: unjust and lying accusers (35:3, 7, 11-12, 15-16, 19-21, 25); evil conspirators (36:1-4); unjust, malicious schemers (37:1, 7, 12, 21, 32, 35); sickness, alienation, plotting and harassing enemies (38:5-12, 19-20).

Psalm 35 unfolds in three movements (vv. 1-10, 11-18, 19-28), each concluding with praise (vv. 9-10, 18, 28). They tell about the enemy's affront against the psalmist (vv. 7, 11-16, 20-21) who appeals to God (vv. 1-6, 8, 17, 22-27). The first and third movements are dominated by petitions. The poet is in distress and needs help. He or she urges God to rally the military arsenal to the defense (vv. 1-3, six times the imperative singular), to frustrate the adversary (six verbs in the jussive form, "[l]et them be . . . ," vv. 4-6). In the end he or she voices fourteen petitions (vv. 22-27, five negative, nine assertive), repeating expressions from the first part of the poem and using legal language. The repetition of "my Lord," "LORD," and "my God" (two times each, vv. 22-24) reflects confidence and intimacy as well as urgency. The addition of LORD (v. 27) gives a total of seven direct references to God in the third movement. In the central movement the pain worsens with the treason of former friends. The request that God fight the psalmist's enemies and repay them in kind voices the burning desire for retribution which dominates the psalm (vv. 1, 4-8, 19, 26). The poet wants the offenders' crimes and schemes to backfire (vv. 7-8; see Pss 7:15-16; 9:16; 62:12).

Various parties are quoted. God is asked to speak consoling words, "I am your salvation" (v. 3); the poet quotes his or her own prayer, "O LORD, who is like you? You deliver the weak . . ." (v. 10); the oppressor scoffs "Aha . . ." (vv. 21, 25), and this is counterbalanced by the poet's allies who rejoice with him, "Great is the LORD . . ." (v. 27). The contrast is noteworthy; do not let the wicked *say*, but rather, "Let those who desire my vindication . . . *say*" (repeated *ᵓmr*, vv. 25, 27). To add weight to the request the poet asks that God not remain silent (v. 22). In the end he or she is committed to recount God's justice in continual praise (v. 28). The poet is an expert in contrast. Words for rejoicing are *śmḥ* (vv. 15, 19, 24, 26, 27), *gyl*, and *śyś* (v. 9), seven times total. Once the wicked are brought to ruin the poet will rejoice (vv. 8-9); hurtful rejoicing consists of the adversaries' scoffs and jeers (vv. 15, 19, 24, 26). The first and last rejoicing is done by the psalmist who, in the end, is joined by supporters (v. 27). The psalmist *was clothed (lbš)* in sackcloth; in contrast, may the adversary *"be clothed [lbš]* with shame" (vv. 13, 26). The liars are quoted as saying *"our eyes have seen* it *[rᵓh]"*; in contrast, God truly *has seen, rᵓh*, has witnessed, and will not remain silent (vv. 21-22). The repetition of *ᵓsp*, "gathered," gives the impression of a swelling mob (v. 15).

The poet has a body, a soul, and a personality. He or she speaks of the "soul" or the self, *nepeš*, "bones," wearing sackcloth, bosom ("head bowed"). *Nepeš*, which designates the psalmist's "[my] life" or "[my] soul" appears seven times (vv. 3, 4, 7, 9, 12, 13 ["myself"], 17; cf. v. 25,

when the adversary gloats, "we have *our heart's* desire"). The enemy is
physically present, but the accent is on the "eyes" (v. 19), their hearts
(seat of intention), and, even more threatening and offensive, their
mouths (vv. 21, 25). The psalmist imagines him or herself trapped like a
defenseless wild animal with a pit and in a net. The adversary gloats
over the catch; the image of gnashing teeth reduces the hunted
psalmist to bagged meat (vv. 7, 15-16). Ironically, those who persecute
the psalmist act like wild beasts; they ravage like lions (v. 17). Once relieved from the attack, the psalmist's tongue will announce God's justice and praise continually.

The adversary is portrayed as fighters (v. 1), hunters (vv. 7-8), lying
witnesses in a trial (v. 11), a mocking mob (vv. 15-16), lions and ravaging beasts (vv. 16-17), lying and jeering foes (vv. 19-20). May they be
reduced to straw in the wind (v. 5; cf. Pss 1:4; 83:13). In the heat of the
offensive the poet anticipates a happy ending (vv. 9-10). The last Hebrew word of v. 11 and the first in v. 12, in a sonorous internal rhyme,
yišʾālûnî yĕšalĕmûnî ("they accuse me . . . they repay me"), illustrates
the mounting enemy assault.

The repeated verbs *ryb*, "contend," and *lḥm*, "fight," illustrate the
law of retribution (v. 1); may those who sue and oppose me meet with
commensurate justice. May the unjust accusers and false witnesses be
convicted and punished in the same way they intended for the innocent (vv. 1, 4, 7-8). Previously, these aggressors were beneficiaries of the
psalmist's sympathy and attentions (vv. 13-14), which pains one even
more than had they been distant and anonymous. The situation is particularly painful. This poor wretch prayed in sackcloth and fasting for
those who now persecute him or her. The suddenness of their about-
face is aptly described; I tripped, and they laughed and struck me,
cruelly ridiculing me (vv. 15-16). Unrequited compassion is a bitter pill.
The passionate description of the aggressors' malice and the psalmist's
previous attentions in their regard is calculated to move God to intervene. The petition follows, mingled with promises of gratitude and
public praise (vv. 17-18) and followed by a caricature of the enemies'
conspiracy and falseness (vv. 19-21). Verse 23 attracts attention, two imperatives and a complement followed by two addresses and a complement (the NRSV changes the order):

Wake up!	Bestir yourself	for my defense
my God	and my Lord	for my cause

Verse 24 reinforces the plea with an imperative and a complement, literally, "Vindicate me according to your righteousness," followed by
two forms of address, "O LORD, my God." Such doubling and repeti-

tion is typical of this psalm, which at first seems redundant but in reality illustrates growing intensity.

The psalmist has been pitifully alone throughout the trial and prayer, yet is now allied with God against enemies. Finally, other allies are introduced and together they will join in praising God and announcing his justice every day (vv. 27-28). The rescue of the innocent will be the motive for public rejoicing.

Psalm 36
Your Love Reaches to the Heavens

Psalm 36 is a prayer for help in three movements—the vision of the wicked (vv. 1-4), the vision of God (vv. 5-9), and the request (vv. 10-12). The last movement summarizes the previous ones, requesting *ḥesed* (the theme of vv. 5-9) and protection against the wicked (a theme of vv. 1-4). The poem begins with a brilliant description of the wicked from the inside out, from the innermost thoughts to their words. They are turned in on themselves by their faulty vision; "[fear of] God" is not "before their eyes," because "they flatter themselves in their own eyes" (vv. 1-2). This willful blindness is ultimately the cause of their downfall. In effect, they think that God neither matters nor cares. They are jaded by chronic evil. They live in it, talk about it, and even at night lie down and pore over it. Indeed they are on a wrong path (v. 4). Their physiognomy is taken into account—heart (v. 1), eyes (v. 2), mouth (v. 3), foot and hand (v. 11). The wicked imagine oracles which support evil "in their hearts"; in contrast, those who recognize and take God seriously, the "upright of heart," may expect mercy (v. 10).

In the Hebrew text of the first verse, evil is personified as an interior force which delivers oracles against God. The seductive voice of Transgression tempts the human heart. An effective maneuver in sin's favor is to block out loving regard for God. Any such reverence would be an obstacle for sin, and evil flows from such contempt. The heart devoid of reverence loves lying and mischief, in both intention ("while on their beds") and behavior ("a way that is not good"). The result is that Transgression seduces the wicked to wallow in evil.

From the wicked lying on their conspiratorial beds the poet shifts abruptly to God, whose concern and care stretches from heights to depths (vv. 5-6). From the human vantage point, *ḥesed*, faithfulness, and righteousness are as high as the sky, the clouds, the mountain ranges. Divine judgments are as vast as the ocean (*tĕhôm rabbâh*; cf. Isa 51:10). The divine attributes are immeasurable; they exceed spatial dimensions.

Their combined effect is salvation, "you save humans and animals alike." These attributes are invaluable ("precious"). From the vast panorama of the sky and ocean, the poet focuses on the protection in the sanctuary, "in the shadow of your" winged cherubim throne (v. 7). Heavens and clouds are the ceiling of the world. The merism "mighty mountains" (5-6, literally, "the mountains of God," a superlative) and "great deep" delineates the expanse of divine virtue and judgments which, in effect, embrace the universe. Within this scope all people and, curiously, even animals benefit from God's salvation (v. 6; see Ps 104:10-23, 27-28). These pairs cover God's loyalty to those who are related to him (*ḥesed* and faithfulness) and vindication of those who depend on him (righteousness and judgments). Even the wicked who do not fear God are incorporated in divine providence. In opposition to the wicked is God, the source of goodness—transcendent, limitless, but present in the temple with his gifts (vv. 5-9). God is the "fountain of life," the "light" which illuminates and lets creatures "see light" or live (v. 9, Hebrew v. 10; see Pss 4:6; 13:3; 31:16; 49:19). This is articulated in a sonorous phrase *bĕ²ōrĕkā nir²eh-²ôr,* "in your light we see light" (the alliterative *aleph* [transliterated as ²] and *"r"*). The "light" is the encounter with God in the temple, the light of God's face. Humanity, "children of Adam" (*bĕnê ²ādām,* translated "all people" in the NRSV), not just the Israelites, benefit from this life and light. All the benefits flow from God's "house," the temple (v. 8). Because of God's immensity, one can ask him to magnify *ḥesed* (v. 10).

The image of the shelter of God's wings (v. 7; cf. Ps 17:8; 91:4) refers to asylum in the temple, where God is enthroned on the wings of cherubim and the people share the thanksgiving sacrifices as at a barbecue. The irony in this poem, replete with references to the temple and the liturgy, is that the only oracle the evil hear is that they need not fear God (v. 1). Personified evil speaks about God while the psalmist addresses God directly by name, LORD (vv. 5-12).

The poet caricatures the godless oracles as the voice of evil; they advise rebellion against God and treachery against neighbor. The description is psychologically intense. The psalmist is threatened with being stomped on and shoved away (the foot and the hand of the wicked), which amounts to exile and subjection (v. 11). The plight of the wicked worsens and issues in a theological consequence. At first they are lying down, meditating on their crime (v. 4); in the end they have fallen and will be unable to rise (v. 12).

The focusing in the second and third movements is marvelous. The opening scene is vast. Heavens and seas, humans and animals are the beneficiaries. Then, in an unexpected turn, all people find refuge in the sanctuary. Amidst this allusion to ritual and liturgy—shadow of wings, feasting, drinking, light—a "we" emerges, the assembly which is present. Focusing continues to narrow, "those who know you" and "the upright of heart" (v. 10). Suddenly, the psalmist focuses on the present plight (v. 11). The arrogant are personal enemies, ready to trample and strike. In the toss-up between God and the wicked, the psalmist, threatened by one, takes refuge in the other. God wins. The wicked, routed, suffer a total and definitive defeat. They end up immobile, "there," *šam* (v. 12). Where? Unable to rise.

Psalm 37
To Inherit or Be Cut Off from the Land

Psalm 37 is an acrostic. Each set of two verses begins with the successive letter of the Hebrew alphabet. What results is a collection of diverse elements, somewhat disjointed and repetitive. An alphabetic psalm lends itself to anthology, and a number of proverbs and other texts are reflected in this one. Compare

v. 1 and Prov 23:17; 24:1, 19-20; Isa 3:31-32;

v. 5 and Prov 16:3;

v. 16 and Prov 16:5, 8, 16;

vv. 23-24 and Prov 20:24;

v. 24 and Prov 24:16;

v. 28 and Prov 2:22;

v. 29 and Prov 2:21;

v. 31 and Jer 31:33;

vv. 32-33 and Ps 1:6.

The psalm takes the form of personal experiences and testimonies (vv. 25, 35-36), descriptions of behavior (vv. 12, 14, 21, 26, 30-32), and avowals of trust in God, who protects the good and punishes the wicked. The affirmation that God rewards the good is stated in various ways. He will reward their hearts' desire, act in their favor, make their innocence and integrity shine, sustain and protect them, not permit them or their children to go hungry, steady their steps, take their hand, bless their descendants, not abandon or condemn them, give them a future. God, their permanent refuge, helps, frees, and saves them. A dominant expression is they "shall inherit the land" (vv. 9, 11, 22, 29, 34); in contrast, the wicked "shall be cut off" (vv. 9, 22, 28, [34,] 38). Their arms will be broken, what they planned against the just will befall them, and they will fade or melt away. Based on these themes,

Psalm 37 is a sequel to Psalm 36. The truths previously set forth concerning God's ways with the good and evildoers are stated as aphorisms to nurture perseverance and calm even amidst humiliating circumstances (cf. v. 16), "Better is a little that the righteous person has than the abundance of many wicked."

Psalm 37 is stamped with the theological motif of possession of the land and its opposite, expulsion or extermination (literally, being "cut off"). Four times this juxtaposition is repeated (vv. 9, 22, 28-29, 34). The third mention of "possess the land" is in letter *lamed*, "l" (v. 22), a privileged position in the alphabetic arrangement since it marks the beginning of the second half. The theme is illustrated by the sevenfold opposition "righteous" (or "innocent") and "wicked," *ṣaddîq–rāšā͑* (vv. 12, 16, 17, 21, 28-29, 32, 38-40). This opposition has a legal connotation (vv. 6, 33). Counting the verb *yaršî͑ennû*, "let them be condemned" (v. 33), cognates of *rš͑* (evil) are used fourteen times. Counting the substantive *ṣidqekā*, "your vindication" (v. 6), *ṣdq* (good or upright) is used ten times. The opposition concentrates on the equitable returns of the just and the wicked in the covenant community. The wicked are members, but they are agents of division and destruction (v. 12). Thus, "cut off" has the sense of being excommunicated. The theme lends itself to contrasts. Wrongdoers are contrasted with "doing good" (vv. 1, 3, 7, 27); the wicked are stingy while the virtuous are generous (vv. 21, 26). The verb *bqš* is employed with effect; the children of the righteous do not *seek* bread (NRSV, "begging bread," v. 25); the wicked "*seek* to kill" the innocent (v. 32); I *sought* but could not find the wicked (v. 36). The meditation about God's equitable treatment of the good and the wicked is sparked by an apparent injustice. For the moment the wicked prosper, even while they oppress the upright and underprivileged. Yet God demands a life consonant with the land of promise where one dwells, which presupposes conduct in accord with the covenant terms. God blesses and grants the inheritance to the worthy and disinherits the evil ones.

The author employs multiple images, among which are war, plotting, spying, and hunting (vv. 12, 14-15, 32). God "will make your vindication shine like the light," like the noonday sun (v. 6). "Grass" depicts the evildoer's brief flowering and swift withering (vv. 2, 20; cf. Isa 40:7).[25] This metaphor is taken from the rapid drying up caused by the Near Eastern sirocco and the sun. Another image is the tree (vv.

[25] The meaning of v. 20 is uncertain. "Like the glory of the pastures" may be rendered "like the best of the he-lambs," in which case the wicked are likened to the fattest animals chosen for sacrifice (1 Sam 15:9, 15). The point of the comparison is the swift change in fortunes. The best of today is gone tomorrow.

35-36; cf. Pss 1:3; 92:12-14). For a little while it looks like the wicked may prosper like a sturdy tree, but they vanish. The "seed," translated "children" (vv. 25, 28), is from the plant world. These images are suggested by the theme of "the land" (vv. 3, 9, 11, 22, 29, 34), probably the promised land.

The wise elder addresses the disciple (singular), and repeatedly urges him or her to be patient, trust God (vv. 3, 4, 5, 7, 34), and observe human ways, especially fleeting prosperity and the inner and outer workings of evil (vv. 1-2, 8, 10, 27, 37). The disciple must avoid illusory evil and foster a relationship with God, who will eventually set things right (vv. 3-7). The young disciple is urged to ward off the temptation to defect to the ranks of the wicked. Abandoning God wins only illusory delights. The poet reassures the virtuous and asserts that God will save them from the wicked (v. 40). The resounding theme of the possession of the land or earth is held out for all who banish evil from their lives and cooperate with God for a better world.

Initially fourteen imperatives (negative and positive) are used to urge that the disciple espouse this teaching; another seven are found toward the end (vv. 1-8, 27, 34, 37). All the themes are introduced in the initial section. The audience runs the risk of envy and destructive anger (vv. 1, 7, 8); they are bewildered by the incongruence between their faith and rough experience. The first principle of law is to protect the innocent, in imitation of God's justice. Evil is opposed to God (v. 20), a fact which is evident in the free-wheeling ways of the wicked who follow their own path and pursue private interests (vv. 7, 12). They attack the innocent and misrepresent them in legal proceedings (vv. 32-33).

Psalm 37 serves a practical purpose, to exhort the virtuous to trust God amid the manifold temptations from the behavior of the wicked. Temptation is expressed in many ways: anger or envy, poverty or affliction, fear, doubts about God's righteousness, or inconstancy. What must the innocent party do? Avoid all violence of feeling and action, refrain from repaying evil in kind, and avoid wicked ways. The sage counsels self-control—do not envy (v. 1) nor become weary (three times), contain wrath (v. 8), repress anger. In addition, he or she advises positive actions—do good (vv. 3, 27), avoid evil (v. 27), be content with what suffices, be generous (vv. 21, 26). The motivation? Because God loves equity. In other words, live a moral life to please God. An ethical character springs from faith and is not motivated by utilitarian concerns. Nonetheless, a life with God offers a hopeful future, and a blessing of the covenant is a long and tranquil life (vv. 37-40). Without God, life is curtailed and doomed to destruction (see Prov 10:27; 13:9; 14:11).

The dialectic of punishment is expressed in the usual way. Evil rebounds on the wicked, so their murderous designs will boomerang

(v. 15; see Ps 35:8 and the principle stated in Jer 2:19), and their weapons will work against them. Plotting and gnashing of teeth identify their swords and bows as their mouths and words (v. 12). God "laughs at the wicked" (v. 13; cf. Ps 2:4).

The poet skillfully refers to time. Prosperity tempts the impatient person who wants immediate results. But this prosperity is illusory; the wicked will vanish "like the grass . . . like the green herb" (vv. 2, 10, 20, 35-36, 38). "A little while" is allotted to them from God's point of view. They have an appointed end. The "day" (singular) of the wicked, a day of reckoning (v. 13), is in contrast to the "days" (plural) of the blameless, which God provides (vv. 18-19). Only the peaceable have a future (v. 37). In time they will get their desert, and the balance will be restored. The sage aims to safeguard the devout from scandal and thus he or she teaches that the one who rebels against God cannot last.

The "steps" and the "way" suggest a pilgrimage, and the destiny is "the land"; this psalm can be considered an allegory of the journey to the promised land (v. 22-23, 31, 34). It images God's people, individual and collective, moving towards God. Like the chosen people, the good person is to walk, supported by faith in God rather than appearances and reason. The word translated "abide," *škn*, means having a roof over one's head (v. 27). The desert prohibits permanent habitation. The sage nourishes the hope of having a permanent dwelling.

There are points of contact between Psalms 37 and 73. In both an experienced elder reflects how quickly the wicked disappear (v. 10; cf. 73:18-20). "Envy," *qnʾ*, is employed for the possibility of defecting (v. 1; cf. 73:3). The qualitative difference between evil and good is not measured in prosperity nor well-being but in the relationship with God (vv. 16-18, 28, 33; Ps 73:23-28). In Psalm 37 this teaching is automatic and to some extent the rewards are tangible. Psalm 73 makes a greater demand on faith in the experience of God.

Psalm 38
Do Not Be Far From Me

Psalm 38 provides an occasion for Psalm 37, the meditation on the ends of the wicked and the just. The psalmist feels beleaguered by the power and influence of the wicked. Near the center of Psalm 38 the poet pronounces a courageous testimony to the effect that, despite the appearance to the contrary (i.e., the strength and prosperity of the wicked, Psalm 37) and personal misery, he or she can confess loyalty, even in adversity: "it is for you, O LORD, that I wait; it is you, O LORD my God, who will answer" (38:15). In these two poems the poet projects a close-up of the wicked, plotting against life, meditating treachery all day.

The poet of Psalm 38 is obsessed with his or her plight. Repetitions and parallel lines leave the impression of an invalid, fretting over the infirmity. The psalmist repeats the complaint "there is no soundness in my flesh" (vv. 3, 7), the confession of sin (vv. 3, 18), and the anxiety about insult from friend and foe (vv. 11-12, 16, 19-20). The repeated *nḥt*, "sink" and "come down," creates the overwhelming impression of being in over one's head (vv. 2, 4), a sense of desperation and power-lessness. Cognates of *kbd* in "like *a burden too heavy*," illustrates the complications (v. 4). From sickness and pain one feels faint, crushed to bits (v. 8). According to Lev 13:3-4; 14:3 the "affliction," *negaꜥ*, is a skin disease which is feared to be contagious (v. 11). Here it is more complex. The only release from it is prayer, which culminates in the insistent plea (vv. 21-22):

> Do not forsake me, O LORD;
>   O my God, do not be far from me;
> make haste to help me,
>   O Lord, my salvation.

The illness is described with both physiological and emotional symptoms—"no soundness in my flesh," "no health in my bones," "wounds grow foul and fester," "bowed down," uncontrollable weeping, a burning sensation, weak and listless, heart palpitations, eye trouble (vv. 3-10). The critical condition is aggravated by social effects—the friends' avoidance and the critics' abuse (vv. 11-12, 19-20). Who wants to stand up to God and declare him or herself an ally or accomplice of heaven-knows-what outrage that has merited such affliction (v. 11)? The adversary takes advantage of the situation to spread rumors and lies, which increases the sense of abandonment (v. 12), and the poet twice alludes to guilt as the cause of the affliction (vv. 3-5, 18). The repetition of *mipĕnê*, "because of," makes a connection between vv. 3 and 5 and identifies sin with foolishness:

> There is no soundness in my flesh *because of* your indignation;
> there is no health in my bones *because of* my sin. . . .
> My wounds grow foul and fester *because of* my foolishness.

The symmetry connects God's indignation with the poet's guilt. God's wrath is the reaction to sin. Since the anger is not definitive, punishment can move a person to repent, in which case divine anger is experienced as mercy (vv. 1-2). According to the operative theology of the day, sickness reveals the sinful condition. This acknowledgment of guilt is the beginning of healing. Although a person is responsible for personal guilt, he or she can do little to relieve its effects. Interestingly, the psalmist complains but does not request healing. Instead, he or she requests God's closeness, help, and "salvation."

The initial description is similar to that of Job, afflicted with sores, listless and mourning, isolated from people who regard him or her as justly punished. The burning sensation in the loins brings on depression that causes stooping, as the patient bears a heavy heart and the weight of guilt. The psalmist withdraws into the self and bears the frigid rebuff (vv. 13-14), hoping in God, whose help is certain once the confession is made (v. 15). To convince God to intervene, he or she admits the relation between suffering and sin. But the psalmist adds another argument; the enemies will rejoice if the psalmist should fail (v. 16), and God would not want that. Death would be a triumph for the adversary, because their loathing towards the victim is not justified. In fact, they do not reject the poet for being a sinner, but rather for correct and good conduct (vv. 19-20); he or she does not deserve the present disgrace.

The poet ends with an urgent plea for God's intervention (see Pss 22:11, 19; 35:22; 40:13; 70:1; 71:12) and underscores the relation with God, named with increasing insistence ʾădōnāy (Lord), "my God," and LORD (vv. 1, 9, 15, 21, 22). Suffering makes the poet conscious, not only of sin but of God's closeness. All of a sudden, the pronouns, which are emphatic in Hebrew, "I" and "you," narrow the focus on God and the sufferer, who is deaf, mute, and alone (vv. 13-15, 17). The prayer remains open to pardon and salvation. In the final plea the psalmist reiterates the heartfelt request that God not leave him or her alone.

The Hebrew conjunction kî (usually translated "for"; not always apparent in translation) appears seven times and gives the reasons for the plea (vv. 2, 7), the affliction (vv. 4, 17), and the psalmist's response (vv. 15 ["but"], 16, 18 [not present in the NRSV]). An oxymoron is remarkable, literally "my near ones stand far off" (v. 11). Speaking and silence clash with each other. Even though the psalmist complains of being like those who cannot speak and the aggressor speaks of ruin (vv. 12-14), he or she is an eloquent witness to God who will answer the afflicted (v. 15).

Psalm 39
Are Not the Days of My Life Few?

Psalms 38 and 39 deplore the sadness and swiftness of the present life and request relief. In the first the poet complains about how deep he or she has sunk in affliction, then in Psalm 39 the poet reflects on the vanity of life. After a confused medley of diatribe, curse, complaint, and contrition, the poet surrenders with moving submission: "I am silent; I do not open my mouth, for it is you who have done it" (39:9). Both psalms end with a plea for relief (38:21-22; 39:12-13). Psalm 40 is a fitting sequel to their plaintive tone. Psalm 40:1-2 summarizes the affliction and acknowledges the relief requested in the previous psalm. The psalmist, left on the brink of death (39:12-13), speaks of rescue from the fatal pit, the danger of death (40:2). He or she acknowledges that God has bent down and heard the cry (v. 1) and again ends with the request to be restored to safety and health (vv. 11-17). Psalms 38–40 may have been deliberately joined, as the condition of waiting and praying (Psalms 38–39) is to God's saving answer (Psalm 40). Into the poet's silent mouth (39:1-2, 9) God put a new song (40:3). The request for and the assurance of God's deliverance closes Book One of the Psalter (40:13-17; 41:1-3, 11-12).

Each movement of Psalm 39 is thematically distinct: the psalmist's situation (vv. 1-3), life's frailty (vv. 4-6), and the request (vv. 7-13). The last two are linked as the prayer which the psalmist voiced in distress. The poem begins abruptly. The anguished psalmist finds life tense and useless. He or she takes bitter delight in the fragility of human existence, a fistful of days, a fleeting breath, a shadow that passes (vv. 4-6, 11, 13; see Pss 62:9; 90:4-6, 9-10, 12; 144:4). Life is brief, crowned with infirmities, sufferings and frustrations, which are the wages of sin. Even worse is God's punishment (vv. 10-11). Physical pain and spiritual restlessness leave a sense of the futility of all things.

At first the poet is more conscious of the self and the human condition than of God. In the course of venting feelings, references to God become more evident (vv. 7-13). The request is urgent: free me from sins, "[d]o not make me the scorn of the fool," "[r]emove your stroke from me," "[h]ear my prayer . . ., give ear to my cry; do not hold your peace at my tears," "[t]urn your gaze away"—seven imperatives, five positive and two negative (vv. 8-13). The final request leaves the impression of imminent, unavoidable death. This amounts to an urgent appeal and a warning to God who by neglect or slowness to act might see the psalmist reduced to nothing. This poem ends on a dark note (cf. also Job 7:21; 10:2-22). It is unusual for a person to request that God look away, but God may look benignly or angrily, and the latter has frightful consequences (see Job 7:19; 14:6). Even so, the psalmist is conscious of God's closeness (vv. 7, 9, 13). Qoheleth also muses on the futility of life, its empty toil and sufferings (cf. Eccl 2:17-18; 4:8; 6:12). The psalmist, like Job, recognizes that God's hand is behind everything (see, for example, Job 10:20; 13:21). But while Job was innocent, the poet is guilty.

The poet at first resolves to keep quiet, lest the enemy, who is present, find some fault (vv. 1-2). But a person cannot keep quiet; one has to speak (v. 3), which the poet does, to God (vv. 4-13). He or she repeats "I am silent" (vv. 2, 9), but ironically, as in Psalm 39, speaks eloquently. The reason for the silence is not clear. Is it to ward off the possibility of apostasy? Or, rather, that the suffering not be misinterpreted by the wicked (v. 9)? The reflection on life's brevity moves God to intervene. The fourfold repetition of "surely" (ʾak, in Hebrew, vv. 5, 6, 11), followed in each case by a reflection on life's brevity, gives the impression of a sigh or groan. Time is running out; God had better act soon or never. Without God's help this life is limited and futile.

The psalmist advances with progressively more emphatic affirmations. At the summit of the poem, he or she pronounces an act of trust (in other psalms of complaint this is found at the end), which appears to be unconditional. The emphatic wĕʿattâh ("*And now,* O Lord, what do I wait for?" v. 7) signals a change in direction. This heartfelt cry indicates a movement inwards and begins a crescendo, "My hope is in you." With such confidence the poet asks for pardon for the sins which contributed to the suffering (v. 8). The renewed silence is filled with resignation (v. 9). But if God continues to grind the person to dust, he or she will vanish like breath (vv. 10-11). In the final requests for relief, the psalmist likens the personal condition to that of a "passing guest" (*ger*) and a foreigner (*tōšāb*) as the ancestors were in the land (v. 12; cf. 119:19; Gen 23:4; Lev 25:23). God should intervene, for according to law the guest has both rights and obligations which guarantee a safe sojourn once one is received into a tent or house.

The psalmist is a master at shaping imagery. He or she vows to muzzle the mouth in the presence of the wicked, so as not to join ranks with them; the heart burned like a furnace, which finally erupts in speech (vv. 1-3); life represents a handful of toils (vv. 4-5); people wander about like shadows, pursuing phantoms, filling granaries with no guarantee that anyone will enjoy the fruits (v. 6). The poet is afflicted as though God has worn him or her down with repeated blows of the hand (v. 10). Moth-eaten clothes is a symbol of God's action and frail humans are as light as air (v. 11). Metaphors such as "passing guest" and "stranger" convey the tenuous grasp that humans have in the present world (v. 12). If God would pay less attention, the poet could have some relief before he or she vanishes forever (v. 13). In the midst of the multiple themes that span this psalm, the conviction is that the ephemeral appeals to the consistent, what is transitory pleads with the eternal God.

Psalm 40
Here I Am; I Delight to Do Your Will

Psalm 40 has three movements, thanksgiving for rescue (vv. 1-5), sacrifice and God's will (vv. 6-10), request for deliverance (vv. 11-17). Verses 13-17 reappear with few changes as Psalm 70. The first and third movements celebrate God's rescue in the past and request it for the future. In each the trial is referred to in general terms, "the desolate pit, . . . the miry bog," "evils have encompassed me," and "who seek to snatch away my life." In each the poet proclaims God's greatness, expresses praise and rejoicing, and makes a general application of the personal rescue (vv. 3-5, 16). The correspondence between these two is accounted for by the request and thanks for liberation. The inverted order of appearance is unusual; the thanksgiving precedes the request. The connection between the first two movements is logical; the LORD's rescue is celebrated, not just by ritual sacrifice but by a change of life and public proclamation. The connection between the second and third movements is verbal, as shown here:

—God's "will" and the petition "be pleased" (cognates of *rṣh*, vv. 8a, 13a);

—the poet *delights* in God's will while the enemies *desire* his or her hurt (cognates of *ḥpṣ*, vv. 9, 14);

—*ḥesed* and faithfulness which keep the psalmist safe and which he or she does not conceal (vv. 10, 11);

—the poet has not hid "saving help" and an invitation for those who love "salvation" (cognates of *yšᶜ*, vv. 10, 16);

—the poet who does not *restrain* the lips, just as God does not *withhold* compassion (cognates of *klʾ*, vv. 9b, 11a).

In the first movement the passage from the "I" of the psalmist to the "we" of the assembly is natural (v. 5a); the poet is part of "the great congregation," an expression which frames vv. 9-10.

The thanksgiving is an account of the psalmist's experience (vv. 1-4) and an address to God (vv. 5-10). Its public nature is affirmed by the double mention of the "great congregation" (vv. 9-10), the "many" (v. 3), and "your thoughts *toward us*" (v. 5). A plea introduces the third movement (v. 11) and forms a thematic inclusion with the final requests (vv. 13-17). In this part the community's presence is hidden behind the "I" of the poet. The three movements are diverse in tone and theme. What is the relation between them? God's previous benefactions, the poet's readiness to serve, and the public testimony in "the great congregation" are the basis of the psalmist's trust spoken about in the third movement.

The poet opens abruptly with the present situation. What appears to be lack of cohesion in the composition illustrates the psalmist's anxiety. He or she hoped in God who heard the cry and answered. Being stuck in the depths of the "desolate pit" (literally "noisy pit") or "miry bog" (v. 2; cf. Pss 69:1-3, 15; 88:4-7) contrasts with finding footing on rock (cf. 18:36; 27:5). God put a "new song" in the poet's mouth when God rescued him or her, and this permits one to live and praise God (vv. 2-3; cf. Ps 33:3). Many will be amazed at this, which will give them a reason to trust God. The poet draws a comparison between God who intervened in favor of one who was afflicted and the idols which deceive (v. 4). Is this an implicit confession of having nearly fallen into idolatry?

The whole person is involved in the prayer, as illustrated by the body parts mentioned: "my feet" (v. 2), "my mouth" (v. 3), "[my] ears" (v. 6), "Here I am" (v. 7), "my heart" (*mē'eh*, v. 8), "my lips" (v. 9), "my heart" (*lēb*, vv. 10, 12), "hairs of my head" (v. 12), "my life" (*nepeš*, v. 14), "I" (emphatic, v. 17). In the second movement there is a pleasant correspondence. God does not desire sacrifice and offering, while the psalmist delights in God's will. Repetition of a Hebrew word is used with effect. Sacrifice and offering "you do not *desire*" (*ḥpṣ*, v. 6); on the contrary (v. 8),

> I *delight* [*ḥpṣ*] to do your will, O my God;
> your law is within my heart.

As the friendship between God and the psalmist is forged with the word *ḥpṣ*, the enemies lurk in the background and "*desire* my hurt" (*ḥpṣ*, v. 14). God has given him or her, literally, "open *ears*," the law is deep in the heart, and he or she does not restrain the lips.

The psalmist asserts that the divine *tôrâh* is in the "heart" (the innermost parts, *me'āy*, v. 8); he or she has not hidden God's "saving help within [his or her] heart" (*libbî*, v. 10), and requests that God not withhold his "mercy." The word translated "mercy," *reḥem*, literally "womb," also refers to an intimate organ. The interweaving of these concepts formulates the petition. May God, who is in the devout poet's heart, not close his most intimate and life-giving part from him or her. Later, as a motive for God to intervene, the psalmist's "heart" (*libbî*, v. 12) fails. He or she is barraged with complaints ("iniquities") which number more than hairs on the head (v. 12; cf. Ps 69:4). Only here does the psalmist refer explicitly to the affliction. The connecting link between vv. 10 and 11 is the repetition of "your steadfast love and your faithfulness," *ḥasdĕkā wa'ămitĕkā*. The rationale of the plea is evident. "I have not concealed your steadfast love and your faithfulness from the great congregation," so may they protect me always. Nine times the divine name (LORD) occurs, and four times "God" with a pronominal suffix, translated "our" (v. 3) or "my God" (vv. 5, 8, 17). An additional *ʾădōnāy* (v. 17, "my Lord") results in a total of fourteen explicit references to God. Furthermore, the emphatic pronoun "you" (*ʾattâh*) is employed four times in reference to God (vv. 5, 9, 11, 17). The intense, intimate relation between the poet and God dominates the psalm.

The two verbs "see," *rʾh*, and "fear," *yrʾ*, reproduce a sound effect in Hebrew, framing the word "many," *rabbîm* (v. 3b), literally, "*seeing, many will fear*," *yirěʾû rabbîm wěyîrāʾû*. The unusual Hebrew word translated (NRSV) "proud," *rěhābîm* (v. 4), echoes the "many," *rabbîm*. God "multiplies" (literally, "makes many," Hebrew *rabbôt*, v. 5) his deeds and attentions. Their countless number places in relief the ineffectiveness of idols. The evils which encompass the psalmist are "without number" ("*more than* hairs" and "*more than* can be counted," v. 12, repetition of *ʿṣm*, v. 5).

The psalmist claims that fidelity to God is superior to sacrifices (vv. 6-8). This estimates the value of liturgical practices and affirms the necessity of interior relations with God. The poet, like the prophets, criticizes material sacrifice which is devoid of listening and a heartfelt content (cf. 1 Sam 15:22-23; Pss 50:8-15; 51:16-19). Sacrifice is worthwhile only insofar as it expresses the inner disposition, the law "within my heart" (v. 8; cf. Jer 31:33). There is no automatic connection between sacrifice, human integrity, and God's pleasure. Thus, the psalmist counterpoises the expiatory sacrifice for sin and the sincere obedience to God's commands, "I delight to do your will." By such obedience a person sacrifices the self before God. To make sense of the difficult formulation of v. 7, we may see it in relation to v. 8. The two statements are parallel, as shown here:

I said:

| Here I am | it is written of me as in the text of a book |
| I delight to do your will | your law is within my heart. |

"Here I am" corresponds to "I delight to do your will" and "it is written of me as in . . . a book" corresponds to "your law is within my heart." The psalmist's point is the readiness to perform the right sacrifice, which is the self over the material offerings in the liturgy. What is inscribed with indelible ink on the heart is equivalent to the personal disposition; rather than an external obligation this is a desire that springs from within. The voluntary sacrifice of the will to God is the most costly and thus the most desired offering.

There are numerous references to speaking. Initially the psalmist speaks repeatedly ("my cry," "song in my mouth," "proclaim and tell," "I said," "I have told the glad news," "I have not restrained my lips," "I have spoken"). In the third movement, first the wicked scoffers speak ("Aha, Aha!"), and finally those who celebrate the psalmist's deliverance ". . . say continually, 'Great is the LORD'" (vv. 15-16). The psalmist could not be justly accused of keeping quiet about God's *hesed* and fidelity.

Psalm 41
Happy Are Those Concerned for the Weak

Psalm 41 is a thanksgiving for relief from a serious illness. It opens with an adage and a lesson about God's protection of the poor and infirmed (vv. 1-3). But the psalmist's experience contradicts this teaching, because everyone who attends his or her sickbed, enemies and friends, are unsympathetic (vv. 5-9). The poet, who cared for the needy, got sick. God, however, repays the kindness by attending him or her.

The body of the poem is framed by "[a]s for *me*" and, literally, "*and I* [in my integrity]" (*ănî* and *waʾănî*, vv. 4 and 12, NRSV), and "O LORD, be gracious to me" (vv. 4 and 10, NRSV). Within this frame the crisis and prayer unfolds, beginning with the confession of sin and a request for physical and spiritual healing (v. 4). According to a prevailing notion at the time, suffering was caused by sin. But the real motive for the request is physical infirmity. The psalmist portrays the enemies' incredulity, as they "wonder in malice when I will die, and my name perish"; they do not expect recovery from this "deadly thing" (literally, "a thing of *bĕlîyaʿal*"), some fatal misfortune (v. 8; cf. Deut 13:13; Ps 18:4). The poet remembers a table companion, a covenant ally who sided with the detractors, which makes the isolation more painful (v. 9). This is reminiscent of Job's trials; however, unlike Job, the poet acknowledges God's justice and views sickness as a consequence of sin. The recital of the rejection by enemy and friend is aimed to persuade God to act. In the end, the poet is admitted into God's "presence," pardon and healing have been granted, and the poet is restored to community life and worship (vv. 11-12).

The composition contains some beautiful poetic elements. When people visit the invalid, they speak insincerely as they enter and leave the sickroom (v. 6). Cognates of the verb *šlm* form a wordplay: at first the false friend, *ʾîš–šĕlômî* (literally, "the man of my peace," from *šlm*; cf. 37:37), was trusted; the psalmist will *repay* (verb, *šlm*) him or her after the recovery (vv. 9-10). The vocabulary for support includes "keeps . . . alive," *ḥyh* (v. 2), "sustains," *sᶜd* (v. 3), uphold, *tmk,* and set, *nṣb* (v. 12). The adversaries suppose that the infirm will not *arise* again, *qwm* (v. 8), while God will *raise up, qwm* (v. 10), and place him or her in the divine presence forever (v. 12).

Sickness and hostility generate the vocabulary of this poem. Enemy (vv. 2, 5, 11), "[a]ll who *hate* me" (v. 7), and "friends" (though false or fair weather, v. 9) all deepen the wound of affliction. The illness confines one to bed (vv. 3, 8). The two hemistichs of v. 3 (Hebrew v. 4) are parallel. The question is, what does the second part mean? The second hemistich, literally, "in his illness you change all his bed," is related to the first.

> The LORD sustains them on their sickbed;
> all his bed you change in his illness.

"Sickbed" and "bed" are parallel. Does this refer to changing the bedding and making the patient more comfortable? Or is it a complete transformation of the prostrate patient, a healing (NRSV)? One desires healing relief, *rpʾ,* because one has sinned.

The poet requests, literally, "Have mercy on me; heal my soul for I have sinned against you" (v. 4). The sin is not specified. If we understand, as the poet does, that there exists a commensurate relation between sin and suffering, healing is an act of mercy. Sickness, incumbent on sin, is relational, and so the social dimension of the illness is divulged in vv. 5-9, the reactions of friends, acquaintances, and enemies. As so often in the Psalter, the sick person inspires aversion rather than compassion. It is not a far cry from the reaction to victims of AIDS in some areas of contemporary society. The invalid's description is realistic—courteous, empty platitudes of some visitors to the sickroom, idle gossip in public. The patient imagines him or herself a burden, feeling that perhaps it would be better to die. The sickness isolates a patient psychologically and physically, to the extent that he or she imagines hostility. But God can be approached for pardon. The enemy, for whom the psalmist's demise is just a matter of time, is less compassionate. The complaint about the enemy's and acquaintance's mistreatment is a motive for God to intervene. The critics wish the worst, that the psalmist's name be blotted out, which would obliterate the descendants (v. 5).

Healing is an irrefutable proof of God's favor. Rescue is necessary so the enemy may not triumph (v. 11). Besides, the psalmist regains innocence, once the confession of sin has been made and pardon granted. According to the internal logic of the poem, formulated in the initial beatitude, the psalmist deserves divine protection, because God cares for the sick. Persons who aid the weak are happy because God in turn will aid them, according to the law of commensurate returns. But a strict application of this principle inspires the psalmist to express an indecent desire for revenge (v. 10). When friends turn accusers, the poet challenges God to act. In the end, because God has defeated the foes, the wronged but now reformed sinner is reinstated in the divine presence. The psalm concludes with God and the poet alone together.

The first and the last psalms in Book One begin with beatitudes: happy the person who meditates on God's *tôrâh*, and happy those who show concern for the infirm. Psalm 41 concludes with a doxology,

> Blessed be the LORD, the God of Israel. . . .
> Amen and Amen,

which has little to do with the psalm, but closes Book One. Similar doxologies are placed at the end of the succeeding books (72:18-20; 89:52; 106;48). Psalm 150 serves double duty, as a doxology of Book Five and the entire Psalter.

Book Two

(PSALMS 42–72)

Psalm 42
Longing for God's Presence

Two series in the Psalter are ascribed to the family of Korah, Psalms 42–49 and Psalm 84–85, 87–88. Each opens with nostalgia for the sanctuary, as though the psalmist had been banished from the temple (Psalms 42–43 and 84). Psalms 42–43 are linked by their liturgical character, and two refrains, a major (42:5, 11; 43:5) and a minor one (42:9; 43:2). Psalm 43 has no superscription, and this absence links the two psalms more closely. The first and third strophes of this complaint begin with an address of God (42:1: 43:1-3). The final "my God" (43:5) ends the paired psalms which began with a question to "God" (42:1). The company of jeering, godless people is common to both (42:3, 9-10; 43:1-2). Psalm 42:1-5 (first strophe) refers to the temple and the liturgy: the throng, the procession, the house of God, thanksgiving songs, a festival. In 43:1-5 (third strophe) liturgical references are again prominent: "your holy hill," "your dwelling," "the altar of God," and "praise . . . with the harp." Between these two an emotional transformation takes place, as occurs in many psalms of complaint. At one level of consciousness nostalgia and confusion predominate, while at a deeper level confidence and hope emerge. The psalmist feels God's painful absence yet dimly perceives his presence and addresses him.

Psalm 42 is divided evenly between two strophes and a refrain. The deer is engraved on the first strophe, which presents the troubled soul while the mocking question "Where is your God" (v. 3) pierces to the depths. In the second, the poet projects the self onto the physical terrain, although the image of the deer continues to resonate in the description of mountains, underbrush, waterfalls. The soul's affliction is mirrored in the landscape. A counterpoint to the water is the confident prayer to God, the rock (v. 9), which expresses the sense of God's abandonment, oppression, and the certainty of God's aid. The taunt "Where is your God?" (v. 10) is more sharply felt in the second strophe than the first.

Exile from God weighs on the poet and the adversary's catcalls isolate him or her. The nostalgic poet remembers participating in the liturgy, walking with the throng, leading the "procession to the house of God," the joyful chorus. Momentarily the bitter present ceases to weigh on the poet as he or she visualizes the ascent to God's temple; nonetheless the sense of separation and distance gives vent to feelings about physical separation from Zion. The imagination transports one to the steep, brushy canyons and raging torrents in upper Galilee, a projection of the terrain of a soul alienated from God. The focus shifts from the river Jordan to two mountains, Hermon and Mizar, and returns to the Jordan's cascading tributaries. The depths of the searching soul echoes in the hollows of mountains and gorges. The billowing torrents of affliction flood the spiritual terrain (cf. Pss 32:6; 69:1-2, 14-15). A person who had once enjoyed God's presence is pained by the separation. God sends *ḥesed* and the poet responds with prayer, like the rhythm of day and night, which sustains a glimmer of confidence (v. 8). The adversary's taunts stab to the heart.

The poet expresses the desperate condition of unslaked thirst, which is like the soul without God (Pss 63:1; 143:6; Isa 41:17; 55:1). He or she is restless, anxious, like a thirsty animal in a desert looking for water (cf. Joel 1:20, same verb *ʿrg*, "long" or "cry"). Liquid tears, imaged as solid food (v. 3; cf. Pss 80:5; 102:9), give shape to the distress and alienation. Water is life-giving, thirst-quenching, although tears are not satisfying. In the second strophe water is deadly and threatening (v. 7). Thus, the images collide as one thirsts for God, gulps down nostalgia, and is threatened with drowning. The waves and breakers are painful reminders of God (*"your* waves"). The sarcastic barb "Where is your God?" more cutting than the exile itself, intensifies the nostalgia. The foreigner's wrenching sadness is often that he or she cannot vent feelings with anybody who understands. Thus the turning in to the self: "as I pour out my soul" (v. 4). Tears for bread *"day* and night" (v. 3a) is reflected by the continual mockery, literally, "all *day* long" (v. 3b). The contrasting use of *day* is picked up in the second strophe; the consoling *ḥesed* and prayer "by *day* . . . and at night" (v. 8) clashes with the adversary's continual taunts (v. 10; literally, "all *day* long" as in v. 3b). The poet is torn between confidence and despair. Hope shines through with the mention of *ḥesed* and the psalmist's prayer (vv. 8-9). To find the resolution, one must consider the following psalm and the two together (see below).

Psalm 43
Send Your Light and Your Truth

The poet requests that God take up the cause and rescue him or her from the ungodly (see 7:6-11; 26:1; 35:1). This is not a legal claim but an ardent desire, springing from faith, that God's righteousness prevail. The material proof of vindication will be the return to the temple which guarantees God's closeness (vv. 3-4). God possesses two attributes with which to aid the needy, light and truth (v. 3). The poet usually appeals to *ḥesed* and faithfulness ("truth," as in Pss 25:10; 40:10-11; 57:3, 10; 61:7; 85:10; 86:15; 89:14; 115:1; 138:2); here, *ḥesed* is replaced by light which emanates from God's presence in the temple (cf. 4:6; 44:3; 89:15). Earlier the poet requested that God bestow *ḥesed* at *dawn* (42:8). In the night he or she requests the dawn, as well as truth. From a monologue (Psalm 42), the poet suddenly addresses God. The petition is explicit: send me your two scouts, Light and Truth, to accompany me—note the geographical progression and focusing—to the holy hill, God's dwelling, the altar, the harp. Near the altar the poet can thank ("praise") God in the liturgy with musical accompaniment. From exile, the journey back home took place in prayer, which colors what began as a woeful refrain with hope.

Two Psalms in One?

Psalm 43 is interwoven with Psalm 42. The identical refrain, along with other artifices, form three strophes. Psalm 42 complains of God's absence and ardently longs for his presence. But even though absent, how present God turns out to be! God is mentioned fourteen times (*ʾĕlōhîm*, plus LORD once), followed by eight additional mentions in Psalm 43. The titles with which God is invoked speak of a personal relationship between the poet and God: "the living God," "the face of God," "your God," "my help and my God," "the God of my life," "my rock," "God in whom I take refuge," "God my exceeding joy." God is omnipresent in a poem which complains of his absence. The drama is played out on two levels. On one, nostalgia and sadness dominates; on another, hope gradually transforms the poet. God's absence is painful, but, ironically, the pain of separation is a way of feeling the presence. God haunts the poet even while the foe glares and mocks that God is non-existent or disinterested. The poet is hungry for God, in the same way that separation from home and loved ones makes memories more intense and the empty feeling makes the presence more painful. The question "why?" introduced by the Hebrew *lāmmâh* or *mâh*, appears ten times in Palms 42–43, and adds to the wistful tone. The mountains of the second strophe are in contrast to the holy hill of Ps 43:3. Six times the word *nepeš* ("soul") refers to the poet's deep self. He or she describes the *nepeš* melting away (translated in the NRSV "is cast down within me," from *šyḥ*, v. 6). A seventh appearance is in the refrain of Psalm 43. The psalmist asks when he will *"come [bwˀ]* and behold the face of God" (42:2), a Hebrew idiom meaning "to visit the temple" (Ps 11:4, 7; Exod 23:17; Deut 31:11). Again in Ps 43:3 the psalmist prays that God's twin messengers, Light and Truth, may *transport* ("bring," *bwˀ*) him or her to God's dwelling. The double use of *bwˀ* embraces the problem and the solution of the psalmist's condition.

A thematic progression links Psalms 42 and 43. Together they are the prayer of an individual who feels separated from God's presence, which is associated with the temple. The distance may be real, or the psalmist may have employed geophysical images to express a state of mind, a sense of guilt, or the assault of jeering, godless people (42:3, 9-10; 43:1-2). Likewise, the mocking adversary may be real or a verbal projection of the nagging doubts. The poet hopes to return to the divine presence. Each strophe varies slightly in theme and tone. The poet focuses on the past (42:1-5), describes the present (42:6-11), and envisions the future (43:1-5). As the prayer crescendos the poet grows more assured, even as the enemy gradually assumes a definite shape. At first the picture is dim, and longing for the temple dominates. Figurative language depicts the experience, and the enemy is vague. The second strophe is gloomy, the complaints more emphatic, and for the first time God is addressed directly (v. 9). The adversary comes gradually into focus and the taunts are more audible. In the intense third strophe introspection explodes in a fervent appeal to God. The poet is hopeful about the future, and the enemy is described more concretely than in the previous strophes: "defend my cause against an ungodly people; from those who are deceitful and unjust deliver me!" (43:1). The poet's reminiscence, complaint, and hope are more explicit in Psalm 43 than in the previous two strophes.

The refrain plays a prominent role in the dynamic of these two poems, and there is an unmistakable progression from its first appearance to the last. At first it is timid and stilted. Then it becomes more affirmative, almost like a reproach to arouse the soul. The third time approaches a shout of triumph. Without changing the lyrics, the refrain changes key, given the different context of each strophe, as longing is transformed into hope. This refrain expresses mixed anguish and hope, as the poet questions his or her mood and attempts to rally the spirits. The way from darkness into light is expressed in the words "Hope in God." The tension of the poet's life is born by a faith which does not see yet knows that deliverance will not be denied. The word *again* accents the nostalgia.

In a soliloquy the worshiper questions God and quotes the enemies who interrogate him. This comes out in a secondary refrain which finds an echo in the mocking questions (42:3, 10), "Where is your God?" In the third strophe the reader can almost hear this repeated "Where is your God?" in the enemy's taunts (43:2), although it is not explicit.[1] The complaints (42:9 and 43:2), "Why have you forgotten me?" (cf. Ps 22:1) or "Why have you cast me off?" and "Why must I walk about mournfully because the enemy oppresses me?" are also secondary refrains. These repetitions further solder the links between the three strophes.

At approximately the center of the three strophes, hope is expressed (v. 8): "By day the LORD commands his steadfast love, and at night his song is with me, a prayer to the God of my life." Between two double qinahs[2] a change of meter sets this verse in relief. Only here the poet calls God by name, LORD, and *ḥesed* recalls the covenant. The growing confidence finally flowers in the third strophe. God responds to the prayer with grace, to which the psalmist in turn responds with prayer or praise. The rhythm of day and night illustrates the prayer and its answer in the form of divine *ḥesed*.

Psalm 44
Why God's Favor in the Past and Not in the Present?

Israel's humiliation and defeat (44:9-16) is a thematic link with the doublet Psalms 42–43 where the poet expresses alienation from the sanctuary. The impassioned confession of loyalty to God and the peoples' longing (44:17-22, 23-26) is similar to the motif in Psalms 42–43. Psalm 44 is the first group complaint and request for national deliverance in the Psalter. It shares a spirit with Psalms 42–43, also "of the Korahites," in which fond memories augment the present sorrow. There are four movements: glorious times past (vv. 1-8); the present complaint in the face of cruel devastation (vv. 9-16); plea of innocence of any breach of the covenant (vv. 17-22); the urgent request that God rise up from indifference and act (vv. 23-26). The theme and language are similar to Psalms 74, 78, 79, 80. Psalms 44 and 80 share in common the group complaint, the questioning, and two metaphors, vine and shepherd.

The poet claims that God abandoned an innocent people to the ravages of the enemy, who sacked their cities and brought them to the brink of destruction. Like Psalm 73 and the book of Job, the poet treats the mystery of the innocent suffering, but here it is the nation's suffering

---

[1] In all the occurrences of "Where is your God?" in the Hebrew scriptures, the stereotyped question appears in liturgical context (Ps 79:10; 115:2; Joel 2:17; Mic 7:10), where it expresses a foreigner's or enemy's needling.

[2] The meter 3 + 2 in vv. 7, 9 (vv. 8, 10, Hebrew).

rather than an individual's. The psalmist attributes the past victory to God, lest the people fall into the presumption against which Moses warned them (cf. Deut 8:17; Judg 7:2). Why did God fight for his people? We (I, they—the subject keeps changing), trusted in God rather than trust in our own forces, and God acted on our behalf, because he "delighted in them" (v. 3; cf. Ps 18:19). Meanwhile the people continually boasted of their God (v. 8). But conditions changed drastically. As the poet describes the present crisis, he or she adopts vocabulary and motifs from the first movement and reverses them (vv. 7, 9-10). The author of victory has become the cause of defeat. God abandoned the people and let the enemies conquer, scorn, and shame them. The people have become an object of derision, a "wagging of the head" (NRSV translates this "laughingstock," v. 14). Alliteration of the letter "m" and assonance ("e") calls attention to the enemy (v. 16; Hebrew v. 17), culminating in the description: *miqqôl měḥārēp ûměgaddēp mippěnē ʾôyēb ûmitnaqqēm,* "at the words of the taunters and revilers, at the sight of the enemy and the avenger." The shepherd led the people to slaughter, sold them at a loss, left them dispersed and landless (vv. 11-12, 22). No commensurate cause explains such a drastic change. Usually the psalmist admits laxity and guilt as the cause of the humiliation (as in Psalms 78, 79; 106; 107, etc.), but in the present instance he or she insists on the people's innocence (cf. Job 31; this theme is developed at length in Psalm 139). God caused the disgrace, just as earlier he brought them victory (vv. 3-7, 22). The crux is that the people find no real cause for this change of mind. The theological dark night is as tormenting as political oppression or physical affliction.

The critical situation presses the psalmist to the final, heartrending appeal, which is composed of imperatives, agonizing questions, the complaint of helplessness, and the covenant allusion, "your *ḥesed.*" "Rouse yourself" and "Awake" are bold metaphors, implying that God is inactive or asleep (v. 23; compare Pss 7:6; 35:23; 59:5; 78:65; 1 Kgs 18:27; Isa 51:9). The picture of a sleepy God does not agree with the description of God's intense activity in the first two movements. God's silence is dreadful for an innocent sufferer (cf. Pss 10:1; 22:2). In the end, the people have no recourse but to deliver an ultimatum and appeal to God who treats them so badly. The request is insistent: wake up, get up, do not reject us, look how we have been humiliated, do not forget! The light of God's countenance guided the ancestors—do not hide your face now (vv. 3, 24; cf. Ps 10:11). The people wallow in their natural substance, their bellies on the ground (v. 25). The final appeal "Rise up" contrasts with the psalmist's serious condition, which is low in the underworld. This cry is associated with the ark of the covenant which journeyed with Israel (v. 26; cf. Num 10:35; Ps 68:1). Finally the people, in desperation, give the clinching incentive for God to intervene, because of God's *ḥesed*, covenant loyalty and love. The psalm has a tragic ending, except for the guarantee of *ḥesed*.

The peculiar agony of Psalm 44 is that creeds, rituals, and traditions collapse before senseless suffering. This poet voices profound human questions, and in the end attests to a God who might be moved by interest in the people's welfare. (Psalm 73 treats a similar theme and concludes with a marvelous new perception of God's ways with the human.) Ironically, faith in God's interest and compassion precipitates the agonizing quandary. The poet struggles with God's silence, while the people are thoroughly tested. None of the questions are answered, yet to vent them shows that the poet has not given up on God. Experience tests Israel's faith and endurance on a deep level. Israel can rely on the covenant, but at times God's silence poses a crisis. At the end of the day the psalmist requests God's intercession simply because of "your *ḥesed*" (v. 26).

The poet mounts a convincing argument for God to intervene. First, God has rescued the people before, so he can do it again (vv. 1-3). Considering the people's crisis, presumably exile, the benefice of the promised land acquires particular force (v. 3), for it proved God's love. The second motive is the present crisis (vv. 9-16). In the second movement God is the subject of ten verbs. The poet expresses a profound theological conviction. If God saves, he can likewise allow the enemy to triumph. But the mood is aggravated because God deserted the people while they were faithful to him and the covenant (v. 17). The poet images a shepherd who scatters sheep with no regard for their welfare (vv. 11, 22), conditions reminiscent of the exile. "You . . . scattered us among the nations" is appropriate to the period after 722/21 (the fall of the northern kingdom of Israel) or after 587 (the fall of the kingdom of Judah and the Babylonian exile). God, who might have sold them for a higher price, settled for less (v. 12). Thus, enemies despise them and the disgrace is aggravated (vv. 13-16). What a way for the shepherd to treat the flock! The description represents a return to chaos (v. 19). The "haunt of jackals," an uninhabited wilderness, is understood by the LXX as a "place of misery." The principle commandment is the exclusive worship of God (vv. 20-21), but the present outrage is that the people are persecuted for their faithfulness, a bitter pill to swallow. Israel's suffering is a reason for God to intervene.

The "days" of the ancestors (v. 1) contrast with the "day" of the community's present trial ("all day long," vv. 15, 22); the same expression *kōl–hayyôm*, translated (NRSV) "continually," describes the community's public devotion to God (v. 8). The adversary is said to have been shamed (v. 7, "put to confusion," *bwš*); later, the "shame," *bwš*, covers the suppliant (v. 15). A nagging psychological pain results from a gross injustice. The people's heart has not *turned aside* (*ʾḥr*, v. 18) yet God has routed the people ("You made us *turn back*," *ʾḥr*, v. 10). This creates a crisis for the psalmist. The people are undeserving of this disgrace, for they have not *forgotten* God who, for his part, has *forgotten* the people (*škḥ*, vv. 17, 20, 24). By the light of God's *countenance, pāneyka,* the people were saved; now God hides his *face, pāneyka* (vv. 3, 24). Finally, the people, prostrate in the dust, request that God "Rise up" (vv. 25-26).

It is tempting to assign Psalm 44 to the historical setting of the siege and conquest of Jerusalem which led to the Babylonian exile (cf. Psalm 74, which gives explicit details and mentions Zion and the temple). The present psalm makes no mention of the city or temple and the descriptive details are generic; military defeat, flight, plunder, slaughter, and captives do not afford a precise identification. The poet has eliminated identifying features and thereby made it applicable to many circumstances. This brings the theological quandary, the mystery of suffering, to the fore.

Psalm 45
Wedding Song

Between the dedication (v. 1) and the blessing (v. 17), Psalm 45 may be divided in two movements, the eulogy of the groom (vv. 2-9) and the encomium of the bride and nuptial ceremony (vv. 10-16). The poet addresses the king (vv. 2-9, 16-17), the bride (vv. 10-12), and describes the procession, with reminiscences of the Song of Songs (3:6-11; 5:10-16) and 2 Samuel 7.[3] First the groom enters, dressed splendidly (vv. 2-5). He is applauded as God's choice (vv. 6-7) and attended regally amidst fragrant perfumes and chamber music (vv. 8-9). The royal bride is wooed with promises of devotion, wealth, and renown (vv. 10-12). The trait the two share in common is their beauty, *yph* (vv. 2, 11). Among the

---

[3] The poet addresses the king by "god" (*ʾĕlōhîm*, v. 6; so the NRSV and the LXX, "Your throne, O God, endures forever"), although the king's subordination to "God, your God" is clear (v. 7). David was compared to a messenger of *ʾĕlōhîm* (2 Sam 14:17, 20), or Samuel is termed an *ʾĕlōhîm* when he comes up from Sheol (1 Sam 28:13). This title is applied to the messiah (Isa 9:5), to judges (Exod 22:8; Pss 58:1; 82:1, 6), and to the house of David (Zech 12:8). Various translations are proposed to facilitate the understanding of this expression, e.g., "your divine throne" (NJPS) or "your throne is from God" (NJB).

wedding guests are wealthy sovereign states, notably Tyre. The lovely princess enters with her royal retinue (vv. 13-15). Descriptions of the bridegroom's and bride's wedding garments are parallel (vv. 8, 13-14). A blessing for posterity is pronounced (v. 16). The poet laureate ends as he or she began, honoring the king by the memorable composition.

"King" or "kings" appears seven times. Framing is a trait of the poem. The scribe's "heart" and "tongue" frame the king (v. 1), whose poise and sword frame God (vv. 2-3). Regalia (throne, scepter, and garments) frame the declaration "God, your God has anointed you" (vv. 6-8). The king is framed between two foreign people, the bride's family and the people of Tyre (vv. 10-12). The poem is framed in a dedication, the poet's own part in the ceremony (vv. 1, 17).

The author compares the tongue, which will "write" the song, with the stylus of a deft scribe. The king is supremely handsome and eloquent ("grace is poured upon your lips," v. 2). He owes this to God's blessing which will sustain bravery in battle for the cause of truth and justice. God appoints the king to champion "righteousness" and reject evil. For that reason God "anointed" (the verb *mšḥ,* from which is "messiah" derived) and adopted him (see Psalms 2 and 110). The poet applies to the king expressions which are elsewhere used for God: "glory and majesty" (v. 3; cf. Pss 96:6; 104:1; 111:3), the "dread deeds" *(nôrāʾôt)* of his right hand (v. 4; cf. Pss 44:3; 98:1; 118:15-16), "love righteousness and hate wickedness" (v. 7; cf. Pss 33:5; 37:28, etc.). Likewise he or she emphasizes dominion over foreign states and the stability of the reign. The "sword" and "scepter" symbolize two royal responsibilities, to fend off aggression and administer justice (vv. 3, 6). The description of the military activity is of disproportionate length in comparison to the allusion to just governance—a majestic steed, offensive maneuvers, sharp arrows, a victorious battle. The battle and the government have a trait in common, "the right" and "righteousness" *(ṣedeq,* vv. 4, 7).

The specifics of the marriage protocol are vague and the specific roles and postures are to some degree unidentifiable. The poem is redolent of the exotic fragrance of the royal attire and glimpses of the nuptial ceremony complete with decorated rooms, musical accompaniment, bridesmaids, the queen mother in her opulent gown at the king's right hand, the poet laureate glorifying the occasion. The bride is a foreign princess who renounces her own people. Exquisitely dressed amidst an entourage of maids of honor, she receives splendid gifts. The wedding scene is electric with glitter, music, and gaiety. In a final flourish, the poet boasts that he or she "will cause your name to be celebrated in all generations"—without ever mentioning the king's name!

Psalm 46
The LORD of Hosts Is With Us

God's dwelling in Zion is treated in Psalm 46, a hymn to Mount
Zion, site of the temple, the bulwark where God is present among the
people (cf. Psalms 48, 76, 84, 87, 122). The theme, God as refuge, is
stated at the outset and repeated in the refrain (vv. 7, 11). Human security is grounded in the transcendent sovereignty of God, whose capital
is Zion. The theme is developed in three strophes, the second and third
of which have a choral refrain. The two lines of the refrain are in a
chiastic relation to each other; literally,

A	B
The Lord of hosts	(is) with us
B^1	A^1
a refuge for us	(is) the God of Jacob

"Refuge," *miśgāb*, is a defensive fortress against attack. God is a sure
and inaccessible defense against enemy siege and he is on the poet's
side ("with us"). The opening verse concurs with the refrain: "God is
our refuge [*maḥăseh*] and strength [*ʿōz*]." Three references to war are apportioned among the strophes: the primeval war against chaos (vv.
1-3), international strife (vv. 4-6), and the eschaton of all wars (vv. 8-10).
God, who conquered the primeval and historical adversaries, will conquer war itself. The divine oracle is the finale (v. 10).

The threat is couched first in cosmic then in human terms. The verbal repetitions in the first and second strophes accent the contrast between secure city and unstable cosmos and history. Both oceans and
nations "roar," *hmh*, and both mountains and monarchies "totter," *mwṭ*,
but God's city is not to "totter." The delightful river and refreshing
streams gushing from the temple and symbolizing God's serene presence contrasts with the chaotic waters (vv. 3-4). The contrast between
the stream and the untamed waters is reminiscent of Isa 8:6-8, where
the people will be flooded with the torrential waters of Assyria as a
punishment for refusing the gently flowing waters of Shiloah. The fury
of the waters has a sonorous effect (vv. 2b-3a): *yammîm yehĕmû yeḥmĕrû
mêmāyw* (". . . the sea; though its waters roar and foam"). What really
roars and foams are the enemy nations and threatening rulers. But
God's presence guarantees the city's safety from the first rays of the
dawn (v. 5). There is commotion everywhere, yet a focus of stability
persists, "the city of God" with God in its midst. Descriptions of movement and instability (vv. 2-3, 6) frame the still point (vv. 4-5). Zion, the
firm anchor, holds the warring forces in check. The spatial focusing in

these two verses is remarkable: "the city of God," the dwelling of the Most High, God in its midst; this is the opposite progression from Ps 20:1-2 (cf. 43:3-4). Raging nations and unstable kingdoms, images of historical chaos, are more menacing than cosmic instability; yet a progression is evident. To the cosmic uproar (vv. 2-3) and international unrest (v. 6), God brings a halt (vv. 8-9). This is the point of the repetition of vocabulary used for seas and nations, mountains and kingdoms. The LORD of hosts is sovereign over national powers as well as cosmic.

God is the permanent refuge. Even though the whole universe may quake, the faithful rest secure. Earthquakes and natural disasters express an awesome, uncontainable power and signify any hostile force, human or superhuman, that might endanger God's people. Amid such terrifying threats, like a counterpoint, the refrain states that God is a "refuge" or "fortress" (see Ps 48:3). The title "LORD of hosts" is associated with the ark, the Israelite standard during the conquest; "God of Jacob" emphasizes God's relation to Israel since patriarchal times.

God repels the aggression with a thunder-like voice that makes the earth melt (v. 6b), a motif of the divine warrior theme (see Ps 18:7-15 and Psalm 29). When the refrain first sounds peace has already been established in creation and the international arena. The scope widens to include the whole world. God's defense of the city is a battle of universal significance and consequence; "earth" appears three times in the third strophe, echoing its earlier appearance (vv. 2, 6). The poetic language is allusive rather than direct, drawn from a vision of the cosmos and history based on the belief that God as sovereign chose Jerusalem as the universal capital. In the last part the poet concentrates on God's continual wonders, notably the definitive end of war, imaged in breaking the weapons. Suddenly God announces the surrender of all contending forces and demands universal recognition. Fear is useless. What could any human power do against one who has such a God on his side (see Ps 56:4, 11)?

To look on God's dwelling is to lift the gaze to God. The poet employs images of God's mythic battle against the primordial ocean and the underworld, which threaten the stability of the terra firma (vv. 2-3). Even though the earth quakes, mountains fall into the ocean, unruly chaos rages, God's presence is a guarantee against disaster. There is no need to fear for God is a "refuge," "strength," and "help" (v. 1). The poet also draws on mythical language to portray the transcendent meaning of Zion, "the city of God" (vv. 4-6). The life-giving river, which gushes forth at the center of the earth and irrigates paradise, signifies that God is "in the midst" of Zion.

The climactic third strophe opens with an invitation to contemplate God's awesome deeds, listed specifically. The raging nations of the previous strophe are recalled in the broken weapons. Considering God's universal sovereignty, international military activities are in vain. Above the tumult of cosmic upheaval and preparations for war God's voice echoes, uttered by a priest or prophet (v. 10). This divine oracle ("Be still, and know") can be misunderstood as a summons to quiet meditation. Rather, the Hebrew imperative (from *rph*, Hiphil) means "desist," commanding the forces opposing God's sovereignty to surrender. The mention of nations and the earth alludes to the battles God has won against chaos and against threatening nations (vv. 2-3, 6, 9). God's residence in the city removes it from the instability of creation and history. The capital city will not totter; even in its temporal locale it represents a transcendent reality. The hymn affirms that God is a bulwark against the prevailing tide of mortal ills. Trust in one's own resources jeopardizes one in the battle against inimical forces.

Psalm 47
All Peoples, Clap Your Hands

In Psalms 46 and 47 the ancient name "Most High," *ʿelyôn*, is used for God (46:4; 47:2).[4] The final acclamation of 46:10 (before the refrain), "Be still, and know that I am God! I am exalted among the nations [*gôyîm*], I am exalted in the earth," is echoed in Psalm 47: "all you peoples" (*ʿammîm*, in place of *gôyîm*, which occurs in v. 8) and "all the earth" (vv. 1-2). "Jacob" (46:7, 11) appears in 47:4.[5] Psalm 46 introduces its sequel, which invites the nations to acknowledge God's universal rule.

Psalm 47 celebrates God's coronation as sovereign (see also Psalms 93, 96–99). Divine sovereignty is the central idea, whatever the precise setting may have been in Israel's liturgy. The "pride of Jacob" bespeaks northern Israel connections (cf. Amos 6:8; 8:7). The psalm was sung in a religious ceremony, probably connected with the ark. The ascension ("has gone up," *ʿlh*, v. 5) ushers the emblem of God's presence into the temple. Another possible interpretation is that this is part of the liturgical renewal of the introduction of the ark into the Jerusalem temple (2 Sam 6:15). The sound of trumpets is characteristic of royal coronation (2 Sam 15:10; 2 Kgs 9:13) and the feast of Sukkoth (Ps 81:3; Num 29:1).

[4] This occurs elsewhere in consecutive psalms (Hebrew) 77:10 and 78:17, 35, 56; 82:6 and 83:18; 91:1, 9 and 92:1.

[5] Jacob (thirty-five times in the Psalter) occurs elsewhere in consecutive psalms (Hebrew) 75:9; 76:6; 77:15; 78:5, 21, 71; 79:7; 84:8; 85:1; 146:5; 147:19.

The sense of celebration is imposing: applaud, shout, sing praises (five times in vv. 6-7)—seven imperatives in all—as well as the sound of joy, a shout, a trumpet peal, and the *maśkîl* (v. 7, a kind of song or psalm). The two panels of the structure are symmetrical:

vv. 1-5	vv. 6-9
v. 1, invitation	v. 6, invitation
v. 2, motive: universal sovereign	v. 7, motive: universal sovereign
v. 3, he subdues peoples	v. 8, international sovereign; throne
v. 4, choice of Jacob, the elect	v. 9a, foreigners as Abraham's family
v. 5, God ascends	v. 9b, God is exalted

The horizontal plane, "all you peoples" and "all the earth," is cut by the vertical axis, "God has gone up," "he is highly exalted," and "peoples under us, and nations under our feet." The poem commemorates Israel's election and international recognition of God. The repeated sequence consists of a summons to praise (vv. 1, 6) followed by the content of praise (vv. 2-5, 7-9). An account of how God established his rule follows the first summons. A description of God enthroned in his court follows the second. What results is a vibrant hymn to God's historical and, above all, eschatological reign over "all the earth" (vv. 2, 7) and "over the nations" (v. 8). The use of "peoples" and "nations" (Hebrew, *ʿammîm, ʾummîm, gôyîm*, vv. 1, 3, 8, 9) is synonymous. The perspective is universal, yet the focus is on Israel among whom God is enthroned.

The Hebrew particle *kî* ("for," vv. 2, 7, 9) introduces three reasons for praise, each affirming God's sovereignty. The first introduces God's universal power and the election of a people (vv. 2-4). The proof of God's dominion is drawn from history, the conquest of Canaan ("our heritage") for Israel. The second invitation to "sing praises" (v. 6) is followed by the second *kî*, which introduces the royal motif, God occupying the temple throne (vv. 7-8). From there he establishes universal rule. The third and final *kî*-clause (v. 9b) reaffirms God's universal sovereignty. God's rule is illustrated by the fourfold occurrence of "king," *melek* or *mlk* (in Hebrew, v. 8, the verb "rules," translated "God is king," is a cognate of *mlk*). The acclamations and trumpet peals accompany the ascension of the divine sovereign. Seven times the absolute form of God, *ʾělōhîm*, appears, with the additional "the Lord, Most High," "Lord," and "God of Abraham." Ten references to the divine illustrate God's universal rule. "[S]hields of the earth" is clarified by its parallel position with "princes of the peoples" (v. 9; cf. Pss 84:9; 89:18). The chiefs gather to what purpose? The question is not the subjection of the peoples to Israel (as in v. 3), but Israel's and all peoples' submission to the divine sovereign. The international assembly is addressed in the invitatory verse (v. 1).

"God of Abraham" alludes to the promise (v. 9; Gen 12:1-3) according to which all peoples will be beneficiaries of the covenant. Here the election of God's people finds its most profound meaning. God chose Abraham so that all nations may be blessed. As the international rulers unite with the descendants of Abraham, they will be blessed (Zech 8:20-23). From the exalted throne God establishes dominion over all nations, uniting the gentiles with the children of Abraham and preparing the definitive reign. In the end the "people of the God of Abraham" are constituted, not by ethnic or national identity, but by recognition of God's sovereignty.

Psalm 48
The City of God

Psalm 48 is a song of Zion in praise of God (see Psalm 46). It celebrates God's rule and victory over chaos and all enemies, a victory commemorated at the fall festival of Sukkoth. The scope, like that of the previous two psalms, is universal, the whole earth (vv. 2, 10). The poem has four movements: praise of God and the city where he dwells (vv. 1-3), the frustrated foreign aggression (vv. 4-8), the ripple effect of the celebration (vv. 9-11), procession around the city walls (vv. 12-14). The opening line, "Great is the LORD and greatly to be praised," is a liturgical formula (cf. Pss 96:4; 145:3). The setting may be a temple liturgy (v. 9), in which case the city's siege in the second movement illustrates the city's impregnability.

Jerusalem's importance derives from the temple, God's dwelling, situated near the northern perimeter of Mount Zion, one of the hills upon which the city is built; hence no claim can be too extravagant. God's "holy mountain" is distinguished in beauty, "the joy of all the earth" (see Lam 2:15; Isa 60:15; 65:18; 66:10), impregnable because God is there (vv. 1-3; Pss 46:4-7; 76:1-2). In "the far north" translates an uncommon phrase, *yarkĕtê ṣāpôn*. The association with the sacred mountain of the Canaanite pantheon, Zaphon in the Ras Shamra texts, was well known, and thus the poet intends a double entendre which links the two holy mountains (cf. Isa 14:13). God is the most effective "defense," *miśgāb* (v. 3; the NRSV renders this Hebrew word as "refuge" in Ps 46:7, 11), within the "citadels." Invincible Zion inspires panic in the enemy but exultant pride in the people (vv. 4-11; cf. Ps 2:4-9). The poet ranges earth's kings against the divine king in the capital and reports that on *seeing, rʾh,* it they panicked (v. 5). Presumably they saw God or some sign of his presence, like the waters that *saw* God and trembled (cf. Pss 77:16; 114:3). In turn, the assembly has heard and *seen (rʾh),* but the poet does not specify the object (v. 8).

The psalm begins and ends with praise of God and descriptions of the city (vv. 1-3, 12-14), which frame the contrasting reactions of the assailants (vv. 4-7) and the faithful (vv. 8-11). A concentration of action verbs moves the enemy along: assembled, came on together, saw, were astounded, were in panic, took to flight (vv. 4-5). The agents suddenly become passive recipients, seized by fear, shipwrecked as by a strong wind (vv. 6-7). In contrast, the reaction of the devout is more tranquil; they "ponder" God's *ḥesed* and rejoice in God's judgments (vv. 9, 11). What began in the temple as a silent meditation reverberates to the distant reaches of the earth as rejoicing. The sequence of verbs, hear–see–ponder–rejoice, draws the assembly into a more conscious celebration.

In Psalm 48 the political site becomes a theological premise, and thus the poet employs vocabulary that does not correspond to the physical and political reality of Jerusalem. The low ridge on which the city sits is called a "holy mountain," beautiful in its towering height, visible and central to the whole earth. Jerusalem is not mentioned, but, surprisingly, Mount Zion is located not in the southern Judean hill country but "in the far north." The poet celebrates not the city of David but the capital of "the great King," who rules over all and who has founded and sustains the city. Thus the poet endows Jerusalem with a new identity, acquired when the ark of God was brought into its walls. The horizon is ample: city, holy mountain, all the earth, Mount Zion, the far north, citadels (vv. 1-3)—it is no wonder the foreign aggressor fled at the sight (vv. 4-7). The spatial description continues: God's temple, Mount Zion, towers, ramparts, citadels (vv. 9-13). God makes the holy city beautiful *(yāpeh),* a "joy of all the earth," "a sure defense," (established) forever. It is so beautiful that it terrifies its assailants, because of the just government that radiates from there (v. 11).

The congregation confesses that the defender of the city gives them something to ponder as they worship in the temple —God's *ḥesed* and *ṣedeq* ("victory"), displayed in his judgments (vv. 9-11). As the assembly celebrates the historical experience, they are reconfirmed in their faith. From the temple the name of God fans out and is praised. From there the congregation meditates God's *ḥesed,* which reverberates in glad tones throughout the earth. The chiastic arrangement of four hemistichs is well devised (vv. 10b-11). Gladness and rejoicing is embraced by justice, *ṣedeq* (translated in the NRSV as "victory"), and judgments, *mišpāṭîm,* as a more literal translation shows:

A justice *(ṣedeq)* fills your right hand

   B let Mount Zion rejoice

   B' let the towns of Judah be glad

A' because of your just decisions *(mišpāṭîm)*

Zion and the neighboring Judean cities rejoice over God's "judgments," understood in terms of saving deeds in favor of God's people (cf. Ps 97:8).

In defiance of the "great King" (v. 2), competing "kings assembled" to besiege God's city (v. 4). The Hebrew for "assembled" *(nôʿădû,* Niphal perfect of *yʿd)* recalls the claim of v. 3b, which could be translated literally, "God has made himself known [*nôdaʿ,* Niphal perfect of *ydʿ*] as a fortress."[6] The pun emphasizes the contrast. God is the most remarkable of the city's architectural splendors. Two similes that depict the sudden disaster that overtook the invaders clash (vv. 6-7); the enemies are seized as with birth pangs and as a hurricane that destroys ocean freighters. Labor pains portrays spasms caused by terror. The second simile evokes a storm that smashes cargo ships which haul metal products from Tarshish, possibly identifiable with a site in Spain (Tartessus) or Sardinia (see 1 Kgs 10:22; Jonah 1:3).

The poet concludes with five imperatives which rally the assembly to tour the defense works (vv. 12-13). The third, central imperative invites the worshipers to "count" *(spr)* Jerusalem's towers so they may "tell" *(spr)* the future generation about God's strength. One views the city's fortifications and acclaims the God within, who is the real defense (v. 3). The visible city is a witness to the invisible God. The earthly reality is estimated in terms of the heavenly, the temporal in terms of the eternal. As a paean to Zion, Psalm 48 glorifies God's greatness and beneficence at the beginning, the end, and at the center (vv. 1, 10, 14). Thus in glorifying a city God is honored. Walking around the city, counting its towers, considering its ramparts and its citadels reflects a greater, more solid reality: "this is God, our God forever." The poet does not cease to surprise the reader. The mighty stronghold reflects God, "our guide forever." In the real world a fortress does not guide a flock or a pilgrim people, but God is both the most stable defense and the surest guide.

[6] For the Niphal of *ydʿ* in the sense of God's epiphany, cf. Exod 6:3; Isa 19:21; 66:14; Ezek 20:5, 9; 38:23; Pss 9:17; 76:2.

Psalm 49
They Will Take Nothing With Them When They Die

True to the role of sage, the poet of Psalm 49 addresses the universal audience (vv. 1-2), and identifies the poem as ḥōkmôt, tĕbûnôt, a māšāl, and a ḥîdâh ("wisdom," "understanding," "a proverb," and a "riddle"; vv. 3-4). The introduction is composed in parallel lines (vv. 1-4). The body is divided in two parts which treat the theme in different ways (vv. 5-12, 13-20). Each part closes with the refrain. The solemn introduction is reminiscent of Proverbs 1–2, and 8, and the Elihu speeches in Job 32–37. The matter is of general interest. The poet speaks with the *mouth*, meditates with the *heart*, inclines the *ear*, and solves the "riddle to the music of the *harp*" (vv. 3-4), and thus the musical instrument is related to physical organs; together they aim to approach the wisdom theme, in pursuit of which the poet is fully engaged. The instruction is broadcast to rich and poor, high and lowborn, wise and foolish (vv. 2, 10), and considers their common destiny, death. What results is a persuasive reflection on the abrupt, bleak end of the wealthy. As in Psalms 1 and 37, not a line is addressed to God, who is only mentioned twice (vv. 7, 15). The sage first tells of how he or she learned to deal with a serious problem (vv. 5-15), before exhorting the congregation (singular) to emulate the lessons which life teaches (vv. 16-20). The truth boils down to the fact that humans, no matter who they are or how hard they try, cannot save themselves. No wealth can ransom one from death (vv. 5-9); even the wise and famous are destined for the grave. An unforgettable image is expressed tersely, "Their graves are their homes forever" (v. 11). Any other house is provisional. Even though their memory is preserved in place names, famous people emigrate to a perpetual dwelling, Sheol. A name cannot guarantee permanence. The verb *lyn*, "abide," in the refrain suggests this theme of a permanent home (v. 12). The poet is preoccupied with Sheol, the grave, and the realm of the dead (vv. 11, 14-15, 19), a place of unrelieved darkness, "the land of gloom and chaos, where light is like darkness" (cf. Job 10:22). He or she sums up the reasoning of the wicked. Content with their comfort, intelligence and power, they do not need God (v. 13). In the end the teaching takes the form of an exhortation. Let not wealth lead the good astray. Just wait, and the law of gravity will bring down the wicked, for the destiny of the wealthy is dingy Sheol (vv. 16-19).[7] The lengthy description of inescapable death suddenly stumbles on the disjunctive ʾak,

---

[7] The ending of v. 14 is uncertain. The MT reads the "upright shall rule" over the wicked, which is contrary to the usual view of the Hebrew Scriptures.

"but," and the surprising declaration, "But God will ransom my soul, [he will take me] from the power of Sheol" (v. 15). Then, again abruptly, the finale reverts to the theme of the futile efforts to avoid death.

The poet, who belongs to the powerless class, holds the key to the riddle. Experience teaches that only God saves, even from the threat of death, "for he will receive me" (v. 15). Does the poet expect life after death? Deliverance from Sheol is formulated in an analogy; God will "receive" or "take," *lqḥ*, him or her as he "took" Enoch (Gen 5:24) and Elijah (2 Kgs 2:3, 5, 9-10; cf. Pss 6:10 [Hebrew]; 73:24, "receive me with honor"). This interpretation contrasts with the earlier statement that a person cannot ransom his or her own life (v. 8),[8] and the use of *lqḥ* which states that the wealthy are unable to *take, lqḥ* (v. 17, "carry"), anything with them when they die. Another interpretation is that God will deliver the poet from threatening death (literally, "the hand of Sheol"). This may be a mortal illness or a wicked plot (v. 5; see Pss 30:3; 86:13). In any case it would be possible to enjoy life after God rescues one from the present crisis. It is doubtful that the poet believes in an afterlife with God. The psalm is too early in the development of Israel's thought to formulate such a belief.[9] What is certain is that the poet is sure of a destiny in God's hands (see Pss 37:37-40; 73:23-28).

The imagery is original. Life is a prisoner of death; the jailer is God, and no price will suffice to pay the ransom (vv. 7-8). The poet contrasts the one who is threatened with *seeing* the grave and *looking at* the wise die (vv. 9-10, the same verb *rʾh*). Death shepherds everyone into Sheol, a terrible lodging (v. 14). Their graves will be their perpetual dwelling, where total darkness reigns, where they will join their ancestors (vv. 11, 17-19). The author portrays someone at ease congratulating him or herself (v. 18; cf. Lk 18:11, the religious person seemingly praying to the self).

The problem is stated in the refrain that compares humans to animals. The poet begins, "I will incline my ear to a *proverb [māšāl]*" (v. 4); the refrain echoes this with a cognate: "they *are like* [from *mšl*] the animals that perish" (vv. 12 and 20). Thus, cognates of *mšl* appear in the beginning, middle and end, and weave together the composition. This is as if to pose a riddle, that the wealthy "are like the animals that per-

---

[8] The NRSV of v. 7 has followed a few Hebrew manuscripts in transcribing the opening word *ʾāk*, "truly" (as in v. 16, Hebrew), instead of *ʾāḥ*, "brother." The meaning of the saying is clear. The pronunciation of *ʾāḥ* suggests a double duty homonym, "brother" and "truly," as in *"Not even a brother can ransom a sibling."* The only real ransom is with God (v. 15).

[9] Clearly the psalmist demonstrates a belief in existence after death, even in the present psalm (v. 19, "the company of their ancestors"); but existence in Sheol does not constitute life.

ish." Even more valuable than wealth is life itself, which riches cannot guarantee—the premise in a nutshell. A variant in the refrain attracts attention. What reads first "Mortals cannot abide in their pomp; they are like the animals that perish" (v. 12), is read the second time (literally), "For all their wealth, mortals do not understand; they are like the animals that perish" (v. 20). The "not abide" becomes "not understand" by the change from *yālîn* to *yābîn*. The person who does not reason along these lines is as good as beasts that perish. The theme that the human is no better than a beast fascinates the poet. Once mortals have been compared to "animals that perish," the image of Death, shepherding them into Sheol, is poignant. The essence lies in what the similarity between humans and animals implies.

The poet addresses "all the inhabitants of the *world [ḥāled]*" which designates not exactly "the world" (usual word *tēbel*) but a [limited] lifetime, which is transitory (cf. Ps 39:6 [Hebrew]), and thus, by metonymy, the world inhabited by transitory guests. By an inversion of consonants, *ḥdl* for *ḥld*, the sense of ending or perishing is understood. Such allusions are understandable in a wisdom composition. In the refrain "they are like the animals that perish," the verb *dmh*, "perish," is a homonym of *dmh*, "imitate" or "be equal to." Along with double meanings, differences in interpretation leave the impression that the poet was playing with metathesis:

ḥld (living world) and *ḥdl* (perishing), v. 1

qbr (grave) and *qrb* (interior, mind), v. 11

qbr (grave) and *bqr* (morning, daybreak), v. 14

"Their graves," *qirbām* (v. 11), becomes, by an inversion of letters "r" and "b," "their interior" or "their mind," *qibrām*. The NRSV opted in v. 14 for a translation based on an inversion of letters; *labbōqer*, "in the morning" is understood as *laqqeber*, "to the grave." The Hebrew "the upright shall rule over them at daybreak" is understood by the NRSV as "straight to the grave they descend."

The sage addresses the problem of how people orient their lives to acquire wealth. The error is not wealth in itself but how people let it disorient their relation with God. With a legal idiom the sage analyzes what happens in such cases, which amount to an attempt to use wealth as a "ransom of life" (see the term *pdh*, "ransom," in vv. 7-8, 15). In certain legal cases where the death penalty was stipulated, the guilty party could pay a "ransom of life" (Exod 21:28-32). The idiom implies that behind the fascination with wealth is a denial of death, the notion that riches can ward it off. The sage meditates on this problem not to denounce the rich but to instruct and comfort the faithful. When the wealthy use their riches to take advantage of others, the faithful are tempted to "fear" (vv. 5, 16), which amounts to anxiety about the meaning and end of life, an unsettling reaction to the influence the wealthy wield over the powerless. Such fear disorients a person from the reverence for God which is the first step in a life of faith (Prov 1:7).

Death is inevitable for everybody. Those who thought they needed no divine guide end up with a shepherd whose name is Death, who herds them into Sheol to dwell forever (v. 14). Mortals can do nothing to ransom their lives from death. Even the wealth thought to be a ransom is lost in death along with their fame (vv. 11, 17). The sage is relentless in the recital for he or she intends to debunk those who suppose riches are the key to life and its destiny. He or she exposes the ultimate pretension of striving after wealth and power that disturbs the faithful.

Psalms 37 and 73 also deal with the problem of the prosperous wicked, but the answers are different there. The teachers assure the faithful that the wicked will be undone during the present life, while the righteous will be vindicated. Psalm 37 is materialistic in the reward of good people, while Psalm 73 emphasizes the quality of a relationship with God. In Psalm 49 the resolution is universal death. The theme is the prosperity of the wicked and the harm they do. The traditional teaching that it will go well for the good people (Psalm 37) is contradicted by these self-sufficient wicked who are boastful and violent.

A rhetorical question (v. 5) affirms that one need not fear the wicked. They will die anyway and neither wealth nor power can exempt them from the common lot. Death is the great equalizer; even the wise die. No one can take anything beyond the grave (repeated in vv. 10, 17). Comfort, opulence, power, like life itself, are all transitory (see Ps 39:6). The address "Do not be afraid" (v. 16) is typical of the wisdom school where the sage addresses the disciple. However wealthy a person might be, if one is so foolish as to forget God and not reckon with death, he or she is no better off than a beast.

Psalm 50
God Arraigns the People

By their theme and development Psalms 50 and 51 belong together, as two parts of a lawsuit. Psalm 50 is a prophetic reprimand, couched in the form of God's arraignment of Israel ("his people," v. 4) on the grounds of a breach of the covenant and her liturgical and moral formalism (as in Isa 1:10-17; Isaiah 58; Jeremiah 7; Amos 5:21-24; Mic 6:6-8; Ps 40:6-8; Sir 34:21–35:20). The prophet, speaking for God and probing the people's religious conscience, indicts them publicly (Ps 50:7-21). An introduction describes God's arrival and summons the witnesses and the accused (vv. 1-6; see Isa 1:2); the prosecution follows. The proceedings are clear: opening statement, establishing God's legal right to sue (v. 7), denunciation of liturgical practice (vv. 8-15) and the moral life (vv. 16-21, the singular "you" opens each line; cf. Pss 44:11-15 [Hebrew]; 74:13-17; 89:10-14 [Hebrew]), finally, God urges a restoration of religious practice with a warning, a threat, an exhortation and promise of salvation (vv. 22-23). The process is not complete until the accused party answers, which is the plea of guilty in Psalm 51.

God is the offended party, prosecutor, and judge. Three names ("mighty one" [*ʾēl*], God [*ʾĕlōhîm*], the LORD) identify him whose authority reaches from one horizon to the other (v. 1). God resides in Zion, the seat of government, where he radiates forth (*hôpîaʿ*, see Deut 33:2; Pss 80:1; 94:1). He will "testify against" the people and proceed against them (vv. 7, 21). What in the preceding wisdom psalm is an invitation to learn becomes in the present a call to order in the proceedings ("Hear," v. 7; cf. Pss 49:1; 95:7). To listen, hear, is the desired attitude before God, who presents the case. The resonance with the first word of the credo of Israel is poignant ("Hear, O Israel," Deut 6:4). The covenant is the basis of the legal action, because it forges the relationship and formulates the privileges and responsibilities of each party, including the right to accuse (v. 5). The witnesses embrace created reality; horizontally, from east to west (v. 1), and vertically, heavens and earth (v. 4). Their function validates the process. The sky announces the judge's "righteousness" (v. 6; cf. Ps 19:1). The judgment will take place in Zion, the seat of the supreme court and God's dwelling, "the perfection of beauty" (v. 2; see Pss 48:2; 122:5). The divine prosecutor appears in grandiose style, flamboyant and tempestuous (v. 3; see Pss 18:7-15; 97:2-5). He summons the accused party, and the irony of "my faithful ones" is clear. They are being indicted for a breach of the covenant. The poet announces the commencement and introduces the judge (v. 6).

The divine accuser begins with an appeal in which he introduces himself, "I am God, your God," and recognizes the covenant partner, "my people" (v. 7; for the complete formula cf. Exod 6:7; Lev 26:12; Deut 4:20, etc.). God does not accuse them of malpractice in the liturgy, although he asserts that worship alone is insufficient. The people ratified the covenant with a sacrifice (v. 5), but now their ritual offerings are all bogus. God cannot be placated with animals for food or drink; being sovereign, he needs nothing (vv. 8-12). Furthermore, the sacrificial animals have no material value for they already belong to God. The list represents a totality—tame and wild animals, large and small, forest and steppe, field and sky. Rather, the acceptable and sincere sacrifice is praise, fulfillment of promises, turning to God in danger, following the right path (vv. 14-15, 23). Any expression of one's interior disposition is worth more than material offerings. God desires that the people "fulfill" the covenant obligations, and invoke him, so he can deliver them. What is absent from the liturgy, is "praise," which implies confession of sins, fidelity to the covenant, good neighborly conduct. How dull the people must be to follow recipes in their relation with God, maker of heaven and earth, while failing to see that God actually governs creation (v. 12)! God does not accuse the people of lack of form; in that regard they are impeccable. Rather, it is lack of content.

The second part of the discourse is more explicit about the violations of the covenant (vv. 16-21). The accused are called "the wicked." The fault is hypocrisy, reciting the commandments verbally and not practicing them, especially with respect to the neighbor ("kin" or "your own mother's child," v. 20). The crimes are thievery, adultery, slander and deceit, an illustrative, not an exhaustive list. Sins against proper speech are particularly odious. Should God be indifferent toward such gross behavior (v. 21)? A God, silent before this incongruity in the people's lives, would be an accomplice. Worship is genuine only if the covenant stipulations concerning public conduct are observed.

The finale offers the accused two alternatives (vv. 22-23). If they do not convert, they will be chastised. Conversion ("sacrifice of thanksgiving," vv. 14, 23) and change of behavior ("the right way") lead to pardon and salvation, to which the human response is to honor or glorify God (verb, *kbd*, vv. 15, 23). The desired outcome of the suit is conversion and reconciliation. The last phrase, "the salvation of God," shows how the divine word, even when it accuses and convicts of sins, is a grace (cf. the same ending in Ps 91:16). What remains is for the accused to respond to the charges (cf. Psalm 51).

Psalm 51
Offering the Broken Heart

The confession of guilt of Psalm 51 complements the legal indictment begun in Psalm 50. The sacrifices which do not please God (51:16) are alluded to in 50:9-13. The poet is not a slave to the external forms of religion. He or she was schooled in them—ritual washing (v. 2), purification with hyssop (v. 7), burnt offerings (vv. 16, 19)—but denounces them insofar as they do not constitute an intimate relationship with God. The appropriate sacrifice is "a broken and contrite heart" (v. 17). Once the penitent is forgiven, he or she rejoins the worshiping community (vv. 18-19). Repentance and forgiveness amount to rebuilding Jerusalem.

Psalm 51 has three movements: request for personal cleansing (vv. 1-9), request for personal renewal and right sacrifice (vv. 10-17), and restoring the city and the liturgy (vv. 18-19). The careful use of language clarifies the structure. In the opening lines three verbs are used metaphorically, "blot out" *(mḥh)*, "wash" *(kbs)*, and "cleanse" *(ṭhr)*. They recur in reverse order (vv. 7, 9, "I shall be clean," "wash," "blot out"), framing the first movement. A second frame is the repetition of "heart" and "spirit" (vv. 10, 17). In the first movement the verb *ḥṭʾ* ("sin" and cognates) is repeated six times, and once in the last two (v. 13). Other expressions for sin or sinner occur six times in vv. 1-9 and again once in v. 13 (transgressions, iniquity, evil, guilty, iniquities, transgressors). Thus, fourteen times vocabulary for wrongdoing is employed. In inverse proportion "God" is named once in the first movement (v. 1) and six times in the remainder of the poem (seven times total as in the NRSV). Sin, remarkably present in the beginning, gradually disappears and is replaced by God in the latter part. To be more precise, sin disappears in the second half in the same ratio that God appears; thus, with the confession sin is replaced by God's presence. The poet literally and literarily is emptied of sin and filled with grace. Furthermore, the whole psalm and particularly the opening lines are rich in a vocabulary of forgiveness, with a preference for words for cleansing.

The initial requests (vv. 1-2) are supported by a reflection and motives for God to respond, as the poet describes the personal trouble (vv. 3-5). A second set of requests (vv. 6-12) is concluded by a promise to testify to God's ways (v. 13). The requests amount to one, that the poet be thoroughly purged. He or she pleads for a solution that will restore praise of God (vv. 14-15) and gives the reason (vv. 16-17). The rebuilding of Zion will be honored by the resumption of sacrificial worship (vv. 18-19).

Fifteen imperatives move vv. 6-15: "teach," "purge" and "wash me," "let me hear" and "let [the bones] rejoice," "hide your face"[10] and "blot out," "create" and "put a new," "do not cast me away" and "do not take . . . from me," "restore" and "sustain," "deliver"; the finale is "Lord, open my lips." Two more imperatives follow, "do good to Zion" and "rebuild the walls" (v. 18). Adding the four requests in the opening lines, "have mercy," "blot out," "wash," and "cleanse" (vv. 1-2), the sum is twenty-one in all. This intentional concern for multiples of seven shows that the poet desires a total reordering of life.

The repetition of cognates of *ṣdq* articulate God's negative and positive reactions to the guilty party. The psalmist admits that God is

---

[10] God's "hiding" or "turning away" his face, given the parallel with "blot out," is an idiom for forgiveness (v. 9), which is distinct from its usual meaning (cf. Pss 69:17; 88:14).

"*justified [tisdaq]* in your sentence" (v. 4), but later affirms "and my tongue will sing aloud of your *deliverance*" (*ṣidqātekā*, literally, "your adjusting things right," v. 14). Two forms of the verb *ydꜥ* function differently; the guilty poet "knows" or acknowledges personal guilt (v. 3) but wishes to *know* [NRSV, "teach"] "wisdom in my secret heart" (v. 6). Different forms of *šwb* ("return," "restore") outline the process of salvation; once God has "restored" *(šwb)* the penitent's joy of salvation, he or she desires to teach others how to "return" *(šwb)* to God (vv. 12-13). The word translated "contrite" *(dkh,* with reference to the heart, v. 17) is a cognate of "crushed" (v. 8). The psalmist wishes forgiveness to be able to return to "joy," *śāśôn* (vv. 8, 12).

"Spirit," *rûaḥ*, is repeated four times in the second movement (vv. 10-12, 17). To receive a new spirit, live with God's spirit (cf. Ps 104:29-30), and have a generous spirit requires the sacrifice of a "broken" spirit. The "clean" heart afforded by God's new creation will be the "broken and contrite heart" which the poet offers to God. "Heart," parallel to "spirit," is not the seat of emotions as might be thought in English (in Hebrew that would be "kidneys" or "bowels"). Heart is akin to the mind and will, the font of decision, action, and loyalty. The divine action in a person, God's "holy spirit," saves and keeps one faithful (v. 11; see Isa 63:10-14). God's spirit (or breath) was infused into humankind at creation (Gen 2:7). "Heart" and "spirit" figure in another way. God accepts the "broken spirit" and "a broken and contrite heart" as a sacrifice (v. 17). Broken or crushed spirit and heart are metaphors for the mind and will humbled by God's action. The idiom "let the bones that you have crushed rejoice" (v. 8) is a metaphor for the self and its conscious reaction to God's grace. The poet desires both internal holiness and an expressive spirit—a clean, contrite heart; a new, right, willing, broken spirit. Once the individual is forgiven, the community can rejoice, "Let me hear joy and gladness" (v. 8), a reference to reintegration in the worshiping community. He or she promises to evangelize and praise as a response to God's recreating grace (vv. 13-15).

The theology of Psalm 51 is born of the elaborate use of language and metaphor. The major chord "[h]ave mercy" sets the tone from the beginning. The poet does not appeal to personal efforts at penitence, tears or remorse, but to God's *ḥesed* and "abundant mercy" (*raḥămîm*, v. 1). Rather than turn inward, wallow in regret over failure and guilt, the poet reaches outward to God and grace. The opening lines include a profound awareness of guilt, "Against you, you alone, have I sinned." Sin is a personal offense against God not an abstract violation. But, according to the indictment in Ps 50:18-20, the real sin constitutes injustice against the neighbor; furthermore, the caption claims that this is David's psalm following the Bathsheba affair. In this context the poet presents the theological tenet that any sin is an offense against God, the author of our human relationships. When David recognized his guilt, he said, "I have sinned against the LORD." The superscription of Psalm 51 is likely to have been added late in the redactional process. The scribe applied the poem to a sensitive moment in David's life, perhaps because of the verbal connection between v. 4 and 2 Sam 12:13. When the poet writes "Against you only have I sinned," he or she did not mean that David committed no wrong against the murdered Uriah and his wife. But David's adultery and murder constitute a crime against God. The meaning is profound. A crime against the neighbor is an offense against God. Furthermore, the poet confesses the condition of sinfulness, not simply external actions. The extensive vocabulary of sin illustrates the thoroughness of the confession. Even the line, "Deliver me from bloodshed *[dāmîm]*" (v. 14),[11] which connotes homicide, in the present context means guilt. Ultimately, every sin is related to killing, curtailing someone's life. This choice of vocabulary was the grounds for assigning this psalm to David (see 2 Sam 12:9).

The present guilt causes the poet to discover the roots of the sinful condition in humankind. He or she reviews life from its inception in the womb and confesses that the whole span stands under God's scrutiny. The reference to a sinful conception and birth is sheer exaggeration and may be a poetic attempt to abase oneself so as to win God's mercy, almost as if to say "I had no choice in the matter; I could not help it." The request is not just that God pardon a particular wrong but that God deliver one from the deep-rooted predicament of the self. Such a confession conditions the request for God's creation of a new self (vv. 10, 14-15). The verb "create," *brʾ*, expresses God's act of calling the world into existence out of chaos (v. 10; Gen 1:1). Isaiah uses "create" to speak of God's transformation of reality so what emerges is something new and different (Isa 41:20; 45:8, 12; 65:17-18). By this choice of vocabulary the poet asks God to bring into existence what was not there before. "Put a new" or "renew," according to the principle of parallel lines, is a synonym of "create."

The request that God show good will toward Jerusalem by rebuilding its walls (vv. 18-19) corresponds to the petition that God create a clean heart and renew the spirit. As the individual is recreated, the whole community is restored and the city is built anew. Both individual and civic restoration are works by which God removes people from guilt and renews them. In the restored city, inhabited by the pure in heart, right sacrifices and meaningful liturgy can be resumed. Some

---

[11] Other instances where *dāmîm* is translated "bloodshed" are in Ezek 22:3, 4, 6, 9, 12-13; Hos 12:15. These occurrences refer to a crime of corporate Israel.

features suggest that Psalm 51 was composed during or after the exile and used in Israel as a penitential prayer. Its language and thought are connected with that of Jeremiah, Ezekiel, and Isaiah 40–66. It resonates with the promises of a new heart and spirit in Jer 24:7; 31:33; 32:39-40 and Ezek 36:25-27. In this exilic context some of the prayer's difficult points make theological sense, and the reference to the reconstruction of the city's demolished walls and the restitution of temple worship form an appropriate conclusion. In any event the idea of rebuilding Jerusalem has been transposed from a literal to a metaphorical sense.

The verb "create" marks the beginning of three verses which Alonso Schökel likens to an epiclesis, because they comprise a triple invocation of the spirit. As at creation, the divine spirit hovered over the ocean when the cosmos was taking shape, here a triple spirit recreates the penitent psalmist. The three references are in parallel positions:

> . . . a right spirit renew within me
>
> . . . your holy spirit do not take from me
>
> . . . a willing spirit sustain in me

The spirit in each case is the direct object of an imperative verb; two positive requests frame a negative ("do not take"). The Niphal participle *nākôn*, translated "right," connotes stability, firmness, which at first seems strange when applied to a wind, breath, or spirit, but this means a firm resolve or strong will. The second qualifier, "holy," refers to God's breath which is in the living creature (Gen 2:7; 7:22). If God were to withdraw the divine breath, life would stop (see Ps 104:29-30). The third qualifier, "willing spirit," denotes the virtue of generosity. The penitent requests not just exterior conformity to God's design but interior resolve and transformation. Together the three aspects display a completely transformed person, with firm resolve, based on God's life which breathes in and through him or her, and which expresses itself in a virtuous life, thus producing a new person. In the simple and sincere act of confession a person is renewed.

Psalm 52
Why Do You Boast of Wrongdoing?

Psalm 52 is framed by "the godly," "steadfast love" and "the faithful," all cognates of *ḥsd* (vv. 1 and 8-9).[12] In three movements the initial

---

[12] The Hebrew text could be understood as "Why do you boast of evil, O mighty one? God's kindness endures all day long" (v. 1).

accusation against the wicked (vv. 1-4) is followed by the verdict (vv. 5-7) and the poet's personal commitment to God (vv. 8-9). The psalmist opens with the address to an anonymous person or a typical character and concludes by addressing God. In the style of a prophetic denunciation (recall Pss 50:16-21; 82:1-4), a "mighty one" or "warrior," *gibbôr*, is denounced for plotting and falsehood. The term here is derisive. Dominant in the accusation are the multiform evils of the tongue, which is "a sharp razor" and uses "words that devour." Lying and deceit are conceived in a perverse mind, premeditated *(ḥšb)*, and are the product of a basic choice, to "love *[ʾhb]* evil more than good" and "love *[ʾhb]* all words that devour." The poet relishes the destiny of the wicked and their punishment will bring relief to the oppressed (vv. 5-7). The poet pledges a public thanksgiving.

The contrasting vegetal images are vivid (vv. 5, 8; cf. Ps 1:3-4); the wicked will be uprooted, while the good ("I") are [planted] "like a green olive tree in the house of God." The tree symbolizes a life rooted in God which draws on the resources which the temple represents and provides (cf. Ps 92:12-14). The images take on greater vigor when they are compared. The big shot dwells in a tent, speaks offensively and deceitfully, trusts in material things, lives contentedly and hoards possessions. Without warning he or she will be violently destroyed, as by a swift desert raid or a tornado out of nowhere. The counterpart, represented by the poet, is planted in fertile soil like a healthy tree that enjoys the nourishment and growth which sturdy roots afford. The poet wastes no words on the uprooting of the self-assured. The green, flourishing olive, an emblem of prosperity, lives long and is resilient even after pruning. It is rooted where it will be well-tended, in the temple plaza, while the wicked are ruined because they have no roots. The poet contrasts the object of "trust," *bṭḥ* (vv. 7 and 8). The wicked trusts in riches and he or she vanishes, while the poet trusts in God's *ḥesed*, will celebrate in the temple and enjoy a lasting friendship with God. The wicked will be removed "from the land of the living," while the poet will thank God forever. The irony is poignant. The wicked, so evident at the beginning, completely disappear from the text. After a lengthy address to the wicked (vv. 1-5), the psalmist turns to God, thanking him "because of what you have done" (v. 9), which amounts to exterminating the wicked and curbing their oppression of the faithful. The evil speech contrasts with the poet who will "proclaim" (Hebrew, "wait for") God's goodness.

The poet poses a typical situation. A person enjoys power and influence on the basis of wealth, but is inconsiderate and cruel. What is more, he or she vaunts the abuse of power, presuming immunity from danger. The tongue is the lethal weapon used to entrap, deceive, and slander (see Pss 10:7; 12:2; 50:19; 55:9, 21; 57:4). The offended poet holds the mirror close to the wicked face and the distinguishing features become clear—a razor tongue, loving "evil more than good, and lying more than . . . the truth," loving "words that devour" (vv. 2-4). Such heinous dispositions and conduct merit immediate destruction, which is described energetically. The righteous will see, fear and laugh (v. 6). Their terse speech identifies the source of the criminal behavior. Their adversaries "would not take refuge in God, but trusted in abundant riches" (v. 7). The end of the wicked is God's triumph and liberation of the faithful.

The deserved punishment is concentrated in images. A green olive tree in the house of God is opposed to the nomadic "tent" of the wicked and being uprooted. The images gain strength by the verbs. A person lives secure in a dwelling, has a position in society, is content and guards his or her possessions. Suddenly the violent wind snatches everything away. A person who is apparently rooted in fertile ground is torn up by the roots to dry or rot. The olive grows around the temple (v. 8). This is a simile of the vitality of a devout person. The temple is the soil wherein the olive grows its roots and which nourishes its lush, green growth, in marked contrast to being yanked out by the roots.

According to the superscription Psalm 52 is set in David's life when Doeg the Edomite tattled to Saul that the fugitive had sought help from the priest Ahimelek at Nob (1 Samuel 21–22; especially 21:7 and 22:9). This report resulted in the murder of ("devouring" of, v. 4) many of the Nob priests. Doeg is supposed to typify the "mighty one" addressed. This application is contradicted by the mention of the temple. Nonetheless the psalm can be transposed to any generation by heeding the poet's warning and taking Doeg's as a typical behavior to avoid.

Psalm 53 (parallel to Psalm 14)
O That Deliverance Would Come from Zion!

Psalm 53 presents few changes from its double, Psalm 14. The superscription adds "according to Mahalath" and "a Maskil." The designation "LORD" (14:2, 4, 7) is altered to "God" (53:2, 4, 6) as one would expect from psalms of the elohist section of the Psalter. The copy of Psalm 14 breaks down in Ps 53:5:

53:5	**14:5-6**
There they shall be in great terror, in terror such as has not been.	There they shall be in great terror; for God is with the company of the righteous.

For God will scatter the bones of
   the ungodly;
they will be put to shame,
   for God has rejected them.

You would confound the plans of the
   poor,
but the LORD is their refuge.

The main difference is that the punishment and rejection of the wicked (53:5, the Hebrew text is unclear) occupies the place of God's protection of the just. Counting this alteration, the negative particles (*ʾên* and *lōʾ*) total seven, whereas there are only six negations in Psalm 14. The change also creates a sonorous triple repetition of cognates of the verb *pḥd* (v. 5), literally, "They *shall be terrified* with *terror*, such a *terror* as has not been." The image of God scattering the bones of the wicked contrasts with Israel's rejoicing in the final verse. The shame and God's rejection of the wicked is told in a single breath, which emphasizes their previous denial of God and refusal to do good (53:1, 3). Although the text of Psalm 14 has been altered in Psalm 53, there are in each seven direct references to God. Both represent prophetic pronouncements.

Psalm 54
God Holds Me Up

The complaint in 53:4, they "do not call upon God," is echoed in 54:3, "they do not set God before them." Psalm 54 has the typical elements of a complaint. The three parts comprise a call for help followed by the reason (vv. 1-3), an expression of trust with a request (vv. 4-5), and the thanksgiving for the rescue (vv. 6-7). The superscription refers to an incident in David's life when he was a fugitive from Saul (1 Sam 23:19; 26:1). The calls for help and motives are generic—"save me," "vindicate me," "hear my prayer," and "by your name" and "by your might" (vv. 1-2). The trouble is "the insolent" (the Hebrew *zārîm* may be better translated "foreigners" or "strangers") and "the ruthless," *ʿārîzîm*, who ignore God and plot against the psalmist's life (v. 3). The uncommon expression "[they] seek my life," *biqĕšû napšî*, is in contrast to "the upholder of my life," *sōmĕkê napšî* (v. 4). Originally *nepeš* ("life") meant breath and neck, so *bqš nepeš* meant to hunt the neck (like a head hunter), the opposite of seeking the face, which refers to a friendly visit. Likewise, *smk nepeš* means to hold up the neck, to raise the head, a sign of benevolence or protection. In these two expressions the first *nepeš* refers to the life and the second the person. The general plight can be applied to any incident in which ignoring God results in violence against one's neighbor. In effect, snubbing God is an affront against the source of life. The poet requests a pay back of what the adversary intended against the innocent, which amounts to their annihilation (v. 5).

The poet uses three designations for God, *ʾĕlōhîm, ʾădōnāy* (literally, "my Lord"), and the divine name, LORD, in meaningful sequence. The initial *ʾĕlōhîm* (vv. 1, 2, 3, 4) is transformed to "my Lord" (v. 4), which accentuates the growing intimacy between the supplicant and God. In the resolve to thank the divine rescuer, the poet writes "I will give thanks to your name, O LORD" (v. 6). "[B]y your name" was part of the initial appellation (v. 1). The three words for God, along with the alternating modes of address (God is addressed [vv. 1-2, 6] and spoken about [vv. 3-5, 7]) have a dramatic effect. Parallelism is the basic structure, and the lengthening of a line and departure from parallel lines emphasizes the scandal, "they do not set God before them" (v. 3). The continuation of this phrase with the beginning of v. 4 produces the only interesting stylistic feature of this poem; "they do not set God before them" is followed by "But surely, God is . . .," *lôʾ śāmû ʾĕlōhîm lĕnegdām. hinnēh ʾĕlōhîm.* It is like a wake up call to the obvious.

Psalm 55
Complaint about a Friend's Betrayal

Inclusions frame the two movements of Psalm 55. The first opens with the distraught poet's insistent cry to God and closes with the assurance of God's intervention (vv. 1-2, 16). References to time, "Evening and morning" and "half their days," frame the second movement (vv. 17, 23). Four imperatives set the plaintive tone. The shifting focus captures, alternately, two sets of actors, the poet and God (vv. 1-2, 16-19), the poet and the enemy (vv. 3, 9-15, 20-21). The poet's plight and introspection is the theme of vv. 4-8. The finale contrasts the enemy's desert and the poet's trust in God (vv. 22-23). Emphatic Hebrew pronouns ("But you" and "But I") corrals the opposition, "the bloodthirsty and treacherous," and forges the alliance between the poet and God, stated concisely, "But I will trust in you."

In the expression "I *am troubled* in my complaint" (v. 2; cf. Gen 27:40) the Hebrew verb *rwd* connotes uncontainable restlessness. This interior disposition is aggravated by the adversaries' angry noise, which pierces to the heart (vv. 3-4). The pressure finds a vent in the complaint. The poet's "heart is in anguish," and terror avalanches upon *(npl)*, invades *(bwʾ,* NRSV "come upon"), and covers *(ksh)* him. Together the verbs *bwɔ* and *ksh* express saturation with and submersion in fear, within and without, as four synonyms for fear demonstrate (vv. 4-5). The person quakes in fear ("horror overwhelms me," cf. Ezek 7:18), is scared to death, and longs for a fantastic escape from the enemies' rampage—to get wings like the dove and fly; even the hostile wasteland would be more hospitable than the ravaging storm (vv. 6-8).[13] Israel's memory idealizes the desert sojourn as a time of special divine protection. The escape is purely mental, because the clamor of the wicked penetrates the thin wall of refuge.

The Hebrew reads "Confuse, O Lord, confound their speech" (v. 9a), alluding to Babel (Gen 11:6-9), where God divided the people by creating a communication barrier. This brief curse implies that the offensive weapon against the poet is speech. The city is overrun by sinister personalities. The psalmist exchanges one fantasy for another. This time he or she surveys the city and finds "Violence and Strife" patrolling the walls, "Iniquity and Trouble" occupying the city, "Ruin," "Oppression and Fraud" commanding the commercial center—seven personifications in all (vv. 9-11). The city is completely infiltrated by nefarious forces, which reflect the multiple faces of social evil. Anarchy and civil disturbance foment treason even of religious allies (vv. 12-14). The state of emergency is intensified by a friend's betrayal (cf. Ps 41:9), a stab deepened by the memory of conviviality. The contrasts, friend and enemy, before and now, aggravate the pain. The psalmist addresses the friend directly, "But it is you, my equal. . . ." The "house of God" identifies the city as Jerusalem. The holy precincts, with its religious throng, intensifies the contrast between the holy city and one completely populated by violence and crime. The psalmist could have coped with persecution, but the blow to the heart is the betrayal of a fellow worshiper. Multiple synonyms for "friend" emphasize the enormity of the treason. This personal affront of friend-turned-foe is enveloped by the curses (vv. 9 and 15). One matter is enemy assault; even worse is the betrayal of a friend in the sanctuary—damn them all! In contrast to God's dwelling, the adversaries' homes and hearts house evil (v. 15). The alliterative phrase in *aleph* (transliterated ɔ, v. 16, Hebrew v. 17) marks the end of the first movement: *ɔǎnî ɔel-ɔĕlōhî ɔeqrā* ("But I call upon God"), as God and the poet meet in prayer, which eases the tension and calms the imagination.

The poet waits for God to answer the insistent appeal (vv. 16-17). "Evening and morning and at noon" are prayer times but together they mean "continually." (The day was reckoned to run from sunset to

---

[13] The raging wind and tempest form a hendiadys (alliterated *sōɔâh* and *sāɔar*, v. 8).

sunset.) Another expression of time refers to a long life, proof of God's favor (v. 23; cf. Pss 21:4; 91:16). The sign of God's displeasure with the wicked is a premature end, they "shall not live out half their days." The enemies gradually take shape; they resist change and "do not fear God" (two negative aspects); they assaulted a friend and violated a pact (two offensive positions); their speech is "smoother than butter," their words "softer than oil" (two comparisons), while in reality the "heart [is] set on war" and their words are "drawn swords" (vv. 19-21). The contrasts are forceful—buttery speech and warring heart, well-oiled tongues which stab like swords. Suddenly a voice interrupts the discourse, either a liturgical oracle or an inner voice (v. 22). The final comparison resolves the tension. The adversary will be cut down in mid course, while the psalmist's trust in God wins life. Even amidst anarchy and passion the psalmist finds a moment of repose (v. 23b).

There is a paronomastic display of cognates of *qrb*, "within," "in its midst"; the heart, literally, pounds *in the breast* (v. 4); the malice and mischief is *within* the city, "in its *midst*" (vv. 10-11). An example of focusing is "evil is in their homes and *in their hearts*" (v. 15). Finally God intervenes to rescue "from the battle," *miqqărāb* (a cognate of *qrb*, v. 18). Another cognate, *qārōb*, refers to the enemies' "heart *set on war*" (v. 21). The play on expressions derived from *qrb* illustrates the tension. Contrast heightens the drama. The poet is scared to death but reassures him or herself (vv. 4-5; note the contrast with the self-assurance of v. 23). "Fear," *yrʾ*, overwhelms the poet, while the enemy has no fear, *yrʾ*, of God (vv. 5, 19). The desert retreat (v. 7) contrasts with the dense urban violence and strife (vv. 9-11). The poet describes that "ruin is in its midst *[qereb]* and oppression and fraud do not depart from its marketplace *[rĕḥôb]*" (v. 11), a merism which embraces blind alleys, the public square, and everything between. The "house of God" is juxtaposed to Sheol where God is absent (vv. 14-15). The enemies' "clamor" contrasts with the psalmist's "voice" (*qôl*, vv. 3, 17). The sequence, God will "hear" and "humble" (*ʿnh*, "oppress, afflict," v. 19), is surprising. Usually one expects "God will hear and answer" (another verb *ʿnn*). A friend turned out to be false (vv. 13-14, 20-21), while God is the true support (v. 22). God will not "permit the righteous *to be moved*," *mwṭ* (v. 22), yet the "terrors of death *have fallen [mwṭ]*" upon the psalmist (v. 4). The emphatic phrase "But . . . you" (*wĕʾattâh*, vv. 13, 23) contrasts God and human, which is to say the false friend and true God.

The poet looks inward, while upset by the outside voices. He or she returns inside, overwhelmed by deadly terror (vv. 1-5), looks for a mental escape, a flight to the desert, but the civil unrest is all too apparent, and is aggravated by treason. The poet inhabits two regions, the external situation and introspection. All around is social disorder, while in-side is agitation and fear; outside a friend turned traitor, while inside the poet quakes with fear. The interior self corresponds to the city's conditions (vv. 4, 10). The point of departure is the present social un-rest, which moves the poet to introspection, and there too the poet finds disorder. He or she seeks an open place like a desert because the city walls, instead of protecting, imprison him or her. All this finds a resolution in the poet's prayer, which amounts to a united front in the face of opposition, the poet and God.

Psalm 56
Trust in God

Psalms 56–60 all have "Of David. A *Miktam*" in the captions. The imprecations in 54:5; 55:9, 15, 23 link them with 56:7, "repay them for their crime; in wrath cast down the peoples." In both Psalms 55 and 56 the psalmist is endangered or persecuted; in each he or she voices a complaint and a request. Psalm 56 unfolds in three movements. An ini-tial plea, "Be gracious to me, O God" (cf. Pss 51:1; 57:1), and complaint is followed by an affirmation of trust (vv. 1-4). Another complaint, an imprecation, a petition, and an affirmation of trust follow (vv. 5-11). The concluding vow celebrates God's intervention (vv. 12-13). A refrain stamps the psalm with a tone of trust and closes the first and second parts (vv. 4, 10-11).[14] Opposition is couched in the verbs "to be afraid" and "trust" and the nouns "God" and "flesh" *(bāśār)* or "mortal" *(ʾādām)* (vv. 3-4, 11), as is shown here:

"I am afraid" — "I trust . . .

in God";   — "what can flesh [or "mortals"] do to me?"

The rhetorical questions "what can flesh do for" or "against me?" admit that human threat or aid is indifferent (vv. 4c, 11b; cf. Ps 60:11; Isa 40:6). The sequence and repetition of verbs is concentric (vv. 3-4):

A	B	C	B'	A'
I fear [yrʾ]	trust [bṭḥ]	praise [hll]	trust [bṭḥ]	do not fear [yrʾ]

---

[14] The alliteration with *aleph* (transliterated with the symbol ʾ) calls attention to the refrain, *ʾîrāʾ ʾănî ʾēleykā ʾebṭāḥ* (v. 3).

Initially the fear inspires one to confide in God, the object of praise; with such trust, fear vanishes. The plotting of the attackers who seek the poet's life is more dangerous than an open assault (vv. 5-6). May God repay them (v. 7).[15] The poet is confident that prayer is a sure offensive against assailants (v. 9). The second appearance of the refrain is amplified with God's name, LORD (vv. 10-11).

The foes are persistent, "all day long" (repeated, vv. 1, 2, 5). They are numerous, cruel, and obsessed with harming the poet. They trample, oppress, fight against, seek to injure, stir up strife, lurk, track—evidently aiming to do away with him or her (v. 6). But the poet does not lose hope. The repetition of "day" gives the answer to the plight. The psalmist says "When [literally, "on the *day*"] I am afraid, I put my trust in you" (v. 3) and "my enemies will retreat in the *day* when I call" (v. 9). Fear (vv. 3-4, 11) neither paralyzes nor blocks him or her from turning to the divine rescuer and reviving the trust in God's word, which is effective (vv. 4a, 10; Pss 106:12; 119:41-42; 130:5). God's solicitude is so tender that it collects and counts every tear (cf. Matt 10:30) and treasures them because the pains they represent are precious; thus they are not wasted. The "bottle" is a leather flask. God's "record" book of life appears in Pss 69:28; 139:16; Exod 32:32-33.

Confident of a divine hearing, the poet closes with thanksgiving for rescue from death and a return to life in God's presence, the guiding light (vv. 12-13; cf. Pss 27:13: 52:5; 116:9). The "light of life" is opposed to darkness in Sheol (cf. Job 10:21-22). Earlier the psalmist complains that the enemy watches his or her "steps," *'ăqēbay* (v. 6). Feet can stumble or be caught in a net (cf. Pss 9:15; 25:15). God guards the feet, *raglay*, from the fall or a false step so the psalmist "may walk before God" (v. 13; cf. Pss 66:9; 91:12; 94:18; 116:8; 121:3). His or her life is summed up by the "wanderings" (NRSV, "tossings") and tears, which God records. Life is spent roaming without a specific aim and weeping, but God's interest infuses the sad wandering with purpose and thus ends the prayer.

The superscription sets Psalm 56 in the context of 1 Sam 21:11-13, when David was "in the hands" of the servants of the Gath king. The LXX understood the unclear phrase "according to The Dove on Far-off Terebinths" as "for the people far removed from the sanctuary," and adopted a personal complaint for corporate use (so also the title in the Targum). The request that God "cast down the *peoples*" (v. 7) may indi-

---

[15] The NRSV conjectures "repay them for their crime," *'al-'āwen pallet-lāmô* (v. 7; Hebrew v. 8). Literally the verb *plt* asks God to "preserve them" or "set them aside" (cf. Mic 6:14; Ps 91:14), which does not make sense in the present context, except in view of a judgment and eschatological punishment. A literal translation of the Hebrew is "For their evil preserve them; in anger cast down the peoples, O God."

cate that the composition in the singular was composed for congregational use or it was revised.

Psalm 57
Let Your Glory Appear Over All the Earth

The identical beginning, "Be gracious [merciful] to me, O God," and
the promise of thanksgiving (cognates of *ydh*, 56:12; 57:9) link Psalms
56 and 57. The poet opens with confidence that God will provide
refuge from danger (vv. 1-3). The second part begins with a statement
that anticipates the adversaries' downfall; they have fallen into the pit
they dug (v. 6), which is cause for rejoicing (vv. 7-11, repeated in 108:1-
5). The refrain, which interrupts the description and closes the psalm,
adds a communal dimension to what began as an individual complaint
(vv. 5, 11).

"[I]n the shadow of your wings" refers to refuge in the presence of
the ark of the covenant (v. 1). The cherubim wings atop the ark was
God's throne (see 17:8; 36:7; 61:4; 63:7; 91:4). The poet trusts in God's
intervention, who from the heavens has always favored him or her and
will continue to send help (vv. 2-3). The poet describes the difficult
straits with the typical images of a storm, a stampede, wild beasts, and
the hunt (spears, arrows, swords, the net and the pit; vv. 1, 3-4, 6). The
attackers are like lions, and the image is fantastic. With spears and
arrows for teeth and sharp swords for tongues, they devour humans[16]
(v. 4; see 7:2; 10:9; 17:12; 22:13, 21; 35:17). The leonine identity suggests
that they are royalty or governors. The persecution consists of abusive
speech or false accusation, poignantly imaged by these savage beasts.
The picture of a person ambushed by animals is replaced by that of a
hunted animal. The trapper lays the net, digs a pit, and camouflages
them in hopes of catching the prey. These assailants are bound to fall
into their own traps, a picturesque statement of retributive justice (v. 6;
cf. 7:15-16; 9:15-16; 35:7-8).

The repeated expression "He [God] will send . . ." brackets "he
will put to shame those who trample on me" (v. 3). God's deputies
commissioned to protect the psalmist, *ḥesed* and faithfulness (*ʾĕmet*),
reappear in immense proportions, "high as the heavens" and "to the
clouds" (v. 10). Altitude is likewise applied to God (vv. 3, 5, 11). *ʾĕmet* is

[16] The Hebrew *lhṭ* (NRSV, "greedily devour") really means "burn, be aflame for"
(cf. Ps 104:4), and is used figuratively. The alliteration of "*ḥ*" focuses on the dangerous image: *ḥănît wĕḥiṣṣîm . . . ḥereb ḥaddâh*, "spears and arrows . . . sharp sword."

employed frequently for God's fidelity, and it signifies something firm, lasting, a reliable guarantee, someone on whom we can always count. *Ḥesed* often accompanies *ʾĕmet* and adds a connotation of mercy and kindness to reliability. The poet believes that *ḥesed* and faithfulness, traits of the divine rescuer, are as big as the universe (v. 10; cf. 36:6), and he or she trusts that God will delegate *ḥesed* and faithfulness to do his will (v. 3b; cf. 43:3; 85:10-13; 89;14).

The transition from the poet's personal danger to the adversaries' failure is marked by a refrain (v. 5), which interrupts the description and creates two scenes. The effect is a drastic mood change. In a peal of excited introspection, the poet rallies himself (*kĕbôdî*, "my soul"; cf. 7:6 [Hebrew]; 16:9; 30:13 [Hebrew]) and the musical instruments to awaken the dawn. He or she erupts in a morning thanksgiving song (vv. 7-10). The word *kĕbôdî* contrasts with the expression "your glory" (*kĕbôdekā*, in reference to God, vv. 5, 11). The psalmist is a reflection of God's glory.[17] He or she, awaking, rouses God and the musical instruments, with the aim of waking the dawn. All are to awake hurriedly to participate in the thanksgiving. In the refrain heavens and earth are converted into a majestic scene as they honor God who gives salvation to the faithful. The thanksgiving is a public proclamation "among the peoples" or "nations" (v. 9) which extends beyond the limits of the chosen people, "over all the earth" (vv. 5, 11).

Psalm 58
Dethroning Unjust Rulers

Psalm 58 is an energetic invective against corruption and injustice, leveled at the guardians of social justice and human rights. It is distinguished for its opening line, which addresses the wicked. The poem has three movements: accusation against the judges and wicked (vv. 1-5), curses (vv. 6-9), the triumph of the good (vv. 10-11). It is framed by the repetition of words and cognates (in Hebrew): *ṣdq* ("right" or "righteous") and *špṭ* ("judge," vv. 1, 11); *ʾereṣ* ("earth," vv. 2, 11); *rāšaʿ* ("wicked," vv. 3, 10). Right judgment, bad and good, and the place where evil and judgment is effected frames the poem. What began as an address to the wicked "on earth" ends with the recognition of "a God who judges on earth." Psalm 82 is similar to Psalm 58 in intensity. Both are community appeals for the righting of systematic evil.

[17] The luminous quality of *kābôd* is recognized in texts like Exod 16:10; 24:17; Isa 60:1; Ezek 1:28; 3:23; 10:4.

The opening is a blunt and passionate denunciation of rulers. Judges and governors are supposed to collaborate with God in the maintenance of a just order (cf. Ps 82:2-4). If they do not, God will have to intervene (as in Psalms 7, 18, 140). The present appeal moves God to do just that. The identity of the *ʾēlem*, "you gods" (v. 1), is vague, and its interpretation determines the understanding of the psalm. It accuses either the lesser divinities or human authorities for delinquency in administering justice. The vocative "you gods" is derisive, like "mighty one" of Ps 52:1. The answer to the question is all too evident; no, they definitely do not employ their office and influence to maintain a just society. The unjust power mongers are dedicated to wicked inside and out, "your hands" and "your hearts" (v. 2). The verb *pʿl*, "to work, devise," is employed for the unjust machinations of the heart or mind (cf. Mic 2:1). The earnest desire is that God, the real judge, unseat the corrupt practitioners (v. 11; e.g., 7:11; 9:7-8; 11:4-7; Psalms 96–99).

The imagery is masterful. Although the translation is uncertain, the metaphor in v. 2 is of rigging the scales to one's advantage (Hebrew v. 3; the root *pls* means to adjust scales, to weigh or calculate). The allusion to "Adam" (NRSV "people" is, literally, "children of Adam," v. 1) and the serpent (v. 4) recall the fall of Genesis 3. The vendors of justice are bad to the core (v. 3; cf. Ps 51:5; Isa 48:8); their entire lives even from their fetal origins are consecrated to wickedness—a hyperbole. They are liars who bite, poison, and can kill. The venom is their speech. Bestial images are fitting for these people who act inhumanely. Their complicity with evil is diabolical. A "serpent" injects its venom which spreads like a deadly virus through the wicked allies.[18] Their evil is so potent that they are unmoved by the charmer's spell which is meant to control it (v. 5; cf. Jer 8:17; Sir 12:13). The poet erupts in a curse against this inimical force which works injustice and violence. The defanging (v. 6a) refers back to the image of the venomous serpents and ahead to "the fangs of the young lions." The poet savors the vitriol with seven terrible curses (vv. 6-9). This, which amounts to a plea that the wicked be aborted (cf. v. 8), is as violent as the victory celebration is graphic— may the feet of the righteous be bathed in their blood (v. 10). This latter idiom expresses the desire for the enemies' utter defeat in battle (cf. Ps 68:23; Deut 32:42) and for participation in God's victory. The Hebrew text of vv. 8-9 (NRSV vv. 7-8) is unclear, but the intention is brutal. The snail leaves its empty shell and hence appears to dissolve. The sum of these images is no more drastic than that in Ps 52:5 which calls for the swift and total annihilation of wicked in God's world. The oriental

---

[18] John the Baptist and Jesus spoke of a "breed of vipers" (Matt 3:7; 12:34; cf. Rev 12:9).

curse is expressed in eloquent, exaggerated terms (cf. Pss 109:6-20; 137:9), and thereby the poet leaves an unforgettable impression.

Psalm 58 opens with the painful realization that the institution which is set up to safeguard justice and human rights is corrupt. It concludes with the assertion that God cares and will right the scales of justice (v. 11; cf. Ps 37:28). This joins other psalms which deal with the problem that prosperous evil poses for the good who trust in God's providence and observe the law (cf. Psalms 9–10, 11, 12, 14, 17, 37, 49, 73, 91, 94).

Psalm 59
Complaint Against Bloodthirsty Enemies

Both Psalms 58 and 59 are complaints, which alternate between descriptions of the wicked or enemies (58:3-5; 59:3-4a, 6-7, 14-15) and a curse (58:6-9) or prayer for vindication reminiscent of a curse (59:1-2, 4b-5, 10b-13). The injustices of the powerful (58:1-2) become the source of the poet's suffering (59:1-4).

A refrain (vv. 9, 17) divides Psalm 59 into two parts (vv. 1-9, 10-17) in which the drama of trial and liberation is acted out.[19] A second refrain (vv. 6, 14) places roving dogs in the background of the psalmist's crisis. Evil speech and false accusations are lethal weapons against the psalmist. The prayer begins with four imperatives for divine intervention—deliver (*nṣl*, repeated), protect, save me, followed by the motive, introduced by *kî* "[e]ven now." Three more imperatives are spoken before the dogs refrain—rouse, see, awake. This septet is rounded off by a negative imperative, "do not have mercy" (*ḥnn*, NRSV "spare none"), and the description, "those who treacherously plot evil" (v. 5). The adversary gets progressively worse: "my enemies," "those who rise up against me," "those who work evil," "the bloodthirsty," "they lie in wait for my life; the mighty stir up strife against me" (vv. 1-3). The "mighty" tags them as part of the ruling class. The present persecution, described as a military maneuver (v. 3a; *gwr* means "to lie in wait for, to besiege," cf. Isa 54:15; Pss 56:7 [Hebrew]; 140:3 [Hebrew]), cannot be justified because the psalmist is innocent (vv. 3b-4). He or she calls on "my God," LORD, "LORD God of hosts . . . God of Israel," "my strength," "my fortress," "Lord, our shield," "refuge" (vv. 5, 9-11, 16-17). With such terms the psalmist accentuates God's loyalty, summed up in the word *ḥesed* (vv. 10, 16-17). He or she shows how the people

---

[19] The repetition "O my strength, I will *watch for [šmr]* you" (v. 9) becomes "O my strength, I will *sing praises to [zmr]* you" (v. 17), by the change of a single letter.

will know that God really governs. That the wicked get what they deserve will prove God's existence and providence, and answer their doubts. The psalmist tries to awaken God, as if he were asleep, had distanced himself or averted his gaze, "Rouse yourself . . . to my help and see!" (vv. 4-5; see Pss 35:23; 44:23).

The psalmist prays to be "lifted out" (*śgb*, v. 1; NRSV "protect") of reach of the foes, and God is said to be the "fortress" (*miśgab*, "acropolis, high spot," from *śgb*; vv. 9, 16-17), the answer to the emergency. The instability and sneakiness of evil is contrasted with God's stability and clarity ("fortress"). The imagery is ingenious. Human adversaries are reduced to being stray dogs roaming the city streets at night, howling, following their sinister instincts (vv. 6-7, 14-15). "Dogs" is a derogatory term, emphasizing their voracious, subhuman conduct. They are filthy, aggressive, insatiable and they even feed on corpses (cf. 1 Kgs 14:11; Isa 56:10-11; Ps 22:16, 20). The second occurrence of the refrain is expanded, which leaves the impression of this band of strays all night, growling and looking for food. The first time the no-good animals are "bellowing with their mouths," with dagger-like words on their lips (v. 7). It is unclear whether the question "Who will hear us?" represents the acerbic skepticism of the "dogs" (the NRSV has opted for this by adding "they think") or the questioning of the incredulous psalmist, complaining that the prayer may fall on deaf ears. The tongue is their weapon; calumny and, possibly, a blasphemous question, "Who will hear us!" imply a denial of God's hearing.

The poet is impressed with the foes' ferocity, but God laughs at their supposed strength and derides them (v. 8; cf. Pss 2:4; 37:13). The psalmist pictures him or herself as a sentinel on the watch for God (v. 9). Typical of Psalm 59 is the arsenal of military images (see vv. 3a, 5, "lie in wait," "LORD God of Hosts"), "my strength" and "my fortress" (vv. 9, 17), "our shield" (v. 11b). The curse is no less vivid than that in the previous psalm (vv. 11-13; cf. Ps 58:6-9), requesting that every trace of the enemy be obliterated. They will be "consumed" by the heat of God's wrath. The root of their malice, pride, is doubly framed:

A	B	C	B'	A'
sins	words	their pride	cursing	lies
of their mouths	of their lips			

The adept use of cognates illustrates both the cause and the resolution. At first the adversary is termed "the mighty" (*ʿazîm*, v. 3). The refrain calls on God, "my strength, *ʿuzzî* (from the same *ʿōz*), and the poet is certain to "sing of your [God's] might" (*ʿuzzekā*, from *ʿōz*). Instead of waging a battle the poet finds refuge in prayer.

The time change is significant. The dogs range freely in the evening (vv. 6, 14), but in the morning God's *ḥesed* brings relief (v. 16; cf. Ps 30:5). In the evening or at night the psalmist is on the lookout, watching for God (v. 9). Normally in the Psalter God watches over the psalmist (cf. Pss 12:7; 146:9). The poet wishes that God would awake, *ʿwr* and *qyṣ* (vv. 4, 5; cf. Pss 35:23; 44:23; Hab 2:19). Only God can tumble the enemy, bring them down, consume them (vv. 11, 13). At daybreak, the poet will be able to "look" at their defeat (v. 10), and thus in the morning he or she will celebrate God's *ḥesed* (v. 16). From one day to the next, evening to morning, the drama of liberation unfolds. "In the morning" may be morning prayer, or it may state metaphorically that the night of sorrow and fear is over. Morning is the usual time for thanksgiving sacrifices.[20] The promise of thanksgiving closes the poem. If unpredictable dangers, projected in the figure of roving dogs, is proper to the night, God will scatter and destroy them at dawn, and the psalmist will gratefully praise God's action.

The superscription gives a clue to a setting of Psalm 59 in the history of David (1 Sam 19:11). The suppliant represents the community. God is addressed as "God of hosts" and "God of Israel" and petitions seek action against "all the nations" whose pretensions God derides (v. 5). God's intervention is to be a revelation "to the ends of the earth" that God is ruler over Israel (v. 13). To pray this psalm "in David" is to voice the sentiments and needs of all the oppressed of God's reign.

Psalm 60
Complaint after Defeat in Battle

The military language woven throughout Psalm 59 is even more in evidence in Psalm 60. Psalm 60 is a national complaint. The structure is simple: the people's defeat because of God's rejection (vv. 1-3); prayer for victory (vv. 4-5); a divine oracle in which the nation is claimed for God (vv. 6-8); continued prayer for victory and confident assurance (vv. 9-12). Verses 6-12 appear again in Ps 108:7-13. The opening lines register Israel's trauma when military defeat deprived them of control of the promised land. Has an angry God reneged on the promises of old (cf. Deut 26:5-10; Josh 24:2-13; cf. Ps 44:9-16)? The people is God's personal property and charge, yet he has allowed this defeat and treated them harshly, confused them (v. 3). The disaster is described in seismic and

---

[20] A liturgical action concludes several psalms in Book Two; e.g., 50:23; 52:9; 54:6-7; 57:9-10; 61:8.

military terms (vv. 2, 9-12). One hopes that God will not be indifferent to "those who fear you," "those whom you love" (vv. 4-5).

To the solemn appeal "answer us" (v. 5), a divine oracle responds (vv. 6-8) in which God is imaged as a warrior distributing booty. The inherited and occupied territories are arranged first as geographical regions, then tribes, and finally nations. All Canaan and the Transjordan belong to God, just as they were once parceled out under Joshua. The event is associated with the northern capital of Shechem in the territory of Ephraim, where Joshua made a covenant with the local inhabitants (Josh 8:30-35; 24:1, 25). The territories were Israelite at the time of David and Solomon, and God reclaims them all. They are mainly the Rachel tribal areas (Ephraim, Manasseh), Judah, and the Transjordan. Succoth is located in the lower stretch of the Jabbok Valley east of the Jordan where Jacob had built a sanctuary after meeting Esau and before his return to Shechem (Gen 33:17). Gilead is the fertile region also east of the Jordan between the wadis Arnon and Yarmuk. Moab and Edom, southeast of the Jordan, and Philistia on the west coast were David's and Solomon's vassals. In the oracle Ephraim and Judah have specific functions. The helmet is the headgear (protection of vital parts), and the scepter is the emblem of government. The reference to the "washbasin" means that Moab performs the menial task of carrying water used for ritual ablutions. Or this may be an ironic allusion to the Dead Sea. David subdued Philistia and Edom (2 Sam 8:12-14) and the symbolic action "hurl [one's] shoe" represents taking possession (see Deut 25:9-10; Ruth 4:7-8), or it could be where the devout person keeps the footwear in order to pray (Exod 3:5; Josh 5:15). Israelite victory over Moab and Edom included the expansion of Israel's worship to military outposts there. Several candidates fit the bill of "the fortified city" (v. 9), but parallel lines indicate that it is one of the capitals of Edom, Bozrah, or Sela (the Greco-Latin name for which is Petra). Once the eastern neighbors have been subdued, the author turns westward, "over Philistia I shout in triumph." A voice speaking for the king ("me") asks a rhetorical question, whether the divine authority will cooperate in the victory or has there been a definitive rejection (vv. 9-12; cf. Ps 44:9). But confidence in divine aid is certain, for only God can relieve Israel from foreign domination.

The superscription reflects David's wars and conquests from southern Edom to northeastern Euphrates (2 Sam 8:2-3, 13-14; par., 1 Chr 18:2-3, 12-13). With this background the psalm serves as a pledge and prophecy that the geographical extension of David's reign will again be realized. It is not necessary to suppose that the poet refers to a particular defeat, although the double reference to Edom suggests trouble on that front.

The images are expressive. God's rejection imposes a difficult test (v. 1; see Ps 66:10-11). It is like the earthquake that cracks open the earth and totters the house (v. 2). The seismic imagery is reminiscent of God's judgment as in Isa 13:13; 24:18-20; Jer 4:24, and later becomes an apocalyptic trait. So God is asked to remedy the evils, repair the cracks in the earth and fight for the people. Once God got the people drunk on drugged wine that made them dizzy, unsteady, and undid them (v. 3; cf. Isa 51:17, 21; Jer 25:15-16; Ps 75:8). The banner God set up and to which the people rallied is the signal for retreat and, consequently, defeat (v. 4). The paradox is that even though God has rejected the people, he has not stopped loving them, and the psalmist appeals to this love so that God intervene and save them (v. 5).

Psalm 61
The Monarch's Prayer in Time of Danger

Both Psalms 60 and 61 speak of "those who fear you" or "your name" (60:4; 61:5). After the initial cry, the poet of Psalm 61 elucidates the situation. He or she feels distant from God, spiritually deflated, and the enemy threatens (vv. 2-3). Even so, he or she is confident in God. The motif of continual praise reflects the certainty of God's response and anticipates the vows to be fulfilled, which are thanksgiving sacrifices for the prayers answered and gifts received. A prayer for longevity and divine protection for the king (vv. 6-7) is framed between the certainty that the vows have been heard and the promise to keep them ("my vows," *nĕdāray*, vv. 5, 8). Does the poet utter this psalm in the sovereign's behalf as might be the case in Pss 28:8-9; 63:11; 84:9? A more likely interpretation is that the voice of the presider, who might also be the king, is ratified by the voice of an official who intercedes for the king. A super-humanly long life ("to all generations") is requested, a stable and unending reign under God's protection, which is to say, under the shield of God's *ḥesed* and faithfulness (*ʾĕmet*) (v. 7; cf. Ps 57:3, 10 etc.), personified as bodyguards. These two link the divine and human rules.

The psalmist employs metaphor, which makes the specifics of the external situation and the complaint difficult to pin down. The "enemy" remains indefinite (v. 3). Instead of "lead me back to the sanctuary" the poet says "Lead me to the rock that is higher than I" (v. 2). Instead of "protect me" he or she chooses an image from the sanctuary, "Let me . . . find refuge under the shelter of your wings" (v. 4). The urgency is compelling, as the poet calls from "the end of the earth," a metaphor for a last ditch effort to get help. The "faint heart" means that courage and resolve are exhausted. Here and in Ps 27:3-6 the poet weaves together military images with the sanctuary. The two titles for God, "refuge" and "strong tower," refer to God's presence and protection (v. 3); the latter likens God's presence in the sanctuary to an inaccessible fortress. To dwell in God's tent draws on the laws of hospitality and protection (v. 4; cf. Ps 23:6), but here it refers to God's presence in the ark of the covenant. Normally a tent is a temporary residence, but God's tent, which houses the ark, affords permanent asylum and immunity from danger. The Hebrew word *sēter*, "shelter," implies a hiding place, refuge. The wings are those of the cherubim throne which adorns the lid of the ark. As shelter they are a metaphor for God's sanctuary protection (v. 4 and Ps 91:1; elsewhere "shadow," *ṣēl*, cf. Pss 17:8; 57:1).

Temporal expressions refer to continuous, unending time. The poet requests permanent residence in the sanctuary (v. 4); intercessions are made for the monarch's long life and unending rule, and the poet promises always to praise and fulfill the promises of sacrifice (vv. 6-8). Relation with God, as expressed in proximity to the sanctuary and participation in the liturgy, comes with a lasting guarantee.

Psalm 62
My Soul Waits in Silence for God

Psalm 61 employs images of strength and stability for God—*ṣûr*, "rock," *maḥseh*, "refuge," *migdāl-ʿōz*, "strong tower" (vv. 2-3); Psalm 62 has similar appellations (*ṣûr*, "rock," *miśgāb*, "fortress") with the assurance of stability *lōʾ-emmôṭ rabbâh*, "I shall never/not be shaken" (vv. 2, 6), and again *ṣûr-ʿûzî*, "my mighty rock," and *maḥsî*, "my refuge" (vv. 7-8); it concludes with "power belongs to God," *kî ʿōz lēʾlōhîm* (v. 11), a fitting declaration after the images of strength. Verbal correspondences between the two psalms include *ḥesed* at the end of both psalms (61:7; 62:12) and *šlm* ("paying" [vows], 61:8; and "repay," 62:12). Links between Psalms 62 and 63 are the psalmist's "soul" (*napšî*, 62:1, 5; 63:1, 5, 8, 9 ["my life"]) and *ḥesed* (62:12; 63:3). Shared motifs are the soul's closeness to God, longing for God, the insignificance of earthly life, and the waning concern for enemies.

Psalm 62 has two movements: trust in God and perplexity about the enemies (vv. 1-7); invitation to trust in God and advice (vv. 8-12). The beginning of the second movement is marked by a change of address, "Trust in him at all times, O people" (v. 8). The first is framed by the

verbal and thematic refrain (vv. 1-2, expanded in vv. 5-7), a brief monologue, as the poet rallies him or herself. Repetitions which frame this
movement are the sense of tranquility and the compatibility between
God with "my soul"; this is followed by three titles—"my rock," "my
salvation," "my fortress" (vv. 1-2, 5-6). In each movement descriptions
of humans and typical conduct evoke trust in God (vv. 3-4, 9-10). Six
Hebrew lines begin with the emphatic expression *ʾak* (vv. 1, 2, 4, 5, 6,
9—not translated in the NRSV), which unifies the poem.

The poet speaks throughout, and the drama is evident in the way he
or she switches the addressee, as shown here:

    —the introspective poet speaks to him or herself (vv. 1-2)
    —the poet addresses and describes an adversarial group (vv. 3-4)
    —the introspective monologue is repeated and expanded (vv. 5-7)
    —the poet exhorts the present assembly ("God is a refuge *for us*," vv. 8, 10)
    —the poet speaks about God (v. 11)
    —and addresses the Lord directly (v. 12)

The exasperation expressed publicly and the description spring from
the interior monologue. A second monologue inspires an address to the
present assembly. The order changes in the end when the poet reflects
on God which switches suddenly to direct address, "*ḥesed* belongs to
you, O Lord. For you repay to all according to their work" (v. 12). A
psalmist who struggled to meditate finally gives God free rein in the
meditation. After underscoring the divine protection, he or she teaches
and comforts others with wisdom and briefly exhorts them (vv. 8-11).
The enemies are liars whose hearts are not in accord with their mouths
(v. 4). The poet does not use the usual word for "heart" for the wicked;
"inwardly they curse" is, literally, "in their viscera" (v. 4, *bĕqereb*). It is
as though they have no heart. On the contrary, the one who trusts in
God does (two Hebrew words, *lēb* and *lēbāb*, vv. 8, 10)—"pour out your
heart before" God and "do not set your heart on" riches. Wisdom has
licensed the teaching on equitable rewards (v. 12; see Pss 28:4; 94:2;
137:8). The reflection on transitory human life concludes aptly, "if riches
increase, do not set your heart on them" (vv. 9-10; cf. Pss 39:4-6; 90:3-10,
etc.). Rich and poor are lumped together (also in Ps 49:2) and together
they are weighed against a breath of air; the whiff weighs more than all
humanity (cf. Isa 40:15, 17). The play on cognates of *hbl* makes the
image more pointed. Humanity amounts to less than a *"breath," hebel,*
and the poet urges that they *"set no vain hopes* [*ʾal–tehbālû*, from *hbl*] on
robbery." The person, who is essentially empty, gains nothing by steal-
ing. The psalm concludes with an aphorism, introduced by the numer-

ical formula "once God has spoken; twice have I heard this" (cf. Prov 30:15, 18, 21). In contrast to the pretended human devices, the poet states that God is powerful, loyal, and good. Parallel lines connect God's power with *ḥesed* (vv. 11b-12a).

> . . . power belongs to God,
> and *ḥesed* belongs to you, O Lord.

God, *ʾĕlōhîm*, occurs seven times, plus once *ʾădōnāy*, "my Lord" (v. 12; "O Lord" in the NRSV). Of note are the divine predicates, many repeated. The sense of mutual belonging and intimacy grows and blooms in this final stroke, where "God" becomes "my Lord," whom the psalmist addresses unexpectedly and only this once. The literal translation "my Lord" is preferred to the NRSV "O Lord," because it echoes the multiple use of "my" in earlier divine references ("my salvation," "my rock," "my fortress," "my deliverance and my honor" (vv. 1-2, 6-7). The poet, speaking for the people, expands and applies this, "God is a refuge *for us*" (v. 8). The predicates identify God as the source and future of life, "Trust in him at all times, O people" (v. 8). Four times the poet repeats that God is "my salvation," three times God is "my rock." Trust in God makes even a decrepit wall an impregnable defense.

The personal assault is registered like the battering to fell a shaky wall or fence. Humanity's innate mendacity is underlined—"They take pleasure in falsehood *[kāzāb]*" (v. 4) and they are "but a breath, . . . a delusion *[kāzāb]*" (v. 9). The aggressor does not just tell lies, but he or she is a lie. The consistency which comes from and is God (salvation, rock, fortress, refuge, power, *ḥesed*) is in great contrast with the human who is essentially unstable and inconsistent (leaning wall, tottering fence, a breath, a delusion). The juxtaposition is drawn more explicitly by the repetition of the particle *ʾak*, which in the refrain introduces "For God alone . . .," and "He alone," and elsewhere introduces the human inconstancy, "Their only plan" and "'but a breath."

What kind of silence is referred to in the refrain (vv. 1, 5)? The meaning may be akin to "Be still, and know that I am God" (Ps 46:10, although there the form of the verb *rph* has the military connotation of "surrender"), which expresses the soul's quietness, an inner tranquility that comes with entrusting anxieties and insecurities to God. The first movement ends with the confession that God is "my refuge," (v. 7), a word which links with the next part, in which the poet invites the people to trust in God, "a refuge for us" (v. 8). The expression "pour out your heart before him" invites prayerful trust. For God to be a refuge, one needs to "pour out" the heart. One cannot trust in humans, even the most powerful, not because they are mean (Jer 17:5-6) but because human nature is essentially weak and ephemeral. Neither can one trust in criminal acquisition or wealth. The repeated words "heart" and "trust" ("put . . . confidence," *bṭḥ*) frame vv. 8-10 and alert the reader to the contrast—trust in and commit the heart to God; do not trust in shady behavior nor commit the heart to wealth. In this poem, silence and trust walk hand in hand as one approaches God and lives secure.

Psalm 63
Love Song

Psalm 63 can be charted in two movements, nostalgia for and intimacy with God (vv. 1-8), followed by the certainty of the enemies' defeat and the king's and his allies' fortune (vv. 9-11). From the beginning intimacy and intense feeling dominates. The psalmist exclaims, "O God, you are my God" and confesses a thirst for God like dry ground, sun-baked and cracked from prolonged drought (cf. 42:2). The word translated "soul," *nepeš*, can be understood as "throat" or "neck," as in "the waters have come up to my *neck*" (69:1). The soul thirsts for God like a parched throat for water. Just as water is fertility for dry ground, so God will revitalize the poet (cf. 36:8-9). Without the divine presence the soul cannot live. The encounter with this presence in the temple has previously met this need and sated the soul as with rich food, the rich banquet of praise which is savored by lips and mouth (v. 5). Lips (and mouth) offer praise (vv. 3, 5), whereas the lying enemy is one who assaults with the mouth (v. 11). That divine *ḥesed* is valued more than life is not surprising, for it gives and sustains life. The "shadow of your wings" refers to the cherubim throne on the ark (v. 7; cf. Ps 17:8, etc.). Exquisitely tender is the image of the soul clinging to God whose right hand steadies him or her (v. 8). Union with God is a deep, lasting experience and, in contrast, "those who seek to destroy my life" are in a precarious position (v. 9; cf. Pss 35:4; 38:12; 40:14, etc.). They will descend to the realm of the dead, "the depths of the earth." The poet expresses the confident hope that the king's enemies will become battle casualties, left as carrion for scavengers ("jackals"), while those loyal to God and the king will be victorious (vv. 10-11).

Nostalgia intensifies as the psalmist recalls the intense experience of the temple, when the person comes to "look upon" or "behold" God's "power and glory" in the liturgy (v. 2). One recalls the contemplative satisfaction of which the poet of Psalm 73 is the beneficiary. Upon past experience can be built a future of praise and expectation of renewed delights that come from the liturgy, which includes blessings, upraised hands, invocation, communion sacrifices (vv. 4-5; cf. Ps 65:4). The tone of intimacy and joy resounds (vv. 6-8). The psalmist muses on God at night and in the light of his or her contemplation the enemies lose their clout. Psalm 63 has various oppositions: the thirsting soul and the soul "satisfied as with a rich feast," intimacy with God and human hostility, meditation and song, the fainting human and God's power, lying in bed and raising the hands.

The poet does not stop with desire. The fervent confession, "You are my God" (v. 1), is followed by an energetic assertion that God hears and the resolve to praise God forever. He or she is unsettled by the present, which keeps one awake at night (vv. 6-8). The nostalgia is softened because, after contemplating a happy future and remembering God's help in the past, he or she feels that God is already near and has always been so. Joy and a sense of security, couched in beautiful imagery, invade the poet—"in the shadow of your wings," clinging to God, sustained by God's right hand, fearing nothing. What more could one desire! The past experience and the certainty of the future transforms the present into a jubilant celebration of God's presence.

Psalm 63 is dominated by personal pronouns, you and I, in reference to the poet and God. Only in the end does the horizon expand to include the adversary. The suffix *–ka* ("you," "your"), referring to God, is added to eight verbs and seven nouns. The suffix *–î* ("I," "me," or "my") is added to nouns or prepositions fourteen times. The relation between the psalmist and God is intimate, expressed in primarily corporal terms—"I seek," "thirst," "[my flesh] faints," "is satisfied," "[as I lie] on my bed," "meditate," "[my soul] clings," "your right hand upholds me," "lift up my hands." The experience transcends the physical and symbolizes a spiritual experience. Eyes look toward the sanctuary, but contemplate the "power and . . . glory" of the incorporeal God (v. 2). The throat thirsts, the flesh faints, for God. The desire "is satisfied as with a rich feast" (v. 5), which refers to the liturgical banquet following a sacrifice. God's right hand upholds; the psalmist's "soul clings to" God.

From this sublime note the key suddenly changes and God is referred to in the third person (vv. 9-11). Unexpected actors enter the drama—the assailants, the sovereign and God's adherents ("who swear by him"), and liars. Far from being alone in exile the poet is persecuted by unidentified enemies. But armed with trust won by an experience of God and without fear, he or she is certain of their defeat. They will die violently and remain without burial, which is the worst disgrace. Meanwhile the joy that invaded the poet will invade the king and God's allies (v. 11). In Psalm 63 a sovereign, presiding at the liturgy, with intimate language and complete trust, confesses that help and prosperity are from God. The title locates the psalm in David's life when he had to live in the desert. An editor connected the dry land with the Judean desert and recalled texts that report that Saul sought David's life there (1 Sam 23:14; 24:2).

Psalm 64
Hide Me from the Plots of the Wicked

The ending of Psalm 64 echoes that of Psalm 63 (linking words "rejoice" *[yiśmaḥ]* and "exult" or "glory," from the root *hll*, 63:11; 64:10). The reference to threatening speech links them (63:9, 11; 64:1-3). Together they provide an ironic illustration of retribution with the repetition of "sword," *ḥereb*: "they shall be given over to the power of the sword" (63:10), "who whet their tongues like swords" (64:3).

Psalm 64, the voice of an individual, has two movements. The request for divine aid and a description of the wicked (vv. 1-6) is followed by the record of divine intervention and the reaction of the faithful (vv. 7-10). The psalmist is the victim of a plot and asks God for asylum (v. 1-2a). The persecutors' weaponry consists of lying and calumny, which they use with impunity (vv. 2b-6). The counterattack occurs with the same weapons as the attack. Suddenly God comes to the rescue, shooting arrows at those who shot poisoned-tipped words. This ruins those who sought to ruin others. In the end the righteous proclaim God's action in the defeat of the wicked and rejoice. Everyone will fear God and testify to the happy outcome.

An urgent plea, "Hear my voice," is addressed to God, and the poet tells about the adversary's vicious speech—"secret plots" or confidential speech *(sôd)*, "tongues" *(lāšôn)*, "bitter" or poison words *(dābār mār)*, "evil purpose" *(dābār rāᶜ)*, "they talk" *(spr)*, "thinking" or saying *(ᵓmr)*. The description points to the damage to a person's reputation and security by slanderous speech (vv. 2-5). Among the weaponry is a preference for archery—"whet their tongues like swords, . . . aim bitter words like arrows" (v. 3), "they shoot" (v. 4), "laying snares" (v. 5), "God will shoot his arrow" (v. 7). The last word from the vocabulary of speaking tells of their ironic but fitting end, "Because of their tongue [God] will bring them to ruin" (v. 8). The verb "shoot," *yrh*, and the word *suddenly*, *pitᵓôm*, depict both the crime and punishment. The wicked *shoot* arrows *suddenly*, without *fear* (v. 4); this vicious act will rebound on them, for God will *shoot* at them *suddenly*, with the result that all will *fear* (vv. 7, 9). "Swords" and "arrows" are metaphors for calumny (cf. Pss 57:4; 120:2-4). But God's arrows are shot and in the confusion their own tongues destroy themselves (vv. 7-8). Assonance marks the enemies' volley of arrows, *yōrūhû wĕlōʾ yîrāʾû*, "they shoot . . . without fear" (v. 4).[21] The poet adds a positive word about speech: "Then everyone will fear; they will *tell* [*ngd*] what God has brought about" (v. 9).

The enemies' secrecy is underscored. The wicked plot secretly *(sôd)*, shoot "from ambush" *(mistārîm*, from *str), hide* traps secretly *(str liṭĕmôn)*, conceive cunning plots. Their heart is *ʿāmōq*, "deep" (v. 6). In response the poet wishes *to be hidden, str* (v. 2), and take refuge *(ḥsh)* in God (v. 10). Cognates of *str* pose the problem and propose a solution. In this assault and resulting fray the poet need not act, but only trust in God who acts in his or her behalf. The repetitions show a correspondence between the two combatants:

evil *doers, pʿl*, v. 2b	"God *has brought about," pʿl*, v. 9a
their tongue, *lĕšônām*, v. 3a	their tongue, *lĕšônām*, v. 8a
arrows, ḥēṣ, v. 3b	his *arrow, ḥēṣ*, v. 7a
suddenly, pitʿôm, v. 4b	*suddenly, pitʿôm*, v. 7b
without *fear, yrʾ*, v. 4b	everyone *will fear, yrʾ*, v. 9a
who can *see, rʾh*, v. 5b	all who *see, rʾh*, v. 8b
"mind" *[heart]* deep, *lēb*, v. 6b	"upright in *heart," lēb*, v. 10b

The language shows that God is up to the challenge and responds swiftly and in kind. The adversary is called "the wicked" *(rĕʿîm)* and "evildoers" *(pōʿălê ʾāwen)*, while the psalmist is "blameless" *(tām*, v. 4) and "righteous" *(ṣaddîq*, v. 10), and is among "the upright of heart" *(yišrê–lēb*, v. 10). A double conversion occurs. The wicked braggadocio is silenced, and the fearful *(paḥad*, as in "*dread* enemy," v. 1) psalmist ends up rejoicing *(śmḥ*, v. 10). The *fearless* enemy finally disappears, and as a result "everyone *will fear*" *(yrʾ*, vv. 4, 9). Thus Psalm 64 illustrates the boomerang effect of evil (see Ps 7:16). God sees, acts, and punishes the wicked with their own weapons and according to their methods,

---

[21] The two forms of the verb *yrh*, "shoot," are intentional and form an alliterative word play with "[without] fear," *yrʾ*, as in *yōrūhû wĕlōʾ yîrāʾû*, "they shoot and do not fear" (v. 4; Hebrew v. 5). The ancient Syriac version understood another play on words, "look" *(yērāʾû)* instead of "fear" *(yîrāʾû)*.

turning their arrows against them and making them victims of their own swords (vv. 7-8).

Psalm 65
Song of Springtime Joy

The thanksgiving Psalm 65 appears to be isolated from the preceding psalms, although its mention of "[t]hose who live at earth's farthest bounds *are awed [yrˀ]*" (v. 8) links it with the preceding (64:9, "fear," which translates the same form of *yrˀ*). Psalm 65 is a hymn with three movements. A congregation celebrates God's mercy in the temple (vv. 1-4), God's creative power (vv. 5-8), and the bountiful gifts of rain and harvest (vv. 9-13). Each movement is concluded by a description of the effects of God's activity—for the congregation (v. 4), for the world (v. 8), for the earth (vv. 12-13). Each develops a theme. God hears our prayer and forgives sins, thus we are drawn to the temple (vv. 1-4); the creator and savior subdues chaos (vv. 5-8) and visits the world with life-giving water (vv. 9-13). The spatial focus shifts from the temple to earth's horizontal and vertical limits, the seas and mountains, and finally to pasture and farmland. The center is Zion, the source of all divine benefactions, where God dwells, listens to prayers, and forgives sins (vv. 2-3).

This structure is reinforced by the threefold appearance of God, *ˀĕlōhîm*, in the first line of each movement. The sequence is "God, in Zion," "God of our salvation," and "the river of God." The first two movements embrace near, *qrb*, and far, *rḥq*—"near . . . in your courts" and "the farthest seas" (vv. 4-5). The initial focus on Zion and the temple widens to the "gateways of the morning and the evening." The second and third movements have the verb *kwn* in common (vv. 6, 9); in giant strokes God "*established* the mountains," "*provide[s]* the people with grain," and *prepares* the earth. "Earth," *ˀereṣ*, is cosmic, "all the ends of the earth" (v. 5), and local, the cultivated land (v. 9). God's attention encompasses the great and small; he tames the roaring seas and peoples and cultivates the soil. The first and third movements share the word *ṭûb*, which at first refers to the "goodness" of God's temple and afterwards to God's "bounty" that crowns the year (vv. 4, 11). The connection is understandable because the "vows" (v. 1) are thanksgiving offerings selected from the harvest. The earth teems with divine gifts which in turn are offered to God; the person who offers at the temple partakes of them in a communion banquet with God. The worshipers receive material "satisfaction" (v. 4b) when they share them with others (cf. Jer 31:12, 14, where similar vocabulary is used, and the "goodness" [ṭûb] of God's house is specified). The holy exchange of fulfilling vows and being satisfied with God's bounty parallels Ps 22:25-26 (cf. 116:12-14).

God is addressed throughout the poem. The first movement uses God once, ʾĕlōhîm, and seven pronominal references—to you (three times), "you forgive," and your courts, your house, your temple. One expects an opposition between sinfulness and God. But a wonderful truth couched in the first movement is that the "deeds of iniquity" and "transgressions" occasion God's approach in the temple. The power of sin and God's power to engineer mountains are expressed with cognates of gbr, "deeds of iniquity overwhelm us" and "girded with might" (vv. 3, 6). The text moves from personal forgiveness to universal recognition of God, from the Jerusalem temple to the surrounding countryside and the world. References to God unify the psalm and show how he becomes increasingly more involved in the people's life: "you . . . listen to prayer" (from šmʿ; the NRSV reads "answers," v. 2); "you answer us" (v. 5); "[y]ou visit the earth" (v. 9). From vast horizons, "earth's farthest bounds," the poet turns to examine God's material benefits in detail. The creator and savior retires from the public arena to agricultural life. How marvelous that the architect and engineer of mountains also stoops to survey the land! The custodian of oceans and empires also irrigates the pasture and fertilizes fields. The poem gravitates toward this simple finale. Psalm 136 represents a similar gravitational pull, celebrating the creator and savior, who distributes food daily to all flesh (cf. 136:25).

The geographical concentration on Zion of the first movement contrasts with the distant mountains, seas, nations, sunrise and sunset of the second. The liturgical capital is converted into the center of universal contemplation. The vision embraces the earth and seas and is subsequently divided into mountains and water (vv. 5-7). The restless sea and peoples are in tumult. God holds everything in check. The poise and serenity of the mountains are in contrast to the thundering rage of the ocean (v. 7). A correlation exists between oceans and farm irrigation, between mountains and fertile fields, between the ocean roaring and the song of the first fruits.

The psalmist hesitates, repeats "the roaring of the seas," before introducing the peoples' tumult (vv. 5, 7). Then the focus expands to the distant population, which is overpowered by God's "signs." The day is filled with joy even to the doorways of sunrise and sunset. The last movement celebrates the divine bringer of rain, which prospers the fruits and flocks. The poet weaves a tapestry of the land's beauty and bounty—all this because God looks after the earth and waters it. The primeval seas are harnessed into "the river of God" and fertile rains (vv. 9-10). God's material gifts to the land are "visit the earth," "water it," "enrich it," "provide the people with grain," "prepare it," "water its furrows," "soften it," "bless its growth" described with seven finite verbs (vv. 9-10).[22] This is answered by seven verbs ("wagon tracks overflow," "pastures overflow," "hills gird," "meadows clothe," "valleys deck themselves," "they shout and sing," vv. 11-13), depicting the earth's response. The scene bursts with anthropomorphisms—fields, pastures, hills and nature all celebrate the end of the year. "Wagon tracks" is unusual, but one may imagine the cart carrying the ark of the covenant crossing the fields. Or this may be a metaphor for the wagon load of blessings God brings when the rains arrive. Three verbs for attiring tell that everything dresses up for the fiesta. The hills "gird themselves" with rejoicing (v. 12), which consists of shades of green of vines and fruit trees; "the meadows clothe themselves with flocks"— white polka dots on green, sheep which attire pastures before clothing people with their wool; "the valleys deck themselves with grain," a sequined outer garment. At the new year celebration everybody, brightly attired, chimes in rejoicing. The clothing images are not lost on the reader who has already met God "girded" with strength (v. 6; cf. 93:1). The divine preparation of the land is exuberant. God's chariot leaves wagon tracks as it travels with the rains that fertilize the earth; joy girds the hills, and the fields and valleys sing! Nature's joyful, symphonic shout concludes a psalm which began with the worshiping assembly in Zion.

An inclusion (vv. 5, 8), "the awesome deeds" with "signs" and "the ends of the earth" with "the gateways of the morning and the evening," frames the second movement. God is universal sovereign, creator and savior. Based on parallel lines, the poet builds an analogy between the commotion of the sea and that of the peoples (v. 7), between the remotest inhabitants and the sunrise and sunset (v. 8). God's marvelous works in creation, history (vv. 5-7) and human life (vv. 3-4) are "signs" (v. 8). Among them is included the rhythm of the agricultural cycle (vv. 9-13). "Signs" of what? They point to God, the protagonist of nature's prodigious cycle. The universal touches are underlined, and God, who has no geographic or temporal limits, is sovereign over everything cosmic and human. All can rejoice in his gifts—"all flesh" (v. 2), the

---

[22] Alliterative rhyme in the phrase "you provide the people with grain, for so you have prepared it," *tākîn dĕgānām kî-kēn tĕkînehā*, emphasizes God's care for the people (v. 9).

ends of the earth and the distant peoples (vv. 5, 7), the earth's eastern and western limits (v. 8).

On Zion God hears prayers and pardons sins, hymns are intoned and vows fulfilled (vv. 1-4). To live in God's company, sated by his benefactions, is the greatest blessing. "[A]ll flesh" (v. 2) has a prophetic dimension as in the last chapters of Isaiah or Zechariah. Israel, the chosen representative, confesses sins and the chosen people worship in the temple (vv. 3-4). God responds to prayer with prodigies of salvation which reverberate to "all the ends of the earth" (v. 5). God's "awesome" deeds *(nôrā'ôt)*, usually a reference to saving deeds, include creation (vv. 6-7). The universalism makes itself felt and organizes the people in the future messianic reign. A mixture of fear ("awed") and joy invades the distant inhabitants (v. 8).

The poet mixes remarkably dissimilar themes: sin and pardon, entrance into the temple, establishing the mountains and victory over the seas, the gift of rain and harvest. This and the phrase "You crown the year" (v. 11) suggests a liturgical context like the New Year festival. The annual agricultural cycle is "crowned" with the bountiful harvest. What is missing in the New Year hymn is the reference to God's sovereignty. Psalm 65 possibly occupied a place during the feast and fast days of the month of Tishri (our September–October), the head of the Hebrew calendar at a late stage of its development. The themes are reminiscent of the high holidays from Yom Kippur (the Day of Atonement) on the tenth of Tishri to the octave of Sukkoth starting on the fifteenth, which includes thanksgiving for the harvest and prayer for rain to end the long dry season.

There is textual ambiguity in the opening words. In accord with the ancient Greek and Syriac versions, the opening line is usually understood, as in the NRSV, "Praise is due to you" (understanding a participle of *dmh*). Yet the Hebrew may be read, "For you silence is praise, O God, in Zion." Thus Jerome translated this text: *"Tibi silens laus, Deus, in Sion."* The context argues for silence; God stills the tumultuous seas and peoples, and east and west personified resound with silent joy. The same Hebrew word, *dumîyâh,* is elsewhere understood as "silence" (cf. Pss 39:3; 62:1). One may recall the cosmic clamor in Ps 19:1-4, in which, amidst much speaking and proclaiming, no sound is audible, yet the message is broadcast throughout the world. The assembly's awe-filled silence on Zion may be a quiet echo of God's subtle managing of the natural world (vv. 9-13). One is reminded of the silent beauty of the awakening world at dawn, viewed from the hill overlooking a valley. From there the visible horizons reach even more distant as the monks quietly wake and warm their hearts for morning praise.

Psalm 66
How Marvelous Your Works

Psalm 65 sets the stage for Psalm 66. Verbal links are *bêtekā*, "your house," in reference to the temple (65:4; 66:13), and fulfilling vows (65:1; 66:13). Psalm 65 ends with the earth wondrously clothed, receiving plenteous gifts from God, celebrating joyfully (*šîr*, v. 13), an image repeated in 66:4 as all the earth sings *(zmr)*. Whereas Psalm 65 celebrates the growing season and harvest (vv. 9-13), the motive for a feast, Psalm 66 recalls God's deliverance at the Exodus (v. 6), celebrated at the early harvest festival, for which the poet pledges appropriate thanksgiving sacrifices (vv. 13-15). This pair is framed by reference to God who listens to the psalmist's prayer, *šmᶜ* and *těpillâh* (65:2; 66:18-20). The "awesome deeds," *nôrā᾿ôt* and *nôrā᾿* (65:5; 66:3, 5), and "all flesh" or "all the earth" and "peoples" strengthens the bond (65:2; 66:1, 4, 8).

Psalm 66 is a hybrid between what appears to be a community hymn (vv. 1-12) and individual thanksgiving (vv. 13-20), and it reproduces two movements in a liturgy. The direct address of God bridges the two movements (vv. 10-12, 13-15). "Come *[lěkû]* and see" or "hear" invites the general audience to contemplate God's prodigies (vv. 5, 16; cf. Ps 46:8). Another unifying factor is how recent (vv. 10-12) and particular acts (vv. 17-19) complement the rescue begun in the Exodus. The poem begins like Psalm 100, "Make a joyful noise to God, all the earth" (v. 1; cf. 98:4; 100:1), and the universal dimension of praise is reiterated in the first part (vv. 4, 7, 8).

The poet invites everyone to appreciate God's benefits. In the preceding psalm the "awesome deeds," *nôrā᾿ôt*, are salvation and creation (cf. Ps 65:5); here God's deeds are "awesome," *nôrâh* (vv. 3, 5), notably the transformation of the sea into dry land and the people's crossing the river into the promised land without getting their feet wet. These two Exodus frontiers encompass the desert sojourn (v. 6; cf. Ps 114:3). Another invitation introduces the people's thanksgiving for a recent rescue (vv. 8-9). The communal thanksgiving of the first movement is complemented by the individual before God and the assembly in the second (vv. 13-20). The expression "pay my vows" refers to fulfilling the promised and prescribed liturgies (cf. Pss 22:25; 50:14; 56:12; 65:1; 116:14). The liturgy links God's initial intervention with subsequent ones in an over-arching plan of salvation.

The hymn recalls the rejoicing "there" among the people at the sea (vv. 6-7; cf. Exodus 15) which reveals that God reigns forever over all. In the Hebrew lines of v. 9 *nepeš* (throat) and foot are in parallel positions, literally:

He has kept our necks among the living
and has not given to wavering our feet.

Without God, one false step and we are dead. God allowed the poet to be tested just like the people (vv. 10-12, 14, 17-19), but in every instance he kept them safe. The language describing the trial is similar to how the prophets describe the afflictions of the exile (metal refinery, v. 10; cf. Isa 48:10; Jer 6:29; 9:7; Zech 13:9; Mal 3:3; the net, v. 11; cf. Ezek 12:13; 17:20). One examines for rust or corrosion so as to remove it (cf. Pss 12:6; 17:3; 18:30). God allowed the people to fall into a net; he made them bear heavy burdens, endure slavery. The picture of the tyrant mounted on the necks and shoulders of those who are no better than beasts of burden is original (v. 12a). The figure of "through fire and through water" summarizes all kinds of trial (v. 12; cf. Isa 43:2).[23] God ends the summary of trials with rescue, "you have brought us out to a spacious place";[24] this is traditional language, implying something like the Exodus. Thus concludes the first movement, the community hymn.

The leader identifies him or herself as the recipient of the gift, and responds with the present thanksgiving. The burnt animal sacrifices, a hyperbole, are whole offerings (v. 15). Nobody had to offer that much in thanksgiving rituals. The poet calls with the voice (mouth, *pî*) and extols with the tongue, but if he or she saw *(rʾh)* or intended evil in the "heart, the LORD would not have listened *[šmʿ]*." An opposition is drawn between "mouth" and "heart," "see" and "hear." Psalm 66 closes with praise for God's *ḥesed*.

A symmetry exists in the relationships: what Israel is to the nations (the first movement), the individual is for the devout community (the second movement). The individual invites the community to recognize God (v. 16), just as the community invites the peoples to praise (v. 8). Meanwhile, in the first movement opposition is felt with the mention of "your enemies" (v. 3), "the nations" and "the rebellious" (v. 7), and an oppressive ruler (v. 12). The perspective of the first movement is God's awesome deeds for humanity, the memory of the chosen people,

---

[23] The alliteration of the letter "b" *(beth)* links the testing and the promise with sacrifices of thanksgiving—*bāʾnû-bāʾēš ûbamayim* ("we went through fire and through water," v. 12) and *ʾābôʾ bêtěkā běʿôlôt* ("I will come into your house with burnt offerings," v. 13).

[24] Here the NRSV follows the Greek text. The Hebrew (the noun *rěwāyâh*) connotes satiety or saturation. The Targum, Greek, and Syriac versions understand a different Hebrew word, *rěwāḥâh*, which means relief, respite (cf. Exod 8:11; Lam 3:56) or, here, "a spacious place."

and ordinary providence or government. Then God's actions for Israel are contemplated. God is now "our God" (v. 8), who protects and rescues, although he also tests the people. In the second movement the invitation to an audience and the dialog with God alternate, while the horizons narrow and focus on the individual, as the poet describes salvation in the particular case. Our God is "my Lord" (v. 18), who listens to the poet, affirms innocence and shows mercy. From "all the earth" and "peoples" (vv. 1, 8), the focus narrows to "all who fear God" (v. 16)—from all humanity, to devout Israel, to the psalmist as representative of all.

Psalm 67
May God's Face Shine Upon Us

Psalm 66 ends with the phrase *bārûk ʾĕlōhîm*, "Blessed be God" (v. 20), and Psalm 67 begins "May God . . . bless us" and ends "our God, has blessed us. May God continue to bless us" (*brk*, vv. 1, 6-7). A refrain (vv. 3, 5) divides Psalm 67 into three parts (vv. 1-2, 4, 6-7). It begins and ends by invoking God's blessings (God is spoken about, vv. 1, 6-7); the middle verses address God directly. The movement is from "us" to "all the earth" (vv. 1, 7). God's face illuminating the people implies generosity and material favor (cf. Pss 4:6-7; 27:8, etc.).

The poet requests God's favor, so all may "know" God's "way" and "saving power" (v. 2). The objective is universal (the earth and the nations). The divine benefits consist of equitable government and universal guidance, centrally positioned (v. 4; see Pss 9:8; 82:8; 96:10, 13; 98:9), and an abundant harvest (v. 6; see Pss 65:9-13; 72:16; 85:12). As a response to God's blessing "the earth has yielded its increase." The blessing is, above all, rain and fertility, which is both a blessing and the grateful response to the heavenly gift. In the prophets the future blessings, even messianic ones, are portrayed with harvest imagery (cf. Isa 45:8; Amos 9:13; Zech 8:12). As at the beginning, the final blessing is requested for the congregation ("us"), which is the channel of blessing to "all the ends of the earth" (v. 7). The parallel lines of v. 6 argue for the translation "May the earth yield its produce," in which case the congregation prays for rain and fertility as it would during the feast of Sukkoth. The "earth" in vv. 4b and 7b shows another relationship. God guides "the nations upon the earth" who in turn "revere him." Thus, divine governance constitutes the blessing to which the appropriate response is universal recognition of God. The epiclesis, "May God . . .

bless us," is related to the Aaronic blessing (Num 6:24-26). Whereas the substance of the blessing was "peace," *šālōm,* the present blessing embraces the land's fertility, a just government, and universal salvation.

Psalm 68
A Triumphal Parade

Psalm 68, renowned for posing difficulties in interpretation, is a hymn to God's power and majesty. It is composed of an introduction (vv. 1-3) and a body comprised of various styles of praise and prayer (vv. 4-35), bracketed by a summons to "sing to God," the cloud rider, and the mention of God's dwelling (vv. 4-5, 32-35; cf. Pss 18:9-10; 104:3). Another inclusion, "Blessed be the Lord" or "God" (vv. 19, 35), divides the body in two major sections (vv. 4-18 and 19-35). A concentric design can be appreciated:

A hymnic invocation (vv. 4-6)

   B from Sinai to Zion (vv. 7-18)

      C acclamation and oracle (vv. 19-23)

   B' procession toward the temple (vv. 24-31)

A' conclusion (vv. 32-35)

"God" and "LORD" appear with unusual density in the middle section.

The poem opens with a reflection about the distinct reactions of the good and the bad in God's presence (vv. 1-3). The wicked flee, disperse, perish; the just rejoice, exult, leap for joy. Three verbs reflect each group's reaction to God's ascension. This recalls the ritual of raising the ark (Num 10:35; Ps 132:7-8). The images of the swift disappearance of the wicked are remarkable—smoke that is driven away and wax that melts. Fire is a divine element, and by association come the images of smoke and wax.

God is praised for parenting orphans and protecting widows. Motifs of the Exodus, the conquest, Jerusalem, the land's fertility, and vanquishing enemies are developed in the Sinai to Zion section, which is an impressionistic portrayal of the Exodus up to the housing of God on Mount Zion. It focuses on the march from Sinai through the desert and the battles with nations who opposed God's and Israel's progress toward the temple, the center of God's universal rule. The battle never comes into focus, but the results are clear—retreat, booty, scattering of enemy forces, taking captives, vassal tribute. God appears in single-handed combat. He has chosen Zion instead of the hostile and "jealous," more prominent Bashan mountains (vv. 15-16). Repeatedly the focus is on God's presence and rule in the temple (vv. 5, 16-18, 24, 29, 35). In the conclusion God's power is manifest in the storm—the thunder voice, majesty, power (vv. 33-35; see Pss 18:7-15; 29:3-9; 93:3-4; 97:2-5).[25] The last verses are dominated by nouns derived from the root ʿwz, "strength," "might," "power," "mighty" (vv. 28, 33-35).

Psalm 68 has an unusual number of uncertain lines, rare words, and uses allusive language and shifting styles, which makes it impossible to arrive at a commonly accepted translation. Furthermore, the images, details, and references are enigmatic. In the Zion to Sinai section salvation history is projected as a solemn procession where God advances in front of the people, making the arid land fertile, dispersing enemy kings and armies, dividing booty among the people and protecting Mount Zion. The procession extends over a vast geographical surface, from Egypt through Sinai and enigmatic Zalmon to Bashan, the northern mountains of the Transjordan (vv. 14-15; mentioned again in v. 22). The overall impression is of a triumphal parade which culminates on Zion. The detail of taking captives is found only here in the biblical text (v. 18).

Two northern and two southern tribes are named, all directed to the temple of Jerusalem (v. 27; cf. Ps 122:4). Benjamin, the youngest, goes first. This is explained by the fact that Saul was a Benjaminite, and according to the book of Joshua Benjamin's territory was first to be occupied. Gilgal, Jericho, Ai, and Gibeon all lie within the Benjaminite domain (Joshua 4–9). The description of the victory parade is simplified: singers, musicians, and in the middle the tambourines (vv. 24-28). Benjamin is followed by the tribe of Judah, from which David came. Zebulon and Naphtali are northern tribes. The mention of four tribes signifies universality. The mention of girls in the procession does not surprise us, as everybody participated in the victory celebration (v. 25; see Exod 15:20-21; Judg 11:34; 1 Sam 18:7; 21:12; 29:5).

The poet makes forty-two (six times seven) direct references to God (ʾĕlōhîm or ʾēl), LORD or Lord (ʾădōnāy). The affirmations about God are many. The God of Sinai, of Zion, of Israel—shepherd, warrior, father, savior—appears in nature, in history, in the temple. God saves and gives victory, in the past, the present, and the future. The address shifts as the poet speaks alternately to and about God, addresses the faithful,

---

[25] The assonance and alliteration of v. 33 (Hebrew v. 34) leaves an impact, *lārōkēb bišĕmê sĕmê–qedem hēn yittēn bĕqōlô qôl ʿōz.*

the kingdoms or nations. In an apostrophe the poet addresses the mountains (v. 15). This change of address is characteristic of liturgical compositions. For all its ambiguity, the poem can be applied to any generation of God's chosen people, as they reflect on their history and the mystery of their relation to God.

Psalm 69
Waters up to My Neck

Psalm 69 is an individual complaint in which pleas for help (vv. 1-29) conclude with a vow to offer thanksgiving and a prayer for Zion (vv. 30-36). The first part opens and closes with the request for salvation; cognates of $yš^c$ form an inclusion, translated "[s]ave" and "salvation" (vv. 1, 29). This part is composed of petitions (vv. 1a, 6, 13-18, 22-25, 27-28, 29b) which alternate with descriptive motives for an answer (vv. 1b-5, 7-12, 19-21, 26, 29a). The weave looks like this:

v. 1a	save
vv. 1b-5	deep waters, desolation, adversary, personal guilt
v. 6	**let them not be shamed**
vv. 7-12	for God's sake the poet has borne personal suffering
vv. 13-18	**fifteen imperative requests**
vv. 19-21	the desolate psalmist has borne insult and assault
vv. 22-25	**request for vengeance on the aggressors**
v. 26	for they afflict the afflicted
vv. 27-28	**blot out the aggressor**
v. 29a	"I am lowly and in pain"
v. 29b save	

The psalmist is ill and unjustly accused. The cause for alarm is described, beginning with the heartrending cry: "Save me, O God, for the waters have come up to my neck." The distress is projected in images of drowning—deep, ebbing waters; bottomless marsh; an undertow dragging a person down; no firm footing. Yet the throat is parched and the sight fails from so much waiting and calling on God (vv. 1-3; cf. Ps 42:1-2). The waters, synonymous with Sheol, symbolize the assault of death (vv. 1-2, 14-15; see Pss 18:16; 32:6; 124:4-5). The poet admits the distress is related to personal sinfulness (v. 5), but this punishment brought on by false accusation is not commensurate with the guilt (v. 4; see Ps 35:11). He or she is spurned, hated, abandoned by family, and is the butt of criticism for being zealous for God and practicing penance (vv. 7-12). Public disgrace and insult crush the poet who was initially stricken by God (vv. 19-21, 26, 29). Everyone—elders at the gate who administer justice and even drunks—makes sport of him or her (v. 12). The theme of reproach (shame, insult, dishonor) is prominent.

"Answer me" opens a series of seven positive imperatives (answer [twice], turn, make haste, draw near, redeem, free, vv. 16-18; "[d]o not hide," v. 17, is negative). Another seven positive and negative requests precede it (answer, rescue, let [me] not sink, let [me] be rescued, let not [the flood] sweep, let not [the deep] swallow, let not [the Pit] close, vv. 13-15).[26] The psalmist asks that two divine attendants, *ḥesed* and "faithful help," *ʾĕmet,* rescue him or her (v. 13; cf. Ps 57:3, 10 et al.), confident of a hearing on the basis of the divine *ḥesed.* The request closes by recalling the gravity of the situation and the psalmist's complete helplessness (vv. 19-21).

The real problem is that countless adversaries falsely accuse the psalmist, innocent of the alleged crime. God, before whom there is no pretense, knows all (v. 5)—a nice way to start a confession. The poet appeals to him to intervene on behalf of those who would be scandalized at the undeserved suffering (v. 6). If an innocent person were convicted, others who trust in God would be disheartened. A compelling reason for God to act is that the psalmist's pious zeal has brought on alienation and public insult (vv. 7-12). The request is well argued—the right moment ("an acceptable time"), stuck in the mud, deep waters, the devouring Pit, a heart broken from insult, devoid of comforters, poisoned food, vinegar to drink (vv. 13-21). The diet, poison and vinegar, are images of personal estrangement (v. 21; cf. Pss 42:3; 102:9).

Rather than take matters in his or her own hands or expect someone else to right the wrong, the poet appeals to the just judge with an eloquent, violent curse (vv. 22-28). It begins with the wish that the adversaries' banquets be a snare for them (v. 22). The transference from "table," *šūlḥān,* to "trap," *paḥ,* is understandable when one thinks of a banquet reclining on rugs and cushions, rather than a table and chairs. Snares, traps, and nets were concealed to catch birds and other animals (cf. Pss 91:3; 119:110; 124:7; 140:5; 141:9; 142:3). The ardent wish is that the wicked be ensnared at their own sumptuous banquets. Fire and liquid are brought together in the images of "pour out" and "burning anger" (v. 24). At first the wrath is poured on them from above and then it flares up and consumes them. The curse amounts to a request

---

[26] The translations often do not reproduce the Hebrew imperative forms literally.

for the extinction of the family, an empty home (v. 25). A strong personal faith ascribes everything that happens to God's knowledge, plan, and power, even the suffering, which has incited this enemy assault (v. 26). The force of the anathema demands that the adversary be excommunicated from the community of the devout (vv. 27-28). Retributive justice is passionately invoked. Just as the enemies desired his or her death, so too may their names be blotted from "the book of the living" (v. 28; cf. Pss 56:8; 139:16). Because they served poisoned food and vinegar to drink, "Let their table be a trap for them" (vv. 21-22). "[L]et no one live in their tents" (v. 25), contrasts with the desire for the good, "God will . . . rebuild the cities of Judah" and their peaceful habitation (vv. 35-36). In the end, the poet pledges to an internal disposition which corresponds to the sacrifices (vv. 30-31, as in Ps 50:8-15). The description "a bull with horns and hoofs" is neat. The horns bespeak strength and maturity; the hoof is the mark of kosher approval (Lev 11:3). These are the horns and cloven hooves of the sacrifice. The song is worth more than the material sacrifice, because thanksgiving, *tôdâh*, is foremost in the liturgy. Finally, hope rises and the psalmist, forgetting him or herself, encourages the oppressed and needy and praises God (vv. 32-36).

The images are memorable. Those who hate the psalmist without cause are more numerous than hairs on the head (v. 4). Siblings regard him or her as a stranger (v. 8). Zeal for God's house consumes one, and insults against God fall on the faithful psalmist. The adversaries sit at the gate getting drunk and composing sarcastic lampoons (vv. 9-12). Both "God" and the divine name are remarkably present at the beginning but disappear from the text when the psalmist pleads "Do not hide your face from your servant" (v. 17; cf. Ps 10:11).

The psalmist is God's "servant" (v. 17), one of the lowly (v. 29; Hebrew *ʿānî*). He or she should be counted among God's ministers (v. 35), "the oppressed" (*ʿănāwîm*, v. 32), those "who *seek* God" (vv. 6, 32), who rejoice. The verb *hll*, "praise," frames a thematic unit (vv. 30-34). The psalmist invites the created world to join him or her in praise. Initially the waters *(maym)* "come up to" *(bwʾ)* the neck; then the poet declares "I *have come [bwʾ]* into deep waters *[maym]*" (vv. 1-2). This enveloping sea creates the impression of desperate straits. The poet has lost foothold, security is gone, he or she is in danger of being gulped down by the undertow. In the end, the poet will invite "the seas and everything that moves in them" to praise (v. 34)—how complete the rescue! Threatening waters have been tamed. The complaint is concluded with the hope for Zion, the cities of Judah, and the present and future generations of the devout (vv. 35-36). Along with Psalm 22 this psalm is frequently quoted in the gospels in relation to Christ's suffering.

Psalm 70
Lord, Hurry to Help Me

Psalm 70, with few variations, reproduces Ps 40:13-17. It has its own Hebrew title, "for the memorial offering," which it shares with Psalm 38. The urgency with which the psalmist opens the plea evolves into a curse against the enemy who pursues him or her to death and pokes fun (vv. 2-3). He or she prays for God's allies and reiterates the plea for rescue (vv. 4-5). The trajectory from misery and cursing to joy is traversed, and the poem concludes on the note with which it began, "hasten" and "do not delay."

A call for fast relief is marked by a chain of repetitions. The psalm is framed by an invocation, repetition of the divine name (both LORD and God), and "make haste" (*ḥûšâh*), which is reinforced by "do not delay" and cognates of *ʿzr*, "to *help* me" and "my *help*" (vv. 1, 5). Cognates of *bwš* (noun and verb, vv. 2-3) request that God put the enemy to "*shame.*" Verbal contrast is remarkable; for example, the repeated participle *mĕbaqĕšîm*, "who *seek* my life" (v. 2) and "all who *seek* you" (v. 4). The first group of seekers should be disgraced and shamed; the second gladdened. Three terms express the opposing gladness—"*desire* [enjoy] to hurt me" (*ḥpṣ*, v. 2), "*rejoice* and *be glad* in you" (*śyś* and *śmḥ*, v. 4). Cognates of *ʾḥr* request relief and illustrate the tension between the adversary and God, "Let those be turned *back*" and "*do not delay*" (vv. 2, 5). In Hebrew, the emphatic "I" and "you" juxtapose the petitioner's dejection with God's benefice (v. 5). Another opposition is "Those who *say*, 'Aha!'" and those who *say*, "God is great" (*ʾmr*, vv. 3, 4). Several repetitions are arranged symmetrically around the first Hebrew expression in v. 3, "turn back" (*šwb*), which is like a hinge in the composition. In the chart on page 169 the Hebrew verse numbering is used.

This individual complaint is a plea for speedy rescue from the enemies' taunts. "God" is preferred to the divine name, LORD, which appears twice, probably for reasons of symmetry (the opening and closing verses). One would expect that the divine appellation "God" be used more frequently here (*ʾĕlōhîm*) in the elohist psalms (Psalms 42–83; see Appendix Two). In comparison to the polished style of Psalm 70, Ps 40:13-17 is rough and disconnected. It is uncertain which serves as the model for its twin.

The adversary is those "*who seek* my life," those "*who desire* to hurt me," and "those *who say*, 'Aha, Aha!'" The description embraces action (seek), intent (desire), and words. The ardent request is that they be completely frustrated—put to shame and confusion (*bwš* and *ḥpr*),

v. 2   ʾĕlōhîm   a

     yhwh   b

     . . . help . . . (ʿzr)   c

     "make haste" (ḥûšâh)   d

v. 3   "put to shame" (bwš)   e

     "who seek my life" (mĕbaqĕšîm)   f

     "Let those be turned back" (ʾḥr)   g

     "who desire to hurt me" (ḥpṣ)   h

v. 4   "Turn back" (šwb)   i

     "their shame" (bwš)   e

     "those who say, 'Aha . . .'" (ʾmr)   j

v. 5   "rejoice and be glad" (śyś and śmḥ)   h

     "all who seek you" (mĕbaqĕšîm)   f

     "say . . ., 'God is great'" (ʾmr)   j

v. 6   ʾĕlōhîm   a

     "hasten" (ḥûšâh)   d

     . . . my help . . . (ʿzr)   c

     yhwh   b

     "do not delay" (ʾḥr)   g

turned back and brought to dishonor (swg ʾāḥôr and klm), routed because of their shame (šwb . . . bwš). In contrast, one whose life is sought joins forces with "all who seek" God (bqš). May those who "love" (intention or desire) salvation one day say (ʾmr) "God is great" and clash with "those who say, 'Aha, Aha.'" The threefold rejoicing and acclaiming augments the adversaries' frustration. Their action, intent, and speech is directed against the poet; in contrast, the deed and intent of the faithful is directed toward God.

The psalmist describes the distress in vague terms. One "poor and needy" (v. 5) who identifies with "all who seek" God (v. 4)[27] is taunted by enemies who want him or her dead (vv. 2-3). Thus he or she joins the ranks of the defenseless (ʿānî, singular, from the poor, ʿănawîm, who have a right to God's rescue) and prays that rejoicing will come soon.

---

[27] The sonorous word play ʾănî ʿānî, "I am poor" (v. 5), occurs elsewhere in (Hebrew) Pss 69:30; 86:1; 88:16. The alliteration continues to the following words wĕʾebyôn ʾĕlōhîm.

Personal privilege is mirrored in the direct address of God, "Lord" and "my help and my deliverer." Psalm 70 amounts to a heartfelt sigh. Will the enemy triumph or will God intervene and help? The repeated use of *ḥûšâh* (vv. 1, 5), "make haste" and "hasten," leaves no doubt about the state of emergency. The ending is terse, "do not delay," and the *orante* is left hanging.

Psalm 71
Do Not Forsake Me Now That I Am Old

Psalm 70 was set intentionally with Psalm 71, which lacks a superscription. Both begin with an urgent plea for rescue (70:1; 71:1-4), and the verb *bwš* ("shame") occurs in both (70:2, 4; 71:1, 13, 24). "O my God, make haste to help me" (71:12) is nearly identical to "hasten to me, O God! You are my help" (Ps 70:5). Synonymous expressions "who seek my life" and "who desire [seek] to hurt me" recur (70:2; 71:13, 24).

A prayer which begins in the present with a request for relief (vv. 1-5), remembers the past (v. 6), concentrates on the present (vv. 7-13) and expresses certainty of a future with God (vv. 14-16). Then memory (v. 17) and the present condition (vv. 18-20) culminate in the assurance of a joyful future (vv. 21-24). The infirm, elderly poet reflects on how time impacts his or her life. The prayer is composed like a diptych. Twice the elder remembers God in whom, from infancy, youth, and throughout life, one has trusted and whose wonders admired (vv. 5-6, 17). Twice the poet contemplates the advancing years and weakness and asks God not to abandon one when help is most needed (vv. 9, 18). Twice the poet describes the present situation. First the focus is on the wicked who surround, murmur, and try to take advantage of the situation (vv. 10-11). He or she briefly recalls that one has seen many evils and disgraces during a long life (v. 20). The first description inspires an urgent plea and a curse against the detractors, and requests divine justice (vv. 12-13; see Pss 22:11; 35:22; 38:21-22; 70:1). The poet is sure of the restitution of honor with its attendant comfort (vv. 20-21). Finally, the poet pledges continuous praise and the broadcast of God's "righteous" works of rescue (vv. 14-16, 22-24). The two panels can be charted like this:

first panel	second panel
vv. 5-6a, recollection: birth	v. 17a, recollection: youth
vv. 6b-8, present praise	vv. 17b, 19, present praise
v. 9, may God not forsake one in old age	v. 18, may God not forsake one in old age

vv. 10-11, description of present assault
vv. 12-13, request for help and curse of enemies
vv. 14-16, promise of praise for the rescue

v. 20a, reference to past trouble
vv. 20b-21, confidence in God's intervention
vv. 22-24, promise of praise for the rescue

There are fourteen references to God. The intimate relation between him and the poet is illustrated by the possessive (not always evident in translation), "my God" or "my Lord" (vv. 4, 5, 12, 16, 22). Once personal faculties and dignity have been depleted by advancing years, the poet composes a tribute to the value of a lasting friendship with God. Burdened by the years, he or she is also sick and pursued by enemies or at least by people who suppose that God has abandoned one to such a decline.

Psalm 71 is framed by the repetition of *ṣidqāteka*, "your righteous [ness]," and *bwš*, "shame" (vv. 1-2, 24). In the middle, the author takes up the theme of "shame," and thus the sequence:

v. 1, "let me never be put to shame"

v. 13, "let my accusers be put to shame"

v. 24, "those who tried to do me harm have been put to shame"

"Righteous[ness]" is repeated five times; first, pleading for help "[i]n your righteousness" (v. 2), and later as the object of praise (vv. 15, 16, 19, 24). God's righteousness, which reaches to the heights, is opposite the depths from which the poet asks to be raised (vv. 19, 20). Relief from current despondency will issue in the continuous ("all day long") proclamation of God's "righteous acts" or "help" (vv. 15, 24).

The imperative form gives an urgent tone to the beginning. The poet nearly despairs over the attack from enemies who scheme and interpret the infirmity as God's punishment or abandonment (vv. 4, 7, 10-11, 13). The progressive stages of human life are reviewed. God has always sustained the poet, even from the womb (vv. 5-6). God controls all life, including the mysterious stage which is spent in the maternal womb when the poet was just an embryo of hope (see Pss 22:9-10; 139:13, 15-16; Job 10:8-12), embrace all horizons, "My praise is continually of you" (v. 6; cf. v. 14). A second stage in life is youth and apprenticeship. Looking back, the poet confirms that the guide has been constant, "O God, from my youth you have taught me" (v. 17). He or she reminds God of all the activity and interest invested throughout life and requests that God not abandon one in old age (vv. 9, 18). From experience the psalmist knows the appeal will be heeded. One looks to a future full of praise (vv. 8, 14, 22-23).

The aged eyes shift from present to past and future. The fact that God continually sustained and protected one serves as a revelation ("portent") to others and a motive for praise (v. 7). Appearances do not bear this out, and the people are bold about declaring, "for there is no one to deliver" (v. 11). The enemies' speech contradicts the poet's praise and discourse (vv. 8, 15-16, 24). It will not be like this for much longer, the poet proclaims, trembling, because just as it was a sign of God's help in the past, one hopes to survive long enough that it be so again (v. 18). God, in whom the poet has always trusted, will intervene again. In the fullness of years, the inevitable physical and mental consequences will not signify God's abandonment but a life crowned with blessings, cared for by the affection of an elder God, who will live forever.

The poet punctuates the request with praise, beginning with the assertion, "My praise is continually of you" (v. 6). The ample vocabulary is telling:

praise, *těhillâh*, vv. 6, 8, 14

glory, *tipʾeret*, v. 8

"my mouth will tell," *pî yěsapēr*, v. 15

I will praise, *ʾazkîr*, v. 16

I proclaim, *ʾaggîd*, vv. 17, 18

praise, *ʾôděkā*, v. 22

sing praises, *ʾăzaměrâh*, v. 22

shout for joy, *těrannēnnâh*, v. 23

will tell, *tehgeh*, v. 24

Already in the opening verse *ʿôlām*, "never," hints of a concern for time. What the NRSV translates "Be to me a rock of refuge, a strong fortress, to save me" (v. 3, on the basis of an echo of Ps 31:3), the Hebrew reads, more literally, "Be for me a rock of refuge, come continually *[tāmîd]*; you have commanded my rescue." The psalmist finds God always accessible, has always *(tāmîd)* confided in God (v. 6), keeps *(tāmîd)* hoping (v. 14). A related expression is "all day long," *kōl–hayyôm* (vv. 8, 15, 24), referring to praise. The phrase "to all the generations to come" adds a future sense (v. 18). To the threefold use of *ʿad*, "still," "even," "until," referring to time (vv. 17-18), is added a fourth usage in the expression "your righteousness . . . [to] the high heavens" (v. 19). The lesson learned throughout life about God's far-reaching righteousness will be proclaimed even in old age.

Psalm 72
Judge the Poor with Justice

Psalm 71 is the prayer of an old person, not explicitly David (as the captions in Psalms 68, 69, 70 suggest). According to the superscription Psalm 72 is of David's youthful successor, Solomon. It consists of a request on behalf of the king (v. 1), followed by intercessions for the new monarch which include prosperity and equity in the reign (vv. 2-7); a vast domain (vv. 8-11); wealth and prosperity (vv. 15-16); renown and blessing (v. 17). Specific responsibilities form the basis of the intercessions (vv. 12-14). Blessings on the sovereign are matched by blessings on the people, as shown here:

Blessing the king . . .	redounds on the people
v. 1, justice and righteousness	vv. 2-4, justice and righteousness, prosperity, defense for the needy
vv. 5-6, longevity	v. 7, righteousness and peace
vv. 8-11, universal dominion and international recognitions	vv. 12-14, rights and favor for the defenseless classes
v. 15, longevity and prayers	v. 16, fertility of land and people
v. 17a, renown	v. 17b, blessing for the nations

The opening imperative requests the gift that befits the royal office, God's "justice" (plural in Hebrew) and righteousness. The ruler's first responsibility is to ensure law and order and defend the rights of all levels of society, particularly the helpless and poor. This is as much a part of the natural order as mountains, hills, the sun, moon, and climate. May such an ideal rule attain universal proportions (vv. 5-8) and may the enemies be defeated (vv. 9-11), because the monarch protects the defenseless and rescues them from violence (vv. 12-14). May the reign be blessed abundantly (vv. 15-16); may the ruler's fame spread in space and time (v. 17). The doxology closing Book Two (vv. 18-20), is woven into the psalm by the repetition of "name" and "bless" (vv. 17, 19).

God, the true judge, ensures a just order and defends human rights by exercising justice personally or delegating authority to the human regent. God's deputy guarantees divine justice, which is exercised in the service of society, preeminently among those who cannot fend for themselves (vv. 1-2). The benefits which will be harvested from an equitable rule are like the mountains and hills flowing with peace ("prosperity," translating šālôm) and righteousness (vv. 3-4; a similar hyperbole is found in Isa 32:15-20). The poet requests an endless reign, immeasurable in time and space (vv. 5, 8; cf. Zech 9:10). The poet draws an analogy of the sovereign's benevolence which penetrates the peoples' hearts (v. 6). Equitable rule will quench the people's spiritual thirst just as showers moisten the ground. The analogy grows. As a result of the shower of the monarch's benevolence, equity and peace will bud and blossom until the end of time (v. 7; cf. v. 3) and universal sovereignty will vanquish all rivals. In effect, the monarch's dominion is as vast as God's, whose agent he is on earth. The hyperbole, "enemies lick the dust," underscores the submission of contending earthly power (vv. 9-11; cf. Isa 49:23; Mic 7:17). The sovereign does not jostle for power. His moral force benefits the helpless and oppressed (vv. 12-14). The poet recapitulates the theme of long life and foreign tribute (v. 15; cf. vv. 5, 10), and the blessing is manifest in the abundant harvest (v. 16, an echo of vv. 6-7). The "tops of the mountains," usually barren, will also yield crops. The beneficent sovereign is a channel of material blessings for land and people. The sovereign's name and fame will be perpetuated, and the promise to Abraham will flow to all peoples through him (v. 17; cf. Gen 12:2-3). Curiously, the poet is silent about the name which is to be celebrated forever (cf. Ps 45:17).

In the Israelite mentality the monarch is God's agent, his adopted child, anointed or "messiah," responsible for effecting divine rule on earth. The present prayer asks that God participate in the policies of the crown, so that he may govern with equity, above all in behalf of the lowly and defenseless (vv. 2-4, 12-14; see Job 29:12). This implies the removal of oppressors and the rescue of their victims. The people request those qualities that should accompany a government that represents God's rule—a long reign, prosperity like the rain (vv. 5-7); victory and universal dominion over all the known lands (Spain, the Mediterranean, Arabia, vv. 8-11); wealth, fame and blessing for all the constituents (vv. 15, 17). The poet also requests material prosperity which is linked to good government, fertile lands and abundant crops, almost as if nature contributes to the success of the reign (v. 16). The sovereign is the channel of righteousness, well-being *(šālôm)*, fertility, and victory, who saves the helpless when they call; he is served by nations and his fame endures forever. The poor, humble, and handicapped are the main beneficiaries of the government's attention, precisely because they are principal in the divine eyes. This psalm has a special place among the psalms which speak of a messiah who is to save the downtrodden and establish God's reign of peace and justice on the earth.

Book Three

(PSALMS 73–89)

Psalm 73
The Trial of the Just

Psalm 73, the experience of an individual "I," introduces Book Three, which is dominated by communal psalms of complaint (Psalms 74, 79, 80, 83, and parts of 85 and 89). Psalm 73 recalls Psalms 1–2. The wicked are prominent in both (1:1, 5, 6; 73:1-12). The beginning of Psalm 73 echoes Psalm 1, and the end echoes that of Psalm 2 with the repetition of "refuge" (2:12; 73:28). Psalm 73 summarizes the lesson of Psalms 1–72, that personal beatitude has less to do with prosperity than with the assurance of God's presence amidst peril.[1]

Psalm 73 examines one of life's mysteries, the prosperity of the wicked. The plot is straightforward. A devout intellectual pondered a difficult question, which led to frustration and doubt about the religious values he or she has lived. The doubt expands the context beyond the scope of reason, when it finally opens to God's presence and perspective. Attachment to God and conviction of the divine presence replaces the initial sense of estrangement. The poem is a community instruction about the disparity between faith in God and experience in life.

An inclusion frames the poem, which begins and ends with declarations of God's goodness (vv. 1, 28).[2] The word *good, ṭôb*, is repeated, and the final phrase "But for me," *waʾănî* (v. 28), echoes the psalmist's precarious position at the start (v. 2; also vv. 22, 23). The seven explicit references to God, LORD, and *ʾădōnāy* predominate in the second half.

---

[1] I am indebted to J. Clinton McCann, *A Theological Introduction to the Book of the Psalms* (Nashville: Abingdon, 1993) 143, for this observation. Walter Brueggemann ("Bounded by Obedience and Praise: The Psalms as Canon," *JSOT* 50 [1991] 81) writes ". . . in the canonical structuring of the Psalter, Psalm 73 stands at its center in a crucial role . . . theologically as well as canonically."

[2] Most contemporary versions, including the NRSV, adjust the Hebrew text of v. 1 to create a neater poetic line. They translate "the upright" *(layāšār ʾel)* instead of "Israel" *(lĕyiśrāʾēl)*.

God is addressed in v. 15 ("your children"), which marks a turning point in the personal drama.

Initially the psalmist was on slippery ground (vv. 1-3), while the wicked seemed secure (vv. 4-12). In the end the reverse is true; the wicked are slipping (vv. 18-20) and the psalmist is stable (vv. 21-28). The graphic description embraces their appearance, speech, and thoughts. Two terms are repeated in inverse order to describe the comfort of the wicked in contrast to the poet's affliction, *ʿml* and *ngʿ*:

they are *not in trouble [ʿml]* (v. 5)

they are *not plagued [ngʿ]* (v. 5)

all day long I *have been plagued [ngʿ]* (v. 14)

it seemed to me *a wearisome task [ʿml]* (v. 16)

The wardrobe of the wicked consists of a necklace of arrogance and the finery of violence (v. 6). They are evil to the core; their hearts spill over with evil (v. 7). Metaphors of height are used to describe their haughtiness ("pride," v. 6; "loftily," v. 8; "against heaven," v. 9, and scoffing against "the Most High," v. 11). Blasphemy has free rein; "[t]hey set their mouths against heaven, and their tongues range over the earth" (v. 9). The merism "heaven" and "earth" appears again in v. 25. Obtuseness nearly undermined the poet, making him or her a brute, oblivious to God's presence (vv. 2, 21-22). Temporal expressions are employed to contrast the poet and the wicked. The wicked are "always *[ʿôlām]* at ease"; the psalmist is troubled continuously, "all day long" and "every morning" (vv. 12, 14); the wicked vanish suddenly, like a dream (vv. 19-20); the union between God and psalmist is "continually" and "forever," *ʿôlām* (vv. 23, 26).

"[T]heir *end*," *ʾaḥărît*, is in contrast with "*afterward [ʾaḥar]* you will receive me with honor" (vv. 17, 24). The repetition of the Hebrew *šyt*, "they *set*," "you *set*," "I *have made [set]*" (vv. 9, 18, 28), juxtaposes where the wicked have set their mouths and where the good find refuge. The poet speaks of the evildoer's inconstancy and God as a solid rock (vv. 18, 20, 26). The two uses of the *ʾmr*, "say," juxtapose the wicked speech and that of the psalmist (vv. 11, 15). The repetition of *spr* teaches a lesson (vv. 15, 28). To talk along these lines is untrue to the poet's deepest instincts and it might scandalize somebody; to "relate" all God's works includes the testimony to God's presence acquired through prayer. "Heart" is repeated with effect. More basic than the "pure in heart" and keeping one's "heart clean" (vv. 1, 13) is the assurance that God is the "rock [strength] of my heart," even when the heart seems to fail (vv. 21, 26). The word *lbb* ("heart" or "mind") is associated with other body parts—eyes (v. 7), hands (v. 13), soul [literally, "kidneys"] (v. 21), flesh (v. 26). Interiority is expressed in corporal terms, embracing perceptions and actions, passions and imagination, leaving an impression of wholeness.

The expletive ʾak, "Truly," announces the traditional doctrine, the start of the meditation. It may be no more than an aphorism. Repetition calls attention to a paradox, for another ʾak introduces the antithesis, after considering the apparent blessedness of the wicked, *Truly* "in vain I have kept my heart clean" (v. 13, not translated in the NRSV). The third ʾak introduces a reappraisal, and confirms that the wicked will indeed slip, which affirms the initial thesis, "*Truly* you set them in slippery places" (v. 18).

At first "they" are dominant, as viewed by the poet (vv. 2-12; "I," v. 2). In the critical moment, as the poet struggles to comprehend, "I" dominates (vv. 13-17). In the resolution "God" ("you") dominates and determines "their" destiny (vv. 18-20). The final verses express the union between "God" and "me" (vv. 21-28). The repeated "you" (ʿimāk or ʿimĕkā, vv. 22, 23, 25; partially evident in the NRSV) for God emphasizes this union.

God's goodness is the starting point to investigate the problem of merit and reward. The initial affirmation is echoed in the conclusion (vv. 23-28), and the final ṭôb, "good," ratifies the poet's initial exclamation. This repetition describes what God's goodness consists of, which is not estimated in terms of temporal benefits. The value is to be near God, an everlasting inheritance. The problem is explored in images (vv. 3-12), not all of which are clear, but they amount to the disregard of God by those who suppose he is removed from mundane matters (v. 11). The question is not merely academic; it assaults the poet's faith, "my feet had almost stumbled" (v. 2). Are the poet's efforts to live with integrity in vain (vv. 13-14)? People get bored with God, above all when disappointment, disillusionment, and prolonged silence challenge the faith and tempt them to look elsewhere. In light of this the psalmist questions the value of practicing the faith and fulfilling religious duties (v. 13; cf. Ps 26:6; Deut 21:6). The temptation to disregard God is real (v. 15). But to relinquish faith would betray that community of devout and scandalize the younger generation. What prevents the psalmist from defection is the sense of obligation to the community.

The answer comes in the form of a religious experience. The translation of v. 17 is literally "until I entered the divine sanctuaries." If we understand here pagan shrines, the psalmist's eyes were opened when he or she entered the shrines and realized the folly of idolaters. Another interpretation is that this refers to a contemplative experience of God and not an actual sanctuary at all.

Intelligence alone does not provide an adequate solution to the problem of evil (v. 16). Only God can unveil the mystery and invite one into communion, the fruit of religious experience. The human is invited to view reality from God's perspective, which contemplates the people's destiny (v. 17). The wicked, trapped in their own deceit, disappear quickly (vv. 18-20). Suddenly the psalmist is transported to the future and sees the path of evil coming to an abrupt halt (see 37:35-36; Isa 29:8). Compared with this sublime truth, human intelligence seems foolish and vain (vv. 21-22).

The poet does not solve the problem, but an intimate relationship with God is reassuring and the problem dissolves. The bitter failure to understand is answered by the assurance of God's presence (vv. 23-24). The psalmist has an insight into the lot of the good, which is companionship with God (vv. 25-26, 28). Does "*receive* me with honor" or "to glory" (v. 24) indicate that the relationship extends beyond death? Many argue that it does, citing the technical use of the term *lqḥ*, "receive," as with Enoch and Elijah, who were "received *[lqḥ]*" (Gen 5:24, translated "God *took* him"; in 2 Kgs 2:1-10 *lqḥ* is translated in the NRSV "took" or "taken" for the assumption of Elijah; cf. Ps 49:15, "God will ransom my soul from the power of Sheol, for he will *receive* me"). The terms "continually" and "forever" (vv. 23, 26) do not settle the question. The Hebrew vocabulary does not connote infinity but rather indefinite duration. "Heaven" is above the firmament, in contrast to the "earth" (v. 25). For the Hebrew this affirms that the poet is delivered from evil and impending death. In the end God will "receive" him or her with glory. Thus the affirmation moves beyond the immediate problem into a confidence which lies beyond experience (vv. 25-26):

> Whom have I in heaven but you?
>   And there is nothing on earth that I desire other than you.
> My flesh and my heart may fail,
>   but God is the strength of my heart and my portion forever.

The psalm closes with a contrast between alienation from and refuge in God (vv. 27-28).

As in Job and Psalms 37 and 49, the poet of Psalm 73 meditates on the question of reward and punishment. In accord with wisdom literature generally, Psalm 37 offers a conciliatory answer, that there are equitable returns on virtuous and wicked behavior. Psalm 49 shows a disdain for material goods and avoids the question. Psalm 73 confronts the difficulties and concludes that nothing in heaven or on earth can compare with God. Unusual for wisdom literature, Psalm 73 hesitates on the threshold of belief in personal immortality, introduced by piety rather than by doctrinal discourse. The poet admits life's unfairness and puts the question squarely before God, as did Jeremiah (Jer 12:1). This theme appears frequently in wisdom reflections which examine the uncertainties of experience and the mysteries of life. Like Job, the poet is skeptical about God's ways and has a firm grasp of reality. In the end God's presence does not solve the problem but it gives an assurance which the intellectual alone cannot grasp.

The answer to the wisdom problem withdraws into contemplation. Failure was necessary for the psalmist to perceive reality differently, as a gift of God. When a person relinquishes control in prayer, God expands the perception to a new level. Verse 25 approaches a spiritual summit in the first Testament, along with Jacob's wrestling with the angel and Elijah at Horeb (Gen 32:22-32; 1 Kgs 19:11-13; cf. Deut 30:11-14). A personal encounter with God outweighs everything. The wicked assailed heaven and earth, which in the end do not even matter in the psalmist's new view of things.

Psalm 74
Do Not Deliver Your Dove to the Wild Animals

Psalm 74 ponders the situation of Psalm 73, why does God reject his flock, inheritance, and dwelling? It opens with a crisis (vv. 1, 3), the sanctuary has been entered, sacked, and desecrated (vv. 3-8); this could be a motive for the psalmist's questioning in Psalm 73. Ps 74:12-17 fulfills the pledge made in 73:28 to proclaim God's works. "Sanctuary," *miqdāš*, is a link word (73:17; 74:3-4, 7).

Psalm 74 has three movements. The first begins and concludes abruptly with agitated questions (vv. 1, 10-11). The introductory and secondary cries (vv. 2-3, 9) frame the city's destruction and the invaders' wreckage (vv. 4-8). The second movement, the heart of the psalm, recalls God's power in creation and the Exodus (vv. 12-17). The poem closes with the request that God defend himself (vv. 18-23). The image of God, absent from or angry at the people, is not consistent with past experience. It is not good for God to undo what he has accomplished, reject the chosen, repudiate the rescued, move into a house and then burn it down, consecrate and then desecrate a temple. The initial complaint and description are convincing arguments for God to intervene.

Plural address distinguishes the opening chorus, "Why do you cast *us* off forever?" from the individual query, for example, in Psalm 22, "why have you forsaken *me?*" The divine shepherd is angry with the flock. The anxious, questioning tone "Why?" (cf. Pss 10:1; 22:1; 44:24; 79:10, etc.) is followed by the imperative, "remember" (v. 2; cf. vv. 18, 23). God's destiny is allied with that of the people among whom he dwells. The poet sees in the burning temple God's smoking anger (vv. 1, 7). The graphic description of the city's ruin is convincing. The disappearance of the people's rallying points, "emblems" and "prophet," adds weight to the plea (v. 9). The same word "emblems," *ʾōtôt*, refers to the enemies' military standards (v. 4) and God's saving instruments, which include prophets, as can be surmised from the parallel lines shown here (vv. 4, 9):

> Your foes have roared within your holy place;
>> they set up their *emblems* [= military standards] there.
> We do not see our emblems;
>> there is no longer any prophet. . . .

The "emblems," the prophets, are the signs of God's presence, which are as real as the military standards the enemy set up in the destroyed temple. The congregation fearfully asks whether the present humiliation augurs the shape of the future —why? how long? (vv. 1, 9-11, 23). Various expressions for lasting time stand out—"forever" (*lāneṣaḥ*, vv. 1, 3, 10, 19), "from of old" (v. 12), "all day long" (v. 22), "continually" (v. 23).

The description of the temple's destruction magnifies the offense against God. The word *redeem, gʾl*, implies a close bond, usually of blood, an idea that continues in the phrase "your heritage" (v. 2). This recalls Israel's redemption from Egypt. The second imperative "Direct your steps" introduces the scene in which God, like an absent or forgetful landlord, is invited personally to inspect the ruins (v. 3). The poet describes the total destruction, the result of insatiable violence, audio and visual (the enemy "roared" and "set up their emblems," v. 4). The verb *šʾg*, "roar," suggests the aggressors' savagery. The poet goes so far as to read their intention, "We will utterly subdue them" (v. 8). He or she projects the brutality with which an assailant wrecked the temple's wealth and beauty, leaving it profaned and smoldering (v. 7; cf. Lam 2:2-3; 4:11; Isa 64:11).

The people's isolation reaches critical proportions. Even communication with God, which was accomplished by means of the prophetic oracles, has been severed (v. 9; see, Lam 2:9, "her prophets obtain no vision from the LORD"). The complaint reflects God's silence as well as a decline of respect for prophets, many of whom have prostituted their service for personal gain (cf. Hos 4:4-6; Mic 3:5-7). Amidst such pathos the psalmist attests to a faith in God who governs all and even allows the present outrage (v. 11): "Why do you hold back your hand?" The hand which could be used for defensive fighting is inactive.

The expression "God my King" presumes an intimate relation between those who pray and the divine sovereign (v. 12). This movement is punctuated with the emphatic pronoun "you," *ʾattâh* (seven times in Hebrew), which forges a relation between the poet and God (vv. 12-17; cf. Pss 44:9-14; 50:16-21; 60:1-3; 89:9-13). The heart of this complaint praises God, the only one who can send relief. The vivid description evokes the Exodus (vv. 13-15):

> You divided the sea by your might . . .
> You cut openings for springs and torrents;
>   you dried up ever-flowing streams.

In a few strokes the poet alludes to the crossing of the Sea of Reeds, the Jordan crossing and the water from the rock (Exod 17:2-7; cf. Ps 107:33-35). The poet also evokes creation (vv. 16-17):

> you established the luminaries and the sun.
> You have fixed all the bounds of the earth. . . .

God is acclaimed governor of all time, "*Yours* is the day, *yours* also the night" (v. 16). God who programmed the rhythm of day and night and the seasons is a cause of amazement. He is supposed to be interested as long as time follows a certain pulse (cf. Gen 8:22), and this makes his silence even more critical. The description convulses with the battle of primeval sea monsters, and reveals God's control of earth, its seasons and fertility. The monsters personify the sea ("dragons" *tannînîm* and Leviathan, cf. Ps 89:9-10; Isa 27:1; 51:9-10),[3] which God subdued. The reference to the "heads of Leviathan," who serves "as food for the creatures of the wilderness," leaves the reader in awe at the image of God dealing with the primeval enemy (cf. Jer 7:33; 16:4; Ezek 32:4). With the merism day–night, "the bounds of the earth," summer–winter, the psalmist embraces the diversity created by God (vv. 16-17).

Once again a destructive force menaces God's creation, destroys the temple, and it is inconceivable that God remain silent and passive.

---

[3] According to a creation myth, God subdued the monsters of chaos, which personify the restless sea, before he began creation. The poet employs this myth of the divine warrior's victory over the multi-headed dragon to portray dividing the sea to redeem a people from chaos. This rescue was also an act of creation. The double perspective of creation and Exodus echoes in these lines.

The incentive for him to intervene is the slander of the divine *name* (vv. 10, 18; the divine name LORD is pronounced only once, v. 18) and the threat of genocide (v. 19). God is ultimately the target. Another argument for God's intervention is the people's defenselessness and the repeated use of "the poor," *ʿānî* (vv. 19, 21). This along with nuanced terms like "the sheep of *your* pasture (v. 1; see 79:13; 95:7; 100:3; Jer 23:1; Ezek 34:31), *your* congregation, "the tribe of *your* heritage" (*šēbeṭ naḥălâh;* cf. Jer 10:16; 51:19), "*your* foes," "*your* holy place," "*your* sanctuary," "the dwelling place of *your* name" (vv. 2, 4, 7) imply dependence on God and are designed to induce God to intervene. The repetition of "your name," *šĕmekā* (vv. 18, 21), poses a contrast. While "an impious people reviles *your name*," the poet requests that "the poor and needy praise *your name*." This is in inverse order from the first part, "the dwelling place of your name" and "the enemy . . . revile your name" (vv. 7, 10).

The theme of remembering and forgetting is condensed in the last movement (vv. 18-23), which is dominated by seven imperatives (positive and negative) urging God to act. They culminate in the appeal, "Do not forget" (cf. vv. 2, 18, 19, 22, 23). The positive formulations refer directly to God—*your* name, *your* [Hebrew "the"] covenant, *your* cause (vv. 18, 20, 22); the negative ones refer to the chosen people in their misery—*your* dove (cf. Ps 68:13), *your* poor, *your* foes (vv. 19, 23). The tug of war is especially evident in the opposition between God's foes and the afflicted people. Is there any question about who needs God's assistance? The opposition is graphic (Hebrew):

the enemy—an impious people—wild animals—

   your dove—

   your poor—the downtrodden—the poor and needy—

the impious—your foes—your adversaries.

Literally and effectively the poor and afflicted are surrounded by the heavy-weight enemies.

A national disgrace inspires a liturgy requesting rescue. The description, evocative of the destruction of Jerusalem by the Babylonians in 587 B.C., can be applied to any national disgrace. Psalm 74 is almost as significant for what it does not say as for what it says. Nothing is mentioned of the sins of Israel which had provoked the catastrophe nor is there any request for pardon. While the poet recalls the temple's destruction, the annihilation of the population, and the siege of the city, he or she is silent about exile. Like other psalms with "of Asaph" in the caption (Psalms 50, 73–83), Psalm 74 is vigorous and blunt.

Psalm 75
At the Appointed Time I Will Judge with Equity

Psalm 75 is a fitting sequel to the appeal for help in Psalm 74. The link word *môʿêd* is understood as "holy place" or "sanctuaries" and "the set time" (74:4, 8; 75:2). The relation is even closer. In the first God is "my King" and in the second God appears as judge (74:12; 75:2, 7). The poet requests that God "plead your [his] cause" or judge (74:22). The question is asked "[h]ow long?" and the answer comes "[a]t the set time" (74:10; 75:2). Both psalms advert to Hebrew cosmogony; in Psalm 74 the poet appeals to God's victory over chaos and in Psalm 75 affirms that God steadies the pillars of the earth. "[T]he tribe of your heritage" becomes [the God of] "Jacob" (74:2; 75:9). In Ps 74:13-17 "you" (emphatic), with reference to God, is repeated, and God answers with an emphatic "I" (75:2-4). "Your name," in reference to God, appears in 74:7, 10, 18, 21; 75:1.

Change of address and number signals a liturgical celebration. The congregation begins (v. 1), God speaks an oracle (vv. 2-5), the poet tells about God (vv. 6-9), and the poem closes with an oracle (v. 10). The faithful thank God, as they review his "wondrous deeds" *(niplāʾôt)*, which in this context are God's verdict against the wicked who have misused power. The psalmist affirms God's universal dominion, warns of impending punishment (vv. 6-8), and pledges continual praise (v. 9). God reiterates the determination to execute judgment (v. 10; cf. v. 7). The concentric pattern that links the poet's affirmation to God's oracle looks like this:

  A I will judge with equity (v. 2)

    B the earth with all its inhabitants (v. 3)

      C I say to the boastful, "Do not boast" (v. 4a)

        D to the wicked, "Do not lift up your horn" (v. 4b)

        D' "do not lift up your horn on high" (v. 5a)

      C' "or speak with insolent neck" (v. 5b)

    B' not from the east, the west or the wilderness (v. 6)

  A' God is judge (v. 7)

God is the world's creator and sustainer. Neither earthquake nor human uprising alters what he has established. "I who keep its pillars steady" refers both to the foundations of the moral order and its geophysical stability (v. 3; cf. Pss 11:3; 82:5; 104:5; Job 9:5-6; 38:4-6). The author depicts the earth like a dish which is set on columns in the primeval ocean. Human injustice causes these foundations to totter, but God steadies its pillars. Right conduct or justice is of a piece with the cosmic order.

The horn is an image for power and, by extension, the potent evil of pride. The repeated image of lifting up is significant (vv. 4-7, 10)—"Do not *lift up* your *horn*"; "not from the wilderness comes *lifting up*"; God "put[s] down one and *lift*[s] up another"; "the *horns* of the righteous *shall be exalted.*" The repetition focuses on the attitude of the wicked, while "lifting up" is a divine prerogative. When the wicked lift their horn, they preempt the right of God, who will exalt the righteous. The vertical slant continues; the "horns of the wicked," previously raised, will be cut off, while "the horns of the righteous shall be exalted." The incomplete drawing of the compass leaves an opening for a double entendre. "Lifting up" comes from on high, where God is, so "north" is understood along with east, west, and south (wilderness), in the denial of "lifting up"; but Mount Zaphon, associated in mythology with God's residence, is in the north, so the reader is left with an allusion. Even so, the judgment has an earthly, horizontal dimension (vv. 6, 8). Only in lifting the gaze to the judge on high is balance and justice maintained.

The metaphor of the cup of drugged wine is used by the seventh and sixth century prophets to dramatize judgment (v. 8; cf. Ps 60:3; Isa 51:17; Jer 25:15-29; 49:12; Ezek 23:32-34; Hab 2:15-16). God has a cup which augurs the destiny of those under judgment, and he will pour a draught from it for "all the wicked" to drink. The judgment has an eschatological dimension. The psalmist, in the community's name, proclaims the intention to praise God continually for the defeat of sinners and the victory of the good (v. 9).

Psalm 76
God is Awesome

Three divine attributes delineate the tripartite structure of Psalm 76: God, manifest to his people (vv. 1-2), victorious in war (vv. 3-6), awesome in judgment (vv. 7-12). An inclusion frames the third part (the verb *nôrâ*, "awesome" and "inspires fear," vv. 7a, 12b). The direct address ("you") bridges the latter two parts (vv. 4-8). The revelation of God frustrates opposing powers, a truth repeated four times as shown here:

v. 1   God is known, his name is great
v. 3   God broke the weapons of war

v. 4   God is glorious, majestic
v. 5   spoils were lost; horse and rider stunned

v. 7   God is awesome
v. 8   human dissent is judged and sentenced

v. 12a   human dissent is cut off
v. 12b   God is awesome (awe inspiring)

The fourth time the usual order, revelation followed by the effects, is reversed.

The parallel lines argue for an identification between Salem and Zion as well as Judah and Israel (vv. 1-2; cf. 114:2). God wins a military victory in Jerusalem ("there," v. 3) or, more broadly, among his people (in Judah, which is a territory within larger Israel). The victory may be historical or it may be God's general victory over the enemies of justice (see vv. 7-12). A third possibility is the eschatological victory, which can be surmised from historical happenings. (Psalms 46 and 48 are similar to the present psalm in this regard.) The final verses articulate the theological interpretation, which is the triumph of divine justice. God is an awesome judge for those who attack his inheritance. God, who sends forth his spirit or breath, can also withhold it and stop the respiratory process; he "cuts off the spirit of princes" or leaves them breathless and in awe after the blitzkrieg (v. 12; cf. Ps 104:29-30; Gen 2:7).

God penetrated history through Abraham and his descendants Israel and Judah. God chose a geographical center where he could approach the people, Salem (an older name for Jerusalem, Gen 14:18), Zion. War is a symbol of power and rendering accounts. Israel is a warring people, but never in such vast proportions as depicted here. The motif of breaking weapons suggests that God alone achieves victory (v. 3; Ps 46:9). All arms, both offensive and defensive (arrows and shield), of long or short range (arrows and sword) are broken. The sleep of the vanquished is torpor (vv. 5-6); they are stunned by the sight of the "awesome" *(nôrâ*).[4] This is a realistic picture of the strong who are "stripped of their spoil" because they fell asleep and, suddenly jolted awake, could not defend themselves. The NRSV reading, "none of the troops was able to lift a hand," *wĕlô° māṣĕ°û . . . yĕdêhem,* could be

---

[4] An inversion of consonants produces a play on words. The repeated *nôrâ°* appears as *nā°ôr,* ("resplendent" or "glorious," v. 4). A related wordplay occurs in v. 11, *môrā°,* "awesome."

understood literally "they did not find their hands." The "rider and horse" alludes to the crossing of the Red Sea (v. 6), which typifies all God's victories in the people's behalf. Heavens and earth, a merism which embraces creation, are witnesses of God's judgment (v. 8; cf. Ps 50:4). When God "rises" in judgment, the verdict will save "all the oppressed of the earth" (v. 9; Pss 7:6; 12:5; 74:22; 82:8; cf. Isa 2:19).

The opposing forces are illusory and not fully developed. At first the weapons appear, but with no one to wield them (v. 3). In the second place the opposing troops, suddenly awakened, are in the ridiculous position of being unable to find even their hands. Awestruck, God's enemy ("the spirit of princes" and "kings of the earth") is neutralized (v. 12). God, on the other hand, is presented not as a warrior defending a fortress but simply "dwelling" on Zion, in the temple. God needs no other battle plan than recognition in Zion.

Psalm 77
Has God Changed?

"Shepherd of Israel" and the appeal for the "flock" is a recurrent theme in Psalms 77–80 (77:20; 78:70; 79:13; 80:1), which narrate God's miracles in Israel's history. Psalm 77 is composed of two movements, the complaint of God's abandonment (vv. 1-10) and the memory of God's past action (vv. 11-20). A troubled sleeper bemoans the present crisis and reflects on the glorious past. The repeated phrase "in the night" adds weight to the anxiety (vv. 2, 6). Night is a symbol of internal unrest, the seeming futile search for a hidden God. The insomniac is restless and frets over God's absence and silence. Troubling questions aggravate the condition. The poet declares that he or she pleads ceaselessly, yet the pleas are not to be found in the psalm. Even the thought of God, which ought to bring consolation, magnifies the pain and keeps the psalmist awake. The question burns, has God really finished with us, changed his mind about us (vv. 7-10)? Was the eternal covenant conditioned? The poet identifies with the people, and anguish worsens as their suffering is meaningless. How does the present situation score with the past? Has God's everlasting *ḥesed* expired? The worst scenario is a definitive change of heart on God's part—"forever," "never again" and "for all time" (vv. 7-8). If God has forgotten, the repercussions will be definitive, and there is no hope. God's forgetfulness is reminiscent of the capital sin of the people, who chronically forgot God's deeds in their favor (cf. Ps 78:11; Psalm 106). The unsettling questions which began, "Will the Lord spurn forever, and never again be favorable?" culminate with the possibility that God has changed his mind about the people (v. 10). His right hand is vigorous (cf. Pss 44:3; 89:13; 118:15); has he become left-handed (cf. 74:11)? The expression "the right hand of the Most High" evokes past triumphs and the questioner proceeds with an impressionistic review of the Exodus (vv. 11-20), a painful reminder yet a hope.

Amidst this intense drama, the psalmist addresses God ("you" and "your"), which narrows the distance between God and the people. The poet narrates in general terms (vv. 11-15), before spotlighting the pre-eminent miracle of the sea (vv. 16-19).[5] The result is an original version of redemption. God appeared in the storm, and the waters recognized him (cf. Ps 18:7-15; 114:3-5). God opened a highway through them yet remained enshrouded in mystery (v. 19). Analogously, the psalmist cannot track God in the present crisis. Like writing on water, God works miracles but erases the traces. The final assertion, "You led your people like a flock," lightens the initial morose mood. The divine shepherd dominates the scene, as his deputies Moses and Aaron guided the tranquil flock. The ending is so abrupt that the psalm seems incomplete. Based on the experience of God's favor, more palpable than the present quandary, the poet can reasonably anticipate deliverance.

The poet's predicament represents the community's, as one would expect of an Asaph psalm, which is typically collective. The poet laments God's abandonment of the people. There is no explicit mention of an adversary. The poet's anguished "day" (v. 2) is analogous to the people's distress before the Exodus. As he or she reviews God's intervention, the implied request is that this miraculous rescue be commuted to the present.

In the first movement God is spoken of in the third person, with one exception, when the poet unexpectedly addresses God (v. 4). In the second movement the poet addresses God. The reader becomes easily involved in the descriptions of the anxiety and the miraculous rescue. The psalmist's anxious "voice" is drowned out by God's "thunder" (*qôl*, vv. 1, 18). The poet's tossing and turning is forgotten in the earthquake which contributed to the people's liberation (vv. 16, 18). The initial description of trouble, with God interspersed among verbs of reflection—remember (*zkr*, "think," vv. 5, 9, 11), meditate, consider, commune with, search, call to mind, muse—is resolved (vv. 3, 5-6, 11-12), and this brings to a climax the theme of reflecting on the past. The repeated *śyḥ*, "meditate," marks the poem as a meditation (vv. 3, 6, 12; cf.

---

[5] The "descendants of Jacob and Joseph" is an anomaly, because the descendants of Joseph (Ephraim and Manasseh) are also grandsons of Jacob. In the partition of the land they inherit along with their uncles.

Ps 143:5). The poet ponders a painful possibility, "Has God *forgotten* to be gracious"? (vv. 9-10). Then he bolsters himself by *remembering* (v. 11, twice) and recounting God's deeds as epitomized in the Exodus.

Anxiety touches every part of the poet. He or she cries aloud, outstretches the hand; the soul is restless, fainting; one moans, can neither sleep nor speak. Day and night, but especially at night, anxiety weighs on one. The complaint about God's silence, the futile questioning, is followed by speaking to God as the poet stands in contemplative awe of past wonders. The plaintive tones give the impression that God has abandoned the people. This is reminiscent of Psalm 73 where the poet poses the problem of the apparent triumph of evil. There the problem was answered by a contemplative experience which widened the focus (73:16-17). The present problem is answered by deeper meditation and the recollection of God's action. Psalms 73 and 77 are alike in the way they depict the inquiring soul. The pain gnaws to the point that one is tempted to doubt God's interest or involvement (vv. 1-10; cf. 73:1-16); one seeks deeper, in the memory, to contemplate God's miracles (vv. 11-20; cf. 73:17-28). In the end, the problem is not solved, but rather dissolves in the light of a more profound experience of God.

The poet understands that God's extraordinary actions and unprecedented reversals are history. In the present, victories belong to those who reject God, and this results in the backsliding of those who trust God. The psalmist is in a dark night (v. 2) and the congregation is sympathetic. But by remembering the Exodus the night is illumined, just as the pillar of fire accompanied the people through the desert. The contemplative experience is underscored by the phrase "your footprints were unseen" (v. 19). Just as God mysteriously guided the people and their leaders, he continues to open a path through the turbulent waters. It is left to the poet and the people to follow God through the storm, the lightning, the earthquake, and the hurricane, where only God knows the way.

Psalm 78
A New Beginning in Zion and David

Psalm 77 is joined to Psalm 78 by shared vocabulary, God's "might" or "power," *ʿōz* (77:14; 78:26); "Most High," *ʿelyôn* (77:10; 78:17, 35, 56); God's "right hand" (77:10; 78:54; the "strong arm" of 77:15 saved Israel in the past). The theme of the Exodus and motifs of forgetting and remembering are shared (77:11-20; 78:11-72). Psalm 77, which reviews the Exodus and God's favors, is a fitting introduction to the epic psalm, which expands this miniature of history as it reviews God's favor and the people's chronic failure. The psalmist plunges deeper into meditation (77:2-6) and promises to remember God's great works (77:11-12, 16-20), which he does in Psalm 78.

A historical psalm may take any of various forms.[6] Psalm 78 begins like a wisdom poem (vv. 1-4; cf. Ps 49:1-4; Prov 3:1; 5:1). The history of God's "glorious deeds"[7] and the people's unfaithfulness aims to instruct the present assembly, "that they should not be like their ancestors . . ., whose spirit was not faithful to God" (v. 8). Continuity is underscored by the repetitions, ancestors (vv. 3, 5, 8), children (vv. 4, 6), generations (vv. 4, 6, 8), "tell" (vv. 3, 4, 6), "know" or "teach" (vv. 3, 5, 6). The lesson can be summed up in the following terms: fidelity to God brings blessings, sinfulness invites punishment, but God's mercy prevails and affords a new beginning. As in Psalm 106 the poet emphasizes the people's chronic disobedience and ingratitude. Ephraim's defection, for which God rejected the northern tribes in favor of Judah, frames the account (vv. 9-11, 67). This colors the historical background, serves as an example of behavior to avoid, and justifies the rejection of Joseph (Ephraim) and the election of Judah, David, and Zion. Ephraim's sin which merited impeachment is described (vv. 9-11):

> The Ephraimites . . . did not keep God's covenant,
>   but refused to walk according to his law.
> They forgot what he had done,
>   and the miracles that he had shown them.

The poet returns to this at the end, stating the punishment (v. 67):

> He rejected the tent of Joseph,
>   he did not choose the tribe of Ephraim.

Memory reaches back, first to the recent experience in the promised land, then to the remote desert sojourn, and even farther to the Exodus. A repeated motif, the people's forgetfulness (vv. 11, 42), and a thematic refrain (vv. 17, 32, 40, 56) organize the historical reconstruction. Three locations are surveyed, the promised land, the desert (vv. 12-41), and

---

[6] Psalm 105 is a thanksgiving hymn, which scans Israel's history to emphasize God's fidelity. Psalm 106 retells history and laments the people's infidelity.

[7] Acts of God, niplāʔôt, "wonders" (v. 4), are either cosmic or historical achievements, and they are beyond human capabilities. The importance of the miraculous for faith is not that it occurred but that its happening reveals God's hand to the faithful. God performs wonderful acts of mercy (Pss 71:17; 75:1; 77:12; 98:1; 145:5).

Egypt (vv. 42-53). The desert sojourn is framed by the repetition of "Egypt" and "the fields of Zoan" (vv. 12, 43). After the abbreviated account of the plagues, the poet jumps ahead to the settlement of the land (vv. 54-66). Sacred history reached a critical moment, owing to the unfaithfulness of northern Israel ("the tent of Joseph . . ., the tribe of Ephraim"). The sanctuary of Shiloh was abandoned, but God elected David and chose Zion where God dwells (vv. 67-72). Psalm 78 teaches that God will reject those who spurn his favors. A setting in the temple liturgy is plausible.

The poet introduces the reflection as a parable *(māšāl)* and "dark sayings" *(ḥîdôt)* or enigmas (v. 2). He or she intends to review God's benefactions, the people's failure to respond adequately, and God's loyalty (vv. 3-6). Tradition is, besides a lesson, a "decree" of God, who revealed himself and intended this revelation to be handed on. The purpose of the instruction is that the next generation not repeat the past but rather stay loyal to God (vv. 7-8), that they not "forget" but "remember" (vv. 7, 11, 35, 39, 42). To "forget" God is a capital crime and the major theme of this psalm. The poet's memory is jarred by some recent failure (vv. 9-10, the vague "on the day of battle"), a defeat brought about by a breach of the covenant. The dominant tribe of Ephraim simply *forgot,* which had serious consequences. If wisdom is the fruit of the collective memory so as to avoid repeating past mistakes, forgetting dooms one to repeat past errors. Analogously, forgetfulness of God's benefits is tantamount to their nullification, while remembering them reactivates God's wonders for the present and stimulates the people's faith and faithfulness.

The people remember the redemption from slavery, the passage through the sea, and the desert trek (vv. 12-16).[8] The unprecedented occurs, water solidifies like a dike and rock liquefies. Nothing is out of God's reach, neither in time (cloud by day and fire by night) nor in substance (water and rock). In spite of this the people "sinned still more" (v. 17). This expression causes one to wonder about the former sins, as this is the first one mentioned. The report of miracles in the desert follows no particular order. The Israelites "tested" God, when they demanded material proof for their faith (v. 18). This enkindled God's rage (vv. 21-22), but instead of acting on impulse, God provided food in an even more astonishing fashion than the water, "raining" "grain of heaven" on them (vv. 24, 27; cf. Exod 16:3-8; Num 11:4-15). Both water

---

[8] The verb used for dividing the sea (v. 13, literally, "to split open") occurs again for splitting the rock to provide water, which surges up "abundantly as from the deep" (v. 15). The Hebrew *těhōmôt* is associated with the primeval waters that surround the earth and are prominent in creation (see Pss 46:2-3; 104:5-9).

and food came from the same storehouse. The punishment of the satisfied people is unexplained (vv. 29-31; cf. Num 11:33-34).

The poet meditates on the dialectic of sin, conversion, and backsliding which characterize human life (vv. 32-39). He or she is obsessed with the fickleness and insubstantiality of human life, just a breath of air, only flesh (*bāśār,* vv. 33, 39; cf. Pss 39:5; 90:3-6; 144:4), which is synonymous with weakness. The theme of transitory life brackets this interlude. God's punishment made the people's days vanish like a breath, but their frailty became a motive for God's mercy (vv. 33, 39). This section is distinct from the rest of the poem in that it describes spiritual dispositions, insincerity and unfaithfulness, and represents a theological position, that sin warrants punishment. The historical schema is simple—liberation, rebellion, punishment, mercy, and this time and again. Remorse leads the people to call for help and repent. God, patient and loving, can be relied on to pardon. The description of God is memorable (vv. 38-39):

> Yet he, being compassionate,
>   forgave their iniquity,
>   and did not destroy them;
> often he restrained his anger,
>   and did not stir up all his wrath.
> He remembered that they were but flesh,
>   a wind that passes and does not come again.

God never forgets the human condition. People remember God, who responds by remembering the people (vv. 35, 39). To be forgotten by God is akin to annihilation.

History repeats itself (v. 40). The root of sin is forgetfulness (v. 42), which plunges the people into another chapter of sinfulness and infidelity. The poet returns to events prior to the Exodus. A free rendition of the plague tradition,[9] the "signs" and "miracles" (*ʾōtôt* and *môpĕtîm*), culminates in the last one (vv. 49-51). With poetic license the poet reorders and condenses seven plagues (a totality; cf. Ps 105:28-36), and only alludes to the flight from Egypt (vv. 52-53; cf. vv. 12-13). He or she skips the desert sojourn treated earlier and moves directly to the conquest. The line, "He drove out nations before them; he apportioned them for a possession" (v. 55), places God's seal of approval upon Israel's conquest.

---

[9] The number and order of the plagues differ from the Torah traditions. For example, according to the present hail and frost strike vines and sycamores (v. 47); in Ps 105:33 God wipes out the vines and fig trees; in Exod 9:31 hail hits the barley and flax.

Once again, the people "tested" God with idolatry (vv. 56-58; cf. v. 18). The image of a twisted bow which does not shoot straight is apt (v. 57; cf. v. 9). In anger God chastised the people and abandoned the northern shrine at Shiloh, which was within the boundaries of Ephraim (vv. 59-60).[10] The poet sums up the Philistine's victory (vv. 61-64), when the ark of the covenant passed into enemy hands. Reverence for the ark is felt in the language, "[he] delivered his power to captivity, his glory to the hand of the foe" (v. 61; cf. 1 Sam 4:11, 22). The completeness of the tragedy is evidenced by the pairs young men and girls, priests and their widows (vv. 63-64). The men are all slaughtered and the tragedy is that the women cannot respond appropriately to their station in life, marriage for the girls and weeping for the widows. The defeat embraced the battlefield and home life, secular and sacred, young and old, illusions of youth and experience of age, male and female.

A meditation concludes the psalm (vv. 65-72). The rejection of Shiloh did not mean the end. God's sudden change of heart is compared to a drunken warrior who suddenly shakes off the drowsiness and routs the enemy. God took decisive action, altered the plans, and chose Judah and Zion to replace Joseph. The poet boasts that the restored temple will have a cosmic dimension, as stable as the earth, as high as heaven. The preference of Zion and David is a theme dear to the deuteronomic school (cf. 1 Kgs 8:15-16). The passage reflects the tension between north (Israel or Ephraim) and south (Judah) which ended in schism.

The present generation is a continuation of the history of Moses, the desert and the occupation of the land. The cycle is like that of the deuteronomic preface to Judges: wealth can bring selfishness and sin, which brings punishment. Affliction awakens the sense of guilt and the request for mercy which God grants (Judg 2:11-23). This historical cycle lasts until the messianic era. The people no longer worship at Shiloh; even the ark was destroyed. With reference to the election of David and Mount Zion, the messiah and Jerusalem in its eschatological dimension are evoked by Christians when the Church celebrates the liturgy.

Psalm 79
Do Not Remember the Iniquities of Our Ancestors

Psalm 78:68-69 ends with the sanctuary in Jerusalem and David's election, and 79:1-3 opens with the devastation of Jerusalem. A link is

---

[10] The enemies' victories during the Philistine wars (capturing the ark and the destruction of Shiloh) are explained by Israel's infidelity. The tragedy of Shiloh is mentioned elsewhere only in Jer 7:12-14 and 26:6 (cf. 1 Sam 4:1-11).

the word *naḥălâh*, "inheritance" (78:71; 79:1). Psalm 79, an Asaph psalm, is the only communal prayer for help in the Psalter that includes a confession of sin. As in Psalm 74, the poet describes the state of emergency in the city (vv. 1-4), appeals to God on behalf of the oppressed population and admits that both past and present generations have erred (vv. 5-9), and requests sevenfold (complete) vengeance against the aggressor (vv. 10-12). In return, the sheep of God's flock (cf. Pss 77:20; 80:1) pledge themselves to thank God continually for the rescue (v. 13).[11] The rhetorical questions (vv. 5, 10) divide the composition into three parts.

The repeated use of the pronoun "your" shows that God is an interested party; the offense deals with "your inheritance," "your holy temple," "your servants," "your faithful" (vv. 1-2). God has to act "for the glory of your name" (v. 9; cf. 74:18-19), because the enemies, like wild beasts, have devoured the people of Jacob (v. 7). God's prestige is threatened (vv. 9-10). Furthermore, the people, captive and condemned to death, can do no more (vv. 8, 11), and in essence God is the offended party because of the special relationship between them. The neighbors' ridicule of the people is really directed at God (vv. 4, 6, 12). In response, God must show that one cannot attack the chosen with impunity. The plaintive tone is evident as the poet questions God (v. 5),

> How long, O LORD? Will you *be angry* forever?
> Will your jealous wrath *burn like fire?*

The connotation of heat in "be angry" (*teʾĕnap* is related etymologically to the warm breath from nostrils) becomes a metaphor of burning wrath. The assembly pleads not that God cool down but rather redirect the anger from the people to the offensive nations. Why should God intervene? They have massacred Jerusalem and defiled the temple (vv. 1-4); they are irreligious, aggressive (vv. 6-7); they despise and insult God (vv. 10, 12). The cry "Why should the nations say, 'Where is their God?'" (v. 10; cf. Pss 42:3, 10; 115:2; Joel 2:17; Mic 7:10) is the last straw. It sparks the prayer for vengeance and the request for favor.

The relation between crime and punishment appears in the repeated vocabulary, shed blood and avenging shed blood (vv. 3, 10). Bodies were left unburied; blood spilled and unburied cries out to heaven (vv. 2-3; Jer 7:33, 14:16). This demands reparation (v. 12; see Gen 4:10, 15). The image "sevenfold into the bosom" is derived from the ample folds of the garments that served to gather and carry things, and hence it is

---

[11] The title "sheep of your pasture" recurs in two classic shepherd texts (Jer 23:1; Ezek 34:31), in a related psalm (74:1) and two hymns (95:7; 100:3).

an appropriate metaphor for generous punishment. Retributive justice is seen again in the repetition of "taunt," *ḥerpâh:* "We have become a *taunt*" and "Return . . . the *taunts* with which they *taunted* you, O Lord" (vv. 4, 12). After venting their spleen in the request for vengeance, the congregation promises in return to praise and thank God forever.

Psalm 80
Prayer to Restore God's Vineyard

Psalms 79 and 80 form a pair. Psalm 80 addresses the "Shepherd of Israel, you who lead Joseph like a flock," a theme met in 79:13, "we your people, the flock of your pasture." These two communal complaints tell of destruction and pray for restoration. The community bemoans the national disaster and requests God's favor. Like other psalms of Asaph, Psalm 80 can be situated in the northern tradition, represented by Hosea and Deuteronomy. The vine is applied to Israel (Jer 2:21; Hos 10:1) and Jerusalem (Ezek 15:6). The situation is a military defeat which is not identifiable and therefore applicable to any analogous plight.

The message is encapsulated in a choral plea for help (vv. 3, 7, 19), a response to the leader's intonation of the rest of the psalm. The irregular intervals of the refrain divide the psalm as well as illustrate the psalmist's agitation. Furthermore, this refrain is expanded with each repetition, "God," "God of hosts," "O LORD God of hosts." The prayer expresses longing to return to normal relations between God and the covenant people. The refrain is reinforced by the recurring theme of God's care and protection (vv. 2, 8-9, 14-15, 17). The altered version attracts attention (v. 14). The poet requests God's inspection of the whole situation and the plantation's condition. Instead of "Restore us" (Hiphil of *šwb*), the poet requests "Turn again" (Qal of *šwb*); instead of "let your face shine" he says "look down from heaven, and see; have regard for this grapevine." In the end the congregation vows never again to turn away (v. 18).

Four initial imperatives ("give ear," "shine forth," "stir up," "come") impose a sense of urgency which is magnified by the request for the radiant divine face.[12] An inclusion (vv. 4, 19), "O LORD God of Hosts," frames the body of the poem. This begins with the typical complaint, "How long?" The questioning plea is accusatory (vv. 4-5), how long

---

[12] The image of a radiant, benevolent divine face is well-known from the priestly blessing and other liturgical texts (Num 6:25; cf. Pss 31:16; 44:3; 67:1; 89:15).

will God vent anger, while the people suffer? God's "anger" connotes punishment. The beleaguered people sense God's rejection, and their neighbors are jeering. The centerpiece is the allegory of the vine, which symbolizes Israel's history up to the present tragic hour. The allegory is framed by the repetition of "vine" and "planted" (vv. 8, 14-15). The intensity of the plea is evident, "have regard for this vine, the stock that your right hand planted." In contrast to the present when God appears to be absent, he was once intimately involved with prosperous Israel (vv. 8-11). May he not leave this work unfinished. The planting evokes the Exodus and the conquest, which is the basis for the earnest prayer. The poet curses those who would ravage the vine (vv. 12b-13, 16). The allegory finished, the poet appeals to God's attention to the people (v. 17). It concludes with petitions and a promise of fidelity and praise if the congregation is granted life (vv. 14-18).

What appears to be three generations, Israel, his sons Joseph and Benjamin (by Rachel), and his grandsons Ephraim and Manasseh, are really a single nation, Israel. Jeremiah alludes to the misfortunes of the northern tribes by evoking Rachel's children (Jer 31:15-20). Uncle Benjamin is framed between the twins, Ephraim and Manasseh. The name Benjamin means "son of the right hand," which is echoed in the mention of "your right hand" (vv. 15, 17). The "one at your right hand" alludes to the preference for Israel rather than a specific person like Benjamin, David or Zerubbabel.[13] In the end the relationship between God and people is emphasized (v. 18). Having learned from this punishment, the people promises to amend and invoke God's name, which amounts to conversion.

The use of imagery and metaphor is rich. The invisible God, the shepherd, is enthroned "upon the cherubim," the protective, winged creatures, half-human and half-animal, associated with the ark. God's inactivity in state affairs is imaged in terms of sleep, "Stir up your might" (v. 2; cf. 78:65). The metaphor of fire or smoke (verb *'šn*, "fume," translated in the NRSV "be angry") is employed for God's reaction to the people's guilt and for the nations' destruction of the vine (vv. 4, 16). The diet is solid "bread of tears" and liquid "tears to drink"—pain, humiliation and ridicule (v. 5; cf. Job 3:24; Pss 42:3; 102:9). God's deliverance is outlined in terms of a vine transplant. The people invoke God as vinedresser (v. 8; cf. Isa 5:1-7), substituting the initial shepherd metaphor. The verb *ns'*, "brought out," usually indicates leading a march (the Hiphil is rare). Here it has the nuance of uprooting, transplanting, yet with a definite allusion to the Exodus. The image is amplified in

---

[13] A passing reference to the king is suggested by the word "stock" (v. 15; see Isa 4:2; 11:1).

three phases, planting, destruction in the present crisis, and the request for a return to divine favor (vv. 8, 12, 14b-15a). Three synonyms for the branches (*ʿānāp, qāṣîr, yôneqet,* vv. 10-11) illustrate the rapid growth of the transplant from Egypt, which received God's care in the planting. The vine will cover mountains and giant cedars, an exaggeration born of national pride and expansionism. The influence will extend north into Lebanon (the "mountains" and "mighty cedars") and east to the River, from the Mediterranean to the Persian Gulf (vv. 10-11; cf. Ps 72:8). The extension of the vine signifies the triumph of the lowly over the great. So why would God destroy the hedge and leave the field open to trespassers and passers-by? The implication is that its fruit has spoiled. The boar is not kosher and it symbolizes Israel's national enemies. A contrast is drawn by cognates of *rʿh* (vv. 1, 13); God is the "shepherd," *rōʿēh,* of Israel, and the beast is "feeding" (*rʿh,* pasturing) on the vine, Israel. God finds the vine burned and cut down (an inverted order from reality). The coherence between this description and Isaiah 5 (cf. Jer 6, 9) calls to mind the people's sinfulness. The refrain recognizes implicitly that Israel is at fault ("restore us"), which is confirmed, "Then we will never turn back from you" (v. 18).

The two images, shepherd and vine, do not mate easily. Here God shepherds a vine. (In the love poetry of the Song of Songs the male is a shepherd and the female is a garden or vine.) The pastoral image is operative in the background to v. 5 where he waters the flock (with tears). The vine image is exploited with surprising force as it spreads in gigantic proportions, higher than cedars and mountains, extending over nations, from the sea to the river. As with the pastoral image, the allegory of the vine has inconsistencies, the boar and wild animals devour the vine which has covered mountains and cedars (v. 14).

Psalm 81
If Only You Would Listen to Me

Psalms 80 and 81 single out the Joseph tribes (80:2; 81:5). Psalm 81 has two parts, a summons to celebrate a festival (vv. 1-5a) and God's address to the people (vv. 5b-16). This structure is similar to Psalms 50 and 95. It opens with a call to praise with musical accompaniment during Israel's festival day (vv. 1-3) and cites God's authorization for the feast (vv. 4-5a).[14] The "God of Jacob" represents the ideal Israelite com-

---

[14] This coalesces with the tradition recorded in Numbers 29 and Lev 23:23-43 concerning the institution of the feasts of the seventh month. The duration of nearly three weeks embraces both the new moon and the full moon (v. 3; Lev 23:24, 34).

munity, before the schism. A transition to the divine oracle (v. 5b) introduces the two-part speech, which reviews God's relationship with Israel (vv. 6-10) and expounds the crisis created by Israel's unfaithfulness (vv. 11-16). At the center of each part is God's appeal that the people listen and pay attention, the unifying theme (vv. 8, 13). The first appeal is accompanied by the review of God's deliverance in the past (vv. 6-7) and the command to worship one God (vv. 9-10a). The second is accompanied by recalling the people's rebellion (vv. 11b-12) and the consequences for compliance or noncompliance with the command (vv. 14-15). The promise to fill Israel's mouth (v. 10b) anticipates the promise of the finest wheat and honey from the rock (v. 16; cf. Deut 32:13-14). The structure of the oracle can be simply charted, noting the repetitions:

A (v. 5b-7) "I hear *[šmᶜ]* a voice *[šĕpat]* I had not known"; deliverance

    B (v. 8) God's appeal: "Israel . . . listen to me," *yiśrāʾel . . . šmᶜ lî*

        C (vv. 9-10a) command to worship "the LORD your God"

            D (v. 10b) "Open your mouth and I will fill *[mlʾ]* it"

A' (vv. 11-12) "My people did not listen *[šmᶜ]* to my voice *[qôl]*"; rebellion

    B' (v. 13) God's appeal: "listen to me . . . Israel," *šmᶜ lî . . . yiśrāʾel*

        C' (vv. 14-15) consequences of compliance or non-compliance

            D' (v. 16) "feed . . . and satisfy *[śbᶜ]* you"

C and C' repeat the sacred name (LORD); to *bow down* (verb *šḥh*) before a foreign god is prohibited (v. 9), and the punishment for rejecting God is to *cringe (kḥš)* before him.

The celebration begins with gusto with five invitations to worship (sing aloud, shout for joy, raise a song, sound, blow), and five musical ways to celebrate (choral and instrumental). The song has a full orchestral accompaniment, strings (lyre and harp), percussion (tambourine), and wind instruments (trumpet). Suddenly the majestic voice resounds, which chills the initial enthusiasm as it unveils the radical falseness of such musical celebration. God formally denounces the people who celebrate the liturgy without listening to him or following his path. Praise and liturgical celebration without corresponding action is meaningless. Five times the word "hear" or "listen" resounds, which the people know as the first word of their credo (Deut 6:4). The psalmist "hears" the oracle, which recalls the command to "hear" and "listen" (vv. 5, 8); the people refused to "listen" (v. 11, and the synonym "submit," *ʾbh*).

Given another chance, if they "listen" (v. 13), God will care for them in wondrous ways. The connection between hearing and obedience is illustrated in the parallel lines of vv. 11 and 13:

> "But my people did not listen to my voice;
>   Israel would not submit to me. . . .
> O that my people would listen to me,
>   that Israel would walk in my ways!"

The essence of Israel's identity as God's people is found in the ability to listen. For not listening Israel was punished (v. 12). If only she would again listen, God would rescue and provide for her (v. 14).

The oracle spans the past, present, and future. Based on God's past involvement with the people, if they but listen and heed the word in the present, they may anticipate a secure future. A change of address is present in the Hebrew in this oracle. God both speaks about the people (v. 6) and to them (vv. 7-10). The Hebrew of v. 7 [NRSV v. 6] reads "I relieved *his* shoulder of the burden; *his* hands were freed from the basket." The consequences are terrible; once God abandons the people to their caprices, they have no chance of survival. God desires a happy, prosperous future, but it all depends on the people's attitude and action (vv. 8, 13; see Ps 95:7).

The liturgical celebration has its origins in the Exodus (vv. 4-5). Once the people have assembled, a prophet pronounces a divine oracle, literally, "a tongue I do not know." God's voice, authoritative and unlike the human, introduces the suit against the people (cf. Num 24:4, 16, "the oracle of one who hears the words of God"). God freed Israel from slavery (the "basket" is for carrying clay bricks), appeared in "thunder" at Sinai, and tested her (vv. 6-7). Oddly, Meribah is remembered as a place where God tested Israel, which reverses the tradition that the people tested God there (Ps 95:8-9; Exod 17:7; Num 20:13). The term translated (NRSV) "admonish," *ʿwd* (v. 8; cf. Ps 50:7), is juridical in the present context, meaning "testify against," and it amounts to a warning to correct a relationship that has gone bad (cf. 1 Kgs 21:10, 13; Mal 2:14; Job 29:11). The covenant relation implied with the expression "my people" legitimizes the divine claim (v. 8). The accusation is based on the decalogue (vv. 9-10, as in Psalm 50), with explicit reference to the first commandment, which outlaws idolatry and prescribes exclusive worship. The speech reminds the people that the outcome of the liturgy is that they resume their status as a listening people of God.

Nonetheless, they erred by not listening (v. 11). The punishment? God abandoned them to their own designs (v. 12). There is no more bitter desert than to live with the consequences of one's bad decisions, in this case the hardness of one's own heart.[15] But even this severe chastisement is corrective rather than merely punitive. God desires that the people face their foolishness and convert (v. 13); once they do, God will respond with protection and providence. The psalm ends with the renewed invitation to convert, in order to receive the covenant benefits, victory over enemies and agricultural bounty.

The feast of Sukkoth is a moment of rededication and decision, and it situates the present assembly with Israel at Sinai to hear God's voice and in Moab to hear Moses before crossing the Jordan (Exod 19:3-5; 20:1-3; Deut 5:1-6). The aim of the festival is for the people to decide whether they will continue their recalcitrance or listen anew to God and walk in his ways. Not listening is a chronic malaise in Israel's history, and the oracle reminds the assembly of this, and that it warrants God's punishment. As long as God's voice is heard among the people, even though they may be convicted as guilty, God will not abandon them. Salvation approaches as the divine word, which denounces the people's error, is heard and taken to heart.

Psalm 82
The Downfall of Unjust Gods

Psalm 81:5b-16 is a prophetic accusation of God's people who refused to obey, and Psalm 82 denounces those who have misruled. Psalm 81:1-5a, a liturgical introduction, corresponds in theme to 82:1. Psalm 82 constitutes the legal process (cf. Psalms 50, 58, 81, 94; Isa 3:13–4:1), in which the Most High sues for law and order in society. The "divine council" or "gods" (v. 1b) are judges or governors who share God's responsibility to administer justice and protect the rights of the downtrodden and defenseless (cf. Exod 21:6; 22:8; 2 Chr 19:5-6). The convocation of the gods under the presiding major deity ("Most High") is a recurring motif (1 Kgs 22:19-20; Isaiah 6; Job 1–2). God accuses those who are charged with the maintenance of the social order (vv. 2-4). To the extent that these functionaries do not fulfill their commission, are corrupt and violent, the earth's foundations are destabilized. After the verdict of guilty, God condemns the wicked incompetents. The punishment is loss of their "divine" privilege; they will die like ordinary humans (v. 7). The concluding request is that God assume his role as

---

[15] The diagnosis of the "stubborn heart" appears in Jeremiah, where the context defines its character (Jer 7:24; 9:14; 11:8; 13:10; cf. Deut 29:19).

universal judge and thereby reestablish order in the international arena and the cosmos (v. 8). Deuteronomy 32:8 provides a setting for Psalm 82, for it mentions the Most High apportioning international boundaries according to the number of the lesser deities. Aspects of this psalm are reminiscent of Gen 6:1-4, where the sons of deities were said to have cavorted with human women. For this violation of a divinely appointed order, the life span was curtailed in both Genesis 6 and Psalm 82.

The drama is the opposition of good and evil. The repetition of "the wicked" (*rĕšāʿîm*, vv. 2b, 4b) illustrates the dichotomy; the evil potentates are unfair in their dealings with the defenseless. The "gods" support the oppressors instead. They are arraigned on the basis of a single norm, whether or not they had done their duty. This criterion was a feature of government expected of all who exercised power in the Near East. The powers that control a society where the rights of the defenseless are violated or neglected are unmasked as failures. Darkness is their residence and serves as a metaphor for social disorder (Ps 11:2; Isa 59:9). This social disturbance tilts the cosmic balance ("all the foundations of the earth are shaken," v. 5), engenders darkness, is akin to a regression to chaos. The connection between injustice and the physical world is expressed also in Pss 75:2-3; 96:10; Isa 24:1-6; Hos 4:1-3. This is like the effects of the first sin in Genesis, where the consequences fan out to every level of relation, including the human with the environment. Once leaders prove unworthy of their responsibility, their divine privilege is removed, and they are condemned to the ultimate fate of humans, death.

God's posture ("has taken his place," literally, "stands," and "[r]ise up")[16] brackets the legal proceedings (vv. 1, 8). The Most High, judge and prosecutor, indicts the "gods" for their corruption (v. 1). Cognates of *špṭ* are repeated four times, underscoring the judicial theme, "holds judgment" (v. 1), "judge unjustly" (v. 2), "give justice" (v. 3), "judge" (v. 8). According to the context, the aim of "justice" is to promote salvation, for example, for the "weak and the orphan" (v. 3). With four imperatives the prosecutor reviews the leaders' commission to protect the defenseless (vv. 3-4; cf. Lev 19:15; Deut 1:16-17; 16:19; 24:17). The alliteration of the initial *aleph* (Hebrew) in the pronouncement (v. 6a, "I say, 'You are gods,'" *ʾănî–ʾāmartî ʾĕlōhîm ʾattem*) solemnizes the verdict (v. 7). Once the sentence is pronounced, the people summon God to

---

[16] God stands; elsewhere the posture of judges is sitting (Exod 18:13; Judg 4:5; Isa 28:6; Joel 4:12; Pss 9:4, 7; 122:5; Prov 20:8; cf. Job 29:7, 12-18; Dan 7:9-10). God rises because the legal proceedings are over, and the pronouncement of the sentence is awaited (Isa 3:13; 33:10; Zeph 3:8; Pss 7:6; 74:22; 76:9; 94:2). The posture also suggests imminent action (cf. Pss 3:7; 9:19; 10:12; 12:5; 17:13; 35:2; 44:26; 68:1).

take charge (v. 8). The psalm ends on a universal note which will be played out in the latter part of the Psalter. The LORD is sovereign of all the nations, not just Israel, because the foreign gods, the corrupt judges and ministers who represent them, have been impeached for not performing their duty.

Psalm 83
Prayer Against Any Who Wish Evil

Psalms 82 and 83 are coupled by the use of ʿelyôn, "Most High" (82:6; 83:18). Psalm 83 opens with the contrast between God who is quiet and the nations in tumult. The poet portrays the conspiracy to rob God of his people. The threefold plea that God not withdraw (v. 1) is followed by a sketch of the present crisis (vv. 2-8). The nations have formed a dreadful coalition against God and the people. The plot to eliminate them from history and their name from memory is an assault on God's plan for the world. The roster against Israel is comprised of neighboring states and tribes (vv. 6-8), but this coalition is an anachronism and a geographic puzzle. Ten foreign aggressors represent a totality. In the north with Tyre, where one would expect Sidon, is Gebal (or Biblos). Amalek is south. Eastern Ammon is mentioned with Gebal in the north and Amalek. To mention "the children of Lot" rather than their names, the Ammonites and the Moabites, is a poignant recollection of the incestuous union between Lot and his daughters (Gen 19:36-38). The southern and southeastern alliance is an unusual grouping, bedouin encampments of Edomites, Ishmaelites, Moabites, Hagarites. The latter as an entity separate from the Ishmaelites is only found in 1 Chr 5:10, 19-20. Nine of those named are neighbors and relatives, and as an allied force they never attacked Israel. The list concludes with imperial Assyria, understood, like Babylon elsewhere, as a cipher for the archetypal enemy who opposes God's plan (for example, Lam 5:6; Zech 10:11). Mighty Assyria is reduced to an ally of the lesser powers, "the children of Lot." The poet thus typifies Israel's enemies. First, he or she requests that God do what he has done in comparable crises in the past (vv. 9-12). Finally, in an apparent contradiction, the poet roundly curses the enemy with the desired result that they recognize God, "so that they may seek your name, O LORD" (vv. 13-18).

The initial address in Hebrew is framed by two forms of the divine name (ʾĕlōhîm and ʾēl), requesting God to withdraw the silence (v. 1; see Pss 35:22; 39:12; 109:1). The compelling reason for God to intervene is that his enemies are conspiring and threatening genocide, which would wipe out knowledge of God (vv. 2-4). Parallelism intensifies the description.

A   your enemies

  B   are in tumult

A' those who hate you

  B' have raised their heads

C   against your people

  D   they lay crafty plans

  D' they consult together

C' against those you protect

This parallel structure juxtaposes God and the people with the repetition of the pronoun "you" or "your" (the Hebrew suffix –*kā*), "*your* enemies," "who hate *you*," "*your* people," "those *you* protect." The enemies are stormy like the sea (*hmh*, "in tumult," is commonly used to describe the sea), and they raise their heads in a gesture of superiority. The enemies' direct quote continues the parallel structure (v. 4):

E   let us wipe them out

  F   as a nation

E' let not be remembered

  F' the name of Israel

The chosen people hear the hateful declaration with horror.

The ten-nation alliance corresponds to a decade of curses, which advances in three waves. First, the poet recalls victories and asks that they be repeated (vv. 9-12). The battle cry "Let us take the pastures of God for our own possession" shows that a threat against the people is an affront to God. Then, the poet requests the enemies' annihilation (vv. 13-15) and, finally, that their defeat effect the recognition of God's sovereignty (vv. 16-18). He draws on famous defeats of the past, Sisera and Jabin at Wadi Kishon (cf. Judges 4–5); Oreb and Zeeb (Judg 7:25); Zebah and Zalmunna (Judg 8:5-21). Gideon against the Midianites is in the background of the latter two. The accumulation of comparisons is noteworthy (the prefix *k*-), seven persons ("like" Midian, Sisera, Jabin,

Oreb, Zeeb, Zebah, Zalmunna) and four elements of nature ("like" dust, chaff, fire and flame). It is as if the requested divine intervention follows a predetermined pattern, while the enemy's plans are frustrated. At first the curses are descriptive, but as the poet builds up steam, he or she lets off a final blast of four in a single breath. The adverb "forever" is artfully sandwiched between two sets of verbs, literally (v. 17),

A   Let them be shamed and dismayed

  B   forever

A' let them be disgraced and perish

What begins with plant images, "chaff before the wind" and a brush fire, mounts to hurricane proportions (vv. 13-15; cf. Isa 17:13; 40:24). This may refer to the east wind, the sirocco, which scorches the countryside in certain seasons. The fire destroys the underbrush in the mountains and evokes God's wrath. The order of calamities is here reversed from the initial order, which went from generic to concrete (vv. 2-8). In the curse section, from the historical (vv. 9-12), the poet moves to the generic punishment (vv. 13-17). Essentially he or she requests the same total destruction that was wished upon Israel in v. 4.

At first the enemy is strong, a multi-national alliance with a plan to conquer God's people. In the end the opposition is confused, defeated. The enemy's rise is described with seven verbs ("are in tumult," raised, lay plans, "consult together," say, come, wipe out, vv. 2-4). Similarly, the enemy's fall is encapsulated in seven verbs (pursue, terrify, fill, put to shame, dismayed, be disgraced, perish, vv. 15-17). The contrast of two "names" illustrates the tension of the composition: "let the *name* of Israel be remembered no more" (the enemy's intention), "that they may seek your *name*, O LORD," and "Let them know that you alone, whose *name* is the LORD, are the Most High over all the earth" (vv. 4, 16, 18). Seven references to the divine punctuate this poem (vv. 1 [twice], 12, 13, 16, 18 [twice]).

The curse offends any sensitivity to violence. It expresses the desire that God retaliate against the wicked. To what end? That the chosen be rescued and that God's enemies may convert, "so that they may seek your name, O LORD" (v. 16). This expression is unique; normally, one seeks God or the divine face (cf. 27:8). The mention of God does not appear in the initial part which describes the enemies. As the curse gains force the poet appeals to "O my God" and concludes with "LORD" and "Most High over all the earth." The distance between God and the poet narrows as confidence increases and even as the curse is pronounced.

Psalm 84
Prayer of a Pilgrim to Jerusalem

Psalm 84 has three movements, a pilgrimage hymn (vv. 1-7), intercession for the king (vv. 8-9), and a declaration of the value of God's
presence (vv. 10-12). "LORD" appears seven times, four in the expression "LORD of hosts." Likewise, God, *ĕlōhîm*, occurs seven times, plus
once the denomination *ĕl-ḥāy*, "the living God" (v. 2). The intimate relation is underscored by the possessive pronouns, *my* God and *my* king.
The psalmist praises the temple, even as he or she expresses nostalgia
for arrival (vv. 1-3). The temple is God's dwelling and a human refuge,
surveyed with a shifting scope—"dwelling place," "courts of the LORD,"
birds nesting, "your altars," those who live in God's house.[17] Soul,
heart, and flesh, representing the spiritual, intellectual and physical
aspects—in a word, the whole person—desires life from "the living
God," which the physical condition of finding a home within the
temple signifies. The little birds also project the spiritual condition. The
psalmist's longing, fainting, and singing imitate the birds, dipping,
soaring, and nesting in the temple precincts.

The image is a happy one, darting sparrows who attach their mud
nests in the temple and graceful swallows playing in the cloister and
nesting under the eaves. The psalmist likes birds and uses them elsewhere—fleeing like a bird to the mountains (11:1), flying away with
wings of a dove (55:6), "an owl of the wilderness," "a lonely bird on the
housetop" (102:6-7). Nesting is a metaphor for settling in (Num 24:21;
Obad 4; Hab 2:9), and it symbolizes the security of the devotees in the
temple. Enthusiasm abounds; even one day in the temple is better than
a thousand elsewhere (v. 10).[18] The threshold of God's dwelling is better
than the tents of the wicked. The comparison of the "wicked" is unexpected, but it affirms that they cannot enjoy God's nearness. They live
in tents, while the psalmist has access to God's "house." The divine
presence confers an incomparable value on the temple.

To appreciate the sentiments about God's "house," one can recall
those of the poet of Psalm 122 and what God's dwelling means for the
psalmist (cf. 50:2; 74:2; 76:2; 87; 132:13-18). It is the protection, shelter,
and place of celebration (cf. 27:4-5; 46; 48; 125:1). Nesting there and
caring for the young connects with another image of those who take

---

[17] The Solomonic temple had two "altars," one in front for burnt offerings and the
smaller incense altar before the sanctuary.

[18] The comparison of one to a thousand is conventional (e.g., Deut 32:30; Josh
23:10; Isa 30:17; Ps 90:4; Eccl 7:28).

refuge "beneath the shelter of the wings" of God (17:8). "Happy" those who live in God's house (v. 4; see, for example, 65:4; 91:1-10). Some people dwell in the temple; priests who celebrate the liturgy are characterized as praising God always (v. 4). Others are fortunate because they arrive in pilgrimage. God strengthens them to set out and accompanies them along the way (v. 5). Nature joyfully heralds the blessings which the pilgrims will receive in the temple (vv. 6, 11). This depicts the autumnal pilgrimage, around the time of Sukkoth, when the first annual rains are awaited.[19] Zion is the goal, the holy place where God is met (v. 7; see 63:2). The transformation of the road to Zion is an image dear to Isaiah as well (Isa 35:6-7; 41:18). The Hebrew is vague in vv. 7-8 (NRSV vv. 6-7). The words translated "strength" (v. 5, ʿōz; v. 7, ḥayl) leave the interpreter wondering whether the latter are geographical locations ("from strength to strength"), like forts along the highway, or rather the inner rush one feels in journeying toward a beloved place (cf. Isa 40:29, 31). The NRSV retained the RSV translation of this ambiguous phrase, which, because it complements the verb "they go," would be better understood as "from fortification to fortification," military outposts on the way to Zion. Along highways and through the Baca valley the psalmist approaches Zion, and the way is miraculously transformed as in the return from exile sung by Deutero-Isaiah. The location of the Baca valley is unknown (v. 6); the Latin tradition understood this as "the valley of tears," suggestive of the desolate places which the pilgrim must traverse to arrive at God's dwelling, the end of the psalm.

The psalmist requests a hearing (vv. 8-9) and petitions God on behalf of the anointed king or priest (called "our shield"), the guarantor of safety for pilgrims and citizens (cf. 61:6-7). The parallel lines of v. 9 pray for the human protector,

A	B
Behold	our shield, O God;

A'	B'
look	on the face of your anointed

Elsewhere God is "our shield," and in the present psalm the metaphor is also applied to God, called "sun and shield" (v. 11; cf. Ps 3:3; 18:2; 28:7),[20] a combination which bespeaks glorious light and reliable protection.

---

[19] The Greek caption reads "for the wine-presser," which has a connection with the autumn feast.

[20] Nowhere else in the Hebrew scriptures is God called "sun" (v. 11; the Targum reads "bulwark"), but God's solar attributes appear in Deut 33:2; Isa 60:19-20; 62:1-2; Mal 4:2; Ps 57:5, 11.

Once the pilgrimage has arrived to the sanctuary, petitions are offered, foremost among which are prayers for the welfare of the anointed human sovereign or protector, who, after the exile, is the priest.

What anchors the poet to the temple and unleashes such tenderness and sense of belonging? God who dwells there and the benefits he gives (128:5-6). The divine sun and shield enlightens, enlivens, defends the faithful. God listens and gives grace. The ethical dimension appears, with the image of walking, coherent with the rest of the psalm; the beneficiaries are "those who walk uprightly" (v. 11; see Ps 15:1-2). The poet congratulates them, calls them blessed, as he or she did earlier with those who "live" in the temple and those who are on pilgrimage toward it (v. 4-5, 12).

The poet is in relation to the temple. Longing connotes distance, birds nesting connotes closeness or presence. The gap is bridged with aspects of the pilgrimage—the highways, the valley flooded with rain. The journey is focused in three movements, crossing a wet valley, going "from strength to strength," arriving at the presence of God in Zion (vv. 6-7).[21] The fainting soul's distance from the temple, God's protection, and right walking are a spiritual reflection of the geographical pilgrimage (vv. 2, 11). The insistence in the pronoun "your" (with reference to God) makes the divine presence palpable in the longing ("your dwelling," "your altars," "your house," "your praise," "strength is in you," "your anointed," "your courts"). The pilgrim arrives, and union with God at the temple is expressed in right conduct (v. 11). The real pilgrimage becomes an image of the spiritual in the repetition of *hlk* ("go" or "walk," vv. 7, 11); the walk "from strength to strength" is echoed in God who withholds nothing good "from those who *walk* uprightly." The poet signals a physical distance from the "courts" (v. 2); later he or she expresses presence, "a day in your *courts* is better than a thousand elsewhere" (v. 10). The sparrow at "home" *(bayt)* and the "doorkeeper in the house" *(bayt)* links the two actors, the psalmist and the sparrow. Between the two, a beatitude, "Happy are those who live in your *house*" (v. 4). Another beatitude amplifies the thought, "Happy are those whose strength is in you" (v. 5). The first is about dwelling, the second about journeying, and together they embrace a totality (merism), all human life with God. These are summed up in a third, "happy is everyone who trusts in you" (v. 12). The second and third beatitudes begin the same, *ʾašrê ʾādām*, literally, "blessed is the one." Once again the tension between rest and movement visits the psalm.

---

[21] That "God . . . will be seen" is blasphemous (v. 7; cf. Exod 33:20; but recall 33:10). This must refer to a spiritual vision or reassurance, like Ps 73:17-26.

The opening is tender and well translated, "How lovely." The Hebrew term, *yĕdîdôt*, from *dwd*, is found elsewhere in the Bible. Psalm 45 is a "love song," *yĕdîdôt*. God's beloved, *yĕdîdîm*, plea for help (Ps 60:7, Hebrew). God "gives sleep to his beloved *[yedîd]*" (Ps 127:2). Benjamin is beloved (Deut 33:12); Isaiah sings a love song (Isa 5:1), and Jeremiah accuses an unfaithful, beloved wife (Jer 11:15). The prophet Nathan speaks of Solomon with this term, and the name David is a cognate of the verb *dwd*. In a word, the poet is in love with the temple.

Psalm 85
Ḥesed and Faithfulness Meet; Righteousness and Peace Kiss

Psalm 85 moves from thanksgiving (vv. 1-3), to complaint (vv. 4-7), to an oracle and its fulfillment (vv. 8-13). The verb *šwb*, "restored" and "turned" frames the first movement (vv. 1, 3), and *yšᶜ*, "salvation," the second (vv. 4, 7). Cognates of *šwb* provide a leitmotif—"you *restored*," "you *turned*," "*restore again*," "*again*" (v. 6), "who *turn*" (v. 8). The poet affirms "you restored" only to plead "Restore us again" (vv. 1, 4). Past deliverance is a motive for God's future intervention. The repetitions which stitch the first two movements together are "restore," "anger" (vv. 3, 5), and "your people" (vv. 2, 6). Ḥesed and "salvation" are repeated in reverse order (vv. 7, 9-10). The divine name (LORD) and (Hebrew) *ᵓereṣ*, "land" or "ground" (vv. 1, 9, 11, 12), recur four times each. The beginning "your land" becomes "our land" (vv. 1, 9, 12). The insistence makes one think of a drought. Several verses follow a parallel pattern (vv. 1-5, 7, 10-13). The prophetic oracle (vv. 8-9) departs noticeably from the parallel lines of the composition.

The poet recalls the past that was rich in pardon for Jacob; God's renewed wrath is a tangible reality (v. 4). In the NRSV the interpreter may see an incongruity between the celebrated rescue and the present need. In this respect, Psalm 85 is a companion to Psalm 126. The people suffered a setback by God's punishment of their guilt (vv. 1-3). The restoration was not definitive, and the effects of God's anger and, consequently, their guilt, are still felt (vv. 4-7). In parallel lines the people request that God quell his anger and be merciful. The rhetorical questions add an urgent tone (vv. 5-6). The third movement is a divine oracle which confirms the hope; God announces peace, *šālôm*, which is more than pardon and surpasses human hopes (vv. 8, 10). God's gift embraces both divine and human realms (love, salvation, fidelity, glory); it touches human relationships (justice, love, peace), and fans out to include the natural world (heaven and earth, rain and harvest).

Universal reconciliation is promised (vv. 10-13). The qualities of *ḥesed* and fidelity, fairness and peace are personified as God's attendants (cf. Pss 43:3; 89:14; 96:6), and they meet and greet each other enthusiastically. This allegory is the opposite of Isa 59:14-15, where the noble virtues are barred from the city overrun by injustice (cf. Ps 55:9-11). The poet contemplates a triumphal retinue, heavenly and earthly personages starting out and arriving, meeting, embracing, and kissing. Sky and earth are encompassed. Just as human waywardness results in disharmony, human and cosmic (see Genesis 3; Hos 4:1-3), God restores harmony and fertility (Pss 67:6-7; 126:4-6; Hos 10:12).

The delightful picture of heaven and earth meeting and embracing is explicit in the similar vocabulary and marriage imagery of Hos 2:19-23. The virtues are divine gifts on behalf of the people's welfare. Righteousness kisses Peace, looks down from the sky (v. 11) and opens a path for the LORD. Salvation approaches on the horizon and the divine Glory will take up residence in the land. Righteousness bends down and faithfulness sprouts up, heaven meets the earth—righteousness like rain and faithfulness like the crops that "spring up from the ground." A sign of God's favor toward Israel is the land's fertility and abundant rainfall. Productive land is a feature of salvation oracles in Amos 9:13; Isa 30:23-25; 32:15-18; 45:8; 55:10; 61:11; cf. Lev 26:3-6. What a marvelous harvest of virtues and a plentiful crop in the fields (cf. Ps 72:6-7, 16)! Surprisingly, the psalm ends on the road; "Righteousness *will go [hlk]* before him and will make a path for his steps." The focus of the finale is the divine glory dwelling in the land and the wonderful effects. The dynamic movement shows that God continues to open a path and move into the future.

The theology of Psalm 85 is traced in the repetition of key words. A prayer for rain focuses on the renewal of the covenant through Israel's confession of guilt. God's forgiveness is expressed in the rain. Key aspects of this reconciliation are *šwb* (see above), land, peace (twice), salvation (three times), and the covenant virtues. The "glory" which departed the temple at the exile is destined to return (Ezek 11:23). The attendants in the arrival of "salvation" are *ḥesed* and faithfulness, righteousness and peace.

Psalm 86
Abounding in Ḥesed to All who Call upon You

Psalm 86 is an anthology. Expressions borrowed from or alluding to other psalms are numerous (compare v. 1a and 102:2b; v. 1b and 40:17a;

v. 2 and 25:20; v. 4b and 25:1; v. 11a and 27:11a; v. 14 and 54:3; vv. 5, 15 and 103:8; Exod 34:6, etc.; v. 16a and 25:16a). The poet opens with requests and vocatives supported by statements about self and God (vv. 1-7). Repeatedly the particle *kî* ("for" or "because") appears, reiterating the grounds for God's intervention or the declaration:[22]

v. 1	answer me	for I am poor
v. 2	preserve my life	for I am devoted to you
v. 3	be gracious	for . . . I cry all day
v. 4	gladden the soul of your servant	for to you . . . I lift up my soul
v. 5		for you . . . are good
v. 7	I call	for you will answer
vv. 9-10	nations . . . shall glorify your name	for you are great
vv. 12-13	I will glorify your name	for great is your *ḥesed*
v. 17	[let them] . . . be put to shame	[for] you . . . have helped me

Seven requests (imperative and jussive forms, vv. 16-17, turn, be gracious, give strength, save, show a sign, that they may see and be shamed) precede the final *kî*, "*because* you, LORD, have helped me and comforted me" (v. 17). The poet ends on a pleasant note.

Seven times the emphatic pronoun "you," *ʾattâh* (not represented in English; vv. 2, 5, 10, 10, 12, 15, 17) punctuates the poem entirely directed to God. The frequency of the use of divine names is unusual for such a short piece. The psalmist calls God "O Lord" (*ʾădōnāy*, literally, "my sovereign") seven times. The sum of *yhwh* and "name" is also seven. Statements with "God" make an impact—"You are my God" (v. 2); "you alone are God" (v. 10); "I give thanks to you, O Lord my God, with all my heart" (v. 12). God's presence is felt, as well as the intimate relationship between the poet and God. The poet is "poor and needy" (v. 1). He or she is named "your servant" three times, strengthened finally with "child of your serving girl" (v. 16; cf. Ps 116:16), a word which refers to one who has been born into life-long servitude. This expresses total devotion, the fundamental relation the human has with God. All the more reason for him to respond quickly, lest his own property be damaged. The sovereign Lord, omnipresent in the psalm, is also present whenever a devout person needs attention, care, and love.

A concentric disposition of phrases and themes frames a nucleus of praise and the central declaration of universal recognition of God (vv. 8-10):

---

[22] L. Alonso Schökel, *Salmos II* (Estella: Editorial Verbo Divino, 1993), 1117.

A   request; imperatives "incline your ear," "answer," "preserve," "save" (vv. 1-2)

 B   "save [yšᶜ] your servant"; "be gracious to me [ḥānnēnî]" (vv. 2-3)

  C   You Lord (ʾattâh ʾădōnây), abounding in love (wĕrab-ḥesed) (v. 5)

   D   "the day of my trouble" (v. 7)

    E   incomparable greatness of God's being and action (v. 8)

     F   international homage (v. 9)

    E'   the greatness of God's being and works (v. 10)

   D'   "the insolent rise up" (v. 14)

  C'   You Lord (ʾattâh ʾădōnây), abounding in love (wĕrab-ḥesed) (v.15)

 B'   "be gracious to me [ḥānnēnî]"; "save [yšᶜ] the child of your serving girl" (v. 16)

A'   request; imperative "show" (v. 17)

The undivided heart is able to thank God wholly (vv. 11-12). The prayer closes as it began, repeating the opening expressions, your servant, have mercy, save (vv. 2-3, 16). The frame around the central verses sets in relief the excellent form of prayer, praise. Psalm 86 reaches great heights and depths, from God's glory seen by all nations to the depths of the nether world, a metaphor for the psalmist's distress (vv. 9, 13).

Psalm 86 opens like a typical complaint; a cry for help, almost like a litany, is formulated with imperatives and motives for God to intervene. The danger or disgrace is indeterminate. The motives are the psalmist's misery, devotion, trust, persistent prayer, and God's nature (vv. 1-5). The latter, "you . . . are good and forgiving, abounding in steadfast love to all who call on you" (v. 5), resounds like a liturgical formula that finds a variant in v. 15. Other motives are God's goodness, indulgence, immense mercy, and swift response to the anguished prayers of all who call upon him. The requests for help are resumed at the end where the tone of confidence prevails. The poet contemplates God and gets lost in the fascinating reality, forgets the disgrace in the vista of broader horizons (vv. 8-10). God is not just any god among others but the great God, the one and only (see Pss 40:5; 71:19; 77:13; 83:18), incomparably marvelous. A personal motive is added, God's attention and rescue when the psalmist was in serious danger (v. 13). In this psalm which soars in the heights of praise and universal recognition of God, one must not forget the affliction. The "sign," ʾôt, which the poet requests is double edged; favor for the poet is defeat for the adversary (v. 17). The poet seeks not only deliverance from trouble but also formation of the self, "give me an undivided heart to revere your name" (v. 11). He or she acknowledges that even faith and faithfulness depend on instruction and personal integration.

Psalm 87
City of God and Mother of Peoples

With Psalm 87 the poet ushers the reader onto the stage of prophecy as Zion is proclaimed the home for all nations. The structure is straightforward: God's choice of Zion as a dwelling (vv. 1-3) and Zion, the birthplace of all (vv. 4-7). The roll call of all who recognize God as universal sovereign begins, surprisingly, with Judah's classic arch-foes, Egypt (the mythical Rahab; cf. Isa 30:7) and Babylon, the oppressors of the Exodus and the exile. These two, located opposite one another with Israel in the middle, embrace the fertile crescent. Once they have completed their historical mission, they too will "know" or "recognize" God. Jerusalem's universal destiny will attract them to her, as citizens of a remodeled world. The same applies to the historical enemies, warring Philistia, proud and wealthy Tyre, and remote Ethiopia (*Cush* in Hebrew), who join the parade of the citizens in Zion. Ironically, each name is fraught with negative memories. The psalmist strips them of their foreign status, and, shockingly, makes them naturalized citizens. The emphatic repetition of "this one was born there" refers either to diaspora Jews or to gentiles, no matter where they live, who acknowledge God and thereby have a birthright in Zion. Other texts speak of foreigners or immigrants incorporated into Israel (e.g., Isa 14:1; 56:3, 6-7). Closer to Psalm 87, a late prophetic text reads, "Many nations shall join themselves to the LORD on that day, and shall be my people" (Zech 2:11; cf. 14:16-18). Jerusalem will be an open, universal capital, consolidated in the worship of one God, enjoying predilection as God's dwelling. The newcomers' true home is the place where God has bestowed preferential love.[23]

The city is addressed, "O city of God," *ʿîr hāʾĕlōhîm*. Based on this distinction, the city of the one true God, Zion enjoys universal prominence. The psalmist has a taste for the plural—(holy) mountains (v. 1; NRSV reads a singular), gates, dwellings, glorious things, peoples, singers and dancers, springs. All this is concentrated on one God, one city, a parade of individual (representative) nations passing by in single file for registration. The relation of birth with Zion, that is, full citizenship,

---

[23] Verse 7 is elliptical and the meaning uncertain, literally, "Singers like dancers, . . . all my water-sources [or origins] are in you."

erases the differences of race, culture and language, religion; Philistines, Tyreans, Ethiopians are converted into brothers and sisters, family members of Israel, against whom they were previously hostile. This psalm erases even the origins marked by oppression and impurity like those of Egypt and Babylon, personifications of violence, brutality, injustice. Almighty God, who takes the census, inscribes these unlikely partners as faithful, with birth rights in the capital.

Psalm 88
My Companion Darkness

Psalm 88 has three movements: call for help with the description of affliction and social ostracism (vv. 1-9); a barrage of questions (vv. 10-12); another call with a description which ends in isolation (vv. 13-18). The third movement parallels and projects graphically the anguish of the first. The points of contact are evident:

vv. 1-2, opening plea	v. 13, renewed plea
vv. 1, 9, day (in Hebrew)[24] and "night"	vv. 13, 17, "morning" and "day"
vv. 3-6, the dead and its regions	v. 15, the dead, *gwᶜ*
vv. 6, 9, "regions dark" *(maḥšāk)* and "eye grows dim"	v. 18, "darkness" *(maḥšāk)*
v. 7, "your wrath," *ᶜălay . . . ḥămātekă*	v. 16, "your wrath"; *ᶜălay . . . ḥărônekă*
v. 7, flooding	v. 17, flooding
v. 8, companions shun, *ḥrq* (Hiphil)	v. 18, society shuns, *ḥrq* (Hiphil)

The poet, who prays day and night (vv. 1-2, 9b, 13), is insistent because darkness and death are closing in and there may be no tomorrow.

Intense physical pain, death's imminence, and psychological duress engrave Psalm 88 with a definite texture. Suffering is an effect of God's anger (vv. 6-8, 14-16, 18). As if this were not enough, the poet is deprived of human compassion (v. 8, 18). The troubled soul, which wanders ceaselessly along the frontier of death, demands a hearing. The word *nepeš* is translated "soul," but not as a Greek philosophical concept, the person's spiritual component. It refers to the individual as a living, breathing person, and highlights the aspects of desire and affection, just as, elsewhere, *bāśār*, translated "flesh," highlights the carnal

---

[24] The reference to day has been left out of the NRSV; literally the elliptical expression might be translated "By day I cry for help; at night [I cry] in your presence" (v. 1).

aspect. The range of vocabulary associated with death is remarkable, and the images are lively and pathetic: the threshold of the abyss (Sheol), en route to the pit, a sickbed among the dead, forgotten by God, in murky darkness (literally, "in the dark places, in the depths," v. 6), drowning in the breakwaters of God's wrath, repugnant to acquaintances, shut in, eyes clouded over with sorrow. The tug of gravity is real, and the poet senses death's company, where a relation with God is unthinkable (vv. 3-6). In eloquent, impressionistic strokes the poet intermingles the psychological and physical symptoms.

God must intervene, because if the patient dies God's praises will be lessened (v. 10; cf. Pss 6:5; 30:9; 115:17). God's providence does not reach the dead, "they are cut off from your hand" (v. 5). This line of reasoning is etched vigorously in the parallel rhetorical questions in which death appears with various images (vv. 10-12), the dead, shades, the tomb, Abaddon (the realm of the dead; cf. Job 26:6; 28:22; Prov 15:11— even the name sounds ominous), darkness, the land of the forgotten (a unique expression). In this wave of anguish the psalmist wonders, as he or she convinces God to intervene, whether *ḥesed* and faithfulness (*ʾĕmûnâh* or *ʾĕmet*), God's deputies, reach death's realm (v. 11; cf. Ps 57:3, 10), whether God has any power there. This challenges God to act quickly. The worst tragedy would be existence in Sheol. Silence reigns there, oblivion and darkness. The dead "go down to the Pit," they "lie in the grave" (vv. 4-5). In Sheol or Abaddon, "regions dark and deep," people are cut off from God's memory or providence. Furthermore, death is a process experienced even in life. It is a consuming fire ("wrath," *ḥārôn*, v. 16), and a flood which rushes on, envelopes and swallows its victim (vv. 7, 16-17). Death is a big vacuum, a dark world with no exit, a "land of forgetfulness," where *ḥesed* is not found and praise is not heard (vv. 10-12). The inhabitants of Sheol lie in the grave, do not get up, do not praise. From youth the psalmist has been terrified of such an inert existence (v. 15). God is the actor in this deadly drama—"you remember no more," "[y]ou have put me in the depths," "[y]our wrath lies heavy upon me," "you overwhelm me," "[y]ou have caused my companions to shun me; you have made me a thing of horror," "you cast me off," "you hide your face from me," "[y]our wrath has swept over me; your dread assaults destroy me," "[y]ou have caused friend and neighbor to shun me" (vv. 5-8, 14, 16, 18). With all this in the poet's scope, another aspect of God comes into view— "your *ḥesed*," "your faithfulness," your wonders, your saving help (vv. 11-12).

The expression translated "I am like those who have no help" (v. 4b) is more poignantly understood "I am like a hero without strength." The Hebrew word *geber*, "hero, warrior," connotes strength and courage, which results in the oxymoron, a strong man without strength. The repeated expression, "You have caused . . . to shun me" (*hirḥaqtâ . . . mimmennî*, vv. 8, 18), doubles the poet's loneliness. The terrible question, why? is repeated; "hide your face" expresses divine unconcern or even anger (v. 14; cf. Ps 10:11). "Fire" and "water" is an unlikely pair. In Hebrew *ḥārôn* means literally "fire," and the metaphorical meaning is "[heat of] anger" or "inflamed wrath" (v. 16; cf. Jer 25:38). Together fire and water symbolize the misfortunes which God sent. In v. 7, *ḥēmâh*, a different word translated "wrath," is again in conjunction with "fire" (cf. Pss 66:12). These composite images aggravate the mental pain and create the sensation of drowning (vv. 7, 16-17). Each has a great capacity for destruction. Fire sweeps through and ravages, waters envelop and drown. The anguished poet feels like the object of this impersonal cosmic destruction. He or she concludes with a sense of desolation and darkness from which there is no relief. The phrase is elliptical in Hebrew, reading, literally, "my companions . . . dark place." It is necessary to supply a verb "are." A personification nicely satisfies the context, "my companion is darkness" (v. 18; cf. vv. 6, 9, 12).

Each reference to time—day and night (v. 1); "by day [Hebrew]" (or "all day," v. 9); "in the morning" (v. 13)—is associated with a cry for help ("all day long," v. 17, is the exception). The first verse is badly translated in the NRSV, "when, at night, I cry out in your presence." This is a case of a double-duty verb, "I cry out," and a double-duty preposition, "in your presence," and thus a translation should represent the insistence of the prayer, "by day I cry out [in your presence], at night [I cry] in your presence." The earnest hope is that the prayer "come before" God, that God "incline [his] ear" (v. 2). The psalmist is watching the clock, yet the suffering is so intense that one is unable to discern God's approach. Morning is the propitious time to receive God's favors (v. 13; cf. Pss 5:3; 30:5; 57:8). But dawn for the poet does not bring the light of God's face.

This complaint is one of the most desolate in the Psalter. The sustained tone from beginning to end is like that in Psalms 39 and 120. According to the caption, where the words *Mahalath* and *Leannoth* might be translated, this is a prayer during an illness. It reflects the anguish of a critically ill patient at the limit of physical and spiritual energies. In the theology of much of the Hebrew scriptures sickness is attributed to God's anger, provoked by guilt (see, for example, Ps 38:1-8). However, in this case there is no reference to guilt, which heightens the anguish as the poet prays insistently for help and for God to reveal the reason for this plight. The absence of the motif of a certain hearing, typical of the complaint, is conspicuous. The ending is tragic, a sick person, desolate and depressed. The prayer ends on the grim note, "darkness"

(v. 18; cf. Job 10:21-22), and gives no hint of God's response. Only the hope that God will act, the "God of my salvation" (v. 1), sustains the desperate patient.

Psalm 88 is distinguished for what is lacking. The absence of any confession of guilt, either explicit or implicit, means the personal tragedy is unjustifiable. There is no real description of the adversary or hostile action. Is the reader to suppose that God is the source of aggravation? The content of the request is not specified. There is no pledge of a thanksgiving offering, because where the suppliant is going it would be unthinkable. Psalm 88 is neither an anguished, uncontrolled cry nor an urgent, emotional outburst of an agonizing poet; it is a carefully composed poem pleading with God to intervene. The psalm ends. Light was the first of God's creation; the poet's last encounter is with darkness.

Psalm 89
Complaint Over God's Promise to David

Verbal connectors between Psalms 88 and 89 are steadfast love (*ḥesed*) and faithfulness (*ʾĕmûnâh*) (88:11; 89:1, 2, 14 [*ʾĕmet*], 24, 33, 49). The questioning tones (with the repetition of *str*, "hide"), addressing God's distance, are similar (88:14; 89:46). Psalm 89 concludes Book Three and has a prominent position in the Psalter. It stands as the counterpart to Psalm 2 with its divine decree that the anointed is God's answer to the hostile nations, that human leadership has failed.

The king in Psalm 89 represents the community in the request for deliverance from oppressors. A hymn acclaiming the God of the covenant ends as a complaint about Israel, whose king and people have been abandoned by God. Do the victims at first wish to forget their disgrace by singing (v. 1)? God's *ḥesed* is manifest in the covenant (vv. 3-4, an oracle). The universal sovereign founded the world with incomparable acts of *ḥesed* (vv. 5-18). God anointed David as king and promised *ḥesed* to his descendants (vv. 19-37, a second oracle). However, the present crisis contradicts God's loyalty to this covenant which seems to have been canceled (vv. 38-45). What was forever chosen has been rejected. The king prays that God remember him and the promise to David's line (vv. 46-51). The plot of Psalm 89 is this reversal of fortune, which reaches its climax in the final reproof.

An inclusion frames the psalm, the expression "sworn [or "swore"] to David," *nišbaʿ lĕdāwid* (vv. 3, 49; cf. v. 35), reinforced by *ḥesed* and "faithfulness" (vv. 1, 49). The pair *ḥesed* and *faithfulness* (*ʾĕmûnâh* and the synonym *ʾĕmet*) appears seven times. Parallelism confirms their synonymy, and thus the connotation of *ḥesed,* translated "steadfast love," is loyalty. God's favors are literally acts of *ḥesed.* These attributes and the interwoven themes of vv. 1-37 are absent in the description of the present crisis (vv. 38-51), until the question, "Where is your *ḥesed* . . . your *faithfulness* you swore to David?" (v. 49). Because these are divine attributes, associated with durability and consistency, the final plea becomes more poignant.

The language for God's sovereignty weaves the first parts together: "forever," *lĕʿôlām* (vv. 1, 4; cf. vv. 28, 36, 37); "as firm as" and "establish," *kwn* (vv. 2, 4; cf. v. 37); synonyms *śym,* "stand firm," and *ʾmn,* "endure" (vv. 28, 29, 37); "established" and "build," *bnh* (vv. 2, 4); and "to [for] all generations," *lĕdōr wādōr* (vv. 1, 4). Two pairs of attributes characterize God's rule, righteousness and justice, *ḥesed* and faithfulness. The first is the platform of the divine throne (v. 14; cf. 97:2); the second, God's royal escort, which accompanies the king (cf. vv. 14, 24). The longevity of the royal line is based on *ḥesed* and fidelity. God, not human merit, guarantees its permanence (vv. 3-4, 14, 24, 28-29, 36-37). The theme "forever" and "all generations" makes God's silence particularly painful.

The first part is symmetrical, and the language highlights the central declaration. The oracle is introduced with *ʾāz,* "then," and continues (vv. 19-20):

> Then you spoke in a vision to your faithful one, and said:
> "I have set the crown on one who is mighty,
> I have exalted one chosen from the people.
> I have found my servant David;
> with my holy oil I have anointed him."

The concentric structure can be charted:

A   vv. 1-2, *ḥesed* and faithfulness (*ʾĕmûnâh*)

   B   vv. 3-4, God's eternal covenant; "I have sworn to David"

      C   vv. 6-8, God's incomparable rule

         D   vv. 9-10, God's rule and "mighty arm" (*zerôaʿ*); the "sea," *yām*

           E   v. 13, God's mighty arm (*zerôaʿ*), hand (*yād*) and right hand (*yāmîn*)

              F   v. 14, *ḥesed* and faithfulness (*ʾĕmet*), God's escort

                 H   vv. 19-20, beginning of the oracle which consecrates David

E' v. 21, God's hand *(yād)* and arm *(zerôaʿ)*

     F' v. 24, faithfulness *(ʾĕmûnâh)* and *ḥesed,* the king's escort

       D' v. 25, David's rule, his hand *(yād)* and right hand *(yāmîn);* the "sea," *yām*

         C' v. 27, David, first among earthly rulers

       B' vv. 28-37, God's eternal covenant; "I have . . . sworn to David" (v. 35)

    A' v. 33, *ḥesed* and faithfulness *(ʾĕmûnâh)*

The structure shows that David's sovereignty is derived from God's. As God defeated and crushed (verb *dkʾ*) his enemies, so he will defeat and crush (verb *ktt*) David's (vv. 10, 23). Repeated assertions about the permanence of the covenant and David's rule (vv. 28-29 , 33-37) frame the conditions of civil disobedience which warrant punishment (vv. 30-32):

> If his children forsake my law . . .,
> then I will punish their transgression with the rod. . . .

A major division follows the oracle. The negation is signaled by "But now" (adversative *vav,* v. 38), followed by the emphatic "you" (Hebrew *ʾattâh*),[25] as the poet faces the painful reality which contradicts the oracle about David (vv. 38-45). Fourteen verbs express God's decisive action against the anointed (you have spurned, rejected, angered, renounced, defiled, broken, ruined, exalted, gladdened, turned back, removed, hurled, cut short, covered), plus one negative action, which is equivalent to the others, "you have not supported him" (v. 43). The overthrow implies that righteousness and justice, the foundations of the divine throne, have not been operative in the king's rule (v. 44).

Psalm 89 concludes with two grievances, expressed as interrogatives, and a plea to "remember" (vv. 46-47, 48-51). The first interrogative, "how long?" is accusatory; it questions whether this measure of God's wrath is justified, given the brevity of human existence in comparison to God's eternity. Another question ("where" is *ḥesed?*) and the imperative "remember" presses God to consider the suffering God's enemies heaped on the king. The aim is to convince God to withdraw the anger and act in the king's favor. The use of pronouns shows that an affront against David is an attack on God—"your" servant, "your"

---

[25] In the first part the emphatic pronoun "you" (Hebrew *ʾattâh*) occurs seven times as an address to God (vv. 9-26).

enemies, and "your" anointed.[26] These grievances painfully conclude this psalm.

God's cosmic activities are acclaimed (vv. 9-13; cf. 74:13-15). The psalmist identifies Rahab, chaos personified, with the Red Sea, which opposed Israel's liberation. Like Leviathan (Ps 74:14; Isa 27:1; see also Isa 51:9-10), Rahab is a legendary marine monster which God defeated when he created and organized the world. Sky and earth embrace the universe. The polar extremes, another merism, embrace the horizontal plane. "North and south" in Hebrew are proper names, Zaphon and Yamin, two mountains in the Lebanon. If their memories are associated with the pagan shrines on them, their mention implies the subordination of their deities to God. The mountains Tabor and Hermon (both in Galilee, but not specifically Jewish) intone the hymn.[27] In these verses (except v. 12) the pronoun "you," *ʾattâh,* opens successive lines (as in 74:13-17). God is complete strength, arm and hand ready for action.[28] After the cosmic display of power, the psalmist considers Israel's election (vv. 15-18). God guarantees royal prerogatives (vv. 19-37; cf. 2 Samuel 7, which describes David's coronation), anointing, protection, victory, adoption, personal and dynastic security. Individual kings may be punished, but the dynasty will continue.

God speaks twice (vv. 3-4, 19-37); the symmetrical structure adds formality to the oaths:

A	B	
I made a covenant	with my chosen (v. 3a)	
A¹	B¹	
I have sworn	to David my servant (v. 3b)	
C	A²	B²
forever	I will establish	your descendants (v. 4a)
A³	C¹	B³
I will build	for all generations	your throne (v. 4b)

---

[26] The Hebrew text reads "remember, O LORD, the taunt of your servants [plural]" (NRSV translates a singular "servant"), and then shifts to the singular, "I bear in my bosom the insults of the peoples" (v. 50). The shift from "servants" to "I" exemplifies the solidarity between the people and the anointed.

[27] The poet likes pairs. Others are the left and right hands (vv. 13, 25), righteousness and justice (v. 14), sea and rivers (v. 25), sun and moon (vv. 36-37), scepter and throne (v. 44).

[28] God's mighty arm and hand acts in creation and history (vv. 10, 13, 21); the spread of the king's hands embraces the territory (v. 25); the hands ("power") of Sheol and the enemy threaten the king's life (vv. 42, 48).

The verbs of v. 2 are repeated in reverse order (v. 4)—*bnh* (establish), *kwn* (NRSV "as firm as"), *kwn* (establish), *bnh* (build). The symmetry of the oath is repeated in vv. 19-20, which celebrates David's coronation:

A	B
I set the crown	on a warrior (v. 19a)
A^1	B^1
I exalted	one chosen from among the people (v. 19b)
A^2	B^2
I found	David my servant (v. 20a)
A^3	B^3
with holy oil I anointed	him (v. 20b)

Symmetry imposes solemnity. Also in vv. 28-29 the poet establishes a congruence between David ("him"), the "covenant," "his line," and "his throne," all of which are guaranteed "as long as the heavens endure" (v. 29).

Four synonyms for "law" are parallel in the casuistry of vv. 30-31. The structure is

A	B
If his children forsake	my law
B^1	A^1
and according to my ordinances	they do not walk
B^2	A^2
If my statutes	they violate
B^3	A^3
and my commandments	they do not keep

In the apodosis, the punishment (parallel lines) is inflicted "with the rod" and "with scourges" (v. 32); both are calibrated and programmed. The people will be punished for noncompliance, but the covenant will not be revoked, a promise reinforced by parallel lines of another quatrain (vv. 33-34):

A	B
my *ḥesed*	I will not remove from him
B^1	A^1
I will not be false	to my faithfulness
B^2	A^2
I will not violate	my covenant
A^3	B^3
and what went forth from my lips	I will not change

The oracle concludes with a return to the theme of the perpetual dynasty (vv. 35-37; cf. vv. 4, 29). The dynasty's disappearance would be akin to breaking the contract with the sun and moon in respect to time.

The poet contrasts the present, depressed situation with the glorious promise (vv. 38-45). In jarring contradiction to the preceding oracle, the poet describes complete destruction. He or she even accuses God of allying with the enemy; the expression "exalted the right hand of his foes" is the opposite of what God is supposed to do (v. 42; cf. vv. 13, 25). The scepter and throne refer to the king (v. 44). The change of clothing (verb *ʿṭh*, "to clothe," v. 45; cf. 104:2; 109:19, 29; Zech 3:4-5) in the expression "you have covered him with shame" signals a change of dignity, the change of state from ruler to conquered or slave. The complaint aims to move God to intervene.

Ḥesed and faithfulness are as enduring as the heavens. The humiliating present does not negate their effective outreach. It is easy to sing of God's eternal *ḥesed* when everything is going well. The difficulty is to sing of it in adversity. This is the paradox of Psalm 89. A quantum leap separates the opening "I will sing of your steadfast love, O LORD, forever" and the ending, "where is your steadfast love of old, which by your faithfulness you swore to David?" Thus, in a negative way and with a rebuke, the initial song of God's *ḥesed* continues. The theme is constant, even if the song is transposed to the minor key of a complaint. Psalm 89 is about the anointed, David's legitimate descendant, and the poet expresses an unquenchable hope based on the divine promise and fidelity. Thus, the psalm lends itself to messianic and eschatological interpretations.

A doxology attached to the psalm closes Book Three of the Psalter (v. 52; cf. Ps 41:13).

Book Four

(PSALMS 90–106)

Psalm 90
God's Eternity and Human Frailty

The plaintive question "How long?" bridges Books Three and Four (Pss 89:46; 90:13). Psalm 90 occupies a crucial position in the Psalter. After Books One—Three have charted the failure of the Davidic covenant, Book Four opens with an emphasis on God's sovereignty,[1] with the resounding acclamation that the LORD reigns. The dominant collection is Psalms 93, 95–99, which affirms God's sovereignty (93:1; 95:3; 96:10; 97:1; 98:6; 99:1). Formulaic expressions and other similarities are common to these psalms.

Psalm 90 is the only psalm attributed to Moses in the caption (cf. the song of Moses in Deut 31:30). The term "man of God" is applied to Elijah, Elisha, and Moses, each of whom represented hope and fidelity to his contemporaries. The poem is framed by the divine designations LORD (ʾǎdōnāy) and God (ʾēl or ʾělōhîm). The final request, "prosper the work of our hands," forms a thematic inclusion with the initial mention of God's creative works, the mountains, the earth, and humankind (vv. 1-3, 17). At the beginning the poet unfolds three concepts and repeats them in reverse order, framing them by the emphatic Hebrew "you," ʾattâh (vv. 1, 2):

A	B	C
"you" (God)	"in all generations" (time)	"mountains" (place)

C'	B'	A'
"earth and the world" (place)	"everlasting" (time)	"*you* are God"

God's eternity is contrasted with fleeting human life. The assembly laments the troubled lot of the individual ("us," ʾěnôš) and the species

---

[1] McCann, *Theological,* 1993, 155. The caption of Psalm 90 attributes it to Moses, who appears seven times in Book Four, (cf. 99:6; 103:7; 105:26; 106:16, 23, 32), and elsewhere in the Psalter only in 77:20.

("mortals," *běnê–ʾādām*). The dust from which God formed the human never loses its hold on us (v. 3; Gen 2:7; 3:19; Sir 14:17-18), and the divine sentence evokes Adam's sin. From God's telescopic perspective a millennium is ephemeral, like "yesterday" and a night watch (v. 4). A whole day passes with the mention of night watch and "dream," dawn *(bōqer)*, morning *(bōqer)*, evening (vv. 4b-6).[2] The four verbs focus on the transitory plant which flourishes, is renewed, fades, and withers (v. 6). As unexpectedly as life sprouts, it disappears; this makes God's intervention urgent.

"[Y]our anger" (*bĕʾappekā* and *ʾappekā*) and "your wrath" (*baḥămātĕkā* and *ʿebrātekā*), frame the second section (vv. 7-11). Chronic guilt sparks the divine wrath, thus making time even more of a cause for mortals fretting. The allotted seventy or at most eighty years is almost nothing, and even a long life passes quickly and wearily (the theme of Ecclesiastes 1–2; cf. Sir 18:8-10), while God precedes creation and embraces all time.

The imperative mood dominates in the third section (vv. 12-17)—teach, turn, have compassion, satisfy, make us glad, manifest, prosper (repeated). Suddenly, the poet turns from addressing God to speaking about God, "Let the favor of the Lord our God be upon us" (v. 17a). He or she requests knowledge, relief, compensation for bad days, favor, and prosperity. The repetition of *šwb* articulates both the complaint and the appeal to humans and God to repent; "You *turn* humankind back to dust," "*Turn back,* mortals," and "*turn,* and have compassion on your servants" (vv. 3, 13).[3] Reckoning life's brevity is akin to obtaining wisdom (v. 12; cf. Ps 39:4-6) and amounts to knowing how best to negotiate life's span without incurring God's wrath which shortens life even more. The poet asks God to refresh the diminishing life at daybreak *(bōqer)* with love and joy, to compensate for the sad days and years (vv. 14-15). The concluding plea is urgent because life is so brief. This line of reasoning is also developed in Ps 102:9-14, a prayer for Zion's restoration.

The poet employs a remarkable range of metaphors—the birthing of the created world (v. 2), the return of mortals to dust (v. 3), frail human life compared to a night watch or a dream that disappears upon waking (vv. 4-5; cf. Ps 73:20), and grass that grows and withers in the same day (vv. 5-6; cf. Pss 102:11; 103:15-16; 129:6; Isa 40:6-8). God is a search light from which not even secret sins can be hidden (v. 8); human life is as ephemeral as a weary sigh (v. 9b). Temporal duration gradually shrinks; from perpetuity ("in all generations" and "from everlast-

---

[2] In vv. 5-6 the MT is obscure, but the brevity of human life is affirmed; cf. Ps 102:11.

[3] The mortal returns to dust (a cognate of *dkʾ*), which is related to "contrition" (Ps 34:18; Isa 57:15) and has a double meaning in the present text.

ing to everlasting") the focus gradually narrows to "a thousand years," yesterday, "a watch in the night," morning, evening (vv. 1-6). Then the focus expands, "our days," our years, the life span (vv. 9-10). After posing the question "How long?" the scope again expands from morning to "all our days" and the days and years of affliction (vv. 14-15). The human shrinks before God's immensity. The parallelism of days and years illustrates how quickly a lifetime passes. The supplicant requests that "all our days" and "our years" under God's anger receive equal consideration in divine favor ("as many days . . . as many years," vv. 9, 15). Adverbs "before," "soon," "[h]ow long?" and verbs bespeak fleeting time ("is past," "sweep [them] away," "fades and withers," "are consumed," "come to an end," "are soon gone," and "fly away"). Even so, the poet requests that his or her works be solid, enduring; "prosper [*kwn*] . . . the work of our hands" bespeaks stability and firmness. To the divine work, *pā‘āl*, glorious power, *hādār*, and favor, *nō‘am*, responds the prosperity of human work, *ma‘ăśîm* (vv. 16-17). God's action gives human work consistency and success.

It is meaningless to apply the usual ways that humans measure time to God who is limitless duration (v. 4). The morning of God's *ḥesed* opens to countless days (v. 14). The introductory themes continue throughout the composition, but God's compassion and *ḥesed* work a metamorphosis, transforming dust into rejoicing. In the end, this is the poet's hope. In contrast to the incessant changes and life's swift course, God is a perennial, unchanging current which relieves misery. The psalmist surveys the horizons of time, looks back and ahead, but fixes on the present, "You are" (v. 2). He or she does not request pardon but rather wisdom to accept the human lot and divine compassion for human misery. God has set the limits to human life; it is left to the human to give it meaning. God's short speech commands the human to return, and the command moves in two directions, "Turn back, you mortals"—to the earth from which you were formed or to God whose image you are. The spatial image is unusual; God is a permanent "dwelling place" *(mā‘ôn)*. God, our dwelling place, invites us to return (v. 3).

Psalm 91
Security Under God's Protection

Psalm 91 has two movements. First the poet addresses the individual and invites trust in God (vv. 1-13). Reassurance comes in the form of a divine oracle (vv. 14-16). Something happens in the composition after v. 8. The poet addresses God with the emphatic "Because you," *kî-ʾattâh,* and repeats vocabulary from the beginning, "refuge" *(maḥsî),* Most High and LORD (vv. 1-2, 9). The divine epithets, *ʿelyôn,* "Most High," and *šadday,* "the Almighty," are secondary to the personal relationship with God whom the *orante* knows by name, LORD (v. 2), and all these designations inspire confidence. The poet invites the person who lives in God's presence to take refuge in him and receive guaranteed protection from all dangers (vv. 3-8, 10-13)—hostile attacks (vv. 5-6), pestilence right and left (vv. 7, 10), animal threats and all they symbolize (v. 13). Expressions like "who live in the shelter of the Most High" signal a temple setting.

The divine oracle (vv. 14-16) endorses the trust of those who find refuge in God. The affirmation "I will be with them," *ʿimmô-ʾānōkî* (v. 15), is centrally positioned amidst seven verbs: I will deliver, protect, answer, "I will be with them," rescue, honor, satisfy, show. Thus the poet describes God's response to those who love, know, and call on God's name. The oracle is solemnized by the chiasm (v. 14):

A	B	C
[me]	one who loves	I will deliver him/her

C'	B'	A'
I will protect him/her	who knows	my name

Love, ḥšq, is affectionate (cf. Gen 34:8; Deut 21:11); to "*know* my name" is to enjoy a personal relationship, so that one can *call* on God. Those who commend themselves to God can be utterly transformed. A striking formula for God's commitment to adherents is "When they call to me, I will answer them; I will be with them" (v. 15). The people take the initiative and God's response is guaranteed. None of life's threats will prevail. The martial language "rescue" and "protect" clashes with the intimate term *(ḥšq)* which connotes cleaving, yearning, desiring and binds God to the poet.

Initially the poet employs four divine titles, the Most High, the Almighty, the LORD, my God. This anticipates another foursome and dominates them. They pose a considerable threat, and their sequence follows a design, as shown here:

A	B	A	B
terror by night	arrow by day	pestilence in the dark	destruction at noon

Some ravages operate under cover of night; others like a well-aimed arrow, need the light of day. Altogether they pose a round-the-clock threat. Another foursome is comprised of two groups of lions (animal royalty) and the sinister "adder" and "serpent" (v. 13). Other threats are "the wicked," a generic reference to human assault, "evil" and "scourge" (vv. 8, 10). The dangers include premeditated entrapment, epidemic, night and day demons, ambush or military assault, stumbling, lions, the serpent. Some are quaintly specific, as "the snare of the fowler" or "dash your foot against a stone" (vv. 3, 12). These perils, which represent every possible assailant, correspond to angels which ensure protection along the way, an allusion to the Exodus (v. 11; cf. Ps 34:7). The angel metaphor can be explained by Exod 19:4; Isa 63:9, whereas to "dash your foot" simply alludes to the perils of travel along the rocky terrain in Palestine (Pss 35:15; 37:31; 38:16; Prov 3:23). With the expressions "near your tent" and "all your ways" the poet claims that God protects any sojourner who inhabits or traverses danger zones (vv. 10-11). Divine protection is articulated by two motifs, shelter and path. A well-protected, inaccessible shelter means help, shade, wings, shield, and immunity. The temple is an image of a secure relation with God, the best guarantee against any threat. The complement to this is the path for which God sends a special escort. Evil spirits besiege the shelter as an arrow may be shot in the open; wild beasts stalk along the path and more sinister animals can bite or sting in the shelter. In the temple God provides the protection; while traveling the angels do the same (cf. Exod 23:20; 32:34; 33:2). Pitfalls may be spiritual or physical. In either case God is a refuge, a shield, a sanctuary, and he provides angelic guards. The traveler will be unscathed from any threat, for God is both guard and escort, and the wicked will be duly punished (v. 8). This psalm reflects no notion that suffering is divinely inflicted or the reward of wickedness.

Metaphors bespeak God's protection (v. 4). The feathers and wings cover and protect (the verb *skk*) and, referring to a bird, they symbolize solicitude and intimacy (cf. Deut 32:11). But there is more. The wings are those of the cherubim atop the ark, a place of asylum and legal immunity (cf. Pss 17:8; 36:7; 57:1; 61:4; 63:7). Their outspread wings are the visible throne of the invisible God, an image which gives the poem a liturgical flavor. As God's winged throne covers the ark, so God protects the faithful. God as "dwelling place" (v. 9; cf. Ps 90:1) recalls the opening verse, "the shelter of the Most High," and alludes to the asylum God offers. The image enlarges the horizon beyond time and space. Anyone who trusts in God has the right of asylum. Thus, any person within the faith community may be addressed. The sanctuary is transcended (v. 9); "the Lord" and "the Most High" is our refuge and support. A single image in God's oracle, to "show them my saving power," tells of God's rescue, and possibly refers to a contemplative experience (v. 16, as in Ps 50:23). The declaration "in whom I trust" sets the tone for the poem. In the end, God's oracle confirms the poet's words and guarantees the protection that the poet has announced. Those who love me and know my name I will protect, and, even more, I will answer when they call, I will be with them, rescue and honor them, give them long life and salvation. What more can a devout person desire?

Psalm 92
Thanksgiving for God's Just Governance

Psalms 91 and 92 are of equal length. Psalm 91 ends (vv. 14-16) with God's oracle and in Psalm 92 (after the caption) the psalmist extols giving thanks to God. "Most High," *ʿelyôn,* is common to both (91:1, 9; 92:1). Psalm 91 expands the theme of God as refuge (vv. 2, 9; see v. 4) and Psalm 92 ends with confidence in God, the rock (v. 15).

Psalm 92 is the only psalm assigned by the Hebrew caption to a particular occasion, the Sabbath. The sevenfold repetition of the divine name and an inference of creation may be the reason for this connection (vv. 4-5). The Sabbath anticipates the final rest, the eternal Sabbath, when creation is complete and God's enemies are defeated, a victory which Psalm 92 anticipates and celebrates. It may be divided into three movements, introduction (vv. 1-4), the contrast between the wicked and the psalmist (vv. 5-11), and the announcement of the recompense of the just (vv. 12-15). In the first two the psalmist addresses God, then he or she turns to the assembly and reaffirms trust in "our" God (vv. 12-15). The psalm is framed by an inclusion, it is good to *declare* the LORD's *ḥesed* and faithfulness, and the just like the trees *declare* ("show") "that the LORD is upright" (vv. 2, 15; *ḥesed* and "faithfulness" are synonymous with "the LORD is upright"). The joyful tone is introduced by "It is good," followed by affirmations that broadcast God's splendid works. The affirmation, "you, O LORD, are on high forever," is framed between the prediction of the destiny of "evildoers," *pōʿălê ʾāwen* (vv. 7, 9).[4] These two verses with three lines each frame the central declaration:

—the wicked sprout like grass

—evildoers flourish

—they are doomed forever

—you, O LORD, are on high forever

—your enemies, O LORD

---

[4] The fourth of seven occurrences of the divine name is in v. 8 (central). The designations for God, *ʿelyôn* (v. 1) and *ʾĕlōhîm* (v. 13), steady the frame.

—your enemies shall perish

—all evildoers shall be scattered

The poet describes the rapid growth and destruction of the wicked and, in the middle position, the LORD appears, sublime and eternal. Opposition to God will perish and with it the poet's enemies. The psalmist is allied indisputably with God, and he or she calls God's adversaries "my enemies," those who attack "me." The repeated use of *pʿl* heightens the contrast between God's great *works* and the transitory evil *workers* (vv. 4, 7, 9). The contrast is further intensified by the images of flourishing grass and God's "highness." Meanwhile, the devout continually give thanks and praise, "in the morning" and "by night" (v. 2). Musical accompaniment, notably strings, underscores the joyful mood (vv. 3-4). That these are references to liturgy is incontestable (morning and evening sacrifices, liturgical instruments; see Num 28:4; Ps 141:2; Psalm 150).

The images clash with each other, "the strength [literally, "horn"] of a wild ox" and delicate, aromatic ointment (v. 10). The horn symbolizes strength (cf. Pss 75:5, 10; 89:17), while oil represents the refreshment offered a guest or the consecration of a royal figure (Pss 23:5; 45:7). As in wisdom literature the poet contrasts the destinies of the wicked and the just (vv. 5-6). To the plant image of the wicked corresponds the plant image of the righteous (repetition of *prḥ*, "flourish" or "full of sap," vv. 7, 12, 14). The wicked flourish like grass, but the just flourish like the palm and cedar, contrasting transience and stability. The tree compared with the just occurs also in Pss 1:3; 37:35; 52:8; Jer 17:8. What is unique about the image here is that the palm tree and the Lebanon cedar are transplanted to the temple. The foolish cannot understand God's profound purpose, that the wicked are destined for punishment, while the just flourish and bear fruit even in old age (vv. 7, 9, 12-14). Just as the wicked thrive, their tragic and sudden end has been determined, and this is in sharp contrast to the righteous destined for God's loving regard. The poet is an ear and eyewitness to this fact (v. 11).

The palm and the Lebanon cedar are as beautiful as they are distinct from each other. The palm, straight and knot-free, supple and graceful as a jet stream with an umbrella top, fruit-bearing and long-lived, contrasts with the sculpted beauty, resilience, and opulent needles of the majestic cedar. Both trees evoke the idea of transplanted, fresh growth, fertile throughout the years. By an optical trick the poet superimposes the arboreal image on the upright person in the temple, and tree and person fade into each other and exchange features. The just person in God's house is sturdy, thrives and bears fruit even in advanced maturity. Just so the palm and the cedar take root, flourish, bear fruit in old age, and proclaim that "the LORD is upright." The cedar has no fruit, a fact which accentuates the interplay of image and reality. In the end the poet tells how the good people will be rewarded, in comparison with the fate of the wicked, who have an amazingly quick growth but wither just as quickly. The conclusion underscores the main idea; God's just governance is a guarantee for those who trust in him.

Psalm 93
The LORD Is Sovereign, Girded with Strength

The poet of Psalm 93 acclaims the eternal sovereign (v. 1), the stability of the world and God's throne (v. 2), God's effective rule over rebellious chaos (vv. 3-4), and the permanence of God's rule and the lasting holiness of his house (v. 5). The sovereign is both spoken about (vv. 1, 4) and addressed directly (vv. 2-3, 5), and this change of address echoes alternating solo and choral voices in the liturgy. In the end the poet declares the implications for humanity that flow from God's nature.

Both static and dynamic qualities, "majesty" and "girded with strength," apply to God (v. 1a). The heavenly throne corresponds on earth to the temple where God dwells. Permanence is imprinted on the make-up of the stable world, which is befitting of holiness, for God's house is there. God's governance of the world corresponds to the heavenly order. By divine decree the covenant is reliable in ordering human life.

Framed within the references to stability[5] and unbounded time (vv. 2, 5) is what is most unstable yet immense and ageless, the thundering breakers of chaos which constantly threaten to destroy creation but are checked by divine power (vv. 3-4).[6] The firmness of God's throne guarantees security against unpredictable chaos. The poet compares the primeval floods to God's majestic power because they represent the chaos from which the world was brought forth and established (Ps 24:1-2; Job 38:8-11). The composition is marked by an exceptional number of triplets—three times God is clothed, girded (v. 1); there are three declarations of stability in reference to the world, the throne, and divine decrees (vv. 1-2, 5); the clause "the floods have lifted up" (v. 3) is repeated three times; expressions for time, "from of old," "from everlasting," and "forevermore" or, literally, "for length of days" (vv. 2, 5);

---

[5] The expressions "established" and "never to be moved" (*kwn*, vv. 1-2) and "very sure" (*ʾmn*, v. 5) are synonymous.

[6] An image of mythic origins, the primordial ocean opposes the order imposed by God. In Israel's creation story God's effective word replaces the battle. An image of God's dominion is control over chaos, symbolized by the sea (see Pss 74:13-14; 89:9-10).

the cosmic strata, consisting of the world (*tēbēl*, the continental mass that rests on the earth's pillars), the sea, and the heavens ("on high," *mārôm*); the majestic, rising flood, the sea's awesome strength, and God (v. 4); God's appurtenances, "your throne," "your decrees," and "your house." To the three assertions of the world's firmness, the stability of God's throne, and God's agelessness correspond the concluding triplet, God's sure decrees, the holiness of "your" house, and "LORD, forevermore" (vv. 1b-2, 5). The repetition and tripling of parts adds to the solemn tone of the celebration.

The poem is replete with images and metaphors. God is garmented with majesty and might (v. 1; cf. Isa 51:9; 52:1; 59:17; 61:10; Ps 104:1; Job 40:10). In the poet's cultural climate ordinary apparel was free-flowing, and energetic activity required gathering and tying up the folds of the tunic to ease movement. To be "girded" means to be ready for action. God's reign is not measured in years but exists both before and beyond them (v. 2). The "throne" is a metaphor for sovereignty and justice (Pss 9:4; 89:14; 122:5). God is "on high," *bammārôm*, beyond the space measured by humans (v. 4c). The temple expresses holiness, because God resides there (v. 5). The word *ʾaddîr*, translated "majestic," may also designate a robe (v. 4c; Josh 7:21, 24; 1 Kgs 19:13, 19; 2 Kgs 2:8, 13; Jonah 3:6; Zech 13:4), but the sea where the Egyptians perished is also *ʾaddîr*, "mighty" (Exod 15:10). Thus the multivalent word associates God's robe of strength and the divine power over rebellious powers.

This hymn celebrates God's victory over chaos and the world's foundation. The royal theme dominates. The LORD is sovereign, inhabits a palace, is enthroned, clothed regally with power, pronounces immutable decrees. As a liturgy Psalm 93 contemplates the created world and the laws which govern it, and this inspires the poet to recognize and extol the divine sovereign. It was probably sung in connection with some festival, perhaps the fall Sukkoth, which recalls creation, praises God's sustenance and extols divine sovereignty. In the LXX the caption designates Psalm 93 as the hymn for the day before Sabbath when, according to Genesis 1, the world was populated. The LXX and the Talmud understand it as unifying the themes of creation and God's reign, and thus it is a fitting transition to the following psalms which celebrate God's reign.

Psalm 94
"Rise Up, O Judge of the Earth" (v. 2)

Psalm 94 is divided by the beatitude "Happy," *ʾašrê* (v. 12). The two halves are related to each another as crisis to relief. This division is strengthened by eight explicit references to God in each half. A thematic inclusion frames the poem—"give to the proud what they deserve" and "repay them for their iniquity" (vv. 2, 23). Repetitions and correspondences give a sense of coherence to the whole (vv. 5, 14; vv. 6, 21). Drama is felt as the poet alternately addresses and speaks about God. He or she asks rhetorical questions (vv. 3, 8, 9, 10, 16, 20) which lend a tone of impatience to the poem. The question "how long [ʿad– mātay] shall the wicked triumph?" is echoed in the scolding, "fools, when [mātay] will you be wise?" (vv. 3, 8). The poet addresses the fools (vv. 8-11) and enters into an introspective monologue with God very close by, "Happy are those whom you discipline, O LORD . . ." and "your steadfast love, O LORD, held me up" (vv. 12-13, 18b). The concluding plural "LORD *our* God" supposes a communal setting (v. 23).

The double address "God of vengeance" is unique. God is the court of final appeal (v. 2, as in Pss 50:1-6; 82:8; cf. 7:6; 9:7-8, 19). Anadiplosis, or repetition of words or phrases, is a regular feature of Psalm 94. Besides the opening epithet, other examples are the agonizing questions "how long?" and the unwavering confidence that God "will wipe out" the wicked (vv. 3, 23). Such emphatic repetition gives prominence to key lessons on the nature of God, the intolerable nature of human suffering, and certainty about the ultimate downfall of evil.

The wicked who thwart justice boast about their crookedness (vv. 3-7). They cheat the defenseless, and the height of their pride is their sneer that God is oblivious, that he neither sees nor understands (rʾh and byn, v. 7). On the contrary, God, who made the eye, sees (nbṭ) and knows (ydʿ) (vv. 9-11). The poet rebukes these dullards and rallies the devout to faithfulness (vv. 12-15). Then, in a startling leap expressed in a rhetorical question, the poet represents the people's complaint of "the righteous" (vv. 16-19). Just as God has defended, rescued and comforted the poet, so may the divine judge vindicate the oppressed righteous. Previously God intervened to prevent one from descending to "the land of silence" (v. 17). In the end one is confident that human injustice can neither compete against nor ally itself with the judge of the earth; in a decisive moment God will intervene to annihilate its perpetrators. It is not really "vengeance" that the poet desires, but a rigid application of justice in human relations and the righting of an order that had been seriously violated.

The wicked are a focus of special concern. They are "the proud," "the wicked," "dullest of people," "fools," "evildoers," "wicked rulers." Their arrogant words and deeds are given prominence; they boast, "crush your people," "kill the widow and the stranger, . . . murder the orphan," "contrive mischief by statute," "band together . . . and condemn the innocent to death." The judges are unjust and partial, and the legal system is corrupt (vv. 15, 20; cf. Psalms 58 and 82). The victims are identified as the usual classes of the defenseless in society, who are assaulted openly and without recrimination (vv. 5-6, 21). The wicked conceive of an absentee God who created the world yet stays aloof from human affairs (vv. 8-10; cf. Pss 10:4, 11, 13; 14:1). But in reality, the "God of vengeance" and "judge of the earth" designed and molded the ear and the eye, disciplines nations, teaches humankind, discerns secret thoughts, consoles and protects. Far from being inactive, God assumes a decisive role in righting the wrong and will abolish the wicked with their wickedness (v. 23).

The poet reasons that the creator cannot be inferior to creation and must possess the same faculties that he confers on humans. History confirms that God disciplines nations. The reasoning, "He who disciplines the nations . . . does he not chastise?" recalls the prophetic oracles, which teach that violation of the moral law is a recipe for disaster. The repetitions of "discipline" *(ysr)* and "teach" *(lmd)* articulate the meaning. The poet, like Job, does not believe in a correlation between suffering and sin. On the contrary, he or she holds the view that God allows the innocent to suffer. The delay in God's judgment is explained. God disciplines his people and teaches them with the law, while a pit is prepared for the wicked who live in apparent prosperity (vv. 12-13). The "land of silence" refers to a place where there is no possibility of calling on God (v. 17; cf. 88:10-12). Ironically, what the poet feared for him or herself is actually the destiny of the wicked. God disciplines like a parent (Deut 8:5; Prov 3:11-12). The Hebrew root that underlies the translation "knowledge," *daʿat* (v. 10) refers to religious and moral instruction, not just to the development of intellect. Rather than a penalty for sin, suffering may express God's parental love, which tests one's character and provides the moral fiber to bear adversity. But the psalmist is confident that the wicked will be repaid and tyranny overthrown. Even as the anguished poet asks "how long?" he or she knows that God tells time and perceives human urgencies differently.

The Greek caption (not in Hebrew) reads "A psalm of David for the fourth day of the week." Rabbinical tradition assigns Psalm 94 to the temple liturgy on Wednesday. It shares a theme with Psalm 82, the liturgy for Tuesday, and supplements it. Both psalms treat of the systemic evil that leaders inflict on society. Psalm 94 grapples with the lack of transcendent vision and, consequently, the lack of a lofty destiny of the unprincipled power mongers. In contrast, those whom the Lord disciplines and teaches are beatified.

Psalm 95
Today Listen to God's Voice

Psalm 95 opens in a festive mood, with procession and joyful praise. The scene is set and suddenly, God, the one who is being celebrated, speaks and chills the festive air. Thus ends the psalm. Psalm 95 has two kinds of discourse, invitation (vv. 1-7) and oracle (vv. 8-11). It begins like a hymn with invitations to join the celebration (vv. 1-2, 6), followed by the reasons for doing so (vv. 3-5, 7a). Two imperatives, "Come," mark the beginnings of two strophes, in which seven invitations (a number signifying totality) are extended to the assembly. The invitations are rendered mostly in the NRSV with "let us." The Hebrew of v. 6 has three, "let us worship . . . bow down . . . kneel." In each strophe the motive for worshiping is explicit. After four invitations the first motive, introduced by *kî*, "for," focuses on the creator (vv. 3-5). God created everything on the vertical axis, "the depths of the earth" and "the heights of the mountains," and his hand formed the horizontal plane, consisting of the sea and dry land. The second motive is that (*kî*, "for") "he is our God and we" the flock he tends, an Exodus theme (v. 7a). Among the invitations is the phrase "the rock of our salvation," another echo of the Exodus (v. 1). The final invitation is grounded in the fact that God made us, which sums up the creation motif (v. 6b). This is followed by the covenant formula, "he is our God, and we are the people of his pasture," which connotes salvation (v. 7a; cf. Lev 26:12; Deut 7:6; Hos 2:23; this formula occurs mostly in the exilic prophets). Thus, the themes are presented in parallel fashion:

A	B	C
v. 1, "come, let us sing . . .	to the rock of our salvation"	vv. 4-5, God's majesty in creation

A	C	B
v. 6, "come, let us worship . . .	the LORD, our Maker"	v. 7, covenant allusion

The oracle recalls events during the Exodus. The initial chorus, which is accompanied by music and choreography, contrasts with the sober mood of the oracle.

The assembly is rallied to hear God's voice, which is introduced by "O that today you would listen to his voice" (v. 7b). The oracle advises against doing what Israel did in the desert. Unresponsive and calloused, the Exodus generation did not listen to God, which caused them to be denied admission to their promised home. The implication is clear for the present generation which is covenanted with God. God is "the great king," creator of the universe and shepherd of the people; if they heed the divine voice they will be the beneficiaries of the promise.

A contrasting use of language marks the poem. Two poetic lines are framed by "hand[s]," *yād* (vv. 4-5). The NRSV of v. 7 follows the Hebrew and reads "the sheep of his hand." The first two hand references portray God's comprehensive embrace of the cosmos and God's closeness to sculpted creation. The panorama is traced with depths and heights, sea and land. If the earth's depths are in his hand, if the dry land was shaped by his hands, how much more the chosen people, his flock. Synonyms for the verb *make* are employed effectively. God made *(ʿśh)*, fashioned *(yṣr)*, the sea and dry land and created *(ʿśh)* us, the pinnacle of creation (vv. 5-6); the ancestors rebelled, even though they had seen God's *works* (*pĕʿālîm*, a synonym of "make," v. 9), which comprise creation and redemption.[7] There is a wordplay with "Massah," which means "testing." The clause "that *today* you would listen to his voice" is menaced by "the *day* at *Massah* [testing]" when "your ancestors *tested* me" (vv. 7b-9). The past serves as a corrective warning, "Do not harden your *hearts [lēbāb]*, as at Meribah," a generation whose *hearts [lēbāb]* strayed (v. 10). (Meribah means "discord"; thus "at Meribah" makes one think of "that place of discord.") The real threat is that the same will happen to the present generation if the people do not mind their hearts. Finally, there is a contrasting use of *bwʾ*, "come" or "enter" (vv. 6, 11). At first it invites the worshiper into God's presence, and finally it denotes the worst fate of God's people, "They shall not *enter* my rest."

The imagery is exquisite. The "rest" meant originally the promised land, which is God's resting place (cf. Deut 12:10; 25:19; 1 Kgs 8:56). In the present context it connotes peace with God, as the people are reminded where their true rest is. "Anger" (v. 11) is a metaphor which expresses God's incompatibility with evil of any kind, manifested in the punishment of the guilty. It images the all-holy God's reaction against all that infringes on the divine majesty and perfection. In Ezek 16:42, it is described as a passion which must be satisfied before it can be quelled. The Israelites attributed to God all the calamities that befell them; God's "anger," far from an emotional outburst, is the divine justice which automatically punishes sin (2 Chr 19:2; Nah 1:6).

Worship implies an attitude of listening and right disposition, and carries with it a severe warning against imitating the behavior of ancestors who had experienced the greatest wonder of all, deliverance at the Red Sea, and yet paid no attention. That generation was eliminated

---

[7] "My work" (v. 9) possibly refers to the miracle of water at Meribah, but, because it is a plural form, more plausibly it includes all God's mighty deeds in saving and sustaining Israel. The LXX also uses the plural form, *ta erga mou* ("my works").

from the promised land. The forty years of desert sojourn is the punishment of God disgusted with the people's noncompliance in the divine plan. What is implied is that residence in the land and the divine protection is conditioned by the people's disposition of listening. Their obtuseness will cause them to forfeit the inheritance. The author of the New Testament Letter to the Hebrews (3:7–4:11) quotes Ps 95:7-11 to warn against the danger of weariness, hardness of heart and giving up, as the poet urges believers to trust in God.

Psalm 96
Praise of The Creator, Sovereign of the Universe

Verbal connections between Psalms 95 and 96 are "great" is "the LORD," *gādôl yhwh* (95:3; 96:4); "the LORD . . . king," *yhwh melek* (95:3; 96:10); "above all gods," *ʿal–kol–ʾĕlōhîm* (95:3; 96:4-5). Each voices the (plural) invitation to approach God for worship (95:1, 6; 96:1-3, 7-10). The invitation is followed by the motive introduced by *kî,* "for" (95:3, 7; 96:4-5). The repeated exhortation of Psalms 96–99 is to celebrate God as sovereign.

A version of Psalm 96 appears in the context of David's bringing the ark to Jerusalem (1 Chr 16:23-33). It has a definite shape. Three times the summons (vv. 1-3, 7-10a, 11-12) is followed by the reason or content of praise (vv. 4-6, 10b, 13). The flow of the psalm is better appreciated in Hebrew than in the NRSV; there are three waves of invitations, as shown here:

vv. 1-3	invitation with six imperatives, sing (three times), bless, tell, declare
vv. 4-6	*kî* (twice), followed by the motive, which consists of titles, attributes, and attendants
vv. 7-10a	invitation and eight imperatives, ascribe (three times), bring, come, worship, tremble, say
v. 10b	the world is firm, and the government is just (introduced by *ʾap*)
vv. 11-12	five jussive forms invite: let . . . be glad, rejoice, roar, exult, sing
v. 13	double *kî,* followed by the motive, which amounts to God's universal rule

The humans are rallied with imperatives; the natural elements (heavens, earth, sea and field with everything in them, trees) are summoned with jussives ("let . . ."). In sum, God is the greatest, and the universal government is equitable. Creation, which attests to the goodness and power of the creator, is to join humanity in praise. God's reign is the motive for all creatures to rejoice. Rival gods are nil (vv. 4-5; cf. Pss 115:3-8; 135:5-7, 15-18). Divine attributes are personified as escorts and courtiers (v. 6; cf. Ps 89:14, 24). God made the heavens, which are summoned to rejoice (vv. 5, 11); may the earth be caught in the joyful praise as well (vv. 9, 11). Based on the LXX, an alternate understanding of the difficult text of v. 9a, translated "in holy splendor," is "in his sanctuary," understanding the created world. Parallel lines would argue for this:

> Worship the LORD in his sanctuary;
> tremble before him, all the earth.

The composition turns around the number seven and its multiples. Fourteen imperatives invite the assembly to worship (vv. 1-10), and the use of the synonyms "peoples" and "nations" (ʿammîm and gôyîm) totals seven. After the proclamation "The LORD is king" (v. 10), the effects of this reign are described in seven facets, which encompass the world's stability, fair government, heavenly and earthly rejoicing, and the echoes through sea, field, and forest. The word kôl, "all," resounds seven times—all the earth, peoples, gods, trees, and all that fills the sea and field. Everything and everyone is included in the praise, all except the gods, who are mere nothings.

The liturgical phrase "a new song" signifies the renewal of praise (v. 1; cf. Pss 33:3; 40:3; 96:1; 98:1; 144:9; 149:1; Isa 42:10). Various actions comprise the invitation—sing, bless, tell, broadcast, revere, acknowledge, offer, worship, tremble, say, exult, rejoice, resound, sing joyfully. Some verbs are pure praise; others are oriented towards proclamation or underscore the effect which God and the divine attributes produce in creation. The act of salvation to be broadcast is not specified (v. 2). Although sovereign forever, God is manifest in decisive action and establishes a just reign in the world (v. 13). Besides praise of the universal sovereign, this beautiful poem breathes the religious universalism which Isaiah announces, the gospel of salvation to be proclaimed. Praise and proclamation go hand in hand.

Psalm 97
The Universal Sovereign

The verb špṭ, which means "to judge equitably" or "to set things right," is a verbal link with the cognate mišpāṭ, "judgment" or "justice"

(96:10, 13; 97:2, 8). Psalm 96 has five invitations ("let . . .") which rally creation to celebrate (vv. 11-12); the two invitations of Ps 97:1 complete the septet which began in 96:11. Psalms 96 and 97 are related as the arrival (97:2-6) is to the news of the arrival (96:13). Link words between these two are "his glory," *kĕbôdô*, in each case in the multinational arena ("nations," *gôyîm* and "peoples," *ʿammîm*, 96:3; 97:6) and *ʾĕlîlîm*, "idols" and "all gods," *kol–ʾĕlōhîm* (96:4-5; 97:7, 9). The land (earth or mountains) reacts before God's presence (96:9; 97:5). Together in the two psalms the explicit references to God total twenty-one, a multiple of seven, which designates fullness.[8]

Psalm 97 is framed by inflections of *śmḥ*, rejoicing and gladness, and cognates of *ṣdq*, righteous[ness] (vv. 1-2, 11-12; cf. v. 6). It begins with a double invitation to rejoice and ends with a double invitation, addressed to the righteous, to rejoice and thank God's name (v. 12; cf. v. 8). The division is tripartite: an invitation to praise and a description of God's apparition (vv. 1-5), diverse reactions and the frustration of the idols (vv. 6-9), and a reflection and the concluding invitation to rejoice (vv. 10-12).

The poet first turns to the horizon and invites the earth's farthest reaches, the "coastlands" or "islands," to rejoice at the proclamation of the LORD's reign. The repetition of "[all] the earth" (vv. 1, 4, 5, 9) and the reaction to God's sovereignty forms a picture of a world which is gradually brought under the sway of the eternal sovereign. The meteorological twins, clouds and darkness, parallel the ethical twins, righteousness and justice, and the effect is a symbolic portrait of God's sovereignty (v. 2). In Ps 89:14 these two are the foundation of God's portable throne (cf. Ps 9:4, 7-8). In naming these two as the throne's platform, the poet highlights what the prophets understood as the qualities of God's rule, right order and correct behavior, which sustain the world's equilibrium and are concrete realities to build on. Remove these and the world is shaken to its foundations (cf. Ps 82:5).

Heaven heralds God's righteousness to which all peoples are witness and before which idolaters are shamed (vv. 6-7). The proclamation ("righteousness") is made in Zion and echoes throughout Judah (v. 8a). The poet does not suppress the enthusiasm and in a singular exclamation addresses God—"because of your judgments, O God"—essentially summing up the content of the proclamation, God is the universal

[8] To the seventeen occurrences of the Tetragrammaton are added twice "his name" (96:2, 8), once "Lord," *ʾădôn* (97:5), and Most High, *ʿelyôn* (97:9). What the NRSV translates "his holy name" (97:12) is literally "to the memory of his holiness," or "his holy memory," *lĕzēker qodšô*.

sovereign and "exalted far above all gods" (vv. 8b-9). The benefits of this rule are announced in five phrases, God loves, guards, rescues, illuminates, and gladdens (vv. 10-11). In the initial theophany, the effects of God's actions were perceived rather than God himself, who was surrounded by thick darkness and clouds, from which fire and lightning emanated. In the end, "light dawns" for the righteous,[9] "and joy for the upright of heart."

God is seated on a throne set on righteousness and justice, which is canopied by darkness. One can see the principles of this rule but cannot gaze on the divine face. The chain reaction to the announcement "The LORD is sovereign" reverberates through clouds, lightning, mountains and even touches the sky (v. 6).[10] Fire shoots out from God and consumes all opposition. Lightning, earthquake, and melting mountains shake up the scene.[11] Lightning is linked to the earthquake as cause to effect. The cosmos registers the aftershock. God's power is manifest in the storm and in volcanic eruption, which commonly accompany a theophany. The spotlight moves vertically to the heavens and back to the horizon from which peoples view the cosmic quake (v. 6). The description of God and his surroundings (repetition of *sbb,* translated "all around" and "on every side") is extensive, registering seven cosmic reflexes, a plenitude (vv. 2-5), which culminates in the heavens announcing God's righteousness and the people caught in admiration of the "glory" (v. 6; cf. Ps 19:1). The unusual doublet attracts attention; the heavens *proclaim* and the peoples *see* (one would expect "hear"). In the righteousness or, better, right order, which is imprinted in the heavens, all peoples can contemplate God's glory. Reactions are mixed; with rejoicing for some and shame for others. The adversaries are unnamed; they might be the idolaters or the wicked (vv. 3, 7, 9-10). In any event, little space is ceded to the idols. Clearly if the cosmos and the peoples react with such enthusiasm, any agent of dissent will be shamed. All God's comings image the principal coming, the advent of the Messiah. It is easy to apply this psalm to the definitive moment of the Messiah's triumph—a final epiphany, frightening for some, light and joy for others, when justice and right conduct will extend to all corners of creation.

---

[9] By a change of one consonant, the Hebrew "light *is sown,*" *zrˁ,* becomes "light *dawns,*" *zrḥ* (v. 11).

[10] Water, so often leagued with chaos and death in Hebrew thought, is noticeably absent.

[11] Typical features of a theophany are found in Judg 5:4-5; Pss 18:7-15; 50:1-3; 77:16-19; Hab 3:4-6; fire, lightning, earthquake and mountains melting symbolize God's unearthly glory and majesty.

Psalm 98
The Coming of the Divine Sovereign to Judge

Psalm 98 has two movements. An opening invitation to sing (v. 1a) is followed by a well-argued motive (vv. 1b-3); a second invitation to natural elements accompanied by musical instruments (vv. 4-8) is concluded by the motive (v. 9). The first movement gives more space to the motive; the second movement cedes more to the participants and instruments of the choral praise.

God is fully present in the text, six times designated as "LORD" and once as "our God"—seven times in all. Like its near cousin Psalm 96,[12] this "new song," is stamped with seven plural imperatives, invitations to celebrate the LORD as sovereign (vv. 1-6; v. 4b might be translated, literally, "break forth *[pṣḥ]*, shout joyfully *[rnn]*, praise *[zmr]*"). In addition, the poet uses three jussives ("[let . . .] roar . . . clap . . . sing," vv. 7-8) to invite the created world to join in widening ripples of praise. A total of seven verbs invites the whole world to praise, with special mention of the sea, marine creatures, floods and hills, accompanied by three musical instruments (lyre, trumpets, and horn). The motivation for this solemn celebration is expressed in seven action verbs ("done [marvelous things]," "gotten [him] victory," "made known," "revealed," "remembered," "is coming," "will judge"). What began with Israel, reverberates to all earth's inhabitants and the natural world.

The first invitation has a universal scope, as it announces God's victory or *salvation* (cognates of *yš'* occurring three times) on Israel's behalf. This was the exclusive work of God, his "right hand and his holy arm" (cf. Ps 89:13), images that portray the victor in military guise. It is not clear what constitutes the victory, but the parallel lines of vv. 2-3a give a hint, "he has revealed his vindication in the sight of the nations." The word translated "vindication" (NRSV) is *ṣĕdāqâh*, which connotes "justice" (Gen 18:19; Isa 5:16). This may refer to a specific act of deliverance as in the Exodus or the liberation from Babylon, or it may be a general term for divine interventions throughout history. Nothing prevents it from referring to eschatological intervention on God's part. Whatever the case, it is clear from the following verse that God "has remembered his *ḥesed* and faithfulness to the house of Israel," that God has fulfilled the ancient promise.

The second invitation has an orchestral interlude. The choice of musical instruments is telling. The lyre is an instrument strummed by David and the Levites. The shofar ("ram's horn") announces the begin-

---

[12] Compare Pss 98:1a and 96:1a; 98:7-9 and 96:11-13.

ning of a feast or the arrival of the Sabbath and was principally used by the Levites. The shofar and trumpets appear together only here and in Hos 5:8. Trumpets, too, had a liturgical function at a later period (cf. Sir 50:16-19). They were used in the service of the temple and were played by priests or Levites (2 Kgs 12:13; 1 Chr 16:42; 2 Chr 5:12). Thus, this celebration has a universal, choral, and liturgical dimension. In the continuation nature is invited to chime in, water, the world *(tēbēl)* with its inhabitants, and land (vv. 7-9). The sea's constant, undulating din, the clapping sound of rapids, and the soft strains of breeze in the hills are incorporated into the music, like water or wind as a background to Gregorian chant or classical music. Inanimate creatures are personified in the floods' and hills' applause which echoes the clamor of the sea. The climax is God's arrival to judge the world with righteousness and fairness.

The declaration, "He has remembered his steadfast love and faithfulness to the house of Israel," is framed by the word *victory (yĕšûʿâh)*, the public domain, and the verb "revealed" or "seen," as shown here (vv. 2-3):

a his victory, *yĕšûʿâh*

    b in the sight of the nations

        c he has revealed

            d . . . his *ḥesed* and faithfulness to the house of Israel . . .

        c' have seen

    b' all the ends of the earth

a' our God's victory, *yĕšûʿâh*

This psalm represents a tension between the particular and the universal, the preeminence of Israel and its acknowledgment in the international arena. In Psalm 96 God was "the LORD," without other determinations, that is, the absolute and universal sovereign. In Psalm 98 God is also "LORD," but at a certain moment he is "our God," clearly the God of Israel (v. 3). Israel's victory is coherent with the divine nature. God is faithful to the promise, and his abiding *ḥesed* for Israel is revealed to all the world (*ḥesed* and faithfulness are God's escort in Ps 89:14). God's power is irresistible, and the victory will have an effect in the international theater. God's arrival will bring about a just and fair government for all people.

Psalm 99
Praise the Holy Sovereign, Our God

The first and last words of Psalm 99 can be fused together to state the theme, the LORD is sovereign and our God is holy. The interchange between speaking about God and the people, addressing God, and addressing the people, is constant, as can be seen here:

vv. 1-2   declaration about God and the people

vv. 3-4   address to God, with the exception of "Holy is he"

v. 5   invitation to the people

vv. 6-7   declaration about the people and God

v. 8   address to God

v. 9   invitation to people (repeated substantially from v. 5)

The assembly responds with a solemn acclamation ("holy") three times. The change of address is typical in liturgical texts.

Before God's stable reign the nations and the earth quake (v. 1). Yet, in contrast to the universal outlook of the previous psalm, Psalm 99 is decidedly Israel-centered. The poet extols the greatness of the divine sovereign for equity and justice in Jacob's behalf (vv. 1-5; compare v. 4 and Ps 98:9). The scope narrows in naming the famous leaders, the pillar of cloud, and the holy mountain where the liturgy is celebrated (vv. 6-9). The earthquake and the "holy mountain" recall the Sinai revelation and actualize that experience for the present worshipers "in Zion" (vv. 1-2). The focus is on the place of worship. God's throne and footstool is the cherubim above the ark in the temple (vv. 1, 5, 9; cf. Ps 80:1; Exod 25:18). From here God's governance fans out to embrace the world.

The triple repetition of "Holy is he," expanded the third time, and the triple invitation to praise and extol God is a basic liturgical refrain built into the structure of the psalm (vv. 3, 5, 9), dividing it into three strophes. Parallel lines argue that God's "footstool" is identified with the "holy mountain" where the cherubim throne is in the temple (vv. 5, 9). God is thrice holy, in his majestic rule, in giving the law, and in administering justice and mercy. The initial portrayal shows God enthroned on Zion, sovereign over the earth and all its peoples (vv. 1-3). The continuation concerns God's relation to Jacob (Israel), the first to call him "our God" (vv. 5, 8, 9). Psalm 99 is seven times punctuated with the name of the LORD, which four times forms part of the phrase

"LORD, our God." The remarkable use of pronouns with reference to God (not required by normal Hebrew syntax), four third person and three second person—seven in all, is also unusual: *"he* [is exalted]" (v. 2), "[Holy is] *he"* (vv. 3, 5), *"you* [have established equity]; *you* [have executed justice]" (v. 4), *"he* [answered them]" (v. 6), *"you* [answered them]" (v. 8). "Holy" appears four times, and there are four proper names, Jacob, Moses, Aaron, and Samuel, of which three are privileged ministers in the divine king's court. For the enigmatic threesome, the simplest explanation may suffice. Moses is mediator of the law, Aaron represents the priesthood, and Samuel the prophets. The three are "priests . . . who called on his name" (v. 6), and each exercised an intercessory role between God and the people.

The foundations of God's throne, justice and equity, are established in Jacob (v. 4; cf. Ps 97:2), the funnel of God's benefactions to the whole world. From God's transcendence (vv. 1-3), to Jacob's election (vv. 4-5), to the human intermediaries in the gift of the law and the guidance of the people, God's holy presence is experienced most intensely in forgiveness and punishment, whereby God disciplines the people, erases the residue of sinful conduct, and offers them a participation in divine holiness (v. 8). God, who inspires fear and awe, is at the same time near, forgiving and just. God's distant holiness is accessible through human intermediaries.

Psalm 100
Know That the LORD *Is God*

Psalm 100 is distinct from the preceding six psalms which speak of God's sovereignty. But in its present location it may be considered the seventh in a series. Besides, it has the following points of contact with the preceding: v. 1 quotes 98:4a; the verb *r^{cc}* ("make . . . noise," v. 1 and 95:1-2); the tone of gladness ("sing," v. 2 and 97:11-12); the verb *rnn* (v. 2 and 95:1; 96:12; 98:4, 8); the entrance (v. 2 and 95:6; 96:8); sheep and pasture (v. 3 and 95:7); "thanksgiving," *tôdâh* (v. 4 and 95:2); enter the courts (v. 4 and 96:8); bless his name (v. 4 and 96:2); *ḥesed* and faithfulness (v. 5 and 98:3).

According to the caption Psalm 100 is for *tôdâh,* "thanksgiving," which refers both to the thanksgiving sacrifice and accompanying praise. Seven imperatives (a plenitude) invite "all the earth" to join the liturgy. The weight is on the fourth, the central doctrine, as shown here:

make . . . noise—worship—come

"Know that the Lord is God"

enter—give thanks—bless

God's personal name Lord occurs four times. Two parts are parallel and are composed similarly, the invitation (vv. 1-2, 4), followed by the motive clauses (vv. 3, 5). The liturgical climate is festive, although the careful composition sustains a solemn tone. The symmetrical structure consists of four plural invitatory imperatives (make . . . noise, worship, come, know) followed by *kî*, and the complement, "[that] the Lord is God"; then three more imperatives (enter, give thanks, bless) are followed by *kî*, "for," and the reason, "the Lord is good." A chart demonstrates the careful composition:

vv. 1-2   make noise, worship, come, know

v. 3   that *[kî]* the Lord is God
           he made us and we are his . . .

v. 4   enter, give thanks, bless

v. 5   for *[kî]* the Lord is good
           his *ḥesed* forever; his faithfulness to all generations

The dependent clauses of "know," introduced by *kî*, "that," are statements about God, he made us and "we are his people," his flock (v. 3; cf. Ps 95:3-5, 7). The clauses following "the Lord is good" are amplifications of this goodness, *ḥesed* and faithfulness.

The verb *ʿbd* in the expression "[w]orship [serve] the Lord" may refer to the peoples' homage toward God, or, more specifically, the liturgy (cf. Exod 3:12; 2 Sam 15:32; Isa 19:21). The imperative "come into his presence," an invitation into the temple, supports the latter (cf. Pss 95:6; 96:8; Isa 1:12). The aim and spirit of the worship is "gladness" in God's presence, the attitude of someone who has received God's blessing (v. 2). Later, the poet invites the congregation to enter the temple with thanksgiving, once again referring to the liturgy of those who have been blessed as God's people (v. 4).

The clustering and sequence of personal pronouns and (in Hebrew) pronominal suffixes is striking, as a literal translation illustrates (v. 3): "Know that the Lord, *he* is God, *he* made *us* and *his we* are, *his* people, the sheep of *his* pasturing."[13] The awareness of God awakens in the

---

[13] The Hebrew tradition preserved two alternative readings for what is translated "and we are his." The RSV, NRSV, RNAB, NJPS follow the *qere* variant supported by the Targum and some ancient Greek translations, while the *ketiv* along with the LXX and

worshiper the sense of creaturehood, and thus human self-sufficiency vanishes. As with Psalm 95 the overwhelming insight is that God is our origin, who cares for us according to a freely bestowed covenant, and thus our destiny is with God. Rather than the genesis of the human species, the formation of God's people in the Exodus is underscored (cf. Isa 29:23; 43:1, 21; 44:2; 60:21). The abbreviation of the classic covenant formula boils down to "You are my people and I am your God" (Hos 2:23; cf. Exod 6:7; Lev 26:12; Ps 95:7). The LORD's goodness consists in *ḥesed* and faithfulness (v. 5). *Ḥesed* is part of God's essence, and thus acts of grace are not the expression of some affectionate whim. The people's reliance on God is justified by God's covenant loyalty. That is what the term "faithfulness" means in the present context. The joy of worship springs from the knowledge of God's *ḥesed* and faithfulness.

Who is called to worship in Psalm 100? In this respect a relationship exists with another brief composition, Psalm 117, which addresses, "all you nations." The invitation has universal scope, "all the earth" (v. 1; cf. Pss 47:1; 66:1; 96:1; 98:4; the wording in 66:1 and 98:4 is the same as here, except for the substitution in Psalm 66 of "God" for "the LORD"). This general address is specified, "we are his people." One may recall the initial promise to Abraham and the choice of a people to be the channel of blessing for "all the families of the earth" (Gen 12:3). A choral response, "his steadfast love endures forever" (cf. Pss 106:1; 107:1; 118:1-4, 29; 136:1-26), concludes the poem. This liturgical formula transcends parochial, temporal limits and announces God's never failing *ḥesed* and fidelity.

Psalm 101
Plan of Life and Holiness

The divine name frames Psalm 101. The outline appears simple, an introduction (vv. 1-2a), followed by the poet's commitment to right behavior (vv. 2b-8). On second glance a division after v. 5 provides a thematic correspondence between two parts. As shown here, the repetitions occur in nearly the same order:

Syriac represent the alternative "and not we ourselves." The present interpretation is consistent with and better suits the context. The phrase "the sheep of his pasture" is in synonymous parallelism with "and we are his" (cf. Pss 74:1; 79:13; 95:7; Isa 40:11; Jer 23:1-2; Ezek 34:31).

A   "the way that is blameless," *bĕderek tāmîm* (v. 2a)

  B   "within my house," *bĕqereb bêtî* (v. 2b)

    C   "not set *before my eyes* anything . . .," *lĕneged ʿênî* (v. 3a)

      D   "the work [*ʿśh*] of those who fall away" (v. 3b)

        E   "evil," *rāʿ* (v. 4b)

          F   "I will destroy," *ʾaṣmît* (v. 5a)

A   "the way that is blameless," *bĕderek tāmîm* (v. 6b)

  B   "in my house," *bĕqereb bêtî* (v. 7a)

      D   "who *practices* [*ʿśh*] deceit" (v. 7a)

    C   "no one . . . shall continue *in my presence*," *lĕneged ʿênî* (v. 7b)

          F   "I will destroy," *ʾaṣmît* (v. 8a)

        E   "wicked," *rĕšāʿîm* (v. 8a)

The symmetry between two parts and the repetitions frame the central affirmation (vv. 5b-6a),

> A haughty look and an arrogant heart
>   I will not tolerate.
> I will look with favor on the faithful of the land,
>   so that they may live with me.

Each part opens with the positive good (vv. 2, 6) which is followed by the negative element to be avoided and from which the poet divorces him or herself and the efforts to eliminate evil from society (vv. 3-5, 7-8). The alternation of positive and negative elements deserves mention (vv. 2- 5):

"I will walk" (v. 2b)	"I will not set" (v. 3a)
"I hate" (v. 3b)	"it shall not cling to me" (v. 3c)
"Perverseness . . . shall be far" (v. 4a)	"I will know nothing of evil" (v. 4b)
"I will destroy" (v. 5a)	"I will not tolerate" (v. 5b)

This pattern is concluded by a double affirmation and a double negation (vv. 6-7). In this way the psalmist's decisive action is juxtaposed to the behavior to be avoided.

Like Psalms 15 and 24, which articulate the conditions for entering the temple, Psalm 101 formulates a renewal program, possibly of a ruler. It concentrates on the worshiper's attitude (vv. 2b-3, 6a). God's loyalty *(ḥesed)* and justice *(mišpaṭ)* are the foundation and model of human virtue (v. 1a), and these standards of the Mosaic covenant are confided to the interested party. The "way" is the revelation of the law (v. 2a); it is "perfect" (*tāmîm*, translated "way that is blameless") because God designed it. The opposite of "integrity of heart" (v. 2b) is "perverseness of heart" (v. 4; Prov 11:20), meaning conduct inconsistent with inner conviction, here expounded in general ("evil") and specific terms (slander, deceit, haughtiness, and arrogance). A sound heart is able to steer clear of illusions ("before my eyes," v. 3a) and avoid bad influences ("it shall not cling to me," v. 3b). After considering the attitude, the poet considers public action, insisting on the virtue of integrity and the rejection of lies and slander (vv. 4-5). The "haughty *look*" contrasts with "I will *look*," which in Hebrew is, literally, "haughty *eyes*" as opposed to "my *eyes* are on the faithful . . ." (vv. 5b, 6a; cf. Ps 123:1). Broadness of heart, *rĕḥab lēbāb*, and haughty ["on high"] eyes, *gĕbah–ʿênaym*, signify pride, avarice, ambition. The psalmist will promote the faithful and demote the deceitful (vv. 6-7). Among the list of offenses, those who commit evil with the tongue are singled out; those who slander and lie are near, "in my house," and the poet consciously distances him or herself from their crookedness. The repetition of *yšb* ("live" or "remain," vv. 6a, 7a) illustrates the contrast. The faithful will "*live* with me"; deceitful sycophants will not "*remain* in my house." The poet alludes to decisive participation in the legal proceedings (v. 8; cf. Ps 127:5), and morning is the usual time for this and for renewing one's resolve to do good (2 Sam 15:2; Job 38:12-13; Jer 21:12). His or her actions have an impact on society, "cutting off all evildoers from the city of the LORD." The psalmist implies that every honest person is pledged to preserve and enhance the integrity of the society in which he or she lives, which entails decisive exclusion of the wicked. This action begins with expelling liars and evildoers from "my house," then "in the land" and "in the city."

The opening words forge the theme, *ḥesed* and justice (*mišpāṭ*). Micah 6:8 combines these two terms in God's design for human life. "[T]he way that is *blameless*" (*tāmîm*) and "*integrity [tām]* of heart" are related verbally (v. 2). The repetition of *tām* suggests that a steady, blameless walk is born of a blameless heart. With regard to conduct, integrity refers to acts that are consistent with basic values, which in the present context are God's *ḥesed* and justice.[14] The emphasis on *heart* shows that the evils amount to more than external wrongs (vv. 2, 4, 5). The heart is emblematic of character, the moral fiber from which conduct emerges. The poet begins with praise that acknowledges a dependence

---

[14] "Integrity," *tōm* and *tāmîm*, are the primary terms in the description of the king's righteousness in Pss 18:20-30 and 78:72.

on God by which he or she can be virtuous and act with integrity. The strange question in v. 2 does not really fit with the rest of the psalm, and interpreters are uncertain about its meaning. What the NRSV translates as "When shall I attain it?" is clearer than what can be said of the Hebrew, which reads, literally, "When will you come to me?" apparently addressing God. There is a trade-off here. Just as the disciple of the "way" in v. 2a approaches God by personal dedication, he or she awaits God's response. According to this interpretation the poet relies on the source of goodness and appeals for God to reveal himself. The rest of the poem articulates the personal commitment to practice virtue, to support those in one's realm who do and oppose those who do not.

The original setting may be the ruler's acknowledgment of the responsibility as judge to promote justice in society (v. 8) and this becomes a basis for the worshiper's examination of his or her own adherence to such a standard. The responsible citizen does not simply pledge to keep the rules and oppose the unruly. He or she is committed to develop character and practice what is morally consistent, as is evidenced by references to integrity, honesty, keeping good company, and even humility (the opposite of arrogance, v. 5). The effect is the project of an ideal city and government from which evil is absent, because it is God's city.

Psalm 102
It Is Time God Had Mercy on Zion

The poet of Psalm 102 meditates on God's eternity and the salvation God offers. The setting is a national crisis, although the unique Hebrew title, "A prayer of one afflicted, when faint and pleading before the LORD," ascribes this complaint to a person on the verge of collapse. The victim is Zion, and the poet speaks for the community, like the voice of Jerusalem in Lamentations.

The first word in Hebrew, LORD, targets God. After pleading for relief (vv. 1-2), the poet energetically and at length describes the distress, which includes the enemies' scorn, personal depression, and God's rejection (vv. 3-11). The repetition of life "withering like grass" and "my days" frames the first movement (vv. 3-4, 11). After the initial petitions, God is eclipsed as the introspective poet concentrates on the present plight and laments passing existence, merely alluding to God as the remote author of the distress ("your indignation and anger," v. 10). Normally, God's anger is a reflex to sin. In the present case there is no inference of the speaker's guilt or anything that might merit such affliction. God's face is hidden, his voice drowned out by the psalmist's agitation. In Hebrew the emphatic "I" in v. 11b concludes a section which concentrates on the first person (I, me, my). The poet states emphatically, *"and I [wa'ănî] wither like grass,"* and follows with *"But you [wĕ'attâh],* O LORD, are enthroned forever." Human frailty encounters divine permanence.

At the beginning of the second movement (vv. 12-22), the emphatic "But you" (vv. 12, 13; also vv. 26, 27) signals God's reentry into the line of vision. In this movement the divine name occurs seven times, making God totally present. This insistence forges an intimacy between the afflicted and God. But unexpectedly the gaze turns to the city, Zion, beloved and equally afflicted. The repeated mention of Zion and Jerusalem provides a liturgical context (vv. 13, 16, 21), as the individual praises the everlasting sovereign, who will rebuild Zion and thus demonstrate his rule to the nations in response to the prayer of the destitute (vv. 13-17). The poet dictates an epitaph of the deliverance so that God will be praised in Zion by future generations (vv. 18-22). Repeated motifs register the pulse of the prayer—God's intervention to rescue Zion (vv. 13, 16), God's people in Zion (vv. 14, 17, 20-21), and international recognition (vv. 15, 22).

In an interlude the anguished poet repeats the reference to punishment and pleads that God relent (vv. 23-24). Finally, the poet praises the creator whose longevity guarantees future generations (vv. 25-28). In contrast to the first movement where time is encased within the poet's brief life, God's time is limited. The psalmist does not ascribe to a belief in immortality but desires the survival of God's people and their worship in the rebuilt sanctuary.

The description of the affliction includes fever, loss of appetite, weight loss, depression, insomnia, and social abuse. The malaise is compounded by the impression of God's caprice and the swiftness of life's passing (vv. 3-11, 23). Groaning gives voice to the sickly, depressed state which results in emaciation (vv. 4-5; cf. Job 33:19-21). An unclean bird (v. 6, listed in Lev 11:13-19; Deut 14,12-18) in a desert habitat is a projection of the poet's inner state, and it anticipates Jerusalem in ruins (vv. 14, 16). The bird images are ironic, because wings and birds usually symbolize freedom and flight (cf. 55:6-7), while a lonely owl in the wilderness or a sparrow twittering on the roof captures the sense of desolation, aridity, and futility and underscores failing energies, spiritual emptiness, and numbness caused by grief. Aggression magnifies the sense of isolation, and the height of insult comes when the poet's fate (his name) is wished on others as a curse (v. 8; Jer 29:22; Lam 3:14). Synonymous parallelism has a focusing effect and intensifies the impression; for instance, "I am like an owl of the wilderness, like a little owl of the waste places" (v. 6). It also magnifies the description, as in "For my days pass away like smoke, and my bones burn like a furnace" (v. 3). Where there is smoke, there is fire, and as the poet compares the passing days to smoke, he or she feels the bones weaken and likens the sensation to fire. Mourning, signified by the ashes and tears, is as much a part of life as eating and drinking (v. 9; cf. Pss 42:3; 80:5). The similes are concentrated in the first part and reappear in the last:

—my days [like] smoke (v. 3)

—my bones like a furnace (v. 3)

—my heart, withered like grass (v. 4)

—I [like] an owl . . ., like a little owl (v. 6)

—like a lonely bird (v. 7)

—ashes like bread (v. 9)

—days like lengthening shadow (v. 11)

—I wither like grass (v. 11).

—they wear out like a garment (v. 26)

—you change them like clothing (v. 26)

How can God, who is so big, resist this pathetic plea on behalf of the afflicted one who is here today and gone tomorrow?

The motif of time runs throughout the poem. The lengthening shadow (v. 11), which portends evening, symbolizes the closeness of death, even though the poet's life has only reached its mid-point (v. 24).[15] Other similes, smoke and grass, capture the sense of a swift life and an abrupt end (vv. 3, 11). How inconsistent and brief life is! It is only a shadow, less than smoke, like a breath or a sigh leaves not a trace behind (v. 3; cf. Ps 144:4; Job 8:9). Suddenly the end, which God's anger has authored (vv. 10, 23), is at hand. Human life has an expected course, and the poet has a nagging sense that he or she has not fulfilled the assigned task. God's perpetuity contrasts with ephemeral human existence ("my days," vv. 3, 11, 24 [translated as "my life"]). Relentlessly, "all day long," the poet is the butt of the enemies' taunts (v. 8). To this can be added other "day" expressions, "in the day of my distress" and "in the day when I call" (v. 2). The poet uses a special language for time; "it is *time [ʿēt]* to favor it [Zion], the *appointed time [môʿēd]* has

---

[15] The expression "My days are like an evening shadow," *yāmay kĕṣēl nāṭûy* [or *nāṭāyû*], is better understood, "my days stretch out like a shadow" (verb *nṭh*). The image is unclear, but the parallel line "I wither away like grass" gives the clue; the afternoon shadows, my days, approach evening when they will disappear.

come" (v. 13). These words signal the opportune time to intervene. In contrast to transitory creation, the eternal God outlasts earth and heavens, which can be changed like worn out clothing (vv. 12, 25-27; cf. Isa 51:6 and Psalm 90). Brief segments of time, counted off by days, contrast with longevity in the final plea (vv. 23-24; cf. Lam 5:19-21). As the psalmist contemplates life cut off in mid course, he or she petitions that the children of the faithful may continue. Because God never ages, a person can pray for mercy, for present and future security.

The individual's plight mirrors that of the city, which has been reduced to dust and ruins. The prayer of the lowly corresponds to that of the afflicted poet (vv. 1, 17); those doomed to die are like the one about to be taken in mid-life (vv. 20, 24). The poet personifies Zion's destitute population and anticipates Zion's restoration as the answer to prayer. This inspires the meditation about God's permanence, which gives hope of relief for Zion (vv. 13-17). The personal anguish makes the poet more sensitive to the national disaster, or, contrariwise, the public disaster becomes more poignant in personal suffering. In either case, both dimensions are present and because the psalm is part of a liturgical repertoire, the individual is a stand-in for the community (cf. Psalm 66). Both are found in deteriorated states and both need rescue and restoration. From v. 13 on the two are intermingled, identifying the afflicted one as Zion. The personal appeal becomes a request for Zion's restoration, so the nations may pay homage to God in Jerusalem (vv. 21-22), where God chose to be present as sovereign for the people to manifest his rule to the nations. So God's servants cherish the very stones and dirt of Zion (v. 14), where eternity touches finitude.

Psalm 102 is a prayer for help for captive Israel. It is a complaint about suffering which turns confidently to God. The poet is more concerned with the people's fate than with personal destiny. He or she, like a spokesperson, associates the individual in critical condition with the people's state. The individual's sufferings are symptomatic of the ills of the contemporary age. The cure of the whole people will have resounding effects in the individuals' lives.

Psalm 103
In Praise of Ḥesed

Psalms 102 and 103 reflect on God's eternity (102:12, 25-27; 103:17), and in each transient human life is compared with dried grass (102:3-4, 11, 23; 103:15-16). Psalm 103 begins with the individual and fans out to the community of Israel, God's dealings with humankind, and finally

to all creation. It can be divided by style and content into four movements, each of the first three featuring *ḥesed* (vv. 4, 8, 11) and mercy or
compassion (cognates of *rḥm*, vv. 4, 8, 13). Self-address and God's dealings with an individual consolidate the first movement (vv. 1-5).
Human life is the sphere of God's saving activity. The *nepeš* ("soul" or
"self") is summoned to bless the LORD, who effectively transforms life's
pains in accord with divine *ḥesed* and mercy, revitalizing the self like
the proverbial eagle, a symbol of perennial vigor and the renewal of
life. The style shifts and the poet focuses on God's ways with Israel (vv.
6-10). Thus, the close of the second movement after v. 10 is preferable to
that of the NRSV after v. 14. The third movement begins with three comparisons which elaborate the claims of the first two (vv. 11-13), then
amplifies the motif of the brevity of human existence (vv. 15-18, introduced in v. 14) and contrasts it with God's eternal *ḥesed* (inclusion,
"those who fear him" and *ḥesed*, vv. 11, 17).[16] In the final movement, introduced by a shift in subject, the poet announces God's sovereignty
over the cosmos and appeals to the celestial court and all creation to
join in blessing God (vv. 19-22). Twenty-two lines (verses), the sum of
letters in the Hebrew alphabet, hint at a wisdom motif and a comprehensive composition. The repetition of "all," *kôl*, several times at the
beginning and end reinforces the sense of completeness—"*all* that is
within me," "*all* his benefits," "*all* your iniquity," "*all* your diseases,"
"*all* who are oppressed," "over *all*," "*all* his hosts," "*all* his works," "*all*
places of his dominion." The initial warning "do not forget" states the
purpose of the psalm, to remember, celebrate, reactualize. The concluding invitations addressing angels, hosts, ministers, and all creatures,
place the psalmist in good company. The finale reiterates the opening
note, "Bless the LORD, O my soul." The poem which opened as a soliloquy ends with the soloist chanting the universal acclaim of God.

The imperative "bless," twice at the beginning and four times at the
end, frames the poem. Initially the psalmist rouses him or herself; in
the end he or she is joined by a marvelous chorus. Mercy (*raḥămîm*,
raḥûm) and *ḥesed* show up together (vv. 4, 8) and are repeated (vv. 11,
13, 17). Cognates of *gml* are repeated (vv. 2, 10), God's "*benefits*" and
God does not "*repay us according to our iniquities.*" The word *ʿôlām* is

---

[16] "Those who fear him" appears twice as an identification of the assembly ("us")
to whom the psalm is applied (vv. 11, 13); the third appearance formulates the
axiom that God does for the present generation what he does in every age (v. 17).
"Those who fear the LORD," along with the servants of the LORD, designates those
who accept God as the focus of their lives (e.g., 25:12, 14; 31:19; 34:7-10; 85:8-9). This
fear is understood as reverential love, expressed in a life consonant with the devotion to God.

repeated, denying that God's anger is *forever*, asserting that God's *ḥesed* is (vv. 9, 17). Repetitions weave the composition together and identify the major themes.

As in the previous psalm, comparisons stand out (introduced with the Hebrew particle *k-*). Verses 15-16 develop the well-known simile, "like grass" (cf. Ps 102:4, 11); but here rather than God's perpetuity, the psalmist focuses on the lasting quality of *ḥesed*. Two comparisons are altitude and distance. How high is the sky above the earth? That is the measure of God's *ḥesed* to the faithful (cf. 36:5; 57:10). How far is east from west? God will separate us from our guilt by that much. God's paternal tenderness is moved by the knowledge of our humble origins (vv. 13-14). The image of a potter is brought to mind by the verb *yṣr*, "fashion," and *ʿāpār*, "dust" or, better, "clay."[17] God fashions us from a lump of clay. Thus, no one knows better than the divine potter our fragile earthenware substance. Unless sustained by God, the human is in danger of returning to clay or dust (cf. Ps 104:29). The poet brilliantly associates the notions of creation and covenant. The brevity of the human life, like grass, contrasts with the longevity of the *ḥesed* manifest concretely in the covenant (vv. 15-18; cf. Isa 40:7-8). Tenderness rather than anger surges in the divine heart in the face of human frailty. The comparison with the eagle, which according to legend constantly renews its vigor by changing its wings (v. 5; cf. Isa 40:31; Job 29:18), is the opposite of the grass which sprouts and quickly dries and dies. The eagle is free and flies high; grass is ephemeral and earth-bound.

Ḥesed is expressed in all God's dealings, personal and communal (vv. 2, 7). The poet testifies to God's *ḥesed* and compassion in two ways. The first is a litany of benefits which stem from God, who is forgiver, healer, rescuer, the one who crowns and satisfies, and worker [of vindication] (vv. 3-6), a description composed of six participles and their complements. Forgiveness is first because the infirmities are understood as a consequence of sin. The second testimony speaks of God's ways revealed to Israel through Moses, which shows for all time how God effects justice for the oppressed. The poet alludes to Exodus 33–34, where Moses asked for a manifestation of God's "ways" (v. 7; cf. Exod 33:13), and quotes from God's self-revelation to Moses after the Israelites had committed idolatry (v. 8; see Exod 34:6-7).[18] Moses received the guarantee that, despite Israel's fickleness, God would accompany the

---

[17] The metaphor of the potter and ceramics in Gen 2:7; 3:19; Job 10:9 is apt. A potter normally works with clay, not dust. On *ʿāpār*, "clay," rather than "dust," see also Pss 7:5; 22:15; 30:9.

[18] This classic formula is quoted in Pss 86:15 (cf. also v. 5); 145:8; Num 14:18; Joel 2:13; Jonah 4:2.

people and ensure their future. In Exodus the complement is "merciful," which occurs in Psalm 103 as a noun, adjective, and verb (from *rḥm*). This liturgical formula summarizes the experience of living with God. The poet expounds the theology; God's *ḥesed*, more durable than his anger at wrongdoing, is why sinners hope for forgiveness.[19] *Ḥesed* so abounds that it surpasses time and space, as high as the heavens above the earth, the unimaginable distance between east and west, as lasting as eternity (v. 17). God's compassion or mercy *(rḥm)*, in relation to sin, checks divine anger and affords forgiveness (Pss 51:1; 77:9; 78:38; 102:13). A parent's anger at a child's failures does not last and compassion prevails (v. 13; cf. Isa 49:15). The paradox is noteworthy. What is apparently weak is stronger than what resists it. God's grace frees from sin.

God's *ḥesed*, greater than anything deserved, provides the motive for worship. The language which echoes the prophecy in Isaiah 40–66,[20] suggests that the poet has more in mind than Israel's foundation story. God's ways revealed to Moses are confirmed in the restoration after the exile. *Ḥesed* endows the individual's life, the history of the people, even the cosmos with ultimate meaning. God's forgiveness purifies and sustains the people's response to the covenant and their following God's law (v. 18). *Ḥesed* is the basis of relationship with God and the motive for living in accord with the divine will. How can what was essentially clay not respond to a love of such grand dimensions, as high as the sky, which removes sins as far as east is from west and whose tenderness and affection are as profound as a mother's and a father's for their little children. The last image in the psalm articulates the permanency, "The LORD has established his throne in the heavens" (v. 19).

Psalm 104
Send Forth Your Spirit and Renew the Earth

Psalms 103 and 104 are each framed by "Bless the LORD, my soul" (103:1, 2, 22; 104:1, 35), the only instances of this phrase in the Psalter. Psalm 103 tells of God's bountiful *ḥesed* whereas Psalm 104 speaks of the innumerable creatures sustained by God's wisdom. Together the

---

[19] Besides *ḥesed* and mercy, the theme of sin appears (vv. 3, 10, 12), and the thread of God's relation to sinners is woven throughout. Three different words for "sin" are used, *ʿāwōn*, *ḥṭ*, and *pšʿ*.

[20] Compare v. 5 with Isa 40:31; v. 9 with Isa 57:16; v. 11 with Isa 55:9; vv. 15-16 with Isa 40:6-8.

pair praise God, the savior who forgives and the creator who provides. Included among their themes is God's sovereignty (103:19-21; 104:1-4), which links them to the theme of Zion's salvation in the previous psalm (102:12-22). In Psalms 103–104 the divine name *yhwh* occurs twenty-one times, including the abbreviated form *halĕlû– yāh* (104:35). In the Hebrew Psalter three *hallelujah* psalms conclude Book Four (Psalms 104–106).

Psalm 104 celebrates God's goodness reflected in the awesome symmetry and majesty of creation. It makes no reference to Israel or her history. The scope is similar to Isaiah (cf. Isa 40:12-17) and God's whirlwind speeches in Job 38–41. The poet telescopes the *ʾereṣ*, "earth," in a sevenfold repetition. Not counting the frame "Bless the LORD, O my soul" (vv. 1, 35) and the final "Praise the LORD," the divine name *yhwh* appears seven times.[21] Between the initial and final summons, the poet intersperses declarations about God among the instances when God is addressed. The personal relation between the poet and God is apparent. He or she calls the creator "my God" twice (vv. 1, 33). The poet makes an inventory of creation, catalogues everything and assigns it all to God. Following a brief introduction (v. 1a), the poet considers God, the creator of heaven and the earthly habitat (vv. 1-9). Wildlife (vv. 10-12, 16-18) frames the domestic concern (vv. 13-15). The poet then contemplates the rhythm of day and night and their proper activities (vv. 19-23). After a transitional verse (v. 24), the poet gets lost in the description of marine activity (vv. 25-26), God the dispenser of food (vv. 27-28), the mystery of life and death (vv. 29-30), praise of God (vv. 31-32), the poem's dedication to God (vv. 33-34), and denunciation of the wicked (v. 35). What results is not a logical composition, but the poet's impressionistic contemplation.

The description is amazing. God is outfitted with cosmic accessories: a cloak of light (v. 2),[22] a palatial tent of the sky with pillars set in the primeval sea (v. 3), a cloud and the wind's wings as vehicles of transport, messenger winds and lightning servants (vv. 2-4). Creation unfolds. The waters clothe the earth and its mountains (v. 6). The dry ground is made visible by the draining away of the water which had covered it, and the law of gravity is defied as water flows up mountains and down valleys until it gathers into the bowl of the ocean (vv. 7-8). God establishes order with a "thunder" voice. The poet's gaze shifts to animal and human life (vv. 10-18). The unruly flood is commissioned to irrigate creation and provide food and drink for all creatures.

---

[21] In the Greek versions this "Praise the LORD" is placed at the beginning of the following psalm. It is the first "Praise the LORD" (*hallelujah*) in the Psalter.

[22] Light is a cloak which reveals God's majesty and conceals the divine nature.

The mention of wild animals, birds, bread, wine, oil, goats, and humans is a delicate touch. The details are picturesque. Wild asses drink, birds nest and sing, mountains are sprayed, animals are fed, humans relax with wine and refresh their skin with oil, firs are planted for storks to nest and badgers ("coneys") find their homes in the rocks. Rain has a special place among God's blessings, and it irrigates the huge trees not planted by humans. The poet freely orders reality, and thus the sun "knows" when to set, and darkness and night are separate but collaborative realities (vv. 19-20). Sun and moon mark time so wild animals can prowl and growl at night and humans till the soil by day (vv. 19-23). Thus the two are not a threat to each other. The final point in the creation recital is human labor (v. 23). Rather than a burden or curse, labor is consonant with God's work. As the poet admires God's wisdom, what catches the eye are the land and marine animals (vv. 24-26). In other contexts Leviathan is hostile to God; here it is God's toy (cf. Job 41). God is principally a provider of food (vv. 20-21, 27-28), for besides being well-ordered and awesome, creation is daily dependent on God's sustenance, presence, and breath. God creates and regulates the pulse of life and death by his *rûaḥ* or "breath" (vv. 29-30; cf. Gen 2:7; Eccl 12:7). God breathes, and creatures live; God stops breathing and they die.

The author speaks of God's joy in creation, a reflection of the divine glory. After taking a last look at the earth, convulsing under God's touch (v. 32), the poet dedicates the hymn (v. 34). Just as God's creation is pleasing to the poet, so may this poem be pleasing to God; an agreeable exchange. God who imprints the world with glory is, in turn, glorified by the human's recognition. The harmonious order of the universe is disrupted only by the flaw of sin and sinners; may they be anathema (v. 35). The last verse is a surprise. Earlier, untamed waters assaulted the land and were held back (v. 9; cf. Job 38:8-11). The discordant wish that the wicked vanish from the earth jars with the sublime hymn. Sinners and the wicked live in God's world and benefit from divine providence as all other creatures do, but their presence mars the exquisite panorama. The created world is a gift from God, but it comes at a price. In this amazing world the creator's will is to be honored in the arrangement of social life (cf. Ps 145:20). The curse against sinners surges from a desire for a peaceful world, in which divine justice is manifest and sin is no more.

In the Jewish tradition Psalm 104 is sung on the morning of Yom Kippur, as a pledge that new life will emerge out of penance and sorrow. It is chanted on the evening of the new moon, thus consecrating another month to God. It is recited from the Sabbath of the feast of Sukkoth to Passover (i.e., throughout the winter), in anticipation of new life in the spring. In the Orthodox tradition Psalm 104 is chanted at vespers at the setting of the sun, with the lighting of lamps, the beginning of the new day. Orthodox worshipers open this liturgy with this hymn which praises God's providence in all aspects of creation.

Psalm 105
God's Fidelity to the Promise

Psalm 104 is to Psalms 105–106 as Genesis 1–11 is to the rest of the Torah, creation and the history of God's people. Psalm 104 contemplates the creative acts of God up to the present day. Psalm 105 gazes at the history of God's people and is open-ended. Together these two psalms envision God who has a hand in creation, history, and an interest in the present. Likewise, Psalm 136 embraces creation and history under the operation of God's *ḥesed*.

Psalm 105 is an historical recital which celebrates two foundational acts of salvation, freedom from Egyptian slavery and the donation of the promised land. At the beginning and end the poet appeals to God's memory (*zkr*, vv. 8, 42), which is the guiding factor in God's activity and frames the body of the psalm. Besides, the people are told to "*Remember* the wonderful works he has done" (v. 5). The theme of the "word" (promise, covenant, law) dominates the poem. God arranges and is manifest in the events of salvation, and this is significant for the present generation which commemorates the history. The relationship between the "children of Jacob" and the present generation is reinforced by two terms, "servant" and "chosen" (vv. 6, 25-26, 42-43). The phrase "seek his presence continually" (v. 4) has a psychological impact, to desire God's presence, and a liturgical force, to celebrate the liturgy in the temple, where his presence is experienced in a special way. The liturgy actualizes the past wonders and adapts their meaning to the present. Psalm 105:1-15 appears in the liturgy David assigned to the Asaphites when he brought the ark into Jerusalem (1 Chr 16:8-22).

The introduction invites the audience to acknowledge God's saving deeds (vv. 1-6). The invitation is formulated with ten imperative forms: "give thanks," "call," "make known," "sing," "sing praises," "tell," "glory," "seek" (*drš*), "seek" (*bqš*), "remember." (In addition, there is one verb in the imperfect form, "let the hearts . . . rejoice," v. 3.) The congregation is comprised of "those who seek the Lord" and, more concretely, Abraham's and Jacob's descendants (vv. 3, 6). God is "Lord our God," but his decisions and deeds have universal significance, "among the peoples" and "in all the earth" (vv. 1, 7). The poet reviews

Israel's foundation history, the covenant with Abraham and his descendants (vv. 7-11), including the divine protection during their Genesis wandering (vv. 12-15; cf. Gen 12–36);[23] the Joseph story (vv. 16-22); the miracles on Israel's behalf, which culminate in the Exodus (vv. 23-38), and the provision in the desert (vv. 39-41). This liturgical recital follows the sequence of the credo (Deut 26:1-9), with no mention of the Red Sea passage nor Sinai and the gift of the law. The desert sojourn is telescoped into three events, the miraculous guidance (the pillar of cloud and fire, cf. Exod 13:21-22), the food (manna and quail, cf. Exod 16:13-15), and water from the rock (cf. Exod 17:6). The summary of the joyous departure and the gift of the land tells how God remembered "his holy promise" or, literally, "his sacred word," to Abraham (v. 42; *dābār* as in vv. 8, 19). The final verse discloses that God had a purpose, the shaping of a people obedient to divine statutes and laws.

Following the concise covenant allusion, "the LORD our God," the poet stresses the pact which God made with the patriarchs. The beginning of salvation is God's initiative; he gave his word, established a covenant with the people forever. Synonyms are employed—"covenant" (*bĕrît*, vv. 8, 10), "word" (*dābār*, v. 8), "sworn promise" (*šĕbûʿâh*, v. 9), "statute" (*ḥôq*, v. 10). The divine initiative ("he summoned famine against the land") is emphasized in the Joseph story (vv. 16-22) and throughout the recital. The same theology that is operative in Genesis 37–50 is at work here, that behind the events of history, even the messy business of selling a brother into slavery, is God's inscrutable hand which orchestrates everything for the people's benefit (cf. Gen 50:20). The theme of God's effective word is evident. God's prediction *(dābār)* and the "word" *(ʾimrat)* recall the covenant (v. 19). The poet summarizes Joseph's prediction, the interpretation of the dreams in prison and his teaching in Pharaoh's court. Egypt represents a land which respected sages and wisdom (v. 22).

In vv. 29-36 there are fourteen Hebrew suffixes referring to Egypt: "*their* waters," "*their* fish," "*their* vines and [*their*] fig trees," etc. Seven of these refer to "*their* land" and synonyms "*their* country" or "*their* ground." Egypt's illusory strength is defeated. The author relates, "then he brought *them* [the NRSV reads "Israel," which is not in the Hebrew] out with silver and gold" (v. 37). Furthermore, "Egypt was glad at *their* departure, for dread of *them* . . ." (v. 38). Egypt is superseded by Israel at the Exodus.

[23] The patriarchs are called "anointed" by virtue of their divine call, "prophets" by virtue of their reception of God's word which was in turn transmitted to others (v. 15; cf. Gen 20:7). In the present psalm they are called, in addition, "servant" and "chosen ones" (v. 6). All these terms idealize the patriarchal era.

The provision in the desert results from the "promise" *(dābār)* to Abraham (v. 42), a detail which connects the Exodus with the initial promise. God fulfilled the covenant by *giving (ntn)* Israel "the lands of the nations, . . . the wealth of the peoples" (vv. 44; see v. 11). The description of that poor strip of rocky soil on the eastern Mediterranean seaboard seems exaggerated, except from the point of view of one who has no land or who is viewing it from the perspective of God's continual benefactions to the chosen people. The gift of the land as the fulfillment of the promises to the ancestors is the unifying theme. This promise opens and closes the body of the psalm (vv. 6-11, 42-45). The historical stages are considered between these two moments, contemplated from the perspective of God's fidelity to the divine word. All history is converted thus into a continual march toward the fulfillment of the promise and aims toward the goal, the land. In return Israel must be faithful to the covenant by obeying God's laws, otherwise they will forfeit God's providence (v. 45). This conclusion rallies the people to be faithful to the covenant.

As a historical memory, Psalm 105 is similar to Psalms 78, 106, and 136, but it has its own purpose. It praises God's fidelity, trustworthiness, and constancy. A suitable response on the people's part, besides praise and limitless trust in God, is to observe the laws. This amounts to a grateful response for God's faithfulness and the continuous miracles God works for and with the people.

Psalm 106
A Story of Love and Forgiveness

Psalms 105 and 106 form a thematic pair, as they interpret the Torah narrative. Psalm 105, which invites trust, is mostly concerned with the patriarchs Abraham, Isaac and Jacob and the covenant in their regard. Psalm 106, inviting repentance, focuses on Israel's chronic failure; the Mosaic theme introduced in 105:26 is resumed in 106:23, 32. Thus, the two stand in dialectical contrast. In the first, Israel possesses the land of Canaan because God kept the promise to Abraham; in the second, Israel lost the land because of the failure to trust and obey. The praise of Ps 106:1-2 continues that of the historical recital of the previous psalm. But early in the poem Psalm 106 changes key to a somber complaint which reviews the people's history, while emphasizing their chronic perversity and obtuseness. The poet confesses Israel's sins and recalls the rebellion during the Exodus (vv. 7-33) and conquest (vv. 34-46). He or she reflects on the current punishment, inserts it into a history of sinfulness, confesses Israel's guilt (v. 6), and prays for restoration (v. 47). "Praise the LORD," a liturgical refrain, frames the psalm.

The opening verses are diffuse. The summons to thank God is followed by a question which serves as a dedication, "Who can utter the mighty doings of the LORD . . ." (v. 2). Before participating in the liturgy, the faithful must prepare themselves by observing the law (v. 3; cf. 105:45). The logic of the beatitude, "Happy are those who observe justice," is elusive, but it may answer the question, that those who act rightly are qualified to review God's history and praise. This beatitude formulates the ethical teaching. Then the speaker asks to be remembered when God grants Israel relief (vv. 4-5; cf. 105:8, 42), a remarkable testimony of solidarity between the individual and nation. This introduction sets the scene for the history of God's pardon. It is set against the background of a national catastrophe with hope for rescue, anticipating the request for deliverance from the present plight. A thematic statement confesses the present sin in the context of the history of sinfulness from the Exodus to the conquest (vv. 6-46, the body of the poem). The Hebrew reads "We have sinned with our fathers," synchronizing past and present (v. 6; cf. Ezra 9:9-15; Neh 9:5-37; Bar 1:15–2:10; Dan 9:4-19). The sin is "ours," but it is a repetition and a prolongation of the ancestors' sins. This initial confession corresponds to the closing prayer "Save us" (v. 47), where the poet asks for a repeat performance of God's saving power, which he or she has rehearsed. The final section about Israel's corruption by the nations reflects her conduct before the exile (vv. 34-46). The historical recital, ending on the note of God's kindness, grounds the hope for deliverance. History blends into the present as the poet adverts to the diaspora and requests, "gather us from among the nations" (v. 47). Once again pardoned, the people will be able to celebrate the liturgy. The body reviews Israel's ingratitude after repeated rescues. A psalm that opens with a formula invitation to praise God for *ḥesed* closes with a request for the restoration of praise. The doxology closes Book Four of the Psalter (v. 48; see note on the doxology of Psalm 41).

The plea to be remembered *(zkr)* by God introduces a leitmotif (v. 4). In the confession the poet writes that "they did *not remember* the abundance of your steadfast love" (v. 7), that "they soon *forgot* his works" (v. 13), that "they *forgot* God, their Savior" (v. 21). What underlies every sin is the failure to accept God's words and deeds as the basis of life. Finally, after an impressive list of crime and correction, the poet recalls "he *remembered* his covenant, and showed compassion according to the abundance of his steadfast love" (v. 45), before he or she closes with the request for rescue.

The author reviews seven capital (and historical) sins of the Exodus generation before they entered the promised land (vv. 7-33). They are typical sins which threaten any relationship with God. At the same time the poet reviews the history of God's rescue or mitigation of punishment. The seven do not receive the same treatment; for example, not everyone is forgiven. Besides, the reason for the pardon varies in each case. In the first sin God pardons "for his name's sake, so that he might make known his mighty power" (v. 8). God forgives the fourth sin because of Moses' intercession (v. 23), and the sixth because Phinehas intervened (v. 30). This account is followed by a single transgression after the entry into the land (vv. 34-39). The present generation's solidarity with the past, the goods received from God, the sins committed and God's successive pardons infuse the present with hope for divine intervention.

The first sin is the breach of faith at the Red Sea (vv. 7-12; see Exod 14:10-14). Even though the people had experienced the miracles, they did not *remember* God's *ḥesed* (v. 7). God took the initiative in the passage from sin to grace (v. 8). After this miracle the Israelites "believed" (v. 12; see Exod 14:31). The second sin is the lack of faith when the people craved food (vv. 13-15; see Exod 16:1-3 and Num 11:4-6, 31-35; Ps 78:26-31). They weighed the situation in human terms and lost sight of divine grace. God heard the people's grumbling and granted their request, feeding them manna and quail. Their punishment was their gluttony (cf. Num 11:19-20). The third sin is the rebellion of the Dathan and Abiram faction against Moses and Aaron and the consequent punishment (vv. 16-18; see Num 16:1-14). The punishment was definitive, a violent death, presented in two images, the fire of God's anger and being devoured by the earth (Num 16:31-33, 45-49). Fourth and central in a list of seven, the most serious sin, is idolatry (vv. 19-23; see Exod 32:1-6). This event is not in the same chronological sequence as in the Torah, and its central position makes it prominent. God's "glory" must be worshiped without images; the Israelites, on the contrary, traded their God for a portable idol, a grass-eating ox—the disparaging tone is evident. In response to this capital sin, which amounts to forgetting the divine guidance and past miracles, God decided to annihilate the people, but Moses' intercession rescued them. The fifth sin is lack of trust (vv. 24-27; see Num 13:25–14:12). Nearing the promised land and having learned of the indigenous people's military strength, the Israelites refused to enter. They accused God of wanting them dead and they would rather perish than fight in Canaan. God heard the prayer, and— the poet collapses the historical account—after forty years of wandering, this generation died in the wilderness. The punishment is described in terms which fit the Babylonian exile, "disperse their descendants among the nations" (v. 27). Exile is an appropriate punishment for those who "despised the pleasant land" (v. 24). The Baal of Peor apostasy is the sixth sin (vv. 28-31; see Num 25:1-9). After their long desert sojourn the Israelites were seduced by fertility cults. A plague broke out among the people and caused the death of twenty-four thousand people. The bloody act of expiation which averted God's anger is attributed to Phinehas. Seventh, and last in the list of sins, Israel rebelled when water was lacking (vv. 32-33; the Meribah scandal, Num 20:2-13; compare Exod 17:1-7; Pss 81:7; 95:8). This time Moses is implicated in the guilt. No tradition adequately explains why, but for this he would be barred from the promised land. Here it is said that Moses spoke rashly; in Num 20:12 it is said that Moses did not trust God.

What follows is a condensation of sins in the land, which is a summary of Israel's apostasies during the period of the judges (vv. 34-39; cf. Judg 2:11-19). History is conceived globally, from the entrance into the promised land to the Babylonian exile. The whole trajectory is marked by the people's disobedience. The Israelites did not do what God commanded but instead they mingled with the pagans. They adopted idolatrous practices even to the point of child sacrifice, and thus profaned the land. The punishment corresponds to the crime. Just as they served foreign gods, they will be enslaved to foreigners (vv. 40-42). This pattern finally culminates in the present exile (cf. v. 47).

The theme throughout the psalm is clear. Israel has been chronically unfaithful in response to God's deeds in her behalf (vv. 7, 13-14, 19-21, 24-25, 28-29, 32-33, 34-39); nonetheless God has repeatedly forgiven her and shown mercy (vv. 8-11, 15, 23, 30, 44-46). The punishment is not definitive, because it is linked to the divine promise and covenant. There is every reason to hope for divine intervention. The allusions to the exile and to a betterment of conditions are unmistakable (vv. 46-47).

> He caused them to be pitied by all who held them captive.
> Save us, O Lᴏʀᴅ our God, and gather us from among the nations.

This theological reflection teaches how God rescues the people from sin and returns them to a right relationship with God. The line of argument is that God has always been merciful in the past, mitigating the punishment which Israel's sins deserved. May God do so again. After the confession, the present assembly prays to be delivered from displacement and exile which results from sinfulness. The psalm ends like a love song, lauding the persistence of a faithful lover, trusting God's tenderness, patience, and indulgence toward a beloved people.

Book Five

(PSALMS 107–150)

Psalm 107
God the Savior of Those in Distress

The fact that their beginnings are identical argues for the positioning of Psalm 107 after 106 before the division of the Psalter into five books and the current placement of the doxology at 106:48. Even more convincing is the correspondence between the summary of the people's experience as it is described in 106:40-46 and the refrain of Psalm 107 (vv. 6-8, 13-15, 19-21, 28-31). Book Five opens with a hymn rallying those whom God has rescued and gathered from the four winds so that they might join together in God's praise. Then the psalmist, committed to praise, bids the soul rouse musical instruments to join in this universal chant (108:1-3). The symphony announced at the beginning of Book Five will be performed in the grand finale of Psalms 148–150.

Psalm 107 celebrates God's ḥesed for those who are afflicted. The invitatory formula labels it a thanksgiving liturgy (v. 1; see 106:1; 118:1; 136:1; 1 Chr 16:34; Jer 33:11). The concluding meditation has a wisdom motif and the final summons urges the wise to meditate on God's ḥesed (v. 43; cf. Hos 14:9). In a unanimous response, peoples rescued from adversity converge from the four points of the compass, giving the psalm a universal scope (vv. 2-3). In successive movements four groups are arranged according to the adversities they have suffered—desert wanderers are led into the city and nourished (vv. 4-9), prisoners and the oppressed are freed (vv. 10-16), the sick are healed (17-22), and storm-battered mariners are rescued (vv. 23-32). How and where should they celebrate a thanksgiving? With sacrifice and the joyful broadcast of God's deeds in the liturgical assembly of people and elders (vv. 22, 32). The different groups represent all those who experience God's rescue. The poem closes with a meditation (vv. 33-43).

The four typical episodes are marked off by two refrains and shaped similarly—summary of adversity, cry for help, rescue, and thanksgiving for God's ḥesed and wondrous deeds (niplā'ôt). The refrains are the report of the cry and rescue (vv. 6, 13, 19, 28) and the summons to thank God for his ḥesed (vv. 8, 15, 21, 31). In the second and third movements the poet adds the causes of distress, the people's guilt and rebellion

(vv. 11, 17). The descriptions are picturesque: the desert, devoid of clear paths and adequate provisions; the physical and spiritual hunger of the desert wanderer; the dark dungeon with iron shackles, forced labor, metal doors and bars; the sick or dying person's disgust for food; the pitch and roll of a ship at storm; the mariners' fright, seasickness, and the unsteadiness on their feet. Two descriptions, "hungry and thirsty, their soul fainted within them" and "prisoners in misery and in irons" focus on the physical and spiritual affliction and bonds (vv. 5, 10). The calming of the storm moves from high winds and waves to calm waters and God guiding the ship to port (vv. 29-30).

The language is evocative of the Exodus (vv. 4-9), the archetype of national distress, and is reminiscent of the exile, during which the royal leaders were imprisoned (vv. 10-16). The sickness is described in a typical fashion. Its cause is sin, and it inspires repentance (vv. 17-22). The poet paints a seascape and masterfully details a voyage from the outbreak of the storm to safe arrival in port. The seafarers experienced God's wonders in the abyss ("in the deep," *bimṣûlâh*; v. 24), and the storm evokes God's battle with chaos, the sea, which was defeated (v. 29).

The poet specifies the invited, the "redeemed from trouble and gathered in from the lands" (vv. 2-3). The beneficiary of God's miracles is all humanity (vv. 8, 15, 21, 31), and the poet does not hint of a privileged relation between Israel and God. Repeatedly the call for help sets God's *ḥesed* in motion and brings relief. The point of the concluding meditation is that God reverses and transforms the order of things (vv. 33-41; cf. 1 Sam 2:4-8; Job 5:11-15; Isa 35:5-7). These reversals can be boiled down to these four: fertile terrain becomes a wasteland, the desert becomes wetland, the hungry prosper, and oppressive governors are exiled. These reversals gladden the upright and silence the wicked (v. 42).[1] God's way with humans is described in terms of aid for the hungry and needy (vv. 36-38, 41). Meanwhile, God takes action against the wicked governors (v. 40). The conversion of "fruitful land into a salty waste" is an allusion to Sodom and generalizes the threat (v. 34). One who so dramatically transforms the natural world can also soften the human heart to consider the oppressed (vv. 39-41).

Ḥesed is introduced as the content of praise (v. 1), reiterated as the reason for praise (vv. 8, 15, 21, 31), and proposed as the subject for meditation by the wise (v. 43). The singular and plural of *ḥesed* indicates that God's eternal reality is revealed in temporal acts of salvation (vv. 1, 43). The term translated "wonderful works," *niplāʾôt*, refers to these acts of *ḥesed* and summarizes God's salvation of the people. Both

---

[1] Motifs from the first narrative (vv. 4-9) appear (compare vv. 4 and 33, vv. 5 and 36, vv. 4 and 40, vv. 7 and 36).

individual and corporate salvation are the result of *ḥesed*, and praise and meditation go hand in hand. The psalm is instructional; the "upright see" God's *ḥesed* at work and rejoice, and the voice of wickedness is silenced (v. 42).

Psalm 108
Confidence in God's Victory

The poet rearranges previous liturgical texts to reflect a new situation. Psalm 108 is composed of Pss 57:7-11 (vv. 1-5) and 60:5-12 (vv. 6-13).[2] The thanksgiving of Psalm 57 has been placed at the beginning. In its other context vv. 6-13 responds to the situation described in the opening verses of Psalm 60, a communal complaint and petition for help. In Psalm 108 the two parts function differently. Initially, confident in God, the poet determines to sing and play music. The petition for help (vv. 5-6, 12) frames the divine oracle (vv. 7-9) and the complaint about God's rejection (vv. 10-11). The poet concludes with confidence, a tone similar to the one with which the psalm began. The fusion of two poetic fragments has transformed the complaint into a hymn of trust.

Joy fills the night, as the poet rouses the musical instruments to awaken the dawn and praises God among the nations (vv. 2-3). Divine *ḥesed* and faithfulness *(ʾĕmet)* is limitless (v. 4). The poet scans the vertical range, pondering God in relation to the earth (v. 5), then considers the horizontal, requesting rescue for the beloved people (v. 6).

The second half is the clue to the poet's interest and purpose and reflects the unresolved conflict of the postexilic community with its neighbors, particularly Edom, whose treachery had contributed to the fall of Jerusalem. The description delineates the territorial expanse (vv. 7-10). Shechem with a large part of Manasseh west of the Jordan is claimed as well as Succoth together with Gilead east of the Jordan. Northern Ephraim will serve as a military helmet and southern Judah as scepter. The oracle confirms Israel's rights over three longstanding enemies, as the divine warrior claims neighboring Moab in the southeast, Edom in the south and coastal Philistia. A desire for the defeat of Israel's enemies may have inspired the present composition (v. 11).

[2] At first glance, it appears that, like Psalm 116 (Psalms 114 and 115 in Greek and Latin versions) and Psalm 147 (Psalms 146 and 147 in Greek and Latin), Psalm 108 could be treated as two separate units. Together the two form a new composition, with the accent on trust in God.

Psalm 109
Ritual Curse

As the poet riddles the adversary with curses, it is easy to forget that Psalm 109 begins "O God of my praise" and concludes with a promise of praise (v. 30, penultimate verse). The poet expounds the reason for the appeal (vv. 2-5). He or she is accustomed to doing good without looking to personal gain, yet is now unjustly accused and calumniated. This is clear in the poet's summary, "they reward me evil for good, and hatred for my love" (v. 5).

The unresolved problem of Psalm 109 is knowing who pronounces the curse (vv. 6-19). It might be the "wicked and deceitful mouths" and "lying tongues" of those who speak "words of hate" against the psalmist (vv. 2-3). This is the interpretation of the NRSV, which places the speech in quotation marks, and introduces it with "they say" (v. 6). This interpretation, however, does not quench the psalmist's thirst for revenge against the accusers, as he or she prays to deflect the curses against their originators, "May that be the reward of my accusers from the LORD" (v. 20). Furthermore, it is unlikely that the wicked would accuse the psalmist of oppressing the defenseless and loving the curse (vv. 16-19). Another interpretation emerges when one divides the speech into two parts, that of the adversary (vv. 6-15) and that of the psalmist, who defends him or herself and invokes the law of retribution against the assailant (vv. 16-20). The Hebrew text argues for a division of the curse after v. 15. In the initial cry for help and the final petitions, the enemy is couched in the plural, as in "They beset me with words of hate" (v. 3; see vv. 2-5, 20, 25-31); the object of the curse is singular (vv. 6-19), with the exception of v. 15. A third interpretation is that the innocent psalmist pronounces the curse in passionate and exaggerated terms as the ritual curses attached to the covenant are pronounced (cf. Deut 27:15-26; 28:15-46). I incline toward this third option. The structure, revising the NRSV, is, then,

vv. 1-5   appeal to the supreme court and presentation of the case

vv. 6-20   the psalmist's ritual curse of the aggressor

vv. 21-29   the request for vindication

vv. 30-31   concluding promise of praise

The repeated cognates of *hll*, "praise," form an inclusion (vv. 1, 30).

The curse is deployed with eloquent hyperbole. The evils envisioned are that the wicked be found guilty in an unjust trial; that he die prematurely leaving wife and children ruined, helpless and unable to hold onto their possessions; that his posterity and name be obliterated, and that his ancestors' sins be charged against him (vv. 6-15). True to form, the heat of anger is such that the invective does not reflect the apparent contradiction, that neither the offender nor his orphaned children be treated kindly. The eradication of the family group is the maximum punishment for the Israelite, for whom there was no concept of eternal life beyond the family memory and prayers. The brunt of the injured poet's request is "may they be wrapped in their own shame as in a mantle" (v. 29; cf. v. 19). To move God to act, the psalmist describes his or her own battered state, which is compounded by the enemies' jeers (vv. 22-25). Some of the strongest images include the pierced heart, the evening shadow that vanishes with the light, a bothersome insect which can be brushed off, an emaciated person who inspires scorn and disgust.

The legal terminology is clear. Cognates of *špṭ*, "is tried" and "condemn" outline the legal process from arraignment to condemnation (vv. 7, 31). God's silence is in contrast to deceitful speech (vv. 1-2) and is met with eloquent testimony of the psalmist's faith (vv. 21, 26, 30-31). It is hoped that an unprincipled *"accuser [śṭn] . . . on his right,"* *ʿmd* *ʿal–yāmîn* (v. 6; cf. v. 4) prosecute the poet's guilty *"accusers"* (*stn*, vv. 20, 29), while God will be *"at the right hand [ʿmd ʿal–yāmîn] of the needy,"* assuming the defense position in a lawsuit (v. 31). The ardent wish is that the accusers' curse redound on the hostile witnesses and those who desire an unjust verdict (vv. 2-4, 6-7, 17, 20, 28-29). The unlawfully accused poet asks that the defender (rather than the judge!) of the wicked be crooked and be found guilty (vv. 6-7); God, in contrast, is the legal champion of the defenseless (v. 31). In a largely optative composition ("may such-and-such happen to so-and-so") the poet appeals for God's intervention (vv. 20-21), which would include calamity on the accusers and rescue for him or herself, the afflicted. Like "the poor and needy," *ʿānî wě²ebyôn*, "the broken *hearted"* (v. 16), the poet is "poor and needy," *ʿānî wě²ebyôn*, and his *"heart"* is pierced (v. 22; cf. v. 31, "needy," *²ebyôn*). The indictment is clear. The accuser deserves death (v. 8) because he or she pursued others to death (vv. 16, 31). One who mistreats the poor deserves to be impoverished (vv. 8-11, 16). One who curses others deserves to be cursed (vv. 17-19, 28-29). As the accused outlines the crimes, he or she requests retributive justice (vv. 16-19, 29). May all blessings, in which the accursed took no delight, depart. A string of opposites illustrates the contrasts, to love *(²hb)* and not to like *(lō²–ḥāpēṣ)*, curse *(qělālâh)* and blessing *(běrākâh)*, to "come on him" *(bw²)* and "be far from him" *(rḥq m–)* (v. 17). The contrast is formulated in a nutshell (v. 28),

> Let them curse, but you will bless.
> Let my assailants be put to shame; may your servant be glad.

The poet pleads that the punishment fit the crime. He or she previously extended *ḥesed* to the assailants (vv. 4-5). The enemies deserve no kindly treatment because they showed no "kindness" (vv. 12, 16, *ḥesed*). God is bound to show *ḥesed* to the afflicted (vv. 21-22, 26). May God *remember* their parents' guilt so that their *memory* might be banished (vv. 14-15). The emphatic "you" (*ʾattâh,* vv. 21, 27, 28) distances the enemy from God and puts the psalmist and God face to face.[3] The divine name *yhwh* occurs seven times in the latter part, coloring a composition in which God's presence is implicit (vv. 2-13) with a plenary presence (vv. 14-31). The adversary's name, *šēm* (v. 13), to be obliterated, is opposed to the divine name, *šēm* (v. 21). In the end, the contrasts are clear. The wicked curse and consequently are shamed and dishonored; the innocent psalmist is blessed, rejoices, gives thanks and praises God. The unbridled curse amounts to a spiritual or psychological cure. Without taking real measures against the perpetrators of injustice, the devout person who has been sorely wronged can find release and relief in praying in this manner.

Psalm 110
God Appoints both King and Priest

Psalm 110 provides a sequel to the prayer against the wicked in Psalm 109, "The LORD is at your right hand; he will shatter kings on the day of his wrath" (110:5). It has two parts, each opened by a formula introducing an oracle, "The LORD says" and "The LORD has sworn" (vv. 1a, 4a). In these oracles God invests the earthly sovereign as vice-regent and confers on him the priestly office (vv. 1b, 4b), and together they portray a glorious future. Each oracle is amplified by a description of the sovereign who shares God's power and the announcement of the sovereign's victory which God gives (vv. 2-3, 5-7). The amplifications develop the theme "*until* I make your *enemies* your footstool" (v. 1), a metaphor for their subjection to the sovereign's rule.[4] The "enemies"

[3] Other emphatic pronouns, "I" (vv. 22, 25) and "they" (v. 28), are much in evidence in the psalmist's request.

[4] The Hebrew text of v. 3 is subject to hypothetical reconstruction and in v. 7 it is unclear about whom and what are spoken. Conjectures about the meaning are multiple and indecisive.

are the nations and their rulers, and "until" looks forward to "the day of his wrath" when the divine sovereign quells resistance to his rule. Monarchs and nations are foes, not because of some conflict with Israel, but because they owe fealty to other gods and their claims are an exception to God's universal dominion. Thus they are doomed to judgment and defeat.[5]

The poet instinctively or intentionally etches polar contrasts. The beginning and end embrace the king's activity, seated and on the go ("by the path"); there are local and universal concerns, "from Zion" and "among the nations" (vv. 2, 6). The phrase "at my/your right hand" represents a change of perspective rather than position. The king is seated at the LORD's right hand and the LORD fights at the king's right side (vv. 1, 5). The "day" of battle and "day" of wrath are in contrast to the perpetuity of the priesthood (vv. 3-5). The *foot* stool of the enemies contrasts with the king's raised *head*.

The psalm begins with an oracle, presumably given in the temple during a coronation or anniversary celebration, during which an officiating priest or prophet addresses the monarch as "my lord," a royal title. Thus, God invites the sovereign to take the throne on God's right. It is astonishing that a human could share the divine throne. Central to this is the belief that all power derives from God, and that the Israelite monarchy was a divinely appointed office. Whoever sits at the sovereign's right on formal occasions is next in rank and is empowered to represent the sovereign and carry out state policy. The first oracle authorizes a Davidic ruler to assume that position. The divine commander-in-chief will conquer hostile nations and force enemies to acknowledge the king; they will prostrate before the conqueror's throne who will place a foot on their necks as a symbol of dominance.[6] God forges the monarch's scepter, so guaranteeing the submission of pretending rulers and aggressors (v. 2).

The second oracle ordains the priest as the representative and intercessor of the people. As part of the royal appointment God installs the monarch in the priestly office by means of an oath which cannot be taken back ("will not change his mind," v. 4). In the monarchical traditions

---

[5] The description of God's slaughter on "the day of his wrath" shares the tradition of God as warrior that is heard in the prophetic pronouncements about how rebellious nations are treated (Isa 5:15; Jer 9:21; Ezek 32:5-6).

[6] This is exemplified in Josh 10:24, and examples are cited in Othmar Keel, *The Symbolism of the Biblical World: Ancient Near Eastern Iconography and the Book of the Psalms* (New York: Crossroad, 1985), 254–55. The phrase "your enemies your footstool" recalls the footstool of Tutankhamen's throne, which was inlaid with the nine traditional enemies of Egypt, *ANEP*, Fig. 417.

observed in Canaan, the ruler was the principal mediator between God and people. Melchizedek, the Canaanite predecessor of the Davidic sovereign in pre-Israelite Jerusalem, was just such a priest-king (Gen 14:18). The monarch is confirmed as the successor to Melchizedek, who blessed Abram in the name of the Canaanite God, *El Elyon*, "God Most High." When David became ruler of the city the two offices were conferred on him and his successors.

The oracle has an eschatological flavor, reminiscent of oracles of Isaiah and Zechariah. The speaker promises the ruler God's protection, "at your right hand" (v. 5), which insures God's victories over hostile powers. At the judgment of the nations and their rulers, the warrior God will stride across corpses, crushing whoever gets in the way. The text of the last verse is clear, but what does it mean, to "drink from the stream by the path"? What ritual, what stream? The obvious reference is to the tired soldier who refreshes himself with a drink before the ultimate triumph. Another possibility is that this refers to a ritual where the ruler drinks from a sacred font of life, which symbolizes an empowerment in the office. Psalm 110 represents a liturgical celebration, the coronation of an earthly sovereign who is to incorporate the universal divine rule. The oracles authorize the event and endow the human office with the divine purpose. What is said of the Davidic sovereign is visionary language about God's intention to employ human rule to effect his sovereignty over other nations and their rulers. Others who make claims to autonomous existence and power render themselves God's enemies. For Judah, the coronation of a Davidic king answered the question about who is ultimately in control of history and what will come of the hostility among the worldly powers.

By their use of hyperbolic language, Israelite court poets magnified the regent's office beyond the political realities of the modest Davidic monarchy.[7] Such ritual court flattery was eventually applied to a future king, the messiah, as the royal psalms were retained for worship long after the monarchy disappeared from Israel's history in 587 B.C. Psalm 110 portrays a messianic king who perfectly embodies power that derives from God, the divine representative who will come in the fullness of time to reign on earth. The apocalyptic movement saw the messianic victory over the nations as the climax of a drama played out in a universal context. The day of God's wrath was envisioned as the climax to world history.

---

[7] As regards form, subject matter and probably also the occasion of its origin, Psalm 110 is related to Psalm 2. The features of these two psalms show that they were composed for use in rituals concerning the kings of Judah. The human king is also the subject of Psalms 18, 20, 21, 45, 72, 101, 132.

In the postmonarchic period, when the final revision of the Psalter took shape, many psalms were attributed to David, who was regarded by the people as the type of the true king, who represented them before God and mediated the divine rule on earth. They prayed the psalms "in David," so to speak. The New Testament citation of the psalms shows that early Christians prayed the psalms "in Christ," whom they believed to be the anointed one of David's lineage who fulfilled the prophecy of this psalm (cf. Matt 22:44).

Psalm 111
Praise of God's Goodness to Israel

Psalms 111 and 112 are companions, as shown by their external forms. Each is an acrostic of twenty-two Hebrew lines. The short, rhythmical measures tend to be composed of three Hebrew words or tightly formulated expressions; the half-lines begin with successive letters of the Hebrew alphabet. Both psalms begin with the liturgical acclamation "Praise the Lord."[8] The "s" (penultimate) line of Psalm 111 begins with a *śin*, while in Psalm 112 the "s" line begins with a *šin*. The *vav* line (v. 3b in each) is identical (see also 112:9b), "and his [their] righteousness endures forever." Also the *ḥet* line, v. 4b, is similar in both, repeating "gracious" and "merciful," *ḥannûn wĕraḥûm*. Thus, words, phrases, and an entire clause from Psalm 111 are repeated in Psalm 112 as shown here: *yrʾ*, "fear" (111:5, 10; 112:1, 7, 8); *ḥpṣ*, "delight" (111:2; 112:1); *yĕšārîm*, "upright" (111:1; 112:2, 4); *lēb, lēbāb*, "heart" (111:1; 112:7); *sāmûk*, "established" or "steady" (111:8; 112:8); *ntn*, "provides" or "distributed" (111:5; 112:9). Psalm 111 ends "The fear of the Lord is the beginning of wisdom" (111:10; cf. v. 5a), and 112:1 opens, "Happy are those who fear the Lord." Psalm 111 praises those who fear God, and Psalm 112 charts the consequences of such reverence in life. In either case *ṣĕdāqâh*, "righteousness" (111:3b; 112:3b, 9b), endures forever. Both God and his adherents are gracious and merciful (v. 4b); they act generously and rightly (111:5; 112:6). As the divine work is honorable (111:3),

---

[8] *Hallelujah* is the opening word in each of Psalms 111–113. The concluding *hallelujah* of Psalm 113 may belong to Psalm 114 (with the Greek versions), thus providing an identical beginning. The sequence in Psalms 114–117 is complicated because of the varying manuscript traditions and divisions in Hebrew and Greek. Many LXX, Latin, and Syriac manuscripts join 114–115 into one (Psalm 116, LXX). By combining 114 and 115 and shifting the *hallelujah*'s of 115, 116, and 117 to the opening lines of 116, 117 and 118, the LXX results in seven psalms, each beginning with *hallelujah*. The Hebrew tradition lacks this repeated *hallelujah* beginning.

so the horn of those who fear God is honored (112:9). This correlation between praise of God and commendation of the devout teaches that God's works shape lives, and thus Psalm 111 provides the theological basis for the moral conviction of 112. The world is coherent because the creator remembers and commands the covenant (111:5, 9), and its obedience brings benefit (Psalm 112). If Psalm 112 is wisdom, Psalm 111 is the sage's hymn of praise—teaching by example.

Echoes of biblical phrases are heard in Psalm 111, which is like an anthology. The poet praises God and recounts his deeds (vv. 1-9) and ends with a proverb about wisdom (v. 10; cf. Prov 1:7; 9:10; Job 28:28). The praise is private, "with my whole heart," and public, "in the congregation" (v. 1), because God's deeds are great, worthy of study (*děrûšîm*, v. 2), full of honor and majesty (cf. 45:3; 96:6; 145:5), permanent, memorable, powerful, faithful and just. In light of what follows, "wonderful deeds," *niplāʾôt*, is code language for God's marvelous deliverance and the formation of his people (v. 4; cf. Exod 3:20; 34:10). The predicated "gracious and merciful" is the classical designation of God from the time when Israel made the golden calf (cf. Exod 34:6; Ps 145:8-9). The poet alludes to the great moments of history, food in the desert (Exodus 16; Num 11:31-32; Pss 105:40; 106:14), the occupation of the land, redemption and covenant (the parallel lines of v. 9). God's works are "faithful and just," *ʾĕmet* and *mišpaṭ* (v. 7), two nouns which could be translated "faithfulness and justice." The covenant is that of Exodus 19–24 and Deuteronomy and its content is the law. The precepts are "to be performed with faithfulness and uprightness," *ʾĕmet* and *yāšār* (v. 8).

This psalm is intoned by an individual in a public gathering, and the attitude is stressed in the phrase "with my whole heart," a covenant phrase (v. 1). The "works of the LORD" (v. 2) should be "studied" *(drš)*, a word that is used later for the study and explanation of Sacred Scripture. The one who contemplates nature perceives God's glory in the divine rule (v. 3). The ensuing catalog of divine blessings suggests that "generosity" is a preferable translation of *ṣedeq* (NRSV, "righteousness," v. 3).[9] By "renown" or, literally, "memorial" *(zēker, v. 4)*, the poet has in mind the Exodus traditions and the covenant to which the following verses allude. "Memorial" or "commemoration" keeps alive the people's historical identity and her relationship with God; it is an essential element in the liturgy.

Unity is forged by the sevenfold use of cognates of the verb *ʿśh* and its synonym *pʿl*, "work[s]" or "deed[s]" (vv. 2a, 3a, 4a, 6a, 7a, 8b ["performed"], 10b ["practice"]). God's works, foremost among which is the

---

[9] *Ṣedeq* signifies justice, legal rightness, success. Often when it refers to God, it connotes generosity.

covenant (vv. 5, 9), are "[for]ever," *lāʿad* or *lĕʿôlām* (vv. 3b, 5b, 8a, 9b); the response is perpetual praise (v. 10c). "Food" or nourishment (*ṭerep*, an uncommon word) refers to the manna and quail in the desert (v. 5). The promised land, "the heritage of the nations," is God's material gift to the people (v. 6). After the mention of the saving acts comes the praise of the law (vv. 7-8). "Precepts" (*piqûdîm*, v. 7, referred to in Psalm 112 with a different word, *miṣwôt*, "commandments"), a reference to the laws of the Torah, are the revelation of the divine will, the foundation of the human order. The people must keep them with exactness (v. 8). In the summary statement redemption is ordered along the lines of the covenant. The constant praise responds to God's perpetual "righteousness" or generosity (vv. 3, 9). After contemplating and praising divine works, the psalmist turns toward God and concludes that not deeds but rather their author is deserving of study and praise.

The concluding statement, "The fear of the LORD is the beginning of wisdom," seems out of place. The preceding clause says of God, "Holy and awesome is his name." What is translated "awesome" and "fear" are cognates; fear corresponds to God's awesome reality. The following clause reads "all those who practice it [Hebrew "them"] have a good understanding." "Them" is a synonym for "fear of the LORD," plural because its antecedent is the "precepts" that express faithfulness and justice. Fear of the LORD comprises the covenant decrees, the motive to do them, and their performance. The poet believes that wisdom comes from learning and living the Torah, God's instruction. The human who *practices* the "fear of the LORD" is wise, a nice transition to the following psalm.

Psalm 112
Like God, Like the God-Fearer

The content of Psalm 111 shows that it is distinct from Psalm 112. The former begins and ends with praise and is dedicated to God; the latter beatifies the good person and describes his or her conduct. Several qualities attributed to God in Psalm 111 are attributed to the just person in Psalm 112. For example, "righteousness endures forever" is predicated of both God and the human (111:3b; 112:3b, 9b). God's precepts are forever *stable* and the heart of the good person is *steady* (*smk*, v. 8 in each psalm). God provides or "gives" food and the good *give* freely to the poor (*ntn*, 111:5; 112:9). The good person shares God's perpetuity (*lĕʿôlām*, 111:5b, 8a, 9b; 112:6; *ʿōmedet lāʿad*, 111:3b, 10c; 112:3b, 9b). Psalm 111 ends with the classic statement "The *fear of the* LORD is the beginning of wisdom" and Psalm 112 begins with "Happy are those who fear the LORD."[10]

Written in an acrostic style like the preceding psalm, Psalm 112 portrays the ideal wise person who might utter Psalm 111; thus these two were placed side by side with the linking phrase "fear [of] the LORD." They share the wisdom motif, but each has its own accent, as it amplifies in its own way God's moral design of the world. Psalm 112 is divided into two strophes; the beatitude "[i]t is well with those," *ṭôb–ʾîš* (v. 5), parallels "Happy are those," *ʾašrê–ʾîš* (v. 1). Following each is a description of a blessed life and its practical outcome. God created the world so that human attitudes and actions have consequences, as is illustrated in the following schema:

attitude and conduct	consequences
those who fear the LORD and delight in the law (v. 1)	will have descendants in the land, will be blessed, wealthy and upright; they shine with kindness and virtue (vv. 2-4)
those who are generous and conduct affairs rightly (v. 5)	will be stable, remembered, unafraid; they will triumph (vv. 6-8)
they are generous with the poor (v. 9a)	their goodness is permanent and they triumph (v. 9b-c)
the wicked see, get angry, "gnash their teeth and melt away" (v. 10a-b)	they amount to nothing (v. 10c)

The sequence is meaningful; piety ("fear of the LORD") is expressed in generosity toward the needy and has abundant rewards. The wicked are allotted all the space they deserve, a single verse.[11]

Psalm 111 provides the theological basis for the present conviction. The world is morally coherent because the creator is mindful of the eternal covenant (111:3-9). The argument of Psalm 112 explores the initial proposition, that "those who fear the LORD," which is akin to observing the covenant ("commandments"), will live a full and integrated life. This well-being includes numerous descendants (v. 2), material prosperity (v. 3), sound and luminous life style (v. 4), and a steady

[10] The verb *yrʾ*, "fear," occurs a total of seven times in the two psalms (111:5, 10; 112:1, 7, 8a-b, 10).

[11] Psalm 112 is similar in content to Psalm 1, affirming the contrasting destinies of the godly and the wicked, although Psalm 112 is more concerned with the rewards of virtue (vv. 1-9). The first and last words of Psalm 112, "Happy" and "will perish," are identical to the first and last words of Psalm 1.

heart, undismayed by adversity and constant (vv. 6-8). The key phrase which describes such a person is "righteousness," *ṣĕdāqâh*, which includes the notions of stability, generosity, and integrity (vv. 3, 9; cf. v. 6). The righteous help keep the world right.

In any context the term "righteous" or "righteousness" needs qualification. "Righteous" stresses innocence and uprightness, a certain kind of behavior. In addition to conducting one's affairs with equity, the righteous one lends and gives generously (vv. 5, 9). This hints that "generosity" or "beneficence" may be a more apt interpretation in the present context, particularly given the parallelism in the first part of v. 9. Here I depart from the NRSV in favor of a more literal translation:

> Freely they have given to the poor
> their *righteousness* endures forever.

The moral integrity of the blessed is in harmony with God's nature, forever "gracious and merciful" and righteous (112:3b, 9b; cf. 111:3b, 4b). The poet knows God as a person, not as a program, and recommends conduct based on the divine image. Thus human integrity has to do with upholding an equitable world order.[12] Life is well ordered because there is harmony between the creator and the creature. Such a relation with God makes a concrete claim, the generosity toward the poor and needy (v. 9), and this ensures personal constancy. In addition to the words "forever" (vv. 3, 6, 9), the poet traces "mighty" posterity (v. 2), wealth "in their houses" (v. 3), the righteous "will never be moved" (v. 6), "firm" and steadfast heart (vv. 7-8). "Horn" is a symbol of strength and triumph (v. 9). The quality of character and conduct ("righteousness") is evident in the way a person relates to others, practicing justice and caring for the poor, as God does. Virtue is relational.

In contrast, the wicked (singular in Hebrew) makes but a cameo appearance (v. 10; as in 104:35; 145:20). He or she sees how it goes with the just and is angered, but does not change and so wastes away in torment. The lasting blessedness contrasts with the anger of the wicked, whose desires are doomed. This is retributive justice. The wicked resists the good life and is miserable. He or she does not trust God's generosity and so cannot act generously. The play on the word *rʾh* is poignant: the just will *look* on the downfall of their foes; the wicked will *see* the righteous vindicated (vv. 8, 10; cf. 54:7; 118:7).[13] The last reward

---

[12] This is also the thrust of Job's claim on God in chapters 29–31.

[13] The wordplay on *yîrāʾ*, "they will not *be afraid*," and *yirʾeh*, "they will *look* in triumph" (v. 8), is common in biblical poetry (for example, Pss 52:8; 64:5-6; 102:16-17; 118:6-8; 119:74; Job 37:24 [all cited according to the Hebrew versification]).

mentioned is the honor which the just person receives; a person who behaves like this will always be able to hold the head up in society and before God, who provides inspiration and guidance. The author wastes no words on the wicked and briefly tells of their destiny, which is unrelieved failure.

Good conduct is based on a relationship with God which is manifest in delighting in the divine law. The object of "reverence" or "fear" is "the Lord," and the God-fearing subject is blessed and need not fear misfortune (vv. 7-8). The godly person is not immune from evil rumors and from malicious accusations; but trust in God gives one a confident heart so as not to fear people. The rewards are typical of those promised elsewhere by the sages. By one's blessedness a person partakes of the divine nature. In turn, the blessed become a blessing to others (vv. 4-5). The light which dawns in the darkness is the shining example of the wise, who are a living testimony to God's mercy, grace, and righteousness.

Psalm 111 starts off by speaking of God's works in human life and ends by identifying the fear of God as the beginning of wisdom. So Psalm 112 treats of the person who makes this fear the rule of life. This fear is not negative; it is reverential love or loving reverence with God as its object. Humans fashioned in God's image reflect the divine character and qualities. Through loving reverence one becomes more and more like God. Love for God flourishes in genuine love in human relations.

Psalm 113
Majesty is Manifest in Mercy

Following the initial call to praise (vv. 1-3), the poet of Psalm 113 acclaims God's majesty (vv. 4-6) and mercy (vv. 7-9). The word *name* and the divine name (there are six occurrences of Lord), are prominent in the first half, which culminates with the question, "Who is like the Lord our God?" (v. 5a; cf. Exod 15:11; Mic 7:18). "Our God" is the seventh explicit reference to the divine person, not counting the initial and final *hallelujah*, which frames the poem. The poet declares God's incomparability (vv. 4-9), a theme focused in the question. Everything builds up to this question, and what follows answers it, without naming God.

The praise is to embrace limitless time and space, "from this time on and forevermore" and "from the rising of the sun to its setting." Verses 2-3 are composed in chiastic parallel lines:

A (praise)   B (time)
May the name of the LORD be blessed   now and forever

B' (space)   A' (praise)
From the rising of the sun to its setting   the name of the LORD is to be praised

Sunrise to sunset is not a temporal reference but rather spatial, embracing the sun's movement over the whole earth. God's greatness transcends human activity and the created universe (v. 4). From the horizontal plane, the poet draws the vertical axis which frames the central question.

God is "high [rwm] above all nations" (v. 4), "is seated [yšb] on high," but he "looks far down [Hiphil, špl, literally, makes himself low in order to look] on the heavens and the earth" (v. 6).[14] God's self-abasement has consequences. God "raises [qwm, Hiphil] the poor from the dust, and lifts [rwm, Hiphil] the needy" (v. 7). The repetition of rwm is meaningful; the exalted one bends down to raise up the lowly. God is praised because, in spite of the infinite distance from the created world, he is not cut off from creation but rather is inclined toward it. God bends down to observe and care for creatures, especially the defenseless. Also cognates of yšb pose a contrast. God, who "dwells" or "is seated [yšb] on high" (v. 5), raises the poor to seat them (yšb, Hiphil, v. 8) with princes. God, enthroned, gives the poor and needy a seat among the rulers, which amounts to giving them a voice in political affairs. Likewise, God "gives the barren woman a home" (yšb, Hiphil), or a secure position. The repeated use of yšb links "the barren woman" with the preceding description. God is transcendent in essence and immanent in interest. For reaching down and raising the lowly the divine name is even more praiseworthy. Hannah's prayer (1 Sam 2:4-8) and the Magnificat (Lk 1:52-53) acclaim God as turning the tables of the social world; the strong and the weak, the full and the hungry, the poor and the rich exchange places by God's doing. The poet announces God's care for the poor, proof that majesty is manifest in mercy.

Psalm 114
The God Who Transforms

Psalm 114 sings of the people's liberation. It says that God is the holy presence in Israel's midst and shows how he took possession of them. The tone is playful; the structure is chiastic:

---

[14] The two forms hammagbîhî, "on high," and hammašpîlî, "looking down," produce a rhyme which is echoed in other Hiphil and plural forms of vv. 7-9.

A   vv. 1-2, Israel, Jacob, Judah—God's sanctuary and dominion

   B   vv. 3-4, sea, Jordan, mountains and hills

   B' vv. 5-6, sea, Jordan, mountains and hills

A' vv. 7-8, presence of the LORD, . . . the God of Jacob

The eight double lines (verses) are composed in synonymous parallelism. The first doublet connects Israel's Exodus from Egypt with Judah as God's sanctuary; it embraces both the foreign point of departure and permanence in the homeland. The second doublet reports the effect of the Exodus on the natural world (vv. 3-4). The Sea and the River Jordan, bracketing the desert sojourn, retreated as if defeated in battle; mountains and hills skipped like lambs. The third doublet questions the cowardly response and pokes fun at the natural order (vv. 5-6). The last one summons the earth to convulse in the presence of God who turns "rock into a pool of water." Thus the physical world, which seems so stable and reliable, is called to react to the divine presence. The doublets embrace opposite poles (merism)—Exodus from Egypt and settlement in the promised land (slavery and freedom), the receding waters of the sea and the Jordan (first and last crossings; cf. Josh 4:23), water and land, the LORD of the earth and the God of Jacob (universal and particular).

In reaction to the Exodus the sea takes flight and the Jordan flows upstream. The author rearranges the historical account. The land, signaled by the mountains and hills, leaps in response to Israel's liberation. Creation is embraced by water and land, and what is stable convulses. Remarkably, the sea flees without a fight. This represents the suppression of primeval chaotic forces hostile to God. The mythic background is the battle between a god and the sea (cf. *ANET* 130–131; Hab 3:8; Pss 77:16; 104:7). Natural elements are addressed and personified (vv. 5-8; cf. Ps 68:16); the sea "looked and fled," the Jordan "turned back," the mountains, hills, and earth quake. The poet builds up to the miracle of water from the rock, where he or she exaggerates and says that the rock liquefied.

From the poet's perspective, Egypt is a "people of strange language." While they are on the march, God does not have a sanctuary other than the people among whom he dwells (v. 2).[15] The Jordan crossing is paralleled with the Red Sea crossing, forming a synthesis of lib-

---

[15] At first God is not mentioned by name at all (NRSV adds "God" in v. 2), and the designation "Lord," *ʾādôn*, and "God of Jacob" only appears in v. 7. The pronominal references to the divine (v. 2) lack an antecedent, unless the *"hallelujah"* of Ps 113:9 goes with Psalm 114, a reading supported by the LXX.

eration. Likewise, the earthquake is a reaction to the theophany (vv. 4, 7), and appears as simultaneous with the water which sprung from the rock. In these select elements the poet encompasses the miracle of deliverance and all its stages, the difficulties and prodigies which accompanied it. The poet chants of God's glory, the magnitude of God's rescue and dominion over all creation.

When Jacob's enslaved house left Egypt, it was transformed into God's sanctuary and dominion. The natural world registered the change; so sea, river, mountains and hills fled, ran upstream and jumped, mirroring the transformation of the people. The poet addresses the dry, rocky ground, and tells of another transformation: "God . . . who turns the rock into a pool of water." With such a God who transforms reality, there is every reason to hope for the future.

Psalm 115
The Greatness of the True God

In Psalm 115, following a brief introduction (v. 1) and the satire about idolatry (vv. 2-8) is a triple confession of trust (vv. 9-11) and God's corresponding blessing (vv. 12-14), expanded by the memory of creation (vv. 15-16). The psalm ends with the contrast between the silence of the dead (reminiscent of the earlier satire) and the present assembly's ceaseless praise (vv. 17-18). These movements are linked with each other by repetitions—the verb "trust" (*bṭḥ*) in idols and in the LORD (vv. 8-11); the verb "bless" (*brk*, vv. 12-13, 15, 18); cognates of *ʿśh* ("do," "make," "work"). The changing voices can be understood within a liturgical context. The chorus begins (v. 1), somebody questions (v. 2), somebody else answers (vv. 3-8); three choirs are exhorted and respond (vv. 9-11). The congregation ("us" and "we," vv. 12-13, 16-18) is heard, and the priest responds by asking for a blessing on the assembly ("you," vv. 14-15).

Triplets and multiples of three mark the poem. Three groups trust in God, who "is their help and their shield"; to the triple act of faith responds a triple blessing for Israel, Aaron, "those who fear the LORD" (vv. 9-11, 12-13). The divine name, *yhwh*, or its abbreviated form *yh*, occurs twelve times (not counting the final *hallelujah*). Counting "God" (vv. 2, 3), the sum is fourteen. The word *bless* occurs six times (vv. 12-18). The universe is divided into three zones, sky, earth, and underworld (vv. 16-18). The first and the second belong to God; the third is the zone of silence and death. Between the sky and the abyss is the present assembly.

God's glory opposes the blasphemy of the foreigners who deny God's power and presence (vv. 1-2). The nations' ridicule is answered by a confident statement about "our God" (v. 3) and the parody of the ineffective idols (vv. 4-8; cf. Isa 40:18-20; 44:9-20; Jer 10:3-16; Wis 13:10–15:17), which are described with seven physical traits and seven emphatic negations (135:16-17 reproduces the first four). Completely made by hand, they are utterly ineffective, and the deities they represent are impotent frauds. The claim that those who trust what they make become like their handiwork touches on a profound truth (v. 8). If human design sets the boundaries for trust, then those who so trust are hemmed in by possibilities of their own making. Like a computer with its programmer, an idol can do no more than the person who makes it. The polemic is meant to instruct the assembly in support of the first two commandments, the worship of one God and the prohibition of idols. A poignant opposition is drawn with cognates of "do, make" (*ʿśh*): our God *does* what he likes (v. 3); he *made* heaven and earth (v. 15; cf. Pss 121:2; 124:8 134:3; Gen 14:19, 22); the worthless idols are the *work* of human hands (v. 4). The ultimate curse is that the idol makers also become mute, blind, deaf, and immobile cadavers, like the things they fashion. The curse is both cruel and rich with associations. Just as God creates in the divine image and gradually shapes in the divine semblance, so idols reduce their adherents to nothingness. The poet juxtaposes those who "trust" in idols (v. 8) with the choirs of Israel and Aaron (the priests) who "trust" in God (vv. 9-11, 12-13; cf. 118:1-4). Once the idols and their makers are disqualified, the poet rallies the assembly and invokes a blessing. The poet asserts that idols and their devotees are as good as dead and states that "the dead do not praise the LORD" (v. 17). They have descended into silence, opposite the heavens which belong to God. God blesses his adherents who praise him; there is no such exchange between idols and their makers. God, "who made heaven and earth," receives praise and blessing from those who fear and worship him, that is, from the earth (vv. 15-16, 18).

The liturgy centers around the crisis identified in v. 2, where the nations try to undercut Israel's confidence in God (cf. 42:3, 10; 79:10). The people face a perennial predicament because Israel seems to be powerless as a player against the nations and so doubts arise. The assembly's identity and destiny is defined by their trust in a God who is called in question. The plea that God respond, receive glory, reveal himself as sovereign for his own sake (v. 1) is implied. The term "heavens" converts cosmic space into theological meaning. In response to the nations' taunt, "Where is their God?" the liturgy asserts "Our God is in the heavens; he does [*ʿśh*] whatever he pleases" (v. 3). Heaven is not just above in contrast to below, but it is the limitless arena of the rule of God as he wills. "Heaven and earth" comprehends all created reality (Gen 1:1). God is related to but transcends all that exists, all of which is his creative work. He bequeathed the earth to humans. Thus even the capacity to make and worship idols is something which the maker of heaven and earth allows, so everybody, the faithful and the idolater, acts within God's realm. The liturgy summons the assembly to trust in God who has always been "their help and their shield" among the nations (vv. 9-11). The assembly is reminded that God has always "been mindful of" Israel, who can be confident that God will bless them with "increase" (vv. 12-15). In turn, the assembly will "bless the LORD from this time on" (v. 18).

Psalm 116
God Listens to Those Who Call

Psalm 116 expresses the thanksgiving of one whose request has been answered. The poet recalls an experience (vv. 3-4, 10-11), acknowledges God as rescuer (vv. 1-2, 5-9, 15-16), and promises to fulfill his or her vows (vv. 12-14, 17-19), thus weaving past and future into the present gratitude. In the Greek and Latin versions, Psalm 116 is divided in two; vv. 1-9 and 10-19 appear as Psalms 114 and 115. Following this lead, we may divide the poem into two movements. The first incorporates dramatic elements of mortal danger, a cry for help, and God's answer and is the basis for the liturgy celebrated in the second movement. The address "O LORD," *ʾānnâh yhwh*, links the two parts,[16] as does the phrase "call[ed] on the name of the LORD" (vv. 4, 13, 16-17). "You have loosed my bonds" (v. 16) describes the deliverance from "the snares" (v. 3).

The opening "I love the LORD" imprints the poem with an avowal of love.[17] Why? God listens to those who trust in him and grants what they need. Love here means to call on God by name.[18] The repeated phrase "call[ed] on the name" has a double meaning, both to invoke God's help and to offer thanksgiving sacrifices (vv. 4, 13, 17). The soul freed from distress returns to the shelter (a physical space and a psychological reality) that the beloved provides.

---

[16] These are the only direct invocations of God in the psalm.

[17] The declaration is unique, the only direct parallel being the opening of Psalm 18, where a different verb is used. Ps 116:3 repeats Ps 18:4-5 almost verbatim.

[18] The divine name *yhwh* appears seven times in vv. 1-9 and eight times in vv. 10-19 (as in the NRSV).

Death threatened, which plunged the poet into anguish. The metaphor "snares of death" derives from the ancient conception of Sheol. Distressed, the psalmist invoked God, who heard. The recollection makes the experience present, and the poet affirms God's perpetual goodness by the use of adjectives and participles (in Hebrew) and instructs the assembly (vv. 5-6). In a soliloquy the poet bids the "soul" to rest in God (v. 7). This has an intimate ring. God's constant care is a wellspring of trust. The soliloquy may express the intention to visit the temple where God's presence provides relief and security. This interpretation hangs on the understanding of *měnûḥâh* as "rest," but it can also be understood as "resting place" (cf. 132:8, 14). The release from death is illustrated in the tears and stumbling feet, replaced by walking "before the LORD" (vv. 8-9).[19] The mention of "feet" prepares for the "walk" and the metaphor aptly translates the poet's experience. Death tightens its grip on a person by sickness and oppression. What at first is an uncertain walk ends in a life with God and a proposition full of hope, "I walk before the LORD in the land [Hebrew, plural] of the living." Freed from death's clutches, the poet can live with God.

The psalmist kept faith in God, even when he or she was grieved because one could not trust anybody (vv. 10-11). The last part (vv. 12-19) is a pledge to celebrate a thanksgiving liturgy. The rhetorical question admits that God's goodness can never be repaid. The liturgy comprises various rites. A refrain (vv. 13b-14, 17b-18) brackets the declaration, "Precious . . . is the death of his faithful" and the testimony of God's rescue (vv. 15-16). Two ritual actions are singled out, offering the "cup of salvation" (v. 13a; cf. the "drink offering" in Numbers 28) and thanksgiving sacrifice (v. 17a). The cup is either to drink or to offer a libation (see Exod 29:40-41; Num 15:5-7). My "vows" refers to the promised liturgy (possibly in the temple as a public testimony; see Ps 22:25), and it was made when the psalmist was praying for deliverance (see 66:13-15). The poet's dependence on God becomes progressively more emphatic, from "servant" to "the child of your serving girl" (cf. 86:16). Thus, the poet is among those who do God's will and whose death is costly for God.[20]

The poet describes a situation from the point of view of a victim facing the threat of death. Curiously absent are the enemies and the confession of sins or the protestation of personal innocence that is normally found in psalms like this. Rather, the poet soberly narrates how he or she called on God and was heard and gives a reason why God should intervene, that God always proves to be just, compassionate, tender, a

---

[19] "Death," *mawet*, which threatened the poet, appears three times (vv. 3, 8, 15).
[20] See Ps 72:14; the faithful ("their blood") are too precious to be allowed to die.

protector of the little people (vv. 5-6a; see 86:15; 103:8; 111:4; 145:8). The poet graphically describes liberation from death, tears and stumbling. The basis for the present tranquility is the confidence that he or she will walk in God's presence "in the land of the living," in contrast to the abysmal world to which one was on the point of descending (see 27:13; 52:5; 56:13).

Psalm 116, which has an individual flavor, plays a role in the liturgy. The ritual use of a cup and a sacrifice are determinative for its application to the Passover celebration (see *Pesachim*, 10:1-9). Based on this, it becomes the thanksgiving of any believer who celebrates his or her own salvation acquired in the Exodus. For the Christian this psalm was used in the course of the Lord's Supper, the Eucharist, which applies the Exodus to the ultimate redemption found in Christ.

Psalm 117
A Tiny Psalm on a Grand Scale

Psalm 117 calls for world-wide recognition of God. After the initial invitation, the motive and content of the praise is given. The psalm begins and ends with the invocation, "Praise the LORD" (the final invocation is the abbreviated form of the word *hallelujah*, Hebrew). The initial hemistichs are parallel. An invitation to praise is followed by the object (LORD or "him"), followed by the addressee ("nations" or "peoples"). The poet then introduces God's twin attributes, the reasons for the praise, introduced by *kî*, "for." God's *ḥesed* and "faithfulness," *ʾĕmet*, are described in chiastic parallelism ("great" and "endures forever"), literally,

A	B
great toward us	is his *ḥesed*
B'	**A'**
and the LORD's faithfulness	is forever.

These attributes typify God's relationship with the present assembly ("us").

The poet envisages an eschatological horizon when nationality and race distinctions are eclipsed by the unanimous praise of God. Why should all peoples praise God? The theological motive is salvation and hope for the future in terms of *ḥesed* and faithfulness. The present assembly is the recipient of God's kindness. If "toward us" refers to

Israel, the poet invites all humanity to praise God for the *ḥesed* and fidelity shown to the chosen people; in effect, this would equal an invitation to mass conversion on the scale of Isaiah 60. If "toward us" is not exclusively Israelite, the poet testifies to God's faithful *ḥesed* embracing everybody. In either case the thought of Psalm 117 is in harmony with the universalistic current of the first Testament. Believers who recite it are reminded that God's praise is complete only when the intent is to join in concert with all people.[21]

Psalm 118
Ultimate Victory

Psalm 118 is framed between the shortest and the longest psalms (Psalms 117 and 119) and is the concluding psalm in the so-called "Egyptian Hallel" (Psalms 113–118), a collection customarily used at annual festivals and especially during Passover. The collection opens with praise of God who reverses human conditions by lifting up the needy and defenseless (Psalm 113). Psalm 114 recalls the Exodus as the manifestation of God's rule. Psalm 115 contrasts Israel's God with the pagan gods. A theme of death and the world of the dead links 115:17 with 116:3. Psalm 117 invites all nations to praise God.[22] Each of these five psalms anticipates themes and motifs of Psalm 118, and they provide a literary and liturgical context for understanding it as Israel's thanksgiving for the divine *ḥesed* (117:2; 118:1-4, 14-16, 29), which is manifested by God's delivering the people from death.

Psalm 118 is a thanksgiving liturgy which celebrates deliverance. It has two movements (vv. 5-18, 19-28), framed within choral praise of God's *ḥesed* (vv. 1-4, 29). The invitatory is a short litany inviting Israel, priests, and assembly to chant "his *ḥesed* endures forever" (vv. 2-4; cf. the same three groups in 115:9-11; 135:19-20). The term *ḥesed* is not used in the body of the poem. The alternation of individual and choral voices, the repetitions, refrains and explicit references to liturgical actions—the entrance into the temple and the procession (vv. 19-20, 27; see Ps 24:7-9)—make it hard to follow the internal dynamics, but all of this suggests a liturgy on the occasion or anniversary of a major victory.

[21] Paul quotes Psalm 117 as scriptural testimony to expound God's purpose in Jesus Christ (Rom 15:11).
[22] Because of the brevity of Psalm 117, tradition combines it with either 116 or 118. The sixth century monastic rule of Benedict joins Psalms 116–117 for reasons of economy in liturgical recitation.

At first various groups intone the classic formula "his *ḥesed* endures forever" (cf. Pss 106:1; 107:1; 136:1). The presider narrates the experience and rescue. A choral response follows, as in a victory song (vv. 15-16). When the procession arrives at the gate, a verse and response are chanted (vv. 19-20). The liturgy culminates around the altar (v. 27).

The plot is straightforward. The first movement is woven together by recurrent motifs attesting to the victory. The distressed poet called for help to God, who rescued him (v. 5, a drama summarized in vv. 13, 18). The poet contrasts cramped straits and God's spaciousness (v. 5; cf. 4:1; 25:17; 31:8-9):

> Out of my distress [*min–hammēṣar*] I called on the LORD;
> the LORD answered me and set me in a broad place [*bammerḥāb*].

The presider expresses trust in God and draws the conclusion that it is better to take refuge in God than to trust in powerful persons (vv. 6-9; 20:7; 146:3-5). Doublets contrast reliance on God with threat from or trust in "mortals" (Hebrew, *ʾādām*, repeated in vv. 6, 8). What can mere mortals or even a nation do to someone whose protector is God? The moral, "take refuge in the LORD," is broadcast (vv. 8-9). Experience teaches that God is the only reliable helper. The motifs of the besieging nations and their defeat "in the name of the LORD" are grouped together and culminate in the affirmation that God has granted salvation (vv. 10-14).[23] What may have been a victory against national enemies the poet has converted into a cosmic fray, all nations against God's people. The attack is intensified with each repeated phrase but is always rebuffed by the unvarying refrain which represents God's power, help, salvation—in a word, the LORD (vv. 10-11). The enemy ambush is likened to swarming bees in mad frenzy and to dried out brush that is ignited, blazes fast but quickly dies out (v. 12). The assembly can resist the besieging nations because God is an ally. The motif "salvation" is crocheted into the following movement in the phrase "songs of victory [Hebrew, "salvation"]." More like cheers at a rally, the "songs" are repeated three times, and they are a prelude to the triumphal entrance into the temple (vv. 15-16). "The right hand of the LORD" means divine intervention in human affairs (Pss 20:6; 60:5; 98:1). The motif of death

---

[23] The Exodus tradition informs the language of Psalm 118. The pivotal declaration, "The LORD is my strength and my might; he has become my salvation" (v. 14; see v. 21), is the theme of the song of the sea (Exod 15:2; cf. Isa 12:2). Other motifs of the song are God's right hand (vv. 15-16 and Exod 15:6, 12), exaltation of the LORD as "my God" (v. 28 and Exod 15:2b), and *ḥesed* as God's motivation (vv. 1-4, 29 and Exod 15:13).

tells to what degree God has intervened (vv. 17-18); to be said to be near death can serve as an image for any affliction in the Hebrew anthropology.

Individual and choral voices alternate in the second movement. Beginning with a request for entrance the motif of thanks is reintroduced from the beginning.[24] The presider requests entry and announces thanks (vv. 19, 21, 28); attendant ministers respond with conditions for admission, blessing, and the declarations (vv. 20, 26-27). The presider has joined the procession. The porter's response gives the condition for entrance, "This is the gate of the LORD; the righteous shall enter through it" (v. 20). The condition is "righteous," a condensation of the entrance examinations in Psalms 15 and 24.

Framed by the presider's thanksgiving (*ydh*, vv. 21, 28) the assembly acknowledges salvation as God's wondrous act (vv. 22-24) and prays for salvation (v. 25; the cry *hôšî'âh nāʾ*, "Hosanna" means "save us"). The victor (cf. vv. 10-12), who now enters in God's name, is blessed (v. 26). Acclamation is joined to ritual procession, as the faithful approach the altar with branches in their hands (v. 27). The presider and the choir sing alternating refrains (vv. 28-29). Thus, the presider again summons the assembly, "O give thanks to the LORD, for he is good," to which the assembly responds, "for his *ḥesed* endures forever."

The divine name LORD occurs twenty-eight times (both in the Hebrew and the NRSV) and "God" occurs twice (v. 28). Death, *mwt*, has a tenuous foothold in the liturgy, and life is akin to recounting God's deeds (vv. 17-18). The following repetitions give the poem an anaphoric quality: "Let . . . say, 'His steadfast love endures forever'"; "the LORD . . . on my side" (vv. 6-7); "[i]t is better to take refuge in the LORD" (vv. 8-9); "in the name of the LORD I cut them off"[25] and "surrounded" (vv. 10-12); "salvation" or "victory," *yēšûʿâh* (v. 14, 15, 21; the verb *yšʿ* occurs again in v. 25);[26] "righteous[ness]," *ṣedeq*, (vv. 15, 19, 20); "the right hand of the LORD" and "does valiantly [*ḥyl*]" (vv. 15-16); "enter" or "come," *bwʾ* (vv. 19, 20, 26); "we beseech you" (v. 25), you are my God" (v. 28).

---

[24] A plaza inside the gate of a Near Eastern city was a gathering place for civic assemblies (2 Chr 32:6; Neh 8:1). Commercial transactions were effected there (Neh 3:1, 3), and the designation "gates of righteousness" alludes to the fact that legal proceedings were conducted there (e.g., Deut 21:19; 22:24; Ruth 3:11; 4:1, 10, 11).

[25] The translation of the Hebrew *mwl* (Hiphil) is "resist" or "ward off" instead of "cut off" as in NRSV, which depends on the LXX's translation of a verb of uncertain meaning (vv. 10-12).

[26] The cognate usage of *yšʿ* (vv. 14, 15, 21, 25), *ṣdq* (vv. 15, 19, 20), *ḥyl* (vv. 15, 16), and *ṣlḥ* (v. 25), are synonymous, denoting success or victory.

The cornerstone image is derived from the way in which masons choose the stone for key positions of a structure (v. 22). Here it stands for Israel. The analogy represents the doctrine of the remnant taught by Isaiah, who speaks of this tested, righteous remnant as the nucleus of the new Israel (Isa 28:16; cf. Zech 3:9).[27] Though deemed unimportant by imperial neighbors, Israel plays a distinguished role in the architecture of God's reign. "The builders," that is, the nations' rulers, despised the Jews and sought their annihilation. But with the dawn of redemption, all nations will realize that Israel is the "cornerstone" of world redemption.

Psalm 118 was associated with the Jewish festival of Sukkoth (see Lev 23:33-36; Deut 16:13-15) quite early. For Christians, "the day that the LORD has made" (v. 24) refers to the messiah's definitive victory over death, the day of the Resurrection, which transforms the lives of his followers. Read in this way, Psalm 118 becomes the celebration of the risen Jesus and his community. One may think of the resurrected messiah guiding the procession of humanity to give thanks to the Father, inviting everyone to celebrate joy and victory.

Psalm 119
On the Excellence of God's Will

Law, according to the use of the word *tôrâh* and its synonyms in Psalm 119, means wisdom or God's will. This poem represents an understanding of law akin to the *regula* of the ancient monastic tradition, a balanced ordering of human life. Law is a handrail which steadies and guides a person to walk rightly, and it represents divine revelation. Like the Torah, the first five scrolls of the Bible, which recounts God's marvelous acts and regulates human conduct to effect salvation, the law embraces all the movements of human life with God. God's law, an expression of his will, expresses perfection, and the poet gives shape to this sense in the composition of Psalm 119.

This acrostic poem[28] consists of twenty-two strophes, one for each Hebrew letter. In alphabetical order the poet composes strophes of

---

[27] The second Testament interpretation (Matt 21:42; Acts 4:11, etc.) sees an eminent fulfillment in Christ.

[28] Alphabetical acrostics, Psalms 9-10; 25; 34; 111; 112; 119; 145. W. Soll, *Psalm 119: Matrix, Form, and Setting*, CBQMS 23 (Washington: Catholic Biblical Association, 1991) 11–20, surveys biblical acrostics.

eight verses initialized with the same letter. Every verse contains the word *tôrâh* (twenty-five occurrences) or a synonym. Verses 90 and 122 allude to law with uncharacteristic terms, *ʾĕmûnâh*, "faithfulness," and *ʿārōb*, "guarantee." The theological content of Psalm 119 is evident in the well-ordered structure; *tôrâh* is pervasive and all-inclusive. The poem has no well-defined thought sequence, although some strophes are shaded by mood and plot. Motifs of the personal complaint suggest the poet's trials, as, for example, vv. 22-23, 28, 49-54, 61, 81-88, 132-136, 153-158. In this very calculated composition emotions ebb and flow and the drama of a menacing enemy is enacted. References to Israel's history, including the legal corpus and the covenant, are noticeably absent. The anthologic character of the composition is illustrated in the scriptural reference notes in some translations of the Bible. The word *śḥh*, "meditate," urges the disciple of wisdom to linger upon and mutter the *tôrâh* repeatedly (vv. 15, 23, 27, 48, 78, 148). The monotonous structure is intended to help the reader ruminate and thus enable him or her to fully appreciate the *tôrâh* and apply it to daily life. The tireless incantation fosters a contemplative climate which softens the heart and opens it to wisdom. The poet interiorizes God's will with meditation and love (vv. 47-48).

In an overture, two composite beatitudes are directed to the person who walks blamelessly and does no wrong (vv. 1-3). The LORD is in the third person. The rest of the anthology is addressed to God,[29] and the emphatic pronoun "you," *ʾattâh* (v. 4), introduces the change of address. The reader can appreciate the internal design and the poet's choice of language. The frequent use of *derek*, "way, path," a synonym for law, stamps the first half with a pilgrimage or journey motif (vv. 1, 3, 5, 14, 26, 27, 29, 30, 32, 33, 37, 59, 168); other verbs of motion, "walk," *hlk* (vv. 1, 3, 45), "stray, wander," *šgh* and *tʿh* (vv. 21, 118, 176), "run," *rwṣ* (v. 32), reinforce this.

The poet refers to himself thirteen times as "your servant," which betokens a privileged relation with God (vv. 17, 23, 38, 49, 65, 76, 84, 122, 124, 125, 135, 140, 176). In addition, he or she acknowledges that all is at "your service" (v. 91); thus, cognates of *ʿbd* ("serve" or "servant") total fourteen. The author, often badgered by enemies and scoffers, is a sojourner or wanderer, *gēr* (v. 19), an exile in a distant country (v. 54). The Hebrew *gēr* has no right to private property. Here it refers to a person who adopts God as a possession. The migrant poet seeks not prosperity but to know God's will. He or she clings to the dust and needs to be revived so as to cling to the law (vv. 25, 31), asserts the value of per-

---

[29] Exceptions, vv. 57a, 115, 126a. Verse 115 has "my God," the only departure from the use of the divine name *yhwh*.

sonal suffering to appropriate the law (v. 71), and compares the self to a leather flask that gets brittle once it has been drained (v. 83). Emotions are evidenced in the images of melting (v. 28), quaking with fright (v. 120), uncontrolled weeping (v. 136), being consumed (v. 139), anguish and trouble (v. 143). The poet hates, śnʾ, false ways and loves, ʾhb, the law,[30] repeatedly professing that one has not forgotten and will not forget, škḥ, the law (vv. 16, 61, 83, 93, 109, 141, 153, 176), in contrast to the enemies who do forget. The tôrâh is a source of genuine, lasting joy.[31] "Heart" (lēb, lebab) occurs frequently, and denotes whole-hearted devotion to and interiorization of God's will (vv. 2, 7, 10, 11, 32, 34, 36, 58, 69, 70, 80, 111, 112, 145, 161). The poet has a full body, personal experience of the law, as is evident by the mention of the eyes, hands, feet, heart, soul.[32] Day and night the poet meditates or cries out, up to seven times a day (vv. 55, 62, 97, 147–148, 164). He or she is concerned with the threat or possibility of being ashamed (bwš and cognates, vv. 6, 31, 46, 80) and prays that the proud be shamed instead (v. 78). The law is compared with wealth (vv. 14, 72, 127); rejoicing over rich spoil describes the poet's great discovery (v. 162).

The sage reflects on the place of evil in God's plan. It is not clear who the adversary is but twice the implication is that he or she is among the ruling class (vv. 23, 161). The arrogant are digging pits and laying snares (vv. 61, 85, 110). A memorable image is to "grease with lies," to speak with a slick heart, which describes the fat, gross heart of the impious (vv. 69-70). The scandal is the proud and evil who forsake God's commands (vv. 21, 53, 113, 118-119, 136, 139, 158), those who vilify and deride God (vv. 39, 42, 51, 69-70, 78, 122, 141), the wicked who seek to oppress and destroy one (vv. 95, 134, 150, 157). The fray becomes intense. Those who are far from divine teaching close in, but so does God (vv. 150-151). Prominent among the inimical forces which oppose the seeker of God's law is the lie, šeqer (vv. 29, 69, 78, 86, 104, 118, 128, 163).

The composition of some strophes is stamped with a pattern or mood, based on peculiarities of Hebrew language and vocabulary. For example, the initial letter dalet ("d," vv. 25-32) suggests a discourse on the "way" (derek). The journey will be straight if it coincides with the way God traces. The poet asks that God enlarge his or her heart so as to

---

[30] "Hate," śnʾ, appears in vv. 104, 113, 128, 163, cf. 158; "love," ʾhb, occurs in vv. 47, 48, 97, 113, 119, 127, 132, 140, 159, 163, 165, 167.

[31] Verses 16, 24, 47, 70, 77, 92, 143, 174 (šʾʾ); cf. vv. 14, 162 (śwś), 35 (ḥpṣ), 111 (śaśôn).

[32] Organs mentioned are lips (vv. 13, 171), eyes (vv. 18, 37, 82, 123, 136, 148), life or soul (npš, vv. 20, 81, 109, 129), mouth (vv. 43, 103, 131), hands (v. 48), feet (vv. 59, 101, 105, [133]), tongue (vv. 103, 172), flesh (v. 120).

continue along the way (v. 32). Other features of the *dalet* strophe are the verb "to cling," *dbq* (vv. 25, 31, an inclusion), and the contrasting images of personal distress and devotion.

The initial letter *he* ("h") is a preformative of the *Hiphil* conjugation, which has a causative sense. In the *he* strophe (vv. 33-40) seven *Hiphil* imperatives formulate the request to know and follow the law. God is the source of every grace, even the grace to follow him. The true reward is not worldly gain but life in accord with the law (vv. 36-37). This imperative mode is continued in the first verses of the succeeding *vav* ("w") strophe (vv. 41-48), which reinforce the urgent plea (vv. 41-43). Eight times the poet employs the conjunction *vav*, "and" (not usually represented in translation). That God's law is promise and a source of consolation dominates the *zayin* ("z") strophe (vv. 49-56). The significant word *zkr*, "remember," is repeated. May God *remember* his promise (v. 49); the poet, in turn will *remember* the law and the LORD (vv. 52, 55). Six times in the *teth* ("ṭ") strophe the idea of the *good (ṭôb)* is repeated, the initial letter of which is *teth* (vv. 65-72). God is and does *good* (vv. 65, 68). Personal suffering is a *benefit* (v. 71). God's commands are *more precious (ṭôb)* than gold and silver (v. 72).

The intimate relation between the poet and God is underscored in the *yod* ("y") strophe (vv. 73-80). The initial letter forms a series of cohortatives or subjunctives; the tone of supplication, which continues to the end of the poem, is given greater emphasis beginning with v. 76 (i.e., the pleas in vv. 115-117, 132-135, 153-154, 169-173, 175-176, and *he* above). In the *kaf* ("k") strophe (vv. 81-88) complaint dominates, with the motifs of sadness, corporal infirmity, attacks and sneers, impassioned questions and pleas. Here the enemies' presence and action is condensed into four verses; they persecute, set traps, almost get what they want. This makes the need more imperative, which stamps this strophe with a unique tone. A "wineskin in the smoke" projects the psalmist as finished, dried up and shriveled. "[L]anguishes" and the plaintive questions emphasize the point. The adversary appears to be closing in. The *yod* and *kaf* strophes portray the drama poignantly. The intimate relation between the poet and God is threatened by the poet's depression and the enemy attack (vv. 78, 80-87).

The *lamed* ("l") strophe (vv. 88-96) answers this complaint. Here the eternal foundation of the word is compared with the heavens and the earth, both created by God's word. The divine law endures forever and stands true to this day (vv. 89-91). The poet's intimacy with God is expressed briefly (v. 94). The horizon is broadened to contemplation (v. 96). A polemic between law and wisdom is heard in three verses of the *mem* ("m") strophe, as the poet places the law above wisdom (vv. 98-100). In other words, compared to the teaching of the law, the sages and elders who represent tradition weigh less. Comparisons are suggested by the initial *mem*, wiser, *more* insight, *more* understanding. The highest wisdom is to know the divine will. The praise of wisdom is introduced and concluded with exclamations, "how I love your law!" and "sweeter than honey to my mouth!" (vv. 97, 103).

The last verse of the "s" strophe (v. 120) does not agree with the previous declarations about the love, hope, joy, and consolation of fulfilling the commands. Trembling flesh connotes shuddering with fear, hair on end. Given the context, one may think of the balancing act of reverential love. The initial letter in the word "righteous" or "justice," *ṣdq*, is *tsade* ("ṣ" vv. 137-144). God is the source and model of righteousness; for this he reveals equitable laws (vv. 137-138). God's righteousness is eternal and *tôrâh* reflects eternal justice (vv. 142, 144). Even though the poet may feel small and afflicted God's will consoles him or her (vv. 141, 143).

The *tav* ("t") strophe (vv. 169-176) contains a conclusion and dedication and is marked by an accumulation of rhymes and parallels. In six verses the second hemistich begins with *k-* ("according to," "for," "because"). The *-eka* ("you" or "your") rhyme sounds fourteen times in this strophe, placing God and his will in the range of vision. The poet sums up the prayer as a cry and petition (vv. 169, 170), praise (vv. 171, 175), song (v. 172), delight and longing (v. 174). Thus, all prayer is collected in this strophe. In the end, the poet recommends him or herself to the good shepherd (v. 176). This is unexpected. It reintroduces the theme of the path and evokes a pastoral image. But after so many protestations of observance, love, zeal, and fulfillment, how is it that the poet refers to straying, that God has to search to bring him or her back? How could God forget a servant who has so comprehensively meditated the law!

Tôrâh is God's will and wisdom, ordained in the structure of existence, a foundation for moral values. The created world is sustained by God's faithfulness and human attention to how God has ordered creation. Hosea presents a view that violation of the law leads to the undoing of creation (Hos 4:1-3; cf. Ps 82:5). Such a connection between creation and *tôrâh* is evident in the two parts of Psalm 19, a celebration of the wonder of creation (vv. 1-6) and an affirmation of the life-giving *tôrâh* (vv. 7-10). The proper response to God's well-ordered world is a balanced, calm life. In Psalm 119 a dedicated sage meditates and teaches the basics of such an existence. With the *tôrâh* life is ultimately reliable and complete. The *tôrâh* insures the world against a return to chaos. It safeguards humanity and guides persons to a higher satisfaction than a life designed according to self-interest. The meditation can serve as the basis for the moral posture which results in an authentic life in conformity with God's will and a context within which to disperse anxiety. One need not go beyond reflection on the *tôrâh* to live fully and appreciate one's origin, path, and destiny. The poem gradually entices the faithful soul to enjoy such a pleasant life. It also fosters an attitude of circumspection towards mocking persecutors, those who ignore or despise God's wisdom.

The poet praises the law and the fruits to be found therein for the one who "seeks" *drš* (vv. 2, 10, 45, 94, 155). He or she frequently expresses the desire to "learn," "teach," or "be taught."[33] The meticulous poet repeats words and synonyms which demonstrate the dominant ideas. Some patterns of repetition according to the number seven are the following:

—the poet prays for life, *ḥyh* and cognates (fourteen times, vv. 17, 25, 37, 40, 77, 88, 107, 116, 144, 149, 154, 156, 159, 175);

—forms of the verb *šmr*, "to keep, observe," stamp the poem (twenty-one times, vv. 4, 5, 8, 9, 17, 34, 44, 55, 57, 60, 63, 67, 88, 101, 106, 134, 136, 146, 158, 167, 168);

—*ḥesed* (vv. 41, 64, 76, 88, 124, 149, 159);

—"hope," *ḥwl* and *śbr* (vv. 49, 74, 81, 114, 116, 147, 166);

—"serve" and "servant," *ʿbd* (identified above, fourteen times);

—seven times the poet refers to God as "you," emphatic *ʾattâh* (vv. 4, 12, 68, 102, 114, 137, 151).

Given the completeness of the poem, it is not surprising that the poet expresses his or her devotion fourteen times with "continually" and "forever."

Psalm 119 understands that life with God is a two-way street. People who submit to the *tôrâh* can expect commensurate returns. It is the means to harmony with God, not an end in itself. Thus it becomes a port of entry to explore the range of interactions with God and sustain an ongoing relation with God in daily life. This psalm expresses utter trust and submission to God's plan for the universe and the moral order. The similarity between Psalm 119 and a litany is the repetition of a single theme. In both the repeated and continuous pressure massages the consciousness of the *orante* who becomes increasingly relaxed and receptive with each line. Such a prayer focuses the *orante's* heart and mind and directs him or her towards profound meditation. This psalm,

---

[33] Verbs for instruction and understanding are *lmd*, vv. 7, 12, 26, 64, 66, 68, 71, 73, 99, 108, 124, 135, 171; *byn*, vv. 27, 34, 73, 95, 100, 104, 125, 130, 144, 169; and *yrh*, vv. 33, 102.

like a litany, tempers the emotions, views the object of its attention from different perspectives, and adds depth and richness to one's perception.

Psalm 120
Deliverance from Those Who Hate Peace

All the superscriptions of Psalms 120–134 contain the phrase "A Song of Ascents," and possibly this collection was a hymnal prior to its incorporation into the present Psalter.[34] These compositions, except for Psalm 132, are brief. The names Jerusalem and Zion occur with an unusual frequency, twelve times in eight psalms, and "house of the LORD" in two (122:1; 134:1). "Israel" appears with a frequency untypical elsewhere in the Psalter, nine times for the collection. Liturgical components are relatively frequent—benedictions and peace (125:5; 128:5-6; 134:3),[35] summons to confess and hope (124:1; 129:1; 130:7; 131:3), confessional terms (121:2; 124:8; 134:3). The theme of dependence on God amidst adversity recurs. Pairs of psalms share common features (121 and 124; 124 and 129). Psalms 127 and 128 are exhortations in the sapiential style; the beatitudes (initial *ʾašrê*) link two (127:5; 128:1). Both are composed of short sayings which reflect on everyday themes of piety, daily work and rest (127:1-2; 128:1-2) and family blessings (127:3-5; 128:3-4). Psalms 130 and 131 are linked by "O Israel, hope in the LORD," *yaḥēl yiśrāʾēl ʾel–yhwh* (130:7 [absent from the LXX]; 131:3); the subject of each is confidence in God.

The appeal for help, the curse, and the complaint mark the three movements of Psalm 120. The poet summarizes the danger and liberation in a flashback, quoting the cry for help against calumny (vv. 1-2).[36]

---

[34] Recurring features unify the group. Commentators hypothesize about their use as Jerusalem pilgrimage psalms, arranged in a stair-like pattern, from the start of the pilgrimage to the approach to Jerusalem, the entrance into the city and the temple. Another hypothesis is that they were sung on the fifteen steps in the ascent to the temple. There is no evident pattern in their order. Their meaningful arrangement or religious purpose, even their use as a pilgrimage medley, remains hypothetical. For the songs of ascents as a progressive pilgrimage to Jerusalem, see James L. Mays, *Psalms* (Louisville: John Knox, 1994), 358–415.

[35] There is a pronounced vocabulary of blessing (128:4, 5; 129:8; 132:15; 133:3; 134:3), "peace" (120:6, 7; 122:6-8; 125:5; 128:6), and "good" (122:9; 125:4; 128:5 ["prosperity"]; 133:1).

[36] The verbs in v. 1 might better be translated in the past tense (with NJPS, RNAB, REV) instead of the present (NRSV).

Then he or she addresses the enemy and employs the conventional form of a curse framed as a rhetorical question with an answer, expressing the certainty of reprisal (vv. 3-4; see 1 Sam 3:17; 14:44; 25:22). In the end the poet deplores the unhappy situation (vv. 5-7). The combination of the prayer and the recollection of distress juxtaposes the pain of exile and the desire for reconciliation with God. Distress is featured in each part. It first drove the poet to prayer, and it could be surmounted only by dependence on God. The curse reflects exasperation caused by the distress. What does such hostility deserve? Is it not fitting for those who so favor war to undergo the arrows and fire of a siege?

Lying lips and tongue are a personification of the enemy; the neighbors are haters of peace (vv. 2-3, 6). Deceitful speech is often cited in the psalms as a weapon against society (e.g., 5:9; 10:7; 12:1-4; 31:18, etc.). Lies undermine life and, consequently, the soul is insecure and damaged. The poet hopes that the verbal assault, which defies peace and volleys from a distance, will receive a commensurate punishment. This is eloquently portrayed in Psalm 64, where God will turn the enemies' venomous arrows against them (see 7:12-13; 11:6; 64:7-8; 140:9-10). Another image for destruction of the assailant, the consuming brush fire, is derived from the broom plant which burns with intense heat and the roots of which are used for making charcoal. As in Psalm 42, the poet likens his or her state to an exile. Meshech, a warring people of northeast Asia Minor (Ezek 38:2), and Kedar, a belligerent desert tribe from north Arabia (Isa 21:17), are metaphors for exile in alien lands, and they represent any residence beset with personal animosity and social strife. The distress comes from having to live without peace, but the poet is committed to it and thus curses those who hate it.

The connection between this desire and the ways that peace features in the following psalms makes Psalm 120 a good introduction to the booklet of songs of ascent (Psalms 120–134). These psalms represent different stages along the pilgrimage route to Jerusalem, or the ascending steps to the temple, and, thus, they are termed "Gradual Psalms" in the Latin tradition. Indeed, there seems to be a progression, from distance from the temple in Psalm 120, to a concentration on Zion, Jerusalem, and the temple as the goal in subsequent psalms, and the arrival and celebrations in the sanctuary in the last psalms of the series. The songs of ascent share few characteristics in common and do not have the same literary structure or genre. Nothing explains their grouping under this common title, except perhaps their rhythm and brevity, and a concentration on Jerusalem, the object of the pilgrimage.

Psalm 121
The LORD Is Your Guard

The name LORD occurs twice in Psalm 120 and five times in Psalm 121, totaling seven for the two consecutive psalms. "Come" and "coming" (*bwʾ*, vv. 1, 8) frames Psalm 121. The poet answers the initial question "from where will my help come?" and guarantees the divine assistance. The first two poetic lines are composed in the first person, the motif "my help" appearing in both. Then an unidentified voice addresses the psalmist ("you"). Ten times the pronoun suffix (in Hebrew) "your" or "you" reassures the poet—*your* foot, keeper, shade, right hand, life, coming in and going out; "keep[s] *you*" (vv. 3, 7) and "strike *you*" (v. 6). The theme, "my help comes from the LORD" (v. 2), is developed by the assurances that "the LORD is your keeper" (v. 5) and the sixfold repetition of *šmr*, "keep." "Watchman" is more apt than the NRSV's "keeper"; *šmr* also means "preserve," "protect." The assurances of divine protection and the repetitions impose a unity on the psalm. Surely God is the help, the guardian, always vigilant like a dutiful sentry, never overcome by drowsiness (vv. 3-4, the motif "slumber"). God will be the protecting shade from sun and moon, that is, around the clock. The expressions "all evil," "your life," your coming and going" (a merism), and "from this time on and forevermore" embrace the totality. The metaphors about the foot which does not slip and departing and returning frame the main part of the psalm (vv. 3, 8); the image of being abroad day and night is in the center of this frame (v. 6). Not only does God guard the psalmist, but he "who made heaven and earth" guards all the faithful and, in a special way, Israel (v. 4).

The imagery is lovely. The pilgrims ascend the slope that rises to the horizon, which touches the sky or "heavens," where the creator of heaven and earth has a home. A likely location is the hills around Jerusalem (125:2; 133:3). Israel's guardian is everybody's. The assurances of help do not cite specific dangers or details of divine aid; instead, general statements and the repetition of the verb "keep" guarantee God's protection always and everywhere. This is a cousin to Psalm 91, where similar images of danger and protection are used (shade in v. 1, danger day and night in vv. 5-6, all evil in v. 10). The slipping foot is an idiom for unsteadiness (see 38:16; 94:18). Widely differing dangers or threats are suggested here. The phrase translated "your shade at your right hand" evokes a sun screen and a defense lawyer in court or the second in command (cf. 16:8; 110:5). Heatstroke is a real threat in Palestine, and there are superstitions about the moon's effect.

The divine guardian's vigilance is emphasized with four negations, "He will not let your foot be moved," "will not slumber," "neither slumber nor sleep." This amounts to constant vigilance, which is summarized in another negation, "The sun shall not strike you by day, nor the moon by night" (parallel lines). The description is a guarantee especially against nocturnal danger; the night watchman is ever alert. "Who made heaven and earth" is a liturgical formula (v. 2; cf. 115:15; 124:8; 134:3; 146:6). In none of these usages is there a concern about how the world came to be; rather, the context speaks about God who makes a difference for the faithful in the present. Here and in 124:8 and 146:6 the formula accompanies the notion of "help" (*ʿzr*). The one who made heaven and earth, hills and mountains, who designed day and night, is not limited by creation. The world and the psalmist are safe, because the creator can sustain creation while we sleep. The human world, measured by day and night and goings and comings, can trust in the transcendent guard and keeper who neither tires nor falls asleep. Thus, the psalm which began with raising the physical gaze to the heights concludes with a contemplative grasp of reality.

Psalm 122
The *Šālôm of Jerusalem*

The architecture of Psalm 122 is significant. As in Psalm 48, architectural features of the city are prominent—the temple, gates, thrones, walls, and towers. References to "the house of the LORD" bracket the psalm (vv. 1, 9), as if to say that the motivation and destination of the ascent is the temple, and this forms a concentric structure:

A the psalmist and companions ("I" and "us"), "house of the LORD" (vv. 1-2)

    B Jerusalem (vv. 3-4)

        C "the thrones for judgment" and "the house of David" (v. 5)

    B' Jerusalem (vv. 6-7)

A' the psalmist and companions ("I" and "ours"), "house of the LORD" (vv. 8-9)

The structure calls attention to two houses, David's, which derives its authority from the LORD's. The "house of David" is embraced by "Jerusalem" and "house of the LORD." The judgment "thrones," established by God in the temple and the motive for thanks, are steadied by the royal office.

In practically one breath the poet embraces the pilgrimage, the departure for and the arrival in the holy city. From the first word, the song overflows with joy over Jerusalem, being there (vv. 1-2), contemplating its safety and central position in Israel's life (vv. 3-5). The situation is explicit. The pilgrim group has arrived in Jerusalem, their geographical and geo-spiritual goal (v. 2). The name Jerusalem and "house," *bayt*, "peace," *šālôm*, and the divine name, LORD, resound three times. The mental gaze is focused on the city, which has three remarkable traits, compact construction (v. 3), the arrival of pilgrim groups (v. 4), and the royal palace where justice is administered (v. 5). Then the exclamations with the persistent theme *šālôm* are heard. The poem speaks of the city and of peace. The city, *ʿîr*, echoes the sound of the first syllable of Jerusalem, *yĕrû*; the second part of the name is echoed by the word *šālôm*, and together they form Jerusalem, *yĕrûšālaym*, the city of peace. Prayers for Jerusalem and her visitors are summed up in the thrice mentioned *šālôm*. The synonyms "prosper" and "security" (vv. 6-7) strengthen the theme. *Šālôm*, along with an occurrence of *šʾl*, "pray" (v. 6), and two occurrences of *šlh* ("prosper," v. 6, and "security," v. 7), ring with the alliteration of the "sh" and "l" sounds, transliterated *šaʾălû šĕlôm yĕrûšālaym yišlāyû*. The prayer is formulated with care (the English words identify the alliteration in translation):

Pray . . . peace . . . Jerusalem . . . prosper

šaʾălû . . . šĕlôm . . . yĕrûšālaym . . . yišlāyû . . .

. . . . peace . . . . security

. . . *yĕhî–šālôm bĕḥêlēk* . . . . *šalwâh*

Jerusalem is addressed as if the city were receiving the singers' benediction (vv. 2, 6-9).

The poet celebrates the glory of the capital, the place of the supreme court, whence God dispenses justice. Next to God's house is David's palace ("house"). By virtue of parallelism an equation is set up between "the thrones for judgment" and "thrones of the house of David." Right worship implies right conduct, an idea which is not foreign to the psalmist nor the prophets (cf. Ps 50:8-14; Isa 1:10-20; Jer 7:4-7; Amos 5:21-27). The synthesis of all blessing is *šālôm*. The ground for this desired blessing, which is the guarantee of its efficacy, is the LORD's house. Each of the last two verses begins with "For the sake of," *lĕmaʾan*. The poet pledges him or herself to peace and well-being in the human and the divine relations.

Psalm 123
Our Eyes Are on the LORD

Psalm 123 opens with an affirmation of trust (vv. 1-2), which sets the tone for the petition (v. 3a), made more urgent by the scorn the people suffer (vv. 3b-4). The poet speaks directly to God, switching from the singular "I" to the plural "our eyes" (v. 2). The individual represents the group. The ending describes the people's oppression. "Mercy" links the sublime picture of trust (v. 2) to the repeated request, "Have mercy upon us." This calls attention to other repetitions—a double simile ("eyes," v. 2) and the disdain and insult of the leisurely proud (v. 4). The contrast of human contempt and God's grace is aptly illustrated.

Imagery enhances the eloquence of the plea. The throne is a spatial image for God's sovereignty over all creation (cf. 2:4; 11:4; 29:10; 33:13-14; 93:2). Raised eyes express the lifting up of the self in oblation and expectation. The comparison of the alert "eyes" is especially fine; as servants await largesse or a hand signal of "their" master or mistress, so the worshiping assembly looks expectantly to "our" God (cf. 104:27-28; 145:15-16). The verb *ḥnn*, "have mercy" or "be gracious," expresses the superior's favor of dependents, which fits the image of the heavenly sovereign. The analogy is well-chosen because just as servants depend on their patron to guarantee their basic needs and rights, so the faithful pray that God favor them. Contempt and scorn, repeated or continual, does more harm than physical oppression. From such a degraded state the poet raises the eyes to the LORD. This gaze transcends human differences and categories and restores lost dignity. God's "mercy" does this. As in Psalm 121, raised eyes mirror a spiritual elevation and hope.

Psalm 124
The People's Rescuer

In Psalm 124 a memory of rescue (vv. 1-5) ends in praise and an avowal of trust (vv. 6-8). The first part opens with a repeated condition, "If it had not been the LORD," followed by three clauses introduced by "then," *ʾăzî*, telling of the flood. Both the condition and the outcome have parallel "when" clauses, "when our enemies attacked us" and "when their anger was kindled against us" (vv. 1-5). A chiastic arrangement brings the images into focus and illustrates the mounting danger (vv. 4-5).

A + B	the flood and "swept us away"
A^1 + B^1	torrent and "gone over us"
B^2 + A^2	"[gone] over us" and "raging waters"

The negative scenario is dismissed because the LORD is the ally, which prompts the assembly to celebrate that he was and is "on our side." God's commitment to the people frustrates the human assault. The concluding avowal of trust is formulated like the first part, with mention of the rescuing LORD and a chiastic arrangement,

| A + B | "we have escaped" and "from the snare" |
| B^1 + A^1 | "the snare" and "we have escaped" |

A wordplay which links the two parts is lost in the NRSV. The word *nepeš* is employed in two different ways, "up to *our necks*" (vv. 4-5; translated "over us") and *"our necks"* or *"our lives"* (v. 7; translated *"we* [have escaped]"). A final verdict based on the victory (v. 8) hearkens to the beginning (vv. 1-2). The divine name and the theme "on our side" with "our help" frame the psalm. The liturgical character is apparent in the invocation "let Israel now say" (cf. 118:2; 129:1), the formula "[b]lessed be the LORD" (v. 6), and the concluding acclamation (v. 8; cf. 115:15; 121:2; 134:3; 146:6).

The author paints a vivid picture. Fire ("kindled"), evoking a siege, and a billowing flood symbolize the danger and recall the terror. Here, water does not douse the fire. The people were threatened with burning alive or drowning. The climax intones a note of relief, "Blessed be the LORD," but not without recalling the assault from fangs and the fowler's snare. Images of danger are spliced together—being swallowed alive (vv. 2-3), inundated by a raging torrent (vv. 4-5), the prey of a wild animal (v. 6), a defenseless bird in a trap (v. 7). The verb "swallow," *bl*^{c}, connotes drowning in untamed waters. But God harnesses them as at the Exodus. The threat of fangs parallels that of swallowing alive. These images of aggression occur frequently in the Psalter: fire (e.g., 78:63), flood (18:4, 16; 32:6; 42:7; 69:1-2, 14-15; 144:7), savage beasts (7:2; 10:9; 22:12-13, 16, 20-21), the hunter and the net (11:1-2; 18:4-5; 57:6; 66:11; 91:3; 141:9-10). The unlikely conspiracy of fire and water is found in 66:12; the teeth and the net in 57:4, 6. As in many psalms, the real enemy is not identified. Altogether these metaphors create the psychological impact of one who barely escapes. The bird's excited flurry as it escapes from the broken snare aptly projects the excitement of sudden release. The little bird on the wing, being the last image, dominates the others—foaming waters, wild fangs, the snare—images which hunt, kill, and drown life out. The flight shows how free life with God is.

This disciplined psalm celebrates a communal deliverance. Engulfing waters, fire, fangs and snare, depict helplessness in the face of personal or communal assault. Coming to their senses and recovering their calm, the assembly gives God credit for the present and future rescues. At the beginning the LORD's presence is underlined ("If it had not been the LORD"), before the human enemy (*ʾādām*, which the NRSV translates "enemies," v. 2) is even mentioned. Thus, God was there before and is more in evidence than the human assault. The poem begins and ends with unshakable faith in God, the rescuer.

Psalm 125
Israel's Security

Psalm 125 begins with a double statement about a secure place (Mount Zion, Jerusalem) and God's protection of those who trust him. The formulation is chiastic (vv. 1-2):

A	B
"Those who trust in the LORD"	simile: Zion's stability
B¹	**A**¹
simile: mountains around Jerusalem	the LORD around the people

This is followed by an assurance that the wicked will not overpower the good (the Hebrew *kî* introducing v. 3 may be translated as "surely"). The poem ends with a double request for God's retributive justice, good for the good and an end to the wicked (vv. 4-5). The concluding liturgical invocation specifies the theme, Israel's *šālôm*, prosperity (cf. 122:6-8; 128:6).

The landscape of Mount Zion, secure and nestled among the Judean mountains, serves as a background in the portrait of one who trusts in the LORD. God embracing the one who confides in him is like the geophysical terrain around the holy city where mountains hug Zion on all sides (cf. 16:8; 21:7; 46:5; 62:2, 6; 112:6). Evil assaults will not triumph in "the land allotted to the righteous," *gôral haṣṣaddîqîm*, literally, "the allotment of the just," which has a double meaning. *Gôral* refers to the portion of land allotted to each tribe (Josh 15:1; 17:1), but it can also refer to the LORD as the privileged inheritance of those who trust in him. The vocabulary and descriptions delineate two opposing camps:

"Those who trust in the LORD"
"his people"

                                "scepter of wickedness"

"the righteous" (repeated)
"those who are good"
"those who are upright"

                                "those who turn aside to . . . crooked ways"
                                "evildoers"

Israel

The generic terms "righteous," "good," and "upright in . . . heart" are
specified by "who trust in the LORD," "his people," and Israel (seven
designations in all, counting the repeated "righteous" twice). Those
who follow crooked ways is more specific, a reference to apostasy,
which is catalogued among the generic "evildoers." The oppositions
are marked: the good have good hearts; evildoers follow crooked ways.
The poet requests that God reward each according to the standard
norm, which leaves those who travel by crooked paths destined for
perdition (cf. 1:6 and 146:9).

God dwells in the temple on Mount Zion, in the midst of the city,
surrounded by mountains. Just so, he embraces and protects the
people. The mountain symbolizes stability and firmness, especially
Mount Zion, which has the added guarantee which God's presence
affords. Just as a mountain finds its firmness on the earth, so one who
confides in God has a secure place to live. The allotment of the righteous, where the wicked have no sway, is the LORD.

Psalm 126
Reversal of Zion's Fortunes

Psalm 126 opens with a memory of God's incredible favor and the
resulting exuberant gladness. The return seemed like a dream at first.
The manifestation of God's greatness startled even the gentiles. Both
the event and its recollection is one motive for joy; another is the anticipation of deliverance. Joy is God's work, first in the restoration of Zion
and secondly in the renewal of the worshipers. Repetitions divide the
poem in two parts, each introduced by a line that employs the phrase

"restore . . . fortunes" and a simile (vv. 1, 4). The word *then*, *ʾāz* (twice), connects v. 2 with the first word of the psalm, "When." "The LORD has done great things" (repeated) links vv. 2 and 3. In the end weeping and joy line up twice with sowing and reaping.

Vocabulary of laughter and rejoicing imposes an emotional chord on the poem. Three times the poet contemplates an inversion of situations. The first already took place (vv. 1-3); the second is yet to come (v. 4). The request that fortunes be restored alludes to a return to the land (cf. 85:4).[37] The third inversion is either past or something that customarily recurs, encapsulated in a proverb (vv. 5-6). To depict God's renewal the poet draws on the image of the dry, caked wadis of the Negeb desert which the erratic rain transforms into flash floods. Suddenly they become fertile and green. The people's experience is projected into the image of sowing the food stores on the ground with the gamble that all will be lost and then surprisingly reaping an abundant harvest for the coming year. The prayer for restoration, contrasting tears and sowing, reaping and laughter, depicts the desired change. It is almost as if the desert is at first watered with tears and rains follow. Finally, there is another inversion; from the pains and fatigues of sowing, the people celebrate the harvest (see Ps 4:7). The sad face of the sower is exchanged for the thrilling boast of the reaper. We could hardly believe it when the tragedy of exile was replaced by repatriation! May it happen again for the present generation, unexpectedly like a flash flood, with more abounding benefits than the tears that were sown during the tragedy.

Psalm 127
Useless Without God

Solomon, to whom Psalm 127 is ascribed in the caption, is famous for wisdom and building. The psalm can be divided into two strophes according to the themes of building a house and a family (vv. 1-2, 3-5). Repetitions highlight the motifs —"in vain," *šāwĕʾ* (three times in vv.

---

[37] "Restore our fortune" becomes "return from captivity" with a vowel change. This phrase translates a Hebrew idiom found primarily in prophetic sayings where it is used for the radical change from the effects of God's anger to divine favor. It means restoration of an earlier situation between God and people (e.g., Amos 9:14; Joel 3:1; Jer 29:14; Zeph 2:7). The formula has the same meaning in other psalms (cf. 14:7 = 53:6; 85:1).

1-2) and "sons" (twice, plus a synonym, "fruit of the womb," v. 3-5). The first two "in vain" sayings are similar in form, while the third shifts to direct address ("you" plural, v. 2). The lesson is that endeavors like building a house, guarding a city, and daily toil are futile unless they are consonant with God's purpose. The second strophe is composed of an illustrated proverb (vv. 3-4) and a beatitude. "Arrows" and "quiver" link these two.

God is the architect and watchman. Even when humans rest, God's silent activity continues, so that they can eat the next day. The "bread of anxious toil" hearkens to the frustrating labor to which the human is condemned (v. 2; cf. Gen 3:16-17). God is the real provider, regardless of human effort, and this is expressed in the contrast between hard work and sleep; God dispenses as he pleases. Children are received from God, as are houses and safety within the city walls. The basis for the comparison between sons and arrows is the protection they provide a family. Sons support and defend the family honor in the legal suits at the city gate. The two parts of Psalm 127 are related thematically. The building of a city corresponds to the forming of a family. The city's defense works correspond to the defense that male children offer in defending the family. Amidst civic protection, agrarian enterprises and family building, while God's beloved sleeps, the LORD guards and provides. The image of the quiver of arrows is graphic: one is well prepared, and when danger threatens his or her reserves will never fail, thanks to the LORD.

Psalm 128
The Happy Home of the Good

Psalm 128 is a logical conclusion to the preceding psalm. It is governed by two themes, beatitude for the family (vv. 1-3) and blessing on the individual and on Zion (vv. 4-6). The language is select. Framing vv. 1-2 is the repeated ʾašrē, "happy," and the synonym ṭûb, "it shall go well." A cognate ṭôb, "prosperity," links vv. 2 and 5. Verses 4 and 5 are connected by cognates of brk, "bless," and the word *children* is repeated (vv. 3, 6). The phrase "who fears the LORD" (vv. 1, 4) frames the assurances of fruitful labor and family in direct address ("you" is singular). "Thus" (v. 4) identifies the comforts of daily life as God's blessing. The concluding blessing for the one who fears God is elaborated with vocabulary from earlier verses. The following schema gives a snapshot of the components of this poem:

v. 1	Happy					(a)
	everyone who fears the LORD					(b)
v. 2			shall eat			(c)
	You shall be happy					(a)
v. 3				it shall go well with you		(d)
					children	(e)
v. 4			around your table			(c)
	who fears the LORD					(b)
v. 5						bless (f)
						bless (f)
v. 6				prosperity		(d)
					children	(e)

The elemental benefits of the blessing are evident in daily life. In the end, *šālôm*, peace, recapitulates the beatitude and the blessing, which is extended to all Israel.

The poet teaches that the good in life comes from God. Fear of God implies walking in his ways (parallelism, v. 1), which amounts to devotion to the law. Psalm 128 contemplates the saying that, for behaving well—honoring God and conforming to the divine will—a person receives the blessings of fruitful labor, guaranteed sustenance, prosperity, and a happy home. In the Hebrew culture family relations were viewed primarily through the optic of the male figure. The father's role is to provide for the family; the wife and mother creates the home; children bring life to the table, a sacrament of family unity and harmony. Father arrives home, satisfied from a day's work with the fruit of labor in hand. He reclines at table with the children. His wife is attentive to the amenities, and together they enjoy the meal, mutual affection, and happiness. Such a happy home is a blessing for those who honor God.

Two images are derived from horticulture, the vine and olive shoots, which suggest the children's vigor and growth, the mother's vitality and fertility. The fruit of the father's labor is both around and on the table. In the end the poet makes a transposition. The fruitful mother is identified with Jerusalem, a feminine image throughout the Bible, and

her children come to stand for Israel. Thus, the convivial family blessing is transposed to future prosperity for Jerusalem and the one who
honors God (vv. 5-6; see Num 6:23-27). The blessing issues from Zion
(see 14:7; 20:2; 134:3), extends to the holy city, and embraces future generations of Israel. Everyday happiness is condensed in the word *šālôm*
(cf. 122:6-8; 125:5). Jerusalem plays a principle role in the blessing in the
songs of ascent. God blessed the capital of the universal reign, whence all
blessing issues (v. 5; 132:13-15; 133:3; 134:3). May God grant Jerusalem
prosperity and may the faithful live to enjoy their children's children.

Psalm 129
No Blessing for Israel's Enemies

The abundant blessing of Psalm 128 contrasts with the absence of
blessing in Psalm 129. The poet recalls the peril from which God's
people were rescued as he or she prays that present and future hostility
be frustrated. Repetition and the use of the first person singular ("they
attacked me") focus the drama, as the poet relives Israel's conflict (vv.
1-4). A liturgical formula identifies the speaker as Israel personified
("let Israel now say," v. 1b; cf. 124:1; 118:2). The poet roundly curses the
enemies of Zion, the capital of God's universal reign (vv. 5-8). Because
the peace and blessing of the faithful is bound up with the good of
Jerusalem (122:6-9; 126:1-3; 128:5), the faithful pray for the failure of
Zion's enemies.

In the past, "from my youth," Israel was plagued by oppressors,
who subjugated her and opened furrows on her back with their beat-
ings (cf. Isa 1:6; 51:23). But they were unable to triumph, and God severed her bonds (vv. 3-4). The slavery image of the "cords of the wicked"
continues that of the plowers. The poet employs another agrarian simile, grass that sprouts on the earthen roofs overnight and withers without producing even enough to fill a reaper's hand (vv. 6-7). In the end
the grass and the wicked converge into a single focus. Passers-by neither admire nor bless them. In the NRSV, the exuberant greetings "the
blessing of the LORD" (cf. Ruth 2:4) are muted, which is part of the
curse. It is ironic that a blessing that could be repeated is silenced (v. 8).
Psalm 129, which presents the image of ephemeral and sterile life, contrasts with that of the elderly good couple surrounded by children and
grandchildren, the fruit of God's blessing (Psalm 128). The two images,
plowing and reaping, articulate the message: may those who plowed—
not the earth but furrows on the backs of the oppressed with their
whips—wither and disappear before the time for reaping.

Psalm 130
Trust in God's Ḥesed

Psalm 130 is a personal complaint in two movements. First, the poet pleads with God for a hearing (vv. 1-4). Then he or she attests to personal sentiments and exhorts hearers to share them (vv. 5-8). Repetitions are like links in a chain in Psalm 130, as the following schema illustrates:

v. 1	yhwh . . . ʾădōnāy	(a)	(a)	
v. 2	voice (repeated)	(b)	(b)	
v. 3	"watch for" [šmr] iniquities [ʿăwônôt]	(c)	(d)	
	yhwh . . . ʾădōnāy	(a)	(a)	
v. 4	"there is forgiveness [sĕlîḥâh] with you"	(e)		
v. 5	I wait [qwh] for yhwh	(f)	(a)	
	my soul waits [qwh]	(g)	(f)	
	"in his word I hope [yḥl]"	(h)		
v. 6	my soul for ʾădōnāy	(g)	(a)	
	who watch for [šmr] the morning (repeated)	(c)	(c)	
v. 7	Israel, hope [yḥl] in yhwh	(i)	(h)	(a)
	with yhwh there is ḥesed	(a)	(e)	
	power to redeem [pĕdût from pdh]	(j)		
v. 8	redeem [pdh] Israel	(j)	(i)	
	iniquities [ʿăwônôt]	(d)		

Petitions (first person singular, vv. 1-2) introduce a statement about the relation of sinners to the forgiving God (vv. 3-4). The poet cries out and asks for a hearing, but the particular request is never made clear. The avowal of trust takes the form of waiting for God and the divine word (vv. 5-6), comparing the anticipation to sentinels watching for morning. The poet "waits for" or "watches" for God, who does not "look for" (v. 3; Hebrew, šmr; NRSV, "mark") sins. In the end the poet urges the community to hope for God's redemption. The theme of "iniquities" is repeated (vv. 3, 8); they are all forgiven. The first movement concludes as the poet addresses God and avows "[b]ut there is forgiveness with you" (v. 4). The second also ends with an affirmation (vv. 7-8),

> with the LORD there is steadfast love. . . .
> It is he who will redeem Israel. . . .

Such connections underscore the theme of hope that God will show *ḥesed* and redeem Israel from her sins. The eight references to God (five times the divine name *yhwh*, plus three times "Lord," *ʾădōnāy*) are evenly distributed in the two movements.

The poet draws the vertical axis; from the depths he or she raises a cry which reaches up to God. The "depths" is the watery deep (Isa 51:10; Ezek 27:34), chaos, Sheol and the realm of death—as far away as one can get from God. One has a sense of drowning in confusion and sin, being overwhelmed by turbulent waters (cf. 69:1-2; 124:3-5; Jon 2:2-3, 5), an apt image for acute distress. To be sucked into chaos is to be separated from the place where people can praise God and share the faith. Indeed, the distance between God and sinful humanity is so vast that if God were to keep an account of sins, no one could stand with a clear conscience (v. 3). But God's nature is to be faithful to the covenant, which includes immunity for the offender, and so the poet can hope for pardon and redemption, the expression of God's *ḥesed*. Even so, it remains an act of grace, the appropriate response to which is reverence.

As dawn brings light, God sends favor (vv. 5-6). "Hope" is the lifeline in the darkness, as the poet "waits" for God's forgiving word. The verbs for "wait," *qwh*, and "hope," *yḥl*, are synonymous (cf. Isa 51:5). The repetition of "those who watch for the morning" illustrates the protracted waiting. Aware of personal guilt, the psalmist compares the suspenseful wait for God's *ḥesed* to the lonely sentinel in the night. This is repeated in the appeal to Israel to wait for God's generous redemption (vv. 7-8). Hope bridges the gap between the psalmist and God.

The human predicament is dependent on divine grace. In this prayer the individual and the believing community merge into one as the poet speaks with, for, and to the community. He or she embodies the guilt and the hope of Israel. Mercy will dawn and God will redeem the people. As with the individual, so the people awaits the dawn of mercy. The poet is silent about particular sins but admits that guilt is unavoidable in human life. The psalm teaches that "[the] forgiveness" is with God (forgiveness has the definite article in Hebrew, as does "[the] *ḥesed*" [v. 7]). The author encourages the assembly to adopt this attitude, confident of the abundance of divine *ḥesed* and certain that God will free Israel from sin.

Psalm 131
Humble Trust in God

Psalm 131 expresses submission to God and the ordering of life as a model for the community. Initially God is addressed, as the poet attests to a balanced life that depends ultimately on him. Then the poet addresses Israel and urges her to order life in reference to God. Two appearances of the LORD, in the first and last verses, frame the prayer. As in the previous psalm, the individual represents the community of Israel.

The poem has three phases. First, a declaration of innocence is marked by three negatives, with a fourth one understood—not lifted up, not raised too high, not occupied in things too great, [nor] in things beyond me (v. 1). The language encompasses both the vertical axis ("too high") and the horizontal plane ("occupied" is, literally, "walked," *hlk*). The poet neither entertains too lofty illusions nor spreads him or herself too thin, meaning one has moderated the relation with God and others. The mention of "heart," "eyes," "occupied," and "soul" scopes out both interior attitudes and external actions. The method is clear. The poet first mentions the heart *(lēb)*, the seat of thought, intention and decision. He or she next mentions the eyes, which open to the world around and mirror the interior, as they look after desires and seek things small or great. Next is how to proceed or "walk." Rising from the heart, led by the eyes, the person's conduct takes shape. The second phase is the positive counterpart, affirming the serenity of one who trusts in God's parental care (v. 2). My "soul" represents the whole self, the individual who moderates and controls his or her desires and behavior. The young child is not too ambitious. Precious though he or she is, the child is dependent on the mother, someone very big in the child's eyes and heart. This basic relationship is the anchor for all other relations. The weaned child who is not dependent on but still has recourse to Mother is how life is with God. The third phase is marked by a change of addressee, and the poet superimposes the homey image onto Israel, God's children, and exhorts the community to right their relationship with their divine parent.

There are problems with this poem. Why would a prayer begin so emphatically with a denial, unless the opposite were suspect? Does the poet, by denying it, tacitly admit that perhaps he or she tends to trespass the boundaries? Another problem is the age of the child. The Greek translation understood the Hebrew *gāmūl* to be a weaned, three-year-old child, who indeed explores horizons beyond the mother, yet for whom the mother is a conscious point of reference when the little one climbs too high or wanders too far, becomes anxious or threatened. The opposite of the child dependent on the mother is the self-sufficient person. Thus, the domestic portrait provides an affirmation about how Israel should order her life with God. The final exhortation which the author directs to the assembly contains a profound religious thought. Anxieties can find their resolution in God, who offers the only friendship worthwhile.

Psalm 132
The Everlasting Covenant between David and God

Psalm 132 is longer than the other songs of ascent. As a liturgy it is stamped with repetitions, interrelations, and changes of address. It celebrates the twofold election, that of Zion and the Davidic dynasty. The dynasty will mediate between God and the people, and the temple is God's dwelling among the people. The two parallel movements (vv. 1-10, 11-18) are framed with the name of David (vv. 1, 10, 11, 17), and each recalls an oath (repetition of *šbᶜ*, "swore," vv. 2, 11). The first is David's vow to find a resting place for God and the second is God's oath to keep David's throne there (vv. 2-5, 11-12). These in turn are followed by a reenactment of both the way in which David carried out his vow and how God will keep his oath (vv. 6-10, 13-18). Similar language links the two movements (vv. 8-9, vv. 14, 16). Geographical names and locations circumscribe the space: Ephrathah, the fields of Jaar, David's house. The temple is seven times designated by synonymous terms, "a place" *(māqôm)*, "dwelling place" *(miškānôt)*, "his footstool" *(hădôm raglāyw)*, "resting place" *(měnûḥâh)*, "habitation" *(môšāb)*. "This" *(zōᵓt)*, "here" *(pōh)*, and "there" *(šām)* signal the location (vv. 14, 17).

Initially, the poet requests that God bear in mind David's merits (v. 1). David proposes to construct a dwelling for the ark of the covenant (v. 7), the token of God's presence among the people. The oath is solemnized by repetitions, and three negations emphasize the irrevocable decision. God, identified with the ark, is to process to the temple where he dwells. The priestly attendants are clothed with righteousness and salvation (vv. 9; cf. v. 16). The assembly requests that, for the love of his servant David, God not reject the present and future anointed (v. 10).

This is linked to the second movement by the repetition of "David" and the verb "turn," *šwb*. The request that God not "*turn* away the face of your anointed one" is followed by God's assurance that "he will not *turn*" from his oath to David (vv. 10-11). This comprises a request and the response. God promises a perpetual dynasty and the election of Zion as the permanent divine dwelling (vv. 12, 14). This covenant, however, is conditional, unlike that in Ps 89:28-37. One must be loyal to the covenant in order to retain divine support of the dynasty. From the temple God will bless the inhabitants of Zion with abundant provisions; the poor will be fed, the priests will enjoy (be clothed with) salvation, the faithful will fully celebrate, and the Davidic line will have a glorious reign, free from dissent (vv. 15-18). These four declarations represent all the blessings which will be showered on the nation.

Overall prosperity is guaranteed, the liturgical life is ratified, the political structure is assured, which includes absence of dissent or aggression.

The poet uses quotations extensively, which adds to the poem's liturgical resonance: a vow of David (vv. 3-5), the choral processional chant (vv. 6-7), the solemn address to God (vv. 8-10; cf. Num 10:35; 2 Chr 6:41-42), God's oaths concerning the Davidic succession (vv. 11b-12), and Zion's election and the future of David's dynasty (vv. 14-18). The verb *nwḥ* and cognates show a progression, from David's eyes not *resting* (v. 4) to the invitation to God to come to the *resting place* (v. 8) to God's establishment of the *resting place* (v. 14). Sights and sounds, the people's joyful shout, and the vested priests are part of the ceremony (vv. 9, 16). The contrasting use of *lbš*, "clothe," is poignant, "your priests . . . *clothed* with righteousness" or "salvation" and the "enemies I will *clothe* with disgrace" (vv. 9, 16, 18). David's horn and the royal crown are linked by two verbs which ordinarily describe plant growth (v. 17); a horn will sprout (*ṣmḥ*) and the crown will flourish (*ṣyṣ*, translated "gleam," v. 18). The "horn" is David's strength, his descendants, and so also, by virtue of parallelism, is the "lamp" in "I have prepared a lamp for my anointed one."

Verses 1-5 reflect an imaginative, poetic version of the events in 2 Samuel 6–7. No record exists of David's vow to deprive himself of sleep. In the liturgical celebration of this poem the oath was presumably spoken by a priest or court minister. God is the "Mighty One of Jacob," the God of the tribal alliance (vv. 2, 5; Gen 49:24; Isa 49:26; 60:16). Ephrathah evokes the region of Bethlehem associated with Benjamin's birth and Rachel's death (Gen 35:16, 19), with Ruth, David, and his successor (cf. Mic 5:1, Hebrew). The "fields of Jaar" recalls the region of Kiriath-jearim, where the ark rested until David took it up to Jerusalem (1 Sam 7:1-2). The poet dramatizes the descent of a group from central Judah to its western borders to transport the ark to Jerusalem in procession (vv. 6-9; cf. 2 Sam 6:1-19). A choir ("we") liturgically reenacts the story of the ark's recovery, with ritual acclamations inviting God to enter the sanctuary. During the sojourn in the desert God "arose" when the ark was to move. God advances, enthroned on the ark ("his footstool"), born by priests in festive vestments, accompanied by the "faithful." A priest or prophet recites God's promises (vv. 11-16), and the liturgy concludes by reviewing God's twofold promise. It celebrates God's past promises and anticipates a bright future—the new David, the new temple, the eternal reign. This psalm expresses the expectation for the messiah, the guarantor and embodiment of God's dwelling and the continuation of David's line.

Psalm 133
Everlasting Life for a Blessed Community

The divine name *yhwh* occurs seven times in Psalms 132–133, evidence of an editorial design. The motif of blessing, introduced at the end of Psalm 132, is an appropriate entrée for Psalm 133, a liturgy of blessing. Another theme in Psalm 132 and continued in Psalm 133 is the priesthood, a blessing from God, a channel of blessing to the people, and representative of the people (132:9, 16; 133:2). The adverb "there" (132:17; 133:3), evoking where God's presence is felt, also links the two psalms. Psalm 133 shares the motif of Zion, a place of blessing, with the neighboring psalms (v. 3; cf. 132:13-15; 134:3).

In Hebrew Psalm 133 is composed of a single sentence with two main clauses followed by subordinate ones.

> How good, how pleasant, sisters and brothers living together united—
>   fine as precious sacred ointment, streaming down . . .,
>   refreshing as copious dew falling . . .,
> for there the LORD ordains the blessing, life forever.

Two qualifiers, "good" and "pleasant," describe the fraternal unity, where God bestows eternal life. "Good" recalls the created order of Genesis 1. Is the poet describing a past experience that memory and longing has enhanced, eliminating the bad and elevating it to an idyllic plane? Is this poet exhorting the community by reminding them that blessings of life and fertility will abound if they worship together? The phrase translated "live together," from *yšb*, can also be understood to refer to a festal celebration.

The simile from the liturgy is exquisite and suggestive. Sacred oil is poured so lavishly that it streams from the head onto the sidelocks of the beard (a norm for Aaronic priests; cf. Lev 21:5) and onto the vestments. Dwelling or worshiping together is like precious, fragrant oil in abundance, used to consecrate the sanctuary, the sacred vessels, and the priest (Exod 30:23-31; Lev 21:10). The officiating priest wears a vestment, the front of which has a plaque studded with twelve precious stones, which represent Israel's tribal union, upon which the ointment flows. The simile from nature is suggestive of freshness and fecundity. The region of Hermon in the far north of Palestine is remarkable for heavy dew. This is transferred to the desert mountains around Zion, drenching, enriching, and cooling the region where God chose to dwell and where the people gather for their feasts.

The similes artfully blend into one by the thrice repeated *yrd*, "running down" and "falls." Together they form an extravagant picture of the well-being of togetherness. God has ordained "there" the blessing of endless life (v. 3b). The word *šām*, "there," is polyvalent, referring to the assembled fraternity, the collar of Aaron's vestment, and Zion. In all three the divine benediction is present, communicated, and enjoyed. Fragrance and freshness exude from this place. The divine name only occurs at the end of the poem, where the LORD is acknowledged as the hidden source of this well-being.

Once the two images of abundant oil and heavy dew are in place, the poet assigns a name and a function. There in the temple, in the community, God sends the blessing, which amounts to lasting life. In contrast to death, life is fragrant like the perfumed oil; it is refreshing and fertile like dew. Fraternal love is a blessing which keeps on giving in the vitality it fosters and the fragrant atmosphere it gives. Thus the poet attributes the joy of common life and worship to God's generosity. On Mount Zion and in the liturgy personal and ideological differences, which threaten to destroy the group identity, submit to the confession of one God. The poem anticipates the harmony of all people as they live without defenses in God's creation whose care for all is a continually unfolding blessing.

Psalm 134
Night Prayer

Psalm 134 is an invitation to praise and bless God, addressed to those "who stand by night in the house of the LORD" (vv. 1-2), and it concludes with a blessing (v. 3). The faithful assembly is addressed and the summons is framed by the imperative, "bless the LORD" (vv. 1-2), which means to praise and give thanks, one of the noblest of human actions. This is followed by a blessing upon an individual ("you" is singular, v. 3), an individual in the liturgical gathering or the assembly as a corporate entity. Prayer is two directional, as evidenced by the repetition of *brk*; the people are exhorted to *bless* God who, in response, is to *bless* them. The final verse is akin to the priestly blessing (Num 6:24-26; cf. Ps 115:12-15). God's servants remain in the sanctuary all night, like Samuel at Shilo (1 Sam 3:1-6), Jacob at Bethel (Gen 28:11-18), or Solomon at Gibeon (1 Kgs 3:5-15). At nightfall the faithful retire, but they first invite the ministers who lodge in the temple to praise God (cf. Pss 113:1; 135:1-2). The gesture of hands raised toward the sanctuary is liturgical (cf. Pss 28:2; 63:4; 141:2).

The worshipers are caught in a continuous cycle of blessing. God, "maker of heaven and earth," has previously blessed the people. Praise rebounds the blessing to God who in return imparts to the assembly the ongoing blessing and salvation. Thus, Psalm 134 is the literary and the liturgical conclusion of the songs of ascents. It sums up the major concerns of the collection and the purpose of pilgrimage, to praise God and receive blessing (128:5; 133:3), channeled through Zion and through the "servants of the LORD."

Psalm 135
Praise of Israel's Benefactor

Like its neighbor, Psalm 135 addresses the "servants of the LORD, who ["you that"] stand . . . in the house of the LORD" (134:1; 135:1-2). Both psalms feature the blessing in and from Zion (134:3; 135:19-21). *Hallelujah,* and the opening and closing invitations frame the psalm (vv. 1-3, 19-21). The poet opens with a summons to the LORD's devotees to praise him for his goodness and concludes by rallying Israel, the Levites, and the faithful to bless the LORD who resides in Jerusalem (v. 21). The body of the poem has two panels (vv. 5-12, 13-18), and the schema looks like this:

A *hallelujah*

    B invitation (vv. 1-3)

        C election of the people (v. 4)

            D God's superiority (v. 5; cf. 95:3)

                E God's universal authority (vv. 6-7)

                E' God's past action on behalf of the elect (vv. 8-12)

            D' God's unsurpassing renown (v. 13)

        C' benefice to the people (v. 14)

                F nothingness of idols and idolaters (vv. 15-18)

    B' invitation (vv. 19-21)

A' *hallelujah*

Two themes are announced at the outset, God's predilection for Israel (v. 4; cf. v. 14) and God's superiority over all the gods (v. 5; cf. v. 15). God's benefices "in heaven and on earth" and specifically with reference to Israel are the topic of the following verses. God's superiority and unconditional sovereignty is manifest in the supervision of the natural world (vv. 6-7). The poet marvels at how the God of nature can cause the flaming lightning bolts to mix with the rain, which demonstrates his power to design nature and history as he pleases. He subdued the Egyptians and the kings of the Transjordan and Canaan, and gave Israel an inheritance (vv. 8-12). A merism, the plague of Egypt and the entrance to the Promised Land, embraces the Exodus and bespeaks God's power to liberate the people. God's sovereignty, manifest in creation and the rescue of his people, is a guarantee for the present and future generations (v. 14). The themes stress a contrast between God with his people as opposed to the nations with their bogus gods.

Toward the end and before the concluding invitation to praise, idolatry is calmly disclaimed. Four organs sum up the seven of Psalm 115 (vv. 15-17), and the conclusions are the same, "Those who make them and all who trust in them shall become like them" (v. 18; cf. 115:8). Other gods are nothings, cold, lifeless metal dolls. The Hebrew word translated "idols" is a homonym for "toil" or "affliction" (*ʿṣb*) They bring neither delight nor benefit to their devotees. The concluding curse is harsh. May those who fashion and trust in these idols become just like them, inert dummies, mute, blind, and deaf. This section forms an implicit tribute to God, since the idols are powerless and contrast starkly with God's power as acclaimed in the first panel. The idols, made by humans, are inferior to their makers. The LORD, of whom no image is possible, is infinitely superior. Throughout the poem Israel and God contrasts with the nations and their gods.

The setting of Psalm 135, as with the preceding psalm, is the temple, probably on the occasion of a feast (vv. 1-2). This anthologic composition employs texts from the Law, the prophets, and the psalms to address the folly of idol worship. Moses' identification of Israel as God's treasured possession appears in a context that speaks of God's abolition of the nations with their rival gods (Deuteronomy 7; compare v. 4 and Deut 7:6; Exod 19:5). The confession of God's superiority above all gods and idols evokes the psalms of the LORD's reign (v. 5; see Pss 95:3; 96:4-5; 97:7, 9). The poet recalls the contrast between Israel's God and the nations' gods (v. 7b; cf. Jer 10:13; 51:16). As in Ps 136:10-22 the poet reviews God's actions in Israel's behalf (vv. 8-12). The Exodus is summed up in the last plague, the slaying of the firstborn, with an allusion to the other plagues, "signs and wonders" (vv. 8-9). The psalmist embellishes the historical account by unexpectedly addressing Egypt, "into your midst, O Egypt." The events of the Red Sea are not mentioned (cf. Ps 136:13-15), while Sihon, Og, and "the kingdoms of Canaan" sums up the end of the desert sojourn and the conquest (vv. 11-12). The names of the defeated kings are played against God's everlasting name which the poet acclaims in spontaneous praise, "Your name, O LORD, endures forever" (v. 13; cf. Exod 3:15). The assurance that God will vindicate the people quotes from Moses' song, which tells how God will sustain the relation with Israel even among the nations and their gods (v. 14; cf. Deut 32:36). Three choirs, the houses of Israel and Aaron and those "that fear the LORD," appear elsewhere in Pss 115:9-11 and 118:2-4. Given the participants (assembly of priests and people) and the location (Zion and the temple), Psalm 135 supposes a liturgy of considerable weight. Jerusalem and the temple have been rebuilt and are functioning.

Psalm 136
Thanksgiving for God's Everlasting Ḥesed

Psalm 135 praises the Lord who is above all gods (v. 5), a note that is sounded in 136:2-3. Both psalms review Israel's history (135:8-12; 136:10-22), the order of the events being the same. The two are partners which resume the *hallelujah* theme introduced in Psalms 111–118. In the LXX the final *hallelujah* of Psalm 135 is affixed to 136. The structure of Psalm 136 is straightforward: introduction (vv. 1-3); God's *ḥesed* in creating the world (vv. 4-9); God's *ḥesed* in the Exodus, wilderness, and conquest (vv. 10-22); God's continual presence and activity (vv. 23-25), and conclusion (v. 26). The name *yhwh* appears only once (v. 1). The poet opens with a liturgical formula, "give thanks to the LORD, for he is good,"[38] and reiterates the summons, substituting different titles the second and third times (vv. 1-3). The poet states the theme, God's "great wonders" (v. 4, a collective term for God's deeds in creation and history; cf. 78:4; 105:2, 5; 106:2), and launches into a recital, which includes the design of heaven and earth (vv. 5-6), the lights' specific times of governance (vv. 7-9), smiting Egypt, freeing Israel and dividing the Red Sea (vv. 10-15), guiding the people, removing human obstacles to the gift of the land (vv. 16-22). This outline corresponds to the episodes related from Genesis to Joshua. History unfolds like a series of photographs arranged in a gallery of divine interventions. By God's power Israel crossed the sea and the pursuing Egyptians did not. God guided the people through the desert and opened the path to enter the

---

[38] This formula is associated with the Levitical guilds of singers who sang it on various occasions, and it is used in the liturgy (1 Chr 16:34; 2 Chr 5:11-14; 7:1-3; 20:21; Ezra 3:11). It is also heard in the introductory or concluding frame of Pss 100:4-5; 106:1; 107:1; 118:1-4, 29.

land. Each succeeding episode is new, but the refrain chants what is
always the same. A change in syntax in Hebrew marks the ending (cf.
v. 23). The first person appears ("us" and "our") and a relative particle
(translated "It is he who") introduces the present generation's rescue
from a low ebb. He "who remembered us in our low estate" continually "gives food to all flesh," (v. 25; cf. 104:14-15, 27-28; 145:15-16; 146:7;
147:9), another manifestation of *ḥesed*. The final summons forms an
inclusion and adds another title, "the God of heaven" (v. 26). By the
end the refrain has been charged with the content of all the acclamations, as God's eternal *ḥesed* is expounded throughout the litany.

The cosmological picture (vv. 5-9) can be compared to Genesis 1; in
both creation serves as a prelude to salvation history. The cosmos is envisioned in horizontal layers, heavens then earth, spread out on the
deep waters. God creates the cosmos "by understanding" or "insight,"
bitĕbûnâh (v. 5), which connotes the artisan's skill. The heavens are
proper to God, whereas the earth is the theater of divine providence.
Sun and moon are creatures which measure the pulse of the day and
night as well as the course of history. The poet breaks off the narration
after the fourth day and the creation of the lights (v. 9). Once the immutable elements of creation and this celestial clock are in place, the
poet paints the tableaux of the people's history with great sweeps of
God's hand and delicate brush strokes to fill out some details. The
Exodus is collapsed into the final plague (vv. 10-12; the "strong hand
and an outstretched arm," cf. Deut 4:34; 5:15; 26:8) and the events at the
Red Sea (vv. 13-15). God "divided," *gzr*, or "cut [the sea] in pieces," a
rare verb. He "shook off" Pharaoh (v. 15, as in Exod 14:27), as one shakes
off an insect in Ps 109:23. God's guidance in the desert is reduced to a
single phrase (v. 16); the critical events of Sinai remain untouched. God's
ḥesed is trustworthy and vigorous, as illustrated by the narrative which
moves through history to the present. The killing of the first born and
kings (vv. 10, 17) does not seem like "steadfast love," and the victims
did not perceive it as such, but it demonstrates *ḥesed* for an oppressed
Israelite. Each divine act opens onto succeeding ones, which makes the
transition to "us" understandable and gives the hymn a hopeful tone,
which is needed as one enters the world of the following psalm.

A salient attribute governs the divine action and reveals God. It is
easy to understand that God's *ḥesed* effected the people's rescue. From
there one can deduce that *ḥesed* has been active ever since creation and
continues today; it touches all reality and transcends everything. The
attribute "forever," *lĕʿōlām*, confirms its transcendent quality. Why
repeat the same phrase twenty-six times? The unvarying refrain illustrates the content of the phrase "endures forever" and invites the assembly to assimilate its meaning. The term *ḥesed*, translated "steadfast

love," does not correspond adequately to any English term. Neither kindness, mercy, loyalty, benevolence, love, nor even a periphrasis ("committed love," "covenant loyalty," "bonded love") captures the content, so the NRSV's "steadfast love" is as good a term as any. In view of the inadequacy of an English term to match *ḥesed*, it is justifiable not to translate the term that evokes the covenant and connotes God's commitment to a relationship as long as eternity. Thus the congregation is urged to thank God ceaselessly.

Psalm 137
Love Song for Jerusalem

Psalm 137 has no link with the psalms which precede and follow it. Linguistically, the mournful, imprecatory tone and the theme set it apart from its context. The poet vividly remembers and relives the exile. The memory is unsettling and it results in a suffocating nostalgia for abandoned Jerusalem and the destroyed temple. The heart aches just thinking about how it could not celebrate the liturgy; the muted, dangling instruments on the trees share in the musicians' mourning. Onto the aliens' homesickness the captors heaped insensitive jibes, "Sing us one of the songs of Zion!" (vv. 1-3). The exiles were prodded to amuse their captors with their liturgy and thus reduce it to folklore. Such playacting would be akin to forgetting their estrangement from Zion, postponing their mourning, not bearing their disgrace. In reaction the poet denounces the outrage to wake the instruments and neglect the offended love for the temple and the homeland. He or she curses the self, "let my right hand wither!"—the hand with which I pluck the harp; "[l]et my tongue cling to the roof of my mouth"—with which I sang the sacred liturgies. Jerusalem is the greatest of the poet's joys (vv. 4-6). Memory inspires the poet to pray, but passion boils up and spills over into vituperation (v. 7). The "day of Jerusalem" was her downfall, when the Edomites allied with the conqueror and applauded Jerusalem's disgrace.[39] The poet recalls the savage catcalls—may God hold this against them! He or she prays that those who dishonored

---

[39] The Edomites were Babylon's allies in Jerusalem's destruction, in which they cruelly collaborated (Lam 4:21; Ezek 25:12; 36:5; Obad 10-14). Different authors (e.g., Isaiah 34, Ezekiel 35, Obadiah) elaborate on the theme of Edom's judgment, which in part is derived from the tradition of the rivalry between brothers Jacob and Esau, who represent the neighboring nations of Israel and Edom. It is likely that historical conflict contributed to the theme, but in Psalm 137 Edom also serves as a symbol for the world hostile to Jerusalem.

noble Jerusalem get what they deserve (see 129:5-8). Edom's jeers
evoke the image of nudity. What is translated "Tear it down," from *ʿrh*,
means to "strip her naked" or "strip her bare to her foundations," obviously with the shameful nuance implied (cf. Isa 3:17; 47:2-3; Lam 1:8;
4:21; Jer 50:12; Ezek 16:37-39; 23:29). Zion is Mother, and we are to
understand the desired disgrace as the defiling of her dignity. Finally
the exiled community intones the song with sarcastic irony (vv. 8-9).
After invoking the name of the enemy capital, "O daughter Babylon,
you devastator," the poet begins the benediction "Happy." Passion
translates the wish into violent malediction. May God remember Babylon's and her allies' insult and pay them back in kind. The psalm culminates in a reckless desire, to destroy even defenseless babies so as to
deny a future to the enemy (cf. 2 Kgs 8:12; Isa 13:16; Nah 3:10).

Stylistically, the composition is a gem. It expresses unbridled emotion, from melancholy and nostalgia to rage. The poet plays with sounds,
words, and ideas. He or she addresses Jerusalem (v. 5), the LORD (in
v. 7), and Babylon (v. 8), and quotes the taunters (v. 3; cf. Ps 42:3, 10;
79:10) and Edom (v. 7). The sequence of remember–forget–not remember–remember accents the liturgical aspect (vv. 1, 5, 6, 7). Memory
transports the poet into exile, which inspires a curse on the self if he or
she should forget Jerusalem and a prayer for God to remember and
repay the outrage. The irony is that the imprecation constitutes a hymn
of allegiance to Zion. The chiastic pattern of the middle strophe provides emphasis (vv. 5-6):

A   If I *forget you*, O Jerusalem,

  B   let my *right hand* wither!

  B' Let my *tongue* cling to the roof of my mouth,

A' if I do not *remember you*.

Thematically and geographically the poet begins with the self and
the memory (vv. 1-4), moves to Jerusalem (vv. 5-6) and on to the LORD
and Babylon (vv. 7-9). The opposition Babylon–Zion is deftly handled.
The references to place follow a certain order, and Jerusalem occupies
the central position:

A   Babylon

  B   Zion

    C   Zion

      D   foreign land

        E   "you, O Jerusalem"

      C' Jerusalem

      D' Edom

   B' Jerusalem

A' Babylon

The poem begins along the watercourses of Babylon with the tears coursing down the faces of deported Jews and concludes with lifeless Babylon dashed against the bare rock.

This poem expresses the grief of those who were dispirited because the aggressor destroyed the holy city, and it can be appropriated by anyone who strongly feels the present siege of Jerusalem and its theological significance. As a symbol Babylon is transhistorical and appears both in Daniel and Revelation as the world's capital, a city wherein evil resides and from where it continues to assault God's capital and plan for the human race. To the extent that Babylon conquers the human heart she has allies and adopted children. This psalm is prayed as a pledge of allegiance to the holy city, Jerusalem, emblem of the celestial city, and it invokes the triumph of God's saving action in the world. The poem and prayer would be slightly less objectionable without the translation of "little ones" or "children," which obviously needs to be interpreted for this to be prayed in the liturgy (see Introduction).

The cruel beatitudes express the intense devotion to Jerusalem and the profound sense of injustice committed against her by the Edomites and the Babylonians. This is not a program of action, to knock the hell out of Babylon and her children. Rather it is an overflow of feeling beautifully captured in a restrained composition. Certainly the sentiments clash with our morals, and thus these verses are not included in some contemporary liturgical books. But this curse is not to be understood literally. One has to transpose the image of the slain children. If Jerusalem is the symbol of the Church and, more broadly, of the reign of God, Babylon is just the opposite, the personification of evil and all human and inhuman powers which oppose the divine reign of truth, justice, and peace among people (Rev 14:8; 18:1-24). Babylon's destruction augurs the definitive victory against every evil. Much of our life of faith is lived in Babylon, even as we long for Jerusalem.

Psalm 138
Hymn of a Grateful Heart

The last line of Psalm 138, "steadfast love . . . endures forever," is reminiscent of the anaphora of Psalm 136. The thanksgiving of Psalm

138 gradually expands and becomes all embracing. It is individual and choral, and to a degree the two parallel each other. The following schema identifies the corresponding vocabulary:

vv. 1-2	vv. 4-6
I give *thanks (ydh)*	kings . . . *praise (ydh)*
to your name	LORD
your *word (ʾimrâh)*	the *words* of your mouth (ʾimrîm)
for (kî) you *have exalted (gdl)*	*for (kî)* great *(gādôl)* is the glory

The change of address is no surprise. God is spoken to (vv. 1-4, 7, 8b) and about (vv. 5-6, 8a). The repetition of *ḥesed*, "your steadfast love," forms an inclusion (vv. 2, 8). The sevenfold occurrence of the divine name[40] illustrates God's supremacy above rival "gods," before whom the psalmist praises the LORD (v. 1). Vocabulary of communication illustrates the dialogue; the poet *called*, God *answered*, and all kings *have heard* God's *words* (vv. 3-4).

The poem begins with the psalmist's grateful heart, expressed in song and gesture, directed toward the symbol of God's presence, the temple. The psalmist has experienced God's enduring qualities of *ḥesed* and fidelity (vv. 1-3). A personal act of thanksgiving will be broadcast to the international forum, "[a]ll the kings of the earth" (vv. 4-5). To the horizontal plane is added the vertical axis, as the motive of the song becomes explicit; God, who is on high, cares for the lowly, and this extends to the psalmist and all God's works (vv. 6-8). Several elements of this poem are borrowed from other psalms (cf. 5:8; 9:2; 23:5; 57:3; 68:32; 96:4-5; 100:5; 102:16; 113:3-6; 115:1).

The psalmist reflects on God's omniscience and presence. He is both "high," *rām*, "far away," *mimmerḥāq* (v. 6; cf. 113:4-6), and intimately near ("for me," *baʿădî*, v. 8). From a lofty vantage point God surveys everything. The motives for thanksgiving are personal and general —God's love and fidelity (v. 2a), his words and great glory (vv. 2b, 4b, 5b), his attention to the humble (v. 6), and care for the psalmist (vv. 3, 7-8). The poet synthesizes the personal experience with the image of God stretching out a hand to rescue one (v. 7). Supported by this experience, he or she can regard the future with confidence, and therein is born the final request, that God, creator of all, never abandon the work of his hands, a reminiscence of the way in which the human was fashioned by God in Gen 2:7. Another motive is concrete, the greatness of the LORD's glory, which consists in the attention to the lowly. The irony is that God, who is high, is close to the lowly and keeps a distance from the haughty. The juxtaposition of the lowly and the haughty manifests

---

[40] With the textual emendation in v. 1, "O LORD," present in the NRSV.

a political awareness. Then the poet generalizes about his or her own experience, affirms personal trust in God's rescue, and requests that the trust be vindicated (vv. 7-8).

The poet thanks God and wishes, surprisingly, that "[a]ll the kings of the earth" do so, which is a remarkable stroke of universality (vv. 4-5; cf. 22:27-29; 66:1-4, and the LORD as sovereign psalms, Psalms 96–99). The poet does so "before the gods" (v. 1), another universal perspective. In other contexts the Hebrew *ʾĕlōhîm* stands for "gods" or members of the divine court (cf. 82:1; 86:8). Or perhaps the psalmist is a foreigner, awaking to the belief in the one God. Or maybe, distant from the temple, he or she prays in the vicinity of idols, but prostrate in the direction of Jerusalem and the temple. If this is the case, an accent of nostalgia pervades the poem.

Regardless of the precise circumstances, the poet can attest to the universality of God's *ḥesed*. In the end he or she repeats the personal experience, synthesizes it, and gives it permanent value, "your right hand delivers me" (v. 7). Bolstered by this experience, the poet pronounces a touching entreaty. All of life is the work of God's hands; may he who has begun it sustain it forever (v. 8). Because God fulfills his purpose, because the divine *ḥesed* is unending, to abandon the work of his hands would be a denial of the self. The recognition of "your *ḥesed*, O LORD, endures forever" is all the confidence a person needs.

Psalm 139
All-Seeing God Knows I Am Innocent

Psalm 139 is framed by four words or synonyms, which set the tone (vv. 1-2, 23):

ḥqr, "search"	*ydᶜ,* "know"	*byn,* "discern"	*lĕrēaᶜ,* "thoughts"
ḥqr, "search"	*ydᶜ,* "know"	*bḥn,* "test"	*śarᶜappîm,* "thoughts"

The repetition of the word *derek,* "path" or "way" (vv. 3, 24), strengthens the frame. In the end the poet reformulates the initial declaration, "O LORD, you have searched me and known me," as a petition, "Search me, O God, and know my heart." The poem is comprised of four movements, thematically distinct from one another—divine omniscience (vv. 1-6); omnipresence in space (vv. 7-15); omnipresence in time (vv. 16-18); denunciation of God's enemies and final petition (vv. 19-24). The verb *ydᶜ,* "know," occurs six times, plus once the cognate *daᶜat,* "knowledge" (v. 6), seven times in all. In addition, seven synonyms from the semantic field of *knowing*, *ḥqr*, "search" (vv. 1, 23), *bnh*, "discern" (v. 2), *zrh*, "search" (v. 3), *skn*, "acquaint" (v. 3), *rʾh*, "behold, see" (vv. 16, 24), bolster the theme. This vocabulary describes the activity of the divine judge who assesses the human heart (cf. Pss 11:4-5; 17:3; 26:2; Job 7:17-18; 13:9; Jer 9:7; 17:10). The scope of images which describe God's penetrating scrutiny is remarkable: "hem me in," "lay your hand upon me," "you are there," "your hand shall lead me," "your right hand shall hold me fast," "darkness is as light to you," "you knit me together in my mother's womb," your "eyes beheld my unformed substance," "in your book." Such language is used elsewhere to plead innocence, confess sin, and express trust (cf. Pss 17:3; 26:2; 44:21; 69:5; 142:3; cf. Jer 12:3).

What appears to be a sublime hymn developing the theme of God's omniscience culminates in a curse, which in effect is the poet's plea of innocence. His or her purpose is to be exculpated from any alleged guilt, which is attained by the eloquent portrayal of divine friendship, care, and knowledge. While one confesses God's omniscience and omnipresence, one praises him (v. 14), and not the least of God's awesome works is the one who is confessing and praising (v. 13; cf. 138:8). In the first three movements the poet tells how fully God comprehends one's existence. This part of the poem can be charted like this:

vv. 1-5	God's all-pervasive knowledge
v. 6	surpasses me
vv. 7-12	to flee or hide is useless
[v. 14	God's works are wonderful]
vv. 13, 15-16	God's personal knowledge since before birth
vv. 17-18	God's unfathomable thoughts

God knows whatever the poet thinks and does (vv. 1-5), is present wherever he or she is (vv. 7-12), and was even present before birth (vv. 13-16). A thematic refrain registers a progression in the poet's admiration, from God's knowledge (v. 6), to God's works (v. 14), to God's thoughts (vv. 17-18). The three movements are a literary fabric woven of personal pronouns. Every line contains a "you" or "your" and an "I," "me," or "my." God is enmeshed in the poet's existence. The irony is that he who knows the human condition also knows that one is born sinful. After the third movement the harsh request, "kill the wicked, O God" (vv. 19-20), and avowals of allegiance with God, "Do I not hate those who hate you, O LORD" (vv. 21-22), are calculated to put maximum distance between the poet and the wicked. God's total knowledge of the poet, reviewed in the first three movements, is all the proof needed to establish his or her innocence.

God is both intimately close and infinitely distant, within and without, from beginning to end. God encompasses and floods all space and time. The poem is distinguished for the use of merisms and polar expressions—sit down and rise up, path and lying down, behind and before, heaven and Sheol, morning (east) and sea (west), darkness and light, night and day. Verses 2-3, 5 are formulated similarly:

A	B	C
when I sit	when I stand	you discern my thoughts from far away
my path	my lying down	you are acquainted with all my ways
behind	before	you lay your hand upon me

The merism sitting and rising embraces time (v. 2). The "path" and "lying down" (v. 3), "behind and before" (v. 5) are spatial, and this is mapped out by other contrasts—in every part, near or far, heaven or Sheol, where the dawn lives or at the edge of the sea (east and west). God's knowledge is likened to total presence, impossible to escape (vv. 7-12). Even if one were caught up like Elijah (2 Kgs 2:9-11) or sunk to the depths of Sheol like Korah and Dothan (Num 16:29-33), one could not escape the divine reach (cf. Amos 9:2). The psalmist imagines the improbable disguise and flight, utilizing wings of light or hiding in a black cloak loaned by the night to escape from the divine spirit. God does not move from place to place as the poet might, but nonetheless he is invariably present in every place, and every escape attempt is futile. Darkness and light are not opposites from God's perspective, who shines light out of darkness at creation and continues to regulate the light. God is beyond yet present to every detail in the universe.

God's knowledge also extends to the mystery of gestation (vv. 13-16). He is involved in maternal ovulation and, with a delicate, adept touch, knits and weaves the poet, even to the intricate chromosome structure and the complexity of the brain (cf. Job 10:8-12). The "depths of the earth" refers to the secrets of the maternal womb, which reflects the fecundity of mother earth. God foresaw life unfolding and registered all human actions in a book even before they came to be (v. 16; cf. 56:8; 69:28). The vast space of the previous movement is beautifully contrasted with the embryo in the womb and from there the focus expands once again, "my inwards parts," "my mother's womb," "the depths of the earth." The poet's "inward parts" and "frame" are not out of reach of God's "eyes" and "thoughts" (vv. 16-17). Spontaneous praise interrupts the reflection, as the poet sees him or herself as a marvelous part of God's handiwork (v. 14). God's thoughts are weighty and count-less (see Isa 55:8), more numerous than grains of sand on the beach. Even if one could count the prodigies of creation, he or she would still encounter God's immeasurable, infinite mystery.

In the end the poet requests the punishment of the wicked and for-mally dissociates him or herself from them. One desires to be defini-tively separated from those bloodthirsty, deceitful perjurers who aim to vilify God's plan, who *"rise up"* against God (v. 21); the verb *qwm* re-calls the earlier ("rise up," v. 2). Three times the poet mounts hatred against the godless who are hostile to God; those who hate God I hate, those who oppose God I loathe, God's enemies are my enemies. The ha-tred is not emotional but rather the reflex theological response to what is not of God. The psalmist, after describing the intimate relationship with God, retreats as much as possible from the wicked. A concluding request places one completely in God's hands (vv. 23-24). In the un-likely event that the poet's *way* be found crooked, the all-knowing God can bring about a change and lead one "in the way everlasting."

The poet is amazed at God's boundless knowledge, by his vigilant omnipresence, by the greatness and profundity of his designs which surpass human comprehension. For that one thanks God and requests a thorough investigation and guidance along the right path. The re-markable feature of this poem is the sense of intimacy with God. The poet, charged with emotion, speaks with God, using extreme contrasts in his reflections. At first the monologue concentrates on the fact that God penetrates all life, all action, thought and intention, from begin-ning to end. In conclusion the poet pleads innocence of any complicity with evil. The psalmist feels tucked into the divine consciousness and protected; God is always concerned for the poet and, vice versa, he or she for God.

Psalm 140
Prayer for Deliverance and Punishment

Psalm 140 is a personal complaint, structured symmetrically in four movements: a cry for help against attack (vv. 1-5), an act of trust and an appeal for help (vv. 6-8), the wish for the defeat of the enemy (vv. 9-11), and a confession of confidence and thanksgiving (vv. 12-13). In the first two God is called upon seven times to act decisively (imperative and jussive forms, vv. 1-8). The divine name *yhwh* appears seven times (rep-resented in the NRSV), with more resonance in the act of trust; the addi-tional "my God" and "my Lord" *(ʾădōnāy)* strengthen the bonds between the poet and the divine protector. The sevenfold appeal for God's intervention and the *selâh* argue for a division after v. 8, which removes any direct reference to God from the curse (vv. 9-11). In the end the poet is identified with the usual beneficiaries of divine aid, the poor and the needy victims of the schemes of the high and mighty. To "live in your presence" alludes to the temple where one enjoys God's nearness (v. 13; cf. 11:7; 16:11; 17:15; 27:4).

The repeated petition, "protect me from the violent" (vv. 1, 4), identifies the general situation. Following the call for help is a generic description of the assailant, falling under the heading of plotting and calumny (vv. 3, 9, 11), symbolized by the mouth. The insidious plot is conceived in the *mind* (*lēb*, "heart"), expressed in *speech*, and the wicked threaten with their *hands* (vv. 2-4). The poet adopts conventional images—the sharp, snaky tongue and viperous venom (cf. 52:2; 55:21; 57:4; 64:3); traps, nets, and snares (vv. 4-5; cf. 9:15-16; 10:8-9; 31:4; 57:6; 64:5; 119:110; 124:7; 141:9). The second call for help parallels the first, followed by another description of the wicked. The images bespeak treason. In both appeals the "violent," *ʾîš ḥămāsîm*, appear as a kind of refrain, "protect me from the violent" (vv. 1, 4; see also v. 11). Chiastic parallelism appears in vv. 1 and 4 (not evident in the NRSV):

A	B	B¹	A¹
deliver me, LORD	from evildoers	from . . . violent	protect me
guard me, LORD	from the . . . wicked	from the violent	protect me

A schema helps appreciate the care with which the initial verses were composed (underlined words are repetitions in Hebrew):

vv. 1-3 Deliver me LORD from evildoers
         protect me   from *the violent*   who *plot* evil
                                                 stir up wars
                                                 venomous mouths

vv. 4-5 Guard me LORD from the wicked
         protect me   from *the violent*   who *plan* my downfall
                                                have hidden a trap
                                                spread a net
                                                set snares for me

The LORD is an indispensable ally, "my God," recalling the covenant, and the poet appeals to a military alliance where God is rescuer and helmet (vv. 6-7). The "day of battle" may refer to a past rescue when the poet was confronted with false accusations and calumny (in the NRSV), or it may be translated in the present, "you cover my head in the day of battle," as a statement of trust. The standard curse is that evil designs may be foiled; God has no direct involvement in its inner workings as annihilation is brought on by burning coals and a fall into the pit (vv. 9-11; see 7:15-16; 141:10). Hostility is characterized with metaphors of war (v. 2), snakes (v. 3), and the hunt (v. 5). Considering the verbal and thematic repetitions, symmetry and beauty touch even the act of retribution, as the poet hopes that all evil plans will backfire. The elements of the curse recur in the inverse order of their initial appearance, as shown here:

A   ". . . [the adversaries] stir up *wars*" (v. 2)

B   ". . . under *their lips* is the venom of vipers" (v. 3)

C   ". . . who have planned my *downfall*" (v. 4)

D   ". . . hidden *a trap* for me, . . . spread *a net*, . . . set *snares*" (v. 5)

A'   "you have covered my head in the day of *battle*" (v. 7)

B'   "let the mischief of *their lips* overwhelm them" (v. 9)

C'   "Let them be *flung into pits*" (v. 10)

D'   "let evil speedily *hunt* down the violent" (v. 11)

The poet desires retributive justice, that evil turn against its violent accomplice, that the enemy be defeated by their own evil devices. The objective is the defense of the poor and oppressed, the defenseless, then the upright will thank God and dwell in a world governed by the divine presence (vv. 12-13).

Psalm 141
Lead Us Not into Temptation

Psalm 141 is a personal complaint in which the poet prays to be rescued from social pressure to join wicked company. Incense was a prescribed morning and evening offering (Exod 30:7-8). A gesture of uplifted hands accompanies the prayer and symbolizes it (cf. Pss 28:2; 63:4; 134:2). The institution of the "evening sacrifice" is mentioned at Ahaz' reform (2 Kgs 16:15), Ezra's penitential rite (Ezra 9:5), and Daniel's vision (Dan 9:21). The incense rite symbolizes and expresses the prayers

of the faithful, and the poet requests that the present prayer be equivalent to the incense offering and the evening sacrifice (vv. 1-2). One requests deliverance from the idolaters' wiles and worship, so that no
enticement or punishment may induce him or her to join their company (vv. 3-5). Their destruction is anticipated (vv. 6-7), and he or she
concludes with a request for deliverance (vv. 8-10).

In an agitated state the poet prays fervently that God come to the
rescue and that the wicked be frustrated (vv. 1-2, 8-10), even while he or
she toys with the temptation of accepting their offer of friendship: "Do
not turn my heart to any evil"; "do not let me eat of their delicacies";
"[n]ever let the oil of the wicked anoint my head." The expressions "eat
of their delicacies" and "anoint my head" refer to ritual actions offered
by the wicked. The poet feels enmeshed in their nets. The wicked approach the psalmist, and their words and actions are seductive, for the
mouth and heart are liable to move in that direction. One would prefer
harsh fraternal correction from good people to the sumptuous comforts
of the wicked (cf. Sir 22:27–23:6, a prayer to be removed from evil).

First the poet asks to be restrained in speech; but even more profoundly, the heart, where evil is designed, must be curbed (vv. 3-4). The
image of the sentinel at the door of the lips is unique. The guard God
puts there as at the entrance of a fortress will not let bad words pass.
Another psalm will speak of a gag or muzzle (39:1; cf. Sir 22:27). God is
asked to countermand any inclination to evil in the heart. The mouth is
the vulnerable point in the defenses, a gate between the heart and action. This is illustrated in the poem, where the mouth frames attitudes
and behavior (vv. 3-4):

A   set a guard over my mouth . . ., over the door of my lips

    (interior)   do not turn my heart to [speak] evil

    (external)   to do wicked deeds with the wicked

A¹   do not let me eat of their delicacies

Rarely in the Psalter does the poet admit such a temptation (cf. 73:13-
15), and this admission is a convincing reason for God to answer. The
sequence of ideas in the obscure vv. 5b-7 requests distance from and
punishment of the wicked. Hands, mouth, heart, head, eyes—all these
organs appear. The hands and eyes are directed to God. The mouth and
the heart must be protected from evil. The head is to be without the
honors with which the evildoers would reward their accomplices. The
final prayer asks that God protect the suppliant from the traps of the
wicked who, it is hoped, will be ensnared in their own devices (vv. 9-
10; the verb *šmr*, "keep" is repeated from v. 3, "set a guard"), leaving the

psalmist free. That the wicked become trapped in their own snares follows the logic of retaliation (cf. 7:16; 9:16; 35:8; 69:22; 106:36; 140:9-11).

Psalm 142
Rescue Me from Prison

The superscription of Psalm 142 makes one ask, what cave? There are two candidates, that of Adullam, where David fled from Gath to find refuge (vv. 3-4 and 1 Sam 22:1) or the cave of Engedi (1 Sam 24:3-4). Neither of these fits the poet's description, unless the interpreter understands that David, fixing his eyes so firmly on God, lost sight of his fair-weather comrades.

With an insistent invocation composed of four expressions, the poet introduces the complaint (vv. 1-2), before he or she describes the desperate straits, spiritual collapse, persecution, and lack of human support (vv. 3-4). This description is intended to move God to act. In the Hebrew text, the initial regular rhythm changes after v. 4. A second movement begins with another invocation, signaled by the repetition of "I cry" and "Lord" (v. 5; cf. v. 1). This time the poet adds the reason, his or her only "refuge" and "portion in the land of the living" is God (cf. Ps 17:14; Eccl 9:9). The author employs the term *ḥēleq*, "portion," which elsewhere refers to the inheritance when the land was apportioned. It is used metaphorically with reference to the Levites, for whom God is the "portion" or "inheritance" (Num 18:20; Deut 10:9; see, analogously, Ps 16:5). Two realities are in play. A person lives on a parcel of land and makes a living on it. Those who dwell in "the land of the living" live on God. The motif of persecution is reiterated. The prison is a metaphor for distress, like the trap, "the Pit" or Sheol (cf. Lam 3:7-9; Ps 88:6). The image is apt. The poet is faint, threatened with entrapment, ignored, devoid of help, depressed, and persecuted. In this narrow, closed condition he or she calls to heaven, which opens an escape hatch to a broader reality. The assailant is unidentified, "they have hidden a trap for me" (v. 3). Who are they? "[P]ersecutors . . . too strong for me" (v. 6). What began as painful isolation is relieved by a celebration of deliverance in the community of the "righteous." The final stroke registers a surge of confidence.

To an ordinary invocation the poet adds an original element, the venting and "pouring out" of a complaint before God (v. 2; cf. 62:8). The poet has a flair for the dramatic. The intensely personal tone (vv. 1-3a) reads literally,

My voice, I cry to the LORD;
  my voice, I entreat the LORD;
I pour out before him my complaint;
  I declare my trouble before him;
when my spirit is faint within me,
  you know my way.

With an emphatic shift the poet jumps to God, attesting to his knowledge, "*you* [ʾattâh] know." He or she appeals to what God already knows. The poet vacillates between complaint and trust—flagging energies, trust in God (direct address), and treacherous path (v. 3). The penetrating solitude contrasts with the enthusiastic company brought by the rescue. The poet is alone and no one cares, literally, "for my soul," *napšî* (v. 4); once released (again, *napšî*), he or she will be surrounded with a community of the righteous (v. 7). It is curious that the poet does not request the adversary's punishment. God's favor effectively wipes out the sense of alienation. In the end the poet presses the plea, this time surcharged with trust and motivated by personal exhaustion and the enemies' strength, and imagines salvation like an exit from a painful, solitary prison. The irony is that the descriptions are of exclusion rather than confinement. The poet speaks of a path, absence of refuge, no one paying any heed. The path of life is a prison from which there is no escape. God is the only relief, the only worthwhile portion in the land of the living.

Psalm 143
My Soul Thirsts for You Like Parched Land

The distressed poet is besieged by enemies (Psalms 142–143). The use of the imperative mood (in each case followed by *kî*, "for," introducing the reason) is identical (142:7; 143:8-10). Common vocabulary links the two—the enemies "pursue" (from *rdp*, 142:6; 143:3); the petition, "save me," *haṣṣîlēnî* (142:6; 143:9); the sevenfold *napšî* (translated "my soul," "my life," or simply "me," 142:4, 7; 143:3, 6, 8, 11, 12) spanning the two, as well as the sevenfold divine name (142:1 [twice], 5; 143:1, 7, 9, 11); an identical phrase, "my spirit is faint [faints within me]" (142:3; 143:4). Personal devotion associates the poet with the Levites, "You are . . . my portion in the land of the living" (142:5) and "I am your servant" (143:12).

An inclusion frames Psalm 143, "in your righteousness," "your servant," "living" and "my life," enemy, and the divine name (vv. 1-3,

11-12). The poet is God's "[your] servant," depends on divine *ḥesed*, and has a claim on God's "righteousness." The poem opens with four pleas, which are followed by a rare admission of the human condition before God. The psalmist does not specify any sin. He or she merely states generally that on one's own no one is innocent ("righteous, *ṣdq*, v. 2; cf. Pss 51:5; 130:3). The two movements are vv. 1-6 and 7-12, their beginnings marked by the sequence, "answer me" followed by a negative request ("Do not enter . . .," v. 2, and "Do not hide . . .," v. 7), and "hear," *šmᶜ* (vv. 1, 8). *Ḥesed* frames the second movement (vv. 8, 12). The fourteen imperatives (positive and negative, without counting the repetition of "answer me") texture the poem like a litany. The basic schema consists of the request followed by the reason, introduced six times by the conjunction *kî*, "for" (cf. vv. 3, 8-10, 12); the last reason is the most convincing, "for I am your servant." There are seven positive and negative requests of God in vv. 1-2, 7; what is translated "quickly" is a verb, "hurry" (v. 7). From "[a]nswer me quickly" to the end the poet sustains a volley of requests for help, bolstered by descriptions of trouble and confessions of confidence. One function of the term *selâh* is rubrical; here *selâh* indicates a pause before the second half is performed (v. 6).

Death and life are juxtaposed, and the psalmist is at the edge of death (vv. 2-4, 6-7). Throughout the poem the self-conscious psalmist is aware of the plight, as evidenced by the vocabulary: *napšî* ("me," "my soul," vv. 3, 6, 8, 11, 12 ["my"]), *rûḥî* ("my spirit," vv. 4, 7), and *libbî* ("my heart," v. 4). The body registers the stress in the shortness of breath and the abnormal pulse (vv. 4, 7), to which is added the sensation that God has hidden his face (cf. Ps 104:29). Death is not far off. This fainting, languishing spirit *(rûaḥ)*, "like those who go down to the Pit," is opposite God's "good spirit" which the psalmist desires (*rûaḥ*, v. 10; cf. 51:10-12).

The imagery is exquisite. "[C]rushing my life to the ground" literally means "grinding the life against the earth" (cf. 3; cf. Ps 7:5). The human is dust and at death will return to the earth from which he or she came (cf. 146:4). This is how the human enters the realm of "darkness like those long dead" (cf. Job 10:21-22). The images of being crushed to the earth and left in darkness recall the pre-creation state. The poet feels the pain of the spirit being extracted (vv. 4, 7) and requests a resuscitation of God's "good spirit." From the dark night of the soul the poet longs for the dawn of *ḥesed* (v. 8; cf. 5:3). The memory of God's saving work among the people is both a consolation and a reason to appeal to God (v. 5; cf. 77:11-15). One longs for God as parched land needs rain. This is not the first time that the poet has "thirsted" for a divine response (v. 6; cf. 42:1-2; 63:1). As one meditates on the works of God's *hands* (of which the poet is one), one raises the *hands* in prayer (vv. 5-6; Pss 44:20; 141:2; Job 11:13; Isa 1:15). The visual images of the hands *stretched out (prš)* to God, the soul *thirsting like dry ground* for God, and the soul *lifted up (nśʾ)* toward God (v. 8b) reflect the poet's condition as it reaches to God. Outstretched hands symbolize a soul stretched out, reaching for God, and lifting up the soul (the self-offering) is a mirror image of the hands raised, which also expresses the lifting of the morning offering. The parallelism between "for in you I put my trust" and "for to you I lift up my soul" argues for a pictorial image of trust, which raises the person toward God.

Psalm 143 is a conventional complaint with unique characteristics. A person, harassed by enemies which push him or her to the brink of the grave, implicitly confesses guilt and pleads for rescue, guidance according to God's will, and the annihilation of persecutors. The final expression is eloquent for its brevity, introduced by an emphatic pronoun, literally, "I, your servant," and expressing utter dependence on God. What is missing is the pledge of thanksgiving. But what is evident at every turn is the trust in the divine salvation and the abandonment of the "servant" into God's hands. How can God resist such a sincere, passionate request which ends with the signature "your servant"?

Psalm 144
Happy the People Whose God Is the LORD

The linking word *lmd*, "teach" or "train," connects Psalms 143 and 144 (143:10; 144:1). Style and theme divide Psalm 144 in two distinct movements. The first is composed in the singular and requests rescue from warfare (vv. 1-11). It begins with a sublime invocation of God in military guise and a meditation about human insignificance. Suddenly, appealing for intervention, the poet asks that God "scatter them" and "rout them," although no adversary had been mentioned (v. 6). A refrain closes the personal supplication (vv. 7b-8, 11). The second movement, in the plural, concerns the people's prosperity (vv. 12-15). The blessings have nothing to do with war but rather with the basics of a happy agrarian society. They include healthy sons and lovely daughters, fertility in field and flock, public security and peace (vv. 13-14). Sons are likened to plants (agriculture) while daughters are compared to pillars (architecture). The list is concluded by a double beatitude for the people, blessed because their God is the LORD (v. 15). This section is awkwardly attached to the earlier by a Hebrew relative particle *ʾăšer* (not represented in translation, v. 12). Verbs are missing in the elliptical formulation, so the clauses either express the desired blessing (NRSV) or a present state of being (NJPS). In an effort to unite the two movements, one might consider the finale as a liturgical response to the foregoing, in which case the conclusion with the double beatitude ("happy," *ʾašrê*) is a priestly blessing.

The wisdom query (vv. 3-4) may be a transition from the initial appeal to the request, but it is odd in the present context. It departs from the initial military tone and jars with the theophany which follows. "[W]hat are human beings that you regard them" echoes Ps 8:4, where the question is answered with an affirmation of the glory God bestows on humans. In the present context the reflection is closer to Job 7:17-18, where the poet suggests God's relentless and inescapable pressures upon the human. The thought expresses both the sense of wonder that God should be so concerned with humans and the question examined in Job, how can there be a relationship between the temporary human and the infinite God. The images of fleeting life are unoriginal—a breath (known from Ecclesiastes as "vanity"), a passing shadow (v. 4; cf. 39:5; 102:11).

Here, as frequently elsewhere in the Bible, turbulent waters symbolize chaos and death (v. 7; cf. 18:16). More specifically, the waters picture the foreign aggressors, liars, false witnesses and perjurers. The "sword" is a metaphor for the sharp, lying words used against the psalmist (v. 11; cf. 57:4; 59:7; 64:3). This interpretation is supported by the refrain ". . . from the hand of aliens, whose mouths speak lies, and whose right hands are false," which the second time is preceded by "Rescue me from the cruel sword." The parallel lines and the alterations focus on the adversary:

vv. 7b-8

| mighty waters | the hand of aliens | lying mouths | false right hands |

v. 11

| cruel sword | the hand of aliens | lying mouths | false right hands |

The right hand accompanied the deceitful mouth in swearing falsely. The threatening evil is foreigners who violate treaties, perjure themselves, and break the peace pact.

Psalm 144 defies efforts at classification. A reasoned explanation is that it is the prayer of a sovereign for him or herself and the people, first for protection against assailants and promises to praise God (vv. 1-11), then for the people's material well-being. The two movements share in common trust in the source of all blessing, who rescues from personal or national crises. Our trust constitutes access to God's support. The final beatitudes are parallel and one derives from the other, the people's prosperity derives from having God as sovereign.

Psalm 145
The Greatness and Goodness of God

Psalm 145, the interlude before the finale, is followed by five hymns, each framed by the liturgical acclamation "Praise the LORD," *hallelujah*. All five echo features and fulfill the promise of Psalm 145, which closes with "[m]y mouth will speak the praise of the LORD" (v. 21). The declaration that "all flesh will bless his holy name forever" (145:21) anticipates the final summons, "Let everything that breathes praise the LORD" (150:6); together these two frame the concluding paean of praise. Psalm 146 summons the soul to praise God and promises lifelong praise (vv. 1-2). After a comprehensive rehearsal of praise and God's benefits, the wicked are brought down in a single stroke (145:20b; 146:9c). Another hemistich treats the wicked (147:6b). A thematic link, God's creative genius, joins 147:4, 15-18 and 148:5-6. The theme of God's chosen people, Israel, connects 147:2-3; 148:14; 149:2, 4. The use of participial forms to describe God's works weaves Psalms 146 and 147 together. A crescendo of praise begins from the "I" (146:1-2), expands in the plural imperative (146:3), and reaches the people centered on Zion (146:10). This includes the dispersed of Israel (147:2), the brokenhearted (147:3), and the angelic and heavenly choirs (148:2-4), indeed, all creation, including rulers (148:7-12). The crescendo reaches God's elect people, *ḥăsîdîm*, Israel (148:14). The people chime in, as the phrase "in the assembly of the faithful *[ḥăsîdîm]*" links 149:1 with 148:14. These two psalms are linked by echoes of praise and motives introduced by *kî*, "*for* he commanded and they were created," "*for* his name alone is exalted," "*for* the LORD takes pleasure in his people" (vv. 148:5, 13; 149:3-4). The kings, princes, and all peoples have a voice in the universal choir (148:11; 149:7-8). Music accompanies singing and praise as instruments and dancing are introduced. These reappear in reverse order in the final doxology (149:1-3; 150:3-4). The superscription identifies Psalm 145 as "Praise [Hebrew *těhillâh*]. Of David," the only psalm so identified. The fact that this is the last caption in the Psalter links it to the group of praise psalms (Psalms 146–150). The ending (v. 21) serves as a prelude to this final series.

Psalm 145 is an alphabetic acrostic.[41] This poetic pattern exemplifies the thoroughness of praise for God's well-ordered creation. The Hebrew word meaning "every" or "all" *(kōl)* is repeated nineteen times (counting v. 13b). The rhetorical use of an indivisible number emphasizes the completeness of the praise and accents God's eternity. An inclusion,

---

[41] The *nun* ("*n*") line (v. 13b) is missing in the MT, but is included in the Qumran, LXX and Syriac versions (as here).

formed by the repetition of *"bless* your [his holy] *name* forever and ever" (vv. 1-2, 21), states the purpose. Three times the poet refers to God's name (vv. 1, 2, 21), the third reference being to "his holy name." The name LORD appears ten times (counting v. 13b), and the addition of "my God" (v. 1) tallies fourteen mentions of LORD, name, and God—a plenary appearance. What begins with the personal intention to bless God concludes by extending the invitation to all living beings. The praise has four movements (vv. 1-3, 4-9, 10-13, 14-21). In the first three the poet praises God and recites the divine attributes, the motive for praise. In the fourth the components are reversed, so that the poem ends with praise. The interplay of praise and motive looks like this:

A	vv. 1-2	praise
B	v. 3	LORD is great; his greatness is unsearchable
A¹	vv. 4-7	praise
B¹	vv. 8-9	LORD is gracious, merciful, good . . .
A²	vv. 10-12	praise
B²	v. 13	God's everlasting kingdom; LORD is faithful, gracious
B³	vv. 14-20	description of God and his actions
A³	v. 21	praise

The growing intensity of praise and Israel's joyous confidence in the creator unfolds and blooms in the final verse, "all flesh will bless . . . forever."

The range of praise widens from the personal "I" (vv. 1-2) to the intergenerational community (vv. 4-7), to all God's works (vv. 10-12). Two voices rebound in choral response, between "they" and "I," declaring, meditating, speaking and giving testimony (vv. 4-7). The last verse mentions the two voices, the poet and "all flesh." The object is "my God" (v. 1), the sovereign who is great and performs mighty deeds. Synonyms designate God's deeds, *maʿăśeh* ("works," "made," "doings," vv. 4, 9, 10, 17), *gĕbûrût* ("mighty acts," "power," "mighty deeds," vv. 4, 11, 12), "wondrous works" (v. 5), "greatness" (vv. 3, 6); to these are added "kingdom" and "dominion" (vv. 11, 12, 13). The poet alters a liturgical formula about God (vv. 8-9; cf. Exod 34:6; Pss 103:4; 111:4) and uses his self-declaration as a source for theological reflection. The qualities—gracious, merciful, slow to anger, abounding in *ḥesed*, good, compassionate—express God's loyalty to the covenant partner, in this case the whole created world. Verses 11-12 feature the chiastic repetition of "reign," *malkûtekā*, and "power" or "mighty deeds, *gĕbûrâh*.

A	B
of *your reign* they will speak	of *your power* they will tell

B¹	A¹
to make known . . . *your mighty deeds*	and . . . *your reign*

The world's reliability is mirrored in God's benefices to people, beginning with those who depend solely on divine providence (vv. 14-20). This constitutes a growing description of God. The common theme is *hesed* which links creation and daily sustenance. This conclusion is derived from the simple fact that God provides the necessities of life.

The shift from regal power to compassion is intentional. God is my "king" and his benefits extend to the needy. His power is characterized by care for the defenseless and those who call on him. All creation is included in this praise, and all dissenting voices of the wicked, who appear only at the end, are destroyed (v. 20b). God's presence has a double impact, to rescue and to judge. Up to this point, the poet has focused on the positive. But now the antithetical parallel is stated in chiastic form.

A   The LORD watches over

  B   all who love him,

  B'   but all the wicked

A'   he will destroy.

The verbs are "watch over" *(šmr)* and "destroy" *(šmd)*. The objects are God's lovers *(ʾhb)* and the wicked *(ršʿ)*. This verse is a sobering qualification of the poet's claims. The tersely promised destruction of the wicked is striking after the eloquent praise. Psalm 146 is similar to this, with the mention of the wicked at the end. It seems that the Psalter, which begins with wicked and good side by side in Psalm 1, ends with only the good and God, since the wicked disappear after Psalm 146 with only a brief mention in Ps 149:7-9.

Psalm 146
God Keeps Faith Forever

Psalm 146 inaugurates the last group of Hallel psalms (see Appendix Two). Every psalm in this series is set within the parentheses of the liturgical acclamation *hallelujah*. Psalm 146 shows a preference for God's name (LORD), which occurs eleven times altogether. The appearance of

God, *ʾĕlōhîm* (vv. 2, 10), forms an inclusion; another *ʾĕlôhîm* (v. 5) totals fourteen direct divine references. The repetition "forever" frames the second part which is initialized by a beatitude, "Happy," and where *yhwh* occurs seven times (vv. 5-10). The soloist introduces the hymn (vv. 1-2), counsels wisely against trusting in humans who are powerless to save (vv. 3-4), and reflects on reasons for trusting God (vv. 5-9). The transition from the introduction to the wisdom reflection is unusual. The underlying logic is that trust in God wins beatitude rather than reliance on the powerful. After recalling creation, the poet recounts deeds which constitute God's governance. An acclamation of God's eternal sovereignty addressed to Zion concludes the hymn (cf. 122:2; 137:5; 147:12).

The poem is instructive. The admonition about human mortality (vv. 3-4) contrasts with the praise of God who can be trusted in every crisis (vv. 5-10). The "powerful" (nobles, princes), despite their apparent influence, are mere mortals, "dust" (see 39:5-6; 90:3-6; 102:11; 144:4), as are their plans.

The catalogue of divine attributes is typically concrete and contrasts with the incompetence of human governors. Five poetic measures with participles as predicates (vv. 6-7a) are followed by five in which God's name is subject of the participles (vv. 7b-9a). God's character is epitomized in a key phrase (v. 6c), he "keeps the faith forever," and the ensuing verses show how. Foreigners, widows, and orphans were defenseless and so protected by law (Exod 22:21-22), but in real life are often neglected. The poet contrasts God's support of the widow and the orphan with the fate of the wicked (v. 9b). It would be senseless to trust human leaders, considering God's trustworthiness.

The juxtaposition of the righteous and wicked (vv. 8b, 9c) is typical of how these two are characterized in the psalms. The pair is viewed in salvific rather than moral terms. If God did not love the righteous and frustrate the wicked, he could not be trusted. A psalm which began with "my soul" praising God "as long as I live," is related to Zion and eternity with the concluding acclamation, "The Lord will reign forever!" (see 48:8, 12-14; 68:16; 125:1).

Psalm 147
God's Word Restores Jerusalem

Psalm 147 begins with the praise of praise, which is "good" and "fitting," before turning to praising God for universal power and providence. What the Hebrew Bible treats as one psalm was regarded by many ancient versions as two, vv. 1-11 and 12-20 (equivalent to Psalms 146–147). But after a close look at Psalm 147, a division of three movements can be made on the basis of the initial imperatives, "sing" and "make melody" (*ʿnh, zmr*, v. 7), "praise" (*šbḥ* and *hll*, v. 12). The first is introduced "How good . . . to sing praises" and "a song of praise is fitting." Thus the tripartite division is praise of God, the restorer of Israel and the caretaker of the stars (vv. 1-6), nature, provided for by God who delights not in human exploits (vv. 7-11), and God's power over nature and care for Zion and Israel (vv. 12-20). Each movement touches both natural and human orders. In the first two the description of God dominates. The third is addressed to "Jerusalem" and "Zion," which is the beneficiary of reconstruction, reinforcement, blessing, peace, food supplies (vv. 13-14; cf. v. 2). The repetition of "Israel" frames the psalm (vv. 2, 19). Counting the abbreviated forms (vv. 1, 20, *hallelujah*), LORD occurs seven times. LORD also frames the third movement. The praise of Psalm 147 is complete.

In the first movement, restoring the city and people and arranging the stars are ranged side by side, which illustrates the parallel between how the world is ordered and how history runs (vv. 2-6; cf. Isa 40:26-29; 61:1-11). Here and in Ps 51:17-18 the broken heart and the reconstruction of Jerusalem appear together. According to tradition, the tribes of Israel on earth and the stars are God's armies. The parallel verbs of the two hemistichs of v. 4 focus the thought:

> He determines the number of the stars;
> he gives to all of them their names.

Naming something, which in the biblical world implies intimate knowledge of that thing's essence, is more specific than counting. The themes of God's wisdom and power appear together, as God knows the stars individually and cares for the humble.

The second movement begins with an invitation to play music to God and from the macroscopic view of the universe the scope narrows to daily sustenance for people and animals. God prepares the weather, convokes clouds, sends rain, and makes grass grow. The poet is in awe of this marvelous activity which ends in feeding animals and ravens (see also 65:9-13; 104:13-14). According to the parallel lines of v. 10,

> His delight is not in the strength of the horse,
> nor his pleasure in the speed of a runner. . . .[42]

[42] Literally, the Hebrew reads "the legs of a man."

Humans and God reckon power differently. Trust in military power and prowess is opposed to fear of God and hope in divine *ḥesed* (cf. 20:7; 33:16-17; 118:6-9; Prov 21:31). Material advantages are of no account; what pleases God are those who reverence him and wait for his kindness. As with the first movement, the recital of God's blessings includes a wisdom reflection.

The invitation of the third movement loops back to v. 2 by mentioning Jerusalem. The poet exalts God because he protects and provides for the people (vv. 13-14), controls winter's arrival and passage (vv. 15-18), and reveals the statutes and ordinances to Israel (vv. 19-20; cf. Deut 4:8). God regulates material benefits and weather conditions. The poet moves from the general to the particular—the strength of the city's gates and the people inside, national prosperity and eating "the finest wheat," the all-powerful word and the commands to change the weather. Nature is domesticated by comparisons "snow like wool," "frost like ashes," and "hail like crumbs." After the wintry snow, frost, hail, and cold, the divine word and the wind come and melt the frozen scene. As in the first two movements, God is attentive to every detail of creation. But the divine word has another dimension, as it reveals God's will to an elect people to order their life aright (v. 19). God's word expresses the exercise of divine sovereignty; it is sent to do God's bidding in the world.

Psalm 148
All Creatures Voice Praise of the Divine Name

The two movements of Psalm 148 (vv. 1-6, 7-14), corresponding to heavenly and earthly theaters of praise, are arranged similarly, as can be seen here:

> *hallelujah*
> invitation to the heavens, "Praise the LORD (seven times)
>   v. 5a, "Let them praise the name of the LORD
>   three phase motive: he commanded, established, fixed (vv. 5b-6)
> invitation to the earth, "Praise the LORD (once)
>   v. 13a, "Let them praise the name of the LORD"
>   three part motive: exalted name, glory, people (vv. 13b-14a)
> *hallelujah*

The poet invites all in the heavens and on earth to praise God and tells why. In Psalm 136 the motives for praise were multiplied; here multiple choirs are enumerated. The motives are clear. All these beings owe their existence and permanence to God's creative action, because his name is sublime and because God has favored Israel (vv. 5-6, 13b-14). The two movements are asymmetrical. After the opening line which designates the heavenly realm (v. 1, parallelism), the conductor signals the entry of seven voices in a sort of fugue (seven imperatives, "praise"), angels, hosts, sun and moon, stars, heavens, and waters above the heavens. Then following a single imperative, twenty-one earthly choirs join one another in unison. The entry of the heavenly choirs is ordered generally from high to low. Those on earth move from the underworld, to natural phenomena, to rational creatures, and finally to Israel. In each movement the refrain, "Let them praise the name of the LORD" (vv. 5a, 13a), closes the enumeration of voices, thus totaling, with the eight imperatives, ten invocations to praise. The motif "all" or "every" *(kōl)* punctuates the roll call ten times and designates an inclusive, universal orchestra, recruiting all heavenly and earthly reality. The scope of the liturgy is from the highest heaven to the earth below (vv. 1, 7) and God's majesty surpasses and thus encompasses everything (v. 13). The poet concludes that God's "glory is above earth and heaven," which summarizes the content of the two movements.

In the invitation to the earthly space, the first voices are "sea monsters and all deeps" (v. 7). The created world is rearranged in this poem. Where one might expect three zones, heavens, earth, and underworld, this poet presents two, with the "deeps" or oceans *(tĕhōmôt)* included in the terrestrial zone. The "earth below" is the opposite end of the vertical axis from the heights. In contrast to the scattered terrestrial creatures (vv. 7-10), the celestial bodies are placed in their orbits and patterns (v. 6). The earthly choirs are grouped according to oceans and their inhabitants, meteorological phenomena, mountains, trees, animals, rulers and their peoples, male and female, young and old. One might expect "mountains and valleys" to represent the lay of the land instead of "mountains and all hills." The fruit trees and cedars stand for all vegetation. Wild animals are contrasted with the tame; winged fowl are paired with crawling things. Even sea monsters, the object of battles in Pss 74:13; 89:9-10; Isa 51:9-10, are tamed to worship God their creator. Humans form a separate choir in the symphony and are named according to office, gender, and age. All are equal in God's sight. The poet's attention narrows from the heavens to the earth, then to the peoples, and finally to Israel. The climax of the summons is "all his faithful" and "the people of Israel who are close to him." "He has raised up a horn for his people" is an idiom for the bestowal of dignity and strength (cf. 18:2; 75:10; 92:10; 112:9; 132:17). A relationship exists between prosperity, power, and praise. Those who are on intimate terms with God can praise him and, thus, they articulate all creation's praise.

Psalm 149
Praise God with Song and Sword

The liturgical acclamation *hallelujah* frames the two movements of Psalm 149, as does the reference to the "faithful" (vv. 1, 9). Of seven invitations to praise, six ("let," vv. 2-3, 5) follow the imperative, "Sing to the LORD a new song" (v. 1; cf. Pss 33:3; 40:3; 96:1; 98:1; 144:9). (The pattern is broken in the NRSV which translates "making melody" instead of "let them make melody," v. 3b.) The first summons (vv. 1-3) is supported by the basis or content of praise (v. 4). The second summons (vv. 5-6) is followed by infinitives which define a course of action (vv. 7-9a). The term "glory" or "honor," *hādār* (v. 9), corresponds to "glory," *kābôd* (v. 5), and forms an inclusion in the second movement and defines its theme, the glory of the faithful. Their divine "King" is victorious over the nations' rulers (vv. 2, 8).

Whereas God by name, title, or pronoun is present in every clause of the first movement, the faithful occupy the second. Israel is "the assembly of the faithful," "children of Zion," "his people" and "the humble" (vv. 1-2, 4). God is identified without exception in relation to Israel. He is the maker and king of Israel, who delights in his people and adorns them with victory. In the second movement the poet describes a ritual dance, in which enthusiasm is displayed in the shouting and brandishing of swords. The dance pantomimes the execution of the divine justice. What brings "glory for all his faithful ones" is their readiness to carry out God's will.

God's faithful are summoned to praise and they cooperate in the defeat of godlessness, which will usher in the final judgment and punishment of God's enemies. The faithful, with praise in their mouths and two-edged swords in hand, avenge nations, punish peoples, arrest rulers and nobles, and execute judgments. The imagery illustrates that praise is stronger than worldly power. This praise corroborates the testimony of Ps 8:2, infants who mysteriously confound God's enemy and avenger. The image of people reclining on couches and praising God with their mouths is in bold contrast to their power with the sword, which executes vengeance and binds the world's powerful in irons. This gives an eschatological, almost apocalyptic, dimension to the psalm as the faithful wage a holy war to settle the conflict between the kingdoms of this world and God's reign. The expectation of an international victory transcends local and provincial conflicts. As the second to the last psalm in the Psalter, Psalm 149 corresponds to the location of Psalm 2, which announces that through the royal messiah God will claim rulers and nations. In Psalm 149 the human instrument is the assembly of the faithful, who function as a messianic community through whom God achieves what was assigned to the Davidic king.

Psalm 150
Final Doxology: Everything That Breathes, Hallelujah

Between the introductory and concluding *hallelujah*, the call to praise of Psalm 150 is tersely structured, with nine "Praise him" phrases following the initial "Praise God." This imposes a rhythm on the poem and seals Book Five and the whole Psalter with a doxology. The object of praise is the LORD's greatness and mighty deeds (vv. 1b-2). Seven different instruments play in the orchestra of nine sets (vv. 3-5). The shofar ("trumpet") or horn was usually sounded by priests and leaders in liturgical settings. The lute and harp were said to have been strummed by David and the Levites, also in liturgies. The tambourine, strings, and flute were instruments which enlivened secular festivities; the tambourine, which accompanies dance or processions, was played by women. Thus, the praise embraces liturgical and secular settings and everybody participates. The enumeration of the wind, string, and percussion instruments along with dance encompasses all the ways by which people express God's praise with the body, the hands, and the throat. This grand finale, with full orchestra crowns the majestic collection of poems honoring the God of Israel.

The change of person, "everything that breathes praise the LORD" (v. 6), sums up the universal command to praise. Breath *(nĕšāmâh)* is the vitality which all beings receive from God (Gen 2:7; cf. Job 32:8; 33:4; Isa 42:5). If God were to withhold the breath, we would return to dust (Job 34:14-15; Ps 104:29). The last line of the Psalter, addressed to all creatures, invites a simultaneity of praise with life. It might be paraphrased with a moral tone, "As long as you breath, praise God." Where? "In his sanctuary," under the mighty dome of the sky (v. 1). The earthly temple reflects God's heavenly dwelling, the pavement of which is the "mighty firmament" which embraces the cosmos. Here the poet makes no distinctions between earth and heaven, and the temple liturgy imitates the heavenly. Why praise God? The whole Psalter formulates the answer, which is summarized, "for his mighty deeds . . . his surpassing greatness" (v. 2). For the Hebrew the "mighty deeds," *gĕbûrôt,* are creation, deliverance from Egypt, the crossing of the Red Sea, the giving of the law at Sinai, the entrance to the Promised Land, the choice of Mount Zion as God's residence on earth—God's historical actions on behalf of Israel and every human. Often the poet sings in general terms of God's goodness and compassion for the humble and, more specifically, of building Jerusalem and of protection and peace for the holy city (cf. Psalm 147). He or she invites all creation to praise God on the grounds that they were created at his command (Psalm 148; cf. v. 5). God is praised as our sovereign, the creator, who gives his people victory over their enemies (Psalm 149). All of this is included in the phrase "mighty deeds."

Psalm 150 closes the Psalter with liturgical and cosmic praise, and it underlines the basic human attitude toward God, to praise, which is inspired by awe that one is not the center of the world. Praise is the joyful recognition that greater than us is someone who loves without limit and on whom we depend for life. Praise rejoices before the mystery of being and before the divine mystery. Praise ultimately looks to God rather than to his gifts. In praise the person loses him or herself in God.

So the Psalter ends. In this book of inspired poems and prayers the devout believer enjoys a new song of joy, and, more profoundly, a love song. Anyone who has loved or tried to love appreciates the new song which has its inspiration in the life one finds in the beloved. Everybody wants to love someone, but the question is, whom to love? The Psalter offers the best option. Here we discover that we can choose because we were first chosen. We love because someone first loved us. The inspiration of these poems is just this, that God loved us first and is dedicated to being the object of our love, so that at every turn he is revealed as the font and the goal of life. Inspired by love, the poet invites the believer to praise and pray to God with the divinely inspired words. The poet invites us, praise God and you will come to know your first lover, for you could not praise had God not first chosen you, loved you, lived in you.

APPENDICES

Appendix I.
Superscriptions

One hundred and sixteen psalms have superscriptions or captions in the Hebrew, ranging from one word to lengthier comments. Nearly all the psalms in Books One–Three are titled, and the majority of untitled psalms are in Books Four and Five. Psalms 1 and 2 function as an opening to the Psalter. Psalms 10 and 43 lack titles because they are linked to the preceding psalms either by an alphabetical acrostic pattern (Psalms 9 and 10) or by a refrain (Psalms 42 and 43). Psalms 33 and 71 lack titles because they are thematically linked to the preceding psalms. Psalms 111–113, 117, 135, 146–150 all begin with "Praise the LORD," which also serves as a title.

Some captions indicate the type of poem. Hebrew *mizmôr* was translated *psalmos* (Greek), which gave the name to the Greek Psalter. *Mizmôr* occurs fifty-seven times, only in psalm captions; thirty-six occurrences in the expression "a psalm of David." "Song" (*šîr*) occurs in thirty captions, at times coupled with *mizmôr*; notably it is used in the captions of the "songs of ascents" (Psalms 120–134). "Praise," *těhillâh*, occurs in Psalm 145 (the plural form provides the Hebrew title for the Psalter, *těhillîm*). "Prayer," *těpillâh*, features in the captions of Psalms 17, 86, 90, 102, 142; it is in the plural form in 72:20 (Hebrew).

Another kind of caption suggests an application of the psalm, and is part of the history of its interpretation and use. Psalms 38 and 70 are designated "for the memorial offering," and Psalm 92 "[a] song for the Sabbath Day";[1] Psalm 100 is "[a] Psalm of thanksgiving." The lengthy caption of Psalm 60 includes "for instruction." However, it is not always evident how the caption should be applied. According to content, Psalm 30 is suited for an individual giving thanks after recovery, while the superscription suggests its use as "Song at the dedication of the temple."

---

[1] In the LXX Psalm 24 is assigned to Sunday, Psalm 94 to Wednesday, Psalm 93 to Friday.

There are some notable differences between the captions in the LXX and those in the Hebrew. Some LXX captions bear the names of persons —David, Ezekiel, and Jeremiah (Psalm 64 [65, Hebrew]), David, the sons of Jonadab and the first captives (Psalm 70 [71, without super-scription in Hebrew]), David and Zechariah (Psalms 137 and 138 [138 and 139]). Psalm 136 (137) is entitled "For David. By Jeremiah at the time of the captivity." Some captions mention David during the captivity (Psalms 64, 95, 136, 138, [65, 96, no Hebrew title; 137, no Hebrew title; 139]). The LXX captions of Psalms 145, 146, 147, 148 (146, 147, 148; the Hebrew Psalm 147 comprises the LXX 146–147) include the names Haggai and Zechariah (like Psalm 137 [138]). The initial "Alleluia" is under-stood in the LXX as a superscription. Psalm 113 (114) bears the caption "Alleluia," as do Psalms 114 and 115 (equivalent to one Hebrew psalm, Psalm 116, without title), 116, 117, and 118 (117, 118, 119). In some of these cases what was the final word in the Hebrew psalm is ascribed to the first position in the LXX (e.g., the *hallelujah* of Psalm 104 appears as the first word "Alleluia" in Psalm 105). While the superscriptions were not part of the original compositions, they provide clues to the inter-pretation and the use of the psalms in the worshiping community.

The Hebrew Bible attributes seventy-three psalms to David, twelve to Asaph, eleven to the Sons of Korah, two to Solomon (Psalms 72 and 127), and one each to Moses (Psalm 90) and to Ethan (Psalm 89).[2] The rest are anonymous. In the Greek Psalter eighty-five psalms are attrib-uted to David. The tendency in the LXX to attribute more compositions to David stemmed from a desire to impress the poems with his author-ity and bring the saint closer so as to pray as he prayed. The LXX attrib-utes Psalms 32, 42, 70, 90, 92–99, 103, and 136 (Hebrew, 33, 43, 71, 91, 93–100, 104, and 137) to David, though it omits mention of David in the titles of Psalms 121 and 123 (122 and 124).

The superscription "Of David" hints that a private prayer has been transposed to the public domain. David, king and priest, and presider at liturgy (cf. 1 Chr 29:10-22; 2 Sam 6:17-19), represented the commu-nity of Israel. Even the caption of Psalm 51, which assigns it to the in-tense moment of David's self-recognition after committing adultery and orchestrating the death of Uriah, addresses the community in the startling last lines "Do good to Zion in your good pleasure; rebuild the walls of Jerusalem, then you will delight in right sacrifices, in burnt offerings and whole burnt offerings; then bulls will be offered on your altar" (vv. 18-19). In a psalm like this, the caption may have been added to suggest an attitude which the worshiper may adopt in praying it.

[2] Psalm 88, "A Psalm of the Korahites," is, in addition, superscribed "A *Maskil* of Heman the Ezrahite."

After the exile, David embodied the hope of the people who awaited a new king, a second David, who would reestablish the rights of the poor and dispossessed. David was understood as the exemplary champion of the people's rights. From the postexilic, depressed period, the record of 1 Chronicles omitted all David's major flaws except the census (1 Chronicles 21). Yet in representing him in all virtue and integrity the author or theologian projected David as the embodiment of the people's hopes. Many psalms of personal complaint, traditionally termed individual laments, are attributed to David, who experienced suffering, humiliation, abandonment. But he experienced them as a believer, addressing God as one who feels abandoned and yet knows that the prayer will arrive to God.

The captions assign several psalms a context in David's life.[3] Those which allude to a historical event situate certain psalms in contexts in the histories of Samuel. The connection with a historical incident often resulted from a perceived verbal link (e.g. compare Ps 51:4 and 2 Sam 12:13). David's experience provides a pattern for understanding human life, and thus it enables later generations to see their own sentiments and uncertainties in a larger context. Given the extensive and varied Davidic traditions, this hero is a good choice as a model of anyone who has a deep relationship with God. The stories in the books of Samuel paint a vivid personality which even the uncertainties about historical and textual difficulties cannot efface. David's portrait is life-like because of his failings. His figure is marked by virtue and treachery, fleshed out with contrasting moments of exemplary dedication to God and sinister motives. David, the decisive, just ruler, was soft when it came to managing his own family. He nearly lost his throne to ambitious Absalom and he jeopardized it again in his grief at that son's death. Nonetheless, David is credited with moving the court and the cult to Jerusalem, and many psalms can be prayed against the background of his life.

Relating the psalms to a representative David universalized them. The full range of David's virtuosity and inconsistency, victory and defeat, gratitude and complaint enables future generations of worshipers to sympathize. Associated with the life of that exemplary figure of Israel's past, the psalms express the needs and hopes of every worshiper. Insofar as they record David's response to changing fortunes and experiences, they nourish the souls of succeeding generations. Relating the

[3] In the MT thirteen psalms have such historical settings (Psalms 3, 7, 18, 34, 51, 52, 54, 56, 57, 59, 60, 63, 142). The LXX, in addition, ascribes a historical setting to Psalm 142, "When David's son Absalom pursued him," and Psalm 143, "Concerning Goliath" (Hebrew, Psalms 143 and 144).

psalms to David, for example, provides a precedent for the Jewish believer of any age to pray them as a member of a community of faith; it invites the Christian to relate them to Christ as head of the Church.

Appendix II.
Prehistory of the Psalter

Fixed in its present state more than two centuries before Christ, the Psalter is composed of 150 psalms.[4] The different LXX arrangement accounts for the two psalm numberings in modern versions; some Roman Catholic translations are linked to the Vulgate and hence to the LXX tradition, where Psalms 9 and 10 are read as one, resulting in a divergence in numbers by one from that point to Psalms 114 and 115, which are read as one. Psalm 116 is divided into two, and so the shift of one continues until Psalm 147, which is comprised of two psalms in the LXX. The two numbering systems result in the same total, but arrive by different means. The rationale for the psalm order is not clear, although there are traces of a history of psalm groupings. The Psalter is a compilation of prayers, but it is also a collection of previous collections.

The 150 psalms were divided into five books: Psalms 1–41; 42–72; 73–89; 90–106; 107–150. The fivefold division may have been intentionally created to parallel the literary legacies of Moses and David. Support for this conclusion may be found in the compositions of Books Four and Five, which are distinguished by features different from those in Psalms 1–89. Psalms 90–150 are comprised mainly of praise and thanksgiving psalms. The term *hallelujah* only occurs here, and several psalms have no caption, while those with captions contain none of the musical type. The terms *selâh* and "for the leader," *lamnaṣēaḥ*, are rare,[5] suggesting that Psalms 90–150 may have been originally a single col-

---

[4] In important Greek Bible codices and in the Peshitta an additional Psalm 151 bears a special caption noting that it is "outside the number." This psalm appears in the Latin, Coptic, Arabic, Armenian, and Ethiopic versions; in 11QPsᵃ Psalm 151 appears as two separate psalms. The Syriac apocryphal psalms number 151–155, three of which are found in the psalms scroll from Qumran Cave 11 (11QPsᵃ).

[5] "To the leader," *lamnaṣēaḥ*, a term associated with overseeing (Ezra 3:8, 9), occurs fifty-four times in the Psalter, twice in the final book (Psalms 109 and 139). Only four of the seventy-one usages of *selâh* are found after Psalm 89 (140:3, 5, 8; 143:6). The meaning of *selâh*, which occurs seventy-one times in thirty-nine psalms, remains unexplained. In the Greek this term occurs ninety-two times, translated *diapsalma*, which means an instrumental interlude. This particle normally signals a pause rather than an ending, but in Psalms 9, 24, 46 the *selâh* occurs at the end.

lection which was later split in two to create five books. Each book concludes with a brief doxology (41:13; 72:18-19; 89:52; 106:48); Psalm 150 functions as a doxology, both to Book Five and the whole Psalter.

Book One contains a number of memorable poems, dramatic exposés of the soul's struggle with God with comparatively lengthy descriptions and a preference for compositions in the first person singular. The poems in Book Two are more suggestive, less explicit, but they retain the forceful imagery that characterized some poems of Book One. There are more personal complaints than any other type of psalm, and most of them appear in the first two books. Psalms 3–7; 14; 17; 22; 25–28; 31; 35; 36; 38–39; 40:11-15; 42–43; 51; 54–57; 59; 61; 64; 69–71; 86; 88; 102; 130; 140–143. The note at the end of Book Two, 72:20, reads, "The prayers [těpillôt] of David son of Jesse are ended" (Hebrew), although the LXX has read těpillôt as těhillôt, and, thus, "The end of the psalms of David . . ." (RNAB). If the Hebrew is accepted, the foregoing collection is designated "prayers," that is, prayers in time of need, or complaints, while in Books Four and Five, in which the verb *hll* and its cognate *těhillâh* is more in evidence, songs of praise or hymns predominate.

Book Three opens with a poem of intensely personal introspection, but the corpus is marked more by compositions with historical and international references. A number of psalms in Book Three are community complaints (Psalms 74, 79, 80, 83, 85), and most captions in this book associate the psalms with Asaph (Psalms 73–83). In Books Four and Five other thematic collections are not attributed to anyone. Praise dominates in the "reign of God" psalms (Psalms 93; 95–99) and in the hymns (Psalms 103–106) of Book Four. Several psalms begin with the invitation *Hallelujah* (Psalms 105–107; 111–118; 135–136; 146–150).[6] Other features link this collection; Psalms 103 and 104 each begins with "Bless the LORD, my soul"; Psalms 105 and 106 both recite God's intervention in Israel's history, each beginning with "Give thanks to the LORD," and ending with *hallelujah*.[7] With Book Five praise continues up to Psalm 119 (109 is the exception). Psalms of David are grouped at the beginning and toward the end of the book (Psalms 108–110 and 138–145).

[6] In the tradition of psalm study Psalms 113–118 are called the Egyptian Hallel, as distinguished from the simple Hallel, Psalms 146–150. The great Hallel designates Psalms 120–136 (songs of ascents), or Psalms 135–136, or just Psalm 136.

[7] Psalms framed with "Praise the LORD" appear at strategic places. They close a book (Psalm 106) and the Psalter (Psalms 146–150), or conclude a collection (Psalm 100 follows the "reign of God" psalms and Psalm 135 follows the psalms of ascents). In some instances, a psalm framed by *hallelujah* is followed by a psalm beginning "O give thanks" (Psalms 106 and 107; 117 and 118; 135 and 136).

Psalms 120–134 comprise the collection of the "songs of ascents" (so designated by the superscription). A short complaint series is included here (Psalms 140–143), and the Psalter concludes with resounding praise (Psalms 146–150). The guiding principle in the arrangement of these books of disproportionate length is uncertain.

To trace the history further, in Psalms 42–83 God is nearly always referred to in Hebrew as *ʾělōhîm,* while the poet elsewhere prefers to address and speak about God using the personal name *yhwh.* This accounts for the term "Elohist psalms." A comparison of duplicate psalms is instructive. Psalm 53 is nearly identical with Psalm 14, with the replacement of *ʾělōhîm* (53:2, 4, 6) for *yhwh* (14:2, 4, 7). Psalm 70 is a copy of 40:13-17. The designation *yhwh* of 40:14a, 16, is replaced by "God" in 70:1a, 4; the *yhwh* of 40:13b remains *yhwh* in 70:1b, and God of 40:17b is replaced by *yhwh* in 70:5b. The fact that Book Two includes duplicates from Book One might suggest that these two once had a separate existence. This argues for two collections, Psalms 1–41 and 42–83, prior to the pentateuchal division. As the final edition took shape, earlier compositions were touched up and placed in a different context.

Another stage in the formation of the Psalter can be supposed. The text of most psalms furnishes personal names in the superscriptions, which provide hints as to the liturgical setting. Considering these personal names, three groupings can be distinguished, according to the liturgical usage. Did the seventy-three psalms superscribed with "David" once comprise a collection under that name? Such psalms include nearly all those in Book One (Psalms 3–41), and, in addition, Psalms 51–65 and 68–78, 108–110 and 138–145. Most of these, together comprising nearly half the Psalter, are individual supplications, many linked to the royal throne rather than to the temple liturgy.[8]

Twelve psalms are attributed to the sons of Korah (42, 44–49; 84–85; 87–88), and twelve more to Asaph (50 and 73–83).[9] Chronicles identifies these two groups as Levitical. The sons of Korah, introduced in Num 16:1; 26:9-11, were active in David's time (1 Chr 6:22; 26:1) and still served in Jehoshaphat's time (2 Chr 20:19). Asaph was a musician from the tribe of Levi who was appointed by David to provide music when the ark was brought to Jerusalem (1 Chr 6:24; 15:17, 19; 16:5, 7, 37), and

---

[8] Outside the superscriptions, David is rarely mentioned in the poems; e.g., Pss 18:50; 78:70; 89:3, 20; 132:1, 10, 11, 17; 144:10.

[9] The Syriac version includes Psalm 100 among the Asaph psalms. Common features are vivid descriptions of nature, emphasis of divine providence in one's life, history recounted with a didactic purpose, exalted conceptions of God, and a sublime style.

his family was present at the dedication of the temple (2 Chr 5:12), active at the time of Josiah (2 Chr 35:15), and as late as Nehemiah and Ezra in the fifth century, when they were still involved in music and instrumental music (Ezra 2:41; 3:10; Neh 7:44; 11:22; 12:35). The psalms which bear the names of Asaph or the sons of Korah in the captions have a national character and an evident relationship with the temple liturgy; several have Zion as a main interest.[10] They show a tendency toward the use of proper names of individuals or a group. The psalms of Asaph are more somber and dramatic than those of the sons of Korah. The three collections of David, the sons of Korah, and Asaph occupy most of Books One through Three, and may have been collections prior to the final arrangement of the Psalter into five books.

Appendix III.
Literary Types

The scholar responsible for the classification of the psalms according to literary type is Hermann Gunkel. His classification of psalms is foundational, even though some of his conclusions have been modified by other scholars. Since Gunkel's pioneering work, refinements in literary classification have been proposed. Sigmund Mowinckel emphasized the liturgical background of the psalms, both in their later usage and in their compositional stages.[11] He postulated the feast of the Lord's enthronement ("coronation" is a more apt English term), with which he associated about forty psalms, and even though such a feast remains beyond the scope of proof, the idea of the Lord's coronation dominates many compositions (e.g., Psalms 47; 93; 96–99). Claus Westermann regarded the hymn and the complaint as the dominant categories of the Psalter, and he saw the psalms as a movement from complaint to praise, of which the final edition of the Psalter bears witness.[12]

The most frequent literary type are psalms of personal complaint (some forty psalms, usually termed "laments"). Personal psalms are predominant among those captioned "Of David" (Psalms 3–41, 51–72), most of which are complaints. Outside these two collections there are

[10] E.g., Psalms 46, 48, 50, 76, 85, and 87. Psalm 78 contrasts the exit from Shiloh (vv. 59-64) to that of Jerusalem (vv. 68-72).

[11] Sigmund Mowinckel, *The Psalms in Israel's Worship*, 2 vols. Trans. D. R. Ap-Thomas (Oxford: Basil Blackwell, 1962).

[12] Claus Westermann, *Praise and Lament in the Psalms* (Atlanta: John Knox, 1981).

personal complaints only in Psalms 77, 94, 102, 109, and 140–143. The complaint usually begins with a plea for help addressed to God, after which the distress is described—persecution by enemies (38:12-20; 41:5-11), false testimony or accusation (Psalm 7), sickness and death (Psalms 6 and 38), personal guilt (Psalm 51). In most cases the precise reasons for the complaint cannot be discerned, due to the extravagant imagery which is used. Bulls, dogs, the sword, the lion, and wild oxen all inhabit Psalm 22, where the psalmist also complains that he or she is a worm. Such imagery is to the advantage of the readers, who can transfer it to their own distress. The weapons of the enemy, the abyss, and Sheol are all suggestive images. Death and the realm of the dead are envisioned as forces which assault a person's life. A victim, sick or threatened, is in death's grasp, and relief is expressed as "you brought up my soul from Sheol" (30:3).

Agony in the personal complaint is alleviated by cries for help and incentives for God to intervene. The psalmist pleads innocence and pledges fidelity (17:3-5; 26:1-8, 11-12) and trust (13:5; 25:1-2) to motivate God on his or her behalf. Appeals are made to God's *ḥesed*, the loyalty which characterizes God's covenant with Israel.

In nearly all the personal complaints (Psalms 39 and 88 are exceptions), the psalmist changes key and expresses certainty that God has heard the prayer, yet in most cases the reason for the change in mood remains obscure. A striking example is Psalm 22, where the anguished cry, "Save me from the mouth of the lion!" is followed by, "From the horns of the wild oxen you have rescued me. I will tell of your name to my brothers and sisters . . ." (vv. 21b-22). One explanation for this, with widespread support among scholars, is that the complaint is celebrated in the liturgy. An initial complaint uttered in the temple was answered by one of the ministers in a salvation oracle, which inspired a further response, the announcement of relief. There are hints of such oracles in some psalms (12:5; 35:3; 85:8; 91:14-16), but most complaints did not retain the oracle as part of its composition.

The communal or national complaint was celebrated when the community assembled to pray during a crisis, such as drought or military defeat. Most of the elements that characterize the personal complaint are found here as well—a cry for help, the questioning tone, a description of the distress, a vow to praise God (reminiscent of the motif of certainty). Psalms 44, 74, and 79 are generally included in this category. Among the communal complaints, the ending of Psalm 89 sustains the urgency of the plea, and thus ends with the same tone as its neighbor, Psalm 88.

The song of praise or hymn is another major literary type. It begins on a joyful note in which the psalmist invites either the community

(Psalm 117) or the self (Psalms 103 and 104) to praise God. The most concise pattern is "praise the Lord, because. . . ." The reasons for the praise can be boiled down to two, and they constitute the core of the prayer. The first is God's creation. The divine creativity is imaginatively portrayed. The psalmist may recall the effortless creation by the divine word of Genesis 1 or depict God who is personally and intimately involved in creation as Gen 2:7. In the psalms, as elsewhere in the Bible, creation is depicted as the result of a battle with chaos, personified, for example, in Leviathan (Pss 74:14; 104:26), or characterized simply as "Sea." The other reason for praise is God's saving intervention in history, typically the Exodus (Psalms 78, 114; cf. Exod 15:1-18). History is recalled in order to instruct Israel (Psalm 78) or to prompt the people to repentance (Psalm 106). As with the belief in creation, God's intervention in history, rather than just an exercise of the memory, was the motive for liturgical reenactment; thus, it was celebrated in the congregation, for whom it had special meaning and guaranteed a future.

Some hymns can be classified according to content. In the hymns of Zion (Psalms 46, 48, 84, 122) Jerusalem is the focus of praise. God and the holy city, his dwelling place among the people, are inseparable. Israel's greatness was conceived as connected with God who dwells in her midst. Psalms 46 and 48 celebrate the invincibility of Zion. Another type of hymn celebrates God's sovereignty ("the Lord reigns," Psalms 47, 93, 95–99), and here again the themes are God's creative power and rule over history. God's sovereignty is rooted in the past and reenacted in the liturgy.

Another literary type, the thanksgiving psalm, represents the prayer after deliverance from distress—a counterpart to the complaint (e.g., Psalms 18, 30, 40, 66, 116, 118). The thanksgiving begins like a hymn and then acknowledges God as the rescuer, which may be expanded into a testimony for participants or bystanders (see 30:2-3), who may share in the psalmist's thanksgiving sacrifice. By means of a sort of flashback the psalmist may review the crisis which preceded the deliverance (116:10-11).

The classification of royal psalms is derived from content rather than literary factors, and some of the following settings and moods are reflected therein: a royal inauguration or anniversary (Psalms 2 and 72); a royal thanksgiving (Psalm 18); prayers before or after military operations (Psalms 20 and 21); a royal wedding (Psalm 45); a platform for one's reign (Psalm 101). Some psalms which originally featured the monarch as the main figure later were adopted by the private citizen (e.g., Psalms 28, 61, 63).

After the disappearance of the monarchy at the fall of Jerusalem in 587/586 B.C., royal psalms were reinterpreted under the influence of texts like 2 Samuel 7 (cf. Psalms 89 and 132) and found to express the growing messianic expectation. The royal psalms, which in their literal historical meaning referred to the reigning king, were then perceived as open-ended in both Jewish and Christian tradition, a position from which a hope for a messiah was natural. Thus Christian usage finds in them the celebration of Christ the king.

The classification of some of the psalms as wisdom psalms is more conjectural. The vague criteria for this type is the use of wisdom language ("teach" and "fear of the LORD"); acrostic patterns (e.g., Psalms 34 and 37); the juxtaposition of the just and the wicked (Psalm 1); the problem of evil and retribution (Psalms 37 and 73); a meditative style (Psalm 90). It may be preferable to speak of wisdom influence, for instance, in Psalms 1, 32, 34, 37, 49, 73, rather than to assign them to a distinct type.

In the types described above there is a sense of their context and use in the liturgy, but certain poems represent liturgical motifs more specifically, particularly those in which oracles, questions, and litany are in evidence. The gate or entrance liturgies of Psalms 15 and 24 have a liturgical format of question and answer. Prophetic oracles appear in Psalms 50, 75, and 85. Psalm 136 is a litany, with the unrelenting repetition of God's *ḥesed* throughout.

FOR FURTHER READING

Allen, Leslie C. *Psalms 101–150.* Word Biblical Commentary 21. Waco, Tx.: Word, 1983.

Alonso Schökel, Luis and Cecilia Carniti. *Salmos; Traducción, introducciones y comentario.* 2 vols. Navarra: Editorial Verbo Divino, 1992–3.

Alter, Robert. *The Art of Biblical Poetry.* New York: HarperCollins, 1985.

Alter, Robert, "The Medium of Poetry," *The World of Biblical Literature,* 171–90. New York: HarperCollins, 1992.

Anderson, Bernhard W. *Out of the Depths; The Psalms Speak for Us Today.* Philadelphia: Westminster, 1983.

Augustine, Saint. *St. Augustine on the Psalms.* Trans. Scholastica Helyn and Felicitas Corrigan. 2 vols. Westminster, Md.: Newman Press, 1960.

Beauchamp, Paul. *Psaumes nuit et jour.* Paris: Éditions du Seuil, 1980.

Brueggeman, Walter. *Abiding Astonishment: Psalms, Modernity, and the Making of History.* Louisville, Ky.: Westminster/John Knox Press, 1991.

Brueggemann, Walter. *The Message of the Psalms.* Minneapolis: Augsburg, 1984.

Brueggemann, Walter. *Israel's Praise.* Philadelphia: Fortress Press, 1988.

Childs, Brevard S., "Reflections on the Modern Study of the Psalms," *Magnalia Dei.* Ed. F. M. Cross, 377–88. Garden City, N.Y.: Doubleday, 1976.

Collins, Terence, "Decoding the Psalms: A Structural Approach to the Psalter," *JSOT* 37 (1987) 41–60.

Craigie, Peter C. *Psalms 1–50.* Word Biblical Commentary 19. Waco, Tx.: Word, 1983.

Craven, Toni. *The Book of Psalms.* Collegeville: The Liturgical Press, 1992.

Hobbs, T., and P. Jackson, "The Enemy in the Psalms," *BTB* 21 (1991) 22–29.

Holladay, William L. *The Psalms through Three Thousand Years; Prayerbook of a Cloud of Witnesses.* Minneapolis: Fortress, 1993.

Kraus, Hans-Joachim. *Psalms 1–59; A Commentary.* Trans. Hilton C. Oswald. Minneapolis: Augsburg, 1988.

Kraus, Hans-Joachim. *Psalms 60–150; A Commentary.* Trans. Hilton C. Oswald. Minneapolis: Augsburg, 1989.

Kraus, Hans-Joachim. *Theology of the Psalms.* Minneapolis: Augsburg, 1986.

Kugel, James L. *The Idea of Biblical Poetry; Parellelism and its History.* New Haven: Yale University Press, 1981.

Mays, James L., "The David of the Psalms," *Int* 40 (1986) 143–55.

Mays, James L., "The Place of the Torah-Psalms in the Psalter," *JBL* 106 (1987) 3–12.

Mays, James L., *Psalms.* Interpretation. Louisville: John Knox, 1994.

Mays, James L., "A Question of Identity: The Three-fold Hermeneutic of Psalmody," *AsTJ* 46 (1991) 87–94.

McCann, J. Clinton, "The Psalms as Instruction," *Int* 46 (1992) 117–28.

McCann, J. Clinton. *The Shape and Shaping of the Psalter.* JSOTSup 159. Nashville: Abingdon, 1993.

McCann, J. Clinton. *A Theological Introduction to the Book of Psalms; the Psalms as Torah.* Nashville: Abingdon, 1993.

Miller, Patrick D. *Interpreting the Psalms.* Philadelphia: Fortress, 1986.

Miller, Patrick D. *They Cried to the Lord: the Form and Theology of Biblical Prayer.* Philadelphia: Fortress, 1994.

Murphy, Roland E. *The Psalms Are Yours.* New York: Paulist, 1993.

Petersen, David L. and Kent Harold Richards. *Interpreting Hebrew Poetry.* Guides to Biblical Scholarship. Minneapolis: Fortress, 1992.

Sarna, Nahum. *Songs of the Heart: an Introduction to the Book of the Psalms.* New York: Schocken, 1993.

Seybold, Klaus. *Introducing the Psalms.* Trans. R. G. Dunphy. Edinburgh: T. &. T. Clark, 1990.

Soll, Will. *Psalm 119: Matrix, Form, and Setting.* CBQMS 23. Washington, D.C.: Catholic Biblical Association, 1991.

Stuhlmueller, Carroll. *Psalms 1 and Psalms 2.* Old Testament Message 21 and 22. Wilmington: Michael Glazier, 1983.

Tate, Marvin E. *Psalms 51–100.* Word Biblical Commentary 20. Waco, Tx.: Word, 1990.

Westermann, Claus. *Praise and Lament in the Psalms.* Atlanta: John Knox, 1981.

Westermann, Claus. *The Psalms: Structure, Content and Message.* Minneapolis: Augsburg, 1980.

Wilson, Gerald H. *The Editing of the Hebrew Psalter.* SBLDS 76. Chico, Calif.: Scholars Press, 1985.

Wilson, Gerald H., "The Shape of the Book of the Psalms," *Int* 46 (1992) 129–42.

Wilson, Gerald H., "The Use of the Royal Psalms at the 'Seams' of the Hebrew Psalter," *JSOT* 35 (1986) 85–94.

INDEX OF SCRIPTURAL REFERENCES

Note: Biblical books are listed in the order they occur in the NRSV. Scriptural references to the Psalms follow the numbering in the NRSV.

Genesis		Gen 23:4	98
Gen 1	25, 315, 320, 357	Gen 26:3, 24	58
Gen 1:1	131, 285	Gen 27:40	136
Gen 1:26-28	25	Gen 28:11-18	316
Gen 1:27	24	Gen 28:15	58
Gen 2:7	24, 77, 130, 132,	Gen 31:3	58
	187, 226, 255, 258,	Gen 32:22-32	181
	324, 345, 357	Gen 33:17	147
Gen 3	143, 210	Gen 34:8	228
Gen 3:16-17	307	Gen 35:16, 19	314
Gen 3:18	74	Gen 49:24	314
Gen 3:19	226, 255	Gen 50:20	260
Gen 4:10, 15	195		
Gen 5:24	124, 180	*Exodus*	
Gen 6:1-4	202	Exod 2:16, 19	76
Gen 7:22	132	Exod 3:5	147
Gen 8:22	183	Exod 3:12	246
Gen 11:6-9	137	Exod 3:15	319
Gen 12:1-3	120	Exod 3:20	276
Gen 12:2-3	174	Exod 6:3	122
Gen 12:3	247	Exod 6:7	127, 247
Gen 14:18	187, 274	Exod 8:11	161
Gen 14:19, 22	284	Exod 9:31	193
Gen 18:19	242	Exod 12:46	85
Gen 19:24	29	Exod 13:21-22	260
Gen 19:36-38	203	Exod 14:10-14	263
Gen 20:7	260	Exod 14:19	86

Exod 14:24	15	Exod 33:10	208
Exod 14:27	320	Exod 33:13	255
Exod 14:31	263	Exod 33:20	208
Exod 15	160	Exod 34:6-7	255
Exod 15:1-18	357	Exod 34:6	211, 276, 338
Exod 15:2	289	Exod 34:10	276
Exod 15:6, 12	289	Exod 37:7-9	42
Exod 15:10	233		
Exod 15:11	280	*Leviticus*	
Exod 15:13	289	Lev 5:2-4	46
Exod 15:20-21	164	Lev 6:12	15
Exod 16	276	Lev 11:3	167
Exod 16:1-3	263	Lev 13–14	xxxix
Exod 16:3-8	192	Lev 19:15	202
Exod 16:10	142	Lev 21:5	315
Exod 16:13-15	260	Lev 21:10	315
Exod 17:1-17	264	Lev 23:23-43	198
Exod 17:2-7	183	Lev 23:24, 34	198
Exod 17:6	260	Lev 23:33-36	291
Exod 17:7	200	Lev 25:23	98
Exod 18:13	202	Lev 25:36-37	36
Exod 19:3-5	201	Lev 26:3-6	210
Exod 19:4	229	Lev 26:12	127, 236, 247
Exod 19:5	318		
Exod 20:1-3	201	*Numbers*	
Exod 20:3-5, 16	61	Num 5:11-31	xxxix
Exod 21:6	201	Num 6:23-27	309
Exod 21:18	12	Num 6:24-26	163, 316
Exod 21:28-32	125	Num 6:25	196
Exod 22:8	114, 201	Num 6:25-26	13
Exod 22:21-22	340	Num 10:35-36	21
Exod 22:25	36	Num 10:35	112, 163, 314
Exod 23:17	110	Num 11:4-15	192
Exod 23:20	86, 229	Num 11:4-6, 31-35	263
Exod 24:17	142	Num 11:19-20	263
Exod 25:17-22	16	Num 11:31-32	276
Exod 25:18-20	42	Num 11:33-34	193
Exod 25:18	244	Num 13:25–14:12	263
Exod 29:38-40	15	Num 14:18	255
Exod 29:40-41	286	Num 15:5-7	286
Exod 30:7-8	330	Num 15:30-31	46
Exod 30:23-31	315	Num 16:1-14	263
Exod 32:1-6	263	Num 16:1	354
Exod 32:32-33	140	Num 16:29-33	327
Exod 32:34	229	Num 16:31-33, 45-49	263
Exod 33–34	255		
Exod 33:2	86, 229		

Num 18:20	39, 332
Num 20:2-13	264
Num 20:12	264
Num 20:13	200
Num 24:4, 16	200
Num 24:7	76
Num 24:21	206
Num 25:1-9	264
Num 28	286
Num 28:4	231
Num 29	198
Num 29:1	118
Num 35:9-28	21

Deuteronomy

Deut 1:16-17	202
Deut 4:8	342
Deut 4:20	127
Deut 4:34	320
Deut 5:1-6	201
Deut 5:7-10, 20	61
Deut 5:15	320
Deut 6:4	127, 199
Deut 7	318
Deut 7:6	236, 318
Deut 8:5	235
Deut 8:17	112
Deut 10:9	332
Deut 12:10	237
Deut 13:13	102
Deut 16:13-15	291
Deut 16:19	202
Deut 17:12-13	xxxix
Deut 17:12	46
Deut 19:16-21	xxxix
Deut 20:4, 10-20	xxxix
Deut 21:6	179
Deut 21:11	228
Deut 21:19	290
Deut 22:24	290
Deut 24:17	202
Deut 25:9-10	147
Deut 25:19	237
Deut 26:5-10	146
Deut 26:8	320
Deut 27:11–28:68	5
Deut 27:15-26	270

Deut 28:15-46	270
Deut 29:19	201
Deut 29:23	29
Deut 30:11-14	181
Deut 31:6	58
Deut 31:11	68, 110
Deut 31:17-18	75
Deut 31:30	225
Deut 32:8	202
Deut 32:11	229
Deut 32:13-14	198
Deut 32:20	75, 206
Deut 32:36	319
Deut 32:42	143
Deut 33:2	127, 207
Deut 33:12	209
Deut 33:26	42
Deut 33:28	13

Joshua

Josh 1:5, 9	58
Josh 1:8	6
Josh 4–9	164
Josh 4:23	282
Josh 5:15	147
Josh 7:21, 24	233
Josh 8:30-35	147
Josh 10:24	273
Josh 14:1-3	38
Josh 15:1	304
Josh 17:1	304
Josh 18:8-10	38
Josh 23:10	206
Josh 24	5
Josh 24:1, 25	147
Josh 24:2-13	146

Judges

Judg 2:11-19	264
Judg 2:11-23	194
Judg 4–5	204
Judg 4:4-5	241
Judg 4:5	202
Judg 5:4-5	42
Judg 7:2	112
Judg 7:25	204

Judg 8:5-21   204
Judg 11:34   164

Ruth
Ruth 2:4   309
Ruth 3:11   290
Ruth 4:1, 10, 11   290
Ruth 4:7-8   147

1–2 Samuel
1 Sam 1:11-13   140
1 Sam 2:4-8   268, 281
1 Sam 3:1-6   316
1 Sam 3:17   298
1 Sam 4:1-11   194
1 Sam 4:11, 22   194
1 Sam 7:1-2   314
1 Sam 13:9-12   49–50
1 Sam 14:44   298
1 Sam 15:9, 15   92
1 Sam 15:22-23   101
1 Sam 17:45, 47   49
1 Sam 18:7   164
1 Sam 19:11   146
1 Sam 21:7   134
1 Sam 21:10-15   84
1 Sam 21:12   164
1 Sam 22:1   332
1 Sam 22:9   134
1 Sam 23:14   154
1 Sam 23:19   135
1 Sam 24:2   154
1 Sam 24:3-4   332
1 Sam 25:22   298
1 Sam 26:1   135
1 Sam 29:5   164

2 Sam 6–7   314
2 Sam 6:1-19   314
2 Sam 6:15   118
2 Sam 6:17-19   350
2 Sam 7   114, 220
2 Sam 7:14   9
2 Sam 8:2-3,
    13-14   147
2 Sam 8:12-14   147
2 Sam 12   xliv

2 Sam 12:9   131
2 Sam 12:13   131
2 Sam 14:1-24   15
2 Sam 14:17, 20   114
2 Sam 15:2   249
2 Sam 15:10   118
2 Sam 15:32   246
2 Sam 22   41
2 Sam 28:13   114

1–2 Kings
1 Kgs 1:49-53   21
1 Kgs 2:28-34   21
1 Kgs 3:5-15   316
1 Kgs 6:23-28   42
1 Kgs 8:15-16   194
1 Kgs 8:56   237
1 Kgs 10:5   8
1 Kgs 10:22   122
1 Kgs 14:11   145
1 Kgs 18:27   112
1 Kgs 19:11-13   181
1 Kgs 19:13, 19   233
1 Kgs 21:10, 13   200
1 Kgs 22:19-20   201

2 Kgs 2:1-10   180
2 Kgs 2:3, 5, 9-10   124
2 Kgs 2:8, 13   233
2 Kgs 2:9-11   327
2 Kgs 3:20   15
2 Kgs 8:12   322
2 Kgs 9:13   118
2 Kgs 12:13   243
2 Kgs 16:15   330

1–2 Chronicles
1 Chr 5:10, 19-20   203
1 Chr 6:22   354
1 Chr 6:24   354
1 Chr 15:17, 19   354
1 Chr 16:5, 7, 37   354
1 Chr 16:8-22   259
1 Chr 16:23-33   238
1 Chr 16:34   267, 319
1 Chr 16:42   243
1 Chr 17:13   9

1 Chr 18:2-3,	
12-13	147
1 Chr 22:10	9
1 Chr 26:1	354
1 Chr 28:6	9
1 Chr 29:10-22	350
2 Chr 5:11-14	319
2 Chr 5:12	243, 355
2 Chr 6:41-42	314
2 Chr 7:1-3	319
2 Chr 19:2	237
2 Chr 19:5-6	201
2 Chr 20:19	354
2 Chr 20:21	319
2 Chr 32:6	290
2 Chr 35:15	355

Ezra

Ezra 2:41	355
Ezra 3:8, 9	352
Ezra 3:10	355
Ezra 3:11	319
Ezra 9:5	330
Ezra 9:9-15	262

Nehemiah

Neh 7:44	355
Neh 8:1	290
Neh 9:5-37	262
Neh 11:22	355
Neh 12:35	355

1–2 Maccabees

1 Macc 4:52	74
2 Macc 10:1-8	74

Job

Job 1–2	201
Job 3:24	197
Job 5:11-15	268
Job 7:17-18	326, 336
Job 7:17-21	25
Job 7:19	97
Job 7:21	97
Job 8:9	252
Job 9:5-6	186

Job 10:2-22	97
Job 10:3-22	25
Job 10:8-12	171, 327
Job 10:9-10	53
Job 10:9 74,	255
Job 10:20	98
Job 10:21-22	140, 217, 334
Job 10:22	123
Job 11:13	335
Job 13:9	326
Job 13:21	98
Job 13:24	75
Job 14:6	97
Job 15:35	22
Job 23:11	3
Job 26:6	5, 215
Job 28:22	5, 215
Job 28:28	276
Job 29–31	279
Job 29:7, 12-18	202
Job 29:11	200
Job 29:12	174
Job 29:18	255
Job 31	66, 112
Job 31:5-40	20
Job 31:7	3
Job 32-37	123
Job 32:8	345
Job 33:4	345
Job 34:14-15	345
Job 34:29	75
Job 37:24	279
Job 38–41	257
Job 38:4-6	186
Job 38:8-11	232, 258
Job 38:12-13	249
Job 40:10	233
Job 41	258

Psalms

Ps 1–119	xix
Ps 1–118	xix
Ps 1–89	xix
Ps 1–72	xxxviii
Ps 1–2	xix
Ps 1	xix–xx, 9, 10, 123, 278, 339

Ps 1:1, 5, 6	177	Ps 7:5	255, 334
Ps 1:1	10, 11, 37	Ps 7:6-11	108
Ps 1:2	11	Ps 7:6	40, 112, 142, 188,
Ps 1:3	xiii, 93, 231		202, 234
Ps 1:4	88	Ps 7:9	40
Ps 1:6	11, 91, 305	Ps 7:11	143
Ps 2	xix–xx, xxxviii, 26,	Ps 7:12-13	xiii, 298
	115, 217, 274, 344	Ps 7:13	29
Ps 2:4-9	120	Ps 7:14-16	xxxvii
Ps 2:4	94, 145, 302	Ps 7:15-16	26, 87, 141, 330
Ps 2:12	21, 177	Ps 7:16	155, 332
Ps 3–4	xxi	Ps 7:17	32
Ps 3	26	Ps 8	xxviii, xxxviii, 33
Ps 3:2	13	Ps 8:2	xxxviii, 344
Ps 3:3	207	Ps 8:4	336
Ps 3:4	12	Ps 9–10	xxi, 144, 291
Ps 3:5	xxi, 13	Ps 9:2	324
Ps 3:6	26	Ps 9:4	233
Ps 3:7	40, 202	Ps 9:4, 7-8	240
Ps 3:8	xxii	Ps 9:4, 7	202
Ps 4	15	Ps 9:7-8, 19	234
Ps 4:1	289	Ps 9:7-8	16, 143
Ps 4:6	38, 90, 109	Ps 9:8	162
Ps 4:7	306	Ps 9:13-14	74
Ps 4:8	xxi	Ps 9:15-16	141, 329
Ps 5:3	216, 334	Ps 9:15	77
Ps 5:8	324	Ps 9:16	xxxvii, 22, 87, 332
Ps 5:9	xxxv, xxxvi, 298	Ps 9:17	122
Ps 5:10	xxxvii	Ps 9:18-19	21
Ps 5:11	10, 21	Ps 9:19-20	25
Ps 6	74, 79	Ps 9:19	26, 40, 202
Ps 6:1	21	Ps 10	26, 27
Ps 6:2	xxxiii	Ps 10:1	26, 112, 182
Ps 6:2, 9	xxxiv	Ps 10:4, 11, 13	235
Ps 6:3	31	Ps 10:4	33
Ps 6:4-5	26	Ps 10:6	75
Ps 6:5	xxxv, 38, 74, 215	Ps 10:7-10	xxxv
Ps 6:6-8	77	Ps 10:7	134, 298
Ps 6:6-7	xxxiii	Ps 10:8-10	40
Ps 6:7	xxxii	Ps 10:8-9	xxxvi, 28, 329
Ps 6:8	xxii	Ps 10:9	54, 77, 141, 303
Ps 6:9	xxiii	Ps 10:11	112, 216
Ps 6:10	124	Ps 10:12	40, 202
Ps 7–9	xx	Ps 10:17	26
Ps 7	66, 143	Ps 11	144
Ps 7:1	10	Ps 11:1-2	303
Ps 7:2	xxxvi, 54, 141, 303	Ps 11:1	206

Ps 11:2	xxxii, xxxv, 202	Ps 17:6	37
Ps 11:3	186	Ps 17:7	37
Ps 11:4-7	110, 143	Ps 17:8	xiii, 90, 141, 149,
Ps 11:4-5	40, 326		152, 207, 229
Ps 11:4	82, 302	Ps 17:9-12	xxxvi
Ps 11:5	xxxvi	Ps 17:12	xxxvi, 54, 141
Ps 11:6	298	Ps 17:13	202
Ps 11:7	41, 68, 329	Ps 17:14	37, 332
Ps 12	144	Ps 17:15	29, 37, 329
Ps 12:1-4	xxxvii, 298	Ps 18	xxii, 143, 274
Ps 12:2-4	31	Ps 18:1, 31, 46	44
Ps 12:2	134	Ps 18:1-3	xiii
Ps 12:3-4	xxxix	Ps 18:1-2	45
Ps 12:5	xxiii, 21, 49, 52, 188,	Ps 18:2, 46	70
	202	Ps 18:2	11, 207, 343
Ps 12:6	161	Ps 18:4-5, 16	79
Ps 12:7	146	Ps 18:4, 16	303
Ps 12:12	26	Ps 18:4-5	xvi, xxxv, 285, 303
Ps 13:1-2	18	Ps 18:4	102
Ps 13:3	xxxv, 90	Ps 18:6	49
Ps 13:4-5	32	Ps 18:7-15	71, 117, 127, 164,
Ps 13:6	22		189, 241
Ps 14	134, 144	Ps 18:9-10	163
Ps 14:1-4	31	Ps 18:11-14	29
Ps 14:1	235	Ps 18:14	xiii
Ps 14:2, 4, 7	134	Ps 18:16	165, 336
Ps 14:2	28, 82	Ps 18:17-18	xxxv
Ps 14:4	xxxvi	Ps 18:19	112
Ps 14:5-6	134	Ps 18:20-30	249
Ps 14:7	49, 306, 309	Ps 18:20-24	66
Ps 15	248	Ps 18:21, 30	45
Ps 15:1-2	208	Ps 18:22	45
Ps 15:5	37	Ps 18:23, 25, 30,	
Ps 16–17	xix	33	44
Ps 16:5	332	Ps 18:23-24	45
Ps 16:7	40	Ps 18:23	xv
Ps 16:8	75, 299, 304	Ps 18:28	45
Ps 16:9	142	Ps 18:30	44, 161
Ps 16:11	329	Ps 18:36	100
Ps 17	66, 144	Ps 18:50	50
Ps 17:1-12	20	Ps 19	xx, 23, 83, 295
Ps 17:1-5	43	Ps 19:1-4	159
Ps. 17:3, 5	37	Ps 19:1	127, 241
Ps 17:3	21, 37, 64, 161, 326	Ps 19:7-9	xv
Ps 17:4	37	Ps 19:8	3, 31
Ps 17:5, 11	3	Ps 19:10	86
Ps 17:5	37	Ps 19:14	70

Ps 20	xxiii, xxiv, 274	Ps 24:6	29, 68
Ps 20:1-2	117	Ps 24:7-10	73
Ps 20:2	309	Ps 24:7-9	288
Ps 20:4	50	Ps 25	84, 291
Ps 20:5	50	Ps 25:1	211
Ps 20:6	50, 289	Ps 25:8-9	4
Ps 20:7-8	82	Ps 25:10	109
Ps 20:7	289, 342	Ps 25:12, 14	254
Ps 20:9	50	Ps 25:15	77
Ps 21	274	Ps 25:16-20	xxxvii
Ps 21:4	138	Ps 25:16a	211
Ps 21:7	304	Ps 25:17	289
Ps 21:8-12	xxiii	Ps 25:20	211
Ps 21:12	xiii	Ps 26:1-10	20
Ps 22–23	xxi	Ps 26:1	108
Ps 22	xxi, xxiv, xxx,	Ps 26:2-3	21
	xxxiii, 79, 167, 181	Ps 26:2	40, 326, 326
Ps 22:1	xxi, 111, 182	Ps 26:4-5	4, 37
Ps 22:2	112	Ps 26:5	xxxvi
Ps 22:4-8	xxxiii	Ps 26:6	179
Ps 22:9-10	171	Ps 26:8	66
Ps 22:11, 19	96	Ps 26:9-11	354
Ps 22:11	170	Ps 26:9-10	xxxvi
Ps 22:12-14,		Ps 26:12	66
20-21	40	Ps 27	xx
Ps 22:12-13, 16,		Ps 27:2, 12	xxxvi
20-21	303	Ps 27:2	xxxvi
Ps 22:12-13	xvii	Ps 27:3-6	149
Ps 22:13, 22	141	Ps 27:4, 8, 13	29
Ps 22:13, 16	xxxvi	Ps 27:4-5	206
Ps 22:14-18	77	Ps 27:4	329
Ps 22:15	xxxii, 255	Ps 27:5	36, 100
Ps 22:16, 20	145	Ps 27:6	11
Ps 22:17	xxxv	Ps 27:8	205
Ps 22:19	xxiv	Ps 27:11a	211
Ps 22:22-31	32	Ps 27:13	140, 287
Ps 22:25-26	157	Ps 27:14	63
Ps 22:25	160, 286	Ps 28:1	xxxv
Ps 22:27-29	325	Ps 28:2	62, 316, 330
Ps 23	xxi	Ps 28:3	xxxvi
Ps 23:1	xii, xxi	Ps 28:4	22, 150
Ps 23:4	xxi, xxiv, xxxii	Ps 28:6	xxiii
Ps 23:5	xiii, 231, 324	Ps 28:7	11, 207
Ps 23:6	149	Ps 28:8-9	148
Ps 24	xxii, 34, 248	Ps 28:9	xii, 58
Ps 24:1-2	232	Ps 29	xix, 117
Ps 24:4	61	Ps 29:3-9	42, 164

Ps 29:10	302	Ps 34:11	26
Ps 30	79	Ps 34:18	226
Ps 30:1-3	xxxiv	Ps 34:21	xxxvii
Ps 30:3	xxxv, 38, 41, 124	Ps 35	xliii
Ps 30:5	xii, 40, 146, 216	Ps 35:1	108
Ps 30:7	27	Ps 35:2	202
Ps 30:9	xxxv, 18, 38, 215, 255	Ps 35:4-6, 8, 26	xxxix
Ps 30:13	142	Ps 35:4	xxxv, 152
Ps 31	xxii, xxiii	Ps 35:5	xii, 7
Ps 31:1-3	36	Ps 35:6	xxxii
Ps 31:4	329	Ps 35:7-8	22, 77, 141
Ps 31:7-8	xxxv	Ps 35:8	xxxvii, 94, 332
Ps 31:8-9	289	Ps 35:11	166
Ps 31:9	xxxii	Ps 35:15-16	xxxv
Ps 31:9-10, 13	xxxiv	Ps 35:15	229
Ps 31:9-10	xxxiii	Ps 35:17	31, 40, 141
Ps 31:10	xxxii	Ps 35:19	31
Ps 31:11, 19, 24	xxii–xxiii	Ps 35:22	96, 170, 203
Ps 31:11-13	18	Ps 35:23	112, 145, 146
Ps 31:11	xxxiii, 17	Ps 35:25	xxxvi
Ps 31:13	xxxv	Ps 36	92
Ps 31:16	90, 196	Ps 36:1-4	86
Ps 31:18-19	xxiii	Ps 36:4	xxxv
Ps 31:18	298	Ps 36:5	255
Ps 31:19	254	Ps 36:6	142
Ps 31:21	xxii	Ps 36:7-9	38
Ps 32–33	xx	Ps 36:7	40, 141, 229
Ps 32:1-2	81	Ps 36:8-9	152
Ps 32:3-4	xxxiiii	Ps 36:9	68
Ps 32:3	17	Ps 37	xxxvii, 7, 123, 126, 144, 180
Ps 32:6	xxxv, 108, 165, 303	Ps 37:1, 7, 12, 21, 32, 35	86
Ps 32:8	81		
Ps 32:10	xv, 81	Ps 37:9, 22, 28, 38	17, 86
Ps 32:11	81		
Ps 33	84	Ps 37:9, 34	63
Ps 33:3	239, 344	Ps 37:12	xxxvii
Ps 33:5	115	Ps 37:13	9, 145
Ps 33:10-12	xxxv	Ps 37:14-15	xxxvii, 22
Ps 33:13-14	302	Ps 37:14	xxxv
Ps 33:16-19	49	Ps 37:28-29	82
Ps 33:16-17	342	Ps 37:28	115, 144
Ps 33:19	xxxiv	Ps 37:30	6
Ps 34	62, 291	Ps 37:31	3, 229
Ps 34:7-10	254	Ps 37:35-36	180
Ps 34:7	86, 229	Ps 37:35	231
Ps 34:8	81	Ps 37:37-40	124

Ps 37:37	102	Ps 41:5-7	xxxv
Ps 38–40	97	Ps 41:9	xxxiii, xxxiv, 18, 137
Ps 38–39	97	Ps 41:12	38
Ps 38	xxviii, 79	Ps 41:13	222
Ps 38:1-8	216	Ps 41:14	xx
Ps 38:1	17	Ps 42–43	xxi
Ps 38:2	xiii, 79	Ps 42	xxii, 27, 298
Ps 38:5-12, 19-20	86	Ps 42:1-5	110
Ps 38:5-12	xxxiv	Ps 42:1-2	165, 334
Ps 38:6-10	xxxiii	Ps 42:2	29, 68, 110, 152
Ps 38:7	xxxii	Ps 42:3, 9-10	110
Ps 38:10	xxxii, 31	Ps 42:3, 10	110, 195, 284, 322
Ps 38:11-12,		Ps 42:3	166, 197, 252
19-20	18	Ps 42:6-11	110
Ps 38:11	xxxiii	Ps 42:7	xxxv, 303
Ps 38:12	xxxv, 152	Ps 42:8	109
Ps 38:13-14	xvii–xviii	Ps 42:9	111
Ps 38:16	31, 229, 299	Ps 43	27
Ps 38:21-22	97, 170	Ps 43:1-5	110
Ps 39	216	Ps 43:1-3	107
Ps 39:1	331	Ps 43:1-2	107, 110
Ps 39:3	159	Ps 43:1	110
Ps 39:4-6	xxxi, 150, 226	Ps 43:2	111
Ps 39:5-6	340	Ps 43:3-4	117
Ps 39:5	xii, 193, 336	Ps 43:3	109, 110, 142, 210
Ps 39:6	125	Ps 43:5	107
Ps 39:7	63	Ps 44:3-8	49
Ps 39:9-10	79	Ps 44:3	109, 115, 189, 196
Ps 39:12-13	97	Ps 44:9-16	146
Ps 39:12	203	Ps 44:9-14	183
Ps 40	97	Ps 44:9	147
Ps 40:1-2	97	Ps 44:11-15	127
Ps 40:1	63	Ps 44:19	xxxii, 3
Ps 40:2	xxxv	Ps 44:20	335
Ps 40:3	3, 83, 239, 344	Ps 44:21	326
Ps 40:5	212	Ps 44:23	145, 146
Ps 40:6-8	126	Ps 44:24	27, 182
Ps 40:10-11	109	Ps 44:26	202
Ps 40:12	xxxii	Ps 45	209, 274
Ps 40:13	96	Ps 45:3	276
Ps 40:13-17	97, 168	Ps 45:5	43
Ps 40:14-15	xxxix	Ps 45:7	231
Ps 40:14	xxxv, 152	Ps 45:17	174
Ps 40:16	68	Ps 46	120, 187, 206
Ps 40:17a	210	Ps 46:2-3	192
Ps 41	xix	Ps 46:4-7	120
Ps 41:1-3, 11-12	97	Ps 46:4	118

Ps 46:5	15, 40, 75, 304	Ps 52:8	xiii, 231, 279
Ps 46:7, 11	49, 118, 120	Ps 52:9	146
Ps 46:8	160	Ps 52:11	63
Ps 46:9	187	Ps 53	33
Ps 46:10	118, 151	Ps 53:4	xxxvi, 135
Ps 47:1	247	Ps 53:6	306
Ps 48	116, 187, 206, 300	Ps 53:7	33
Ps 48:2	127	Ps 54:3	xxxv, 211
Ps 48:3	117	Ps 54:4	xxiii
Ps 48:8, 12-14	340	Ps 54:5	71, 139
Ps 49	144, 180	Ps 54:6-7	146
Ps 49:1-4	191	Ps 54:7	279
Ps 49:1	127	Ps 55:1	108
Ps 49:2	150	Ps 55:4-5	xxxiv
Ps 49:14-15	xxxiv	Ps 55:6-7	251
Ps 49:15	38, 180	Ps 55:6	206
Ps 49:19	90	Ps 55:8	xxxv
Ps 50	xx, 37, 198, 200, 201	Ps 55:9, 15, 23	139
Ps 50:1-6	234	Ps 55:9, 21	134
Ps 50:1-3	241	Ps 55:9-11	210
Ps 50:2	206	Ps 55:13-14	xxxiii
Ps 50:4	188	Ps 55:21	xxxvii, 329
Ps 50:7	200	Ps 56	xxx
Ps 50:8-15	101, 167	Ps 56:4, 11	117
Ps 50:8-14	301	Ps 56:5-6	xxxv
Ps 50:9-13	128	Ps 56:7	144
Ps 50:14-23	60	Ps 56:8	167, 327
Ps 50:14	160	Ps 56:12-13	32
Ps 50:16-21	133, 183	Ps 56:12	141, 160
Ps 50:16-20	xxxvi	Ps 56:13	xxxiv, 287
Ps 50:18-20	130	Ps 57:1	xiii, 40, 139, 149,
Ps 50:19	134		229
Ps 50:23	34, 146, 229	Ps 57:3, 10	109, 148, 215
Ps 51–72	xix	Ps 57:3	324
Ps 51	xx, xxx, 79, 126,	Ps 57:4, 6	303
	127, 128	Ps 57:4	xxxvi, 40, 134, 155,
Ps 51:1	139, 256		329, 336
Ps 51:5	xiv, 143, 334	Ps 57:5, 11	207
Ps 51:10-12	334	Ps 57:6	xxxvii, 22, 77, 303,
Ps 51:16-19	101		329
Ps 51:17-18	341	Ps 57:7-11	269
Ps 51:17	60	Ps 57:8	216
Ps 52:1-4	xxxvi	Ps 57:9-11	32
Ps 52:1	143	Ps 57:9-10	146
Ps 52:2	xxxv, 329	Ps 57:10	255
Ps 52:5, 8	xiii	Ps 58	xxii, xxxix, 201, 235
Ps 52:5	17, 67, 140, 143, 287	Ps 58:1-2	144

Ps 58:1	114	Ps 63:7	xiii, 40, 141, 229
Ps 58:3-5	144	Ps 63:9, 11	154
Ps 58:6-10	xxxix	Ps 63:10	154
Ps 58:6-9	144, 145	Ps 63:11	148, 154
Ps 59	xxvi	Ps 64	298
Ps 59:1-3	xxxv	Ps 64:2-6	28
Ps 59:5	112	Ps 64:3	329, 336
Ps 59:6, 14-15	xxxvi, 40	Ps 64:5-6	279
Ps 59:7	336	Ps 64:5	xxxvi, 329
Ps 59:8	9	Ps 64:7-8	298
Ps 59:11-13	xxxix	Ps 64:7	xxiii
Ps 59:12-13	xxxvii	Ps 64:8	xxxvii
Ps 59:13	xlii	Ps 64:9	156
Ps 59:16	15	Ps 65–68	xx
Ps 60:1-3	183	Ps 65	23
Ps 60:3	186	Ps 65:1	160
Ps 60:4	148	Ps 65:2	160
Ps 60:5	289	Ps 65:4	69, 153, 160, 207
Ps 60:5-12	269	Ps 65:5	160
Ps 60:6-8	xxiii	Ps 65:9-13	162, 341
Ps 60:7	209	Ps 65:17-18	131
Ps 60:11	139	Ps 66	253
Ps 61–62	xx	Ps 66:1-4	325
Ps 61:1-11	341	Ps 66:1	247
Ps 61:2-4	36	Ps 66:9	140
Ps 61:2	xxxv	Ps 66:10-11	148
Ps 61:4	40, 141, 229	Ps 66:10	30
Ps 61:6-7	207	Ps 66:11	303
Ps 61:7	109, 149	Ps 66:12	216, 303
Ps 61:8	146, 149	Ps 66:13-15	286
Ps 62	xxx	Ps 67:1	196
Ps 62:1	159	Ps 67:6-7	210
Ps 62:2, 6-7	70	Ps 68:1-2, 11, 17,	
Ps 62:2, 6	304	21-23	xiii
Ps 62:2	75	Ps 68:1	112, 202
Ps 62:4	xxxvii	Ps 68:4, 33	42
Ps 62:8	332	Ps 68:4, 8	71
Ps 62:9	xxxi, 97	Ps 68:5	xiii
Ps 62:11	xxiii	Ps 68:9	82
Ps 62:12	87	Ps 68:13	184
Ps 63:1, 5, 8, 9	149	Ps 68:16	282, 340
Ps 63:1, 9-10	xxxvii	Ps 68:23	143
Ps 63:1	108, 334	Ps 68:32	324
Ps 63:2-4	38	Ps 68:33	71
Ps 63:2	69, 207	Ps 69:1-3, 15	100
Ps 63:3	149	Ps 69:1-2, 14-15	xxxv, 41, 108, 303
Ps 63:4	316, 330	Ps 69:1-2	311

Ps 69:1, 15	79	Ps 73:18-20	94
Ps 69:1	152	Ps 73:20	xii, 226
Ps 69:3	xxxii, xxxiii	Ps 73:22	80
Ps 69:4	17, 100	Ps 73:23-28	94, 124
Ps 69:5	326	Ps 73:23-26, 28	38, 51
Ps 69:6	63, 68	Ps 73:24	124
Ps 69:8	xxxiii	Ps 74	111, 114, 185, 195
Ps 69:12	xxxv	Ps 74:1	xii, 195, 247
Ps 69:17	27, 75, 129	Ps 74:2	82, 185, 206
Ps 69:21-22	xxxvii	Ps 74:4, 8	185
Ps 69:22-28	xxxix	Ps 74:7, 10, 18, 21	185
Ps 69:22-23, 25	xliv	Ps 74:10	31, 185
Ps 69:22	332	Ps 74:11	189
Ps 69:28	140, 327	Ps 74:12	185
Ps 70	99	Ps 74:13-17	127, 185, 220
Ps 70:1	96, 170	Ps 74:13-15	220
Ps 70:2-3	xxxix	Ps 74:13-14	232
Ps 70:2, 4	170	Ps 74:13	343
Ps 70:3	xxxv	Ps 74:14	220
Ps 70:5	170	Ps 74:18-19	195
Ps 71:1-3	78	Ps 74:22	185, 188, 202
Ps 71:12	96	Ps 75:1	191
Ps 71:13	xxxix	Ps 75:2-3	202
Ps 71:17	191	Ps 75:5, 10	231
Ps 71:19	212	Ps 75:8	148
Ps 71:20	xxxv	Ps 75:9	49, 118
Ps 71:24	6	Ps 75:10	343
Ps 72	xix	Ps 76	116
Ps 72:6-7, 16	210	Ps 76:1-2	120
Ps 72:10-20	104	Ps 76:2	122, 206
Ps 72:14	286	Ps 76:6	49, 118
Ps 72:16	162	Ps 76:9	202
Ps 72:18-20	xix, xx	Ps 77	xxviii
Ps 73	7, 94, 111, 113, 126,	Ps 77:2-6	191
	144, 190	Ps 77:4, 6	xxxiii
Ps 73:1-16	190	Ps 77:9	256
Ps 73:2	3	Ps 77:10	118, 190
Ps 73:3-4	xxxv	Ps 77:11-20	190
Ps 73:3	94	Ps 77:11-15	334
Ps 73:8-9	xxxv	Ps 77:11-12,	
Ps 73:13-15	xxxvii, 331	16-20	191
Ps 73:16-17	190	Ps 77:12	191
Ps 73:17-28	190	Ps 77:13	212
Ps 73:17-26	208	Ps 77:14	190
Ps 73:17, 23-26,		Ps 77:15	118, 190
28	14	Ps 77:16-19	42, 241
Ps 73:17	181	Ps 77:16-18	71

Ps 77:16	121, 282	Ps 82:6	118, 203
Ps 77:17	xiii	Ps 82:8	162, 188, 234
Ps 77:20	xii, 195, 225	Ps 83	xliii
Ps 78	111, 112, 261	Ps 83:5	xxxv
Ps 78:4	319	Ps 83:9-17	xxxix
Ps 78:5, 21, 71	118	Ps 83:13	xii, 88, 118
Ps 78:11	188	Ps 83:14	xii
Ps 78:17, 35, 56	118	Ps 83:18	212
Ps 78:26-31	263	Ps 84	116
Ps 78:38	256	Ps 84:1	xxii
Ps 78:52	xii	Ps 84:4	59, 69
Ps 78:62, 71	82	Ps 84:8	118
Ps 78:63	303	Ps 84:9	119, 148
Ps 78:65	xiii, 112, 197	Ps 84:11	xiii
Ps 78:68-69	194	Ps 85:1	118, 306
Ps 78:70	188	Ps 85:2	33
Ps 78:71	195	Ps 85:4	306
Ps 78:72	249	Ps 85:8-9	254
Ps 79	111, 112, 195	Ps 85:8	xxiii
Ps 79:5	31	Ps 85:10-13	142
Ps 79:7, 12	xliii	Ps 85:10	109
Ps 79:7	118	Ps 85:12	162
Ps 79:10	111, 182, 284, 322	Ps 86:4	62
Ps 79:12	xxxix	Ps 86:7	xxiii
Ps 79:13	xii, 184, 188, 196, 247	Ps 86:8	325
		Ps 86:13	xxxiv, 124
Ps 80	111	Ps 86:15	109, 255, 287
Ps 80:1	xii, 42, 58, 127, 188, 195, 244	Ps 86:16	286
		Ps 87	116, 206
Ps 80:2	198	Ps 88:1	xvi
Ps 80:4	31	Ps 88:3-6	xxxv
Ps 80:5	108, 252	Ps 88:3-5	xxxiii
Ps 80:8-16	xiii	Ps 88:3-4	41
Ps 80:8-12	xiii	Ps 88:4-7	100
Ps 81	201	Ps 88:5, 10-12	18
Ps 81:1-5a	201	Ps 88:6, 10, 12,	
Ps 81:3	118	18	xxxii
Ps 81:5b-16	201	Ps 88:6-7	41
Ps 81:6-16	xxiii	Ps 88:6	332
Ps 81:7	264	Ps 88:7, 17	xxxv
Ps 82	xii, 142, 235	Ps 88:9	xxxii
Ps 82:1-4	133	Ps 88:10-12	74, 235
Ps 82:1, 6	114	Ps 88:11	5, 217
Ps 82:1	325	Ps 88:14	27, 129, 217
Ps 82:2-4	143	Ps 88:18	xxxiii
Ps 82:5	xxxii, 29, 186, 240, 295	Ps 89	xix
		Ps 89:5-7	71

Ps 89:9-13	183	Ps 92:1	118
Ps 89:9-10	183, 232, 343	Ps 92:2	xv–xvi
Ps 89:10-14	127	Ps 92:8	xxiv
Ps 89:10	xiii	Ps 92:10	343
Ps 89:13	189, 242	Ps 92:12-13	72
Ps 89:14, 24	239	Ps 92:12-14	xiii, 7, 93, 133
Ps 89:14	109, 142, 210, 233, 240, 243	Ps 92:15	70
		Ps 93; 96–99	xix–xx
Ps 89:15	68, 109, 196	Ps 93	xxii, 23, 118, 225
Ps 89:17	231	Ps 93:1	225
Ps 89:18	119	Ps 93:2	302
Ps 89:20-37	xvii	Ps 93:3-4	164
Ps 89:26-27	9	Ps 93:5	xxii
Ps 89:26	xiii	Ps 94	144, 201
Ps 89:28-37	313	Ps 94:1	127
Ps 89:30	xv	Ps 94:2	150, 202
Ps 89:46	31, 225	Ps 94:3	31
Ps 89:47	xxxi	Ps 94:7, 12	xxiii
Ps 89:48	38	Ps 94:9-11	82
Ps 89:52	xx, 104	Ps 94:11	xii
Ps 90–106	xix	Ps 94:12	xxiv
Ps 90	253	Ps 94:18	140, 299
Ps 90:1-3, 5	23	Ps 94:23	xxxvii
Ps 90:1	229	Ps 95–99	225
Ps 90:3-10	150	Ps 95	198
Ps 90:3-6	193, 340	Ps 95:1, 6	238
Ps 90:4-6, 9-10, 12	97	Ps 95:1-2	245
		Ps 95:1	245
Ps 90:4-6, 9	xii	Ps 95:2	245
Ps 90:4	206	Ps 95:3-5, 7	246
Ps 90:7-8	xxxvii	Ps 95:3	225, 238, 318
Ps 90:8	46	Ps 95:6	245, 246
Ps 90:9-10	xxxi	Ps 95:7	xii, 58, 127, 184, 195, 200, 245, 247
Ps 90:11-12	25		
Ps 90:13	31	Ps 95:7b-8	xlv
Ps 90:14	15, 40, 75	Ps 95:8-9	200
Ps 91	144	Ps 95:8	264
Ps 91:1-10	207	Ps 96–99	118, 143, 238, 325
Ps 91:1, 5-6, 10	299	Ps 96	242
Ps 91:1, 9	118, 230	Ps 96:1	83, 239, 242, 247, 344
Ps 91:3	166, 303		
Ps 91:4	xiii, 40, 90, 141	Ps 96:2	245
Ps 91:12	140	Ps 96:3	240
Ps 91:14-16	230	Ps 96:4-5	240, 318, 324
Ps 91:14	140	Ps 96:4	120
Ps 91:15	58	Ps 96:6	115, 210, 276
Ps 91:16	128, 138	Ps 96:8	245, 246

Ps 96:9	240	Ps 102:11	226, 226, 336, 340
Ps 96:10, 13	162, 240	Ps 102:12-22	257
Ps 96:10	202, 225	Ps 102:12, 25-27	253
Ps 96:11-13	242	Ps 102:13	256
Ps 96:11	240	Ps 102:16-17	279
Ps 96:12	245	Ps 102:16	324
Ps 96:13	240	Ps 102:19	28, 82
Ps 97	28	Ps 102:25	xiii
Ps 97:1	225	Ps 103–104	xx
Ps 97:2-5	42, 71, 127, 164	Ps 103:1, 2, 22	256
Ps 97:2	245	Ps 103:4	338
Ps 97:7, 9	318	Ps 103:7	225
Ps 97:8	122	Ps 103:8	211, 287
Ps 97:11-12	245	Ps 103:13	xiii, 67
Ps 97:12	xxii	Ps 103:15-16	226
Ps 98:1	83, 115, 191, 239,	Ps 103:19-21	256
	289, 344	Ps 104	xl, 23
Ps 98:3	245	Ps 104:1	115, 233
Ps 98:4, 8	245	Ps 104:2	68, 222
Ps 98:4	160, 245, 247	Ps 104:3-4	71
Ps 98:6	225	Ps 104:3	42, 163
Ps 98:9	162, 244	Ps 104:5-9	192
Ps 99:1	225	Ps 104:5	xiii, 186
Ps 99:4	82	Ps 104:7	282
Ps 99:6	225	Ps 104:9	xxxv, 255
Ps 100	160	Ps 104:10-23,	
Ps 100:1	160	27-28	90
Ps 100:3	xii, 58, 184, 195	Ps 104:13-14	341
Ps 100:4-5	319	Ps 104:14-15,	
Ps 101	34, 274	27-28	320
Ps 101:3-4	37	Ps 104:16	72
Ps 101:8	40	Ps 104:27-28	302
Ps 102	xxiii	Ps 104:29-30	77, 83, 130, 132, 187
Ps 102:2b	210	Ps 104:29	27, 74, 334, 345
Ps 102:3-11	xxxiii	Ps 104:35	279
Ps 102:3-4, 11-12,		Ps 105–107	xx
24-27	xiii	Ps 105–106	xx
Ps 102:3-4, 11, 23	253	Ps 105	191
Ps 102:3-5, 7-8	xxxiv	Ps 105:2, 5	319
Ps 102:3	xxxii	Ps 105:4	68
Ps 102:4, 11	255	Ps 105:8, 42	262
Ps 102:4-5	xxxiii	Ps 105:26	225, 261
Ps 102:6-7	206	Ps 105:28-36	193
Ps 102:7	xxxiii	Ps 105:33	193
Ps 102:8	18	Ps 105:40	276
Ps 102:9-14	226	Ps 105:45	262
Ps 102:9	xxxiii, 108, 166, 197	Ps 106	112, 188, 191

Ps 106:1	247, 267, 289, 319	Ps 112:7	275
Ps 106:2	319	Ps 112:8	275
Ps 106:5	82	Ps 112:9	275, 276, 343
Ps 106:12	140	Ps 113–118	288
Ps 106:14	276	Ps 113	275, 288
Ps 106:16, 23, 32	225	Ps 113:1	316
Ps 106:36	332	Ps 113:3-6	324
Ps 106:40-46	267	Ps 113:4-6	324
Ps 106:48	xx, 104, 267	Ps 113:9	282
Ps 107	112	Ps 114	275, 288
Ps 107:1	247, 289, 319	Ps 114–117	275
Ps 107:10-11	xxxii	Ps 114–115	275
Ps 107:32	6, 8	Ps 114:2	187
Ps 107:33-35	183	Ps 114:3-5	189
Ps 108:1-5	141	Ps 114:3	121, 160
Ps 108:1-3	267	Ps 114:4	72
Ps 108:7-13	146	Ps 115	275, 288
Ps 109	xxxvii	Ps 115:1	109, 324
Ps 109:1	203	Ps 115:2	111, 195
Ps 109:6-20	144	Ps 115:3-8	239
Ps 109:6-19,		Ps 115:8	318
28-29	xxxix	Ps 115:9-11	288, 319
Ps 109:8-10	xlii	Ps 115:12-15	316
Ps 109:8	xliv	Ps 115:15	300, 303
Ps 109:16	xxxix	Ps 115:17	xxxv, 18, 215
Ps 109:17-19	xxxvii	Ps 116	269, 275
Ps 109:19, 29	222	Ps 116:3	41, 285, 288
Ps 109:23	xii, 320	Ps 116:8	140
Ps 109:26	xl	Ps 116:9	67, 140
Ps 110	xix–xx, 115	Ps 116:12-14	157
Ps 110:2	49	Ps 116:14	160
Ps 110:5	299, 324	Ps 116:15	xxxv
Ps 111–118	xix–xx, 319	Ps 116:16	211
Ps 111–113	275	Ps 117	xxiv, 247, 275, 288
Ps 111	278, 280, 291	Ps 117:2	288
Ps 111:3-9	278	Ps 118–119	11
Ps 111:3	115	Ps 118	275
Ps 111:3b, 10c	277	Ps 118:1-4,	
Ps 111:3b, 4b	279	14-16, 29	288
Ps 111:4	287, 338	Ps 118:1-4, 29	247, 319
Ps 111:5	277	Ps 118:1-4	284
Ps 112	275, 276, 291	Ps 118:1	267
Ps 112:1, 7, 8	275	Ps 118:2-4	319
Ps 112:1	3, 8, 275	Ps 118:2	309
Ps 112:2, 4	275	Ps 118:5	xiii
Ps 112:3b, 9b	275	Ps 118:6-9	49, 342
Ps 112:6	275, 304	Ps 118:6-8	279

Ps 118:7	279	Ps 127	297
Ps 118:8-9	xv	Ps 127:1-2	297
Ps 118:15-16	115	Ps 127:1	xiii
Ps 118:15	189	Ps 127:2	209
Ps 119	xix–xx, 11, 288, 291	Ps 127:3-5	297
Ps 119:1	8	Ps 127:5	249, 297
Ps 119:19-20	61	Ps 128	297
Ps 119:19	98	Ps 128:1-2	297
Ps 119:41-42	140	Ps 128:1	297
Ps 119:74	279	Ps 128:3-4	297
Ps 119:92	3	Ps 128:3	xiii, xiv
Ps 119:105, 130	45	Ps 128:4, 5	297
Ps 119:110	166, 329	Ps 128:5-6	208, 297
Ps 119:176	xii	Ps 128:5	49, 297, 309, 317
Ps 120–136	xix	Ps 128:6	297, 304
Ps 120–134	xix	Ps 129	297
Ps 120	216	Ps 129:1	297
Ps 120:2-4	xxxvii, 155	Ps 129:5-8	322
Ps 120:6, 7	297	Ps 129:6	226
Ps 121	38, 297	Ps 129:8	297
Ps 121:2	284, 297, 303	Ps 130	xxix, 297
Ps 121:3	140	Ps 130:1	xxxv
Ps 121:5	xiii	Ps 130:3	334
Ps 122	xviii, 116, 206	Ps 130:5-6	63
Ps 122:1	297	Ps 130:5	140
Ps 122:2	340	Ps 130:7	297
Ps 122:4	164	Ps 131	297
Ps 122:5	127, 202, 233	Ps 131:2	xiii, 67
Ps 122:6-9	309	Ps 131:3	297
Ps 122:6-8	297, 304, 309	Ps 132	274, 297
Ps 122:9	297	Ps 132:7-8	163
Ps 123:2	xiii, xvi	Ps 132:8, 14	286
Ps 124	297	Ps 132:9, 16	315
Ps 124:1	297, 309	Ps 132:10-18	51
Ps 124:3-5	311	Ps 132:13-18	49, 206
Ps 124:3	xxxvi	Ps 132:13-15	309, 315
Ps 124:4-5	165	Ps 132:15	297
Ps 124:7	166, 329	Ps 132:17	315, 343
Ps 124:8	284, 297, 300	Ps 133:1	297
Ps 125:1	36, 206, 340	Ps 133:3	297, 299, 309, 317
Ps 125:2	xiii, 299	Ps 134:1	69, 297, 317
Ps 125:4	297	Ps 134:2	62, 330
Ps 125:5	297, 309	Ps 134:3	284, 297, 300, 303,
Ps 126	209		309, 315, 317
Ps 126:1-3	309	Ps 135–136	xix
Ps 126:1	33	Ps 135:1-2	316
Ps 126:4-6	210	Ps 135:5-7, 15-18	239

Ps 135:8-12	319	Ps 142:7	333
Ps 135:16-17	284	Ps 143:3	xxxii
Ps 135:19-20	288	Ps 143:5	6, 190
Ps 136	157, 259, 261	Ps 143:6	108
Ps 136:1-26	247	Ps 143:7	xxxv, 75
Ps 136:1	267, 289	Ps 143:8	15, 40, 75
Ps 136:2-3	xv	Ps 143:10	335
Ps 136:10-22	318	Ps 144	xxxviii
Ps 136:13-15	318	Ps 144:1-11	50
Ps 136:25	157	Ps 144:1	70
Ps 137	xxxviii–xxxix, xl	Ps 144:3-4	xxxi, 23
Ps 137:5-6	20	Ps 144:4	xii, 97, 193, 252, 340
Ps 137:5	340	Ps 144:5-6	29
Ps 137:8-9	xxxix	Ps 144:6	xiii
Ps 137:8	150	Ps 144:7	xxxv, 79, 303
Ps 137:9	xiv, xxxix–xl, 144	Ps 144:9	83, 239, 344
Ps 138–150	xix	Ps 144:11	xxxvii
Ps 138–145	xix	Ps 144:12	xiii, xiv
Ps 138:2	109	Ps 145–150	xx
Ps 138:8	326	Ps 145	291
Ps 139	xliii, 112	Ps 145:3	120
Ps 139:1-16	82	Ps 145:5	191, 276
Ps 139:1-3	28	Ps 145:8-9	276
Ps 139:11-12	40	Ps 145:8	255, 287
Ps 139:13, 15-16	171	Ps 145:15-16	xiii, 302, 320
Ps 139:13	xiii, 53	Ps 145:20	258, 279
Ps 139:16	140, 167	Ps 145:21	337
Ps 139:19-22	xxxix, 64	Ps 146–150	xix–xx
Ps 139:21-22	xvii, 37	Ps 146:1-2	337
Ps 139:23-24	21	Ps 146:3-5	49, 289
Ps 139:23	64	Ps 146:3	337
Ps 140	xxxvi, 143	Ps 146:4	334
Ps 140:1-2, 10	xli	Ps 146:5	118
Ps 140:3	144	Ps 146:6	300, 303
Ps 140:5	77, 166	Ps 146:7	320
Ps 140:9-11	xxxvii, xxxix, 332	Ps 146:9	146, 305, 337
Ps 140:9-10	298	Ps 146:10	337
Ps 141:2	62, 231, 316, 335	Ps 147	269
Ps 141:4	xxxvii	Ps 147:1-5	xxx
Ps 141:9-10	303	Ps 147:2-3	337
Ps 141:9	166, 329	Ps 147:2	337
Ps 141:10	xxxvii, 22, 330	Ps 147:3	337
Ps 142:1, 5	333	Ps 147:6	337
Ps 142:3	166, 326, 333	Ps 147:9	320
Ps 142:4, 7	333	Ps 147:10-11	49
Ps 142:5	38, 67, 333	Ps 147:12	340
Ps 142:6	xxxv, 333	Ps 147:19	118

Ps 148:2-4	337		Prov 16:3	91
Ps 148:5, 13	337		Prov 16:5, 8, 16	91
Ps 148:5-6	337		Prov 17:3	30
Ps 148:7-12	337		Prov 18:12	43
Ps 148:11	337		Prov 20:5	76
Ps 148:14	337		Prov 20:8	202
Ps 149:1	83, 239, 337		Prov 20:24	91
Ps 149:1-3	337		Prov 21:31	342
Ps 149:2, 4	337		Prov 22:4	43
Ps 149:3-4	337		Prov 23:17	91
Ps 149:5-7	xxxviii		Prov 23:19	3
Ps 149:6-9	23		Prov 24:1, 19-20	91
Ps 149:7-9	339		Prov 24:16	91
Ps 149:7-8	337		Prov 26:27	22
Ps 150	xx, xxx, 104, 231		Prov 30:15, 18,	
Ps 150:3-4	337		21	151
Ps 150:6	337			
			Ecclesiastes	
Proverbs			Eccl 1–2	226
Prov 1–2	123		Eccl 2:17-18	97
Prov 1:7	126, 276		Eccl 3:20	74
Prov 1:8, 10	85		Eccl 4:8	97
Prov 1:15	4		Eccl 6:12	97
Prov 2:1	85		Eccl 7:28	206
Prov 2:8-9	4		Eccl 9:9	332
Prov 2:21	91		Eccl 12:7	74, 258
Prov 2:22	17, 91			
Prov 3:1	191		*Song of Solomon*	
Prov 3:11-12	235		Song 2:13-14	43
Prov 3:23	229		Song 3:6-11	114
Prov 4:1	84		Song 5:10-16	114
Prov 4:14	3			
Prov 4:18-19	4		*Wisdom*	
Prov 5:1	191		Wis 5:6	45
Prov 5:7	84		Wis 13:10–15:17	284
Prov 6:23	45		Wis 18:4	45
Prov 8	123			
Prov 9:6	3		*Sirach*	
Prov 9:10	276		Sir 1:11-20	84
Prov 10:27	93		Sir 12:13	143
Prov 11:20	249		Sir 14:17-18	226
Prov 13:9	93		Sir 17:1-15	25
Prov 14:11	93		Sir 18:8-10	226
Prov 14:15	3		Sir 22:27–23:6	331
Prov 15:9	4		Sir 22:27	331
Prov 15:11	5, 215		Sir 28:18	xxxvi
Prov 15:33	43		Sir 34:21–35:20	126

Sir 43:2-5	45		Isa 31:1-3	49
Sir 50:16-19	243		Isa 31:4	6
			Isa 32:15-20	173
Isaiah			Isa 32:15-18	210
Isa 1:2	127		Isa 33:2	15
Isa 1:6	309		Isa 33:10	202
Isa 1:10-20	37, 301		Isa 33:14-16	34
Isa 1:10-17	126		Isa 33:14-15	60
Isa 1:12	246		Isa 34	321
Isa 1:15	335		Isa 34:9	29
Isa 2:19	188		Isa 35:5-7	268
Isa 3:12	3		Isa 35:6-7	207
Isa 3:13	202		Isa 36:36	15
Isa 3:17	322		Isa 38	74
Isa 3:31–4:1	201		Isa 38:10	26
Isa 3:31-32	91		Isa 38:11	67
Isa 4:2	197		Isa 38:13	85
Isa 5:1-7	197		Isa 38:14	6
Isa 5:1	209		Isa 38:18	18
Isa 5:15	273		Isa 40:6-8	226, 256
Isa 5:16	242		Isa 40:6	139
Isa 6	201		Isa 40:7	92, 255
Isa 6:3	82		Isa 40:11	58, 247
Isa 8:6-8	116		Isa 40:12-17	257
Isa 8:17	75		Isa 40:15, 17	150
Isa 9:5	114		Isa 40:15	76
Isa 9:15	3		Isa 40:18-20	284
Isa 11:1	197		Isa 40:24	205
Isa 13–23	xxxix		Isa 40:26-29	341
Isa 13:13	148		Isa 40:29, 31	207
Isa 13:16	322		Isa 40:31	255, 256
Isa 14:1	213		Isa 41:17	108
Isa 14:13	120		Isa 41:18	207
Isa 17:13	205		Isa 41:20	131
Isa 19:21	122, 246		Isa 42:1-4	58
Isa 21:17	298		Isa 42:5	345
Isa 24:1-6	202		Isa 42:10	239
Isa 24:18-24	148		Isa 43:1, 21	247
Isa 27:1	183, 220		Isa 43:2	161
Isa 28:6	202		Isa 44:2	247
Isa 28:16	291		Isa 44:9-20	284
Isa 29:5	7		Isa 45:8, 12	131
Isa 29:8	180		Isa 45:8	162, 210
Isa 29:23	247		Isa 47:2-3	322
Isa 30:7	213		Isa 48:8	143
Isa 30:17	206		Isa 48:10	161
Isa 30:23-25	210		Isa 49:1-6	58

Isa 49:9-10	58	*Jeremiah*	
Isa 49:15	67, 256	Jer 1:10	70
Isa 49:23	174	Jer 2:19	94
Isa 49:26	314	Jer 2:21	196
Isa 50:4-9	58	Jer 4:24	148
Isa 51:5	311	Jer 5:16-17	17
Isa 51:6	253	Jer 6:29	161
Isa 51:9-10	183, 220, 343	Jer 7	126
Isa 51:9	112, 233	Jer 7:3-23	37
Isa 51:10	89, 311	Jer 7:4-7	301
Isa 51:17, 21	148	Jer 7:12-14	194
Isa 51:17	186	Jer 7:24	201
Isa 51:23	309	Jer 7:33	183, 195
Isa 52:1	233	Jer 8:17	143
Isa 52:13–53:12	58	Jer 9:7	161, 326
Isa 54:8	75	Jer 9:14	201
Isa 54:15	144	Jer 9:21	273
Isa 55:8	328	Jer 10:3-6	284
Isa 55:9	256	Jer 10:13	318
Isa 55:10	210	Jer 10:16	184
Isa 56:3, 6-7	213	Jer 10:24	17
Isa 56:10-11	145	Jer 11:8	201
Isa 57:15	226	Jer 11:15	209
Isa 57:16	256	Jer 12:1	181
Isa 58	126	Jer 12:3	326
Isa 58:4	12	Jer 13:10	201
Isa 59:2-3	75	Jer 14:16	195
Isa 59:4	22	Jer 16:4	183
Isa 59:9	202	Jer 17:5-6	152
Isa 59:14-15	210	Jer 17:7-8	7
Isa 59:17	233	Jer 17:8	231
Isa 60:1	142	Jer 17:10	326
Isa 60:15	120	Jer 18:7-9	70
Isa 60:16	314	Jer 21:12	15, 249
Isa 60:19-20	68, 207	Jer 23:1-2	247
Isa 60:21	247	Jer 23:1	184, 195
Isa 61:10	233	Jer 24:7	132
Isa 61:11	210	Jer 25:15-29	186
Isa 62:1-2	207	Jer 25:15-16	148
Isa 62:9	56	Jer 25:38	216
Isa 63:9	229	Jer 26:6	194
Isa 63:10-14	130	Jer 29:14	306
Isa 63:14	58	Jer 29:22	251
Isa 64:11	182	Jer 31:12, 14	157
Isa 65:18	120	Jer 31:15-20	197
Isa 66:10	120	Jer 31:28	70
Isa 66:14	122	Jer 31:33	91, 101, 132

Jer 32:39-40   132
Jer 33:5   75
Jer 33:11   267
Jer 42:10   70
Jer 45:4   70
Jer 49:12   186
Jer 50:12   322
Jer 51:16   318
Jer 51:19   184

Lamentations
Lam 1:8   322
Lam 2:2-3   182
Lam 2:9   182
Lam 2:15   120
Lam 3:4   85
Lam 3:7-9   332
Lam 3:14   251
Lam 3:56   161
Lam 4:11   182
Lam 4:21   321, 322
Lam 5:6   203
Lam 5:19-21   253

Baruch
Bar 1:15–2:10   262

Ezekiel
Ezek 1:28   142
Ezek 3:23   142
Ezek 7:18   137
Ezek 10:4   142
Ezek 11:23   210
Ezek 12:13   161
Ezek 15:6   196
Ezek 16:37-39   322
Ezek 16:42   237
Ezek 17:20   161
Ezek 18:8   36
Ezek 20:5, 9   122
Ezek 22:3, 4, 6,
  9, 12-13   131
Ezek 22:12   36
Ezek 23:29   322
Ezek 23:32-34   186
Ezek 25–32;
  38–39   xxxix

Ezek 25:12   321
Ezek 27:34   311
Ezek 28:2   6, 8
Ezek 32:4   183
Ezek 32:5-6   273
Ezek 34:10-16   58
Ezek 34:31   184, 195, 247
Ezek 35   321
Ezek 36:5   321
Ezek 36:25, 27 132
Ezek 38:2   298
Ezek 38:22   29
Ezek 38:23   122
Ezek 39:23-24,
  29   75

Daniel
Dan 7:9-10   202
Dan 9:4-19   262
Dan 9:21   330

Hosea
Hos 1:7   49
Hos 2:19-23   210
Hos 2:23   236, 247
Hos 4:1-3   202, 210, 295
Hos 4:4-6   182
Hos 5:8   243
Hos 5:15   68
Hos 10:1   196
Hos 10:12   210
Hos 12:15   131
Hos 13:3   7
Hos 14:9   267

Joel
Joel 1:20   108
Joel 2:13   255
Joel 2:17   111, 195
Joel 3:1   306
Joel 4:12   202

Amos
Amos 1–2   xxxix
Amos 5:21-27   301
Amos 5:21-24   126
Amos 6:8   118

Amos 8:7   118
Amos 9:2   327
Amos 9:13   162, 210
Amos 9:14   306

Obadiah
Obad 4   206
Obad 10–14   321

Jonah
Jon 1:3   122
Jon 2:2-3, 5 41, 311
Jon 2:2, 6   38
Jon 3:6   233
Jon 4:2   255

Micah
Mic 2:1   143
Mic 3:4   75
Mic 3:5-7   182
Mic 5:1   314
Mic 6:6-8   60, 126
Mic 6:8   249
Mic 6:14   140
Mic 7:10   111, 195
Mic 7:17   174
Mic 7:18   280

Nahum
Nah 1:6   237
Nah 3:10   322

Habakkuk
Hab 2:9   206
Hab 2:15-16   186
Hab 2:19   146
Hab 3:3-15   42
Hab 3:4-6   241
Hab 3:8   282

Zephaniah
Zeph 2:2   7
Zeph 2:3   43
Zeph 2:7   306
Zeph 3:8   202

Zechariah
Zech 2:11   213
Zech 3:4-5   222
Zech 3:9   291
Zech 8:12   162
Zech 8:20-23 120
Zech 9:10   173
Zech 10:11   203
Zech 12:8   114
Zech 13:4   233
Zech 13:9   161
Zech 14:16-18 213

Malachi
Mal 2:14   200
Mal 3:3   161
Mal 4:2   207

GENERAL INDEX

Acrostic, 26, 61–62, 84, 91, 275, 278, 291, 337, 349, 358

Affliction, disease, illness, viii, xxii, xxiii, xxviii, xxx, xxxii–xxxv, xxxvii, xxxix, xliv, xlv, 17, 18–19, 26, 27, 28, 31, 38, 52, 53, 54, 55, 57, 62, 74, 75, 77, 79, 81, 85, 86, 93, 95–96, 97, 98, 100, 102, 103, 107, 108, 112, 124, 138, 154, 161, 165, 178, 184, 194, 212, 214, 216, 227, 250, 251, 252, 253, 254, 267, 268, 271, 272, 286, 290, 295, 318, 356

Allegory, 94, 197, 198, 210

Alliteration, ix, xiv, 18, 112, 139, 158, 161, 164, 169, 202, 301

Alonso Schökel, Luis, 132, 211

Alter, Robert, xvi, xvii

Anacoluthon, 69

Anadiplosis, 234

Aposiopesis, 23

Apostrophe, xxiii, xxiv, 165

Ark (of the covenant), 16, 21, 36, 42, 49, 112, 117, 118, 121, 141, 149, 152, 158, 163, 194, 197, 229, 238, 244, 259, 313, 314, 354

Asaph, xx, xxi, 184, 189, 195, 196, 259, 350, 353, 354, 355

Assonance, xiv, xx, 112, 155, 164

Beatitude, xix, xxiv, 8, 9, 10, 11, 51, 79, 80, 81, 101–02, 103, 177, 208, 233, 262, 278, 297, 307, 308, 322, 335, 336, 340

Beauchamp, Paul, xxxii

Bird imagery, xiii, 28, 30, 206, 229, 251, 252, 254, 303

Brueggemann, Walter, 177

Captions (*see* Superscriptions)

Center, central position (*see also* Concentric pattern), xviii, xxiv, 4, 23, 26, 51, 58, 63, 66, 75, 78, 84, 85, 87, 94, 111, 121, 122, 156, 162, 177, 197, 199, 211, 212, 218, 228, 230, 231, 245–46, 248, 263, 281, 299, 301, 314, 322

Change (Shift) of address, viii, ix, xxi–xxv, 53, 59, 67, 78, 79, 114, 133, 136, 142, 149, 150, 162, 164, 165, 185, 189, 200, 232, 236, 244, 257, 292, 305, 307, 312, 313, 314, 324

Chaos, chaotic, xii, xxxii, xxxv, 43, 72, 113, 116, 117, 118, 120, 123, 131, 156, 183, 185, 202, 220, 232, 233, 241, 268, 282, 295, 311, 336, 357

Chiasm, chiastic, xv, xvi, 4, 14, 18, 41, 43–44, 60, 116, 121, 228, 280, 282–83, 287, 302–03, 304, 322, 329, 338–39

Complaint, xx, xxiii, xxx, xxxi, xxxiii, xxxviii, 11, 15, 16, 22, 26, 27, 31, 32, 34, 39, 52, 76, 95, 96, 97, 98, 103, 107, 110, 111, 112, 135, 136, 139, 140, 141, 144, 146, 148, 165, 167, 168, 177, 181, 182, 183, 188, 190,

196, 209, 212, 216, 217, 222, 226, 234, 250, 253, 261, 269, 292, 294, 297, 310, 328, 330, 332, 333, 335, 351, 353, 354, 355–56, 357

Concentric pattern (*see also* Center), xviii, 30, 34, 62, 63–64, 66, 139, 163, 185, 211–12, 218–19, 300

Consecutive psalms, psalm pairs, xix–xxi, 10–11, 26, 32, 37, 84, 109–11, 118, 126, 196, 203, 256–57, 259, 261, 277–78

Contrast, contrasting imagery, xiii, xxxii, xxxv, 4, 5, 6, 7, 8, 12, 15, 28, 30, 31, 33, 39, 40–41, 65, 70, 74, 76, 77, 80, 87, 89, 91, 94, 109, 116, 121, 122, 134, 135, 137, 138, 151, 152, 157, 166, 167, 168, 169, 178, 180, 184, 197, 198, 203, 205, 227, 230, 231, 235, 244, 249, 251, 253, 261, 271, 273, 279, 281, 283, 284, 287, 289, 293, 302, 307, 309, 316, 318, 343, 344

Covenant, xxxii, 8, 15, 20, 24, 36, 42, 43, 44, 51, 92, 93, 102, 111, 112, 113, 120, 126, 127, 128, 141, 147, 149, 158, 184, 188, 191, 192, 194, 196, 200, 201, 210, 217, 218, 219, 220, 221, 225, 232, 236, 247, 249, 255, 256, 259, 260, 261, 262, 264, 270, 276, 277, 278, 292, 311, 313, 321, 329, 338, 356

Creation, xii, xxx, xxxv, 20, 23, 24, 25, 44, 46, 47, 82, 83, 117, 118, 128, 130, 131, 132, 158, 159, 160, 181, 183, 188, 217, 226, 230, 232, 233, 235, 236, 237, 239, 240, 241, 253, 254, 255, 257, 258, 259, 281, 282, 283, 295, 300, 302, 316, 318, 319, 320, 327, 328, 334, 337, 339, 340, 342, 343, 345, 346, 357

Curse, viii, xii, xxxiii, xxxviii–xlv, 5, 15, 64, 97, 137, 142, 143, 144, 145, 150, 166, 168, 170, 171, 197, 203, 205, 251, 258, 270, 271, 272, 284, 297, 298, 309, 318, 321, 322, 323, 326, 329, 330

Dahood, M., 35

Death, dead, viii, xii, xiii, xvi, xviii, xxx–xxxi, xxxii–xxxvii, xxxix, xlii, xliv, 4, 15, 16, 17, 18, 19, 20, 21, 26, 31, 38, 41, 42, 43, 51, 52, 53, 54, 55, 56, 57, 69, 74, 75, 76, 79, 83, 86, 96, 97, 123, 124, 125, 126, 137, 138, 140, 152, 165, 167, 168, 180, 195, 202, 214, 215, 235, 252, 257, 258, 263, 264, 271, 283, 286, 287, 288, 289, 290, 291, 311, 314, 316, 334, 336, 350, 351, 356

Diapsalma, 352

Disease, illness, sickness (*see* Affliction)

Doubling (*see also* Repetitions), 34, 40, 52, 66, 70, 80, 88–89, 99, 110, 214, 216, 234, 240, 248, 282, 289, 304, 335, 336

Doxology, xx, 41, 104, 173, 222, 262, 267, 337, 345, 353

Ellipsis, elliptical, xvi, 15, 54, 213, 214, 216, 335

Entrapment (trap, snare, net), xiii, xvi, xxxvi, 16, 20, 41–42, 62, 63, 77, 78, 88, 133, 140, 141, 154, 155, 161, 166, 167, 180, 229, 285, 286, 293, 294, 303, 304, 329, 330, 331–32

Exaggeration (*see* Hyperbole)

Exodus, 3, 36, 86, 160, 161, 163, 181, 183, 189, 190, 191, 193, 197, 200, 213, 229, 236, 242, 247, 255, 256, 260, 261, 262, 263, 268, 276, 282, 287, 288, 289, 303, 318, 319, 320, 357

Five (*see also* Numerical pattern), xix, xxiv, 20, 48, 60, 62, 67, 76, 81, 82, 87, 92, 109, 113, 119, 122, 171, 199, 203, 204, 238, 240, 241, 259, 292, 299, 311, 337, 338, 340, 343

Flashback, 74, 297, 357

Focus, xiv, xvii, 8, 21, 24, 25, 33, 44, 45, 49, 51, 54, 55, 60, 70, 76, 78, 80, 82, 89, 90, 91, 96, 108, 109, 110, 116, 119, 136, 138, 141, 156, 157, 162, 163, 164, 170, 186, 190, 208, 210,

226, 227, 236, 244, 251, 254, 255, 261, 268, 280, 296, 301, 302, 309, 336, 337, 341, 357

Four, multiples of four (*see also* Numerical pattern), xix, xxiv, 9, 14, 17, 18, 20, 22, 33, 42, 43, 46, 48, 49, 50, 55, 62, 67, 71–72, 74, 80, 81, 84, 92, 98, 101, 109, 119, 129, 130, 136, 137, 144, 151, 153, 164, 172, 186, 187, 196, 202, 204, 205, 206, 209, 221, 226, 228, 230, 234, 235, 236, 238, 244, 245, 246, 254, 263, 267, 268, 282, 284, 285, 290, 292, 294, 297, 300, 311, 312, 313, 318, 320, 325, 332, 334, 343

Framing, frame, bracket (inclusion), ix, xiv, xix, xxi, xxiv, 4, 9, 10, 13, 14, 15, 17, 22, 23, 28, 30, 34, 39, 40, 41, 43, 48, 50, 51, 52, 54, 59, 61, 62, 63, 64, 65, 66, 68, 72, 74, 77, 79, 80, 86, 99, 101, 102, 115, 116, 121, 129, 132, 136, 141, 142, 145, 148, 149–50, 152, 158, 160, 163, 165, 167, 168, 171, 177, 181, 186, 191, 192, 193, 196, 197, 202, 203, 209, 211, 212, 217, 219, 225, 226, 230, 232, 234, 237, 240, 243, 247, 248, 250, 254, 256, 257, 259, 262, 269, 270, 280, 281, 282, 286, 288, 290, 294, 298, 299, 300, 303, 307, 312, 313, 316, 317, 319, 320, 324, 325, 331, 333, 334, 337, 340, 341, 344, 353

Gunkel, Hermann, 355

Hallel, xxi, 288, 339, 353

Hallelujah, xix, xx, 257, 275, 280, 282, 283, 287, 317, 319, 337, 339, 341, 342, 344, 345, 350, 352, 353

Horizontal plane, 15, 119, 127, 156, 186, 220, 236, 241, 269, 281, 312, 320, 324

Hyperbole (exaggeration), xvii, xxxvii, xxxix, xliii, 10, 19, 33, 75, 131, 143, 144, 161, 173, 174, 198, 261, 270, 274, 282

Idolatry, idolaters, xliii, 5, 14, 37–38, 46, 60, 61, 77, 100, 101, 179, 194, 200, 240, 241, 255, 263, 264, 283, 284, 285, 317, 318, 325, 331

Inclusion (see Framing)

Jacob, xxiii, xliii, 32, 48, 49, 60, 116, 117, 118, 119, 147, 181, 185, 189, 195, 198, 209, 244, 245, 259, 261, 282, 283, 314, 316, 321

Keel, Othmar, 273

King, divine or human (*see* Sovereign, sovereignty)

Korah, Sons of, xx, xxi, 107, 111, 350, 354, 355

Kugel, James L., xiv, xvii–xviii

Lament (*see* Complaint)

Legal proceedings, lawsuit, juridical terminology, xx, 4, 15–16, 20, 21, 38, 39, 68, 87, 92, 93, 108, 125, 126–28, 200, 201, 202, 229, 234, 235, 249, 270, 271, 276, 290, 292, 299, 301, 307

Liturgy, vii, viii, ix, xxi, xxii, xxiv–xxv, xxvi, xxix–xxx, xxxi, xxxix, xl, xli, xlii, xliii–xliv, xlv, 5, 8, 9, 10, 11, 13, 14, 15, 16, 17, 18, 20, 22, 23, 26, 27, 29, 32, 34, 36, 37, 39, 41, 49, 51, 52, 56, 57, 59, 60–61, 64, 65, 66, 68, 70, 72, 73, 81, 83, 90, 101, 107, 109, 111, 118, 120, 126, 127, 128, 129, 131, 132, 138, 146, 149, 152, 153, 154, 157, 159, 160, 165, 167, 184, 185, 192, 194, 196, 199, 200, 201, 207, 212, 229, 231, 232, 233, 235, 239, 243, 244, 245, 246, 247, 251, 253, 256, 259, 260, 262, 267, 269, 274, 275, 276, 283, 284, 285, 286, 287, 288, 289, 290, 297, 300, 301, 303, 304, 309, 313, 314, 315, 316, 317, 319, 321, 322, 323, 330, 331, 335, 336, 337, 338, 339, 343, 344, 345, 346, 350, 354, 355, 356, 357, 358

Mays, James L., 297

McCann, J. Clinton, 177, 225

Merism (Totality), xv, 23, 60, 65–66, 90, 127, 138, 178, 183, 188, 208, 220, 282, 299, 318, 327

Messiah, vii, 44, 50, 51, 57–58, 114, 115, 174, 241, 274, 291, 314, 344, 358

Metaphor, xii–xiii, xxiv, xxxv, xxxvi, xlii, 4, 21, 22, 36, 38, 41, 54, 62, 68, 69, 71, 75, 76, 77, 78, 92, 98, 111, 112, 129, 130, 132, 143, 148–49, 155, 158, 178, 186, 195, 196, 197, 202, 207, 212, 216, 226, 229, 233, 237, 255, 272, 286, 298, 299, 303, 330, 332, 336

Metathesis, 125

Monologue, 18, 109, 150, 234, 328

Moses, xl, 112, 189, 191, 194, 201, 225, 245, 255, 256, 263, 264, 318, 319, 350, 352

Mowinckel, Sigmund, 355

Numerical pattern or sequence (*see* Three, Four, Five, Seven, Ten), ix, xiv, xviii–xix, xxi, xxiv, 150–51

Oracle of God, xvii, xxiii, xxxix, 19, 30, 49, 52, 70, 89, 90, 116, 118, 138, 146, 147, 163, 182, 185, 199, 200, 201, 209, 210, 217, 218, 219, 222, 227, 228, 229, 230, 235, 236, 269, 272, 273, 274, 356

Oxymoron, 96, 216

Parallelism and Parallel lines, xiv–xix, xxxii, xxxiii, 14, 17, 18, 38, 41–42, 43–44, 45, 49, 54, 58, 60, 65, 67, 70, 76, 78, 80, 83, 95, 101, 103, 115, 116, 119, 121–22, 123, 129, 130, 131, 132, 136, 147, 151, 158, 160–61, 162, 182, 187, 200, 204, 207, 209, 214, 215, 218, 221, 226, 227, 236, 239, 240, 242, 244, 246–47, 251, 252, 276, 278, 279, 280, 282, 287, 295, 300, 301, 302, 303, 308, 313, 314, 324, 329, 335, 336, 339, 341, 343

Paronomastic, 138

Personification, personified, xxxix, 41, 42, 45, 61, 74, 89, 90, 137, 148, 159, 183, 210, 214, 216, 220, 239, 243, 253, 282, 298, 309, 323, 357

Pit (*see* Sheol)

Plant imagery, xii–xiii, 5, 6, 7, 72, 79, 80, 92–93, 84, 133, 134, 158, 193, 196, 197–98, 205, 226, 230, 231, 238, 239, 250, 251, 252, 253, 255, 258, 260, 263, 298, 308, 309, 314, 321, 335, 341, 343

Praise, viii, xix, xx, xxiv, xxx, xxxv, xxxviii, xxxix, 3, 8, 17, 22, 23, 24, 25, 26, 32, 38, 41, 45, 48, 50, 51, 52, 53, 55, 56, 57, 66, 69, 71, 72, 74, 75, 76, 81, 83, 84, 87, 88, 89, 99, 100, 107, 109, 111, 119, 120, 121, 128, 129, 130, 139, 140, 146, 148, 149, 152, 153, 159, 160, 161, 163, 167, 170, 171, 172, 183, 184, 185, 186, 196, 197, 198, 199, 206, 208, 211, 212, 215, 231, 233, 236, 238, 239, 240, 242, 244, 245, 249, 251, 253, 257, 259, 261, 262, 267, 268, 269, 270, 272, 275, 276, 277, 280, 281, 283, 284, 287, 288, 295, 296, 302, 311, 316, 317, 318, 319, 324, 326, 327, 336, 337, 338, 339, 340, 341, 342, 343, 344, 345, 346, 349, 352, 353, 354, 355, 356–57

Qinah (meter), 45, 111

Refrain, ix, xx, 23, 24, 27, 33, 107, 109, 110, 111, 116, 117, 118, 123, 124, 125, 139, 140, 141, 142, 144, 145, 150, 151, 162, 191, 196, 198, 244, 262, 267, 286, 288, 289, 290, 320, 326, 329, 335, 336, 343, 349

Repetition, repeated vocabulary (*see also* Doubling), ix, xii, xiv–xix, xxi, xxiv, 4, 11, 12, 14, 15, 20, 24, 26, 28, 29, 30, 32, 34, 35, 38, 39, 40, 41, 43, 44, 47, 48, 52, 53, 55, 60, 62, 66, 67, 68, 69–70, 71, 72, 73, 74, 75, 76, 77, 80, 82, 83, 84, 85, 87, 88–89, 91, 92, 93, 95, 98, 99, 100, 101, 102, 110, 111, 116, 117, 119, 126, 129, 130, 135, 139, 140, 141, 142, 144, 147, 150, 151,

152, 154, 155, 157, 164, 168, 170,
171, 173, 177, 178, 179, 184, 185,
186, 187, 188, 189, 191, 192, 195,
196, 197, 199, 202, 204, 208, 209,
210, 211, 212, 213, 216, 217, 219,
221, 225, 226, 228, 230, 231, 232–33,
234, 235, 240, 241, 247, 248, 249,
250, 251, 254, 255, 257, 262, 268,
270, 275, 281, 283, 285, 288, 289,
290, 292, 293, 294, 296, 299, 302,
304, 305, 306, 307, 309, 310, 311,
313, 315, 316, 320, 324, 325, 329,
330, 331, 332, 334, 335, 336, 337,
338, 340, 341, 358

Retribution, vengeance, retaliation,
xxv, xxxii, xxxvii, xxxviii, xxxix, xl,
xli, xliv, 21, 26, 71, 87, 88, 104, 112,
141, 154, 165, 167, 195, 196, 205,
234, 235, 270, 279, 304, 330, 332,
344, 358

Reversals, xvi, xviii, 11, 44, 53, 54, 75,
112, 129, 178, 187, 190, 200, 205,
209, 217, 221, 225, 268, 288, 305,
306, 337, 338

Rhyme, xiv, 12, 88, 158, 281, 295

Royal psalm, xix, xx, 273–74, 344,
357–58 (*see* Sovereign, sovereignty)

Seven, multiples of seven (*see also*
Numerical pattern), ix, xviii–xix,
xxiv, xliii, xliv, 13, 14, 16, 17, 19, 22,
30, 32, 33, 35, 36, 37, 39, 41, 42, 45,
48, 50, 54, 59–60, 64, 66, 67, 71, 72,
73, 74, 76, 82, 84, 87, 92, 93, 96, 97,
101, 109, 110, 115, 119, 129, 135, 137,
143, 144, 151, 153, 157, 158, 164,
166, 171, 177, 183, 184, 186, 193,
195, 198, 204, 205, 206, 211, 218,
219, 225, 226, 228, 230, 236, 239,
240, 241, 242, 244, 245, 251, 257,
260, 263, 264, 272, 275, 276, 278,
280, 283, 284, 285, 290, 292, 293,
294, 295, 296, 299, 305, 313, 315,
318, 324, 325, 328, 329, 333, 334,
338, 340, 341, 342, 343, 344, 345

Sheol (pit), xiii, xvi, xxxiii, xxxiv–
xxxv, 5, 17, 18, 26, 38, 41, 69, 70, 71,
75, 76, 97, 99, 100, 114, 123, 124,
125, 126, 138, 140, 141, 165, 166,
180, 215, 220, 235, 286, 311, 327,
330, 332, 334, 356

Shift of address (*see* Change of
address)

Soliloquy, 110, 254, 286

Soll, W., 291

Sovereign, sovereignty (divine or
human, king), xix, xxxviii, xliv, 8, 9,
10, 11, 15, 22, 23, 24, 25, 26, 28, 41,
43, 44, 48, 49, 50, 51, 54, 56, 60, 61,
73, 81, 82, 84, 114, 115, 116, 117,
118, 119, 120, 121, 122, 127, 140,
146, 147, 148, 152, 153, 154, 158,
159, 160, 164, 165, 173, 174, 183,
185, 188, 197, 203, 204, 206, 207,
208, 211, 213, 217, 218, 219, 220,
222, 225, 232, 233, 237, 238, 239,
240, 241, 242, 243, 244, 245, 249,
251, 253, 254, 257, 272, 273, 274,
275, 284, 291, 302, 309, 313, 314,
318, 320, 323, 324, 325, 336, 337,
338, 339, 340, 342, 344, 345, 346,
350, 351, 353, 357–58

Speech-wicked speech, lying, slander,
xxxvi–xxxvii, xlii, 15, 16, 23, 30–31,
32, 35, 36, 39, 73, 77–78, 85, 86, 87,
88, 89, 98, 102, 128, 133, 134, 137,
138, 141, 143, 144, 145, 152, 154,
155, 169, 172, 178, 184, 249, 270,
271, 298, 329, 331, 336

Sukkoth, 118, 120, 159, 162, 201, 207,
233, 258, 291

Superscriptions (captions), ix, xix, xx,
xxi, xxiii, xxv, xxvi, 20, 22, 26, 73,
74, 81, 84, 107, 130–31, 134, 135,
139, 140, 146, 147, 170, 173, 184,
207, 216, 225, 230, 233, 235, 245,
250, 297, 306, 332, 337, 349–52, 353,
354, 355

Temple (*see also* Zion), 8, 15, 16, 19,
21, 30, 34, 36, 37, 39, 40–41, 49, 53,
56, 59, 60, 61, 62, 65, 66, 67, 68, 69,
71, 73, 74, 90, 107, 108, 109, 110, 114,
116, 118, 119, 120, 121, 132, 133,

134, 152, 156, 157, 159, 160, 163,
164, 181, 182, 183, 184, 188, 192,
194, 195, 206, 207, 208, 209, 210,
228, 229, 231, 232, 233, 235, 243,
244, 246, 248, 259, 273, 286, 288,
289, 297, 298, 300, 301, 305, 313,
314, 316, 318, 319, 321, 324, 325,
329, 345, 349, 354, 355, 356

Ten (*see also* Numerical pattern), xix,
12, 26, 62, 67, 76, 92, 109, 113, 119,
203, 204, 259, 299, 338, 343

Three, multiples of three (*see also*
Numerical pattern), xv, xix, 5, 16,
17, 19, 22, 24, 31, 32, 34, 35, 44, 45,
46, 47, 48, 50, 51, 59, 60, 64, 67, 68,
76, 80, 81, 82, 87, 93, 101, 109, 116,
117, 119, 127, 129, 132, 135, 136,
144, 150, 151, 156, 157, 158, 162,
163, 164, 168, 169, 172, 186, 191,
197, 198, 203, 204, 208, 210, 211,
225, 230, 232, 233, 236, 238, 242,
244, 245, 246, 254, 255, 256, 260,
269, 280, 283, 286, 288, 289, 294,
295, 299, 301, 302, 306, 311, 312,
313, 316, 319, 325, 328, 334, 338,
342, 344, 345

Time, xii, xvi, xxx–xxxi, 15, 32, 40,
45–46, 56, 75, 76, 77, 82–83, 94, 96,
97, 98, 103, 108, 110, 111, 113, 125,
136, 137–38, 140, 146, 149, 150, 153,
158, 166, 170, 172, 173, 174, 178,
182, 183, 185, 188, 190, 192, 193,
206, 214, 216, 222, 225, 226, 227,
228, 229, 231, 232, 235, 249, 250,
251, 252–53, 255, 256, 258, 274,
280–81, 299, 309, 320, 325, 327

Totality (*see* Merism)

Universality, universal, xix, xxxvii, 8,
10, 21, 24, 25, 30, 46, 56, 60, 90, 117,
118, 119, 120, 123, 126, 142, 146, 157,

158–59, 160, 162, 163, 164, 173, 174,
185, 201–02, 203, 210, 211, 212, 213,
217, 220, 237, 238, 239, 240–41, 242,
243, 244, 247, 251, 254, 258, 259,
267, 273, 274, 281, 282, 283, 288,
296, 309, 317, 325, 327, 337, 340,
341, 343, 345, 351

Vengeance (*see* Retribution)

Vertical axis, 15, 22, 40, 76, 82, 119,
127, 156, 186, 236, 241, 269, 281,
311, 312, 324, 343

Water imagery, xiii, xxxv, 6, 7, 42, 54,
58, 59, 71, 72, 75, 80, 81, 82, 107,
108, 116, 121, 147, 152, 156, 157,
158, 161, 165, 166, 167, 183, 189,
190, 192, 198, 213, 215, 216, 237,
241, 243, 257, 258, 260, 264, 268,
282, 283, 303, 304, 306, 311, 320,
323, 336, 343

Westermann, Claus, 355

Wilson, Gerald H., xx

Wisdom, xxxvii, 5, 8, 9, 25, 45, 61, 62,
81, 82, 83, 84–85, 123, 125, 126, 127,
130, 150, 180, 181, 191, 192, 226,
227, 231, 254, 256, 258, 260, 267,
275, 276, 277, 278, 280, 291, 292,
294, 295, 296, 297, 306, 336, 340,
341, 342, 358

Zion (*see also* Temple), xxiii, 8, 9, 10,
26, 33, 36, 49, 108, 114, 116, 117, 120,
121, 122, 127, 129, 134, 156, 157,
158, 159, 163, 164, 165, 167, 187,
188, 190, 191, 192, 194, 207, 208,
213, 226, 240, 244, 250, 251, 252,
253, 257, 273, 297, 298, 304, 305,
307, 309, 313, 314, 315, 316, 317,
319, 321, 322, 337, 340, 341, 344,
345, 350, 355, 357

INDEX OF HEBREW WORDS

Note: The Hebrew words occur in alphabetical order and in the form in which they appear in the commentary.

ʾbd, 5, 11
ʾbh, 199
ʾebyôn, 271
ʾaddîr, 233
ʾādām, 24, 139, 289, 304
ʾădāmâh, 24
ʾhb, 29, 133, 271, 293, 339
ʾōhel, 68
ʾôt, ʾōtôt, 182, 193, 212
ʾāz, 218, 306
ʾāḥ, 124
ʾḥr, 114, 168, 169
ʾaḥar, 178
ʾaḥărît, 178
ʾōyēb, 41
ʾîš ḥămāsîm, 329
ʾak, 98, 123, 124, 150, 151, 179
ʾak lô, 56
ʾākĕlû, 56
ʾlh, 60, 76
ʾĕlōhîm, 25, 59
ʾĕlîlîm, 240
ʾēlem, 143
ʾlp, 62, 84
ʾŭmmîm, 119
ʾĕmûnâh, 215, 217, 218, 219, 292
ʾmn, 218, 232

ʾmr, 32, 87, 154, 168, 169, 178
ʾimrâh, ʾimrat, ʾimărôt, 30, 260
ʾimrîm, 324
ʾĕmet, 64, 141, 142, 148, 166, 215, 217, 218, 269, 276, 287
ʾenôš, 25, 225
ʾanšē dāmîm, xxxvi
ʾsp, 87
ʾap, ʾapĕkā, 9, 19, 226
ʾōrĕḥôt, 62
ʾereṣ, 142, 156, 209, 257
ʾšr, 3
ʾašûr, ʾašûrāy, 3, 39
ʾašrê, xxiv, 3–4, 10, 80, 81, 208, 233, 278, 297, 307, 336
ʾāttâh, 183, 211, 219, 220, 225, 272, 292, 296, 333

bhl, 17, 18
bwʾ, 65, 110, 136, 137, 167, 237, 271, 290, 299
bôr, 76
bwš, 18, 77, 113, 168, 169, 170, 171, 293
bzh, 55
bḥn, 325
bṭḥ, 63, 76, 77, 81, 133, 139, 152, 283

beṭen, 77
byn, 82, 234, 296, 325
bayt, 208, 301
bal, 51
bĕlēb wālēb, 30
bĕlîyaʿal, 102
blʿ, 303
ben ʾādām, 24, 90, 226
bnh, 218, 221, 326
baʿădî, 324
bqr, 125
bōqer, 226
bĕqereb, 150
bqš, 68, 92, 135, 168, 169, 259
brʾ, 131
bĕrōb, 15
bĕrît, 260
brk, 63, 162, 283, 307, 316
bĕrākâh, 271
bāśār, 38, 139, 193, 214
bitĕbûnâh, 320

gʾl, 182
gbh, 281
gĕbah–ʿênaym, 249
gibbôr, 133
gĕbûrâh, gĕbûrût, 338, 345
gbr, 31, 157
geber, 215
gādôl, 324
gdl, 324
gôyîm, 118, 119, 239, 240
gwr, 35, 144
gôral, 304
gzr, 320
gyl, 87
gll, 32
gml, 254
gāmūl, 312
ger, 98, 292

debîr, 69
dbq, 294
dābār, 83, 154, 260, 261
dwd, 209
dkʾ, 219, 226
dkh, 130

dlh, 75–76
dĕlî, 76
dmh, 125, 159
dāmîm, 131
dumîyâh, 159
dāʿat, 235, 325
drk, 62
derek, 11, 41, 62, 292, 293, 325
dĕrûšîm, 276
drš, 33, 84, 259, 276, 296

hbl, 150
hebel, 150
hgh, 6, 11, 172
hdh, 74, 75
hădôm raglāyw, 313
hādār, 227, 344
hôpîaʿ (ypʿ), 127
hôšîaʿ, hôšîʿâh (yšʿ), 48
hlk, 65, 208, 210, 292, 312
hll, 55, 139, 154, 167, 270, 341, 353
hmh, 116, 204

wĕʿattâh, 98

zēdîm, 46
zkr, 48, 56, 62, 172, 189, 259, 262, 294
zēker, 276
zmr, 74, 144, 160, 172, 242, 341
zʿq, 53
zār, zārîm, 135
zēr, zērîm, 46
zrh, 326
zerôaʿ, 218
zrḥ, 241
zrʿ, 52, 241

ḥdl, 125
ḥwl, 75, 296
ḥôq, 260
ḥûšâh, 168–69, 170
ḥzh, 28, 29, 39
ḥṭʾ, 129, 256
ḥăṭāʾ âh, 80
ḥîdâh, ḥîdôt, 123, 192
ḥyh, 103, 296

ḥayyîm, 21, 51, 67
ḥyl, 290
ḥayl, 207
ḥōkmôt, 123
ḥld, 125
ḥāled, 125
ḥēleq, 332
ḥēmâh, 214, 216
ḥāmās, xxxvi
ḥannûn wĕraḥûm, 275
ḥnn, 18, 19, 63, 144, 212, 302
ḥsd, 132
ḥesed, 16, 18, 19, 32, 44, 50, 51, 63, 64,
    76, 80, 81, 82, 83, 84, 89, 90, 99, 100,
    102, 108, 109, 111, 112, 113, 121, 130,
    133, 141, 142, 144, 146, 148, 149,
    150, 151, 152, 161, 166, 188, 209,
    210, 211, 212, 215, 217, 218, 219,
    221, 222, 227, 230, 242, 243, 246,
    247, 248, 249, 253, 254, 255, 256,
    259, 262, 263, 267, 268, 269, 272,
    287, 288, 289, 290, 296, 310, 311,
    319, 320, 321, 324, 325, 334, 338,
    339, 342, 356, 358
ḥasdĕkā waᵓ ămitĕkā, 100
ḥsh, 10–11, 77, 155, 168
ḥāsîd, ḥăsîdîm, 80, 337
ḥpṣ, 99, 100, 168, 169, 271, 275, 293
ḥpr, 168
ḥēṣ, 155
ḥqr, 325, 326
ḥereb, 154
ḥarôn, 9, 214, 215, 216
ḥerpâh, 196
ḥšb, 133
ḥšq, 228

ṭhr, 129
ṭûb, ṭôb, 156, 157, 177, 179, 278, 294,
    307
ṭerep, 277

yābîn, 125
ygᶜ, 17
yād, 237
ydh, 141, 290, 324
yedîd, yĕdîdôt, 209

ydᶜ, 7, 122, 130, 234, 325
yôneqet, 198
yôšēb, 8
yaḥad, 83
yĕḥîdātî, 55
yḥl, 310, 311
yālîn, 125
ysr, 235
yᶜd, 122
yph, 114
yāpeh, 121
yṣr, 237, 255
yrᵓ, 68, 101, 138, 139, 155, 156, 275,
    278, 279
yrd, 76, 315
yrh, 154, 155, 296
yaršîᶜennû (ršᶜ), 92
yšb, 40, 65, 249, 281, 315
yĕšûᶜâh, 243, 290
yšᶜ, 12, 41, 49, 52, 99, 165, 209, 212,
    242, 290
yšr, 29
yāšār, yĕšārîm, 28, 275, 276
yišrê–lēb, 81, 155

kbd, 80, 95, 128
kabôd, 21, 38, 142, 240, 344
kbs, 129
kwn, 156, 218, 221, 227, 232
kāzāb, 151
kḥš, 199
kōl, 24, 84, 239, 254, 337, 343
klᵓ, 99
kilyôt, 38
klm, 169
ksh, 80, 136, 137
ksp, 40
krᶜ, 40
ktt, 219

lēb, lēbāb, 32, 38, 100, 150, 155, 178,
    237, 249, 275, 312, 329, 334
lbš, 87, 314
lḥm, 88
lyn, 75, 123
lmd, 235, 296, 335
lāmmâh, 109

lamnaṣēaḥ, 352
lāneṣaḥ, 182
lāʿad, 277
lĕʿôlām, 218, 277, 320
lqḥ, 124, 180
lĕrēaʿ, 325
lāšôn, 154, 155

māh, 23, 109
mwṭ, 35, 37, 116, 138
mwl, 290
môʿêd, 185, 252
môpĕtîm, 193
môrāʾ, 187
môšab, 4, 6, 8, 313
mwt, 286, 290
mḥh, 129
maḥăseh, 116, 149, 228
maym, 167
mîšôr, 66
mlʾ, 199
mlk, 119
melek, 119
malkûtekā, 338
mimmerḥāq, 324
mĕnûḥâh, 286, 313
mispad, 75
mistār, xxxvi, 155
mēʿeh, 100
māʿôn, 227
māʾăśēh, maʿăśîm, 70, 82, 227, 338
miṣwôt, 277
miqdāš, 181
maqĕhēlîm, 64
māqôm, 313
miqqărāb, 138
mārôm, 233
merḥāb, 77
miśgāb, 116, 120, 145, 149
maśkîl, 119
mšḥ, 8
mĕšîaḥ, 115
miškānôt, 313
mšl, 124
māšāl, 123, 124, 192
mišpāṭ, 82, 121, 122, 239, 248, 249, 276
mātay, 234

nāʾôr (ʾwr), 187
nbṭ, 82, 84, 234
ngd, 155, 172
neged, 77
ngʿ, 178
negaʿ, 95
nĕdāray, 148
nwḥ, 314
nôrâh, 160
nôrāʾ, nôrāʾ ôt, 115, 159, 160, 186, 187
naḥălâh, 82, 195
nḥt, 95
nṭh, 252
nṭʿ, 6
nākôn, 132
nsʿ, 197
nōʿam, 227
npl, 136
niplāʾôt, 185, 191, 267, 268, 276
nepeš, 17, 18, 21, 61, 83, 87, 100, 109,
    135, 149, 152, 160, 214, 254, 293,
    303, 333, 334
nāpĕšâh, 77
nṣb, 103
nṣl, 21, 52, 76, 144, 333
nśʿ, 60, 61, 71, 80, 335
nĕšāmâh, 345
ntn, 261, 275, 277

sbb, 54, 65, 80, 241
sgr, 76
swg, 169
sôd, 154, 155
sūkkâh, 68
skk, 229
skn, 326
selâh, 329, 334, 352
sĕlîḥâh, 310
sāmûk, 275
smk, 135, 277
sʿd, 103
spr, 52, 122, 154, 172, 178
str, 47, 68, 155
sēter, 149

ʿbd, 246, 292, 296
ʿad, 172

ʿēdâh, 4
ʿad–mātāy, 18, 234
ʿad–ʿānāh, 32
ʿwd, 200
ʿwz, 145, 164
ʿôlām, 172, 178, 254
ʿāwōn, ʿăwônôt, 80, 256, 310
ʿwr, 146
ʿōz, 73, 116, 145, 149, 190, 207
ʿzr, 168, 169, 300
ʿṭh, 222
ʿên, 81, 82
ʿîr, 301
ʿlh, 118
ʿal-zōʾt, 79
ʿelyôn, 118, 190, 203, 228, 230, 240
ʿmd, 63, 82, 271
ʿammîm, 118, 119, 239, 240
ʿml, 178
ʿāmōq, 155
ʿnh, 138, 341
ʿănāwâh, 43
ʿănāwîm, 26, 85, 167, 169
ʿānî, 167, 169, 184, 271
ʿnn, 138
ʿānāp, 198
ʿāpār, 74, 255
ʿṣb, 318
ʿēṣâh, 6
ʿṣm, 101
ʿăqēbay, 140
ʿărōb, 292
ʿrg, 108
ʿārîṣîm, 135
ʿśh, 237, 276, 283, 284
ʿšn, 197
ʿēt, 252

pdh, 63, 125, 310
peh, 68
paḥ, 166
pḥd, 68, 135
paḥad, 155
pî, 161, 172
plṭ, 140
pls, 143
pāneykā, 37, 114

pʿl, 70, 143, 155, 231, 276
pāʿāl, 227
pōʿălê ʾāwen, 155, 230
pěʿālîm, 237
pṣḥ, 242
piqûdîm, 277
prḥ, 231
prš, 335
pšʿ, 256
pešaʿ, 80
pitʾōm, 154, 155

ṣaddîq, ṣědîqîm, 15, 28, 29, 81, 92, 155
ṣdq, 20, 29, 39, 92, 129, 142, 240, 290, 295, 334
ṣedeq, 115, 121, 122, 276
ṣědāqâh, 15, 56, 82, 130, 171, 242, 275, 279
ṣûr, 149
ṣyṣ, 314
ṣēl, 149
ṣlḥ, 290
ṣmḥ, 314
ṣpn, 68, 77

qbr, 125
qeber, 16, 125
qāhāl, 64
qwh, 63, 310, 311
qôl, 71, 138, 189, 199
qwm, 12, 31, 39, 67, 103, 281, 328
qyṣ, 146
qělāhâh, 271
qāṣîr, 198
qrʾ, 53
qrb, 125, 138, 156
qereb, 16, 138
qārōb, 138

rʾh, 33, 82, 87, 101, 121, 124, 155, 161, 234, 279, 326
rab, rabbîm, rabbôt, 12, 47, 80, 82, 101
rgl, 35, 140
regaʿ, rāgaʿ, 18, 75
rdp, 333
rěhābîm, 101
rwd, 136

rûaḥ, 77, 83, 130, 258, 334
rĕwāḥâh, 161
rĕwāyâh, 161
rwm, rām, 68, 76, 281, 324
rwṣ, 292
rĕḥab lēbāb, 249
rĕḥôb, 138
raḥûm, 254
rḥm, 254, 256
reḥem, raḥămîm, 100, 130, 254
rḥq, 52, 156, 271
ryb, 88
remiyyâh, 80
rnn, 81, 172, 242, 245
rāᶜ, 16, 59
rᶜh, 198
rōᶜēh, 198
rōᶜî, 59
rēᶜîm, 155
rᶜᶜ, 245
rpᵓ, 19, 103
rph, 118, 151
rṣh, 99
ršᶜ, 29, 39, 92, 339
rešāᶜ, 16
rāšāᶜ, rĕšāᶜîm, 92, 142, 202

śbᶜ, 37, 199
śbr, 296
śgb, 145
śwś, 293
śḥh, 292
śṭn, 271
śyḥ, 189
śym, 218
śyś, 87, 168, 169
śmḥ, 74, 81, 87, 154, 155, 168, 169, 240
śnᵓ, 41, 65, 293
śapâh, śĕpat, 199
śarᶜappᶜîm, 325
śāśôn, 130, 293

šᵓᵓ, 293
šᵓg, 182
šᵓl, 301
šĕbûᶜâh, 260
šbḥ, 341

šēbeṭ naḥălâh, 184
šbᶜ, 313
šgh, 292
šgḥ, 82
šadday, 228
šāwĕᵓ, 306
šwb, 16, 19, 55, 130, 168, 169, 196, 209, 210, 226, 313
šwr, 16
šḥh, 199
šaḥat, 76
šyḥ, 110
šîr, 160
šîr ḥādāš, 83
šyt, 50, 178
škḥ, 26, 114, 293
škn, 35, 94
šlḥ, 301
šulḥān, 59, 166
šlm, 102, 149
šālōm, 163, 173, 174, 209, 300, 304, 308, 309
šam, 91, 313, 316
šēm, 26, 184, 272
šmd, 339
šmᶜ, 39, 157, 160, 161, 199, 334
šmr, 38, 40, 144, 296, 299, 310, 331, 339
špṭ, 63, 142, 202, 239, 271
špl, 281
šqp, 33
šeqer, 293
štl, 6

teᵓĕnap, 195
tĕbûnôt, 123
tēbel, 125, 233, 243
tĕhôm, tĕhōmôt, 89, 192, 343
tĕhillâh, 172, 337, 349, 353
tôbâh, 167, 245
tōm, 249
tôrâh, xix, 3, 4, 6, 7, 8, 45, 46, 47, 82, 100, 104, 291, 292, 293, 295, 296
tām, 155, 249
tāmîd, 172
tĕmîmâh, 47
tmk, 103
tmm, 47

tannînîm, 183
tᵉh, 292
tipᵉeret, 172

tĕpillâh, 160
tĕrûʿâh, 82
tôšāb, 98